GENDERED LIVES

Communication, Gender, and Culture

TENTH EDITION

Julia T. Wood

Lineberger Distinguished Professor of Humanities
Caroline H. and Thomas S. Royster Distinguished
  Professor of Graduate Education
Professor of Communication Studies

The University of North Carolina at Chapel Hill

WADSWORTH
CENGAGE Learning™

Australia • Brazil • Japan • Korea • Mexico • Singapore • Spain • United Kingdom • United States

WADSWORTH
CENGAGE Learning

Gendered Lives: Communication, Gender, and Culture, Tenth Edition

Julia T. Wood

Senior Publisher: Lyn Uhl

Publisher: Monica Eckman

Senior Development Editor: Greer Lleuad

Assistant Editor: Rebekah Matthews

Editorial Assistant: Colin Solan

Media Editor: Jessica Badiner

Marketing Program Manager: Gurpreet S. Saran

Marketing Coordinator: Brittany Blais

Marketing Communications Manager: Courtney Morris

Content Project Manager: Aimee Bear

Art Director: Linda Helcher

Production Technology Analyst: Tom Stover

Manufacturing Planner: Doug Bertke

Rights Acquisition Specialist: Mandy Groszko

Production Service: Integra

Photo Manager: Dean Dauphinais

Senior Image Researcher: Jaime Jankowski, Pre-PressPMG

Cover and Interior Designer: Rokusek Design

Cover Image: © 2011 Artist Rights Society (ARS), New York/SIAE, Rome

Compositor: Integra

For product information and technology assistance, contact us at
Cengage Learning Customer & Sales Support, 1-800-354-9706
For permission to use material from this text or product,
submit all requests online at **www.cengage.com/permissions.**
Further permissions questions can be emailed to
permissionrequest@cengage.com.

Library of Congress Control Number: 2011930785

ISBN-13: 978-1-111-34648-5
ISBN-10: 1-111-34648-8

Wadsworth
20 Channel Center Street
Boston, MA 02210
USA

Cengage Learning is a leading provider of customized learning solutions with office locations around the globe, including Singapore, the United Kingdom, Australia, Mexico, Brazil and Japan. Locate your local office at **international.cengage.com/region**

Cengage Learning products are represented in Canada by Nelson Education, Ltd.

For your course and learning solutions, visit **www.cengage.com.**

Purchase any of our products at your local college store or at our preferred online store **www.cengagebrain.com.**

Instructors: Please visit **login.cengage.com** and log in to access instructor-specific resources.

Printed in the United States of America
1 2 3 4 5 6 7 15 14 13 12 11

This book is dedicated to Emma Goldman, Alice Paul, Elizabeth Cady Stanton, Susan B. Anthony, Margaret Sanger, Sojourner Truth, Mary Wollstonecraft, Charlotte Perkins Gilman, Frederick Douglass, and other women and men who began the conversation about gender in this country;

and to

Betty Friedan, Ella Baker, Marilyn French, Bill McCartney, Gloria Steinem, Jackson Katz, Ellen Goodman, Michael Kimmel, Evelyn Fox Keller, bell hooks, James Doyle, Sandra Harding, Nancy Chodorow, Robert Bly, Gloria Anzaldúa, Judith Butler, Karlyn Campbell, Mary Daly, Lady Gaga, and other women and men who have added to the cultural dialogue about gender;

and to

Malia Obama, Sasha Obama, Jason Muehlhoff, Niko Pezzullo Striphas, Michelle Wood Wilco, Daniel Wood Wilco, Harrison Wood Wilco, and other boys and girls whose voices will shape the next generation's understanding of women and men, masculinity and femininity, and the meaning of gender in our society.

CONTENTS IN BRIEF

CONTENTS

CHAPTER 6
GENDERED NONVERBAL COMMUNICATION   140

PART 2
GENDERED COMMUNICATION IN PRACTICE

CHAPTER 7
BECOMING GENDERED: THE EARLY YEARS   161

LIST OF EXPLORING GENDERED LIVES BOXES

PREFACE

I originally wrote *Gendered Lives* for two reasons. First, I wanted to introduce students to a rich body of research that informs us about the intricate relationships among communication, gender, and culture. Second, I thought that learning about these relationships would empower students to make more informed decisions about how they personally enact gender and deal with gender issues in their lives as well as how they contribute to cultural perspectives and policies related to gender.

Since writing the first edition of this book in the early 1990s, our understandings of gender have changed and issues related to gender have mushroomed. Society has acknowledged a greater range of options for individual women and men—in the military, in the home, in professional life, and in politics. In addition, transgender awareness has grown, new women's and men's movements have emerged, and media have challenged some gender stereotypes while creating others. Academic researchers have continued to identify and map the ways that communication, gender, and culture influence one another. This new edition responds to social changes in the United States and around the world, as well as to feedback from students and faculty who generously offer ideas for ways to improve this book.

I discuss this book's origins and features in the Introduction ("Opening the Conversation," pages 1–12). Here, I want to offer instructors a summary of changes that make this edition different from the last and a list of supplementary resources available for students and instructors.

FEATURES OF *GENDERED LIVES*, TENTH EDITION

Five specific changes set this edition of *Gendered Lives* apart from its predecessors.

Up-to-Date Research

Understandings of gender and issues connected to it change at lightning speed. To keep up with these changes a textbook must be continuously updated to reflect the most current research. This edition of *Gendered Lives* includes more than 200 new references to publications that have appeared since the ninth edition went to press or that I had not read at that time. Incorporation of substantial new research ensures the currency of this edition.

Continuing Coverage to Cultural and Social Diversity

Beginning with the first edition of this book, I've aimed for content and a writing style that are inclusive. For example, I discuss diverse classes, ethnicities, races, ages, and sexual orientations whenever research is available; I use language that includes all readers: not just women as well as men, but also culturally marginalized groups such as people who are in committed relationships but not legally married; and I punctuate my discussions throughout the book with diverse student voices.

This edition extends my commitment to representing diversity by enlarging coverage of gender issues beyond the United States and beyond mainstream groups. I chose not to write a separate chapter on cultural gender beliefs and practices because I didn't want to separate cultural influences from the discussions about families, education, relationships, and so forth that are covered in this book. Instead, I've woven information about gender in a range of cultures and social groups into each chapter so that students can appreciate how profoundly culture shapes gender in multiple contexts. For instance, Chapter 6 includes information on gendered dress codes in different cultures, and Chapter 9 highlights men's increasing participation in child care. To Chapter 12 I've added new accounts of gendered violence around the globe and of women's and men's challenges to it.

Ongoing Enrichment of Theoretical Framework Long-time adopters of *Gendered Lives* realize that I have incorporated new theories as those developed. For instance, in the eighth edition, I added queer theory and queer performative theory. New to this edition are discussions of gender schema theory (Chapter 2), the gender-linked language effect (Chapter 5), and the "maternal wall," which is discrimination against mothers in the paid labor force (Chapter 10). This edition also recognizes behavioral ecology, which is the heir of sociobiology and evolutionary psychology.

Attention to Timely Issues

As I prepare each new edition of *Gendered Lives*, I try to give particular attention to one or two issues that are particularly timely. For this edition, I gave special emphasis to three. First, I have updated Chapter 2's coverage of third-wave feminism. In addition, Chapter 11, which focuses on media, includes a new section on how third-wave feminists and their age peers are using media to challenge and change cultural views of gender. Second, this edition features expanded discussion of work-family tensions, which pose enormous challenges to increasing numbers of women and men. I've woven this coverage into chapters, discussing it in Chapters 7 (Becoming Gendered), 9 (Close Relationships), and 10 (Gendered Organizations). Third, I note how the recession intersects with gender and cultural life. More men than women have lost jobs, which destabilizes men's traditional role as primary or sole breadwinner for families.

PEDAGOGICAL FEATURES TO ENGAGE STUDENTS

Five features are aimed to heighten students' engagement with the text and issues related to gender. First, each chapter opens with "Knowledge Challenge" questions, which focus on issues that are often misunderstood and which are covered in the chapter. Second, selected Exploring Gendered Lives boxes conclude by asking students' opinion about issues raised in the feature. Third, each chapter concludes with questions for thought and discussion. These may be assigned for students to think about or as journal entries. They may also be prompts for class discussion. Fourth, I've added a new feature, "Gender Online," which appears after each chapter summary. This feature invites students to visit websites related to chapter content and to search online for videos and information about concepts and ideas in the chapter. Finally, at the end of each chapter, I suggest two to four sources—films, articles, books. My criteria for selecting these are that (1) I consider them either classic or especially insightful and (2) they are accessible to undergraduate students.

In making these five changes, I've avoided "page creep"—the tendency of a book to grow longer with each new edition because old material is not deleted to make room for new material. I've eliminated dated coverage and references to make room for more current research and coverage of timely topics. I hope the changes I've described make this edition of *Gendered Lives* a valuable resource for instructors and students who want to explore the complex and fascinating ways in which communication, gender, and culture interact and affect our lives.

SUPPLEMENTARY RESOURCES FOR STUDENTS AND INSTRUCTORS

Gendered Lives, Tenth Edition, offers print and electronic supplements to assist in making the gender communication course as meaningful and enjoyable as possible for both students and instructors, and to help students succeed. Wadsworth Cengage Learning has prepared the following descriptions for your consideration.

Companion Website for Students. This website provides chapter-by-chapter resources to help students understand and apply the text's instruction. The resources include live and updated web links for every URL mentioned in the book; self-quizzes written by Jan W. Kelly at the University of Scranton; key term crossword puzzles and flashcards; and an online glossary.

Instructor's Resource Manual. Written by Sara Hayden at the University of Montana–Missoula, and Julia Wood, the *Instructor's Resource Manual* comprises two main parts, the first titled and addressing Special Issues in Teaching Communication, Gender, and Culture, and the second a Chapter-by-Chapter Guide for Teaching *Gendered Lives*, which provides chapter outlines, activities, and test questions. This manual is also available on the instructor's website and the PowerLecture CD-ROM.

Instructor's Website. The password-protected instructor's website includes electronic access to the *Instructor's Resource Manual,* PowerPoints, and links to Wadsworth Cengage Learning technology resources.

PowerLecture. This CD-ROM contains an electronic version of the *Instructor's Resource Manual,* Exam-View® Computerized Testing, and predesigned Microsoft® PowerPoint® presentations prepared by Pamela Hayward at Augusta State University. The PowerPoint presentations contain text and images, and can be used as is or customized to suit your course needs.

Communication Scenarios for Critique and Analysis on DVD includes communication scenarios covering interpersonal communication, group communication, gender, and culture.

The BBC News and CBS News DVDs: Human Communication, Interpersonal Communication, and Public Speaking provide footage of news stories that relate to current topics in human and interpersonal communication, and footage of famous historical and contemporary public speeches, as well as clips that relate to current topics in speech communication.

Please consult your local Wadsworth Cengage Learning sales representative or cengage.com/login for more information, user names and passwords, examination copies, or a demonstration of these ancillary products. Available to qualified adopters.

ACKNOWLEDGMENTS

One of the most gratifying aspects of writing a book is the opportunity to thank those who have offered support, insight, and advice. First and foremost, I thank my students. The undergraduate women and men in my classes are unfailing sources of education for me. Their questions and ideas, their willingness to challenge some of my notions, and their generosity in sharing their perceptions and experiences have shaped the pages that follow—sometimes in obvious ways, sometimes subtly.

Among the undergraduate students who have pushed me to think in new ways about gender, communication, and culture are Jordana Adler, Cutler Andrews, Brandon Carter, Alexis Dennis, Reuben Gelblum, Diana Iglesias, Dimitri Martinez, and Nisha Verma. Among the graduate students who have influenced my thinking are Katy Bodey, Walter Carl, Katie Harris, Naomi Johnson, Kristen Norwood, Tim Muehlhoff, Natalie Fixmer-Oraiz, Julia O'Grady, Phaedra Pezzullo, and Stace Treat.

My thinking and writing also reflect discussions with colleagues. I am particularly grateful to Professors Steve Duck, the University of Iowa, and Bonnie Dow, Vanderbilt University, for their insights and their unflagging willingness to join me in wrestling with questions about gender, communication, and culture. And I am especially indebted to Lynn O'Brien Hallstein, with whom I taught my first gender and communication class in 1989 and who remains an intellectual well-spring for me.

I am fortunate to have enjoyed the professional and personal support of the invincible Monica Eckman, executive editor for Communication Studies, and Rebekah Matthews, development editor, who made my job as an author far easier and far more satisfying than I had a right to expect. Along with Monica and Rebekah, others at Wadsworth Cengage Learning have contributed in important ways to this edition of *Gendered Lives*. They are Colin Solan, editorial assistant; Jessica Badiner, media editor; Amy Whitaker, marketing manager; Susan Miscio and Aimee Bear, content project managers; and Amanda Groszko, permissions manager. As well, I thank Sue Langguth, who managed the production of this book.

I also thank the individuals who reviewed the first, second, third, fourth, fifth, sixth, seventh, eighth, and ninth editions of this book and who offered generous responses and insightful suggestions, which are reflected in the pages that follow. Reviewers of the first edition were Sandra Albrecht, University of Kansas; Victoria DeFrancisco, University of Northern Iowa; Bonnie Dow, University of Georgia; Valerie Downs, California State University, Long Beach; Cheris Kramarae, University of Illinois at Urbana-Champaign; Larry Lance, University of North Carolina at Charlotte; Suzanne McCorkle, Boise State University; Edward Schiappa, University of Minnesota; and Patricia Sullivan, State University of New York, the College at New Paltz.

Reviewers of the second edition were Dan Cavanaugh, Southwest Texas State University; Judith Dallinger, Western Illinois University; Bonnie Dow, University of Georgia; Kathleen Galvin, Northwestern University; Jim Hasenauer, California State University at Northridge; and Diane Umble, Millersville University.

Reviewers of the third edition were Cynthia Berryman-Fink, University of Cincinnati; Pamela Cooper, Northwestern University; Jill Rhea, University of North Texas; Ralph Webb, Purdue University; and Gust A. Yep, San Francisco State University.

Reviewers of the fourth edition were Bernardo Attias, California State University at Northridge; Pamela Dawes-Kaylor, Ohio State University; Michael R. Elkins, Texas A&M University at Kingsville; Maureen Keeley, Southwest Texas State University; Kelly Morrison, Michigan State University; Trevor Parry-Giles, University of Maryland at College Park; and Carol Thompson, University of Arkansas at Little Rock.

Reviewers of the fifth edition were Rick Buerkel, Central Michigan University; Steve Duck, University of Iowa; Victoria Leonard, College of the Canyons; Jennifer Linde, Arizona State University; Kaye J. Nubel, Saddleback College; Bruce Riddle, Kent State University; and Eva Rose, Chaffey College.

Reviewers of the sixth edition were Lisa M. Burns, University of Maryland; Nancy J. Eckstein, Wheaton College; Lindsay Hayes, University of Maryland at College Park; Pam McAllister Johnson, Kansas State University; and Valerie McKay, California State University, Long Beach.

Reviewers of the seventh edition were Martha Blalock, University of Wisconsin; Carla Harrell, Old Dominion University; Julie Mayberry, North Carolina State University; Valerie McKay, CSU Long Beach; Carol Morgan, Wright State University; and Ralph Webb, Purdue University.

Reviewers who guided me in preparing the eighth edition were Michela Ardizzoni, University of Louisville; Pam Birrell, University of Oregon; Amy Blackstone, University of Maine; Maria Brann, West Virginia University; Kate Cady, Northern

Illinois University; Dacia Charlesworth, Robert Morris University; John Chetro-Szivos, Fitchburg State College; Erica Clarke, Syracuse University; Annie Clement, Rochester Community and Technical College; Joan Conners, Randolph-Macon College; John A. Cook, University of Texas, Brownsville; Christine Courtade Hirsch, SUNY Oswego; Kenneth R. Culton, Niagara University; Andy Dehnart, Stetson University; Lynne Derbyshire, University of Rhode Island; Marcia D. Dixson, Indiana University-Purdue University Fort Wayne; Teresa Drake, University of New Mexico; Lisa Flores, University of Utah; Lisa Ford-Brown, Columbia College; Ragan Fox, California State University, Long Beach; Charles Goehring, University of Iowa; Irene Grau, Christopher Newport University; Trudy L. Hanson, West Texas A&M University; Pamela Hayward, Augusta State University; Gwen A. Hullman, University of Nevada, Reno; Julia Johnson, Southwestern University; Naomi Johnson, University of North Carolina, Chapel Hill; Melva J. Kearney, University of South Alabama; Susan Kilgard, Anne Arundel Community College; Viera Lorencova, Fitchburg State College; Linda D. Manning, Christopher Newport University; Verlaine McDonald, Berea College; Rozilyn Miller, University of Central Oklahoma; Louise F. Montgomery, University of Arkansas; E. David Moss, Mt. San Jacinto College; Heather Nesemeier, North Dakota State University; Stacey Peterson, College of Notre Dame of Maryland; Laura C. Prividera, East Carolina University; Leesha Thrower, College of Lake County; Michelle Trim, Lander University; Suzanne Scott, George Mason University; Curt VanGeison, St. Charles Community College; Amy Veuleman, McNeese State University; Kathryn Sue Young, Mansfield University; and Deborah Walker, Coastal Carolina University.

Reviewers for the ninth edition were Patricia Amason, University of Arkansas; Rick Buerkel, Central Michigan University; Patricia Cutspec, East Tennessee State University; Greg Dickinson, Colorado State University; Peter Frecknall, Georgetown University; Sara Hayden, University of Montana; Adrianne Kunkel, University of Kansas; Victoria Leonard, College of the Canyons; Denise Malloy, University of Memphis; Anne Mattina, Stonehill College; Tracy Meyers, Valdosta State University; Nancy Nichols, Lane Community College; Lynn O'Brien Hallstein, Boston University; Nicholas Palomares, University of California, Davis; Judith Pratt, California State University, Bakersfield; Valerie Renegar, San Diego State University; Karla Scott, Saint Louis University; and Ralph Webb, Purdue University.

Finally, I am indebted to the reviewers for this edition: Belle Edson, Arizona State University; Amanda Frioli, Eureka College; Sara Hayden, University of Montana; Marian Houser, Texas State University–San Marcos; Jan Kelly, The University of Scranton; Denise Malloy, University of Memphis; Lynn O'Brien Hallstein, Boston University; Nicholas Palomares, University of California–Davis; Nancy Pearson, Minot State University; Mary Polce-Lynch, Randolph-Macon College; Elizabeth Tolman, South Dakota State University; and Virginia Westheider, University of Cincinnati.

And, always, I thank Robbie—the love of my life—for his support, criticism, and, most of all, his presence in my life.

Julia T. Wood
The University of North Carolina at Chapel Hill
May 2011

ABOUT THE AUTHOR

Julia T. Wood joined the Department of Communication Studies at the University of North Carolina at Chapel Hill at the age of 24. She is now the Lineberger Distinguished Professor of Humanities, the Caroline H. and Thomas S. Royster Distinguished Professor of Graduate Education, and a professor in the Department of Communication Studies, where she teaches courses and conducts research on gender, communication, and culture, and on communication in personal relationships. During her career, she has authored 17 books and edited 10 others. In addition, she has published more than 90 articles and book chapters and has presented numerous papers at professional conferences. She has won 12 awards for undergraduate teaching and 15 awards for her scholarship.

Professor Wood lives with her husband, Robert Cox, who is also a professor of Communication Studies at the University of North Carolina at Chapel Hill. Filling out their immediate family are their dog, Cassidy, and two kittens, Rigby and Rowdy. When not teaching or writing, Professor Wood enjoys traveling, baking, biking, talking with students and friends, visiting family, and consulting with attorneys on cases involving sex and gender issues.

Destiny is not a matter of chance, it is a matter of choice.
William Jennings Bryan

OPENING THE
CONVERSATION

Knowledge Challenge:

1. When was the term *feminism* first used?
2. How many bras were burned in feminist protests in the 1960s?
3. Are heterosexual men happier in relationships with feminist or nonfeminist women?

Most textbooks open with a discussion of the material that will be covered, but I'd like to launch our conversation a bit differently. I think you're entitled to know something about the person behind the words you'll be reading, so let me introduce myself and explain why I wrote this book.

We tend to think of books as impersonal sources of information. Like anything that people create, however, books reflect the experiences, identities, and historical context of the authors who write them. Authors influence books when they decide to include certain topics and omit others, to rely on particular theories, and to include some issues and exclude others. Choices of topics, writing style, and theoretical stance shape the content and overall meaning of a book. This doesn't mean that books are not informative or reliable, but it does mean that authors' experiences and perspectives have an impact on books. By telling you a little about who I am, what I believe, and why I wrote this book, I am inviting you to think about how my background, experiences, beliefs, and values have shaped the book you're reading.

Let's start with some simple demographic information. I am a European-American, middle-aged, heterosexual, spiritually engaged, middle-class woman who has been in a committed relationship with Robert (Robbie) Cox for 39 years. Yet, if you think about it, this information isn't simple at all. It implies a great deal about my identity and my experiences. For instance, I became an adult when the second wave of the U.S. Women's Movement was ascending, and it influenced my personal life and my thinking about gender and culture. The "simple" demographic

1

information about me also shows that I am privileged in many ways—my race, class, and sexual identity are approved by mainstream Western culture. Yet I am disadvantaged by my sex, because women continue to be valued less than men in Western culture. I did not earn the privileges conferred by my skin color, sexual identity, and class, nor did I earn the inequities that come with being female. That is the nature of much privilege and inequity—they are unearned. They do not reflect the achievements, efforts, or failings of the individuals who enjoy or suffer them.

THE SOCIAL CONSTRUCTION OF INEQUALITY

To speak of being privileged in some ways and disadvantaged in others does not mean I take either for granted. The fact that my sex makes me vulnerable to job discrimination, violence, and other injustices is not something I accept as unchangeable. In fact, one reason I wrote this book is because I believe we can bring about changes in our society. I also do not accept my privileges without reflection. What our culture arbitrarily designates as normal or superior means that sex, gender, race, gender identity, sexual orientation, and class profoundly influence individuals' knowledge, experience, and opportunities (Andersen & Collins, 2007b; Johnson, 2006).

If we don't want to be limited by the horizon of our social positions, we can learn about the experiences, perspectives, and circumstances of people in other social positions: the anger and hurt experienced by transgendered people in a society that defines them as abnormal; the resentment felt by some heterosexual white men toward laws and policies that increase rights and opportunities available to women and minorities; what it means to be a person of color in a sea of whiteness; the sense of restriction many women feel knowing they cannot venture out at night without risking assault; the frustration felt by poor and working-class citizens whose needs and circumstances often are not represented in legislation that claims to help everyone.

We cannot fully understand the lives of people who differ from us. Sensitivity and earnest efforts to understand are important, yet they cannot yield complete knowledge of the daily reality of others' lives. But we can realize that our feelings, identities, values, and perspectives are not everyone's. Recognizing the limits of our own perspective and experiences encourages us to learn from people who have different perspectives and experiences. We do this by respecting the specific conditions that shape their lives and by recognizing that only *they* can define the meanings of their experiences, feelings, thoughts, hopes, beliefs, problems, and needs. We cannot speak for them, cannot appropriate their voices as our own (González, Houston, & Chen, 2007). But to listen is to learn, and to learn is to broaden our appreciation of the range of human experiences and possibilities.

Realizing that inequality is socially constructed empowers us to be agents of change. We don't have to treat light skin, heterosexuality, maleness, and middle-class economic status as superior or normal. Instead, if we choose to, we can challenge social views that accord arbitrary and unequal value to people and that limit humans' opportunities and lives.

FEMINISM—FEMINISMS

Finally, in introducing myself to you, I should tell you that I am a feminist. Many people do not identify themselves as feminists and do not admire feminists or feminism. In some cases, people reject feminism because their understanding of the term has been shaped by media misrepresentations. The word *feminism* was coined in France in the late 1800s. It combined the French word for "woman," *femme,* with the suffix *ism,* meaning "political position." Thus, *feminism* originally meant "a political position about women" (McCann & Kim, 2003). Ironically, although many people in their 20s do not call themselves feminists, they do think that the Women's Movement has improved the conditions and opportunities available to women. This suggests that, for many people, there is greater reservation about the label *feminist* than about the actual goals, values, and achievements of feminism (Schechter, 2005).

When I talk with students who say they aren't feminists, we often discover that we agree on most issues relevant to gender but disagree on the meaning of the word *feminism.* There's good reason for this. First, feminism is not one single belief or political position. Chapter 3 discusses a variety of feminist positions, and Chapter 4 explores the different stances—some feminist, some not—endorsed by men's movements. Second, most people's impressions of feminism have been shaped by media misrepresentations. Beginning with the inaccurate report in the 1960s that feminists burned bras as a protest (which they did not do then), media have consistently misrepresented feminists as man-hating, tough, shrill extremists. Many people, like my student Andrea (see her commentary), say they aren't feminists because they associate feminism with media caricatures that emphasize male bashing, being unfeminine, and engaging in radical protests.

▼

Andrea   *I would never call myself a feminist, because that word has so many negative connotations. I don't hate men or anything, and I'm not interested in protesting. I don't want to go around with hacked-off hair and no makeup and sit around bashing men. I do think women and men are equal and should have the same kinds of rights, including equal pay for equal work. But I wouldn't call myself a feminist.*

Media stereotypes of feminists and feminism don't fit many women and men who define themselves as feminists. Like me, many feminists have good relationships with both women and men. In fact, research shows that men in relationships with feminist women are happier and consider their relationships healthier than men in heterosexual relationships with nonfeminist women. The converse is also true: Women in heterosexual relationships with feminist men are happier and more satisfied with their relationships than women in heterosexual relationships with nonfeminist men (Rudman & Fairchild, 2004; Rudman & Phelan, 2007). Also like me, many women who label themselves feminists are feminine in many ways: They enjoy wearing feminine clothes, experimenting with hairstyles and makeup, and engaging in traditionally feminine activities such as baking bread, watching chick flicks, and caring for children. Being a feminist does not conflict with being feminine, but it does mean being reflective about how we define and express femininity.

Because feminism means different things to different people, I want to tell you how I define feminism. I see it as an active commitment to equality and respect for all forms of life. For me, this includes respecting all people, as well as nonhuman forms of life and the Earth itself. Simply put, my feminism means I am against oppression, be it the oppression of women, men, people with disabilities, people with specific sexual identities, people of particular race-ethnicities or religions, elderly people, children, animals, or our planet. I don't think oppression and domination foster healthy lives for individuals or societies as a whole. I believe there are better, more humane and enriching ways for us to live, and I am convinced we can be part of bringing these alternatives into existence. That is the core of feminism as I define it for myself. During the course of reading this book, you will encounter varied versions of feminism, which should shatter the myth that feminism means the same thing to all people, and which should also invite you to consider where to position yourself among diverse viewpoints.

Feminism does not just happen. It is an achievement and a process. I was not raised to be a feminist. In fact, quite the contrary is true. I was raised to be a traditional Southern woman who deferred to men and devoted herself to home and family. In the 1970s when a friend first introduced me to some readings about discrimination against women, my initial response was denial. I tried to rationalize inequities or repress my knowledge of them, perhaps because recognizing them was painful. When denial failed to work, I entered an angry phase. I was bitter about the ways in which women, including myself, were devalued and denied opportunities. I was also angry at myself for having been unaware of society's devaluation of women and for conforming to the roles assigned to women. This angry and embittered phase was necessary for me to absorb what I was learning, but it could not lead me forward in a constructive sense.

Finally, I was able to transform the anger into an abiding commitment to being part of change, not so much for myself as for future generations. I want our society to become fairer, to respect differences among human beings, and to affirm the entire range of identities that people have. When I began to study gender issues, I learned the path I traveled to achieve my feminist identity is not uncommon. Ignorance, denial, anger, internalization of new values and identities, and transformation to constructive commitment are stages that many individuals go through as they dislodge one identity and perspective on social life and embrace alternate ones.

FEATURES OF *GENDERED LIVES*

Three features distinguish this book and support the views I've just discussed. First, I include discussion of diverse classes, ethnicities, races, and sexual orientations whenever research is available. For instance, the Exploring Gendered Lives box on page 8 identifies a range of ways in which cultures define gender and sexual identities. Although research on many races, sexual identities, and socioeconomic classes is still limited, I include what research exists on the range of people who make up our world. *Gendered Lives* is an effort to reflect the diversity of human beings better than most textbooks.

A second feature of this book is language that aims to include all readers. I use terms such as *he* and *she* and *women* and *men* in preference to *he, mankind,* and *men.* But inclusive language means more than including women; it also means using language that refuses to go along with cultural marginalization of various groups. For instance, I refer to individuals in intimate relationships as *partners* rather than *spouses,* and I generally refer to *committed relationships* rather than *marriages.* I'm not entirely comfortable describing my sweetheart, Robbie, as my *partner,* because that sounds so businesslike. But I'm even less comfortable calling him my *spouse* or *husband,* because not everyone who is in a committed relationship can use those words. The terms *spouse, wife, husband,* and *marriage* exclude lesbians, gay men, and many transsexed, transgendered, and intersexed people because currently there are few places that allow same-sex couples the legal, material, and social legitimacy of marriage. The terms *spouse* and *marriage* also exclude heterosexuals who cohabit but choose not to marry.

A third way in which *Gendered Lives* reflects awareness of my own limited standpoint and my respect for those with different standpoints is the inclusion of student voices that punctuate this book. In the pages that follow, you'll meet a lot of students—some like you, some quite different. In many courses on gender and communication, students keep journals or write reflection papers in which they discuss connections between ideas brought forth in their gender and communication classes and in their personal lives. Many of my own students gave me permission to include their reflections in this book. In addition, students at other campuses around the country have written to me in response to previous editions of *Gendered Lives,* and some of their comments appear in this edition. I've tried to return their generosity by including a range of individuals and viewpoints, including ones with which I personally disagree. In fact, including ideas with which I disagree, from both students and scholars, is necessary if this book is to reflect the range of ideas about gender and communication that circulate in our culture. Hannah, a student from a northeastern college, makes a point in her commentary on this page.

Hannah's comment reflects open-mindedness, which fosters learning. As you read this book, I hope you will think about research findings and students' voices and reflect on how they are similar to or different from your own beliefs and values. I have refrained from evaluating or interpreting the reflections that appear in this book. The students write clearly and eloquently, and I don't want to muffle their voices with my analysis. The student commentaries, my ideas, and your responses to what you read create a tapestry of learning in which we collaboratively explore gender, communication, and culture.

Hannah   *When I was reading* Gendered Lives, *I had to keep reminding myself that you were presenting information and that not all points were your personal values and beliefs. I didn't agree with all of your statements or the ideas of others, like the students in their commentaries, but I learned a lot about the ways others see gender. I also learned a lot about how I think about gender by seeing what ideas I agreed with and disagreed with.*

The Exploring Gendered Lives boxes in all chapters highlight important information about gender. These are meant to stimulate thought and go beyond the basic material in the chapter. Some of the Exploring Gendered Lives features include websites you can visit to learn more about particular topics.

BECOMING AWARE

Reading this book will enlarge your understanding of gender—how it is shaped and expressed in contexts ranging from the political arena to intimate relationships. The awareness you gain will enhance your insight into yourself and your society. At the same time, you may feel unsettled as you read this book.

If you are a woman, you may find it disturbing to learn the extent to which Western culture discounts your experiences and limits your opportunities. I also realize that a number of those reading this book—both women and men—have been raped, sexually abused, sexually harassed, or battered. Some of you have eating disorders; some have suffered job discrimination; some of you have been taunted for not embodying current social expectations for males or females. Reading *Gendered Lives* is likely to stir up these issues. If you don't wish to deal with such difficult issues, then you may choose to forgo or delay study in this area. However, if you are ready to wrestle with serious personal and social matters, then this book should help you understand issues in your life as not only personal but also political. Such issues reflect widespread cultural biases that define unrealistic expectations for both men and women, marginalize women, condone violence and aggression, and promote inequities.

▼

Patrick   *I don't want to be lumped with all men. I am not sexist; I don't discriminate against women; I believe in gender equality and try to practice it in my relationships with women. It really makes me angry when people bash males as if we are all oppressors or something. I don't oppress women or anyone else, and I don't want to be blamed for unfair things that others do.*

If you are a man, reading this book may increase your awareness of ways in which cultural views of masculinity constrain your life choices. You may be uncomfortable learning about social expectations for men to succeed, to be self-sufficient, to repress feelings, and to put work ahead of family. You may also be surprised to learn that your maleness benefits you in ways that you may not have noticed. As a result of what you read, you may become more aware of society's valuing of some people more than others and the effects of this different valuing on the social, political, and economic quality of people's lives.

Becoming aware of inequities in social life may make you critical of practices and attitudes that sustain discrimination and disadvantage. Realize that some people will respond negatively if you make thoughtful criticisms of current social attitudes and practices. Women who speak out against inequities and discrimination are sometimes accused of male-bashing. Men who speak out against discrimination against women are sometimes regarded as wimps or as disloyal to men. Such responses reflect an unwillingness to engage the substance of the criticism. If you want to take an active role in shaping our shared world, you must anticipate struggles with those who are less willing to consider ideas that question familiar perspectives and behaviors.

In his commentary, Patrick makes an important point when he says he personally doesn't discriminate against women. We need to distinguish between the actions and attitudes of individuals and the social practices and values of our culture. This book doesn't suggest that individual men are bad, oppressive, or sexist. The point is that Western culture as a whole has constructed inequalities between women and men, and these inequalities continue in our era.

The problem, then, is not rooted primarily in individual men or women. Rather, it is rooted in the social system that accords unequal value and opportunity on the basis of sex, skin color, sexual identity, and other factors. This kind of prejudice diminishes us all. It limits our appreciation of human diversity by falsely defining a very narrow zone of what is good, normal, and worthy of respect. Regardless of whether you are privileged or oppressed by social evaluations of what is normal and good, your study of gender, communication, and culture may be unsettling. If you are seriously disturbed by what you read, you might find it helpful to talk with your instructor or to visit the counseling center at your school.

WHY I WROTE THIS BOOK

I wrote *Gendered Lives* because I believe that change is needed in how we view and enact gender. I also believe that the knowledge in this book can empower you to think more carefully about your personal identity and our shared world. Since the first edition appeared, I've received many positive responses from students in my classes as well as from students around the nation. I've also received feedback that has helped me rethink and improve the book. I am most gratified when readers like Meghann, who attends a college in the Midwest, tell me that this book has made a difference in their lives.

▼

Meghann   *This book was an eye-opener for me. I'd never thought about how society has shaped my sense of myself as a woman or what that means. Now that I do see how society shapes me—or tries to shape me—I think more about how I want to be. I still agree with some social views of women and men, but there are others that I am starting to question. Because now I think critically about these views and their impact on me, I feel more in charge of who I am and who I will be.*

| EXPLORING GENDERED LIVES | MULTICULTURAL PERSPECTIVES ON SEX AND SEXUAL ORIENTATION |

What's feminine? What's masculine? What's gay? It depends on which culture's perspective you take.

- The Agta people in the Philippines and the Tini Aborigines in Australia see keen hunting ability as a feminine ideal (Estioko-Griffin & Griffin, 1997).
- In Melanesia, young Sambian boys perform fellatio on adult men. The Sambia believe that swallowing the semen of adult men helps boys grow into healthy adult males (Herdt, 1997).
- The Society Islands of French Polynesia have three sex-based classifications: males, females, and *māhū*. A *māhū* is understood to be half woman, half man. Female-bodied *māhū* behave in masculine ways and have sexual relations with *non-māhū* females; male-bodied *māhū* behave in feminine ways and have sex with *non-māhū* males (Glenn, 2002).
- To become a man in some societies, a boy must accomplish at least one of three things: have a vision, kill an antelope, or earn enough money to support himself (Clatterbaugh, 1997).
- In parts of South America, male homosexuality is defined not by male-to-male sex but by whether a man penetrates (not homosexual) or is penetrated by (homosexual) another man (Almaguer, 1993; Cantú, 2004).
- In addition to male and female, India recognizes a category of person who is a female man, called a *hijra*. *Hijras* sometimes remove their external genitalia to appear more womanlike (Herdt, 1997; Nanda, 2004). A similar category exists in the town of Juchitán in Oaxaca, a southern state of Mexico. In addition to males and females, this community recognizes muxes (pronounced MOO-shays), who are biological males who from an early age identify as females and adopt the roles and practices assigned to females in their community. Muxes are accepted, and many residents of Juchitán believe they have special abilities (Lacey, 2008).

I wrote this book because I believe our society urgently needs change. In the chapters that follow, you'll learn about the extent to which gender inequities and discrimination persist and diminish individual and collective life. For instance:

- Is there any way to justify the fact that, each day in the United States, at least four women are killed by their partners or ex-partners?
- Is it fair that men who want to spend time with their families are often evaluated negatively in professional contexts?
- Is it acceptable that a Pakistani court sentenced a woman to be gang-raped because of an offense allegedly committed by her brother?
- Is it right that most of the advances won by women's movements have benefited white, middle-class women more than minority and poor women?

- Is there any reason why a woman working full-time outside the home earns approximately 77 cents for every $1 a man working full-time earns (Short-changing, 2010)?
- Is it fair that mothers have an advantage over fathers in gaining custody of children?

If you don't want inequities such as these to continue, read on. Becoming aware of how our culture establishes and communicates inequities is necessary, but that alone will not lead to changes. In fact, concentrating exclusively on what is wrong tends to depress us and paralyze impulses toward reform. Awareness of inequities must be coupled with understanding that change is possible.

Through individual action and social movements, many blatant sex inequities have been eliminated. In the 1800s, women weren't allowed to vote—they had no voice in the government or in making laws that affected them. They also had no access to a university education, could not own property if they married, and were barred from participating in most professions. Women can now vote, attend universities, own property, and pursue professional careers. Forty years ago, it would have been almost unthinkable for a man to have been a stay-at-home dad. Today, a number of men are stay-at-home dads. In recent decades, sexual harassment, acquaintance rape, and marital rape have been named and recognized as illegal.

Paralleling these legal changes are substantial transformations in how we view ourselves and each other as women and men. Our culture once defined women as too frail and delicate for hard manual or intellectual work. Today, women pursue careers in business, construction, science, education, politics, and the military. Views of men, too, have changed. In earlier eras, our society defined manliness in terms of physical strength and bravery. After the Industrial Revolution, the ability to earn a good salary became the social standard of manliness. Today, many men are challenging social definitions of men as income providers and are seeking greater opportunities to participate in personal relationships. You have options for what you will do and who you will be that were not available to your parents.

Changes such as the ones we've discussed lead many people to think that gender equality has been achieved. Some commentators call this a "post-feminist era" in which all the issues that feminism focused on have been resolved. Many of my students tell me that gender discrimination is history and that sexism has been overcome.

- They tell me that women now have freedom of choice, but they don't seem to recognize that some health insurance companies will not pay for contraceptives and that there are more barriers to reproductive choice in the United States than in some other countries.
- They tell me that sex discrimination is no longer a problem in the workplace, but they can't explain why women earn less than men for equivalent jobs.
- They cite high-visibility politicians such as Barbara Boxer and Hillary Clinton as evidence that the playing field in politics is now level, but they don't seem to realize that women hold only less than 25% of seats in both houses of congress.
- They tell me sexist comments are no longer tolerated. They are at a loss to explain why the 2008 presidential primary brought out bumper stickers that read "Life's a bitch. Don't elect one," or why at a McCain rally one of his

supporters yelled out, "What are we going to do about the bitch?" referring to Hillary Clinton, and nobody at the rally vocally objected to the comment.

- They tell me that the United States opposes discrimination against women, but they don't seem disturbed that the United States—along with a few other nations such as Somalia and Sudan—has refused to ratify the United Nations Convention on the Elimination of All Forms of Discrimination Against Women. Jimmy Carter signed the treaty in 1980, and the Senate has yet to act on it.

Not all of the inequities based on sex and gender are history. We've achieved some major changes. There are more changes to be made before we have a truly level playing field and before all of us—men, women, and children—can live more humane and fulfilling lives.

COMMUNICATION AS THE FULCRUM OF CHANGE

Communication is the heart of social life and social change. Through communication, we can identify and challenge current cultural views that constrain individuals and create inequities. We also rely on communication to define alternatives to the status quo and to persuade others to share our visions. For example, in the mid-1800s Elizabeth Cady Stanton and other early feminists galvanized support for the women's rights movement through their eloquent speeches. Public discourse sparks and guides collective efforts at political reform.

Other kinds of communication also instigate change. Perhaps you talk with a friend about gender inequities, and as a result your friend alters her perceptions. Maybe a teacher discusses sexual harassment with his class, and a student is empowered to bring charges against a man who has been harassing her. You talk with your father about ways in which current leave policies disadvantage working mothers, and he persuades his company to revise its policies. Wherever there is change, we find communication. Through your public, social, and interpersonal communication, you are a powerful agent of change—someone who can transform yourself and the society in which we jointly participate.

Information is the foundation of effectiveness as an agent of change. Before you can define what needs to be different, you must first know what exists and what it implies. Reading *Gendered Lives* will provide you with a great deal of information that you can use to form sound opinions, attitudes, and behavior regarding gender. Then, you can make informed choices about what you believe and about the identity you wish to fashion for yourself. You may decide to change how you define yourself, or you may be satisfied with your identity and the existing gender arrangements in our culture. Either stance is grounded if it is an *informed* choice—but no choice is wise if it is not based on information and serious reflection.

THE CHALLENGE OF STUDYING COMMUNICATION, GENDER, AND CULTURE

Studying communication, gender, and culture requires courage because it involves us in perplexing questions about our society and our personal identities. We must be willing to consider new ideas openly and to risk the turmoil of changing values

EXPLORING GENDERED LIVES

ABOUT "MALE-BASHING": JULIA—THE AUTHOR—COMMENTS

Occasionally, a student tells me that *Gendered Lives* "bashes men." This comment puzzles me, because I don't think of myself as a male-basher. For 39 years, I've been in a committed relationship with a wonderful man; I have many male friends and colleagues whom I like and admire; and I've done as much to mentor male students as female ones. When I ask students to explain why they think the book bashes men, they tell me it gives more attention to discrimination against women than to discrimination against men and that it shows how some men harm women. They are correct in this observation, but what concerns these students is findings from research rather than my own views.

Like any scholar, what I write depends largely on available information. Existing research shows that, although both men and women experience violence from intimate partners, 95% of people who are known to be physically abused by romantic partners are women (Haynes, 2009; Johnson, 2006; Wood, 2004). It would be inaccurate to give equal space to discussion of men who are physically abused by intimate partners. The same is true of sexual harassment: Although members of both sexes are sexually harassed, most victims are women. The only way I could present a gender-balanced discussion of sexual harassment would be to misrepresent facts.

You should also realize that this book includes more information about men and men's issues than any other textbook for a course in gender and communication. In the chapters that follow, you'll learn about men's movements, pressures men face to succeed and conform to stereotypes of masculinity, and consequences, such as depression, of social perspectives that limit men in the workplace and in personal relationships. You'll also learn that men, like women, find it stressful to balance work and family, yet men today are contributing more to raising children than previous generations of men.

Research I've included throughout this book shows how social expectations of women and men can restrict all of us. I hope that, as you read this book, you'll perceive the coverage as fair.

and identities that are familiar to us. Further, with awareness comes responsibility. Once we are informed about gender and communication, we can no longer sit passively back as if they were not our concern. They *are* our concern, both because gender and communication affect each of us directly and because we are part of a collective world. Thus, how we act—or fail to act—influences our shared culture.

Although studying communication, gender, and culture is disturbing, it can be very worthwhile. By questioning constructed inequality, we empower ourselves to do more than unthinkingly reproduce the cultural patterns we have inherited. By involving ourselves in communication that enlarges others' awareness and revises cultural practices, we assume active roles in creating personal and collective lives that are fairer, more humane, and infinitely more enriching than what might otherwise be possible. That is the goal of *Gendered Lives*.

Gender Online

1. The Organization for Research on Women and Communication (ORWAC) publishes the journal, *Women's Studies in Communication*. You can read back issues of the journal online at ORWAC's site: **http://www.cios.org/www/wommain.htm**
2. Terms for online searches: "sex, cultural views of," "feminism," "hijras."

Reflection and Discussion

1. Using my self-description as a guideline, consider how your identity influenced your choice to take this course, as well as how it may affect your perceptions of topics in the book and the course. Have you been privileged or disadvantaged by your race, class, sex, and sexual orientation? How have your privileges and disadvantages affected your opportunities, knowledge of issues, interests, abilities, goals, and so on?
2. What changes do you think are most needed related to communication, gender, and culture?
3. How do you define *feminism?* Write down your definition, and see if it changes during the course of reading this book and taking this class.
4. Interview two people who are from non-Western cultures. Ask them to explain what counts as being a man (or manly or masculine) and what counts as being a woman (or womanly or feminine) in their cultures. How do their cultures' definitions of gender cohere with and depart from those in the United States? Ask them what they find most interesting or surprising about American men and women.

Recommended Resources

1. Peggy McIntosh. (2007). White Privilege: Unpacking the Invisible Knapsack. In P. Andersen and P. H. Collins (Eds.), *Race, Class, & Gender*, 6th ed. (pp. 98–102). Belmont, CA: Thomson-Cengage. This is a classic article that raises awareness of privileges many people enjoy without being conscious of them.
2. Megan Seely. (2007). The F-Word. Introduction to *Fight Like a Girl* (pp. 1–14). New York: New York University Press. Seely is a young woman who asks why so many of her peers say, "I'm not a feminist, but..."
3. Allan Johnson. (2006). *Privilege, Power, and Difference*, 2nd ed. New York: McGraw-Hill. This is an engaging and accessible introduction to thinking about inequalities and how they harm all of us, including those who seem to benefit from them.

We are looking for permission to be more than our society tells us we are.

Starhawk

THE STUDY OF COMMUNICATION, GENDER, AND CULTURE

CHAPTER 1

Knowledge Challenge:

1. How many sexes and how many genders exist?
2. Do all males have the same sex chromosomes?
3. Are transgender people attracted to members of their sex or the other sex?

If you watch popular TV talk shows, chances are good you'll see guests discussing gender and communication. Go to a bookstore, and you'll find dozens of popular advice books that promise to help you communicate better with the "opposite sex." Watch *America's Next Top Model,* and you're likely to see a transsexual contestant, such as Iris on the 11th season. Visit YouTube and you'll find a number of videos that comment on gender and gender relations. The general public's fascination with information about gender and communication is mirrored by college students' interest. Around the United States and in other countries, gender and communication is a rapidly expanding area of study in colleges and universities. Many campuses, like mine, cannot meet the high student demand for these courses.

In this chapter, we will consider how learning about relationships among gender, communication, and culture can empower you personally and professionally. Then, we will explore key concepts and vocabulary that form the framework of this book.

COMMUNICATION, GENDER, AND CULTURE AS AN AREA OF STUDY

Courses in gender, communication, and culture have grown remarkably in the past two decades. One reason for the growth is that research has created a knowledge base for courses. In addition, more and more people today want to learn about this area of personal and cultural life.

RESEARCH ON GENDER, COMMUNICATION, AND CULTURE

Had you attended college in the early- to mid-1980s, you would not have found a textbook like this one. Classes that explore various aspects of gender have become widespread only in the last 20 years. An explosion of interdisciplinary scholarship has occurred, producing hundreds of thousands of articles and books; in 2006, the first handbook of research on gender and communication was published (Dow & Wood). This research provides knowledge about how communication creates, sustains, and changes gender and how gender shapes communication and cultural views of women and men (Dow & Condit, 2005). In *Gendered Lives,* you'll encounter research that will clarify the profound connections among gender, communication, and culture.

Research on gender is conducted by scholars in a range of fields including communication, anthropology, history, philosophy, psychology, and sociology. In doing their research, scholars rely on a broad array of methods. To give you an understanding of the research that informs the field of gender and this book, I'll briefly describe different research methods.

Quantitative research methods[1] gather data that can be quantified and analyze the data to draw conclusions. These methods are most closely associated with the social sciences. Three of the more common quantitative methods are descriptive statistics, surveys, and experiments. Descriptive statistics describe populations, proportions, and frequencies. They answer questions such as: How often do women and men interrupt in conversations? How much are men and women in the same professional positions paid? How many hours of child care do mothers and fathers perform? What are the key concerns of men in their 50s? Surveys, which may be written or oral (interviews) ask people to report their feelings, thoughts, experiences, and so forth. Surveys could ask women and men: What do you do with your close friends? How often do you argue with friends? Experiments are controlled studies that manipulate one thing (called an independent variable) to determine how it affects another thing (called a dependent variable). Experiments have been conducted to find out what happens to women's self-esteem when they look at fashion magazines; whether different images come to people's minds when they see the words "urban man" and "urban people"; and whether people who view pornography are more likely to engage in violence against women than people who do not view pornography.

Qualitative research methods, sometimes called interpretive methods, aim to understand the nature or meaning of experiences that cannot be quantified. These methods have grown out of the humanities and remain most closely tied to humanistic disciplines. Two of the most popular qualitative methods are textual analysis and ethnography. As the name implies, textual analysis involves describing communication texts and interpreting their meaning. Communication scholars have a broad view of texts that includes written, oral, and nonverbal symbolic activities.

[1] Boldfaced terms appear in the glossary at the end of this book.

Textual analyses have illuminated the meaning of the *Declaration of Sentiments* (the speech given in 1848 at the first Women's Rights Convention) and compared political speeches of male and female figures. Ethnography relies on extensive and sensitive observation of human activity to discover what things mean to humans. Ethnography has helped us understand how different cultures define and enact gender and how those enactments support specific cultural values. Ethnography study has also provided precise descriptions of women's and men's flirting behaviors and how they are interpreted.

Critical research methods identify and challenge inequities and problems in social life. In this way, scholars engaged in critical research hope to raise awareness of inequities and problems and to motivate change. These methods are particularly associated with disciplines in the humanities and liberal arts. Critical research has given us insight into ways in which communication practices sustain male dominance in conversations and ways that organizational structures and practices create hostile work environments for women and minorities.

Mixed research methods are exactly what the name implies—a mixture of two or more methods. Some scholars find it useful to combine methods to get multiple types of information. For example, a scholar might document the frequency (descriptive statistic) of men's and women's smiling in social situations and then interview men and women (qualitative method) to learn why they smile and how they interpret smiles from other women and men.

REASONS TO LEARN ABOUT COMMUNICATION, GENDER, AND CULTURE

Learning about relationships among communication, gender, and culture serves three important goals. First, it enhances your appreciation of complex ways in which cultural values and practices influence your views of masculinity and femininity and men and women. Differences between feminine and masculine communication often show up when heterosexual partners have distinct orientations to working through problems; when male and female supervisors differ in how direct and assertive they are; when teachers interact differently with female and male students; when media represent men and women in sex-stereotyped ways; and when female and male political candidates say similar things but the public evaluates them differently. You can increase your understanding of personal, social, and professional life by learning about masculine and feminine communication styles and cultural views of gender.

Second, studying gender, communication, and culture will enhance insight into your own gender, both as it is now and as you may decide to revise it. You will become more aware of ways cultural expectations of gender are communicated to you in your daily life. In turn, this awareness will allow you to think more critically about whether there are cultural expectations that you want to accept or challenge.

Third, studying communication, gender, and culture should strengthen your effectiveness as a communicator. Learning about general differences in women's and men's communication will enlarge your ability to appreciate the distinct validity of diverse communication styles. This allows you to understand and adapt to ways of communicating that may differ from your own. In addition, you will learn how

EXPLORING GENDERED LIVES	JOURNALS THAT FEATURE RESEARCH ON GENDER AND COMMUNICATION
Communication Education *Communication Monographs* *Communication Studies* *Gender and Society* *Journal of Applied Communication Research* *Journal of Cross-Cultural Research* *Journal of Gender, Culture & Health*	*Journal of Men's Studies* *Men and Masculinities* *Sex Roles* *Sexuality and Culture* *Signs* *Women and Language* *Women's Studies in Communication* *Critical Cultural Studies*

your own communication does or doesn't conform to prevailing cultural prescriptions for gender, and this allows you to make more informed choices about how you want to communicate.

GENDER IN A TRANSITIONAL ERA

These days, we hear a lot about miscommunication between the sexes. Men are often confused when women want to continue talking after men think an issue is settled; women may be frustrated when men seem not to listen or don't respond to what they say. We may also be perplexed about where we stand on issues that were clear-cut in previous eras.

CONFUSING ATTITUDES

You probably don't subscribe to your grandparents' ideals of manhood and womanhood. You may believe that both women and men should be able to pursue careers and that both should be involved in homemaking and parenting. You are probably not surprised when a woman knows something about car maintenance or when a man prepares a good meal. These experiences and views depart from those of previous generations.

Yet, if you're like most of your peers, there are also a number of gender issues about which you are confused. Many people believe women should have equal professional opportunities but think women should not be involved in actual wartime combat. Although a majority of young adults believe that both parents should participate in child rearing, most people also assume that the mother, not the father, will be the primary caregiver during the early years of children's lives (Galvin, 2006). You may support equal opportunity but still think that colleges and universities should be allowed to offer more scholarships to male athletes. You may believe that everyone has a right to define their own identity, but feel uneasy when you learn your roommate is transsexual.

When we grapple with issues like these, we realize that our attitudes aren't always clear, even to ourselves. On one level, many of us think that women and men are equal in most respects. Yet, on another level, where deeply ingrained values and beliefs reside, we may hold some very traditional values and beliefs. We may believe that it's wrong to discriminate on the basis of sexual identity, yet find we personally don't want to associate with people whose sexual identities differ from our own. We may think it doesn't matter whether a man or woman in a heterosexual couple earns a greater salary, but feel in our own relationship that the man should be the primary wage earner. We live in a transitional era in which many of us no longer accept traditional views, yet we haven't become comfortable with alternative views and their implications for our own identities and relationships. This makes our lives and our relationships interesting, unsettling—and sometimes very frustrating.

DIFFERENCES BETWEEN WOMEN AND MEN

Are women and men really as different as pop psychologists would have us believe? Certainly, there are some differences between the sexes that we need to understand. There is also substantial variation within each sex as a result of diversity in experience, heredity, sexual orientation, race, culture, and class. And there are many similarities between women and men—ways in which the two sexes are more alike than different (Barnett & Rivers, 2004; Wright, 2006).

Katherine's commentary is important. Because there are similarities between the sexes and variations within each sex, it is difficult to find language to discuss general patterns of communication. Terms such as *women* and *men* are troublesome because they imply that all women can be grouped together and all men can be grouped together. When we say, "Women's communication is more personal than men's," the statement is true of most, but not all, women and men. Certainly some women don't engage in personal talk, and some men do. Many factors, including race, economic class, and sexual identity, shape how specific women and specific men communicate (Zinn, Hondagneu-Sotelo, & Messner, 2007).

EXPLORING GENDERED LIVES	CHANGING NAMES—NOT EQUAL OPPORTUNITY

Although most people say they think it's fine for women to keep their birth names when they marry, fewer than 10% of women actually do so (Suter, 2004). Even fewer men are willing to consider changing their names upon marrying. And those who do may be in for a surprise, as Elizabeth Batton and Garrett Sorenson discovered. In August of 2006, the two New Yorkers married and each wanted to take the other's last name. Elizabeth had no problem changing her surname to Sorenson— she simply put her new name on the marriage certificate. For Garrett, changing names was not so easy. New York, like most states, assumes that men will not change their names when they marry. To do so, Garrett had to petition the court, advertise in a newspaper, and pay a significant sum in legal fees (Porter, 2007).

Katherine   *I am really skeptical of books that describe women and men as "opposite" sexes. They focus on a few ways that most women and most men are different. They totally ignore all of the ways that women and men are alike. Even worse is that they act like all women are the same and all men are the same. People are just such individuals that you can't sum them up as "man" or "woman."*

Thinking and speaking as if there were some stable, distinct essence that is women and some stable, distinct essence that is men is referred to as **essentializing,** ✶ the tendency to reduce something or someone to certain characteristics that we assume are essential to its nature and present in every member of a category, such as men or women. When we essentialize, we mistakenly presume that all members of a sex are alike. Essentializing obscures the range of characteristics possessed by individual women and men and conceals differences among members of each sex. In this book, we will discuss generalizations about women and men, but this does not imply any essential qualities possessed by all members of a sex. We'll also take time to notice exceptions to generalizations about gender.

Michael   *The other day in class, we were talking about whether women should have combat duty. I'm really uncomfortable with where I stand on this, since I think one way, but I feel another. I do think women should have to serve just as much as men do. I've never thought it was right that they didn't have to fight. And I think women are just as competent as men at most things and could probably be good soldiers. But then when I think about my mom or my sister or my girlfriend being in the trenches, having to kill other people, maybe being a prisoner who is tortured and assaulted, I just feel that's wrong. It doesn't seem right for women to be involved in killing when they're the ones who give life. Then, too, I want to protect my girlfriend and sister and mom from the ugliness and danger of war.*

But then, this other part of me says, "Hey, guy, you know that kind of protectiveness is a form of chauvinism." I just don't know where I stand on this except that I'm glad I don't have to decide whether to send women into combat!

In just these opening pages, I've used the words *gender* and *sex* several times, but we haven't yet defined them precisely. The next section of this chapter provides definitions to give us a shared understanding of what sex, gender, and sexual orientation are, how they are shaped by the culture in which we live, and how communication reflects, expresses, and re-creates them in our everyday lives.

▼

Tracy   *The issue of women in combat really troubles me. I have a son who is 17 and a daughter who is 15. I don't want either of them in combat, but I've always known my son could be in combat. Would I argue that my son should be and my daughter shouldn't be? That's like saying I value her life more than his. I can't say that.*

RELATIONSHIPS AMONG GENDER, CULTURE, AND COMMUNICATION

When asked to discuss a particular aspect of nature, John Muir, founder of the Sierra Club, said he could not discuss any single part of the natural world in isolation. He noted that each part is "hitched to the universe," meaning that every part is connected to all other parts of nature. Likewise, sex, gender, sexual orientation, culture, and communication are interlinked, and they are hitched to the whole universe. Because this is so, we cannot study any one of them without understanding a good deal about the others.

SEX

Although many people use the terms *gender* and *sex* interchangeably, they have distinct meanings. **Sex** is a designation based on biology, whereas **gender** is socially constructed and expressed. In most cases, sex and gender go together; most men are primarily masculine, and most women are feminine. In some cases, however, a male expresses himself more femininely than most men, or a woman expresses herself in more masculine ways than most women. Sex and gender are inconsistent for transgendered individuals, who have the physical characteristics of one sex but identify strongly as the other sex. Because sex is the less complex concept, we'll explain it first, and then discuss gender and sexuality.

Society designates people as male or female based on external genitalia (penis and testes in males, clitoris and vagina in females) and internal sex organs (ovaries and uterus in females, prostate gland in males). Genitalia and other sex markers are determined by chromosomes. In most cases, human development is guided by 23 pairs of chromosomes, and only one pair determines sex. What we consider a person's sex is determined by chromosomes, usually a pair. The presence or absence of a Y chromosome determines whether a fetus will develop into what we recognize as male or female. Thus, people labeled female usually have XX sex chromosomes and people labeled male usually have XY sex chromosomes.

You might have noticed that I qualified discussion of genetic determination of sex by using the word *usually*. That's because there are occasional variations in the sex chromosomes. Some people have an XO chromosomal pair. In other cases, there are three, rather than the usual two, chromosomes that determine sex: XXX, XXY, or XYY (Blackless, Charuvastra, Derryek, Fausto-Sterling, Lauzanne, & Lee, 2000; Dreger, 2000). Occasionally, an individual has some XY cells and some XX cells (Gorman & Cole, 2004). All fetuses (and people) have cells with at least one

X chromosome because it carries genes essential to life (Jegalian & Lahn, 2001). Because males typically have only a single X chromosome, they are more vulnerable to a number of X-linked recessive conditions than are females, who have two X chromosomes and are unlikely to have an X-linked recessive condition on both. As long as there is a single Y chromosome, a fetus will develop into what we label male, although an XXY or XYY male may differ in some respects from an XY male.

Some children are born with some biological characteristics of each sex. Traditionally, people whose internal and external genitalia are inconsistent were called **hermaphrodites**, a term from Greek mythology. According to the myth, the god Hermes and the goddess Aphrodite had a son whom they named Hermaphroditos. When the young woman Salmacis saw Hermaphroditos, she immediately fell in love and begged the gods to join her with him so that they would never be apart. Granting Salmacis's wish, the gods joined them into a single body that was both male and female. Today, the term **intersexed** is preferred by people who have biological qualities of each sex.

Sexual development is also influenced by hormones. Every person starts life as an embryo, which has both müllerian ducts that develop into female reproductive systems and wolffian ducts that develop into male reproductive systems (Rosenberg, 2007). About seven or eight weeks into gestation, hormones influence sexual differentiation in the fetus. When pregnancy proceeds routinely, fetuses with a Y chromosome are bathed in androgens that ensure development of male sex organs, and fetuses without a Y chromosome receive fewer androgens, so female sex organs develop. In some cases, however, a genetically female fetus (XX) is exposed to excessive progesterone and may not develop the usual female genitalia. The opposite is also true: If a male fetus is deprived of progesterone during the critical period of sexual differentiation, his male genitalia may not develop, and he will appear physically female (Pinsky, Erickson, & Schimke, 1999).

The influence of hormones does not end at birth. They continue to affect our development by determining whether we will menstruate, how much body hair we will have and where it will grow, how much fat and muscle tissue we will develop, and so forth. Because male fetuses receive greater amounts of hormones than female fetuses, they become more sensitive than females to hormonal activity, especially during puberty (Tavris, 1992).

Biology *influences* how we develop, but it doesn't absolutely *determine* behavior, personality, and so on. Nor does biology stipulate the meaning that members of a culture assign to particular behaviors, traits, and roles—which ones are valued, which ones devalued. More important than whether biological differences exist is how we perceive and treat differences. This moves us into discussion of a second concept: gender.

GENDER

Gender is a considerably more complex concept than sex. There is nothing a person does to acquire her or his sex. It is a classification that society makes based on genetic and biological factors, and, for most people, it endures throughout their lives. Gender, however, is neither innate nor necessarily stable. It is defined by society and expressed by individuals as they interact with others and media in

EXPLORING GENDERED LIVES | **SOCIAL VIEWS OF INTERSEXUALITY**

For many years, infants who were born with ambiguous genitals routinely underwent "normalizing surgery" to reconstruct genitals to be more consistently male or female (Crouch, 1998; Lorber, 2001).

But is it possible that intersexed people don't need to be "fixed"? Recently, a number of scholars, scientists, doctors, and laypeople have advocated acceptance of intersexuality (Gorman & Cole, 2004; Kailey, 2006; Preves, 2004; Rosenberg, 2007; Sheridan, 2001). Adult intersexuals within the transgender movement challenge society's view that they are abnormal. They believe that being intersexed is not a disease or problem but just another form of human identity. In other words, maybe there are multiple—not just two—possibilities for sex and gender.

Actually, intersexuality—or, at least, the claim to that identity—is not a new phenomenon. Deborah Rudacille (2006) found records from 1629 describing Thomas Hall, who lived in the Jamestown settlement and claimed to be both a man and a woman. A number of indigenous groups, including several Native American tribes, historically recognized and celebrated "two spirit" people—those who were both male and female (Rudacille, 2006).

The Intersex Society of North America (ISNA) has three primary missions: (1) to affirm a positive identity for intersexed people; (2) to change social attitudes toward intersexuality; and (3) to stop "normalizing surgery."

Do you think intersexed individuals are a distinct sex?

Visit the website at **http://www.isna.org**. Another site that provides information on intersexed and transgendered people is **http://www.itpeople.org**.

their society. Further, gender changes over time. We are born male or female (sex), but we learn to act in masculine and/or feminine ways (gender). Gender varies across cultures, over time within a given culture, over the course of individuals' life spans, and in relation to the other gender. We'll elaborate these aspects of gender.

Gender, which is sometimes called gender role, involves outward expressions of what society considers masculine or feminine. We demonstrate gender role by how we speak, dress, style our hair, and so forth. A related concept is **gender identity**, which is a person's own identification as male or female. It is the personal perception of one's sex. For many people, sex, gender, gender identity, and sexual orientation are congruent and consistent with social expectations. However, for some people the four are not consistent. Later in this chapter and also in chapters that follow we'll look more closely at people who do not fit neatly into existing categories of sex, gender, and sexual orientation.

What gender means and how we express it depend on a society's values, beliefs, and preferred ways of organizing collective life (Holmes, 2008). Consider current meanings of masculinity and femininity in America. To be masculine is to be strong, ambitious, successful, rational, and emotionally controlled. Although these requirements are perhaps less rigid than they were in earlier eras, they remain largely intact. Those we regard as "real men" still don't cry in public, and "real men" are successful and powerful in their professional and public lives (Kimmel, 2000a, 2000b, 2005).

Femininity in our era is also relatively consistent with earlier views, although there is increasing latitude in what is considered appropriate for women. To be feminine is to be physically attractive, deferential, emotionally expressive, nurturing, and concerned with people and relationships (Spence & Buckner, 2000). Those who embody the cultural definition of femininity still don't allow themselves to outdo men (especially their partners), to disregard others' feelings, or to put their needs ahead of others'. "Real women" still look good, adore children, and care about homemaking.

Gender is learned. From infancy on, we are encouraged to learn how to embody the gender that society prescribes for us. Young girls are often cautioned, "Don't be selfish—share with others" and "Be careful—don't hurt yourself." They are praised for looking pretty, taking care of others (including dolls), and being nice. Young boys, in contrast, are more likely to be admonished, "Don't be a sissy," "Go after what you want," and "Don't cry." Usually, males are reinforced for strength, independence, and success, particularly in competitive arenas.

Bishetta   *I remember when I was very little, maybe 5 or so. My brother and I were playing outside in the garden, and Mom saw us. Both of us were coated with dirt—our clothes, our skin, everything.*

Mom came up to the edge of the garden and shouted, "Bishetta, you get out of that garden right now. Just look at you. Now, what do you think folks will think of a dirty little girl? You don't want people to think you're not a lady, do you?" She didn't say a word to my brother, who was just as dirty.

Although individuals learn gender and embody it, gender is not strictly personal. Rather, gender grows out of cultural ideas that stipulate the social *meaning* and *expectation* of each sex. Because our society's views of gender permeate public and private life, we tend to see them as normal, natural, and right. When society constantly represents women and men in particular ways, it is difficult to imagine that masculinity and femininity could be defined differently. But, as we will see later in this chapter, masculinity and femininity come in many forms across cultures and history.

The fact that the social meanings of gender are taught to us does not mean we are passive recipients of cultural meanings. We make choices to accept cultural prescriptions or to modify or reject them. Individuals who internalize and embody cultural prescriptions for gender reinforce existing social views. People who reject conventional prescriptions and step outside of social meanings for gender often provoke changes in cultural views. In the early part of the nineteenth century, for instance, many women challenged social views that women were not entitled to vote or pursue higher education. In defying their era's definition of women, these individuals transformed social views of women and the rights to which they are entitled.

Today, conventional views of both sex and gender are being challenged by people who define themselves as **transgendered,** trans or gender queer (Hirschfeld & Wolf, 2005; Shepard, 2008; Sloop, 2004, 2006). Many people who define themselves as gender queer reject the binary categories of male and female, masculine and feminine. They value the spaces in between, around, and beyond those two bipolar categories. In Chapter 2, we'll look more closely at queer theory, which gives insight into the entire range of gender identities and ways of performing gender.

Meanings of gender are also changed by personal communication. Role models, for instance, provide individuals with visible alternatives to traditional views. We also influence ideas about gender as we interact casually with friends. When one woman encourages another to be more assertive and to confront her supervisor about inequitable treatment, she may instigate change in what her friend sees as appropriate behavior for women. Similarly, when one man tells another that time with his family is a top priority, his friend has to rethink, and perhaps change, his own views of men's roles. When one person announces that she or he is transgendered, that person may make it easier for others whose sex or gender identity doesn't fit neatly into existing social categories. As these examples indicate, there is a reciprocal relationship between communication and cultural views of gender: Each influences the other to continuously uphold or remake the meanings of masculinity and femininity.

Bob   *What I always thought was unfair in my family was the way my folks responded to failures my sisters and I had. Like once my sister Maryellen tried out for cheerleader, and she wasn't picked. So she was crying and upset, and Mom was telling her that it was okay and that she was a good person, and everyone knew that and that winning wasn't everything. And when Dad came home he said the same things—telling her she was okay even if she wasn't picked. But when I didn't make the junior varsity football team, Dad went bonkers! He asked me what had gone wrong. I told him nothing, that other guys were just better than I had been. But he'd have none of that. He told me I couldn't give up and had to work harder, and he expected me to make the team next season. He even offered to hire a coach for me. It just wasn't okay for me not to succeed.*

A good example of the way we remake the meaning of gender is the concept of androgyny. In the 1970s, researchers coined the word *androgyny* by combining the Greek word *aner* or *andros,* which means "man," and the Greek word *gyne,* which means "woman." As you may know, androgynous individuals embody qualities that Western culture considers both feminine and masculine. For example, androgynous women and men are both nurturing and assertive, both strong and sensitive. Many of us don't want to be restricted to the social prescriptions of a single gender, and we cultivate both masculine and feminine qualities in ourselves. As Miguel points out in his commentary, there is value in the full range of human qualities—those the culture labels feminine and those it labels masculine.

To realize the arbitrariness of the meanings of gender, we need only consider varying ways different cultures define masculinity and femininity. Many years ago, anthropologist Margaret Mead (1935/1968) reported three distinct gender patterns in the New Guinea societies she studied. Among Arapesh people, both women and men conformed closely to what we consider feminine behavior. Both were passive, peaceful, and deferential, and both nurtured others, especially young children. The Mundugumor tribe socialized both women and men to be aggressive, independent, and competitive. Mothers were not nurturing and spent very little time with newborn babies, weaning them early instead. Within the Tchambuli society, genders were the reverse of current ones in America: Women were domineering and sexually aggressive, whereas men were considered delicate and taught to wear decorative clothes and curl their hair so they would be attractive to women.

▼

Miguel   *I like to be strong and to stand up for myself and what I think, but I would not want to be only that. I am also sensitive to other people and how they feel. There are times to be hard and times to be softer; there are times to be strong and times to let others be strong.*

Body ideals for women provide another example of the constructed and arbitrary character of gender. Currently, Western culture regards thinness as desirable in women, particularly Caucasian women. Yet in the 1950s, fuller-figured women such as Marilyn Monroe exemplified femininity and sexiness. Even today, some cultures regard heavier women as particularly beautiful and desirable. For example, in the Islamic Republic of Mauritania (sub-Saharan Africa), young girls are often overfed—even force-fed in some cases—so that they become obese and thereby serve as a living symbol of their family's wealth and status (LaFraniere, 2007).

Some cultures view a person's gender as changeable, so someone born male may choose to live and be regarded as female and vice versa. In other societies, notably some Native American groups, more than two genders are recognized and celebrated (Brown, 1997; Nanda, 2004). Individuals who have qualities of multiple genders are highly esteemed. In the United States, gender varies across racial-ethnic groups. In general, African-American women are more assertive than European-American women, and African-American men tend to be more communal than white men (Rothenberg, Schafhausen, & Schneider, 2000; V. Smith, 1998).

Even within a single culture or social group, the meaning of gender varies over time. Prior to the Industrial Revolution, family and work were intertwined for most people. Thus, men and women worked together to raise crops or run businesses, and both were involved in homemaking and child rearing. Affection and expressiveness were considered normal in men as well as in women (Degler, 1980); industry and strength were attractive in women just as they were in men (Cancian, 1989; Douglas, 1977). The Industrial Revolution gave rise to factories and to paid labor outside the home as a primary way of making a living. With this came a division of life into separate spheres of work and home. As men took jobs outside the home, women increasingly assumed responsibility for family life. Consequently, femininity was redefined as nurturing, depending on men for income, focusing on relationships, and making a good home. Masculinity was also redefined as being emotionally reserved, ambitious, successful at work, and—especially—earning a good income (Cancian, 1989; Risman & Godwin, 2001). In her commentary, Emma, a 58-year-old part-time student, reflects on changes in how women see themselves.

Emma   *In my day, women were a lot different than they are today. We were quieter, and we put other people ahead of ourselves. We knew our place, and we didn't try to be equal with men. Today's women are very different. Some of the younger women in my classes put their careers ahead of marriage, some don't want children, and many think they should be as much the head of a family as the man. Sometimes, I feel they are all wrong in what they want and how they are, but I have to admit that a part of me envies them the options and opportunities I never had.*

The meaning of gender also changes over the course of an individual's lifetime (Kimmel, 2003). Being masculine at 10 may mean being good at soccer or baseball. At 28, however, most men place high priority on a good job as a measure of their masculinity. Similarly, what a 10-year-old girl considers feminine may be bows in her hair, but a 28-year-old woman may define femininity as bearing and raising children. Such changes are not just because we age personally, but also because the social context in which we live changes over time, and that affects our personal sense of gender identity.

Finally, gender is a relational concept because femininity and masculinity make sense in relation to each other. Our society defines femininity in contrast to masculinity and masculinity as a counterpoint to femininity. As meanings of one gender change, so do meanings of the other. For instance, when social views of masculinity stressed physical strength and endurance, femininity was defined by physical weakness and dependence on men's strengths. Perhaps you've read in older novels about women's fainting spells—the "vapors"—and the smelling salts they kept nearby to revive themselves. With the Industrial Revolution, sheer physical strength was no

longer as important to survival, so masculinity was redefined as intellectual ability and success in earning income. Simultaneously, many women's business acumen disappeared. In part, this happened because society relied less on physical strength to distinguish between women and men.

Let's summarize this extended discussion of gender. We have noted that gender is the collection of social, symbolic meanings that a society constructs and confers on biological sex. These meanings are communicated through structures and practices that pervade our daily existence, creating the illusion that there are two and only two sexes, two and only two genders, and the gender prescriptions society embraces are the natural, normal ways for women and men to be. Yet, we've also seen that the meaning of gender varies across cultures and over time in particular cultures, and how we conceive of each gender is related to our views of the other. This reminds us that, even though what our society defines as feminine and masculine may seem natural to us, there is nothing necessary or innate about any particular meaning for gender. By extension, this insight suggests that we have more choice than we sometimes realize in how we view and enact gender in our lives.

BEYOND SEX AND GENDER

Sex and gender are not the only ways to define people. We also define ourselves and others in terms of our sexual orientation and whether we are transgendered or transsexual or gender nonconforming. The United States classifies people by sex (male or female), gender (masculine or feminine) and sexual orientation (heterosexual, gay, lesbian, bisexual, or bicurious). Further, our society assumes connections between these categories such that male, masculine, and heterosexual are linked and female, feminine, and heterosexual are linked. Most people match social expectations for links among sex, gender identity, gender, and sexual orientation. For example, most anatomical males identify as male, act in masculine ways, and are sexually and emotionally attracted to females.

Sexual orientation refers to a person's preferences for romantic and sexual partners. People who have heterosexual orientations are attracted to members of the other sex while gays and lesbians are attracted to members of their own sex. Bisexuals are attracted to members of both sexes. Western society links sex, gender, and sexual orientation so that someone who is male is expected to be masculine and attracted to females whereas someone who is female is expected to be feminine and attracted to males. In our society, it's assumed that our biological sex correlates naturally with our socially prescribed gender and with heterosexuality (Glover & Kaplan, 2009; Jagger, 2008).

The term **cis** challenges the taken-for-granted normalcy of consistency among sex, gender, and gender identity. Cis functions as a prefix—cisgendered—that designates a person who fits conventional categories. For instance a biological woman who identifies as female and feminine and who is attracted to men would be labeled cisgendered. "Trans" means "across of," whereas "cis" means "on the same side of." So people who cross from the gender identity assigned at birth to another gender identity are trans, and people who stay on the same side of the gender identity assigned at birth are cis. The use of this term disrupts the assumption that saying "woman" connotes someone who is female and heterosexual and who identifies as female and feminine. It calls attention to the category just as terms such as *gay man* call attention to that category.

Yet the three don't always go together in the natural, effortless way that society assumes. Think of these departures from the normalized pattern in our culture:

- A man who has a feminine gender identity
- A woman who has a masculine gender identity
- A man who behaves in feminine ways and is sexually attracted to women
- A woman who behaves in masculine ways and is sexually attracted to men
- A man who behaves in masculine ways and is sexually attracted to men
- A woman who behaves in feminine ways and is attracted to other women

Other cultures' views of sexual orientation challenge views prevalent in the United States. For example, the Sambia in Melanesia consider same-sex sexual activity between males to be a normal part of developing an adult masculine identity (Herdt, 1997). In ancient Greece, older men with status often took young men as lovers; this was considered the ideal, the purest love relationship. Older men who had male lovers were regarded as ideally masculine. In Victorian society, friendships between married women often included sexual intimacies that today we might consider lesbian, but that, at the time, were seen as a common part of women's friendships (Marcus, 2007).

Changing views of gender as well as sex are also evident in the increasing recognition of individuals who don't fit conventional definitions of male or female, masculine or feminine. We've already noted that intersexed individuals have biological characteristics of both males and females. In addition, we need to think about transgendered and transsexed individuals. Although trans or transgender is sometimes used to refer to all gender nonconforming people, some researchers distinguished between transgender and transsexual. Transgendered is the term for individuals who feel that their biologically assigned sex is inconsistent with their true sexual identity—that they are women, despite having male bodies, or men, despite having female bodies (Hines, 2006; Howey, 2002; Looy & Bouma, 2005; Sheridan, 2001; Stryker, 1997, 1998; Tyre & Scelfo, 2006). Transgendered people often adopt the dress and behaviors of the gender with which they identify. In the movie *Boys Don't Cry*, Hilary Swank gave a compelling portrayal of a transgendered person. More recently, Isis, a transgendered person was selected for competition on the 2008 season of *America's Next Top Model*.

In general, **transsexual** refers to individuals who have had surgery and/or hormonal treatments to make their bodies more closely match the sex with which they identify (Devor, 1997). Researchers estimate that at least 1 in every 2,500 adult males in the United States has had sexual reassignment surgery (SRS) and has become a postoperative woman (Olyslager & Conway, 2007).

After surgery, transsexuals may describe themselves as *post-transition males to females* (MTF) or *post-transition females to males* (FTM). For example, Dr. Wally Bacon left his campus in Nebraska in the spring of 2005 and returned in the fall of 2005 as Dr. Meredith Bacon. At the age of 59, Dr. Bacon decided to make the change. Since making that decision, she has had a number of surgeries so that her body conforms to how she understands herself (Wilson, 2005c).

Sean   *In high school my closest friend was Megean. Our junior year she tried to kill herself and nobody knew why because she was pretty and popular and smart—the "girl who had everything." Later she told me that she had never felt she was female, that she'd always felt she was a guy and just didn't think she could keep going if she had to live as a girl. If I hadn't been so close to Megean, I would have found it totally weird, but we were close—still are, in fact, although now he's Mark—and what I mainly felt was sad that somebody I loved was so unhappy. He's a much happier person now that he's Mark.*

Most transsexuals are attracted to the same sex before and after transition. For example, people who are attracted to women prior to transition continue to be attracted to women after transition, and people who are attracted to men prior to transition continue to be attracted to men after transition. In other words, sexual orientation does not change just because a person transitions from one sex to another. Some transsexuals stay in their marriages or committed relationships after transitioning. An example of this can be found in Helen Boyd's 2007 book, *Not the Man I Married: My Life with a Transgender Husband.*

The commentary by Christine, a post-transition MTF with whom I've corresponded, gives insight into how it felt for her to be accepted as the person she always felt she was. Christine's commentary appears on this page.

Another MTF transsexual is Deirdre (formerly Donald) McCloskey, a professor of economics. According to her, surgery and hormones changed her sex, but she had to learn gender, had to learn to be feminine. She studied all of the small actions—gestures, facial expressions, postures—that women use and practiced them until they were second nature to her. Reflecting on this, McCloskey (1999) wrote that gender is "an accretion of learned habits, learned so well that they feel like external conditions, merely the way things are. It is a shell made by the snail and then confining it" (pp. 83–84). Because they have experience in being and being seen as more than one sex, transsexuals often gain keen insight into gendered dynamics in cultural life. For example, Ben Barres (2006), a FTM transgendered person wryly commented, "By far the main difference that I have noticed is that people who don't know I am transgendered (female to male) treat me with much more respect. I can even complete a whole sentence without being interrupted by a man" (p. 135).

Christine   *Never did I appreciate how quickly life-changing living as an integrated, authentic self would be. Never in my wildest dreams did I believe that "genetic" women ("gg's"—genetic girls—as the community calls them) would so quickly embrace me, invite me into their private world, and want to help me find my place among them. Being accepted as the girl I am has been my dream from age four or five. In some ways, I'm just now living as a teenager, emotionally and socially.*

EXPLORING GENDERED LIVES | **TRANSGENDER ACTIVISM ON CAMPUS**

If Luke Woodward, a student at Brown University, had written a paper entitled "What I Did Last Summer" in 2003, he would have written that he had surgery to minimize the breasts that were incompatible with his self-identity as a man. Meanwhile, Paige Kruza, who attends Wesleyan University, is biologically female but does not identify as female. Paige prefers that people use transgender pronouns such as ze instead of *he* or *she* to refer to Paige (Bernstein, 2004). And Mykell Miller, a student at Northwestern who is biologically female but identifies as male, claims that not all men were born with male bodies (Rosenberg, 2007).

Recognition of transgendered and transsexed people calls for some changes. In 2003, students at Smith College voted to eliminate female pronouns in the student constitution because some students who were biologically female did not identify as female. At Wesleyan, members of what had been the Women's Rugby team voted to delete the word *Women's* from its name so that students who are biologically female but who do not identify as female could be comfortable wearing the team sweatshirts. Wesleyan's student health services has replaced the boxes "M" and "F" that students once checked with the request, "Describe your gender identity history" (Bernstein, 2004). Major companies such as IBM provide transgender medical care, and 25% of the Fortune 500 companies have policies protecting transgendered employees from discrimination (Rosenberg, 2007).

To what extent does your campus recognize and accommodate transgender students?

In 2008 Thomas Beatie attracted a lot of attention when he gave birth to a girl; he later gave birth to a second child. You read the sentence right: *He gave* birth and he did so through vaginal delivery. How can this be? Thomas is a transgender FTM who is legally male and legally married to a woman named Nancy. Thomas's sex reassignment surgery was limited to chest reconstruction and testosterone therapy, but he kept his reproductive organs. Nancy had had a hysterectomy, so when she and Thomas wanted a child, they decided that Thomas would carry it (Beatie, 2008). Thomas later carried and gave birth to a second child. In Thomas' case we have a person whom the law defines as male relying on female sex organs to carry and deliver a baby. People like Thomas (he's not the first FTM to give birth) make it clear that the links between sex, gender, and sexual orientation are not always clear, stable, or absolute.

Before leaving this discussion, we need to consider one other aspect of gender and sexual identity. Cross-dressers, or transvestites, enjoy wearing clothing of the other sex. Transvestites may wear just one or two articles of clothing associated with the other sex or may dress completely, from underwear to outerwear and accessories, in the other sex's clothing. Cross-dressers act from varying motivations. Some wear the other sex's clothes to express gender identities inconsistent with their sex. Some find the novelty of cross-dressing fun or pleasurable; some find it sexually arousing to wear clothes generally worn by the other sex. The great majority of cross-dressers are

AP Photo/Amie Higbee

Jennifer Finney Boylan was born James Richard Boylan but later had surgery to become female.

biological, heterosexual males, who are sexually attracted to women. In their case, gender role is not consistent with social expectations for heterosexual males.

Josh   *I don't think there really is a category of transpeople. To me, it seems like if someone who is male is attracted to other men, he's gay. When men say they are trans and are really female in their identity and they then get together with other men, maybe they're just trying to avoid being seen as gay.*

Sloan   *It's great that some people finally realize there are more than two sexes and two genders. Ever since I came to college, I found lots of people like me who don't identify as exactly male or female and not as straight or gay. There is so much gray area in between the dualities society has imposed.*

Transgendered, transsexed, and intersexed people challenge the idea that sex and gender are dualities—that is, that male and female, masculine and feminine are opposite, stable, and the only two possibilities (Namaste, 2000). Transpeople also disrupt society's assumption that sex, gender, and sexual orientation correlate in consistent and natural ways. Unlike what Josh says in his commentary, not all transsexuals are attracted to people of their own biological sex. A FTM person may be attracted to men or women; a MTF may be attracted to women or men. I know a MTF person who is attracted to women and, because she sees herself as a woman, considers herself lesbian. I also know a MTF who is attracted to men and, because she identifies as female, considers herself heterosexual. These examples show that sex doesn't necessarily predict gender, and sex and gender don't necessarily predict sexual orientation. At the same time, the presumptive status of assuming sex determines gender—and that together they determine sexual orientation—is reinforced by the fact that most people are heterosexuals whose sex and gender are consistent by social standards.

CULTURE

A **culture** is made up of structures (also called institutions) and practices (also called activities) that reflect and uphold a particular social order. They do this by defining certain social groups, values, expectations, meanings, and patterns of behavior as natural and good and others as unnatural, bad, or wrong. Because gender is central to cultural life, society's views of gender are reflected in and promoted by a range of social structures and practices.

One of the primary practices that structures society is communication. We are surrounded by communication that announces social views of gender and seeks to persuade us that these are natural, correct ways for men and women to be and to behave. We open a magazine and see a beautiful, thin woman waiting on a man who looks successful and in charge; we turn on our television and watch a prime time program in which a husband tells of a big business triumph while his wife prepares dinner; the commercials interspersed in the show depict women cleaning toilet bowls and kitchen floors and men going for the gusto after a pickup basketball game; we meet with a group of people on a volunteer project, and one of the men assumes leadership; we check out a new video game and don't even notice that it, like many videogames, includes women characters who are prostitutes and are supposed to be abused by game players; a working woman receives maternity leave, but her husband cannot get paternity leave. Each of these practices communicates our society's views of gender.

Consider additional examples of cultural practices that uphold Western views of gender. Although no longer universal, the custom whereby a woman gives up her name and takes her husband's on marriage still prevails (Suter, 2004). It carries the message that a woman is defined by her relationship to a man but a man is not equivalently defined by his relationship with a woman. Within families, too, numerous practices reinforce social views of gender. Parents routinely allow sons greater freedom and behavioral latitude than they grant daughters, a practice that encourages males to be more independent. Daughters, much more than sons, are taught to do housework and care for younger siblings, thus reinforcing the idea that women are supposed to be concerned with home and family.

Now think about social structures, or institutions, that uphold gender ideology. One institution is the judicial system. Until recently, a wife could not sue her husband for rape, because intercourse was regarded as a husband's right. Men's parental rights are abridged by judicial views of women as the primary caretakers of children, views that are expressed in the presumption that women should have custody of children if divorce occurs. Thus, it is difficult for a father to gain child custody even when he might be the better parent or might be in a better situation to raise children.

In many respects Western culture, as well as many other cultures, is **patriarchal**. The word patriarchy means "rule by the fathers." In a patriarchal culture, the ideology, structures, and practices were created by men. Because America was defined by men, historically it reflected the perspectives and priorities of men more than those of women. For example, it would be consistent with men's interests to consider women property, which was the case early in America's life. Similarly, from men's point of view laws against marital rape would not be desirable. Today, some of the patriarchal tendencies and practices of American culture have been tempered.

▼

Dympna   *In 1974, I traveled to New York for my college education.... I'm a member of the Ibo tribe of Nigeria, and although I've lived in the United States most of my adult life, my consciousness remains fixed on the time and place of my upbringing.... When I left Nigeria at 18, I had no doubts about who and what I was. I was a woman. I was only a woman.... My role was to be a great asset to my husband.... I was, after all, raised within the context of child brides, polygamy, clitorectomies and arranged marriages.... I've struggled daily with how best to raise my daughter. Every decision involving Delia is a tug of war between Ibo and American traditions (Ugwu-Oju, 2000).*

Through their structures and practices, especially communication practices, societies create and sustain perspectives on what is normal and right for women and men. Because messages that reinforce cultural views of gender pervade our daily lives, most of us seldom pause to reflect on whether they are as natural as they have been made to seem. Like the air we breathe, they so continuously surround us that we tend to take them for granted and don't question them. Learning to reflect on cultural prescriptions for gender (and other matters) empowers you as an individual. It increases your freedom to choose your own courses of action and identity by enlarging your awareness of the arbitrary and not always desirable nature of cultural expectations.

COMMUNICATION

The fourth key term we will discuss is **communication**. Communication is a dynamic, systemic process in which two levels of meanings are created and reflected in human interaction with symbols. To understand this rather complicated definition, we will focus on one part of it at a time.

Communication Is a Dynamic Process   Communication is dynamic, which means that it continually changes, evolves, and moves on. Because communication is a process, communicative interactions have no definite beginnings or endings. Suppose a friend drops by while you're reading this chapter and asks what you are doing. "Reading about gender, communication, and culture," you reply. Your friend then says, "Oh, you mean about how men and women talk differently." You respond, "Not exactly—you see, gender isn't really about males and females; it's about the meaning our culture attaches to each sex." Did this interaction begin with your friend's question, or with your instructor's assignment of the reading, or with other experiences that led you to enroll in this class?

Think also about when this communication ends. Does it stop when your friend leaves? Maybe not. What the two of you talk about may influence what you think and do later, so the influence or effect of your communication continues beyond the immediate encounter. All communication is like this: It is an ongoing, dynamic process without clear beginnings and endings.

Communication Is Systemic   Communication occurs in particular situations or systems that influence what and how we interact and what meanings we attach to messages. For example, suppose you observe the following interaction. In an office building where you are waiting for an appointment, you see a middle-aged man walk to the secretary's desk, put his arm around her shoulders and say, "You really do drive me crazy when you wear that outfit." She doesn't look up from her work but responds, "You're crazy, period. It has nothing to do with what I'm wearing." How would you interpret this interaction? Is it an instance of sexual harassment? Are they coworkers who are comfortable joking about sexuality with each other? Is he perhaps not an employee but her friend or romantic partner? The only reasonable conclusion to draw is that we cannot tell what is happening or what it means to the communicators, because we don't understand the systems within which this interaction takes place.

When we say communication is systemic, we mean more than that its contexts affect meaning. Recall John Muir's statement that each part of nature is "hitched to the universe." As a system, all aspects of communication are interlinked, so they interact with one another. Who is speaking affects what is said and what it means. In the foregoing example, the secretary would probably attach different meanings to the message "You really do drive me crazy when you wear that outfit" if it was said by a friend or by a coworker with a reputation for coming on to women. Communication is also influenced by how we feel: When you feel tired or irritable, you may take offense at a comment that ordinarily wouldn't bother you. The time of day and place of interaction may also affect what is communicated and how our words and actions are interpreted.

The largest system affecting communication is our culture, the context within which all our interactions take place. As we saw in our discussion of culture, a society's view and treatment of men and women changes over time. Thirty years ago, it would have been rude for a man not to open a car door for his date and not to stand when a woman entered a room. Today, most people would not regard either as rude. Just a few decades ago, sexual harassment did not have a name and was not considered cause for grievance or legal action. Today, however, laws and policies prohibit sexual harassment, and employees may bring charges against harassers. The same behavior now means something different from what it meant then. The systems within which communication occurs interact; each part affects all others.

Communication Has Two Levels of Meaning   Perhaps you noticed that our definition of communication referred to meanings, not just to a single meaning. That's because communication has two levels of meaning. Years ago, a group of clinical psychologists (Watzlawick, Beavin, & Jackson, 1967) noted that all communication has both a content level and a relationship level of meaning.

The **content level of meaning** is its literal meaning. If Ellen says to her partner, Ed, "You can't buy that car," the content level of the statement is that he can't buy a car. The content level also indicates a response that is expected to follow from a message. In this case, both Ellen and Ed may assume he will not buy the car. The content level of meaning involves a literal message and implies the appropriate response.

The **relationship level of meaning** is less obvious. It defines the relationship between communicators by indicating each person's identity and the communicators' relationship to each other. In our example, Ellen seems to be defining the relationship as one in which she calls the shots. The relationship level of meaning in her comment also suggests that she regards it as her prerogative to tell Ed what he can and cannot buy. Ed could respond by saying, "I certainly can buy it, and I will." Here, the content level is again clear. Ed is stating that he will buy the car. On the relationship level, however, he may be arguing about the power balance between himself and Ellen. He is refusing to accept her control. If she says, "Okay, then buy it," she accepts Ed's claim that she is not running the relationship or him. She affirms his right to buy what he wants and his prerogative to tell her how he'll spend money.

The relationship level of meaning is the primary level that reflects and influences how people feel about each other. It provides a context for the content level of meaning because it tells us how to interpret the literal message. Perhaps, when Ed says he is going to buy the car, he uses a teasing tone and grins, in which case the relationship level of meaning is that Ellen should not take the content level seriously, because he's joking. If, however, he makes his statement in a belligerent voice and glares at her, the relationship level of meaning is that he does mean the content level. Relationship levels of meaning tell us how to interpret content meaning and how communicators see themselves in relation to each other.

Relationship levels of meaning are particularly important when we try to understand gendered patterns of communication. A good example is interruption. Elyse is telling Jed how her day went. He interrupts and says, "Let's head out to the soccer game." The content level of meaning of this interruption is simply what

Jed said. The more important level of meaning is usually the relationship level, which in this case declares that Jed has the right to interrupt Elyse, dismiss her topic, and initiate his own. If he interrupts, and she does not protest, they agree to let him control the conversation. If she does object, then the two may wind up in extended negotiations over how to define their relationship. In communication, all messages have two levels of meaning.

Meanings Are Created through Human Interaction with Symbols   This premise highlights two final, important understandings about communication. First, it calls our attention to the fact that humans are symbol-using creatures. Symbols are abstract, arbitrary, and often ambiguous ways of representing phenomena. For example, ♀ and ♂ are symbols for *female* and *male,* respectively. Words are also symbols, so *woman* and *man* are symbols for certain physical beings. We rely on symbols to communicate and create meanings in our lives.

Because human communication is symbolic, we have to think about it to figure out what it means. Rather than reacting in automatic or instinctive ways to communication, we usually reflect on what was said and what it means before we respond. To be interpreted, symbols require thought. Symbols can also be ambiguous; that is, their meanings may not be clear. Recall our earlier example, in which a man tells a secretary, "You really do drive me crazy when you wear that outfit." To interpret what he said, she has to think about their relationship, what she knows about him, and what has occurred in their prior interactions. After thinking about all these things, she'll decide whether his comment was a joke in poor taste, a compliment, sexual harassment, or a flirtatious show of interest from someone with whom she is romantically involved. Sometimes, people interpret what we say in a manner other than what we intended because symbols are so abstract and ambiguous that more than one meaning is plausible.

The premise that we create meanings through interaction with symbols implies that the significance of communication is not in words themselves. Instead, in the process of communicating with one another, humans create meanings. Our verbal and nonverbal behaviors are not simply neutral expressions of thoughts; they imply values and judgments. How we express ourselves influences how we and others feel about what we communicate. The statement "You're a feminist" can create different impressions, depending on whether the vocal inflection suggests interest, shock, disdain, or admiration. Calling a woman "aggressive" conjures up an impression that is different from the impression created by calling her "assertive." A man who interacts lovingly with a child could be described as either "nurturing" or "soft," and the two descriptions suggest different meanings. People differ in their interpretations of identical messages. The meaning of communication depends on much more than verbal and nonverbal behavior; it arises from human interpretation.

The fact that symbols are abstract, ambiguous, and arbitrary makes it impossible to think of meaning as inherent in symbols themselves. Each of us constructs an interpretation of communication by drawing on our past experiences, our knowledge of the people with whom we are interacting, and other factors in a communication system that influence our interpretations. Because the meaning we attach to communication is rooted in our own perspectives, we are inclined to project our own thoughts, feelings, desires, and so forth onto others' messages.

Differences in interpretation are the source of much misunderstanding between people. However, you can become a more effective communicator if you keep in mind that people's perceptions and interpretations differ. Reminding yourself of this should prompt you to ask for clarification of another person's meaning rather than assuming your interpretation is correct. Similarly, we should check with others more often than we do to see how they are interpreting our verbal and non-verbal communication.

SUMMARY

In this chapter, we began to explore the nature of communication, gender, and culture. Because each of us is a gendered being, it's important to understand what gender means and how we can be more effective in our interactions within a culture that is also gendered. The primary focus of this chapter was to introduce four central concepts: sex, gender, culture, and communication.

Sex is a biological classification, whereas gender is a social, symbolic system through which a culture attaches significance to biological sex. Gender is something individuals learn; yet, because it is constructed by cultures, it is more than an individual quality. It is a whole system of social meanings that specify what is associated with men and women in a given society at a particular time. We also noted that meanings of gender vary over time and across cultures. Finally, we found that gender is relational, because femininity and masculinity gain much of their meaning from the fact that our society juxtaposes them.

The third key concept, culture, refers to structures and practices, particularly communicative ones, through which a society announces and sustains its values. Gender is a significant issue in our culture, so abundant structures and practices serve to reinforce our society's prescriptions for women's and men's identities and behaviors. To understand what gender means and how meanings of gender change, we must explore the cultural values, institutions, and activities through which the meanings of gender are expressed and promoted.

Finally, we defined communication as a dynamic, systemic process in which meanings are created and reflected in human interaction with symbols. In examining the dimensions of this definition, we emphasized that communication is a symbolic activity, which implies that it requires reflection, and that meanings are variable and constructed rather than inherent in symbols themselves. We also saw that communication can be understood only within its contexts, including the especially important system of culture.

This chapter provides a foundation. In the following chapters, we will examine ways in which individuals learn gender, the differences and similarities in feminine and masculine communication, and a range of ways in which gendered communication and identities punctuate our lives.

Key Terms

The terms following are defined in this chapter on the pages indicated, as well as in alphabetical order in the book's glossary, which begins on page 325. The text's companion website (**http://www.cengage.com/communication/wood/genderedlives10e**)

also provides interactive flash cards and crossword puzzles to help you learn these terms and the concepts they represent.

androgyny 23	intersexed 20
cis 26	mixed research methods 15
communication 33	patriarchal 32
content level of meaning 34	qualitative research methods 14
critical research methods 15	quantitative research methods 14
culture 31	relationship level of meaning 34
essentializing 18	sex 19
gender 19	sexual orientation 26
gender identity 21	transgendered 23
hermaphrodites 20	transsexual 27

Gender Online

1. Wikipedia offers a summary of various research on different cultural norms and personal choices for married names: **http://en.wikipedia.org/wiki/Married_and_maiden_names**. Be sure to check out the "references" section for the works cited, which include several informative articles.
2. Online search terms: "cross-sex communication," "genderqueer," "androgyny."

Reflection and Discussion

1. If you have traveled to other countries and experienced other cultures, what differences in views of women and men and masculinity and femininity did you notice between those cultures and your own?
2. How comfortable are you with current views of masculinity and femininity? Which ones, if any, do you find restrictive? Are you doing anything to change them in society's view or to resist them in how you personally embody gender?
3. Talk with your parents and grandparents or with people of their generations. Ask them what it meant to be a woman or man when they were your age. Analyze how their views differ from yours.
4. Conduct a survey on your campus. Ask 10 people whom you know at least casually:

    • Should the campus provide separate bathrooms for people who are transsexed or transgendered? (Be prepared to define these terms.)
    • Why do you think separate bathrooms should or should not be provided?

    Combine the results of your survey with those of classmates' surveys. What do the data tell you about attitudes on your campus?
5. Scott Turner Schofield is a critically praised transgender performance artist who defines himself as a "gender renegade" (Cooper, 2006). His theater pieces

include *Debutante Balls, The Southern Gents Tour,* and *Underground Transit.* Check with nonprint resources on your campus to see if you can get a copy of any of Scott Turner Schofield's performances. Also visit his website: **http://www.undergroundtransit.com/**

Recommended Resources

1. *Boys Don't Cry.* (1999). Directed by Kimberly Pierce. Distributed by Fox. Even if you have seen this film before, watch it again after reading this chapter. The film offers a stunning portrait of how social linkage of sex, gender, and sexual orientation can oppress individuals.
2. Diane Levin and and Jean Kilbourne (2008). *So Sexy, So Soon.* New York: Ballantine. This book shows how media teach children about sex, gender, and sexuality. The authors' careful analysis of media gives insight into how gender is carefully and systematically constructed.

There is nothing so practical as good theory.
Kurt Lewin

THEORETICAL APPROACHES TO GENDER DEVELOPMENT

CHAPTER **2**

Knowledge Challenge:

1. Are other species exclusively heterosexual?
2. When do most children understand that they are male or female and that their sex is not going to change?
3. Does a person "have" gender or "do" gender?

A student of mine named Jenna recently told me that she didn't like to study theory because it had nothing to do with "real life." But the premier social scientist Kurt Lewin disagreed when he insisted, "There is nothing so practical as good theory." What he meant, and what I tried to explain to Jenna, is that theories are very practical. They help us understand, explain, and predict what happens in our real lives and in the world around us.

THEORETICAL APPROACHES TO GENDER

A **theory** is a way to describe, explain, and predict relationships among phenomena. Each of us uses theories to make sense of our lives, to guide our attitudes and actions, and to predict others' behavior. Although we're not always aware of the theories we hold, they still shape how we act, how we expect others to act, and how we explain, or make sense of, what we and others say and do. In this sense, theories are very practical.

Among the theories that each of us has are the ones we use to make sense of men's and women's behaviors. For instance, assume that you know Kevin and Carlene, who are 11-year-old twins. In many ways, they are alike; yet they also differ.

Carlene is more articulate than Kevin, and she tends to think in more creative and integrative ways. Kevin is better at solving analytic problems, especially ones that involve spatial relations. He also has better-developed muscles, although he and Carlene spend equal time in athletics. How you explain the differences between these twins reflects your implicit theory of gender.

If you subscribe to biological theory, you might note that different cognitive strengths result from differential hemispheric specialization in male and female brains. You might also reason that Kevin's greater muscle development results from testosterone, which encourages musculature, whereas estrogen programs the body to develop less muscle and more fat and soft tissue.

Then again, perhaps you know that researchers have shown that teachers and parents tend to encourage analytic problem solving in boys and creative thinking in girls. Given this, you might draw on social learning theory to explain the twins' different cognitive skills as the result of learning and reinforcement. The same explanation might be advanced for the disparity in their muscle development, because you could reason that Kevin is probably more encouraged and more rewarded than Carlene for engaging in activities that build muscles.

A third way to explain differences is to point out the likelihood that each twin identifies with same-sex role models. If so, we would predict that Kevin imitates the qualities—physical strength and working with spatial relations—of men he chooses as models. Identifying with women, Carlene is more likely to emulate feminine models. These are only three of many ways we could explain the differences between Kevin and Carlene. Each represents a particular theoretical viewpoint—a way of understanding the relationship between gender and people's behaviors and abilities. None of the three is the right theory or even more right than the others. Each viewpoint makes sense, yet each is limited, which suggests that a full understanding of gender relies on multiple theories.

It's important to realize that theories do more than provide explanations. Our theories about sex and gender affect our thoughts and behaviors. How we explain the twins' differences is likely to influence how we treat them. If you think the differences in muscle development are determined by biology, then you probably would not push Carlene to work out more in order to develop muscles. On the other hand, if you think differences result from learning and role models, you might encourage Carlene to build her muscles and Kevin to think more creatively. If you believe that women have a natural maternal instinct (biological theory), then you might not expect fathers to be equal caretakers. A different set of expectations would arise if you theorize that women are taught to nurture and that men too can learn this. If you think males are more aggressive because of their higher levels of testosterone, then you are apt to tolerate rowdiness in boys and men and to discourage it in girls and women.

The theories you hold consciously or unconsciously influence how you see yourself as a woman or man, what you expect of women and men generally, and what possibilities you see as open to each sex. Because the theories we hold do affect our identities, perceptions, behaviors, and expectations, it's important to examine them carefully. That is the goal of this chapter.

There are many theories about how we develop gendered identities. Because each theory attempts to explain only selected dimensions of gender, different theories are not necessarily competing to be the definitive explanation of how gender develops and what it means. Instead, theories often complement one another by sharpening our awareness of multiple ways in which communication, sex, gender, and culture interact. Thus, as we discuss alternative theories, you shouldn't try to pick the best one or the right one. Instead, pay attention to the limitations and insights of each theory so that you can appreciate the strengths of each one and realize how they fit together to provide a richly layered account of how we become gendered and the critical role of communication in that process.

Theories of gender development and behavior can be classified into four broad types: (1) biological, (2) interpersonal, (3) cultural, and (4) critical. Within these broad categories, a number of specific theories offer insight into factors and processes that contribute to the gendering of individuals. As we discuss these, you will probably notice both how they differ in focus and how they work together to create an overall understanding of gender development and performance.

BIOLOGICAL THEORIES OF GENDER

Biological theory maintains that biological characteristics are the basis of gender differences. Biologically based theories focus on how X and Y chromosomes, hormonal activities, and brain specialization influence a range of individual qualities from body features to thinking and motor skills.

One focus of biological theories is the influence of sex chromosomes. As we saw in Chapter 1, most males have an XY chromosome structure. Most females have an XX chromosome structure, because they inherit an X chromosome from each parent. Genetic evidence (Tanouye, 1996) shows that several genes that control intelligence are located only on X chromosomes. This implies that some aspects of males' intelligence are inherited only from their mothers, whereas females, who usually inherit an X chromosome from each parent, may inherit their intelligence from both parents. Genetic researchers have also reported that the primary gene responsible for social skills is active only on the X chromosome (Langreth, 1997). This may explain why women, who have two X chromosomes, are generally more adept and comfortable than men in many social situations. It's also the case that men are more prone to a number of genetic conditions than women because the single Y chromosome that has the gene for a condition is not corrected by a second Y chromosome that does not carry that gene. A person with two X chromosomes, on the other hand, is more likely to have one that overrides a gene for a condition.

X and Y chromosomes are distinct. The X is larger than the Y, and the X holds 1,100 genes whereas the Y holds only about 50 genes (Angier, 2007a, b). In part because of the larger number of genes carried on the X chromosome, it is more of a multitasker than the Y. Yet, very recent research shows that the Y chromosome is evolving faster than any other human chromosome (Borenstein, 2010). The Y chromosome's primary function is determining that a fertilized egg will evolve into a male. The X chromosome, however, controls a lot more than sex determination. In addition, the X carries genes that influence intelligence, some hereditary conditions, and sociability (Angier, 2007a).

The sex chromosomes are even more complex than scientists originally thought. As we've noted, women typically have two X chromosomes, which carry

EXPLORING GENDERED LIVES | CHROMOSOMAL VARIATIONS

Although most humans have either XX or XY sex chromosomes, there are variations.

- About 1 in 2,500 females has Turner's syndrome, which is noted by the presence of a single X chromosome instead of the usual two in most of their cells. Some people with Turner's syndrome have Y chromosomes in their blood cells (Wade, 2009). Girls with Turner's syndrome do not undergo the usual changes at puberty, and they are usually not able to have children. They tend to be shorter than average, have normal intelligence, and often have particular difficulty with math.

- About 1 in 700 males has Klinefelter's syndrome, which is determined by the presence of two and occasionally more than two X chromosomes instead of the usual single X. Boys with Klinefelter's syndrome tend to be taller than average and have normal levels of intelligence. They usually produce less testosterone and have less impulse control than XY males.

- Approximately 1 in 1,500 females is born with three X chromosomes instead of the usual two. Triple X girls tend to be taller than XX girls and have normal intelligence and normal passage through puberty. Without genetic testing, triple X girls are unlikely to be identified (March of Dimes, 2006).

genes. Scientists had assumed that one of the X chromosomes was silenced to avoid toxic effects of double X genes. However, research reported in 2005 shows that the second X chromosome is not entirely shut down (Dowd, 2005; "Study Reveals," 2005). Instead, 15% of the genes (between 200 and 300 genes) on the second X remain active. And in some women, another 10% of the second X's genes showed some level of activity.

A second focus of biological theories is the role of hormonal activity in shaping sex-related behaviors. Sex hormones affect development of the brain as well as the body. For instance, estrogen, the primary female hormone, causes women's bodies to produce "good" cholesterol and to make their blood vessels more flexible than those of men (Ferraro, 2001). Estrogen strengthens the immune system, making women generally less susceptible to immune disorders and more resistant to infections and viruses. Estrogen causes fat tissue to form around women's hips, which provides cushioning for a fetus during pregnancy. And estrogen seems to impede liver functioning such that women eliminate alcohol more slowly than men and thus may react more quickly to alcohol consumption (Lang, 1991).

Male sex hormones, too, have some documented effects as well as some controversial possible influences. Like women, men have hormonal cycles that affect their behavior (Federman & Walford, 2007). Research suggests that males who use drugs, engage in violent and abusive behavior, and have behavior problems tend to be at their cycle's peak level of testosterone, the primary male hormone. Higher levels of testosterone are also linked to jockeying for power, attempts to

EXPLORING GENDERED LIVES | DETERMINING ATHLETES' SEX

A person's sex is not always obvious. Just ask Olympic athletes (Thomas, 2008). At the 2009 Olympics, South African runner Caster Semenya's sex was challeged after she won the 400 meter race (Bearak, 2009; Clarey & Kolata, 2009). A poor woman from a remote, rural village in South Africa, Caster and other South Africans were amazed and insulted. Her birth certificate said she was a female; she had been raised as a girl; and her aunt and mother, who had changed her diapers, said she was female. A year earlier, at the 2008 Beijing Olympics female athletes had to submit to testing in a sex-determination laboratory to prove they were females. (Similar labs were set up at the Sydney and Athens Olympics.)

These laboratories are the latest efforts to prevent countries from gaining advantage by entering male athletes in women's events. The earliest method of determining sex involved having doctors visually examine nude women athletes. By the late 1960s, chromosomal tests were used to verify sex. In 1967 Ewa Klobukowska, a sprinter from Poland, was not allowed to compete because she failed the chromosomal test even though she passed the nude test. Some years later Maria José Martínez, a hurdler from Spain, was barred because tests showed she had a Y chromosome. (A later ruling restored her eligibility to compete as a woman.) When the chromosomal tests disqualified 8 athletes at the 1996 Atlanta Olympics, the tests themselves came under scrutiny. All 8 athletes were allowed to compete as women because it was determined that they had a rare congenital condition which gave them a Y chromosome but did not make them male.

A number of doctors have spoken out against tests that determine sex. They point out that sex is not as clear-cut as we often think. People who appear female and even feminine may have a Y chromosome. People who appear male and even masculine may not have a Y chromosome. Some people who appear female and have a Y chromosome live their lives as women, never suspecting that they, like some Olympic athletes, would fail the sex determination test.

If it were up to you to set policy for the Olympics, would you require sex testing? If so, what sort of test would you require?

influence or dominate others, and physical expressions of anger (Cowley, 2003a; Schwartz & Cellini, 1995). Additional research indicates that hormones influence cognitive abilities including decoding nonverbal communication and judging moving objects (Halpern, 1996; Kimura, 1999; Saucier & Kimura, 1998). Beginning around the age of 30, men's testosterone level declines. Unlike the acute hormonal change that women experience with menopause, men's hormonal change is more gradual with testosterone levels dropping about 1% a year after age 30 (Federman & Walford, 2007). Researchers estimate that about 10 million American men over the age of 50 experience testosterone deficiency, which can lead to decreases in muscle, bone strength, and interest in sex and to increases in body fat, moodiness, and depression (Federman & Walford, 2007).

EXPLORING GENDERED LIVES | THE CLAIMS OF SOCIOBIOLOGY

One of the more controversial theories of sex and gender differences is sociobiology (also called evolutionary psychology) (Barash, 2002; Barash & Lipton, 2002; Segerstråle, 2000; Wilson, 1975). According to sociobiology, differences between women and men result from genetic factors that aim to ensure survival of the fittest.

A key claim of sociobiology is that women and men follow distinct reproductive strategies in an effort to maximize the chance that their genetic lines will continue (Barash & Lipton, 2002; Buss, 1994,1995,1996,1999; Buss & Kenrick, 1998). For men, the best strategy is to have sex with as many women as possible in order to father many children who continue their genetic line. Because men produce millions of sperm, they risk little by impregnating multiple women. Women, however, usually produce only one egg during each menstrual cycle during their fertile years, so the best evolutionary strategy for them is to be highly selective in choosing sex partners and potential fathers of their children.

Sociobiology has at least as many critics as proponents. Some scholars point out that the theory fails to account for sexual behavior that occurs without the goal of reproduction—and sometimes in an active effort to avoid that outcome! Also, note critics of the theory, sociobiology pays too little attention to the ways in which social influences mitigate biological drives (Newcombe, 2002).

A more recent theory, behavioral ecology, advances a less extreme view of the influence of biology and genetics on behavior. According to behavioral ecology, factors in the environment influence sexual behaviors and preferences (Begley, 2009). That's why extremely thin women are considered ideal in some cultures and very heavy women are viewed as ideal in other cultures. This may also explain the "cougar phenomenon" in which older, successful women pick younger men as mates. This emergent pattern reflects changes in women's earning power and social status.

Hormones influence skills and tendencies we associate with gender. Research shows that girls favor trucks over dolls if their mothers had atypically high levels of testosterone during pregnancy, and that males who are given estrogen experience declines in spatial skills, which tend to be greater in males, and increases in verbal skills, which tend to be greater in females (Gurian & Stevens, 2007; Tyre, 2006). Men who have a spray of oxytocin, known as the "cuddle" or "love" hormone, show more empathy and sensitivity to others' feelings (Hurleman, Patin, Onur, Cohen, Baumgartner, Metzler, Dziobek, Gallinat, Wagner, Maier, & Kendrick, 2010).

A third focus of biological theories of difference is brain structure and development, which appear to be linked to sex. Although there are some inconsistencies in research findings, the majority of research indicates that, although both women and men use both lobes of the brain, each sex tends to specialize in one. Men tend to have better development in the left lobe that controls linear thinking, sequential information, spatial skills, and abstract, analytic reasoning (Andersen, 2006; Mealy, 2000). Women tend to have greater development of the right lobe that controls imaginative and artistic activity, holistic, intuitive thinking, and some visual and spatial tasks (Joseph, 2000; Mealy, 2000). Research indicates that women tend to use both sides of their brains to perform language tasks, whereas men are more likely to use only or primarily the left sides of their brains. In women, the prefrontal cortex, which restrains aggression, is larger and develops earlier than in men (Brizendine, 2007; Tyre, 2006), and the insula, which affects intuition and empathy, is larger (Brizendine, 2007). In men, the amygdala, which is the center of emotions such as anger and fear, is larger, which may influence men's greater likelihood of engaging in risky and aggressive behavior (Brizendine, 2007).

A bundle of nerves and connecting tissues called the corpus callosum links the two lobes of the brain. Women generally have greater ability to use this structure and to access the distinct capacities of both lobes (Fausto-Sterling, 2000). For instance, brain scans show that men use mostly the left lobes of their brains when they listen, whereas women use both lobes of the brain to listen ("Men Use Half a Brain to Listen," 2000). This finding does not mean that men listen less fully or less well than women. It means only that women and men, in general, use different parts of their brains to listen.

Are differences in how we use our brains indisputable evidence of the force of biology? Not necessarily. The splenium, a thick, rounded fold of connecting tissues in the corpus callosum, is larger in most women, which may account for their greater verbal abilities (Hines, 1992; Konner, 2003). However, the splenium changes as a result of experience, which implies that we can develop it by using it, just as we use exercise to develop other muscles in our bodies.

The force of biology is evident in cases where doctors try to change a child's biological sex. Perhaps the most famous case is that of David Reimer, which is often called "the case of David/Brenda" (Butler, 2004; Colapinto, 2006; McClelland, 2004). When David was eight months old, a surgeon mistakenly amputated his penis during surgery to correct phimosis, a condition in which the foreskin of the penis interferes with urination. Following doctors' advice, a year later the parents decided to have "normalizing surgery" performed on David. His testicles were removed, he was given hormones to induce female characteristics, and he was renamed Brenda. Brenda did not take to being a girl. Her preferred toys were trucks and guns; she routinely ripped off the dresses her parents made her

wear; and, despite not having a penis, Brenda preferred to stand to urinate. Even hormonal treatments and therapists could not convince Brenda to accept being a girl. Finally, when Brenda was about 15, her father told her that she had been born a boy. For Brenda/David, things now made sense. David had his breasts removed and a penis constructed using muscle tissue and cartilage, took male hormone shots, and began to live as a male. At age 25, David married a woman with children, and he helped raise his three stepchildren. In June of 2004, at age 38, David took his own life.

Luanne   *When I was in high school, I wanted to play football. My folks were really cool about it, since they'd always told me being a girl didn't mean I couldn't do anything I wanted to. But the school coach vetoed the idea. I appealed his decision to the principal as sex discrimination (my mother's a lawyer), and we had a meeting. The coach said girls couldn't play football as well as guys because girls are less muscular, weigh less, and have less dense bodies to absorb the force of momentum. He said this means girls can be hurt more than guys by tackles and stuff. He also said that girls have smaller heads and necks, which is a problem in head-to-head contact on the field. My dad said the coach was talking in generalizations, and he should judge my ability by me as an individual. But the coach's arguments convinced the principal, and I didn't get to play, just because women's bodies are generally less equipped for contact sports.*

In summary, biological theories of gender attribute masculine and feminine qualities and abilities to genetics and biology. Specifically, it appears that chromosomes, hormones, and brain structure may affect physiology, thinking, and behavior. Biological theory is valuable in informing us about genetic and biological factors that may influence our abilities and options. Yet, biological theories tell us only about physiological and genetic qualities of men and women in general. They don't necessarily describe individual men and women. Some men may be holistic, creative thinkers, whereas some women, like Luanne, may have the mental and physical qualities necessary to excel at football.

Although virtually no researchers dispute the influence of biology, there is substantial controversy about the strength and immutability of biological forces. Those who hold an extreme version of biological theory maintain that our chromosomes and other biological factors program, or determine, our abilities and behavior. Yet, increasing evidence (Fine, 2010) indicates that biological differences are actually quite small and do not explain most behavioral differences between women and men. That's why most researchers believe that biology is substantially edited by environmental factors (Fausto-Sterling, 2000; Lippa, 2005; Martin & Doka, 2000; Reiss, 2000). To consider how environmental forces may mitigate biological endowments, we turn to theories of interpersonal and cultural influences on gender.

EXPLORING GENDERED LIVES	BIOLOGICAL DIFFERENCES THAT MAKE A DIFFERENCE

Although men and women are alike in many respects, research (Duenwald, 2005; Ferraro, 2001; Fisher, 2000; Reiss, 2000; Wartik, 2002) suggests that there are some significant biological sex differences:

- Women are more likely than men to experience pain. Their pains are also likely to be taken less seriously by doctors.
- Women are more likely than men to suffer from migraine headaches and lupus; men are more likely than women to suffer from cluster headaches.
- On average, women's brains are smaller than men's; women's brains are also more densely packed with neurons than men's.
- Men's livers metabolize most drugs, including alcohol, more quickly than women's.
- Daily use of low-dose aspirin is helpful in preventing first heart attacks in men but not in women; low-dosage aspirin does seem to offer women some protection against stroke, which is not a benefit that has been demonstrated for men.
- Women and men typically have different symptoms of heart attack. Women's symptoms include shortness of breath, jaw pain, backache, and extreme fatigue. Men's primary symptom is usually chest or arm pain.
- Women are more likely to develop melanoma, but men are more likely to die from this skin cancer.

INTERPERSONAL THEORIES OF GENDER

A number of theorists have focused on interpersonal factors that influence the development of masculinity and femininity. Their work has led to development of three theories that shed light on how individuals become gendered. Psychodynamic theory emphasizes interpersonal relationships within the family that affect a child's sense of identity, particularly his or her gender. Social learning and cognitive development theories stress learning and role modeling between children and a variety of other people.

PSYCHODYNAMIC THEORIES OF GENDER DEVELOPMENT

Psychodynamic theories assume that relationships, especially the earliest ones, are central to human development. For most children, the first important relationship is with the primary caretaker, typically the mother. Psychodynamic theory claims that this first relationship fundamentally influences how an infant comes to define her or his identity, including gender.

Psychodynamic theorists think that infants develop a sense of self and a gender identity as they internalize the views of other people around them during the early years. So, for example, infants who are lovingly nurtured by parents tend to internalize the parents' views that they are valuable and lovable. In addition, parents' tendencies to nurture, compete, cooperate, express affection, and so forth are internalized so that the child develops these capacities as part of herself or himself. Internalizing others is not merely acquiring roles; it creates the basic structure of the psyche—the core self.

Psychodynamic theory explains the development of masculine or feminine identity as the result of relationships that typically exist between mothers and children. According to Nancy Chodorow (1989), a prominent psychodynamic theorist, the key to understanding how family psychodynamics create gender lies in realizing that most of us are nurtured by mothers because "women rather than men have primary parenting responsibilities" in Western society (p. 6). Because the mother herself is gendered, she may act differently toward sons and daughters. Consequently, male and female infants follow distinct developmental paths that reflect sons' and daughters' distinct relationships with their mothers.

Between mother and daughter, there is a fundamental likeness that encourages close identification. Mothers generally interact more with daughters, keeping them physically and psychologically closer than sons. In addition, mothers tend to be more nurturing and to talk more about personal and relationship topics with daughters than with sons. This intense closeness allows an infant girl to import her mother into herself in so basic a way that her mother becomes quite literally a part of her own self. Because this internalization occurs at a very early age, a girl's first efforts to define her own identity are suffused with the relationship with her mother. The fact that girls generally define their identities within a relationship may contribute to women's typical attentiveness to relationships (Lorber, 2001).

Because mother and son are not the same sex, full identification between them is less likely to develop. Theorists suggest that infant boys recognize in a primitive way that they differ from their mothers (Chodorow, 1978, 1999). More importantly, mothers realize the difference, and they reflect it in their interactions with sons. In general, mothers encourage more and earlier independence in sons than in daughters, and they talk less with sons about emotional and relationship matters (Galvin, 2006).

▼

Abe   *I remember something that happened when I was a little kid. Mom had taken me to the playground, and we were playing together. Some other boys started teasing me, calling me "Mama's boy." I remember thinking I had to stop playing with Mom if I wanted those other boys to accept me.*

How do most young boys formulate a masculine gender identity? Because they cannot define it through the relationship with their mothers, as daughters typically do, boys tend to pursue a different path. To establish his independent identity, a boy must differentiate himself from his mother or other female caregiver—he must declare that he is not like her. Whether a boy rejects his female caregiver or merely differentiates himself from her, defining himself as different from her is central to the initial development of a masculine identity (Kaschak, 1992). Keep in mind that we're discussing general—but not universal—patterns of developing gender identities.

Identity, of course, is not static or fixed in the early years of life. The initial self that we construct continues to grow and change throughout life as we interact with others and revise our sense of who we are. Yet, psychodynamic theorists maintain that the identity formed in infancy is fundamental. Thus, as infants mature, they carry with them the basic identity formed in the pivotal first relationship with their mothers. As girls become women, they elaborate their identities in connections with others, and relationships tend to figure prominently in their values and lives. As boys grow into men, most of them elaborate the basic identity formed in infancy, making independence central to their values and lives. This major difference in self-definition suggests that close relationships may mean quite different things to people who define themselves as masculine and feminine. For someone who identifies as feminine, intimate relationships may be a source of security and comfort, and they may affirm her (or his) view of self as connected with others. In contrast, someone who identifies with masculinity may feel that really close relationships threaten the independence essential to a strong identity (Gurian, 2006; Lorber, 2001).

This theory of gender development highlights the importance of relationships in cultivating gender. The next two theories we'll discuss also focus on relationships, although in different ways than psychodynamic theory.

Psychological Theories of Gender Development

Psychological theories also focus on the interpersonal bases of gender, but they do not emphasize intrapsychic processes as do the psychodynamic explanations. Instead, psychological theories of gender highlight the influence of communication on gender.

Social Learning Theory Developed by Walter Mischel (1966) and others (Bandura, 2002; Bandura & Walters, 1963; Burn, 1996), **social learning theory** claims that individuals learn to be masculine and feminine primarily by imitating others and getting responses from others to their behaviors. Children imitate the communication they see on television, films, and DVDs, as well as the communication of parents, teachers, siblings, and others. At first, young children are likely to mimic almost anything. However, people around them will reward only some of children's behaviors, and the behaviors that are reinforced tend to be repeated. Thus, social learning suggests that others' communication teaches boys and girls which behaviors are appropriate for them (Kunkel, Hummert, & Dennis, 2006; Morrow, 2006; Wood, in press, b).

Because children prefer rewards to punishments and neutral responses, they are likely to develop gendered patterns of behavior that others approve. As parents and others reward girls for what is considered feminine and discourage behaviors and attitudes that are masculine, they shape little girls into femininity. Similarly, as parents communicate approval to boys for behaving in masculine ways and curb them for acting feminine—for instance, for crying—they influence little boys to become masculine. Even people who claim to treat boys and girls the same have been shown to have gender biases. When told an infant is a boy (but is really a girl), adults describe the infant as angry. When told an infant is a girl (but is really a boy), adults describe the infant as happy and socially engaged (Elliott, 2009).

Although each of us is born with certain inclinations, it is our social world that amplifies or tones down those inclinations. In other words, tendencies to be

Radius Images/JUPITER IMAGES

Gendered behaviors are developed by imitating role models.

aggressive or nurturing are shaped and elaborated by parents, peers, and other people. A good example of this comes from a report by Deborah Blum, a Pulitzer Prize-winning science writer. Blum calls our attention to studies of girls with a condition called congenital adrenal hyperplasia, which means they have higher levels of testosterone than is typical for girls. These girls are more interested in trucks and toy weapons and they engage in rougher play than most little girls. Yet, as they interact with other girls, their peers socialize them toward behaviors, games, and preferences more traditional for girls (Blum, 1997, 1998).

Derrick   *Over break, I was visiting my sister's family, and her little boy attached himself to me. Wherever I went, he was my shadow. Whatever I did, he copied. At one point, I was dribbling a basketball out in the driveway, and he got it and started dribbling. I egged him on, saying, "Attaboy! What a star!" and stuff like that, and he just grinned real big. The more I praised him for playing with the ball, the harder he played. It was really weird to see how much influence I had over him.*

Media also play a role in teaching children what activities and roles are rewarded for each sex (Jamieson & Romer, 2008). If children are exposed to television programs and computer games that show boys being rewarded for engaging in masculine activities and girls being rewarded for engaging in feminine activities, traditional sex roles are reinforced. However, if a child watches a program in which a man takes care of children and is rewarded for that, the child learns that men can engage in caregiving and learns specific behaviors that are part of caregiving (Romer, 2008; Wood, in press, b). Media may also provide children with response repertoires. Children view television characters behaving in certain ways in certain situations. When those children later encounter similar situations in their own lives, they may draw on stored memories of the television characters and respond in those ways (Rich, 2008).

You may have noticed that social learning theory views children as relatively passive in the learning process. It suggests that they more or less absorb a gender identity in response to external stimuli such as rewards and punishments from parents and other people.

Cognitive Development Theory   This theory also focuses on how individuals learn from interaction with others to define themselves, including their gender. Unlike social learning theory, however, **cognitive development theory** assumes that children play active roles in developing their gender identities. Researchers claim that children pick models to teach themselves competency in masculine or feminine behavior.

Children go through several stages in developing gender identities (Gilligan & Pollack, 1988; Kohlberg, 1958; Piaget, 1932/1965; Wadsworth, 1996). From birth until about 24 to 30 months, they search others' communication for labels to apply to themselves. When they hear others call them a "girl" or "boy," they learn the labels for themselves. By age three or earlier, most children realize that being a girl or boy is not temporary; they realize they will always be male or female.

Gender constancy is a person's understanding that he or she is a male or female and this will not change. Gender constancy may develop as early as age three and almost certainly by age six (Dubois, Serbin, & Derbyshire, 1998; Miller-Day & Fisher, 2006; Warin, 2000). Once gender constancy is established, children become motivated to learn how to be competent in the sex and gender assigned to them (Levy, 1998). Boys and girls now devote themselves to identifying behaviors and attitudes that others consider masculine and feminine and to learning to enact them. They look for cues about what girls do, wear, and say and what boys do, wear, and say (Martin & Ruble, 2004; Wood, in press, b). Same-sex models become extremely important as gauges by which young children figure out what behaviors, attitudes, and feelings go with their gender. For many young girls mothers are the primary source of information about femininity. Likewise, little boys study their fathers and other important males in their world to learn what counts as masculine (Tyre, 2006).

Related to cognitive development theory is **gender schema theory** (Bem, 1983; Frawley, 2008; Martin & Halverson, 1981; Meyers, 2007). Like cognitive development theory, gender schema theory was influenced by Kohlberg and claims that cognitive processes are central to our learning what gender means in our culture and to learning how to perform our gender competently. According to gender schema theory, even before reaching the first birthday, an infant distinguishes between male and female faces and voices. By the age of two, gender schema theorists claim that children use the concept or schema of gender to organize their understandings. A **gender schema** is an internal mental framework that organizes perceptions and directs behavior related to gender. Using gender schemata, children organize clothes, activities, toys, traits and roles into those appropriate for boys and men and those appropriate for girls and women. They also apply gender schemata to themselves and their activities, roles, clothes, and so forth.

▼

Lindsay   *The gender constancy that we read about doesn't happen so easily or "naturally" for everyone. Long before I started kindergarten I knew that I was a boy, but I also knew that I wasn't. Everyone called me a boy, and I knew I had boy genitals, but I also knew that I identified more with girls and women and with girl things like dolls and dresses. So, for me, gender constancy didn't happen—I was caught on a fence between how everyone else saw me and how I saw myself.*

As children mature, they continue to seek role models to guide them in becoming competent at masculinity and femininity (Burn, 1996; Martin, 1997). Perhaps you, like many adolescents, studied teen magazines, watched television, and participated in blogs to figure out how to be successful as a boy or girl. We look for models for everything from how to style our hair and do the latest dances to how to feel about various things. At young ages, boys learn that aggressiveness is masculine and leads to popularity (Good, 2000). Girls learn that it's feminine to dress up, put on makeup, and do other things to be physically attractive (Franzoi & Koehler, 1998). Children quickly figure out gender rules. It's feminine to squeal or scream at the sight of bugs or mice, but boys who do so are quickly labeled sissies. It's acceptable—if not pleasant to everyone—for adolescent boys to belch, but a teenage girl who belches would most likely be criticized. There is also evidence that children who witness violence between their parents may follow the model and enact violence in their own intimate relationships (Mihalic & Elliot, 1997).

▼

Victoria   *When I was little—like four or five maybe—if I got dirty or was too loud, Mama would say, "That's no way for a lady to act." When I was quiet and nice, she'd say, "Now, you're being a lady." I remember wanting Mama to approve of me and trying to act like a lady. But sometimes it was hard to figure out what was and wasn't ladylike in her book. I had to just keep doing things and seeing how she responded until I learned the rules.*

In studying how senses of morality and relationships develop, Carol Gilligan and her colleagues (Gilligan, 1982; Gilligan & Pollack, 1988) theorized that most females are socialized to place high value on connections with others, to communicate care and responsiveness, and to preserve relationships. She also claimed that males are more likely to be socialized to place high value on autonomy and to communicate in ways that preserve their independence from others. Each sex learns what society expects of her or his gender, and most decide to act in ways that are consistent with social views of gender.

In summary, psychological theories emphasize the power of others' communication to teach lessons about gender and to provide models of masculinity and femininity. Once gender constancy is established, most children strive to develop communication, attitudes, goals, and self-presentations consistent with the gender they consider theirs.

CULTURAL THEORIES OF GENDER

A third group of theories focuses on understanding gender from a cultural or cross-cultural perspective. Cultural scholars do not necessarily dispute biological and interpersonal factors, but they do assume that these are qualified by the influence of culture. Because it incorporates other theories, the cultural perspective is a particularly comprehensive approach to understanding what gender means in any society at a specific time (Davis & Gergen, 1997; Deaux & LaFrance, 1998; Unger, 1998).

Of the many cultural contributions to knowledge about gender, we will focus on two. First, we'll look at findings from anthropology to discover what cross-cultural research tells us about the range of ways that societies define masculinity and femininity. Second, we will explore symbolic interactionism, which concentrates on how individuals acquire cultural values so that most of us adopt the identities our culture designates as appropriate for our gender.

ANTHROPOLOGY

Anyone who has been outside the United States knows that traveling prompts you to learn not only about other countries but also about your own. When confronted with different values and ways of doing things in a foreign culture, you see the norms of your own society in a new and usually clearer light. This holds true of gender. Our views of gender in twenty-first-century America are clarified by considering what it means elsewhere—how other cultures view gender and how women and men in other cultures express gendered identities.

Many societies have views of gender that differ from those currently prevalent in the United States. Tahitian men tend to be gentle, mild-tempered, and nonaggressive, and it is entirely acceptable for them to cry, show fear, and express pain (Coltrane, 1996). Australian Aboriginal fathers have no say in their daughters' marriages; that is up to the mothers. A number of Samoan males tattoo their bodies from waist to below the knees as a means of marking the transition from childhood to manhood. A male is not considered a man until he has undergone the painful process of extensive tattooing (Channell, 2002; Cote, 1997). The Mbuti, a tribe of pygmies in central Africa, don't discriminate strongly between the sexes. Both women and men gather roots, berries, and nuts, and both hunt (Coltrane, 1996). The Mukogodo people in Kenya place a higher value on females than on males; as a result, daughters are given greater attention and medical care than sons (Cronk, 1993). And on Orango Island on the western shore of Africa, women choose mates and, a man cannot refuse without dishonoring his family (Callimachi, 2007).

▼

Lynn   *At school, I've gotten to know a woman from the Congo. She can't believe how American girls break up with their boyfriends and wives divorce husbands. She says she could never do that, because she was raised to believe a woman can't leave her man and remain good. I know she is not happy in her marriage, but I also know she'll never leave it.*

What fatherhood means and how involved fathers are with children vary among cultures. In hunter-gatherer tribes such as the Hazda in Tanzania, fathers spend about 5% of their time holding infants. But the Aka, a hunter-gather tribe in the Congo Basin hold their children for as much as 22% of the time. Men in India are near their children three to five hours a day whereas Japanese fathers spend an average of 20 minutes near children each day (Gray, 2010).

EXPLORING GENDERED LIVES | VARIED CULTURAL APPROACHES TO FATHERING

In the United States, the responsibilities of parenting have largely fallen on women. When both parents work outside of the home, women spend 400% more time with children than men (Romano & Dokoupil, 2010).

Other countries have done more to make parenting part of manhood. In 1990, only 4% of Swedish men took any time off when a child was born. The Swedish government decided to use public policy to encourage men to be more involved with children. In 1995 the Swedish government set aside 30 leave days for fathers only; if fathers didn't take them, their families lost the leave. In 2002 the state added a second month of leave that new fathers could either take or lose. Now more than 80% of fathers take four months of leave for the birth of a child (Hegedus, 2010; Romano & Dokoupil, 2010).

Or consider Germany. In 2007, the country passed a law that new fathers were entitled to leave. The percentage of new fathers who take family leave soared 700%.

Japan also provides paid leave to new fathers and honors men who devote themselves to child care as "stars of ikumen" (men who rear children) (Romano & Dokoupil, 2010).

Another example of how cultural attitudes vary comes from a group of villages in the Dominican Republic where it is common for males to be born with undescended testes and an underdeveloped penis. Because this condition is not rare, the society doesn't regard it as abnormal. Instead, boys born with this condition are raised as "conditional girls," who wear dresses and are treated as girls. At puberty, a secondary tide of androgens causes the testes to descend, the penis to grow, and muscle and hair typical of males to appear. At that point, the child is considered a boy—his dresses are discarded, and he is treated as a male. Members of the society call the condition *guevedoces*, which means "testes at 12" (Blum, 1998).

Native American tribes offer yet another cultural construction of gender. According to Angela Gonzales and Judy Kertész (2001), prior to contact with Western Europeans, many (but not all) Native American groups had long-established matrilineal systems of inheritance, property ownership, and social status. These tribes were not necessarily matriarchal (in which females have greater power than males), but they were matrilineal because lines of kinship were traced through females, not males. Many of the tribes also viewed women as relatively autonomous, in direct contrast to the views of the Western Europeans who colonized the United States. Native American tribes also created the category of "two-spirit" for individuals who preferred to mate with others of the same sex. Within Native American traditions, these people were not "gay" or "lesbian," but two-spirit people who were particularly admired (Gilley, 2006). Similarly, in Kruje, an isolated rural society in rural Albania, gender swapping is the solution for families that do not have males. When Pashe Kequi's father was killed 60 years ago, she whacked off her long hair, dressed in her father's clothes, and vowed to live as a man and be a virgin for life, giving up marriage and children. Kequi's community accepted her as a man because it's the custom in Kruje (Bilefsky, 2008).

▼

Sheng   *Growing up, when guests came to our home, my mother and I served them drinks, then went to the kitchen to fix food while the men talked. If another woman was a guest, she came to the kitchen with us. Men ate at their own table. The women either stay in the kitchen or eat at a separate table.*

Perhaps the most important lesson we can draw from anthropological studies is that cultures profoundly shape our understanding of identity and our own sex and gender identities.

SYMBOLIC INTERACTIONISM

Symbolic interactionism claims that through communication with others we learn who we are and how our culture views our identity. Because newborns do not enter the world with a sense of self as distinct from the world, they learn from others how to see themselves. As parents and others interact with children, they literally tell the children who they are. A child is described as big or dainty, delicate

---

EXPLORING GENDERED LIVES | **LEARNING FROM OTHER SPECIES**

Meet Roy and Silo, two chinstrap penguins at a Manhattan zoo. Absolutely devoted to each other, the two male penguins interlock their necks, coo lovingly to each other, and show ecstasy in each other's presence. To the frustration of zookeepers, they reject close relationships with female chinstrap penguins. But Roy and Silo longed for a family. They once put a rock in their nest and sat on it, keeping the rock toasty warm in the folds of their abdomens. A zookeeper finally gave them a fertilized egg that needed to be sat on to hatch. After the usual 34 days of sitting on the egg, a female chick was born, and Roy and Silo devoted the usual two and one-half months to raising her (Smith, 2004a). In the spring of 2004 Roy and Silo were kicked out of their nest by two aggressive penguins. Silo's eye began to wander and early in the 2005 mating season he forsook Roy, his partner of six years, and took up with Scrappy, a female penguin from SeaWorld who had been lounging around the aquarium since 2002.

Roy and Silo's relationship isn't unique in the animal kingdom. Some Bonobos, members of the ape family, don't limit themselves to heterosexual relationships (de Waal, 1998). In fact, non-heterosexual behavior has been documented in 450 species (Bagemihl, 2000).

---

or tough, active or quiet, and so on. With each label, others offer the child a self-image, and children internalize others' views to arrive at their own understandings of who they are. Communication is the central process whereby we gain a sense of who we are; from the moment of birth, we engage in interaction with others, especially parents, who tell us who we are, what is appropriate for us, and what is unacceptable.

Research has shown that views of gender are also communicated through play activities with peers (Maccoby, 1998; Powlishta, Serbin, & Moller, 1993) and through teachers' interactions with students (Sandler, 2004; Wood, 1996b). "You are Mommy's helper in the kitchen," mothers may say to daughters, telling young girls it is appropriate for them to be involved in domestic activities. When young boys move furniture in classrooms, teachers often praise them by saying, "You're such a strong little man." This links strength with being male.

At school, young girls are likely to be reprimanded for roughhousing as a teacher tells them, "That's not very ladylike." Boys engaged in similar mischief more often hear the teacher say with some amusement, "You boys really are rowdy today." Notice that responses from others, such as teachers, not only reflect broad cultural values but also provide positive and negative rewards, consistent with social learning theory. In play with peers, gender messages continue. When a young girl tries to tell a boy what to do, she may be told, "You can't boss me around. You're just a girl." Girls who fail to share their toys or show consideration to others may be told, "You're not being nice," yet this is considerably less likely to be said to young boys. Thus, children learn what is expected of them and how that is related to being masculine or feminine.

An important contribution to a cultural theory of gender is the concept of **role**—specifically, roles for women and men. A role is a set of expected behaviors and the values associated with them. In a classic book, Elizabeth Janeway (1971) identified two dimensions of roles. First, roles are external to individuals because a society defines roles in general ways that transcend particular individuals. Roles are assigned to individuals by the society as a whole. Thus, for each of us there are certain roles that society expects us to fulfill because of society's definition of us.

Within our culture, one primary way to classify social life is through gender roles. Women are still regarded as caretakers and they are expected to provide most of the care for infants, elderly relatives, and others who are sick or disabled (Cancian & Oliker, 2000, Wood, 1994b). Even in work outside the home, cultural views of femininity are evident. Women remain disproportionately represented in service and clerical jobs, whereas men are moved into executive positions in for-profit sectors of the economy. Women are still asked to take care of social activities on the job, but men in equivalent positions are seldom expected to do this.

Men are still regarded as the primary breadwinners for families. Thus, it is seen as more acceptable for a woman than a man not to have an income-producing job. Some women today regard a career as an option, something they may or may not do or might do for a while and then focus full-time on raising a family. Very few young men regard a job as optional. To fulfill the masculine role successfully, a man must work and bring in an income; the feminine role does not require this. The current recession in which more men than women have been laid off is challenging these traditional roles.

Sometimes research also challenges traditional roles and society's views of men and women. Postpartum depression, which is feelings of profound sadness and lack of interest in self or others, has been associated with women. Because women given birth and often spend more time with newborns, it has been assumed that women, but not men, might be susceptible to depression following the birth of a child. Research in 2010, however, shows that 10.4% of men suffer from depression related to a new baby. A few of the men experience depression just before the birth, but the most likely time for the onset of depression in men is three to six months after the birth (Ostrow, 2010). The symptoms of men's depression have been evident before this research, but social views of men as not closely involved with newborns may have prevented us from recognizing postpartum depression in men.

Rachel   *My father is in the Air Force, so he's away a lot of the time. Mom has had to become the head of our family. She does everything from work and take care of us to pay bills and cook. Normally, she sits at the head of the table for meals. But when Dad comes home, he sits at the head of the table. Mom still does everything—he says he's on vacation—but they both seem to think the man should be at the head of the table when he's home.*

Not only does society assign roles, but it also assigns value to the roles. Men, more often than women, are seen as leaders and given opportunities to lead.

Western culture teaches women to accept the role of supporting, caring for, and responding to others. Yet that is a role clearly devalued in the United States. Competing and succeeding in work life and public affairs are primary roles assigned to men, and to those roles prestige is attached.

A second important dimension of role is that it is internalized. For social specifications of behaviors to be effective, individuals must internalize them. At very young ages, girls understand that they are supposed to be nice, put others' needs ahead of their own, and be nurturing, whereas boys understand that they are supposed to take command and assert themselves. As we take cultural scripts for gender inside of ourselves, we learn not only that there are different roles for men and women but also that unequal values are assigned to them. This can be very frustrating for those who are encouraged to conform to roles that are less esteemed. Symbolic interactionism underlines the fact that gender is socially created and sustained through communication that encourages us to define ourselves as gendered and to adopt the roles that society prescribes for us.

Cultural theories broaden our understandings by showing how social expectations and values about the sexes are systematically taught to individuals. Cultural views of gender include two related research traditions. From anthropology, we gain insight into the arbitrary and variable nature of gender by seeing the different views of men and women held in diverse cultures. Symbolic interactionist theory offers an understanding of the key role of communication in socializing new members into the understandings and values of a given culture.

CRITICAL THEORIES OF GENDER

Two theories, standpoint and queer performative theory, go beyond the standard goals of theory, which are description, explanation, and prediction. Critical theories do something else—they direct our attention to structures and practices by which societies classify people into groups and then accord more or less privilege to different groups. Critical theorists are particularly interested in identifying how dominant groups manage to privilege their interests and perspectives and impose them on less powerful groups. At the same time, critical theorists want to understand how oppressed groups become empowered and, in some cases, change dominant patterns and perhaps the ideologies that underlie them. In this sense, critical theories have a political edge.

STANDPOINT THEORY

Standpoint theory complements symbolic interactionism by noting that societies are made up of different groups that are organized in social hierarchies. Standpoint theory focuses on how membership in groups, such as those designated by gender, race, class, and sexual identity, shapes what individuals experience, know, feel, and do, as well as how individuals understand social life as a whole (Collins, 1986; Harding, 1991, 1998; McClish & Bacon, 2002; Wood, 2005; Wood, in press, b).

Standpoint theory dates back to the writings of nineteenth-century German philosopher Georg Wilhelm Friedrich Hegel (1770–1831) and Karl Marx (1818–1883). Hegel (1807) noted that society as a whole recognized the existence of slavery but that its nature was perceived quite differently depending on whether one's position was that of master or slave. From this insight, Hegel reasoned that, in any society where power relationships exist, there can be no single perspective on social life. Marx's (1867/1975, 1977) contribution was to emphasize that the work we do—the activities in which we engage—shape our identities and consciousness and, by extension, our knowledge. Each person sees society as it appears from the perspective of his or her social group and the activities that group engages in, and every perspective is limited. All views are partial because each reflects a particular social location within a culture stratified by power.

But social location is *not* standpoint. A standpoint is achieved—earned through critical reflection on power relations and through engaging in the struggle required to construct an oppositional stance. Being a woman (social location) does not necessarily confer a feminist standpoint, and being black (social location) does not necessarily lead to a black standpoint. Because social location and standpoint are so frequently conflated, let me emphasize the distinction one more time: A standpoint grows out of (that is, it is *shaped by,* rather than essentially given by) the social location of group members' lives. Thus, feminist standpoint, which is particularly relevant to issues of gender, can, *but does not necessarily,* arise from being female.

Members of groups that have power have a vested interest in preserving their place in the hierarchy, so their views of social life may be more distorted than the views of persons who are disadvantaged by existing power relationships. Thus, those in positions of power are unlikely to develop the kind of oppositional politics that standpoint requires. Another reason that those in subordinate groups may have fuller understanding is that they have to understand both their own perspective and the viewpoints of those who have more power. To survive, subjugated people must understand people with power, but the reverse is not true. When members of devalued groups have a critical awareness of their positions, they earn a standpoint that may allow them to see the world with less bias.

Standpoint theory claims that marginalized groups can generate unique insights into how a society works. Women, minorities, gays and lesbians, people of lower socioeconomic class, intersexuals, transsexuals, and others who are outside the cultural center may see the society from perspectives that are less distorted, less biased, and more layered than those who occupy more central social locations. Marginalized perspectives can inform all of us about how our society operates. María Lugones and Elizabeth Spelman (1983) point out that dominant groups have the luxury of not having to understand the perspective of less privileged groups. They don't need to learn about others in order to survive.

Tiffany   *I attended a predominantly white middle-school. My mother made me check my homework twice before I turned it in. I asked her why I had to do that when most of the other kids in the school didn't. She said, "the number of times you check your homework is the same as the number of limitations set up against you—one for being black and two for being a girl." I said that was unfair and she said fairness had nothing to do with succeeding if you're black. I think that was my first lesson in standpoint.*

According to standpoint theory, women and men are likely to develop particular skills, attitudes, ways of thinking, and understandings of life as a result of their membership in socially constructed groups. If they gain and use political consciousness to analyze their locations, they may achieve a standpoint. Patricia Hill Collins (1986, 1998) uses standpoint theory to show that black women scholars have special insights into Western culture because of their dual standpoints as "outsiders within," that is, as members of a minority group (African Americans) who hold membership in majority institutions (higher education). Similarly, in his *Autobiography of an Ex-Coloured Man* (1912/1989), James Weldon Johnson reflected, "I believe it to be a fact that the coloured people of this country know and understand the white people better than the white people know and understand them" (p. 22).

An intriguing application of standpoint logic came from Sara Ruddick's (1989) study of mothers. Ruddick concluded that the demands of their role lead mothers to develop what she calls "maternal thinking," which consists of values, priorities, and understandings of relationships that are specifically promoted by the process of taking care of young children. Ruddick argues that what we often assume is a maternal instinct that comes naturally to women is actually a set of attitudes and behaviors that arise out of women's frequent location in domestic, caregiving roles. Ruddick's finding is supported by the work of other scholars (Bailey, 1994; Bem, 1993), whose research shows that what we view as maternal instinct actually results in large measure from women's location in caregiving roles.

The impact of standpoint on nurturing ability is further demonstrated by research on men in caregiving roles. In her research on single fathers, Barbara Risman (1989) found that men who are primary parents are more nurturing, attentive to others' needs, patient, and emotionally expressive than men in general and as much so as most women. Other studies found that men who care for elderly people enlarge their capacities for nurturing. Armin Brott, an ex-Marine and business consultant, is widely known as "Mr. Dad," the author of eight books for men like him who are stay-at-home dads. According to Brott, women are not born knowing how to take care of babies and children. They learn how to do it by doing it. The same goes for men, says Brott: They learn how to nurture, comfort, and guide children by engaging in the labor of doing so (Lelchuk, 2007). That's the standpoint argument that social location shapes our identities, including our parenting skills.

Standpoint research also calls into question the extent to which biology influences gendered behavior. Some biological theorists claim that men's testosterone levels cause them to be aggressive toward others. Yet these findings must be qualified by noting that not all men behave aggressively, even when their testosterone is at peak level. Thus, we must assume that social factors affect the extent to which males act aggressively. It would be incorrect to think that an individual has a single location and, with that, the potential to develop only a single standpoint. Each of us can earn or develop multiple standpoints that overlap and interact (Andersen & Collins, 2007a, b). For example, an African-American man's knowledge and identity are shaped by race, sexual orientation, and gender, each of which may lead to standpoint and oppositional politics (West, 2007). Because standpoints interact and affect one another, this man's masculine gender identity is different from that of a European-American man.

Standpoint theory's major contribution to understanding gender is calling our attention to how membership in particular socially constructed groups shapes individuals' perspectives, identities, and abilities. Our different social locations provide the possibility of developing different standpoints that reflect a political awareness of social hierarchy, privilege, and oppression.

QUEER PERFORMATIVE THEORY

Perhaps the best way to introduce the last theory is with three examples that raise issues of interest to **queer performative theory**.

1. Munroe identifies as a transgender person, or—in Munroe's words—"the hottest and coolest drag queen in town." Before going out, Munroe shaves twice to remove all stubble, spends an hour applying makeup, chooses one of four wigs, and selects an ensemble from the closet, hoping to hook up with an interesting man.

   - Is Munroe female or male?
   - Is Munroe feminine or masculine?
   - Is Munroe straight or gay?
   - Are men who hook up with Munroe straight or gay?

2. Two years ago, Aimee began hormone therapy to stimulate growth of facial hair, increase muscle mass, and decrease breast size. Over the summer, Aimee had sex-reassignment surgery. Now, with a new name to match the new body, Andy has set up an appointment with the coach for the men's track team at the university in the hope of joining the team. Later, Andy will share the news with his boyfriend.

   - Is Andy male or female?
   - Is Andy masculine or feminine?
   - Is Andy gay or straight?
   - Is Andy's boyfriend gay or straight?

3. Jada, who was born with a penis, testes, and a prostate gland, identifies as female. Since the age of 15, Jada has had several romantic and sexual relationships, all with women.

   - Is Jada male or female?
   - Is Jada masculine or feminine?
   - Is Jada gay or straight?
   - Are Jada's girlfriends gay or straight?

Munroe, Jada, and Andy illustrate both the focus and value of queer performative theories. Each of them defies conventional categories. Each slips beyond and outside of binary views of identity as male or female, masculine or feminine, gay or straight. The identities that they claim and perform don't fit neatly with our taken-for-granted understandings of sex, gender, and sexual identity. According to queer performative theories, Munroe, Jada, and Andy trouble our thinking, and the trouble they provoke is very productive.

Queer theory and performative theory are distinct, yet very closely allied. We'll define each theory and then explore how they interact and how, working together, they offer unique insights into gender, sex, and cultural life.

Queer theory is a critique of conventional categories of identity and cultural views of "normal" and "abnormal," particularly in relation to sexuality. Queer theory argues that identities are not fixed, but somewhat fluid. In our first example, Munroe invests significant effort in creating and performing a female identity. In our second example, Aimee becomes Andy, thereby illustrating the fluidity of identity. In the third example, does Jada's choice of female sexual partners mean Jada is heterosexual because Jada is biologically male or lesbian because Jada identifies as female? Within the context of queer theory, the word *queer* does not refer only or necessarily to gays and lesbians, but to anything that departs from what society considers normal and legitimate (Halperin, 2004, 2007).

Queer theory arose in the context of gay and lesbian studies (Butler, 1990, 1993a, b, 2004; Foucault, 1978; Halperin, 2004, 2007; Sedgwick, 1990). The initial focus of queer theory was **heternormativity**, which is the assumption that heterosexuality is normal and normative and all other sexual identities are abnormal. Yet, it would be a mistake to think queer theory is relevant only to gays and lesbians. Almost as soon as queer theory emerged, scholars realized that it has important implications for our understanding of sexuality, including heterosexuality, as well as race, class, gender, and many other aspects of identity (Sloop, 2006; Zimmerman & Geist-Martin, 2006). Queer theory aims to enlarge appreciation of a wide range of identities and ways of expressing them. To do this, queer theory challenges the ways that a culture defines and polices what is considered normal and abnormal.

Two ideas are central to queer theory. First, queer theory claims that it is not useful to use terms such as "women," "men," "gay," and "straight." Such terms are meaningless because they essentialize by focusing on only one aspect of a person. How much does it tell us about someone if we know that the person is biologically male or female? Identities are shaped by numerous factors, so naming somebody according to any one factor is unavoidably misleading. As well, such terms erase the variation among those who are placed into the categories. Queer theorists point out that there are many different ways of being a woman or man, multiple ways of being gay or straight. Using the term *man* to describe Brad Pitt, Barack Obama, and 50 Cent doesn't acknowledge the very different ways that these three people enact their identities as men.

Second, queer theory assumes that identities are not fixed, but are relatively fluid. Any of us may perform our identities one way in this moment and context and another way in a different moment and context. Andy before hormone treatment is not the same person after the post-hormone-treatment, and Aimee is different from Andy. Jada, Munroe, and Andy may have certain objective features such as sex organs, but these don't determine their identities. Rather, according to queer theory, their identities arise from their choices of how to express or perform themselves within the particular contexts of their lives.

Fluidity of identity means more than being able to switch from one sex or gender to the other. It can also mean refusing to accept any stable sexual identity. Some trans people will not specify their sex or specify being of multiple sexes. For them, defining themselves in terms of the existing categories (male, female, heterosexual, gay) would simply reinforce those categories. Thus, people who are trans may refuse to identify as completely, only, or enduringly male or female, straight or gay (Valentine, 2007).

Performative theory argues that humans generate identities, including gender, through performance or expression. A key theorist, Judith Butler (1990, 2004), explains that gender comes into being only as it is expressed, or performed. The performance, she says, is the thing we call gender. Butler's point, which is central to queer performative theory, is that gender is not a thing we have, but rather something that we do at specific times and in specific circumstances. In other words, for Butler and other performative theorists, gender is more appropriately regarded as a verb than a noun. Gender is doing; without doing—without the action of performance—there is no gender.

According to performative theorists, all of us perform gender, although we may do so in quite diverse ways (Butler, 1990, 1993a, b, 2004). We express, or perform, conventional gender through everyday practices such as dominating or deferring in conversations, offering solutions and judgments or empathy when a friend discloses a problem, crossing our legs so that one ankle rests on the knee of our other leg or so that one knee rests over the other knee, and wearing a dress and heels or a sweatshirt and khakis. Conversely, we resist conventional views of gender if we act in ways that are inconsistent with the sex and gender society assigns to us. Some researchers suggest that gender performances also shed light on why women generally do more housework than men. According to this research, individuals perform (or refuse to perform) household tasks and childcare to communicate their gendered identities. That is, women perform domestic labor as a way of demonstrating their femininity and caring (DeVault, 1990) while men refuse to perform household labor as a way to enact masculinity (De Ruijter, Treas & Cohen, 2005; DeVault, 1990; Natalier, 2003).

But—and this is the second key claim of performative theory—our performances are not solo operations. They are always collaborative, because however we express gender, we do so in a context of social meanings that transcends our individual experiences. For instance, a woman who defers to men and tilts her head when talking to men (two behaviors more often exhibited by women than men) is acting individually, but her individual actions are stylized performances of femininity that are coded into cultural life. Our choices of how to act assume and respond to other people who are either physically or mentally present in particular contexts and times.

Queer performative theories integrate the views of queer and performative theory. The result is a view of queer (remember, in this context that means anything other than what is considered "normal") performances as means of challenging and destabilizing cultural categories and the values attached to them. As communication scholar John Sloop (2006) explains, "queer scholarship works against the ways in which gender/sexuality is disciplined ideologically and institutionally and works toward a culture in which a wider variety of genders/sexualities might be performed" (p. 320).

Particularly important are queer performances that are routine and everyday rather than dramatic and unusual. For instance, a person who attends classes dressed in a lace blouse, necktie, combat fatigues, and stilettos cannot be reduced to only feminine or only masculine. This choice of dress is a performance that challenges and undermines conventional gender categories. Two male friends, each of

EXPLORING GENDERED LIVES | MADONNA

Who is Madonna? Whatever else she may be, she is a lightning rod for views of women, femininity, and power relations between the sexes. She has been called

a feminine icon	a brilliant artist
an immoral opportunist	a gender politician
a knowing virgin	a resister of conventional views of women
a feminist	a traditional sex object
a mother	an exemplar of female-defined sexuality

Perhaps she's all of these and more. She has presented herself as a material girl, traditionally feminine, erotically charged, a submissive victim of male aggression, a dominatrix, a Kabbalist, and a devoted mother. She has performed very traditional femininity and also parodied it; and she has expressed herself in ways the culture classifies as heterosexual and homosexual. She has courted the male gaze, disrupted it, and used it to look at both women and men. Madonna radically varies her performances of gender and sexuality, and subverts any stable notion of femininity. In so doing, she insists that a person can be both dominating and docile, both masculine and feminine, both gay and straight, both "good girl" and "bad girl."

How would you describe Madonna or other popular culture figures who perform different gender identities? Can you identify other artists who perform different sex and gender identities?

whom is sexually attracted only to women, who hold hands in public queer normative understandings of masculinity. Two women who perform disagreement with fist fights instead of verbal arguments queer normative views of femininity. A person who fits the social category of heterosexual and who gives mouth kisses to others of the same sex queers cultural views of heterosexuality and—by extension—of homosexuality. Everyday performances such as these become political tools that unsettle taken-for-granted categories of identity that structure social life and label individuals as "normal" or "abnormal." A contemporary example is Eddie Izzard, a British comedian who performs in women's clothing but is straight. His DVD called "Dress to Kill" is a stand-up routine that he does in drag.

In sum, queer performative theories allow us to understand deliberately transgressive presentations of self as political acts that aim to point out the insufficiency of binary categories of male/female, masculine/feminine, gay/straight, and normal/abnormal.

THEORIES WORKING TOGETHER

We've discussed seven theories, each of which offers particular insights into the processes by which we develop and enact gendered identities. Keep in mind that the theories work together to explain both gender and sex differences. For instance, more girls and women, particularly those who are athletes, suffer knee injuries, especially one known as ACL (anterior cruciate ligament). In an NCAA (National Collegiate Athletic Association) study of ACL problems in basketball players from 1994 to 1998, women players were nearly three times more likely to suffer ACL injuries than men. For soccer players, the risk for females is even greater (Jacobson, 2001; Scelfo, 2002). The fact that women suffer more ACL injuries than men suggests that there may be a sex difference—a biologically based difference between women's and men's knees. However, socialization may also be a factor. Dr. William Garrett, a sports medicine surgeon, has studied films of women and men engaged in sports. In an interview with me (Garrett, 2001), he noted that women and men athletes hold their bodies differently. Men, he says, are looser and tend to move and stand with their knees slightly bent. Women are more likely to keep their legs and knees straight and to maintain more rigid posture. Loose posture and bent knees reduce stress on the knee and thus reduce the risk of ACL injury. Biology doesn't seem to explain the differences in posture and knee positioning. It's likely that both result from early socialization in how girls and boys are supposed to act, stand, sit, run, and so forth. Thus, what seems a purely biological effect may also reflect interpersonal and social influences.

Let's consider another example that shows how theories we've discussed work together in complementary ways. In 2008 Hillary Rodham Clinton ran a strong and nearly successful campaign to be the Democratic nominee for President. Prior to that, she had excelled in a legal career, participated in policy making during the eight years that Bill Clinton was President, and been elected a Senator for the state of New York. After Barack Obama was elected President, Hillary assumed the top-ranking position of Secretary of State. How do we explain Hillary Clinton's interest and success in arenas that are male dominated?

Both social learning and cognitive development theories help us understand Clinton's interests and her success in pursuing them. Growing up, she was rewarded for learning, ambition, living by her faith, and contributing to her community. Learning, ambition, living by Christian values, and serving her country are virtues that are critical in public office. Clinton also chose strong women and men as role models for herself. Being born in the late 1940s allowed Clinton to see that women had fewer professional opportunities than men. However, like many women of her generation, she didn't accept that as right or inevitable. She developed an oppositional standpoint that allowed her to challenge social views of women as less able than men. She went to law school at a time when few women did. She was passionately involved in civil rights struggles through which she learned a great deal about black social location in America. Once she had influence, she often used it to fight for equity for blacks, women, and other groups that have historically been marginalized. Early in Bill Clinton's political career, media criticized Hillary Clinton's appearance—her clothes were drab, her hairstyle wasn't feminine, she looked too serious. Whether she (or we) approve or not, Hillary Clinton realized that she had to perform femininity differently in order to be acceptable to the American public. She had her hair styled, began wearing more stylish clothes, and even submitted her recipe for chocolate chip cookies to show she was familiar with the assumed feminine skill of baking. You can see that multiple theories offer insight into Hillary Clinton's career choices and her achievements. As in this case with Hillary Clinton, multiple theories often work together to give us a fuller, more complete understanding of gendered phenomena than any single theory could.

SUMMARY

In this chapter, we have considered different theories offering explanations of relationships among communication, gender, and culture. Rather than asking which is the right theory, we have tried to discover how each viewpoint contributes to an overall understanding of how gender develops. By weaving different theories together, we gain a powerful appreciation of the complex individual, interpersonal, and cultural origins of gender identity. Adding to this, queer performative theory invites us to understand and perhaps appreciate the ways we can create performances that deliberately provoke and destabilize culturally constructed categories of identity and normalcy.

With this theoretical background, we are now ready to consider contexts in which gender is formed and communicated, as well as ways in which individuals accept or resist cultural directives for masculinity and femininity. The next chapter builds on this one by exploring how communication within rhetorical movements has challenged and changed social views of men and women.

Key Terms

The terms following are defined in this chapter on the pages indicated, as well as in alphabetical order in the book's glossary, which begins on page 325. The text's companion website (http://www.cengage.com/communication/wood/genderedlives10e) also provides interactive flash cards and crossword puzzles to help you learn these terms and the concepts they represent.

biological theory 41

cognitive development theory 51

gender constancy 51

gender schema 52

gender schema theory 51

heternormativity 62

performative theory 63

psychodynamic theories 47

queer performative theory 61

queer theory 62

role 57

social learning theory 49

standpoint theory 58

symbolic interactionism 55

theory 39

Gender Online

1. The Urban Dictionary offers definitions of many terms related to gender, communication, and culture. Visit the site and look up terms such as "cis," "genderqueer," and "ze": http://www.urbandictionary.com/
2. Online search terms: "brain, sex differences," "gender constancy," "guevedoces," "Madonna."

Reflection and Discussion

1. Distinguished anthropologist Ruth Benedict said that "the purpose of anthropology is to make the world safe for difference." Having read this chapter, how would you explain Benedict's statement?

2. Think about your relationship with your parents. How were your connections to your father and mother similar and different? If you have siblings of a different sex, how were their relationships with your parents different from yours?

3. Watch men and women athletes as they play their sports. Do you see the differences in posture and knee position that Dr. Garrett found in his research?

4. Watch the French film *Ma Vie en Rose (My Life in Pink)*. It's the story of a young biological male named Ludovic who does not feel that he is male in any conventional sense. After watching the movie, use at least three of the theories discussed in this chapter to shed light on Ludovic's experiences.

5. How might you engage in queer performance? Describe one way that you could express yourself that would challenge conventional understandings of sex and gender, and the "normal" or "abnormal" judgments that are attached to them.

6. Now that you've read about a range of theories that describe and explain gender, how much do you think gender is due to nature and how much to nurture?

Recommended Resources

1. John Colapinto. (2006). *As Nature Made Him*. New York: HarperPerennial.
2. Lise Elliott, (2009). *Pink brain, blue brain: How small differences grow into troublesome gaps—and what we can do about it*. Boston, MA: Houghton Mifflin-Harcourt.
3. *Ma Vie in Rose* (My Life in Pink), 1997. Alan Berliner, director. Winner of the Golden Globe "Best Foreign Language Film," this is the story of Ludovic, a French child who has a boy's body but identifies as a girl. The story is about not only Ludovic, but also his family and community's responses to his identity.
4. bell hooks. (1990). The politics of radical black subjectivity. *Yearning: Race, Gender, and Cultural Politics*. Boston: South End Press. This is a short seven-page chapter that provides a good example of how some blacks move from black social location to political standpoint.

Citizenship must be practiced to be realized.
Spano

CHAPTER **3**

THE RHETORICAL SHAPING OF GENDER: WOMEN'S MOVEMENTS IN THE UNITED STATES

Knowledge Challenge:

1. To what extent have women's movements in the United States fought for the rights of all women?
2. Are all feminists pro-choice?
3. Who are the Guerrilla Girls?

In the opening chapters, we saw that communication in society influences our understandings of gender and our gendered identities. It's equally true that our communication shapes society's views of masculinity and femininity and, by extension, of women's and men's roles and rights. In this chapter and the next one, we'll look closely at how individuals and groups have changed cultural views of gender and sex.

Think about changes in gender roles in the United States. Once, women could not vote; now they can. Once, women routinely experienced discrimination on the job; now we have laws that prohibit sex discrimination in employment. Two centuries ago few men did housework or took active roles in raising children, but today many men participate in homemaking and child care. Changes such as these do not just happen. Instead, they grow out of rhetorical movements that alter cultural understandings of gender and, with that, the rights, privileges, and identities available to women and men.

Rhetoric is persuasion; rhetorical movements are collective, persuasive efforts to challenge and change existing attitudes, laws, and policies. In this chapter, we will consider women's movements that have affected the meaning, roles, status, and opportunities of women in the United States. In addition, we'll note antifeminist movements that have arisen and continue to arise in response to feminist movements. In Chapter 4, we'll explore men's movements that have affected the meaning, roles, status, and opportunities of men in the United States. As we survey these rhetorical movements, you'll discover that they are anything but uniform. They advocate diverse views of gender and pursue a range of goals, not all of which are compatible. Knowledge of the range of rhetorical movements about gender may allow you to more clearly define your own ideas about gender, as well as how you personally express your gender. Even if you do not join a movement, it's worthwhile to learn about the different beliefs and goals of movements that have changed the cultural landscape.

THE THREE WAVES OF WOMEN'S MOVEMENTS IN THE UNITED STATES

Many people think the Women's Movement in America began in the 1960s. This, however, disregards more than a century during which women's movements had significant impact. It also implies that there is a single women's movement, when actually there have been and are multiple women's movements.

Rhetorical movements to define women's nature and rights have occurred in three waves. During each wave, two distinct ideologies have informed movement goals and efforts at change. One ideology, **liberal feminism**, holds that women and men are alike and equal in most respects. Therefore, goes the reasoning, they should have equal rights, roles, and opportunities. A second, quite different ideology, **cultural feminism**, holds that women and men are fundamentally different and, therefore, should have different rights, roles, and opportunities. We'll see that these conflicting ideologies lead to diverse rhetorical goals and strategies. Also, as we'll learn later in this chapter, each wave of activism for women has witnessed a reactionary backlash against changes in women's roles.

You should realize that the wave metaphor for women's movements has limits (Hewitt, 2010). Although it's helpful to organize the movements chronologically, they don't really fit neatly into generational compartments. Themes that were in the first wave—reproductive rights, for example—were also in the second wave and are part of the third wave. Likewise, some of the goals and tactics of third-wave feminists echo those of the radical feminists during the second wave (Fixmer & Wood, 2005). Thus, as you read about three waves of women's movements, keep in mind that specific concerns and ideologies are not restricted to any single chronological point.

THE FIRST WAVE OF WOMEN'S MOVEMENTS IN THE UNITED STATES

Roughly spanning the years from 1840 to 1925, the first wave of women's movements included both liberal and cultural branches. Ironically, the conflicting views of these two movements worked together to change the status and rights of women in U.S. society.

THE WOMEN'S RIGHTS MOVEMENT

The **women's rights movement** engaged in activism aimed at enlarging women's political rights. We might date the start of this movement as 1840 when Lucretia Coffin Mott was chosen as a representative to the World Anti-Slavery Convention in London (Campbell, 1989a), but she was not allowed to participate, because she was a woman. At the convention, Mott met Elizabeth Cady Stanton, who had accompanied her husband (who was a delegate), and the two women discussed the unfairness of Mott's exclusion. The two women quickly bonded on the personal and the political levels.

In the years that followed, Mott and Stanton worked with others to organize the first women's rights convention, the Seneca Falls Convention, which was held in New York in 1848. Lucretia Coffin Mott, Martha Coffin Wright, Mary Anne McClintock, and Elizabeth Cady Stanton collaboratively wrote the keynote address, entitled "Declaration of Sentiments." Ingeniously modeled on the Declaration of Independence, the speech, delivered by Stanton, proclaimed (Campbell, 1989b, p. 34):

> We hold these truths to be self-evident: that all men and women are created equal; that they are endowed by their Creator with certain inalienable rights, that among these are life, liberty, and the pursuit of happiness.

Continuing in the language of the Declaration of Independence, Stanton catalogued specific grievances women had suffered, including denial of the right to vote, exclusion from most forms of higher education, restrictions on employment, and denial of property rights upon marriage. Following Stanton's oration, 32 men and 68 women signed a petition supporting a number of rights for women. Instrumental to passage of the petition was the support of the former slave Frederick Douglass (Campbell, 1989b).

Although Douglass supported women's rights, this fact does not signify widespread participation of black citizens in the women's rights movement. Initially, there were strong links between abolitionist efforts and women's rights. In fact, Frederick Douglass and Elizabeth Cady Stanton were good friends, both fighting for rights for women and blacks (Beck, 2008). However, those ties dissolved as many abolitionists became convinced that attaining voting rights for black men had to precede women's suffrage. In addition, many black women thought that the women's rights movement focused on white women's circumstances and ignored grievous differences caused by race (Breines, 2006). Forced to choose between allegiance to their race and allegiance to their sex, most black women of the era chose race. Thus, the women's rights movement became almost exclusively white in its membership and interests.

On February 3, 1870, the 15th Amendment was ratified, declaring that the right to vote could not be based on "race, color, or previous condition of servitude." Black men had won the right to vote. Not until 48 years later, on August 26, 1920, would women gain the right to vote after two years of protest. From approximately 1918 until 1920, Alice Paul and Lucy Burns spearheaded a nonviolent protest for women's suffrage. Jailed for protesting, a number of the protesters engaged in a prolonged hunger strike, and the correctional staff force-fed the women. This

EXPLORING GENDERED LIVES | A'n't I a Woman?

Isabella Van Wagenen was born as a slave in Ulster County, New York, in the late 1700s. After she was emancipated, Van Wagenen moved to New York City and became a Pentecostal preacher at the age of 46. She preached throughout the Northern states, using the new name she had given herself: Sojourner of God's Truth. She preached in favor of temperance, women's rights, and the abolition of slavery.

On May 28, 1851, Truth attended a women's rights meeting in Akron, Ohio. Throughout the morning, she listened to speeches that focused on white women's concerns. Here, the historical account splits. Some historians (Painter, 1996) state that Sojourner Truth did not speak at the meeting and that someone else gave the speech that is widely credited to Truth. Other scholars state that Sojourner Truth delivered the speech "A'n't I a Woman?" Whether given by Truth or another person, the speech pointed out the ways in which white women's situations and oppression differed from those of black women. The speech eloquently voiced the double oppression suffered by black women of the time (Campbell, 2005; Clift, 2003; Hine & Thompson, 1998). Truth had been owned by a Dutch master, so English was a second language for her, one in which she was not fully fluent. The following excerpt from the speech is based on Frances Dana Gage's transcription (Stanton, Anthony, & Gage, 1882, p. 116).

> Dat man over dar say dat womin needs to be helped into carriages, and lifted ober ditches, and to hab de best place everywhar. Nobody eber helps me into carriages, or ober mud-puddles, or gives me any best place! And a'n't I a woman? ... I have borne thirteen chilern and seen 'em mos' all sold off to slavery, and when I cried out with my mother's grief, none but Jesus heart me! And a'n't I a woman?

protest and the personalities who led it are splendidly documented in the HBO film *Iron Jawed Angels*. The protest for women's suffrage was only one reason that women finally won the right to vote. Another reason was a different movement circulating in the 1800s and early 1900s in America. We'll look at it next.

THE CULT OF DOMESTICITY

In the 1800s a majority of women did not ally themselves with the women's rights movements. Instead, believing the ideal of "true womanhood" (Welter, 1966) to be domesticity, most women of the time were part of a movement referred to as the *cult of domesticity*. Their focus on good homes, families, and communities led them to participate in efforts to end slavery (abolition), ban the consumption of alcohol (temperance, or prohibition) (Fields, 2003; Million, 2003), and enact child labor laws. These early reformers discovered that their efforts to instigate changes in society were hampered by their lack of a legitimate public voice. They realized that a prerequisite for their political action was to secure the rights to speak and vote so they would have a voice in public life (Baker, 2006; Sarkela, Ross, & Lowe, 2003).

These women reformers did not agree with women's rights activists that women and men are fundamentally alike and equal. Instead, they thought that women were more moral, nurturing, concerned about others, and committed to harmony than men. This view led them to argue that women's moral virtue would reform the political world that had been debased by immoral men. This rhetorical strategy was instrumental in women's struggle to gain political franchise.

Although the combined force of the cultural and liberal women's movements was necessary to win suffrage, the deep ideological chasm between these two groups was not resolved. Nor did securing voting rights immediately fuel further efforts to enlarge women's rights, roles, influence, and opportunities. Few women exercised their hard-won right to vote, and in 1925 an amendment to regulate child labor failed to be ratified, signaling the close of the first wave of women's movements.

After this, women's movements in the United States were relatively dormant for about 35 years. This time of quiescence resulted from several factors. First, America's attention was concentrated on two world wars. During that time, women joined the labor force in record numbers to maintain the economy and support the war effort while many men were at war. Between 1940 and 1944, six million women went to work—a 500% increase in the number of women in paid labor (Harrison, 1988).

This changed in postwar America as men's professional opportunities expanded tremendously, but women's shrank. More than two million women who had held jobs during the wars were fired, and their positions were given to male veterans (Barnett & Rivers, 1996). During these years, only 12% of married women with children under the age of six were employed outside their homes (Risman & Godwin, 2001). In the wake of WWII, the average woman married at 20 and had three children before turning 30. By the time she was 40, all of her children were in school, and mothering did not fully occupy her. By the time she was 50, the children had left home (Collins, 2009b). Commenting on this, a 1960 *Newsweek* article noted that when her youngest child enrolled in first grade, the average woman had "forty-five years of leftover life to live" (Diamond, 1960, p. 58).

Although no clear women's movement(s) emerged between the 1920s and the 1960s, there were changes that affected women's lives. Amelia Earhart showed that women could be bold and adventurous; women's sports teams were established and gained some public following; and more effective and available methods of birth control were developed.

THE SECOND WAVE OF WOMEN'S MOVEMENTS IN THE UNITED STATES

Roughly spanning the years between 1960 and 1995, a second wave of women's movements surged across the United States. As in the first wave, both liberal and cultural ideologies coexisted. Also as in the first wave, the second wave pursued diverse goals and used distinct rhetorical strategies.

RADICAL FEMINISM

The first form of feminism to emerge during the second wave was **radical feminism**, also called the *women's liberation movement*. It grew out of New Left politics that protested the Vietnam War and fought for civil rights. New Left women did the same work as their male peers and risked the same hazards of arrest and physical assault, but New Left men treated women as subordinates, expecting them to make coffee, type news releases, do the menial work of organizing, and be ever available for sex.

In 1964, women in the Student Nonviolent Coordinating Committee (SNCC) challenged the sexism in the New Left, but most male members were unresponsive. Stokely Carmichael, a major leader for civil rights, responded to women's demands for equality by telling them that "the position of women in SNCC is prone." (He probably meant *supine*—"on their backs.") In 1965, women in the Students for a Democratic Society (SDS) also found little receptivity to their demands for equality (O'Kelly & Carney, 1986; Stansell, 2010). Outraged by men's refusal to extend to women the democratic, egalitarian principles they advocated for minorities, many women withdrew from the New Left and formed their own organizations. These radical feminists' most basic principle was that oppression of women is the fundamental form of oppression on which all others are modeled (DuPlessis & Snitow, 1999; Willis, 1992).

Radical feminists relied on "rap" groups, or consciousness-raising groups, in which women gathered to talk informally about personal experiences with sexism and to link those personal experiences to larger social and political structures. Radical feminists' commitment to equality and their deep suspicion of hierarchy led them to adopt communication practices that ensured equal participation by all members of rap groups. For instance, some groups used a system of chips, in which each woman was given an equal number of chips at the outset of a rap session; each time she spoke, she tossed one of her chips into the center of the group. When she had used all of her chips, she could not contribute further, and other, less outspoken women had opportunities to speak. This technique encouraged individual women to find and use their voices and taught women to listen to and respect each other. Consciousness-raising groups as well as working committees were leaderless so that participants would have equal power.

Radical feminists relied on revolutionary analysis and politics along with high-profile public events to call attention to the oppression of women and to demand changes in women's place in society and changes in relationships between women and men (Barry, 1998; Freeman, 2002). Examples of public events they staged include:

- Occupation of the *Ladies' Home Journal* office.
- Speak-outs about silenced issues such as rape and abortion.
- Protests against the Miss America pageants in 1968 and 1969, in which women threw cosmetics and constrictive underwear for women into a "Freedom Trash Can" to protest the view of women as sex objects.
- Guerrilla theater, in which they engaged in public communication to dramatize issues and arguments.

Radical feminism continues in the United States and in other countries. One example of contemporary radical feminists is the Missile Dick Chicks, a political

---

EXPLORING GENDERED LIVES | **THE FAMOUS BRA BURNING (THAT DIDN'T HAPPEN!)**

One of the most widespread misperceptions is that feminists burned bras in 1968 to protest the Miss America pageant. That never happened. Here's what did. In planning a response to the pageant, protesters considered a number of strategies to dramatize their disapproval of what the pageant stood for and how it portrayed women. They decided to protest by throwing false eyelashes, bras, and girdles into what they called the Freedom Trash Can. They also put a crown on an animal labeled Miss America and led it around the pageant. In early planning for the protest, some members suggested burning bras, but this idea was abandoned (Collins, 2009; Hanisch, 1970). However, a reporter heard of the plan and reported it as fact on national media. Millions of Americans accepted the report as accurate, and even today many people refer to feminists as "bra burners."

---

street theater troupe from New York City that presents in-your-face protest performances on the street, in post offices, in Times Square, and any other place that strikes them. During George W. Bush's presidency, the Chicks arrived uninvited and unannounced and identified themselves as "a posse of pissed-off housewives from Crawford, Texas, the home of our beloved President George Walker Bush" (The Missile Dick Chicks, 2004). The Chicks outfit themselves in the colors of the American flag, and each Chick is generously endowed with a phallus that looks like a U.S. missile. In 2008, they produced "Trail of Feathers," a feature-length musical documentary about their work (**http://www.trailoffeathers movie.com**).

Another contemporary radical feminist group is the Radical Cheerleaders (Boyd, 2002). The group originated in Florida, but quickly Radical Cheerleader groups formed and performed throughout the United States, Canada, and Europe, including women, men, trans people, and gender-nonidentified people. The Radical Cheerleaders use the style and often costumes, complete with pom poms, of cheerleaders to promote feminism and other progressive political viewpoints. When I was in Washington, D.C., in 2004 for a protest, the Radical Cheerleaders appeared, complete with bright pink pom-poms, and chanted, "One, two, three, four/Gender roles are such a bore."

Radical feminists are also active in working for the liberation of women in non-Western countries. For instance, some Muslim feminists are adopting strong voices and revolutionary challenges to Islam. In her amazingly brash book *The Trouble with Islam*, Irshad Manji (2005) takes on the promise to suicide bombers that they'll awake in paradise to 70 virgins. Manji likens that to a "perpetual license to ejaculate in exchange for a willingness to detonate" (Dickey & Power, 2004, p. 30). Manji wants to reform Islam so that it provides women with the fairness it pledges but has not delivered.

Demonstrations are one communication tool of rhetorical movements.

Sarah   *I have a lot of sympathy with the Muslim woman who wants to reform her faith. I'm a Catholic, and I am really committed to the Church. At the same time, I think the Church should allow women to be leaders and should speak out publicly against domestic violence. I mean, the Church takes public stands saying homosexuality and contraception are wrong, but it says nothing about the wrongness of beating your wife or girlfriend. I will never give up my religion, but that doesn't mean I won't try to change it in some ways.*

Perhaps the most important outcome of radical feminism was the identification of the structural basis of women's oppression. The connection between social practices and individual women's situations was captured in radical feminists'

EXPLORING GENDERED LIVES | **THE GUERRILLA GIRLS**

The Guerrilla Girls, an anonymous radical feminist organization, campaigns against sexism, racism, and elitism in the art world (Guerrilla Girls, 1995). They first captured public attention in the 1980s when they protested the Museum of Modern Art's exhibit entitled, "International Survey of Contemporary Art." The Guerrilla Girls plastered posters throughout public places in New York City. The posters featured one nude woman from the Met's exhibit, but her head was covered by a gorilla mask. Armed with equal measures of information, sarcasm, and humor, the posters asked, "Do women have to be naked to get into the Metropolitan Museum?" Following the question were statistics on the number of women artists (5%) and women nudes (85%) in the museum's exhibit (Kollwitz & Kahlo, 2003). The press appreciated the media-savvy tactics of the Guerrilla Girls and gave them good coverage. The Guerrilla Girls remain anonymous, insisting that their identities are irrelevant and that they want to focus on the issues, not on themselves. This mystery, of course, enhances public interest in the Guerrilla Girls, who appear on talk shows and give public lectures—all the while wearing masks to preserve anonymity.

To what extent do you think radical groups such as Guerrilla Girls and Missile Dick Chicks are effective? (You may need to define "effective" to answer the question.)

The Guerrilla Girls continue their work to serve, in their words, as "the conscience of the art world." Visit their website at **http://www.guerrillagirls.com**.

---

declaration that "the personal is political." Through consciousness raising and collective efforts, radical feminists launched a women's health movement that taught women to resist sexist attitudes from some doctors and become knowledgeable about their own bodies (Boston Women's Health Club Book Collective, 1976; The Diagram Group, 1977). Although radical feminists' refusal to formally organize limited their ability to affect public policies and structures, they offered—and continue to offer—a profound and far-reaching critique of sexual inequality.

LESBIAN FEMINISM

Radical feminism's rejection of male dominance and sexual exploitation of women paved the way for the emergence of a group called Radicalesbians. Members of this group took the radical feminist idea of putting women first a few steps further to assert that only women who loved and lived with women were really putting women first. Arguing that only women who do not orient their lives around men can be truly free, Radicalesbians embraced lesbianism as a positive and liberated identity.

Not all lesbians are feminists, and not all lesbians who adopt feminism are Radicalesbians. Many lesbian feminists are also committed to political activism designed to improve the conditions of women's lives. They join groups ranging from mainstream to radical (Taylor & Rupp, 1998). However, the Radicalesbians

EXPLORING GENDERED LIVES | **REPRODUCTIVE RIGHTS**

Birth control was and is a priority in many women's movements. In the nineteenth century, Elizabeth Cady Stanton insisted that "voluntary motherhood" was a prerequisite of women's freedom (Gordon, 1976; Schiff, 2006). Margaret Sanger's work as a nurse and midwife made her painfully aware that many women, particularly immigrants and poor women, died in childbirth or as a result of illegal abortions (Chesler, 1992). In speeches throughout America and Europe, Sanger advocated birth control for women. In her periodical publication, *The Woman Rebel,* Sanger declared that a woman's body belongs to herself, not the Church or government.

During the second wave of feminism in the United States, feminists again protested for safe, accessible birth control and abortion for all women. In 1969, a group of feminists disrupted the New York state legislature's hearing on abortion reform—the experts who had been invited to address the legislature consisted of fourteen men and one nun (Pollitt, 2000). The protesters insisted that none of the experts had had personal experience with what reproductive choices mean. Four years later, the landmark case *Roe v. Wade* established abortion as a woman's right. Yet, abortion is still not available to all women who are citizens of the United States.

Reproductive rights have also emerged as a focus of the third wave (Jacobson, 2004a; Smeal, 2004). The March for Women's Lives, held on April 25, 2004, on the Capitol Mall in Washington, D.C., drew hundreds of thousands of marchers who were concerned that rights won with *Roe v. Wade* might be reversed. Voicing their support for the right of women to be in charge of their own reproductive health, the marchers included young men and women, grandmothers, and mothers with babies.

Reproductive rights are central to feminist movements, but not all feminist movements are pro-choice. Groups such as Feminists for Life, of which Alaska's ex-Governor Sarah Palin is a member, are firmly against abortion. They argue that choosing not to have a child is antithetical to feminine values.

There is a widespread assumption that birth control is liberatory for women. In reality, however, efforts to control reproduction have been liberatory only for some women, and they have been decisively disempowering for other women (Gordon, 2007; Rose, 2007). For instance, throughout much of the twentieth century, women who were black, immigrant, poor, mentally challenged, or otherwise "undesirable" were sterilized without their consent. Further, if we understand birth control literally, we realize it is about both preventing and enabling births. Again, we see the liberatory nature of enabling some births is linked to class, race, and ethnicity. Well-to-do women who cannot or do not wish to conceive or carry a fetus, can afford to engage in extensive and expensive fertility enhancement procedures and to hire surrogates to gestate fetuses. Those options are not available to poor women who, in fact, are usually the surrogates.

worked out much of the political philosophy that informs the more general group of **lesbian feminists**. They define themselves as women-identified to distinguish themselves from heterosexual women whom they see as male-identified. Being woman-identified fuels their commitment to ending discrimination against all women, including lesbians.

For lesbian feminists, the primary goals are to live as woman-identified women and to make it possible for women in committed, enduring relationships to enjoy the same property, insurance, and legal rights granted to heterosexual spouses. The rhetoric of lesbian feminists has two characteristic forms. First, lesbian feminists use their voices to respond to social criticism of their sexual orientations. Second, some lesbian feminists adopt proactive rhetorical strategies to assert their value, rights, and integrity.

SEPARATISM

The second wave of U.S. feminism saw the emergence of another branch of feminism. **Separatists** build communities in which women live independently in mutual respect and harmony. Many, although not all, separatists are lesbian. Some women believe, as first-wave cultural feminists did, that women are fundamentally different from men in the value they place on life, equality, harmony, nurturance, and peace. Finding that these values gain little hearing in a patriarchal, capitalist society, some women form all-women communities in which feminine values can flourish without intrusion from men and the aggressive, individualistic, oppressive values these women associate with Western masculinity.

Separatists believe it is impossible—or a poor use of their generative energies—to attempt to reform America's patriarchal, homophobic culture. Instead, they choose to exit mainstream society and form communities that value women and strive to live in harmony with people, animals, and the earth. In adopting this course of action, separatists limit their potential to alter dominant social values. Because they do not assume a public voice to critique the values they find objectionable, they exercise little political influence. Yet, their very existence defines an alternative vision of how we might live—one that speaks of harmony, cooperation, and peaceful coexistence of all life forms.

▼

Regina   *I don't see much to be gained by having equal rights to participate in institutions that are themselves all wrong. I don't believe dog-eat-dog ethics are right. I don't want to be part of a system where I can advance only if I slit somebody else's throat or step on him or her. I don't want to prostitute myself for bits of power in a business. I would rather work for different ways of living, ones that are more cooperative, like win-win strategies. Maybe that means I'm a dreamer, but I just can't motivate myself to work at gaining status in a system that I don't respect.*

REVALORISM

Many first- and second-wave women's movements led to an enlarged respect for the music, literature, and art created by women whose creative, artistic work has been silenced or ignored for centuries (Aptheker, 1998). **Revalorists** are feminists who focus on appreciating women's traditional activities and contributions and increasing society's appreciation of women and their contributions to society. The broad goal of revalorists is to increase the value that society places on women and on the skills, activities, and philosophies associated with women's traditional roles.

Drawing on standpoint theory, which we discussed in Chapter 2, revalorists believe that women's traditional involvement in homemaking and caregiving makes most women more nurturing, supportive, cooperative, and life-giving than most men. Sara Ruddick (1989), for instance, claims that the process of mothering young children cultivates "maternal thinking," which is marked by attentiveness to others and commitment to others' health, happiness, and development. Karlyn Campbell's work, *Man Cannot Speak for Her* (1989a, 1989b), documents women's rhetorical accomplishments that have been excluded from conventional histories of the United States. In documenting women's contributions, revalorists aim to render a more complete history of the United States and the people who comprise it.

Revalorist rhetoric is consistent with the goal of heightened public awareness of and respect for women and their contributions to society. First, revalorists often use unusual language to call attention to what they are doing. For instance, they talk about *re-covering,* not *recovering,* women's history, to indicate that they want to go beyond patriarchal perspectives on history. Second, revalorists affirm the integrity of women and their contributions by supporting exhibitions of women's traditional arts, such as weaving and quilting, and public festivals that highlight women's creative expression. Third, revalorists work to secure unique legal rights for women; for instance, they argue that laws must recognize that only women bear children and thus they have special needs that must be legally protected.

ECOFEMINISM

Sharing the separatists' belief in living in harmony, but not embracing the separatists' ideal of women-only communities are ecofeminists, who unite the intellectual and political strength of feminist thought with ecology's concerns about our living planet. **Ecofeminism** was launched in 1974, when Françoise d'Eaubonne published *Le Féminisme ou la Mort,* which is translated *Feminism or Death.* This book provided the philosophical foundation of ecofeminism.

Ecofeminists in both Europe and America perceive a connection between efforts to control and subordinate women and the quest to dominate nature (perhaps not coincidentally called "Mother Earth"). Rosemary Radford Reuther (1974, 1983, 2001), a Christian and theological scholar, argues that the lust to dominate has brought the world to the brink of a moral and ecological crisis in which there can be no winners and all will be destroyed. According to Judith Plant, an appropriately named advocate of ecofeminism (Sales, 1987, p. 302):

[This movement] gives women and men common ground.... The social system isn't good for either—or both—of us. Yet we are the social system. We need some common ground ... to enable us to recognize and affect the deep structure of our relations with each other and with our environment.

Ecofeminists believe that, as long as oppression is culturally valued, it will be imposed on anyone and anything that cannot or does not resist. Thus, oppression is the focus, and women's oppression is best understood as a specific example of an overarching cultural ideology that esteems oppression. Many animal rights activists, vegetarians, vegans, and peace activists have joined the ecofeminist movement. Prominent first-wave feminists such as Charlotte Perkins Gilman, Susan B. Anthony, and Mary Wollstonecraft thought that vegetarianism and animal rights were integral to a coherent feminist agenda.

Stephanie   *Some of my strongest values involve ending the oppression of animals and living a sustainable lifestyle. Until I read about ecofeminism, I never saw the connection between those beliefs and feminism. But it makes sense, once you think about it, that if it's wrong to oppress animals and the earth, it's wrong to oppress women ... or anyone ... or anything.*

The goals of this movement flow directly from its critique of cultural values. Ecofeminists seek to bring themselves and others to a new consciousness of humans' interdependence with all other life forms. To do so, they speak out against values that encourage exploitation, domination, and aggression and show how these oppress women, men, children, animals, and the planet itself (Beate, 2001; Cudworth, 2005; Warren, 2000). In *Feminism Is for Everybody,* author bell hooks (2002) says it's a mistake to think that feminism is about only women or women's rights. She says feminism is about justice, which she thinks is achieved by ending all kinds of domination and oppression, including but not limited to sexism and racism. For her, all forms of oppression are linked. She thinks that only when nobody is oppressed will it be possible for us to form truly authentic, loving bonds of mutuality.

Radical feminism, lesbian feminism, separatism, revalorism, and ecofeminism subscribe, to varying degrees, to the cultural ideology that women and men are different in important ways. In contrast, a number of second-wave women's movements adopt the liberal ideology that women and men are fundamentally alike. We turn now to those groups to see what they believe and what they accomplish.

LIBERAL FEMINISM

The best-known second-wave feminist movement is liberal feminism, which advocates women's equality in all spheres of life. This movement has its roots in the mid-1900s. At that time, many white, middle-class women were living what they had been told was the American dream: Their husbands earned the income while they took care of the children, maintained their suburban homes with matching appliances, and chauffeured the children in their station wagons. But many of these middle-class homemakers were not happy. They loved their families and homes, but they also wanted an identity beyond the home. So they were not only unhappy, but also they felt guilty that they were not satisfied. Because they felt guilty about their dissatisfaction, they kept their feelings to themselves. Consequently, they didn't realize that many other women also felt unfulfilled.

The liberal feminist movement was ignited in 1963 with publication of Betty Friedan's landmark book, *The Feminine Mystique*. The book's title was Friedan's way of naming what she called "the problem that has no name," by which she meant the vague, chronic discontent that many white, middle-class American women felt. Friedan named the problem and, following the insight of radical feminists, defined it as a political issue, not a personal one. She pointed out that women were not able to pursue personal development because of political or structural factors: American institutions, especially laws, kept many women confined to domestic roles with no opportunity for fulfillment in arenas outside of home life.

It wasn't news to most women that they felt trapped in their suburban lives. When *Redbook*, a popular women's magazine of the era, announced a contest to find out why young mothers felt trapped, 24,000 women submitted essays (Collins, 2009b).

Also fueling changes in women's lives were economic factors and, more specifically, marketing strategies to convince both women and men that it was not only appropriate, but desirable for married women to work outside of the home. The robust economic boom that followed WWII moved unprecedented numbers of families into the middle class, and all of these new middle-class families wanted their own homes, central heating, appliances, and other advantages of wealth. The economy could continue to expand only as long as Americans continued to want and buy more: not just one car, but a second car; not just weekends at home but annual family vacations; and college educations for children. Marketers in the 1960s began emphasizing the two-income family as the American ideal because both incomes were needed to sustain the consumption patterns Americans had developed. Three decades after WWII ended, in the 1970s, working wives provided an average of one-third of their families' income (Collins, 2009b).

Liberal feminism is embodied in NOW, the National Organization for Women. Founded in 1966, NOW works to secure political, professional, and educational equality for women and has become a public voice for equal rights for women. It remains a powerful and visible organization that is effective in gaining passage of laws and policies that enlarge women's opportunities and protect their rights.

Liberal feminism identifies and challenges institutional practices, policies, and laws that exclude women from positions of influence in public and professional life. The rhetorical strategies of this movement include lobbying, speaking at public forums, drafting legislation, and holding conventions where goals and strategies are developed. Initially, liberal feminism focused almost exclusively on issues in the lives of women who were white, middle-class, heterosexual, able-bodied, and young or middle-aged. In response to criticism of this narrow focus, liberal feminism began to pay more attention to and devote more political effort to issues faced by women who are not white, middle-class, heterosexual, able-bodied, and young. As a result, liberal feminism has become more inclusive of diverse women

---

EXPLORING GENDERED LIVES | **ABOUT NOW**

The National Organization for Women was established on June 30, 1966, in Washington, D.C., at the Third National Conference on the Commission on the Status of Women. Among the 28 founders of NOW were Betty Friedan, its first president, and the Reverend Pauli Murray, an African-American woman who was an attorney and poet. Murray co-authored NOW's original mission statement, which begins with this sentence: "The purpose of NOW is to take action to bring women into full participation in the mainstream of American society now, exercising all privileges and responsibilities thereof in truly equal partnership with men." Among NOW's achievements:

- Executive Order 11375, which prohibits sex discrimination by federal contractors.
- Amending the Civil Rights Act of 1965 to include sex, along with race, religion, and nationality, as an illegal basis for employment discrimination.
- Support of federally financed child-care centers to enable women to work outside the home.
- Documenting sexism in media.
- Identification of and publicity about sexism in children's books and programs to enable parents and teachers to make informed choices about media for their children.
- Reform of credit and banking practices that disadvantage women.
- Enlargement of women's opportunities to participate in sports.
- EEOC adoption of a rule that sex-segregated want ads are discriminatory.
- Support for women who seek elective and appointive public office.
- Highlighting gender inequities worldwide, particularly in poorer countries.

---

and the issues in their lives. Today NOW sponsors poster contests on the theme of "Love Your Body" to encourage all women to appreciate the bodies they have instead of obsessing over dieting. NOW's homepage also has a link to its work against racisim and a link to the "Media Hall of Shame" that calls attention to advertisements that are egregiously sexist.

Liberal feminism is not confined to the United States. Feminist groups around the world are committed to equal rights for women. Spain, the country that gave birth to the word *machismo*, is responding to the influence of liberal feminism. Activist work, particularly work done by feminist NGOs (nongovernment organizations) in the third world at the grassroots level, has contributed substantially to global awareness of particular forms of oppression of women, such as sex trafficking (Hegde, 2006; Townsley, 2006; Vargas, 2003). In 2004 in Mumbai, India, record numbers of women participated in The World Social Forum and drew worldwide attention to the urgent and continuing issues of violence against women (Sen & Saini, 2005,). In Iraq, women today have fewer rights than before U.S. troops invaded the country. Women there have created The Organization of

Cartoon by Clay Bennett. Reprinted by permission.

Women's Freedom in Iraq (OWFI: **http://www.equalityiniraq.com**) to fight for women's rights to education, employment, marital choice, and inheritance (McKee, 2006). After a long struggle for suffrage, Kuwaiti women gained the right to vote in 2006 (Fattah, 2006).

Cass   *I really like what NOW is about and how it works. It's not as cool as some of the radical groups, but it makes change happen by working within the system. NOW has changed laws and policies. It's given a national platform for fighting racism and women's self-hatred. It's gotten women elected to office. You can't have that kind of impact unless you get inside the system and figure out how to change it from the inside.*

WOMANISM

Another group of second-wave activists who believe that women and men are alike in many ways call themselves **womanists** to differentiate themselves from white feminists. Beginning in the 1970s, a number of African-American women who were disenchanted with white, middle-class feminism but who were committed to women's equality began to organize their own groups (Smith, 1998). Feminist organizations such as Black Women Organized for Action and the National Black Feminist Organization sprang up and quickly attracted members. Many African-American women see womanism as addressing both their racial and gender identities (Guy-Sheftall, 2003; Radford-Hill, 2000).

Womanists highlight the ways in which gender and racial oppression intersect in the lives of women of color. Black women in America have a distinctive cultural history that has not been well recognized, much less addressed, by the white, middle-class women who have dominated both waves of American women's movements (Cole & Guy-Sheftall, 2003; Parks, 2010). Compared to white women, black women as a group are more often single, have less formal education, bear more children, are paid less, and assume more financial responsibility for supporting families. Many black women don't identify with feminist agendas that ignore their experiences and their strength (Findlen, 1995; Morgan, 2003; Parks, 2010; Roth, 2003).

In addition to focusing on race, womanists attend to ways in which class intersects race and sex to create inequality. Womanist organizations often include working-class women and address issues that keenly affect lower-class African-American women. Their goals include reforming social services to respond more humanely to poor women, and increasing training and job opportunities so that women of color can improve the material conditions of their lives. Womanists' rhetorical strategies include consciousness raising and support among women of color, lobbying decision makers for reforms in laws, and community organizing to build grassroots leadership of, by, and for women of color.

In 1997, African-American women organized a march to celebrate and nourish community among African-American women. Following the second Million Man March, which we'll discuss in the next chapter, the **Million Woman March** was held in Philadelphia on October 24 and 25, 1997. Powered by grassroots volunteers who built support in their localities, the steering committee of the Million Woman March was made up not of celebrities but of average women who worked at unglamorous jobs and lived outside the spotlight. The march deemphasized media hype in favor of woman-to-woman sharing of experiences, hopes,

---

EXPLORING GENDERED LIVES | **TO BE WOMANISH, TO BE A WOMANIST**

Alice Walker is credited with coining the term womanism as a label for black women who believe in women's value, rights, and opportunities. According to Walker, Southern black women often said to their daughters, "You acting womanish," which meant the daughters were being bold, courageous, and willful. To be womanish is to demand to know more than others say is good for you—to stretch beyond what is prescribed for a woman or girl (Collins, 1998). In her 1983 book *In Search of Our Mothers' Gardens,* Walker writes, "Womanist is to feminist as purple is to lavender" (p. xii).

and support. Perhaps the spirit of the Million Woman March is best summed up by Irma Jones, a 74-year-old woman who had marched with Dr. Martin Luther King Jr. from Selma to Montgomery. After the Million Woman March, Jones said, "I'm glad we did this before I died. People say black women can never get together. Today, we got together, sister" (Logwood, 1998, p. 19).

MULTIRACIAL FEMINISM

Building on womanism's critique of mainstream feminism's focus on white, middle-class women, **multiracial feminism** emphasizes multiple systems of domination that affect the lives of women and men (Anzaldúa, 2002; Anzaldúa & Keating, 2002; Collins, 1998; Ryan, 2004). Leaders of this new movement prefer the term *multiracial* to *multicultural* because they believe that race is a particularly potent power system that shapes people's identities and opportunities (Zinn & Dill, 1996).

At the same time, multiracial feminists insist that race cannot be viewed in isolation. Although especially important from multiracial feminists' perspective, race intersects other systems of domination in ways that affect what race means. For instance, an Asian American will experience his or her race differently, depending on whether he or she is a member of the professional class, the working class, or the middle class.

Multiracial feminists insist that gender does not have universal meaning—instead, what gender means and how it affects our lives varies as a result of race, economic class, sexual orientation, and so forth. Gloria Anzaldúa (1999), a Chicana feminist, resists being categorized only according to her sex or her race-ethnicity or her sexual orientation. She insists that, on its own, each category misrepresents her identity because her race-ethnicity affects the meaning of being a woman and a lesbian; her sex affects the meaning of her race-ethnicity and sexual orientation; and her sexual orientation affects the meaning of being a woman and a Chicana. Yen Le Espiritu (1997) makes the same argument about Asian-American women and men, as does Minh-ha Trinh (1989) about Vietnamese women.

Katie   *I like the ideas of the multiracial feminists. I agree that race cuts across everything else. I'm middle-class, but my life isn't the same as a white, middle-class girl's, because I'm Asian American. It's like the issues in my life aren't just about my sex; they're also about my race. I can talk to black or Hispanic girls, and we have a lot in common—more than I have in common with most white girls. You just can't get away from the issue of race unless you're white.*

For multiracial feminists, the key to understanding identity lies in the intersection of multiple categories such as gender, race-ethnicity, sexual orientation, and economic class. This leads multiracial feminists to write and talk, not about women or men as broad groups, but about more precise and complex categories such as black, working-class lesbians, and middle-class, heterosexual Chicanas.

Central to multiracial feminism is emphasis on women's agency. Despite the constraints imposed by systems of domination, women of color have often resisted their oppressions. Even when they operated within abhorrent systems of domination such as slavery, women of color found ways to care for themselves and their families and to contribute to their communities. In recognizing that women of color have resisted oppression, multiracial feminists highlight the strengths of women.

Multiracial feminists have contributed significantly to feminist theory and practice by challenging the idea of a "universal woman" and by showing that many groups are disadvantaged by multiple and intersecting forms of domination. This important insight compels us to recognize how intersections among multiple social locations, or standpoints, shape individual lives and structure society.

POWER FEMINISM

The 1990s gave birth to a new movement called **power feminism**. Writing in 1993, Naomi Wolf argued that it is self-defeating to focus on the social causes of inequities and the harm that women suffer. As an alternative, Wolf advocates power feminism, which contends that society doesn't oppress women, because women have the power to control what happens to them. Wolf urges women to "stop thinking of themselves as victims" and to capitalize on the power inherent in their majority status. Wolf tells women that the only thing holding them back from equality is their own belief that they are victims.

Katie Roiphe is a proponent of power feminism. In her 1993 book, *The Morning After: Sex, Fear, and Feminism on Campus,* Roiphe denied that rape is widespread on campuses and in society. Roiphe asserts that Take Back the Night marches, annual nonviolent protests that began in 1978 to speak out against rape, are self-defeating because "proclaiming victimhood" does not project strength. Roiphe ignores the fact that, for many people, Take Back the Night marches fuel activism, not victimhood.

Folana   *The only people I know who talk the power feminist talk have never been raped and never been slapped in the face with discrimination. They think their success and safety is a result of their own efforts and that any woman or minority person who hasn't achieved what they have just didn't try. I'll bet a lot of them would drop the power feminist line if they got raped. That might make them see that women and minorities don't have as much power as people like Wolf and Roiphe. As for me, I don't think of myself as a victim, but I know I'm vulnerable just because I'm black and a woman.*

Power feminism ignores the difference between being a victim at one moment, on the one hand, and adopting the status of victim as an identity, on the other hand. Bryn Panee, a student of mine, clarified this distinction when she reported on her experiences as a rape crisis counselor: "Every turnaround case, where a woman is able to make the transformation from a helpless victim to an empowered survivor, could not have happened if she did not recognize she was a victim of a horrible crime" (1994, n.p.).

Power feminism appeals to some women who, like Naomi Wolf and Katie Roiphe, are white, financially comfortable, successful, and well educated. It is less helpful to women who do not enjoy those privileges. Perhaps that is why power feminism is embraced mainly by white, heterosexual, middle- and upper-class women who have little or no personal experience with discrimination and violation. Although power feminism has not become a major movement, its emphasis on empowering women has been influential in shaping the third wave of American women's movements.

THE THIRD WAVE OF WOMEN'S MOVEMENTS IN THE UNITED STATES

Many branches of second-wave feminism continue to be active today. At the same time, a third wave of feminism has emerged. Drawing from multiple branches of second-wave feminism, especially radical and multiracial feminism, **third-wave feminism** includes women of different ethnicities, abilities and disabilities, classes, appearances, sexual orientations, and gender identities. Third-wave feminism is less fully formed than other branches of feminism. Groups who identify as third-wave feminists include ones working to end violence against women and MomsRising, which aims to change policies that limit parents' abilities to participate in paid labor. Perhaps because it is new, this wave of feminism has not yet defined a clear center. On the other hand, it could be that the third wave will be characterized by multiplicity and the resistance to any single center (Henry, 2004).

Although the newest feminist movement draws from earlier movements, third-wave feminism is not simply an extension of the goals, principles, and values of the second wave (Fixmer, 2003; Fixmer & Wood, 2005; Hernández & Rehman, 2002; Howry & Wood, 2001; Johnson, 2007). The newest feminists have a distinct historical location that informs their politics and goals. At this early stage, we can identify six features that seem to characterize third-wave feminism.

RECOGNIZING DIFFERENCES AMONG WOMEN

Informed by multiracial feminists' attention to differences among women, third-wave feminists recognize that women differ in many ways, including race, class, sexual orientation, body shape and size, and (dis) ability. Third-wavers, coming of age in an era sharply infused with awareness of differences, are figuring out how to speak about and for women as a group while simultaneously recognizing differences among women (Dicker & Piepmeier, 2003; Fixmer, 2003; Zack, 2005). More than second-wave feminists, third wavers focus on the intersectionality of oppression, pointing out that race, class, sex, sexual orientation, and gender identity are intricately woven together and must be addressed holistically. Eve Ensler's latest book, *I Am an Emotional Creature* (2011) includes monologues from girls all over the world, showing both how they are different and how they have commonalities.

BUILDING COALITIONS

A second defining feature of third-wave feminism is a commitment to building alliances with men and other groups that work against various kinds of oppression. Most previous branches of feminism have focused primarily on the needs and rights of white, heterosexual women, which created tensions between heterosexual women and men and between white, heterosexual women and other women. Third-wavers want to get beyond these divisions and build a movement that not only accepts but celebrates diversity.

According to third-wave writers, recognizing differences can lead to a deep appreciation of the intersections among various forms of privilege and oppression. In third-waver Mocha Jean Herrup's (1995) words, people need to "realize that to fight AIDS we must fight homophobia, and to fight homophobia we must fight racism, and so on.... Oppression is interrelated" (p. 247).

Natalie   *I really appreciate what the sixties women's movement did to make my life better, but I can't identify with it. My life is different than my mother's, and so are the issues that matter to me. Mom fought to get a job. I want a job that pays well and lets me advance. Mom worked really hard to find day care for her children. I want to have a marriage and a job that allow me not to have to rely on day care. Her generation fought to make it okay for women not to marry. My generation wants to figure out how to make marriages work better, more fairly. Different generations. Different issues.*

ENGAGING IN EVERYDAY RESISTANCE

Although appreciative of the achievements of earlier waves of feminism, third-wave feminists insist that the reforms won by the second wave have not been woven into everyday life. Sexism is often more subtle today than in 1960 or 1980, but it still exists; in fact, its subtlety is what makes it so challenging (Bennett, Ellison, & Ball, 2010). According to Shani Jamila (2002), laws no longer permit race and gender to be used as automatic barriers, but women and minorities still experience injustices that are subtle and outside legal censure. This motivates third wavers to embrace grassroots organizing and to challenge racist comments in the workplace and on the street, confront homophobic attitudes, and be willing to reject class privileges, including those that benefit us. Jennifer Baumgardner and Amy Richards (2000) declare that, for third-wave feminists, "our politics emerge from our everyday lives" (p. 18). Personal acts are seen as a key way to instigate change, and local actions are viewed as routes to social change (Bodey & Wood, 2009; Fixmer & Wood, 2005; Sheridan-Rabideau, 2009).

Third-wave feminists insist that their politics must be rooted in personal, bodily resistance to oppressive ideologies. In a stunning essay that explicitly links social constructions of female beauty to eating disorders that jeopardize millions of women's health, Abra Fortune Chernik (1995) writes, "Gazing in the mirror at my emaciated body, I observed a woman held up by her culture as the physical ideal because she was starving, self-obsessed and powerless, a woman called beautiful because she threatened no one except herself" (p. 81). After recognizing the connection between cultural codes for femininity and her own body, Chernik responded in a way that was both personal and political: "Gaining weight and getting my head out of the toilet bowl was the most political act I have ever committed" (p. 81).

BEING MEDIA SAVVY

More than previous generations, third wavers are media savvy. They grew up in a media-saturated world, so engaging media is part of how they define their identities, interrogate politics, and advance a feminist agenda. Third-wave feminists, like other members of their generation, tend to be wired, plugged in, and virtually networked so that they gain information from numerous sources and also create media of their own (Harris, 2004; Kearney, 2006; Johnson, 2007; Nunes, 2006). Third wavers not only read zines, but many of them produce and circulate zines that carry political messages about girls (Piepmeier, 2009; Sheridan-Rabideau, 2009). Whereas second-wave feminists waited for the 6 p.m. news on TV to learn about the day's events, third-wavers are likely to learn immediately of new developments from IMs, text messages, and blogs, and they often post their own videos of rallies and other events on YouTube and other websites. The Exploring Gendered Lives box on MomsRising illustrates how one media-savvy third-wave group organizes for political impact.

Third-wave feminists also use mass and social media to advance their ideas. Singer Tori Amos's songs decry violence against women. Her fans' response to such songs led Amos to found R.A.I.N.N., The Rape, Abuse, and Incest National Network, which is a national hotline. Many other young feminists find their voices on blogs, in zines, and in exchanges on social network websites (Kearney, 2006).

EXPLORING GENDERED LIVES | **THE MOTHERHOOD MANIFESTO**

That's the title of a book cowritten by Joan Blades, who previously cofounded the highly influential MoveOn.org, and Kristin Rowe-Finkbeiner. Behind the title is a fast-growing grassroots movement called MomsRising, which is dedicated to changing government and institutional policies that make it difficult or impossible for parents to simultaneously engage in paid labor and care responsibly for children. Their demands include paid maternity and paternity leave, flexible work hours and locations, and decent health care for children. Blades and Rowe-Finkbeiner collaborate and coordinate their leadership primarily through e-mail messages, and MomsRising relies on cyberspace mobilization to increase membership, keep members informed about issues, and organize members for political impact. More than 85,000 members have joined in just the past year (Seligman, 2007).

To learn more about MomsRising, visit the organization's website: http://www.MomsRising.org.

EMBRACING AESTHETICS AND CONSUMERISM

One implication of living in a media-saturated era is that news and images of celebrities are easy to find and, in fact, hard to avoid. When Britney bares various parts of her body, or Paris goes to prison, gets out of prison, and goes back in, videos are available almost immediately online. Twenty-somethings live in a wired world in which they are bombarded by images and stories of celebrities who are scantily dressed, frequently in trouble with the law, and in and out of various highly publicized sexual relationships. It is unsurprising that many young women see celebrities as role models (Lamb & Brown, 2006; Levy, 2005; Seely, 2007). Some, but not all, women who identify as third-wave feminists embrace traditional "girl culture" by placing a premium on being pretty, feminine, sexy, and having the latest fashions. They argue that there is no contradiction between being feminist and being sexy. Being sexy and feminine, however, takes a lot of energy and money. Thus, some, although not all, third-wave feminists embrace consumerism—spending money to belong to or be seen at the "right" restaurants, bars, spas, and stores and to acquire status symbols, including designer clothes and name-brand products (Chaudhry, 2005; Levy, 2005).

Taken to extremes, commodification may go beyond acquiring commodities and lead to regarding the self—one's own mind and body—as a commodity (Shugart, Waggoner, & Hallstein, 2001). In her provocatively titled book, *Female Chauvinist Pigs* (2005), Ariel Levy argues that many young women today equate sexual freedom with objectifying themselves, particularly by making themselves into sex objects for others' consumption. The availability of sexually explicit and sometimes pornographic materials creates a pressure for women to accept sexual images of women and to imitate exotic dancers in order to feel that they are liberated and to convince others that they are not uptight about sex (Paul, 2006). But, asks Levy, whose version of sexy is at stake when teenaged women trade exposing themselves for a girls-gone-wild T-shirt? Whose pleasure is being served? Rather than using sex as currency, Levy encourages women to explore their sexuality on their own terms.

INDIVIDUALISM

A final characteristic of third wave feminism is a focus on individualism—individual goals, strategies, and identities (Crawford, 2007; Henry, 2004). Third wavers claim that because women are so different and their issues are so diverse, there can be no collective political agenda. Life and identity become DIY (do it yourself) projects in which each woman defines feminism on her own terms and lives her life on the principle that every woman can choose to be whatever she wants to be.

One example of third wavers' emphasis on individualism is autobiographical essays, often posted on blogs or social network pages. Astrid Henry (2004), whose research focuses on women's movements, notes that while autobiographical essays can be a first step in consciousness raising, third-wave feminists have gotten stuck and are unable or unwilling to move "from this beginning consciousness-raising stage of self-expression to developing a larger analysis of the relationship between individual and collective experience, culminating in theory and political

---

EXPLORING GENDERED LIVES | **TWENTY-FIRST-CENTURY FEMINISM**

In a July 9, 2009 interview, a *The Seattle Times* reporter asked Gloria Steinem what twenty-first-century feminism looks like. Here's Steinem's answer: "It looks like you. It looks like each self-respecting woman in the twenty-first century. It's not for me to define; the message of feminism is that each of us, as female human beings, define ourselves. There are some generalities that you can see. It's much more international, I'm happy to say. I think clearly most of the country now understands that women can do what men can do; the problem is that they don't understand that men can do what women can do, which as I was saying, is the reason why women still suffer from having two jobs" (Seattle Times, 2009).

---

action.... for the third wave, identity politics is limited to expression of individual identity" (pp. 43–44). Other researchers (Bodey, 2009; Bodey & Wood, 2009) suggest that third wavers use social media to define their identities and their politics.

The third wave's emphasis on individualism does not cultivate a cohesive political agenda that can help build the structures, which will support their life choices (Crawford, 2007; Rowe-Finkbeiner, 2004). For example, many women in my classes believe that if they do well in school and work hard, they can succeed in any career they choose. Yet, I worry that they may confront obstacles such as lower pay than male peers and discrimination against mothers (Hayden & O'Brien Hallstein, 2010; Williams, 2004; Williams & Calvert, 2005–2007). Obstacles such as these are not removed by individual effort; they require structural change, and structural change grows out of collective political action.

In sum, third-wave feminists use media, particularly social media, to build on and go beyond the ideas and accomplishments of prior feminist movements in an effort to make feminism more inclusive, more engaged with everyday life, and more individualistic. As they voice their concerns and carry out their politics, they will remake feminism to resonate with the priorities of their generation.

ANTIFEMINISM: THE BACKLASH

Challenging and changing women's roles and rights have not gone unchecked. The successes of feminism have led to intense antifeminist efforts, also called the backlash against feminism. A **backlash** against feminism has surfaced in response to each wave of activism for women (Superson & Cudd, 2002).

Antifeminism opposes changes in women's roles, status, rights, or opportunities. Antifeminist movements arose in response to both the first and second waves of women's movements in the United States (Blee, 1998). There is also evidence that a third antifeminist movement is shaping up in reaction to the third wave of feminism.

THE FIRST WAVE: THE ANTISUFFRAGE MOVEMENT

The first formal example of antifeminism was the **antisuffrage movement,** which aimed to prevent women from gaining the right to vote in the United States. Immediately following the Seneca Falls Convention in 1848, vocal opposition to women's suffrage surfaced. Both men and women claimed that allowing women to vote, to pursue higher education, and to own property would contradict women's natural roles as wives and mothers.

By the 1870s, opposition to women's suffrage was formalized in public organizations that were often led by the wives of socially prominent men (Blee, 1998). The best-known antisuffrage organization was the National Association Opposed to Women's Suffrage, which claimed to have 350,000 members (Blee, 1998). The antisuffrage movement reached its apex between 1911 and 1916 and disbanded after women won the right to vote in 1920.

THE SECOND WAVE: FASCINATING, TOTAL WOMAN

A second antifeminist movement emerged in the 1970s when Marabel Morgan launched the Total Woman movement and Helen Andelin founded the Fascinating Womanhood movement, both of which advocated women's return to traditional attitudes, values, and roles. The Total Woman movement (Morgan, 1973) stressed the conventional social view of women as sex objects and urged women to devote their energies to making themselves sexually irresistible to men. One example of advice given to women was to surprise their husbands by meeting them at the door dressed only in Saran Wrap. Fascinating Womanhood (Andelin, 1975) was grounded in conservative interpretations of biblical teachings, and it emphasized women's duty to embody moral purity and submit to their husbands.

Although many people saw the Fascinating Womanhood and Total Woman movements as laughable, more than 400,000 women paid to take courses that taught them to be more sexually attractive and submissive to their husbands (O'Kelly & Carney, 1986). Primary support for these courses and the ideologies behind them came from women who were economically dependent on husbands and who embraced conservative values.

THE SECOND WAVE: THE STOP ERA CAMPAIGN

Another instance of backlash was the STOP ERA movement, which also emerged in the 1970s. This movement was a direct response to the 1972 and 1973 campaign to ratify the Equal Rights Amendment (ERA).

The most prominent spokesperson for STOP ERA was Phyllis Schlafly, who traveled around the nation to persuade people that feminism was destroying femininity by turning women into men. Schlafly opposed the Equal Rights Amendment because she thought it would undermine protections and support that historically had been given to women. She said that, if passed, the ERA would mean husbands did not have to support families (Collins, 2009b). She advised women to return to their roles as helpmates and homemakers and affirmed men's traditional roles as heads of families. Ironically, although Schlafly argued that women should be

EXPLORING GENDERED LIVES	THE TEXT OF THE EQUAL RIGHTS AMENDMENT

Equality of the rights under the law shall not be denied or abridged by the United States or by any State on account of sex.

deferential and that their place was in the home, she didn't take her own advice. Her speaking schedule kept her on the road constantly, so she was unable to devote much time to being a homemaker, wife, or mother.

The STOP ERA movement carried out its work not only through Schlafly's speeches but also through lobbying legislators and courting the media. STOP ERA members warned legislators and the public that passing ERA would undercut men's willingness to support children, allow women to be drafted, threaten the family, and permit women and men to use the same public restrooms (Mansbridge, 1986).

▼

Lyle   *I'm a lot older than most students. I've had a career and my wife and I raised four kids. I should say she raised them because that was her job. Mine was to earn an income for the family. That system worked fine for us, and our kids turned out just fine. I don't understand why so many young people don't want to follow traditional roles. We approve of division of labor in business and government; what's wrong with division of labor (he makes the money, she takes care of family) in our personal lives?*

THE THIRD WAVE: SURRENDERED WIVES AND THE WAR AGAINST BOYS AND MEN

Remember the Total Woman and Fascinating Womanhood movements in the second wave? The same idea resurfaced in the 2001 book *The Surrendered Wife: A Practical Guide for Finding Intimacy, Passion, and Peace with a Man* (L. Doyle). This book, like the earlier two antifeminist movements that it echoes, counsels women to abandon the quest for equality if they want happy marriages (Clinton, 2001). Women are advised to let their husbands lead the family and to accommodate their husbands.

The new millennium has seen other examples of antifeminism. For instance, the gains achieved by second-wave liberal feminism in equality of educational access and achievement for women are now being challenged. In 2000, Christina Sommers published *The War Against Boys,* which challenges decades of research documenting disadvantages that females experience in schools. Sommers argues that it is males, particularly boys, who are at a disadvantage in schools today. Another book, *The War Against Men* (Hise, 2004), claims that women have gained power at the expense of men and that this is contrary to God's commandments, which define the proper relationship between women and men.

THE CONTRADICTORY CLAIMS OF ANTIFEMINISM

In her 1991 book *Backlash: The Undeclared War Against American Women*, Pulitzer Prize-winning journalist Susan Faludi identifies two arguments that characterize the antifeminist, or backlash, movement. Faludi also notes that they are internally contradictory. On one hand, a good deal of antifeminist rhetoric defines feminism as the source of women's problems, including broken homes, tension between spouses, and delinquent children. According to this claim, in encouraging women to become more independent, feminism has turned women into fast-track achievers who have nothing to come home to but microwave dinners. Antifeminists argue that, rather than helping women, feminism has created more problems for them and made their lives miserable. They conclude that the solution to these problems is to renounce feminism.

A second antifeminist claim, which directly contradicts the first one, is that women have never had it so good—they have won the battles for equality, all doors are open to them, and they can have it all. Pointing to the gains in status and opportunities won by feminists, antifeminists assert that all inequities have disappeared, and that there is no longer any need for feminism. This line of rhetoric has been persuasive with some people, particularly women who have benefited from feminism. Yet, if women have full equality, why is one woman in four the victim of assault by a man? If women have full equality, why does the average woman get paid less than a man for doing the same job? If women have full equality, why do they still perform most of the child-care and housekeeping tasks in two-earner families? If feminists have achieved all they want, why is *Roe v. Wade* being challenged in our era?

Many feminists charge that claims advanced by antifeminists are misrepresentations and exaggerations. There is truth to that charge. At the same time, some of the claims made by some feminists have been exaggerated, too. It is productive to have different voices, including feminist and antifeminist ones, to act as checks and balances on each other.

SUMMARY

The issue of whether a person is a feminist is considerably more complicated than it first appears. The "women's movement" is really a collage of many movements that span more than 170 years and include a range of political and social ideologies. The different goals associated with women's movements are paralleled by diverse rhetorical strategies ranging from consciousness raising to public lobbying and zines. Whether or not you define yourself as a feminist, you have some views on women's identities, rights, and nature. Much of the analysis in various women's movements should inform your thinking about women's roles and lives.

Key Terms

The terms following are defined in this chapter on the pages indicated, as well as in alphabetical order in the book's glossary, which begins on page 325. The text's companion website (**http://www.cengage.com/communication/wood/genderedlives10e**)

also provides interactive flash cards and crossword puzzles to help you learn these terms and the concepts they represent.

antifeminism 91	multiracial feminism 85
antisuffrage movement 92	power feminism 86
backlash 91	radical feminism 72
cultural feminism 69	revalorists 79
ecofeminism 79	separatists 78
lesbian feminists 78	third-wave feminism 87
liberal feminism 69	womanists 83
Million Woman March 84	women's rights movement 70

Gender Online

1. Visit the Guerrilla Girls at: **http://www.guerrillagirls.com**.
2. If you'd like a sample of the Missile Dick Chicks' political theatre, visit their YouTube channel: **http://www.youtube.com/user/MissileDickChicks? gl=GB&hl=en-GB**.
3. If you'd like to know more about the Radical Cheerleaders, visit them at: **http://radcheers.tripod.com/**.
4. To learn more about ecofeminism, visit Eve Online at: **http://eve.enviroweb.org** or visit the home page of the ecofeminist organization at: **http://www .ecofem.org/ecofeminism**.
5. Visit NOW at: **http://www.now.org**.
6. To learn more about the third wave and differences and commonalities between it and earlier waves, visit this website: **http://www.3rdwwwave.com**.
7. Online search terms: "ecofeminism," "eve ensler," "separatists."

Reflection and Discussion

1. How have your views of feminism changed as a result of reading this chapter?
2. With which of the feminist movements discussed in this chapter do you most identify? Why?
3. To what extent do you think we should work to ensure that women have equal rights and opportunities within existing systems (liberal feminism) or should work to change the systems to incorporate traditionally feminine values and concerns (cultural feminism)?
4. Write or act out a discussion about whether women should serve in combat roles, which takes place between three feminists: an ecofeminist, a power feminist, and a separatist.
5. To what extent do you think it is possible for women to be both politically engaged feminists and sexy and conventionally feminine?

Recommended Resources

1. *Iron Jawed Angels*. (2004). Directed by Katja von Garnier. Distributed by HBO. This film dramatizes the final stage of the fight for women's right to vote.
2. Marilyn French. (1977). *The Women's Room*. New York: Ballantine. This novel protagonist engages in consciousness raising that allows her to see and challenge her own oppression. The novel represents what many women in the 1960s and 1970s experienced.
3. Anita Harris (Editor). (2004). *All About the Girl*. London: Routledge. Harris is one of the most prominent scholars in the area of girls' studies, which focuses on young women's lives and identities. This book presents a collection of essays, which give insight into consumerist inclinations of third-wave feminists.
4. Gail Collins. (2009). *When Everything Changed: The Amazing Journey of American Women from 1960 to the Present*. New York: Little, Brown & Co. This is one of the most comprehensive and readable histories of the second wave of American feminism. Trained as a journalist, Collins writes in an engaging, accessible style.
5. *Fried Green Tomatoes*. (1998). Directed by Jon Avnet. Distributed by Universal. This film gives insight into constraints faced by women in the early- to mid-1900s. There are also scenes that portray (or satirize) some of the backlash against feminism, including the advice to women that they greet their husbands at the door wrapped in saran wrap.

You must be the change that you wish to see in the world.
Mahatma Gandhi

THE RHETORICAL SHAPING OF GENDER: MEN'S MOVEMENTS IN THE UNITED STATES

CHAPTER **4**

Knowledge Challenge:

1. How does a person perform traitorous identity?
2. Which men's groups ally themselves with feminism?
3. What does wearing a white ribbon symbolize?

Historically, American men have been less involved than women in gender movements. In part, this is because white heterosexual men already have the rights and privileges that many of the women's movements work to gain. During the first wave of women's movements, most men opposed women's efforts to gain rights, although a few, like Frederick Douglass, actively supported women's struggle for basic rights.

During the second wave of American women's movements, a number of men supported liberal feminism; many joined NOW (the National Organization for Women) and other groups to work with women for equality. As well, a number of men began to explore issues in their own socialization. As they did, some men challenged what they had been taught about being "real men" and worked to identify and change the ways masculinity is constructed in America.

Like women's movements, men's movements have diverse, sometimes deeply conflicting, political and personal goals and rhetorical strategies. Some men's groups aim to challenge and change what masculinity means, whereas others want to reinvigorate traditional images of masculinity and safeguard or increase men's privileges. Also like women's movements, men's movements are evolving, with new ones constantly arising. For instance, the Mythopoetic movement, which was quite active in the late 1980s and early 1990s, is no longer prominent. Meanwhile new movements have arisen. In the 1990s, the Promise Keepers and the Million Man March emerged as distinct movements about and for men. Today, interest in the Promise Keepers appears to be diminishing, but some of the movement's ideology seems to infuse grassroots Christian men's movements.

Since the late 1980s, there has been an explosion of research on the cultural shaping of masculinity (Bartlett, 2009; Whitehead, 2006). Journals, such as *The Journal of Men's Studies* and *Men and Masculinities,* now publish research on men and men's lives. There is also a journal on boys' lives and identities, *Thymos,* which began publication in 2007. The growth of research on men and masculinities provides a basis for classes, and many colleges and universities across the United States now offer men's studies courses.

Men's movements are not independent of women's movements. As we will see in this chapter, men's movements often arise in reaction to particular branches of women's movements and particular issues pursued by women's movements. Some men's movements ally themselves with feminist groups and goals, particularly the liberal branches of feminism. Other men's movements fiercely reject feminism and feminists, and they work to bolster traditionally masculine roles, status, and the privileges.

▼

Bill   *I can't remember when I wasn't a feminist. It's as much a part of me as being a man or a Christian. My parents both work, Mom as a lawyer and Dad as an accountant. I grew up seeing my mother as strong and achieving and loving, just as Dad was. I grew up seeing my mother express her ideas articulately and seeing my father respect what she said and did. She listened when he talked; he listened when she did. When I was a kid, sometimes Mom worked late, and Dad was in charge of fixing dinner for me and my brother. Other times, Dad worked late, and Mom was in charge. Both of them took care of us. Both of them were successful outside of the home. I grew up seeing that women and men are equal. How could I not be a feminist?*

PROFEMINIST MEN'S MOVEMENTS

Referred to as **profeminists,** *progressive men,* or **male feminists,** this men's movement emerged in the 1960s. Although many men in left activist organizations like SNCC (Student Nonviolent Coordinating Committee) and SDS (Students for a Democratic Society) ignored women who accused them of sexism, some men involved in the New Left thought the women's criticism was on target, and they were ashamed when confronted with the hypocrisy of their political efforts to end discrimination against blacks while discriminating against women.

These men worked to bring their attitudes and behavior in line with the egalitarian ideology they espoused. They joined forces with women to march and to work for women's rights. Later generations of male feminists, including many men in their 20s today, attribute their feminism to parents and teachers who modeled egalitarian, nonsexist attitudes and practices. One of the more recent anthologies of third-wave feminism (Hernández & Rehman, 2002) includes essays by male feminists who believe that women and men should enjoy the same privileges, opportunities, rights, roles, and status in society. For the most part, these men have linked themselves and their rhetoric to mainstream liberal feminism. Out of this perspective, two distinct concerns emerge, one focused on women and the other on men.

Because they believe in the equality of the sexes, male feminists support women's battles for equitable treatment in society and participate in efforts to increase women's rights. For instance, during the 1972 campaign to ratify the ERA (Equal Rights Amendment), many men gave time, effort, and money to the battle for legal recognition of women's equality. Today, most male feminists endorse equal pay for equal work, an end to discrimination against qualified women in academic and professional contexts, and an increase in parental leaves and affordable child care (Digby, 1998; Jensen, 2007; White, 2008).

One rhetorical strategy used by some profeminist men is performing a **traitorous identity**. In performing a traitorous identity, a group member criticizes attitudes or actions that are common and accepted among members of that group. For example, a Christian man of my acquaintance often speaks out at Christian conferences, criticizing the ways in which many Christians discriminate against gays. Another example comes from Larry May, author of *Masculinity and Morality* (1998a). May notes that, at meetings he attends, male speakers sometimes make sexist jokes or comments. The humor in sexist (and racist) jokes and statements depends on the preexistence of sexist (and racist) attitudes in listeners (Ryan & Kanjorski, 1998). May points out that, if a woman objects to the sexist comments, many men roll their eyes or dismiss her as being overly sensitive or "unable to take a joke." However, when he or other men criticize the sexism, both the speaker and other men in the audience look ashamed. According to May, men find it easy to dismiss women's criticism of sexism but difficult to dismiss the same criticism when it comes from "one of us." People who perform traitorous identity are not really "traitors" to their group. Rather, by challenging certain behaviors, they are challenging the group to become better.

Male feminists also engage in personal persuasion to convince friends and co-workers to alter their discriminatory attitudes and practices. For instance, one of my friends talked with several of his colleagues about his firm's policy of paying women less than it paid men in equivalent positions. He thought the action was wrong, and he used his voice and his credibility to persuade other people. Another man, Scott Straus (2004), used his voice on campus to criticize fraternities. Later, he wrote an article in which he criticized men in the fraternity to which he had belonged for practices such as bragging about who had sex with whom and rating female students' attractiveness.

Raymond   *When one guy isn't playing well, others on the team will say he's playing like a girl. I don't know where that started, but you hear it a lot when a guy's game is off. My girlfriend gets really ticked off about that. She's in sports, too, and she says it's really disrespectful to talk like girls aren't any good at sports. So, last week I was off my game, and one of the other guys shouted that I was playing like a girl; I said "Like Mia Hamm or Venus Williams? Thanks, bro."*

Another interest of male feminists is their personal growth beyond restrictions imposed by society's prescriptions for masculinity. Because they believe that men and women are alike in most ways, male feminists want to develop the emotional capacities that society approves of in women but discourages in men. Specifically, many male feminists claim that social expectations of masculinity force men to repress their feelings, and this diminishes men's humanity and makes their lives less satisfying than they could be (Avery, 1999).

Agreeing with liberal feminist women, men in the profeminist movement regard cultural prescriptions for gender as toxic to both sexes. Whereas social codes have restricted women's professional development and civic rights, they have tended to force men to seal off feelings. Male feminists think that, in constricting men's ability to understand and experience many emotions, society has robbed them of an important aspect of what it means to be human; a major goal of male feminists is to change this. Male feminists encourage men to be more sensitive, caring, open, and able to engage in meaningful, close relationships with women and with other men. Aaronette White (2008) studied black men who define themselves as feminists. In her book, *Ain't I a Feminist*, she offers detailed, engaging sketches of how these men's feminism affects their parenting, friendships, and self-identity.

The profeminist movement includes organized political efforts as well as informal, interpersonal communication. Formal, public action dates back to 1975, when the first Men and Masculinity Conference was held in Tennessee. The conference explores the meaning of masculinity and provides a network of support for men who want to talk about problems and frustrations inherent in our culture's definition of masculinity and the roles and activities appropriate for men (Doyle, 1997; Messner, 2001). We will look more closely at NOMAS and men's antiviolence groups as prototypes of the profeminist movement.

NOMAS

One of the most prominent and long-lasting male feminist organizations is **NOMAS**, the National Organization for Men Against Sexism. This association sponsors workshops to expand men's awareness of ways in which their emotional development has been hindered by restrictive social views of masculinity. In addition, the workshops attempt to help men change this state of affairs by offering

EXPLORING GENDERED LIVES | BUILDING MEN FOR OTHERS

"What is our job as coaches?" asks Joe Ehrmann, former NFL star and current football coach for the Greyhounds at Gilman School in Baltimore. "To love us," chant the football players. "What is your job?" Ehrmann demands. "To love each other!" the players shout back (Marx, 2004, p. 4). Not exactly a typical exchange between coaches and players. But then, Ehrmann is definitely not a typical football coach.

Joe Ehrmann thinks that our society does a terrible job of helping boys become men. It teaches three flawed criteria for manhood: athletic ability, sexual conquest, and economic success. When boys are taught to compete for these three things, they wind up constantly competing with each other. According to Ehrmann, the result is that "it leaves most men feeling isolated and alone. And it destroys any concept of community" (p. 5). In place of what he calls "false masculinity," Ehrmann teaches his players that to be a man is to develop "strategic masculinity," which is defined by relationships with others and having a cause beyond yourself.

He teaches his players that, on the field and in real life, success comes from building and sustaining good relationships, which require men to be able to love and be loved. For instance, one of Ehrmann's rules is that no Greyhound player should ever let another student, whether a teammate or a stranger, sit alone in the school lunchroom. Instead, they are taught to think about how bad it would feel to be eating all alone and to invite that student to their table.

Does Ehrmann's record suggest that his approach can build winning teams? In three of the last six seasons, the Greyhounds were undefeated; in 2002 they were number one in Maryland and number fourteen in national rankings. Ehrmann explains that "winning is only a by-product of everything else that we do—and it is certainly not the way we evaluate ourselves" (p. 7).

Do you think Ehrmann's approach would work for men's competitive sports at the college level? Why or why not?

guidance in becoming more feeling and sensitive. Often, these groups serve as safe testing grounds in which men experiment with talking about their feelings, needs, and problems.

Although members of NOMAS believe that some qualities traditionally associated with masculinity, such as courage and ambition, are valuable in men, NOMAS condemns other conventionally masculine qualities, such as aggression, violence, and emotional insensitivity. One of the major achievements of NOMAS is its Fathering Task Group. This group issues a newsletter called *Brother*, which promotes strong, supportive ties between men.

For more than 30 years, NOMAS has held an annual conference on men and masculinity. Four issues consistently arise as priorities for discussion and action at these conferences. One issue is recognizing and resisting the power and privilege that accompany being men. A second issue is ending violence against women by analyzing the relationship between cultural codes for masculinity and men's violence against women. A third issue is working to end men's homophobic attitudes and the resulting cruel, sometimes deadly, attacks on gays and trans people. The fourth issue is continuing to develop and enrich men's studies at colleges and universities throughout the United States. NOMAS's annual conferences allow members to work on social change through political and educational activism.

Members of NOMAS engage in a variety of rhetorical strategies. One is informal group discussion, in which men explore the joys, frustrations, privileges, and problems of being men and of prevailing views of masculinity. Modeled on the consciousness-raising groups popular with many second-wave feminists, these groups encourage men to talk about what our society expects of men and the problems these expectations create. In this supportive context, men learn to talk openly with other men about feelings, fears, and ways to change attitudes and behaviors they find unworthy in themselves as individual men and in society overall.

BIZARRO © Don Piraro. King Features Syndicate.

Members of NOMAS also speak publicly in support of women's rights and men's personal development. In addition, NOMAS members are often involved in educational outreach programs that aim to raise awareness of issues such as men's violence and persuade other men to become involved with changing destructive views of masculinity. Finally, members of NOMAS often enact traitorous identities to challenge everyday incidents of homophobia, sexism, and devaluation of women.

MEN'S ANTIVIOLENCE GROUPS

As we saw in our discussion of NOMAS, profeminists are committed to ending violence against women. Like Kevin, whose commentary appears on this page, profeminists believe that violence against women is not just a "woman's issue." These men reason that, because the majority of violence against women (as well as men) is enacted by men, it is an issue for men. Two specific men's antiviolence programs deserve our attention.

The White Ribbon Campaign   Perhaps you've noticed that some men wear white ribbons between November 25 and December 6. Those who do are stating that they identify with the **White Ribbon Campaign (WRC)**, an international group of men who work to end men's violence against women (**http://www.whiteribbon .com**, n.d.). Formed in 1991, the WRC is the largest men's antiviolence group in the world.

The WRC began when a group of Canadian men felt they had to respond to an appalling incidence of violence against women. On December 6, 1991, 14 women were massacred in what came to be called the Montreal Massacre. They were students in the Engineering School at the Université de Montreal. The murderer felt that engineering was a man's field in which women had no rightful place, so he removed the women students from the school—and from life. Some male students at the Université de Montreal felt they had to speak out and make it clear that not all men hate women, and not all men would commit or condone violence against women.

Kevin   *If someone had told me five years ago I would say I'm a feminist, I wouldn't have believed it. Four years ago, my little sister was raped. I was enraged, and I felt totally powerless to help her, which was hard for me to deal with. I thought I was supposed to solve the problem, make things right, get the guy who did it. But I couldn't. I went with my sister to the rape crisis center and began to learn how bad the problem is. I began to see that the problem wasn't just the guy who raped her. It's the way that most men are socialized, including me—my wanting to be in control and get the guy who raped her. Gradually, I got more involved with others who want to end violence against women. Ending it has to start with men.*

At first, only a handful of men met about the issue, but the group grew. They defined their mission as taking the responsibility as men to speak out against men's violence against women. Designating a white ribbon as the symbol of men's opposition to men's violence against women, after only six weeks of planning this small group convinced more than 100,000 Canadian men to wear white ribbons. According to the White Ribbon website, "wearing a white ribbon is a symbol of a personal pledge never to commit, condone, nor remain silent about violence against women" (http://www.whiteribbon.com, n.d.).

Since the WRC was founded in Canada in 1991, it has spread to many other countries. Local chapters in some countries select Father's Day and Valentine's Day for WRC events that emphasize men's caring and investment in positive, loving relationships. Many college campuses, including my own, have WRC chapters. Although not often in the limelight, the WRC continues in resolute, steadfast pursuit of its mission to persuade men to take responsibility for ending men's violence against women.

Wearing a white ribbon for one or two weeks a year is not the WRC's only rhetorical strategy. Members also present antiviolence workshops in schools, communities, and places of employment. In the workshops, WRC members demonstrate that violence is overwhelmingly committed by men, and they encourage men to take responsibility for stopping it. Men are invited to become part of the solution to men's violence by speaking out against men's violence and by talking with other men about the issue. The workshops focus not only on physical violence such as battering and rape, but also on emotional violence, sexual harassment, sexist humor, and other practices that devalue and harm women.

A third and distinctive rhetorical strategy of the WRC is to emphasize that they are not "male bashers." On their website, http://www.whiteribbon.com/about_us/ #1, they state:

> The majority of men are not violent. At the same time … many men have come to believe that violence against a woman, child or another man is an acceptable way to control another person. By remaining silent about these things, we allow other men to poison our working and learning environments.

A final strategy of the WRC is to be vocal and active in supporting women's groups, particularly those that address violence in women's lives. The WRC campaign works closely and supportively with a variety of women's groups that focus on violence against women. Yet the WRC does not invite women to join. They see the organization as a campaign of and by men that is aimed at men.

The WRC has been praised by both men and women. A number of men agree with WRC that, because men commit most of the violence against women, men need to take responsibility for stopping it. In addition, many women's groups welcome men's stance against men's violence (Lansberg, 2000).

One criticism that has been voiced is that the WRC doesn't go far enough in its analysis of men's violence. Some of the most prominent spokespeople (Johnson, 2006; Katz, 2000) for ending men's violence argue that the problem is not a few men who are violent, but rather it is that violence is intimately woven into how society defines men and masculinity.

Mentors in Violence Prevention   Jackson Katz has developed a distinct approach to reducing male violence against women. Katz is one of the leaders in men's effort to end male violence against women. He gives workshops and speeches all over the world, and he trains men in mentoring other men to reject men's violence. **Mentors in Violence Prevention (MVP)** aims to educate men about socialization that links masculinity to violence and aggression and to motivate men to reject violence in themselves and other men (Katz, 2000).

Reuben's experience is not unusual. Many young boys want to be kind to others, but peer pressure keeps them from showing any tenderness. Gail Williamson and Jay Silverman (2001) conducted a study to find out whether peer influence is also a factor in heterosexual men's violence against the women they date. They learned that men are more likely to be violent toward dates if they associated with peers who verbally endorse or actually engage in violence against female partners.

▼

Reuben   *I don't like saying that men in general see being masculine as connected to being violent. I really don't. But I can't really deny it either. I mean, when I was growing up, being called wimp or sissy or soft were total insults. I remember there was this one guy that all the other guys didn't like, so they excluded him from our team and totally ignored him. I felt sorry for him and said maybe we should let him play on our team. The guys started saying how "sweet" I was and calling me sissy and worse. So I told the other guy to leave me alone, go away—said it in front of all my friends so they'd know I wasn't soft. It's no different now that I'm in my 20s. It's just that guys get a little more sophisticated about showing how tough they are.*

The MVP program seeks to use the power of peer influence to do just the opposite of what Reuben describes and Williamson and Silverman report. MVP wants to instill antiviolence attitudes in men so that men will teach their male peers not to be violent. The program has two foci. The first is to teach men that aggression and violence are closely linked to cultural views of masculinity and thus part of routine masculine socialization. In other words, the MVP program focuses on normative masculinity—on the ways in which violence is seen as a normal part of manhood in our society (Katz & Jhally, 1999, 2000). From sports to the military, masculine socialization teaches boys that violence is an appropriate means of gaining and maintaining control over others and winning—whether it's winning on the football field or on the battlefield. Becoming aware of normative masculine socialization is the first step in challenging and changing it.

The second focus of the MVP program is to call attention to the role of bystanders in preventing violence. Jackson and other MVP trainers reject the idea that only those who actually commit violence are blameworthy. In many cases, for violence to be committed there must be bystanders who approve, encourage, condone, or just remain silent, claims Katz (2000, 2006). You understand Katz's point if you have seen the film *The Accused,* which dramatizes the true story of a gang rape in

New Bedford, Massachusetts. The men who committed the rape egged each other on and cheered each other's assaults on the victim. Further, there were other men who did not participate in the rape but stood by, doing nothing to stop it. This is what Katz means by *bystander behavior.* He wants men to take responsibility not only for refraining from violence but also for refusing to allow or condone other men's violence.

Profeminist men's groups, including NOMAS, the WRC, and MVP, share the belief that current views of masculinity in Western culture are toxic for all of us, men and women alike. They also share a commitment to challenge and change how the culture and individuals in it define and enact masculinity.

In stark contrast to profeminist groups are those in the masculinist branch of men's movements. We turn now to those.

MASCULINIST MEN'S MOVEMENTS

A number of men's groups fit within the second camp of men's movements. These groups, labeled **masculinist** (Fiebert, 1987), or *promasculine,* believe that men suffer from discrimination because of their sex and that men need to reclaim their manliness (Mansfield, 2007). A primary rhetorical strategy of masculinists is to verbally disparage male and female feminists.

Masculinists also differ from profeminist men in attitudes toward gay men. The issue of gay rights is not a primary concern for most masculinist men, who tend to either ignore or denounce gay men. Profeminist men, in contrast, are committed to supporting gay concerns, challenging men's homophobic attitudes, and eliminating discrimination against gay men.

THE MEN'S RIGHTS MOVEMENT

Among the most conservative branches of the men's movement that subscribe to masculinist ideology are **men's rights activists,** whose goal is to restore the traditional roles of men and women and, with that, the privileges men historically enjoyed. Men's rights groups include MR, Inc. (Men's Rights, Incorporated); the National Coalition for Free Men; and NOM (the National Organization of Men).

One of the more extreme men's rights groups is **Free Men,** a group that aims to restore men's pride in being "real men." By "real men," this group means men who fit the traditional macho image—tough, rugged, invulnerable, and self-reliant. Free Men see male feminists as soft and unmanly and denigrate them with epithets such as "the men's auxiliary to the women's movement" (Gross, 1990, p. 12). According to Free Men, the primary burden of masculinity is the provider role, which makes men little more than meal tickets whose worth is measured by the size of their paychecks and their professional titles. Warren Farrell (1991), for instance, claims that most men perceive earning a good salary as an obligation, not an option. During hard economic times, men may feel that society makes it impossible for them to meet the provider role (Faludi, 1999).

However, specific issues such as the provider burden are subordinate to Free Men's overriding concern that men are being robbed of their masculinity. Targeting feminism as responsible for the loss of masculinity, they claim that "men have been wimpified. They've been emasculated" (Gross, 1990, p. 13). Given this perspective, it's not surprising that Free Men oppose affirmative action and requiring men to pay alimony and child support (Kimmel, 1996).

Men's rights groups want men to regain their rightful places as heads of families and unquestioned authorities. At the same time, they think their status should not be tied to the breadwinner role. To advance their agenda, Free Men's strategies range from lobbying for reform of laws they claim discriminate against men to condemning feminist men and women in public and private communication.

▼

Sam   *I know it's not politically correct these days to say it, but I agree with a lot of what masculinist men believe. I think families were stronger when the man was the head and the woman knew to follow. Families can't work if both spouses want to lead. There can be only one leader. I think the country was a lot stronger, too, before women started getting into business and government. I think women and men have different abilities. They're equal, but they're different. As far as gays go, I'm not homophobic or anything, but I don't see protecting their rights as a priority.*

Men's rights groups, including the Free Men, think that discrimination against men is far greater and more worthy of attention and correction than is discrimination against women. To support their claim that men are oppressed, men's rights groups point to issues such as the military draft, shorter life spans, more health problems, and child custody laws that favor women (Whitaker, 2001).

EXPLORING GENDERED LIVES | **FYI: TIME FOR A NEW MEN'S MOVEMENT?**

Does the traditional script for masculinity still work in contemporary America? The recession that began in 2008 resulted in massive job losses. The losses, however, were not evenly distributed. The hardest hit sectors were manufacturing and construction, two of the sectors that remain heavily male dominated. And many of those jobs aren't coming back. Over the next 10 years, more than 15 million new jobs will be created, and a majority of them will be ones that women have traditionally held—nursing, primary and secondary teachers, home health assistants (Romano & Dokoupil, 2010). Men may find it useful to do what women did during the second wave: consider new ways of defining their identities, figure ways to balance paid labor and contributions to home and family, think outside of the conventional boxes about careers, and reinvent themselves to fit changing constraints and opportunities.

FATHERS' RIGHTS GROUPS

One branch of the men's movement focuses on fatherhood and, specifically, fathers' rights. Fathers' rights groups are angry and hurt that men don't have at least 50% custody of their children after divorce. They claim that courts discriminate against men by assuming that women should be the primary parents.

The highest-profile fathers' rights group is in England. **Fathers 4 Justice** relies on two rhetorical strategies to raise public awareness about the custody rights of separated and divorced fathers. One strategy is to perform dramatic stunts that attract publicity. In one stunt, 33-year-old Jason Hatch, whose wife had left him and taken their two children with her, dressed as Batman, climbed the front wall of Buckingham Palace, perched on a ledge, unfurled a Fathers 4 Justice banner, and held it for more than five hours ("Batman," 2004). A second strategy is humor, which is often mixed into the dramatic stunts. One video used to gain sympathy for fathers shows a Fathers 4 Justice dad playing with his daughter and their pet sheep that he had dyed purple. On another occasion, Fathers 4 Justice members dressed up as Father Christmas and staged a sit-in at a government children's affairs office.

Fathers 4 Justice may be the most spotlighted fathers' rights group, but it isn't the only one. In the United States, there are dozens of father's rights groups, including the American Coalition for Fathers, Fathers and Families, and Children and Dads Against Discrimination. In 2005, class-action custody suits were filed by fathers' rights groups in 40 of the 50 states in America. These suits argue that a father has a constitutional right to be a parent, and thus he is guaranteed nothing less than 50% of the time with his children (Dominus, 2005). So far, Iowa and Maine are the only two states that have encouraged courts to grant joint custody if either parent requests it.

The key questions fathers' rights groups ask are these:

- Can fathers love their children as much as mothers?
- Do children need their fathers as much as they need their mothers?
- Is it blatant sex discrimination to give mothers an advantage when it comes to custody rights?

Many of us would answer "yes" to these questions. However, the issues are a bit more complicated than these questions suggest. *New York Times* reporter Susan Dominus (2005) points out that only 52% of divorced mothers receive the full child support payments the fathers were ordered to make. Dominus also notes that almost half of children are not contacted by fathers following a divorce. Statistics like this make it difficult for judges and family service agencies to be confident that all or most fathers will accept the responsibilities that accompany the rights they seek.

MYTHOPOETIC MEN

Another branch of the men's movement that gained a lot of attention in the late 1980s and early 1990s is the **mythopoetic movement,** founded by poet and former peace activist Robert Bly. Bly blended neoconservative politics with some of the traditional gender ideology to shape the mythopoetic movement, which aims to foster men's personal growth, wholeness, and bonding in all-male gatherings (Bonnett, 1996; Messner, 1997b; Silverstein, Auerbach, Grieco, & Dunkel, 1999). Mythopoetics want men to rediscover the deep, mythic roots of masculine thinking and feeling, which they believe will restore men to their primordial spiritual, emotional, and intellectual wholeness (Keen, 1991).

Mythopoetics agree with feminist women and men that the current male role is toxic, yet they don't agree with feminists about the nature of the toxicity. Mythopoetics argue that the traditional masculine ideal was positive. They claim that ideal manhood existed in ancient times and in the Middle Ages, when men were self-confident, strong, emotionally alive, and sensitive. As exemplars of ideal manhood, mythopoetics cite the Knights of the Round Table, Henry David Thoreau, Walt Whitman, and Johnny Appleseed (Gross, 1990).

Mythopoetics think that men's formerly profound connections to the earth and to comradeship with other men were ripped asunder by modernization, the Industrial Revolution, and feminism. Men were taken away from their land and, with that, from ongoing contact with natural life itself and their roles as stewards of the land (Kimbrell, 1991). At the same time that men were isolated from their earthy, natural masculinity (Gross, 1990), industrialization separated men from their families. When men began to work outside the home, young boys lost fathers who could initiate them into manhood and teach them how to relate spiritually and emotionally to other men.

Although mythopoetics believe that men have been separated from their feelings, their views depart dramatically from those of profeminist men (Keen, 1991; Mechling & Mechling, 1994). Like Free Men, Bly and his followers lay much of the blame for men's emotional deficits on feminism. Bly says that in male feminists "there's not much energy" (Wagenheim, 1990, p. 42). Stating this view more strongly, some mythopoetics charge that "feminists have been busy castrating American males. They poured this country's testosterone out the window in the 1960s" (Allis, 1990, p. 80). This statement illustrates the rhetorical strategy of attacking male (as well as female) feminists.

What do mythopoetics advocate for masculinity? They insist that men need to recover the *distinctly male mode of feeling*, which is fundamentally different from the female feelings endorsed by profeminist men. Men need to reclaim courage, aggression, and virility as masculine birthrights and as qualities that can be put to the service of bold and worthy goals, as they were when knights and soldiers fought for grand causes. Robert Bly's book *Iron John* (1990), which is the major rhetorical text of this movement, explains mythopoetic views and recounts ancient myths of manhood.

Central to modern man's emotional emptiness, argues Bly, is **father hunger**, a grief born of yearning to be close both to actual fathers and other men and to build deep, spiritual bonds between men. In the film *Fight Club*, the narrator, played by Ed Norton, laments not knowing his father and tries, without success, to compensate by building a close relationship with Tyler, played by Brad Pitt. To help men who experience father hunger, Bly and other leaders of the movement urge men to get in touch with their grief and, from there, to begin to rediscover their deep masculine feelings and spiritual energies. To facilitate this process, Bly and other movement leaders hold workshops and nature retreats where men gather in the woods

EXPLORING GENDERED LIVES | RITES OF MANHOOD

Men's rites may be as important as women's rights. Prior to the Industrial Revolution, most American fathers worked at or near their homes, so they spent a great deal of time with their sons, teaching them what it means to be a man. The same sort of mentoring of young boys existed in African tribes. When a boy reached a certain age, the men of the tribe—not just the father—would take the boy away from the village and teach him the tribe's values. When the boy returned to the village, he was recognized as a man.

Building on these traditions of mentoring boys into manhood, Rites of Passage is a program designed for African Americans (McDonald, 2005). Launched in 1990, the program pairs each boy with a male elder in the community, who serves as a mentor and role model. The elder teaches the boy to take responsibility for caring for himself and his community, to eschew violence, drugs, and other things that weaken self and community, and to keep promises to himself and others. When the elder is satisfied that the boy understands what it means to be a man, he gives the boy an African name, which symbolizes that he has become a man.

Do you think our society should have rites to mark the passage into manhood? Why or why not?

to beat drums, chant, and listen to poetry and mythic stories, all designed to help them get in touch with their father hunger and move beyond it to positive masculine feeling.

The mythopoetic movement has received both praise and blame. Naming father hunger highlights the anguish many men feel because they have or had distant relationships with their fathers (Chethik, 2001; Schwalbe, 1996). At the same time, mythopoetics have been charged with unwillingness to confront issues of gender inequality and with participation in sustaining that inequality (Avery, 1999; Schwalbe, 1996). In addition, some think the mythopoetics are elitist, as the membership is largely white and middle class.

If you are observant, you may have noticed that the majority of references in this discussion of mythopoetics were published in the early 1990s. Unlike some men's movements, this one has declined. There are still weekend nature retreats—the Mankind Project—which are attended by established mythopoetics. Few new men are joining the group. It is possible that mythopoetics' focus on personal growth simply wasn't enough to sustain a movement. Without a political agenda, it's difficult to keep a movement charged and vital. Even so, the mythopoetic movement contributed to the culture's overall dialogue about masculinity by naming father hunger.

PROMISE KEEPERS

In 1990, Bill McCartney, who was then head football coach at the University of Colorado, and his friend Dave Wardell were on a three-hour car trip to a meeting of Christian athletes in Pueblo, Colorado. On that trip, the two men conceived the idea of filling a stadium with Christian men. Later that year, McCartney and War-dell motivated 72 men to pray and fast about the idea of men coming together in Christian fellowship. The first **Promise Keepers** event in 1991 drew 4,200 men. Two years later, McCartney achieved his goal of filling the 50,000-seat Folsom Field. In 1994, the Promise Keepers spread out to seven sites, at which more than 278,000 men came together to pray and commit themselves to a Christ-centered life. Promise Keeper events, such as "Stand in the Gap," "Storm the Gates," and "The Challenge," drew thousands of men each year (Shimron, 1997, 2002; Wagenheim, 1996).

▼

Sophia   *A few years ago my dad went to a Promise Keepers event, and it changed him and our whole family. Before he went, he was the stereotype of the absent or uninvolved husband and father. After he went, he totally turned around—he was there for mom and for me and my brother. He started making the family the center of his life. For us, Promise Keepers has been a good thing.*

Bill McCartney founded Promise Keepers because he believed many men had fallen away from their responsibilities as men. Whereas mythopoetics see recon-necting with nature as the way for men to regain their wholeness, Promise Keepers see reconnection to God's commandments as the path. The movement urges men to be the leaders of their families because it reflects the "God-given division of labor between women and men" (Messner, 1997b, p. 30). Following the Christian path requires men to be good husbands, fathers, and members of communities. Each Promise Keeper makes seven promises (Shimron, 1997):

1. To honor Jesus Christ through worship, prayer, and obedience to God's word through the power of the Holy Spirit.
2. To pursue vital relationships with other men, understanding that they need brothers to help them keep their promises.
3. To practice spiritual, moral, ethical, and sexual purity.
4. To build strong marriages and families through love, protection, and biblical values.
5. To support the mission of his church by honoring and praying for his pastor and by actively giving his time and resources.
6. To reach beyond any racial and denominational barriers to demonstrate the power of biblical unity.
7. To influence his world for good, being obedient to the Great Commandment (see Mark 12:30-31) and the Great Commission (see Matthew 28:19-20).

Supporters of Promise Keepers believe that the movement promotes values that build strong families and strong communities. In their opinion, Promise Keepers is a call for male responsibility (Whitehead, 1997). Furthermore, a number of women who are married to Promise Keepers say their marriages have improved since their husbands joined the movement (Cose, 1997; Griffith, 1997; Whitehead, 1997; Shimron, 2002).

Yet, others voice reservations about the Promise Keepers. They ask why women can't attend Promise Keepers' meetings. The Promise Keepers' answer is to quote Proverbs 27:17: "Iron sharpens iron, and one man sharpens another." This reflects Promise Keepers' belief that men should lean on each other, not on women, in their quest to be good men; men can hold each other accountable in ways women can't (Shimron, 2002).

Another question asked by people who have reservations about the Promise Keepers is, Why can't husbands and wives be equals (Ingraham, 1997)? McCartney responds, "When there is a final decision that needs to be made and they can't arrive at one, the man needs to take responsibility" ("Promise Keepers," 1997, p. 14A). Critics charge that "taking responsibility" is a code term for denying women's equality, voices, and rights.

▼

Kathy   *I really don't know what to think of the Promise Keepers. I like what they say about men committing to family values and strong spirituality. I'm Christian, so I agree with a lot of what they stand for. But I don't like the idea that men have to be the leader in relationships. I won't be led by a man, and I don't want to lead a man, either. I want a relationship where we're equal in all respects. This makes me identify with only parts of what the Promise Keepers stand for.*

Another frequently expressed criticism has been that Promise Keepers are elitist. The great majority of Promise Keepers are white and economically middle or upper class. In response to criticism, Promise Keepers has made efforts to broaden its membership to include men of different races and to soften its rhetoric about husbands leading wives. In a move to symbolize the group's racial diversity, in 2003 when McCartney retired from the presidency, the group chose Thomas Fortson, an African American, to head Promise Keepers (Gorski, 2003).

But racial inclusiveness doesn't help Promise Keepers respond to charges of another kind of exclusion. Promise Keepers assert that homosexuality is a sin and that gays therefore are leading immoral lives. Naturally, this makes gays and non-gays who support gays uncomfortable with the movement. A final criticism is that Promise Keepers is more a conservative political movement than a social and spiritual movement (Cose, 1997; Whitaker, 2001).

The Promise Keepers reached its peak in 1997 with the "Stand in the Gap" rally at the National Mall in Washington, D.C. In 1997, the group had a budget of $117 million. By 2003, the budget was $27 million, reflecting a steep decline in membership (Gorski, 2003). In 2004, President Fortson announced that Promise Keepers intended to take its message beyond the borders of the United States. Following in the missionary tradition, Promise Keepers hope to establish a presence in places such as South Africa, New Zealand, and South America. Fortson's presidency also signals the group's desire to get beyond charges of racism (Bartkowski, 2004). The theme for all 2006 Promise Keepers conferences was "Unleashed: Releasing the Raw Power of Your Heart" (Shimron, 2006).

▼

Tony   *The PKs really frustrate me. I am a born-again Christian. I'm also gay. I believe everything that PKs stand for except their condemnation of gays. I'll put my Christian values up against those of any PK, but there's no room for me in the organization.*

Whether Promise Keepers reinvigorates itself or not, its impact continues. Some men who were involved with Promise Keepers in the 1990s have used the movement as a model of ministering to men and have built grassroots men's ministries in churches around the United States (Murphy, 2005). Men's ministries work to make local churches relevant to men. For instance, one group sponsors Saturday morning sports and prayer meetings. Another group has once-a-month "God's Weekend Warriors" retreats, at which men meet for breakfast and prayers followed by two hours of community service (Murphy, 2005).

Promise Keepers' trademark was two-day events, but after the weekend conferences many men who attended did not maintain contact with churches (Shimron, 2007). This points to a broader issue—men's decreasing involvement with churches. Today only 35% of men attend church weekly (Murrow, 2004). Some male Christian leaders believe that men's low involvement in churches results from what they call the "feminization of the church" (Caughlin & Caughlin, 2005; Murrow, 2004;

EXPLORING GENDERED LIVES | **GRASSROOTS MEN'S MINISTRIES**

Would you like to learn more about grassroots men's ministries? Would you like to consider starting one in your community? Two model groups are the Washington Area Coalition of Men's Ministries and the National Coalition of Men's Ministries. On its website, **http://www.wacmm.org**, the Washington Area Coalition of Men's Ministries offers this description of itself:

> We join together as men from local churches and organizations in the Washington D.C. Metro area to encourage every man within the sphere of our influence to pursue a vital relationship with God and with one another, to equip them for servant leadership in the home, workplace, community and world, and to enable them to gather for corporate celebration and edification.

The National Coalition of Men's Ministries **(http://www.ncmm.org)** includes more than 100 grassroots groups that work to connect men with local churches. The group states its mission thusly:

> The National Coalition of Men's Ministries welcomes inquiries from people who are interested in starting a men's ministry in their communities. Contact the group at 180 Wilshire Blvd., Casselberry, FL 32707. Phone Number: (407) 332-7703. Toll Free: (877) MAN-NCMM (626-6266). E-mail: **office@ncmm.org**.

Pinsky, 2007). In his book, *Why Men Hate Going to Church,* David Murrow asserts that the modern church service is weak and emasculated and represents Jesus as a sweet, loving person instead of a warrior whom men would regard as a hero worthy of following. Says Murrow, "Men aren't drawn to sweet, tender, and gentle" (Pinsky, 2007, p. 4E). To draw men back to Christian worship, some churches are replacing Christian praise music with martial hymns such as "Onward Christian Soldiers" and giving shorter sermons about a rebellious, courageous Jesus. Following the advice in Clifford Putney's book *Muscular Christianity* (2003), services stress action over reflection and aggression over gentility.

THE MILLION MAN MARCH

Just as many African-American women feel that feminism doesn't speak to or for them, many African-American men feel that most of the men's movements don't fit their histories and lives (Hammer, 2001). In the fall of 1995, Minister Louis Farrakhan, leader of the Nation of Islam, and the Reverend Benjamin Chavis, Jr., organized the first **Million Man March**. Their goal was for black men of all religions and classes to fill the mall of the nation's capital. The goals of the 1995 meeting were for black men to atone for sins and reconcile with one another. Spike Lee's film *Get on the Bus* (1997) offers a dramatic documentation of this first march.

At the march, organizers encouraged men to pledge themselves to spiritual transformation and political action. Specifically, organizers called for the men to register to vote, to fight drugs in their lives and communities, and to stand against unemployment and violence. Men were asked to recommit themselves to their wives and families and to active involvement in their churches and communities.

Michael   *I attended a Million Man March a couple of years ago, and it was the most important event of my life. It was wonderful to see so many black men in one place—all there to unite with one another and to change our world. The whole mood was one of total brotherhood. It strengthened my pride in being a black man and my feeling that I can build a life around strong spiritual values.*

The Million Man March was not a one-time event. Additional marches were held in years following the first one; each time, the crowd stretched from the steps of the Capitol nearly to the Washington Monument. Those who attended found something they could identify with in this movement—something that could guide their lives and give them meaning. The Million Man March has been widely praised as a positive, uplifting movement for black men. Yet there have been criticisms. One is that women are excluded from Million Man Marches. Some women think there is irony in asking men to leave home and be with other men in order to commit to their wives and families.

Another criticism was advanced by Glenn Loury (1996), who is African American and a professor of economics. He is concerned that this movement encourages

The Million Man March called on black men to commit to spiritual transformation and political action.

black men to base their rage on the racial identity of those who suffer rather than to rage against suffering and inequity no matter who is the victim. Finally, some people criticize the Million Man March for being antifeminist and antigay and for holding overly conservative views of families and women (Messner, 1997b).

The inaugural Million Man March in 1995 became a model for other groups. Since that march, America has seen a Million Woman March in Philadelphia, a Million Youth March in Harlem, a Million Mom March in Washington, and, in 2000, a Million Family March ("Million Family March," 2000). Most recently, in October 2005, the Millions More Movement was launched in the nation's capital. Conceived by Minister Louis Farrakhan, who also led the Million Man March, the Millions More Movement learned from criticisms of Millions marches. From the start, it was defined as an ongoing movement rather than a march. The mission statement focuses on educational, political, spiritual, social, and economic aspects of community development. Also, unlike the Million Man March, the Millions More Movement is inclusive of all sexes, races, and sexualities, although its focus remains on racial disparities that continue to affect blacks negatively (Muwakkil, 2005).

SUMMARY

Men's movements, like those focused on women's issues, are diverse and even contradictory. Some men consider themselves feminists, work with women for gender equality in society, and attempt to become more sensitive. Other men think feminism has destroyed families, twisted women, and caused grief to men. And some men feel threatened by women's progress toward equal status. Men's movements range from efforts to advance women's rights and status to active attacks on women's resistance to traditional, subservient roles. Members of men's movements engage in public and private forms of communication that contribute to the cultural conversation about gender—its meaning and its effect on the individual men and women who live under its edicts.

In this chapter and the preceding one, we discussed a wide range of women's and men's movements, as well as the antifeminist movement. Through communication in private and public settings, these movements delineate multiple versions of femininity and masculinity and seek to persuade us to adopt certain points of view. As the conversation evolves, new voices will join existing rhetorical efforts to define the meaning of masculinity and femininity and the rights, roles, and opportunities available to women, minorities, men, lesbians, and gay men. It's up to you to define your role in the cultural conversation about gender. Some people will be passive listeners. Others will be critical listeners who reflect carefully on the points of view advanced by these rhetorical movements. Still others will claim a voice in the conversation and will be part of active rhetorical efforts to define gender. What role will you choose?

Key Terms

The terms following are defined in this chapter on the pages indicated, as well as in alphabetical order in the book's glossary, which begins on page 325. The text's companion website (**http://www.cengage.com/communication/wood/genderedlives10e**) also provides interactive flash cards and crossword puzzles to help you learn these terms and the concepts they represent.

father hunger 109

Fathers 4 Justice 108

Free Men 106

male feminists 98

masculinist 106

Mentors in Violence Prevention
(MVP) 105

men's rights activists 106

Million Man March 114

mythopoetic movement 108

NOMAS 100

profeminists 98

Promise Keepers 111

traitorous identity 99

White Ribbon Campaign (WRC) 103

Gender Online

1. To learn about the range of men's movements and issues and resources on all of them, visit the Voice of the Shuttle's directory for these: **http://vos.ucsb.edu/browse.asp?id=1810.**
2. If you wish to learn more, visit NOMAS's website at: **http://www.nomas.org.**
3. In fact, Free Men say that profeminist men are not part of the men's movement at all. If you want to learn more about Free Men, visit this website: **http://www.ncfm.org.**
4. To find out more about the Promise Keepers, visit their website: **http://www.promisekeepers.org.**
5. Online search terms: "fathers' rights," "male feminist," "mentors in violence prevention."

Reflection and Discussion

1. Before you read this chapter, did you know that there were so many men's movements with such diverse goals? What does limited knowledge of men's movements imply about biases in media and education?
2. Which of the men's movements are most and least consistent with your views of gender and your values?
3. Write or act out a discussion of whether men should pay alimony and child support as that discussion might transpire between a Free Man, a mythopoetic, and a Promise Keeper.
4. Watch the film *Fight Club*. To what extent does the film portray men as feeling betrayed and locked into meaningless lives? Discuss the meaning of the fight.

Recommended Resources

1. Paul Kivel. (2007). The Act Like A Man Box. In Michael Messner (Ed.), *Men's Lives,* 7th ed. (pp. 148–150). Cranbury, New Jersey: Pearson/Allyn & Bacon. This short article provides a clear way of thinking about how Western society's view of masculinity harms men.
2. *Get on the Bus.* Directed by Spike Lee. (1996). Distributed by Sony. This award-winning film provides a dramatic representation of the first Million Man March and what it meant to black men.
3. Michael Messner. (2008). *Guyland: The Perilous World Where Boys Become Men.* New York: Harper. In his latest book, long-standing feminist Michael Messner examines the pressures, fears, and anxieties facing many young men today.

The tongue has the power of life and death.
Proverbs 18.21

CHAPTER **5**

GENDERED VERBAL
COMMUNICATION

Knowledge Challenge:

1. Do women or men generally talk more?
2. How do childhood games affect adult communication styles?
3. What is conversational maintenance work and who generally does it?

Consider these four statements:

I now pronounce you man and wife.
Bob babysat his son while his wife attended a meeting.
"Leave it to the French girl to make a Wimbledon fashion statement....
    Tatiana Golovin had the hottest pants" (Cassidy, 2004, p. 3B).
Freshmen find it difficult to adjust to college life.

What do these sentences reflect about Western culture's views of women and men? The first sentence designates *man* an individual, whereas *wife* is defined only by her relationship to the man. In the second sentence, the word *babysat* implies that the father was performing a special service, one for which we usually pay. Have you ever heard someone say that a mother babysat her children? The third sentence defines an accomplished tennis player as a child (girl) and focuses on her sexy outfit, diverting attention from her athletic skill. Unless the fourth sentence refers to first-year students at an all-male school, the word *freshmen* erases first-year female students.

In this chapter and the one that follows, we look closely at relationships between communication and gender. This chapter focuses on verbal communication, and Chapter 6 concentrates on nonverbal communication. We will explore how verbal and nonverbal communication reflect cultural understandings of sex and gender. In addition, we will consider how individuals embody or refuse to embody cultural prescriptions for gender—that is, how individual women's and

118

men's communication reflects or challenges cultural prescriptions for femininity and masculinity.

VERBAL COMMUNICATION EXPRESSES CULTURAL VIEWS OF GENDER

Language is one of our most complex symbol systems. The language we learn and use both reflects and reinforces cultural views and values, including those about gender. We'll discuss six connections between language and gender.

MALE GENERIC LANGUAGE EXCLUDES WOMEN

One way that language erases women is through the use of **male generic language**, which purports to include both women and men yet refers only to men. Examples of male generic language are nouns such as *businessman, spokesman, mailman,* and *mankind,* and pronouns such as *he* used to refer to both women and men. Some people think that there is no problem with male generic language and that using inclusive language, such as *he* or *she,* is just about political correctness.

Research makes it clear that inclusive language is about something far more substantial than political correctness. In a classic study of the effects of male generics (Schneider & Hacker, 1973), children were asked to select photographs for a text-book with chapters entitled "Urban Man" and "Man in Politics" or "Urban Life" and "Political Behavior." The children almost always chose pictures of men when the titles included male generic language. When the titles did not refer only to men, the children chose more photographs that portrayed both sexes. The language of the titles shaped what the children thought was appropriate to include in the chapters.

Later research confirmed the finding that male generic language leads many people to assume that only males are included (Gastil, 1990; Hamilton, 1991; Switzer, 1990). In a particularly interesting study, students from first grade through college were asked to make up a story about an average student. When the instructions referred to the average student as *he,* only 12% of students com-posed a story about a female. However, when the instructions defined the average student as *he* or *she,* 42% of the stories were about females (Hyde, 1984).

Because there is convincing evidence that male language is not perceived as generic, all the major dictionaries and national newspapers now have policies requiring inclusive language. In addition, new dictionaries and writing style man-uals caution against other linguistic ways of defining men as the standard and women as the exception. For instance, they discourage **spotlighting**—the practice of highlighting a person's sex. Terms such as *lady doctor* and *woman lawyer* define women as the exception in professions and thereby reinforce the idea that men are the standard.

LANGUAGE DEFINES MEN AND WOMEN DIFFERENTLY

Women are frequently defined by appearance or by relationships with others, whereas men are more typically defined by activities, accomplishments, or positions. For instance, coverage of women's sports frequently focuses more on women athletes' appearance than on their athletic skills. Stories about female athletes often emphasize wardrobes ("Venus is sporting a cool new outfit"), bodies ("She's gotten back in shape and is looking good on the field"), and hairstyles ("She's wearing a shorter cut with highlights"), whereas stories about male athletes focus on their athletic abilities ("He sunk two dream shots").

▼

Andy   *For a long time, it seemed really clear to me that a word like* mankind *obviously includes women or that* chairman *can refer to a girl or a guy who chairs something. I thought it was pretty stupid to hassle about this. Then, last semester I had a woman teacher who taught the whole class using* she *or* her *or* women *whenever she was referring to people, as well as when she meant just women. I realized how confusing it is. I had to figure out each time whether she meant women only or women and men. And when she meant women to be general, I guess you'd say generic for all people, it still made me feel left out. A lot of the guys in the class got pretty hostile about what she was doing, but I kind of think it was a good way to make the point.*

In the opening of this chapter, you read a reporter's description of Tatiana Golovin's hot pants. The same reporter noted that Maria Sharapova's "asymmetrical hemline was slit to the hip, adding a little sauce" (Cassidy, 2004, p. 3B). Can you imagine such descriptions of male athletes? Another example of the emphasis placed on appearance for girls and women came from the 2008 Beijing Olympics. Yang Peiyi won the competition to sing "Ode to the Motherland" at the opening ceremony. Officials, however, decided that although Yang Pei had the best voice, she was not attractive enough. The officials chose third grader Lin Miaoke to stand on stage and lip sync the song while Yang Pei, hidden from view, sang (Yardley, 2008).

Even when describing women who have been raped or abused, there are often extraneous and irrelevant descriptions of victims' appearance or dress (Carter, Branston, & Allan, 1998). A particularly appalling example occurred in a rape trial presided over by Florida circuit judge Gene Stephenson. Looking at the woman who brought the charge of rape, Judge Stephenson said, "Why would he want to rape her? She doesn't look like a day at the beach" ("No Comment," 2004, p. 11). A Spanish judge also focused more on a woman defendant's appearance than on evidence that she had been abused by her husband. Judge Francisco Javaier Pauli Collado released the husband, saying, "His wife was too well dressed to be a victim of such abuse" ("No Comment," 2004, p. 11).

Language also reflects social views of women as passive and men as active when engaged in sexual activity. Have you noticed that people say, "He laid her," "He balled her," "He screwed her," "She got laid," and "He made love to her?" Each of these phrases suggests that, in sexual activity, men are active, whereas women are passive. Perhaps because men are expected to be sexual initiators, inappropriate sexual initiative by men is sometimes described in language that makes it

EXPLORING GENDERED LIVES | PARALLEL LANGUAGE?

Parallel language means equivalent terms. For instance, male and female are equivalent, or parallel. But what about some other allegedly parallel terms?

Masculine Term	Feminine Term
Master	Mistress
Sir	Madam
Wizard	Witch
Patron	Matron

seem acceptable. For instance, why did no one challenge Arnold Schwarzenegger's use of "playful" and "rowdy" to describe the multiple incidents of sexual harassment revealed during his campaign for the governorship of California? And why did Fox news commentator Greta Van Susteren refer to Kobe Bryant's rape trial as a "sex scandal" (Morgan, 2003/2004, p. 95)? A sex scandal is about unconventional or illegal but consensual sexual activity. Rape is not a sex scandal, but an act of violation and violence.

Our language also reflects society's view of women as defined by their relationships with others rather than as independent agents. On prime-time television, even professional women are often depicted primarily in interpersonal contexts, and their appearance is highlighted (Dow & Wood, 2006). Throughout the 2008 Democratic primary contest, commentators commented on Hillary Clinton's appearance—she was being suggestive when she wore a v-necked top; her pantsuits were dowdy; she had crow's feet (Mandziuk, 2008). The male contenders' appearance was not scrutinized in the same way.

In Western culture, a woman who doesn't marry historically has been viewed with sympathy or pity. For years, unmarried American women were called *spinsters* or *old maids* (contrast this with the nonpejorative term *bachelor* for men). In Mexico, people say *Me vale madre,* which translates into English as "It's worth a mother to me" and means "It's not important." In Japan, however, unmarried women are called *leftover, underdog,* and *parasite single* (Onishi, 1998; Retherford, Ogawa, & Matsukura, 2001). In 2007, Japan's Health Minister Hakuo Yanagisawa referred to Japanese women as "birth-giving machines and devices" (Dyer, 2007).

There are a number of alternatives to the traditional ways of naming ourselves (Foss, Edson, & Linde, 2000; Fowler & Fuehrer, 1997). Some heterosexual women choose to retain their birth names when they marry. A number of men and women adopt hyphenated names, such as Johnson-Smith, to symbolize the family heritage of both partners. In some countries, such as Spain, both the mother's and father's family names are used to construct children's family names. Another alternative, one less often practiced so far, is renaming oneself to reflect **matriarchal** rather than patriarchal lineage. (The term *matriarchy* means "rule by the mothers" and generally refers to systems of ideology, social structures, and practices that are created by women and reflect the values, priorities, and views of women as a group.)

EXPLORING GENDERED LIVES | **WHAT'S IN A NAME?**

During the 1970s, several states declared they did not require women to assume their husbands' last names on marrying. Other states, however, insisted that a woman must assume her husband's last name on marrying. Only in 1975 was the issue resolved of whether a woman is legally required to assume her husband's last name. Then, a Hawaiian statute requiring women to give up their birth names on marriage was ruled unconstitutional (Schroeder, 1986).

Research by Laura Stafford and Susan Kline (1996) shows that some men say they would question a woman's commitment if she did not adopt her partner's name. Although men felt more strongly than women about this, a majority of both sexes surveyed favored a woman's taking her partner's last name. Additional research (Kline, Stafford, & Miklosovic, 1996) revealed that women's decisions to retain their birth names or adopt their husbands' last names are influenced by the value attached to heritage and tradition, the importance of professional identity, the desire for a new personal identity, views of marriage and family, and practical issues.

Elizabeth Suter and Ramona Oswald (2003) conducted a study to find out how lesbian couples chose names. They found that, like heterosexual couples, women who placed high priority on social recognition of their relationship preferred that one or both partners change her name. For women who kept their names, individual identity was a higher priority.

Do you have different perceptions of heterosexual women whose choose to keep their birth names and women who choose to take their partners' names on marrying?

This involves changing a last name from that of the father's family to that of the mother's. Because that course of action, however, still reflects male lineage—that of the mother's father—some women use their mothers' first names to create a matrilineal last name: for example, Lynn Franklin's daughter, Barbara, might rename herself Barbara Lynnschild.

LANGUAGE SHAPES AWARENESS OF GENDERED ISSUES

Naming is important. We give names to things that matter to us. We don't bother to name what doesn't matter (Coates, 1997; Spender, 1984a, 1984b). The power of naming is clear with sexual harassment and date rape (Wood, 2008, 2009a). For most of history, sexual harassment occurred frequently but was unnamed. Because it wasn't named, sexual harassment was not visible or salient, making it difficult to recognize, think about, discipline, or stop. If sexual harassment was discussed at all, it was described as *making advances, getting out of line,* or *being pushy.* None of these phrases conveys the abusiveness of sexual harassment. Only when the term *sexual harassment* was coined did the general public recognize it as unwanted behavior that ties sexuality to security and advancement. And only with this awareness were efforts devised to redress sexual harassment.

▼

Brian   *I never considered whether my wife would take my name. I just assumed she would. I'm proud of my family, and I feel tied to who we are, and my family name represents that. I always thought it would be a great honor for a woman to have my family name. But my fiancé doesn't feel the same way. She says she's proud of her name, too, that it's who she is, too. I can understand that in a way, but still it seems like she should want to take my name. She turned the tables on me by asking if I would take her name.*

Similarly, for many years women who were raped by their dates had no socially recognized way to name what had happened to them. Until we coined the term *date rape,* women had to deal with their experiences without the language to define and help them think about grievous violations that often had lifelong repercussions. Naming creates awareness.

As our discussion suggests, language is not static. Instead, we continually change language to reflect our changing understandings of ourselves and our world. When we find existing language inadequate or undesirable, we change it. We reject terms we find objectionable (male generics), and we create new terms to define realities we think are important *(sexual harassment, Ms., womanism).* As we modify language, we change how we see ourselves and our world. Further, we shape meanings of our culture.

▼

Bea   *When we were talking about how naming makes us aware of things, it rang a bell for me. My first semester here, I had a lab instructor who made me really uncomfortable. I was having trouble with some of the material, so I went to see him during office hours. He moved away from his desk and sat beside me. Then, he sort of touched my arm and knee while I was trying to show him my work. I felt really bad. Then he started cornering me after class and suggesting we get lunch together. I didn't know what to do. Finally, one day he stopped me after class and told me that he might be able to help me with my grade if I would go out with him that weekend. And you know what? I still didn't understand what was happening. I knew I didn't want to date him, and I knew he could hurt my grade, but I didn't know it was sexual harassment. If that happened again today, I'd know what to call it, and I'd also know I could do something about it. So I understood the stuff about names being important.*

LANGUAGE ORGANIZES PERCEPTIONS OF GENDER

Two ways in which language organizes perceptions of gender are stereotyping men and women and encouraging polarized perceptions of sex and gender.

A **stereotype** is a generalization about an entire class of phenomena based on some knowledge of some members of the class. For example, if most women you know aren't interested in sports, you might stereotype women as uninterested in sports. This stereotype could keep you from noticing that many women engage in sports and enjoy attending athletic events. Relying on stereotypes can lead us to overlook important qualities of individuals and to perceive them only in terms of what we consider common to a general category. Recall from Chapter 2 that queer performative theories object to the terms *women* and *men* because they erase differences within each category and suggest there are only two categories.

Many people stereotype women as emotional and weak and men as rational and strong. Stereotypes such as these can distort our perceptions. For instance, women's arguments are sometimes dismissed as emotional when in fact they involve evidence and reasoning (Mapstone, 1998). Women who use assertive speech are frequently described as rude or bitchy, whereas men who employ emotional language may be described to be wimps or weak (Rasmussen & Moley, 1986).

The English language may also encourage **polarized thinking,** which is conceiving of things as absolute opposites. Something is right or wrong, good or bad, appropriate or inappropriate. Our commonly used vocabulary emphasizes all-or-none terms and thus all-or-none thinking. English includes few words that indicate degrees and increments.

Queer performative theory challenges polarized language for sex, gender, and sexual orientation, claiming that the polar—or binary—terms obscure the range of genders, sexes, and sexual orientations that humans express. Our culture's binary labels for sex, gender, and sexual orientation encourage us not to notice how much variation there is among women and among men (Lorber, 2001). Polar language for sex erases transgendered people because the only linguistic options are *men* and *women,* neither of which describes their full identities. Likewise, people who are intersexed or who do not identify with any gender don't fit into the male-female dichotomies of our language. Awareness of our language's polarizing tendencies allows us to question dichotomous conceptions of sex and gender and the ways that those labels exclude some people.

LANGUAGE EVALUATES GENDER

Language reflects cultural values and is a powerful influence on our perceptions. Women are often described in trivializing terms. Numerous terms label women as immature or juvenile *(baby doll, girlie, little darling)* or equate them with food *(dish, feast for the eyes, good enough to eat, sugar, sweet thing, cookie, cupcake, hot tomato)* and animals *(kitten, catty, chick, pig, dog, cow, bitch).* Diminutive suffixes designate women as reduced forms of the standard (male) form of the word: *suffragette, majorette.* Calling women *girls* (defined as a female who has not gone through puberty) defines them as children, not as adults. Women who are sexually active may be called derogatory names such as *slut,* whereas men who are equally sexually active are described with terms such as *stud* or *man whore,* which my students say is a compliment.

▼

Anthony   *Until we talked about language in class, I hadn't really thought about the double standard for sexually active girls and guys. Or if I had thought about it, I probably would have said that the double standard doesn't exist anymore. Our discussion got me thinking, and that's not really true. Guys who have sex with a lot of girls are* studs *or* players. *Girls who have sex with a lot of guys are* sluts *or* easy. *It's not as bad as it used to be, but I guess there still is kind of a double standard.*

LANGUAGE ALLOWS SELF-REFLECTION

We use symbols to name and evaluate not only the phenomena around us, but also ourselves. Self-reflection is thinking about yourself—how you name and evaluate yourself. Yet, self-reflection is not just personal. Each of us has society's values in our heads, so we tend to reflect on ourselves from society's perspective. In the 1950s a 5-foot 5-inch woman who weighed 140 pounds would have been considered slender. In 2010, some might see a 5-foot 5-inch woman who weighs 140 pounds as overweight. In 1950 a man would not need to be as muscular as is the current masculine ideal. We live in a celebrity culture (Lamb & Brown, 2006; Levin & Kilbourne, 2008; Levy, 2005), which makes it tempting to define ourselves in comparison to celebrities—or the air-brushed, surgically altered images of them. According to Michael Rich (2008), Director of the Center on Media and Child Health, "exposure to body ideals of impossibly thin women and unrealistically muscular men can contribute to negative self-images and viewers' attempts to alter their bodies through restrictive eating, exercise, or drugs or surgery" (p. 90).

"Masculine" and "feminine" are not the only ways we can label our gender. We may also label ourselves androgynous, a concept we first mentioned in Chapter 1. Androgynous people possess qualities the culture defines as masculine *and* feminine instead of only those assigned to one sex. Androgynous women and men are, for example, both assertive *and* sensitive, both ambitious *and* compassionate (Bem, 1993). Many women and men decide not to limit themselves only to those qualities that society associates with one gender.

Research shows that androgynous individuals tend to be more successful personally and professionally. They are able to communicate in a range of ways and can respond to others with flexible skills that meet the demands of various situations. Androgynous women and men have higher self-esteem and are better adjusted personally than sex-typed individuals (Heilbrun, 1986). In the workplace, androgynous individuals are more flexible and effective in interacting with a range of people (Heath, 1991). Androgynous individuals and feminine-typed individuals of both sexes have happier marriages than masculine-typed individuals (Ickes, 1993) and are more likely to be successful in their professional and personal lives than are sex-typed individuals (Heath, 1991).

GENDERED STYLES OF VERBAL COMMUNICATION

In addition to expressing cultural views of gender, language is a primary means by which we express our gendered identities. In the pages that follow, we'll explore the ways we use verbal communication to perform masculinity and femininity.

Keep in mind that we're looking at *gendered* styles of communicating, not necessarily sex-based styles. In other words, although most girls are socialized to communicate primarily in feminine ways, some boys learn feminine modes of communicating; and although most boys are encouraged to cultivate primarily masculine styles of communicating, some girls learn masculine modes as well. Also, as queer performative theorists would remind us, some people perform genders other than the two conventionally recognized in our society.

GENDERED SPEECH COMMUNITIES

Philosopher Suzanne Langer (1953, 1979) asserted that culture, or collective life, is possible only to the extent that a group of people share a symbol system and the meanings encapsulated in it. Langer's attention to the ways in which language sustains cultural life is consistent with the symbolic interactionist and cultural theories that we discussed in Chapter 2. William Labov (1972) extended Langer's ideas by defining a *speech community* as a group of people who share norms about communication. By this, he meant that a **speech community** exists when people share understandings about goals of communication, strategies for enacting those goals, and ways of interpreting communication.

It's obvious that we have entered a different speech community when we are in countries whose languages differ from our own. Distinct speech communities are less apparent when they rely on the same language but use it in different ways and attach different meanings to it. Yet, as we noted in Chapter 2, belonging to a particular race-ethnicity, economic class, and gender influences what we know and how we communicate.

Research shows that males and females are typically socialized into subtly different speech communities (Coates, 1986, 1997; Coates & Cameron, 1989; Hudson, 2001; Wood, 2009b). To understand these different communities, we will first consider how we are socialized into feminine and masculine speech communities. After this, we will explore divergence in feminine and masculine speech communities. Please note the importance of the word *typically* and other words that indicate we are discussing general differences, not absolute ones. Not all women learn or choose to perform a feminine style of communication, not all men learn or choose to perform a masculine style of communication, and not everyone accepts the cultural assumption that there are two "opposite" genders with associated communication styles.

THE LESSONS OF CHILDREN'S PLAY

A classic study by Daniel Maltz and Ruth Borker (1982) gave us initial insight into the importance of children's play in shaping patterns of communication. As they watched young children engaged in recreation, the researchers were struck by two observations: Young children almost always played in sex-segregated groups, and girls and boys tended to play different kinds of games. Maltz and Borker found that boys' games (football, baseball, war) and girls' games (school, house, tea party) cultivate distinct communication styles.

More recent research on children's play confirms Maltz and Borker's original findings. Sex-segregated groups and forms of play remain the norm for children in the United States (Clark, 1998; Gray & Feldman, 1997; Kovacs, Parker, & Hoffman, 1996; McGuffey & Rich, 2004; Moller & Serbin, 1996; Wood, 2009a). Even children as young as two or three years old (about the time that gender constancy develops) show a preference for same-sex playmates (Martin, 1997; Ruble & Martin, 1998).

Boys' Games   Boys' games usually involve fairly large groups—nine individuals for each baseball team, for instance. Most boys' games are competitive, have clear goals, involve physically rough play, and are organized by rules and roles that specify who does what and how to play (Pollack, 2000; Rudman & Glick, 2008).

Because the games boys typically play are structured by goals, rules, and roles, there is limited need to discuss how to play, although there may be talk about strategies to reach goals. In playing games, boys learn to communicate to accomplish goals, compete for and maintain status, exert control over others, get attention, and stand out (Messner, 1997a). Specifically, boys' games cultivate four communication rules:

1. Use communication to assert your ideas, opinions, and identity.
2. Use talk to achieve something, such as solving problems or developing strategies.
3. Use communication to attract and maintain others' attention.
4. Use communication to compete for the "talk stage." Make yourself stand out, take attention away from others, and get others to pay attention to you.

These communication rules are consistent with other aspects of masculine socialization. For instance, notice the emphasis on individuality and competition. Also, we see that these rules accent achievement—doing something, accomplishing a goal. Boys learn that they must do things in order to be valued members of the team. Finally, we see the undercurrent of masculinity's emphasis on invulnerability: If your goal is to control and to be better than others, you cannot let them know too much about yourself and your weaknesses.

Girls' Games   Many girls today also play competitive games like those that boys favor. In addition, most girls play some games that few boys play. The games played primarily by girls cultivate distinct ways of communicating. Girls tend to play in pairs or in small groups rather than large ones (Benenson, Del Bianco, Philippoussis, & Apostoleris, 1997). Also, games such as house and school do not have preset, clear-cut goals and roles. There is no touchdown in playing house, and the roles of daddy and mommy aren't fixed like the roles of guard and forward. Because traditional girls' games are not highly structured by external goals and roles, players have to talk among themselves to decide what to do and what roles to play.

When playing, young girls spend more time talking than doing anything else—a pattern that is not true of young boys (Goodwin, 2006). Playing house, for instance, typically begins with a discussion about who is going to be the daddy and who the mommy. The lack of stipulated goals for the games is also important because it tends to cultivate girls' skill in interpersonal processes. The games generally played by girls teach four basic rules for communication:

1. Use communication to create and maintain relationships. The process of communication, not its content, is the heart of relationships.
2. Use communication to establish egalitarian relations with others. Don't outdo, criticize, or put down others. If you have to criticize, be gentle.
3. Use communication to include others—bring them into conversations, respond to their ideas.
4. Use communication to show sensitivity to others and relationships.

The typically small size of girls' play groups fosters cooperative play (Rudman & Glick, 2008) and an open-ended process of talking to organize activity, whereas the larger groups in which boys usually play encourage competition and external rules to structure activity (Campbell, 1993). In a study of preschoolers, boys gave

Sonyae/Dreamstime.com

Children's games teach gendered rules of communicating.

orders and attempted to control others, whereas girls were more likely to make requests and cooperate with others (Weiss & Sachs, 1991). In another investigation, 9- to 14-year-old African-American girls typically used inclusive and nondirective language, whereas African-American boys tended to issue commands and compete for status in their groups (Goodwin, 1990).

The conclusion from much research is that girls tend to engage in more cooperative play, whereas boys tend to engage in more instrumental and competitive play (Harris, 1998; Leaper, 1994, 1996). The lessons of children's play are carried forward. The basic rules of communication that many adult women and men employ are refined and elaborated versions of those learned in childhood games (Clark, 1998; Mulac, 1998, 2006). Even in the virtual world, boys tend to favor competitive games and girls favor relationship-oriented games.

Erin made the comment on page 130 when she was a student in my class. She's right that young girls today often play competitive sports and that doing so allows them to learn and use the rules of masculine speech communities. This is consistent with standpoint theory's premise that members of subordinated groups are motivated to learn the standpoint of dominant groups. However, Erin is not entirely correct in saying that children's games are no longer sex segregated. How many boys play house and school? It is much more acceptable and much more common for girls to play traditional boy games than vice versa.

GENDERED COMMUNICATION PRACTICES

We will consider features of feminine and masculine speech that have been identified by researchers. We'll also explore some of the complications that arise when people of different genders operate by different rules in conversations with each other.

Feminine Communication People who are socialized in feminine speech communities—most women and some men—tend to regard communication as a primary way to establish and maintain relationships with others. They engage in conversation to share themselves and to learn about others (Hudson, 2001; Johnson, 1996; Wood, 2011a). For feminine people, talk is the essence of relationships. Consistent with this primary goal, feminine people use language to foster connections, support closeness, and for understanding.

Establishing equality between people is a second important feature of feminine communication. To achieve symmetry, communicators often match experiences to indicate "You're not alone in how you feel." Typical ways to communicate equality would be saying, "I've felt just like that" or "Something like that happened to me, too, and I felt like you do." Growing out of the quest for equality is a participatory mode of interacting in which communicators respond to and build on each other's ideas in the process of conversing (Hall & Langellier, 1988). Rather than a rigid "You tell your ideas, then I'll tell mine" sequence, feminine speech more characteristically follows an interactive pattern in which different voices interweave to create conversations.

Erin   *I played house and school, but I also played softball and soccer. Most of my friends did too. We learned to compete and work with external rules and be goal oriented just as much as boys did. The games children play aren't sex segregated anymore.*

A third characteristic of feminine speech is support for others. To demonstrate support, communicators often express emotions (Guerrero, Jones, & Boburka, 2006; Mulac, 2006) to show understanding of another's situation or feelings. "Oh, you must feel terrible" communicates that we understand and support how another feels. Related to these first two features is attention to the relationship level of communication (Eisenberg, 2002; MacGeorge, Gillihan, Samter, & Clark, 2003). You will recall that the relationship level of talk focuses on feelings and on the relationship between communicators rather than on the content of messages. Conversations between feminine people tend to be characterized by intensive adverbs ("That's *really* exciting") (Mulac, 2006) and questions that probe for greater understanding of feelings and perceptions surrounding the subject of talk (Dunn, 1999). "How did you feel when it occurred?" "How does this fit into the overall relationship?" are probes that help a listener understand a speaker's perspective.

Yolanda   *With my boyfriend, I am always asking, "How was your day? Your class? Your jam session? Did you get such-and-such done? Did you talk to so-and-so?" He answers my questions, usually with just a few words, but he almost never asks questions about my day and my life. When I do talk about myself, he often interrupts and sometimes listens, but he doesn't say much in response. I'm tired of doing all the work to keep a conversation going in our relationship.*

A fourth feature of feminine speech style is conversational "maintenance work" (Fishman, 1978; Taylor, 2002). This involves efforts to sustain conversation by inviting others to speak and by prompting them to elaborate their ideas. Questions are often used to include others: "How was your day?" "Did anything interesting happen on your trip?" "Do you have anything to add?" (Mulac, 2006). Communication of this sort maintains interaction and opens the conversational door to others.

A fifth quality of feminine speech is responsiveness. A feminine person might make eye contact, nod, or say, "Tell me more" or "That's interesting." Responsiveness reflects learned tendencies to care about others and to make them feel valued and included (Chatham-Carpenter & DeFrancisco, 1998). It affirms the other person and encourages elaboration by showing interest in what was said.

A sixth quality of feminine talk is personal, concrete style (Hall & Langellier, 1988). Typical of feminine talk are details, personal disclosures, and concrete reasoning. These features cultivate a personal tone, and they facilitate feelings of closeness by connecting communicators' lives.

A final feature of feminine speech is tentativeness (Mulac, 2006). This may be expressed in a number of forms. Sometimes people use verbal hedges, such as "I kind of feel you may be overreacting." In other situations, they qualify statements by saying, "I'm probably not the best judge of this, but …"Another way to keep talk provisional is to tag a question onto a statement in a way that invites another to respond: "*Midnight in Paris* was a pretty good movie, wasn't it?" Tentative communication leaves the door open for others to respond and express their opinions.

There has been controversy about tentativeness associated with feminine speech. Robin Lakoff (1975), who first reported that women use more hedges, qualifiers, and tag questions than men, claimed that these indicate uncertainty and lack of confidence. Calling women's speech "powerless," Lakoff argued that it reflects women's low self-esteem and socialization into subordinate roles. It's important to note that Lakoff's judgment that feminine speech is powerless was based on the assumption that masculine speech is the standard. If we use feminine speech as the standard, the use of hedges, qualifiers, and tag questions may reflect not powerlessness but the desire to keep conversations open and to include others (Mills, 1999). You should realize, however, that people outside feminine speech communities may use masculine standards, as Lakoff did, to interpret tentative speech.

Masculine Communication   Masculine speech communities tend to regard talk as a way to accomplish concrete goals, exert control, preserve independence, entertain, and enhance status. Conversation is often seen as an arena for proving oneself and negotiating prestige.

The first feature of masculine speech is the effort to establish status and control. Masculine speakers do this by asserting their ideas and authority, telling jokes and stories, or challenging others. Also, men maintain both control and independence by disclosing less than women. Men and boys typically use more I-references ("I have a plan," "I had a good game") than women and girls (Mulac, 2006). One way to exhibit knowledge and control is to give advice. For example, a person might say, "The way you should handle that is …," or "Don't let your boss get to you." On the relationship level of meaning, people socialized in feminine speech communities may interpret advice as the speaker saying she or he is superior—smarter, more experienced, etc.,—in comparison to the other person.

A second prominent feature of masculine speech is instrumentality—the use of speech to accomplish instrumental objectives. Particularly when men think they are knowledgeable about a topic, they may want to show their knowledge to others (Leaper & Ayres, 2007). In conversation, this is often expressed through problem-solving efforts to get information, discover facts, and suggest solutions. Conversations between women and men are often derailed by the lack of agreement on the meaning of this informational, instrumental focus. To people socialized in feminine speech communities, it may feel as if men don't care about their feelings. When a man focuses on the content level of meaning after a woman has disclosed a problem, she may feel that he is disregarding her emotions. He, on the other hand, thinks he is supporting her in the way that he has learned to show support—by suggesting how to solve the problem.

▼

Joanne   *My boyfriend is the worst at throwing solutions in my face when I try to talk to him about a problem. I know he cares about me; if he didn't, he wouldn't use up all that energy thinking up solutions for me. But I'm the kind of person who prefers a good ear (and maybe a shoulder) when I have a problem. I would like it so much better if he would forget about solutions and just listen and let me know he hears what's bothering me.*

A third feature of masculine communication is conversational command. Despite jokes about women's talkativeness, research indicates that, in most contexts, men tend to talk more often and at greater length than women (Mulac, 2006). Compared with girls and women, boys and men talk more frequently and for longer periods of time in face-to-face conversation, on the Internet, and in e-mail discussion groups (Aries, 1987; Crowston & Kammeres, 1998). Further, masculine speakers may reroute conversations by using what another says as a jumping-off point for their own topics, or they may interrupt. Although both sexes interrupt, most research suggests that men do it more frequently (Johnson, 2000; Mulac, Wiemann, Widenmann, & Gibson, 1988; West & Zimmerman, 1983).

Not only do men generally interrupt more than women, they may do so for different reasons. Research indicates that men are more likely to interrupt to control conversation by challenging other speakers or wresting the talk stage from them, whereas women interrupt to indicate interest and respond to others (Aries, 1987; Mulac et al., 1988; Stewart, Stewart, Friedley, & Cooper, 1996). A different explanation is that men generally interrupt more than women because interruptions are considered normal and good-natured within the norms of masculine speech communities (Wood, 1998). Whereas interruptions that reroute conversation might be viewed as impolite and intrusive in feminine speech communities, the out-going, give-and-take character of masculine speech may render interruptions as just part of normal conversation.

Fourth, masculine speech tends to be direct and assertive. Compared with women's language, men's is typically more forceful and authoritative (Mulac, 2006; Murphy & Zorn, 1996; Wood, Christiansen, Hebl, & Rothgerber, 1997). An exception to this pattern is when men talk with someone of high status. In this situation, men with lower status may be less assertive and commanding (O'Neill & Colley, 2006; Palomares, 2008; Palomares, 2010). Tentative forms of speech, such as hedges and disclaimers, are used less frequently by men than by women.

Fifth, masculine speech tends to be more abstract than feminine speech. Men frequently speak in general or conceptual terms that are removed from concrete experiences and personal feelings. Within public environments, norms for speaking call for theoretical, conceptual, and general thought and communication. Yet, within more personal relationships abstract talk sometimes creates barriers to intimacy.

▼

Chris   *Once I decided to live as a woman, I had to learn a whole different way of communicating. Even though I've always identified as female, I've always hung out with guys and I learned pretty much what our textbook describes as masculine speech patterns. To be accepted as a woman, I've had to relearn how to communicate—ask more questions about others, express more feelings, describe my experiences with a lot more detail, be more indirect like saying "Maybe we need to do such and such" instead of "Do such and such."*

Finally, masculine speech tends to be less emotionally responsive than feminine speech, especially on the relationship level of meaning (Guerrero et al., 2006). Men, more than women, give what are called **minimal response cues** (Parlee, 1979), which are verbalizations such as "yeah" or "umhmm." People socialized into feminine speech communities may perceive minimal response cues as indicating lack of involvement (Fishman, 1978; Stewart et al., 1996). Men's conversation also often lacks self-disclosure as well as expressed sympathy and understanding (Eisenberg, 2002; Lynch & Kilmartin, 1999). Within the rules of masculine speech communities, sympathy is a sign of condescension, and the revealing of personal problems is seen as making one vulnerable. Yet, within feminine speech communities sympathy and disclosure are understood as demonstrations of equality and support. This creates potential for misunderstanding between people who express themselves in masculine and feminine ways.

The Gender-Linked Language Effect   We've discussed some gendered tendencies in communication. However, these are not as hard and fast as they may seem at first. An emergent line of research focuses on the **gender-linked language effect** (Mulac, 1998; Palomares, 2008). This research suggests that language differences between women and men are influenced by a variety of factors including topics, speaker status, salience of gender in a communication situation, and other people present. One study (Palomares, 2008) found that women tend to speak more tentatively when speaking about masculine topics (sports and automotive matters were the topics in the study), but men speak more tentatively than women when speaking about feminine topics (shopping and fashion in the study). Another study showed that women communicated in more typically feminine ways when they

SALLY FORTH © King Features Syndicate

were assigned feminine avatars than when they were assigned masculine avatars. The same was true of men: They communicated in more typically masculine ways when assigned masculine avatars. Research on the gender-linked language effect reminds us that gender is not static, but is highly dynamic. The extent to which our communication reflects our gender varies according to context and other factors.

GENDER-BASED MISINTERPRETATIONS IN COMMUNICATION

In this final section, we explore what happens when gendered communication styles meet in conversations. We'll consider five communication misunderstandings that can arise.

Showing Support   Martha tells her coworker George that she is worried about Angie, who has been late to work several days recently. George gives a minimal response cue, saying only, "Oh." To Martha, this suggests he isn't interested, because women make and expect more verbal responses to signal interest. Yet, if George operates according to norms of masculine speech communities, he is probably thinking that, if Martha wants to say anything further or ask his opinion, she will. Masculine rules of speech assume people use talk to assert themselves.

Even without much encouragement, Martha continues by saying she knows Angie has a teenage daughter that has been causing some worries lately. She says, "I feel so bad for Angie, and I want to help her, but I don't know what to do." George then says, "It's her problem, not yours. Just butt out." At this, Martha explodes: "Who asked for your advice?" George is now completely confused. He thought Martha wanted advice, so he gave it. She is hurt that George didn't tune into her feelings. Both are frustrated.

The problem is not so much what George and Martha say and don't say. Rather, it's how they interpret each other's communication—actually, how they *misinterpret* it, because they fail to understand that they are operating by different rules of communication. George is respecting Martha's independence by not pushing her to talk. When he thinks she wants advice, he offers it in an effort to help. Martha, on the other hand, wants comfort and a connection with George—that's her primary purpose in talking with him. To her, George's advice seems to dismiss her feelings. He doesn't offer sympathy, because masculine rules for communication define this as condescending. Yet, the feminine speech community in which Martha was socialized taught her that giving sympathy is a way to show support.

Troubles Talk   Talk about troubles, or personal problems, is a kind of interaction in which hurt feelings may result from the contrast between masculine and feminine styles of communicating. Naomi might tell her partner, Greg, that she is feeling down because she didn't get a job she wanted. In an effort to be supportive, Greg might respond by saying, "You shouldn't feel bad. Lots of people don't get jobs they want." To Naomi, this seems to dismiss her feelings—to belittle them by saying lots of people experience her situation. Yet within masculine speech communities, you show respect by assuming that others don't need sympathy.

EXPLORING GENDERED LIVES | Scholarship versus Popular Psychology

Deborah Tannen (1990a, 1990b, 1995) declares that "communication between men and women can be like cross-cultural communication" (1990b, p. 42). John Gray goes even further, claiming that women and men are so different that it's as though they are from different planets (1992, 1995, 1996a, 1996b, 1998). Both Tannen and Gray have sold millions of books. Should we believe what they say about communication between the sexes?

When trying to determine the worth of their claims, we might first ask about their credentials as experts in communication. Tannen is a linguist who holds a PhD. Gray has no graduate degree from an accredited school. Tannen bases her claims on research that she and others have conducted. Gray relies on anecdotes from his personal experience.

Second, we should compare their claims to findings from sound research. Tannen's claims fare better than Gray's. Although Tannen sometimes generalizes too broadly from limited and unrepresentative samples, her claims do have some credible support. Gray, on the other hand, portrays women and men in extreme and dichotomous stereotypes that are not supported by credible research.

If you want to learn about how these popular psychology books measure up to research, read these articles: Goldsmith, D., & Fulfs, P. (1999). "You just don't have the evidence": An analysis of claims and evidence in Deborah Tannen's You Just Don't Understand. In M. Roloff (Ed.), *Communication Yearbook*, 22 (pp. 1–49). Thousand Oaks, CA: Sage; and Wood, J. T. (2001a). A critical response to Gray's portrayals of men, women, and relationships. *Southern Communication Journal*, 67, 201–210.

Now, let's turn the tables and see what happens when Greg feels troubled. When he meets Naomi, Greg is unusually quiet because he feels down about not getting a job offer. Sensing that something is wrong, Naomi tries to show interest by asking, "Are you okay? What's bothering you?" Greg feels she is imposing and pushing him to expose his vulnerability. Naomi probes further to show she cares. As a result, he feels intruded on and withdraws further. Then Naomi feels shut out.

But perhaps Greg does decide to tell Naomi why he feels down. After hearing about his rejection letter, Naomi says, "I know how you feel. I felt so low when I didn't get that position at Datanet." She is matching experiences to show Greg that she understands his feelings and that he's not alone (Basow & Rubenfeld, 2003). According to the communication rules that Greg learned in a masculine speech community, however, Naomi's comment about her own experience is an effort to steal the center stage from him and focus the conversation on herself.

Jay   *Finally, I understand this thing that keeps happening between my girlfriend and me. She is always worrying about something or feeling bad about what's happening with one of her friends. I've been trying to be supportive by telling her things like she shouldn't worry, or not to let it get her down, or not to obsess about other people's problems. I was trying to help her feel better. That's what guys do for each other—kind of distract our attention from problems. But Teresa just gets all huffy and angry when I do that. She tells me to stuff my advice and says if I cared about her I would show more concern. Finally, it makes sense. Well, sort of.*

Cathy   *When I broke up with Tommy, my dad tried so hard to help me through it. He took me to games and movies, offered to pay for it if I wanted to take horseback riding lessons. He just kept trying to DO something to make me feel better. That's how he's always been. If Mom's down about something, he takes her out or buys her flowers or something. It used to really bother me that he won't talk to me about what I'm feeling, but now I understand better what he's doing. I get it that this is his way of showing love and support for me.*

The Point of the Story   Another instance in which feminine and masculine communication rules often clash is in relating experiences. Masculine speech tends to follow a linear pattern, in which major points in a story are presented sequentially to get to the climax. Talk tends to be straightforward without a great many details. The rules of feminine speech, however, call for more detailed, less linear storytelling. Whereas a man is likely to provide rather bare information about what happened, a woman is more likely to embed the information within a larger context of the people involved and other things going on (Wood, 1998, 2011a). Women include details, not because they are important at the content level of meaning but because they matter at the relationship level of meaning. Recounting details is meant to increase involvement between people and to invite a conversational partner to be fully engaged in the situation being described.

Because feminine and masculine rules about details differ, men often find feminine accounts wandering and tedious. Conversely, the masculine style of storytelling may strike women as leaving out all the interesting details. Many a discussion between women and men has ended either with his exasperated demand, "Can't you get to the point?" or with her frustrated question, "Why don't you tell me how you were feeling and what else was going on?" She wants more details than his rules call for; he is interested in fewer details than she has learned to supply.

Relationship Talk   "Can we talk about us?" is the opening of innumerable conversations that end in misunderstanding and hurt. In general, people who are socialized into masculine style are interested in discussing relationships only if there are particular problems to be addressed. In contrast, people socialized into feminine style generally find it pleasurable to talk about important relationships even—or perhaps especially—when there are no problems (Acitelli, 1988).

The difference here grows out of the fact that masculine speech communities view communication as a means to doing things and solving problems, whereas feminine speech communities regard the *process* of communicating as a primary way to create and sustain relationships. No wonder many men duck when their partners want to "discuss the relationship," and women often feel a relationship is in trouble when their partners don't want to talk about it.

Public Speaking   Differences in feminine and masculine communication patterns also surface in public contexts. Historically, men have dominated politics. Thus, it's not surprising that the assertive, dominant, confident masculine style is the standard for public speaking. Women who are effective in politics tend to manage a fine balance in which they are sufficiently feminine to be perceived as acting appropriately for women and sufficiently masculine to be perceived as acting appropriately for politicians. Women who are considered effective public speakers, such as former Texas governor Ann Richards, manage to combine the traditionally feminine and masculine communication styles (Dow & Tonn, 1993).

These are only five of many situations in which differences between feminine and masculine communication styles may lead to misunderstandings. Many people find they can improve their relationships by understanding and using both feminine and masculine communication styles. When partners understand how to interpret each other's rules, they are less likely to misread motives. In addition, when they learn to speak the other's language, they become more gratifying conversational partners, and they enhance the quality of their relationships.

SUMMARY

In this chapter, we have explored relationships among verbal communication, gender, and culture. We first looked at how language reflects and sustains cultural views of masculinity and femininity. By defining, organizing, and evaluating gender, language reinforces social views of sex and gender. From generic male terms to language that demeans and diminishes women, verbal communication is a powerful agent of cultural expression. We also saw, however, that symbolic abilities allow us to be self-reflective about our definitions of masculinity and femininity in general and our own gender identities in particular.

The second theme of this chapter is that we express gendered identities through our communication. Because males and females tend to be socialized into different gender speech communities, they learn different rules for the purposes of communication and different ways to indicate support, interest, and involvement. This can lead to misunderstanding, frustration, hurt, and tension between people. Appreciation of and respect for the distinctive validity of each style of communication are foundations for better understanding between people. Further, learning to use different styles of communication allows all of us to be more flexible and effective in our interactions with a range of people.

Key Terms

The terms following are defined in this chapter on the pages indicated, as well as in alphabetical order in the book's glossary, which begins on page 325. The text's companion website (**http://www.cengage.com/communication/wood/genderedlives10e**) also provides interactive flash cards and crossword puzzles to help you learn these terms and the concepts they represent.

gender-linked language effect 133

male generic language 119

matriarchal 121

minimal response cues 133

polarized thinking 124

speech community 126

spotlighting 119

stereotype 124

Gender Online

1. Visit this site to learn what sexist language is and why it matters: **http://www. sexistlanguage.com**.
2. Online search terms: "gender-linked language effect," "generic language," "speech community."

Reflection and Discussion

1. Think about naming—specifically, about naming yourself. If you are a heterosexual woman, how important is it to you to keep your name or take your partner's name if you marry? If you are a heterosexual man, how much do you expect (or want) your partner to change hers? What are your preferences if you are gay, lesbian, or trans?
2. Think back to your childhood games. What games did you play? Do you think the games you played affected your style of verbal communication?
3. Read several newspapers. To what extent are women and men represented differently in stories? Are women described by appearance, marital status, and family life more often than men? Are men described in terms of accomplishments and action more than women?
4. The next time you have a conversation in which you feel that gendered rules of talk are creating misunderstandings, try to translate your expectations to the person with whom you are talking. For instance, if you are a woman talking with a man about a problem, he might try to help by offering advice. Instead of becoming frustrated that he doesn't focus on your feelings, try saying, "I appreciate your suggestions, but I'm not ready to think about how to fix things yet. Right now, you could help me work through my feelings about this issue." Discuss what happens when you explain what you need or want from others.

Recommended Resources

1. Dale Spender. (1984). *Man-made language*. London: Routledge and Kegan Paul. This classic book provides strong evidence that the English language was developed more by men and represents men's experiences better than women's experiences.
2. Jessica Valenti. (2008). *He's a Stud, She's a Slut, and 49 Other Double Standards Every Woman Should Know*. New York: Seal Press. This is a somewhat humorous look at a serious issue—double standards in how behaviors are named for women and men.
3. Nora Vincent (2006). *Self Made Man: One Woman's Journey into Manhood and Back*. New York: Viking. Nora Vincent spent a year and a half posing as a man, "Ned." As Ned, she discovered the freedoms and privileges men enjoy come at the cost of suppressing emotions and enduring constant testing.

We first make our habits, and then our habits make us.
John Dryden

CHAPTER 6

GENDERED NONVERBAL COMMUNICATION

Knowledge Challenge:

1. How do women and men differ in their typical use of nonverbal communication to regulate interaction?
2. Is physiology the cause of men's typically lower vocal pitch?
3. How accurately do women and men interpret others' emotions?

The nonverbal dimension of communication is extensive and important. Scholars estimate that nonverbal behaviors carry from 65% (Birdwhistell, 1970) to 93% (Mehrabian, 1981) of the total meaning of communication. That's not surprising when we realize that **nonverbal communication** is all elements of communication other than words themselves. It includes not only gestures and movement but also inflection, volume, clothing, and environmental factors, such as space and color. Like language, nonverbal communication is learned through interaction with others. Also like language, nonverbal communication is related to gender and culture in two ways: It expresses cultural meanings of gender, and men and women use nonverbal communication to present themselves as gendered people. Judith Butler (1990, 2004) claims that gender comes into being in our daily performances. In other words, our communication, particularly our nonverbal communication, continually reproduces or challenges images of femininity and masculinity and male and female.

In this chapter, we will consider how nonverbal communication reflects and expresses gender. As we identify functions and types of nonverbal communication, we will concentrate on gender-related patterns.

FUNCTIONS OF NONVERBAL COMMUNICATION

The three primary functions of nonverbal communication are (1) to supplement verbal communication, (2) to regulate interaction, and (3) to convey the bulk of the relationship level of meaning.

140

To Supplement Verbal Communication

Nonverbal behavior supplements verbal messages in five ways. First, nonverbal communication may *repeat* words, as when you say, "Right!" while pointing to the right. Second, we may nonverbally *contradict* a verbal message. For example, you say, "I'm fine" while weeping. Third, nonverbal behavior may also *complement* verbal communication by underlining a verbal message. The statement "I never want to see you again" is more forceful if accompanied by a frown and a threatening glare. Fourth, sometimes we use nonverbal behaviors to *replace* verbal ones. Rather than saying, "I don't know," you might shrug your shoulders. Finally, nonverbal communication may *accent* verbal messages, telling us which parts are important. "I love *you*" means something different from "*I* love you" or "I *love* you."

To Regulate Interaction

Nonverbal communication can also regulate interaction. We use body posture, eye contact, and vocal inflection to signal others that we wish to speak or that we are done speaking.

There are some sex-related differences in patterns of regulating interaction. Women frequently use nonverbal communication to invite others into conversation—looking at someone who hasn't spoken, smiling when a new person sits down in a group. Men, in general, are more likely to use nonverbal communication to hold onto the talk stage. For instance, if a man who is talking avoids eye contact with others, they are likely to assume he doesn't want them to jump into the conversation.

To Establish the Relationship Level of Meaning

A final and particularly important function of nonverbal communication is to convey the relationship level of meaning that expresses relationships between communicators. The three primary dimensions of relationship-level meaning are *responsiveness, liking,* and *power,* each of which is linked to gender.

Responsiveness   The first dimension of the relationship level of meaning is **responsiveness**, which is showing attentiveness to others and interest in what they say and do. Nonverbal cues of responsiveness include inflection, eye contact, and attentive body posture. Lack of responsiveness may be signaled by yawns or averted eyes.

Research shows that women generally are more responsive communicators than men. If you recall the lessons learned in gender speech communities, you'll realize that greater responsiveness is cultivated in feminine speech communities. Socialized to be affiliative, many women use nonverbal behaviors to indicate engagement with others, emotional involvement, and empathy. Females smile more and maintain more eye contact and direct body orientation, whereas males lean forward, display, and adopt postures congruent with those of the persons speaking (Guerrero, 1997).

There are also general differences in how overtly men and women respond to others. Women tend to be more overtly expressive of emotions than men are—a finding reflective of feminine socialization that promotes listening to others and responding to them (Cegela & Sillars, 1989; Ueland, 1992). Many women also show responsiveness by smiling (Burgoon, Buller, & Woodall, 1996; Hall, 2006), a behavior that says, "I am approachable, interested, friendly," which conforms to cultural ideals of femininity.

Other aspects of identity, such as race-ethnicity, interact with gender to influence responsiveness. For instance, Japanese women usually refrain from smiling in formal contexts, including weddings. The norms of Japanese culture regard smiling as indicating a lack of seriousness (Dresser, 1996). In the United States, African-American women generally don't smile as much as Caucasian women. In general, if a white woman does not smile and maintain eye contact, others are likely to think she is angry, upset, or stuck up. Conversely, people may be suspicious of a man who does smile a lot and keeps steady eye contact because he is deviating from norms for the performance of conventional masculinity.

Liking   A second dimension of the relationship level of meaning is **liking**. We use nonverbal behaviors to signal that we like or dislike others. Nonverbal cues of liking include vocal warmth, standing close to others, touching, and holding eye contact. Because most females are socialized to be nice to others and to form relationships, they tend to employ more nonverbal communication that signals liking, acceptance, and friendliness than do men (Stewart, Stewart, Friedley, & Cooper, 1996). For instance, when conversing, two women typically stand or sit closer together than two men; and women, particularly Caucasians, generally engage in more eye contact than men (Cegela & Sillars, 1989; Henley, 1977).

We can also use nonverbal behaviors to signal that we do not like others. A frown or glare communicates dislike, as does turning your back on someone or moving away from a person who sits next to you.

Power or Control   The third aspect of the relationship level of meaning is **power**, or control. Power refers to the degree to which people are equal to, dominant over, or deferential to others. Control issues in conversations include who defines topics, who directs conversation, who interrupts, and who defers. Although many nonverbal behaviors convey control messages, three are especially important: vocal qualities, touch, and use of space. In all three categories, men generally exceed women in nonverbal efforts to exert control (Major, Schmidlin, & Williams, 1990). For instance, compared with women, men tend to use greater volume and stronger inflection to highlight their ideas and add to the force of their positions. Men also tend to use touch to assert and reinforce status (Henley & Freeman, 1995). In addition, men generally command and use more personal space than women; they take up more space in sitting and standing, a difference not attributable to body size alone. Even at very young ages, boys are taught to seek and command more space than girls are (Mills, 1985).

Nonverbal behaviors may also assert or defer when it comes to territoriality. Women generally are more likely than men to surrender their territory, or space. You can confirm this for yourself by watching people on campus and elsewhere. Notice what men and women do when walking toward each other on a sidewalk. Usually, the woman moves to one side and she often does so well in advance.

Now that we have seen how nonverbal communication functions to supplement verbal communication, to regulate interaction, and to define the relationship level of meaning, we are ready to explore how it reflects and expresses cultural definitions of gender.

FORMS OF NONVERBAL COMMUNICATION

We'll consider six forms of nonverbal communication that reflect or express gender.

ARTIFACTS

An **artifact** is a personal object that can both express identity and influence how we see ourselves. Beginning with the pink and blue blankets used with babies in many hospitals, personal objects for children define them as feminine or masculine. Parents send artifactual messages through the toys they give to sons and daughters. Typically, boys are given toys that invite competition and active, rough play, whereas girls are more likely to be given toys that encourage nurturing, domestic activities, and attention to appearance (Messner, 2000a).

Toy catalogues offer clear messages about cultural meanings attached to the sexes. Even in 2010, as I was writing this book, catalogues for children's toys featured pastel-colored pages titled "For Girls," with play kitchen appliances, makeup, hair accessories, and pink tutu outfits. The pages labeled "For Boys" had bolder colors and showed soldiers, science equipment, swords, shields, and building sets. Researchers Sharon Lamb and Lyn Brown (2006) drew three conclusions from their survey of toy sections in stores such as Toys Я Us or Walmart: (1) Toys are sex-segregated—different aisles for girls' and boys' toys; (2) the boys' section features action toys (Spider Man, NEO-Shifters) whereas the girls' section features toys that involve fashion (wigs and make up), taking care of homes (toy vacuums), and nurturing (dolls); and (3) toys for boys usually come in darker, bolder colors than do toys for girls.

Although clothing has become less sex-distinctive than in former eras, fashions for women and men still differ in the world beyond college. Men's clothes generally are not as colorful or bright as women's, and they are designed to be more functional. Pockets in jackets and trousers allow men to carry wallets, change, keys, and miscellany. The relatively loose fit of men's clothes and the design of men's shoes allow them to move quickly and with assurance. Thus, men's clothing enables activity.

Women's clothing is quite different. Reflecting social expectations of femininity, women's clothing is designed to call attention to women's bodies and to make them maximally attractive to viewers. Form-fitting styles, clingy materials, and revealing cuts encourage women to perform femininity and sexuality. Formal

---

EXPLORING GENDERED LIVES | **INDECENT DRESS FOR WOMEN**

Lubna Hussein, a 30-something Sundanese journalist was arrested for violating Islamic law by wearing "indecent clothing." Her offence? Wearing trousers. In July of 2009, Ms. Hussein and 12 other trouser-wearing women were apprehended in a café and sentenced to a fine and lashing with whips that leave permanent scars. Most of the accused women pled guilty and accepted the punishement, but Ms. Hussein pled not guilty. For defying the court, she was sentenced to more lashes. Ms. Hussein printed invitations and sent e-vites asking people to come to witness her whipping. Embarrased, the government offered to drop the charges if Ms. Hussein would agree not to wear trousers. She refused (Gettleman, 2009b).

---

women's clothing often has no pockets to hold wallets and keys. Further, most women's shoes are designed to flatter legs at the cost of comfort and safety—how fast can you run in stilettos?

Artifacts and what they mean depend on cultural context. This point is well made by Zainab, an international student in California, who e-mailed me a comment about the meaning that she, as a Muslim woman, attaches to wearing a hijab, a headscarf that many Western women regard as a symbol of the oppression of Muslim women.

▼

Zainab   *Most Americans I have met think that the hijab [head covering] worn by Muslim women is oppressive. I must disagree with that. Muslim women who choose to wear the hijab are liberated from the stereotypes of women as sex objects. We are not oppressed by the standards of our culture, which are the standards that we should be judged by.*

Other artifacts communicate cultural views of women and men. Advertisements for food, homemaking, and child rearing feature women, reiterating the view of women as homemakers and mothers and the view of men as uninvolved in parenting. Products associated with heavy work, cars, and outdoor sports feature men (or women in seductive poses who are admiring the strong men). Also, consider the artifacts that women are encouraged to buy to meet the cultural command to be attractive: The cosmetics industry is a multimillion-dollar business in the United States. Girls and women scramble to find products to straighten, curl, color, and style hair and products to create "natural-looking" faces by covering up blemishes and coloring and curling lashes.

▼

Emily   *Why do girls have to look nice all the time? My boyfriend rolls out of bed and goes to class or the mall or wherever. He doesn't have to shampoo and blow his hair or dress in clean, ironed clothes. His clothes are rumpled and his hair isn't even combed some days. Once when I had a really bad cold, I felt so bad I didn't do what I usually do before going out. I showered, but I didn't do my hair or put on blush and eye shadow, and I wore work out clothes. My boyfriend told me I looked like a slob just because for once I looked like he did.*

Some people use artifacts to challenge existing perceptions of masculinity and femininity. For example, some men wear one or more earrings, either because they like the adornment or to signal support of gays, lesbians, and transgendered and gender nonconforming individuals. Women may wear military boots or may dress in ways that otherwise defy conventional performances of femininity.

▼

Raquel   *As a Puerto Rican I often felt like I was always different as a child. My skin was darker and there seemed to be no Puerto Ricans in the media to make me feel more pride in my ethnicity as a child.*

I think it's very sad the things we do to conform to the ideal beauty. I have a friend who is Vietnamese who hates her eyes. She is very beautiful but she would rather have the Western eyes. I have another friend who is Italian and had the large Roman nose but right after high school she had rhinoplasty to "fix" it. When I was younger I wanted lighter skin even though all of my white friends said they were jealous of my "tan."

PROXIMITY AND PERSONAL SPACE

Proxemics refers to space and our use of it. Space is a primary means through which cultures express values and shape patterns of interaction. Different cultures have different norms for how much space people need and how closely they interact. For instance, in Latin-American countries, people interact at closer distances than in more reserved societies like the United States (Samovar, Porter, & Stefani, 1998). In some countries, houses for big families are no larger than small apartments in the United States, and the idea of private rooms for individual family members is unheard of.

Proxemics offers keen insight into the relative power and status accorded to various groups in society. Space is a primary means by which a culture designates who is important and who has privilege. In strongly patriarchal societies, women are not allowed to own property; thus, they are literally denied space. Only in the mid-1990s did India begin to allow daughters to inherit property from parents.

EXPLORING GENDERED LIVES | **GENDERED PROXEMICS**

Virginia Valian (1998) is a professor of psychology and linguistics who is interested in how gender stereotypes shape perceptions. She conducted an experiment to find out whether college students are equally likely to perceive women and men as leaders. Students were asked to identify the leader in photos of people seated around a conference table. When the people in the photo were all men or all women, students overwhelmingly chose the person at the head of the table as the leader. Students also selected the person at the head of the table as the leader when the photo showed both women and men and a man was seated at the head of the table. However, when both women and men were in the photo and a woman was at the head of the table, students selected the woman at the head as the leader only half the time.

Create pictures like those in Valian's experiment, show them to friends, and ask friends to identify the leader in each picture. Do your results concur with those of Valian?

Consider who gets more and less space in our society. Executives have large offices, although there is little functional need for so much room. Secretaries, however, are crowded into cubicles that overflow with file cabinets and computers. Generally, there is a close correlation between status and the size of a person's home, car, office, and so forth. Who gets space and how much space they get indicate power.

Think about the home in which you grew up. Who sat at the head of the table—the place typically associated with being head of the household? In most two-parent, heterosexual families, that space belongs to the man and symbolizes his leadership of the family. Did your father or stepfather have his own room, space, or chair? Did your mother or stepmother? Many men have private studies, workshops, or other spaces, but fewer women with families have such spaces. My students initially disagreed with this observation and informed me that their mothers have spaces. When we discussed this, however, it turned out that many of their mothers' spaces were kitchens and sewing rooms—places where they do things for other people. Students whose mothers had spaces for their own work in the home, reported their mothers generally used parts of other rooms (a corner in the living room) or temporary spaces (using the dining-room table when it's not needed for meals). Many years ago, Virginia Woolf gave a famous speech titled "A Room of One's Own," in which she argued that women's ability to engage in creative, independent work is hampered by not having inviolate spaces for themselves.

Territoriality is personal space that we don't want others to invade. Yet, not everyone's territory is equally respected. People with power tend to enter the spaces of those with less power, but the converse is not true. In general, men go into women's spaces more than women enter men's spaces and more than men enter other men's spaces.

What happens when a person's private territory is invaded? This question has intrigued Judee Burgoon and her colleagues (Burgoon & Hale, 1988; LePoire, Burgoon, & Parrott, 1992). One response to invasion of our territory is behavior that restores our privacy zone. For instance, if someone moves too close for comfort, you might step back. That response accepts the invasion and cedes the territory, something women are more likely than men to do. Another response is the well-known elevator phenomenon, in which people are crowded more closely than they like, so everyone looks up or down as if to say "I'm not trying to intrude into your space." Both sexes use this response at times. A third response is to challenge the invasion—to stand your ground and refuse to yield territory. Men are more likely than women to adopt this response to an attempted invasion of territory.

HAPTICS (TOUCH)

Haptics, or touch, from parents and other adults communicates different messages to boys and girls. Parents tend to touch daughters more often and more gently than they do sons, which teaches girls to expect touching from others and to view touching as an affiliative behavior. Boys are more likely to learn to associate touching with control and power and not to expect nurturing touches from others.

Based on these lessons in childhood, women are more likely than men to initiate hugs and touches that express support, affection, and comfort, whereas men more often use touch to direct others, assert power, and express sexual interest (Pearson, West, & Turner, 1995). Members of female softball teams exchange more team hugs and hand piles than members of male softball teams, particularly after negative game events (Kneidinger, Maple, & Tross, 2001). Because masculine and feminine meanings of touch may differ, women may perceive men's touch and entry into their space as harassing (LePoire et al., 1992; Levy & Paludi, 1997). Touching behaviors also reflect social norms and the constraints they impose. For example, Laura Guerrero, Joseph DeVito, and Michael Hecht (1999) report that gay and lesbian couples may feel less free than straight people to touch each other in public contexts.

> **Roseanne**   *A few months ago, I was out with this guy I'd been seeing for a while. We weren't serious or anything, but we had gone out a few times. Well, we were at his place listening to music when he started coming on to me. After a while, I told him to stop because I didn't want to go any further. He grinned and pinned my arms back and asked what I was going to do to stop him. Well, I didn't have to, thank goodness, because he didn't really push, but just the same I had to think there really wasn't anything I could have done if he had. That's always there when I'm with a guy—he could overpower me if he wanted to.*

Because men are generally larger and stronger than women, they tend to have more physical confidence and to be more willing to use physical force than women (May, 1998a). Some men are unaware of how strong they are, especially in relation to others who are less so.

KINESICS (FACIAL AND BODY MOTION)

Kinesics are face and body movements. Kinesic behaviors more typical of women than men include tilting heads, smiling, and condensing their bodies to take up less space. Kinesic behaviors more typical of men than women include using large gestures, taking up space, and entering others' territories.

▼

Elaine   *I never thought it would be so hard not to smile. When you challenged us in class to go one day without smiling except when we really felt happy, I thought that would be easy. I couldn't do it. I smile when I meet people, I smile when I purchase things, I even smile when someone bumps into me. I never realized how much I smile. What was most interesting about the experiment was how my boyfriend reacted. We got together last night, and I was still working on not smiling. He asked me what was wrong. I told him, "Nothing." I was being perfectly nice and talkative and everything, but I wasn't smiling all the time like I usually do. He kept asking what was wrong, was I unhappy, had something happened—even was I mad. I pointed out that I was being as friendly as usual. Then he said, yeah, but I wasn't smiling. I told him that I just didn't see anything particular to smile about, and he said it wasn't like me. I talked with several other women in our class, and they had the same experience. I just never realized how automatic smiling is for me.*

Western women, particularly Caucasians, smile more than men. Judee Burgoon and her colleagues (Burgoon et al., 1996) observe that, for women, smiling is a basic interactional behavior, whereas for men it is reserved for expressing emotion. In combination, these gender-differentiated patterns suggest that women's facial and body motions generally signal that they are approachable, friendly, and unassuming. Men's facial and body communications, in contrast, tend to indicate that they are reserved and in control.

▼

Duncan   *When I was in high school, I played on the football team. On the day we were taking the team photograph, one of the seniors on the team yelled out before the photo, "if anyone smiles, I'm going to beat your ass." Football is a tough, aggressive game, so you're not supposed to smile when you're playing or having a photo in your uniform.*

Males are more likely than females to use facial and body movements aggressively in social, business, and other contexts (Kinney, Smith, & Donzella, 2001; Timmers, Fischer, & Manstead, 1998). Male athletes engage in nonverbal confrontations with teammates, whereas female athletes are more likely to talk through tensions than engage in physical confrontations (Sullivan & Short, 2001).

Called by poets the "windows to the soul," eyes can express love, anger, fear, interest, challenge—a great range of emotions. Many women have learned to signal interest and involvement by sustaining eye contact, whereas men generally do not sustain eye contact during conversations. An exception to this rule is that men sometimes use eye contact to challenge others and assert themselves (Pearson, 1985). Men in my classes tell me that they would lose face and come across as wimps if they didn't return a stare.

▼

Randall   *It sounds kind of stupid when we talk about it, but it's true that a guy has to return another guy's stare if he wants to hold his own. It's like a staring contest. Sometimes, on a street another guy will meet my eyes. When I notice, then he's locked into holding the stare, and that means that I have to, too. It's like that old joke about the first one to blink loses. It's kind of dumb, but I'd feel strange not returning another guy's gaze. Like a wimp or something.*

PARALANGUAGE

Vocal cues that accompany verbal communication are called **paralanguage**. Although there are some physiological differences in male and female vocal organs (the larynx and pharynx), these do not account fully for differences in women's and men's paralanguage. For instance, the larger, thicker vocal folds of male larynxes do result in lower pitch, but the difference between the average pitch of male speakers and female speakers exceeds that explained by physiology.

To understand why women and men tend to have divergent paralanguage, we must once again consider socialization processes. What vocal cues would you expect of someone taught to be deferential and caring? What would you expect of someone taught to be assertive, emotionally reserved, and independent? Your expectations probably closely match identified differences in male and female paralanguage. In general, women use higher pitch, softer volume, and more inflection. Men tend to use lower pitch and greater volume in order to assert themselves and command the conversational stage.

A classic study sheds light on cultural stereotypes of men and women (Addington, 1968). A researcher asked participants to judge the personalities of people on the basis of vocal qualities, which he experimentally manipulated. Women with breathy, tense voices were judged to be pretty, feminine, petite, shallow, immature, and unintelligent. Men with throaty, tense voices were judged to be mature, masculine, intelligent, and sophisticated. The researcher concluded that, when women are perceived as feminine, other aspects of the feminine gender stereotype—such as being pretty, immature, and unintelligent—are attributed to them. Men who are perceived as masculine are assumed to be intelligent and mature.

PHYSICAL APPEARANCE

Members of both sexes often feel pressured to meet current cultural ideals of physical appearance. Although striving to meet physical ideals is typically associated with girls and women, men are not immune.

EXPLORING GENDERED LIVES | A NEW MODEL FOR MODELS?

The fashion industry has long favored models who are thin—alarmingly thin. For many years, critics have charged that using emaciated models encouraged eating disorders among women. The critics were largely ignored until 2006 when two South-American models died: one from anorexia, and one from heart failure, which can be caused by excessive thinness.

In September 2006, Spain's top fashion show—Pasarela Cibeles in Madrid—required women who wanted to model to have a body mass index of 18 or higher. As a result, 30% of the models who expected to be in the show were rejected as too thin (Woolls, 2006). In December 2006 Milan pledged that it would keep dangerously thin models off its runways (Givhan, 2006). Taking note, in January 2007, the Council of Fashion Designers of America, based in New York, issued a memo suggesting that models should be educated about eating disorders and that healthy snacks should be provided for models backstage during fashion shows.

Currently, Crystal Renn is the reigning plus-size model. But what is "plus-size?" Renn is a size 12; the average American woman is a size 14. Says Renn, "It's simply bizarre that 'normal' is the new overweight" (Wilson, 2010, p. E1).

Do you prefer a range of body sizes or a single size in advertisements?

Some men are dissatisfied with how they look (Davison & Birch, 2001). Yet, significant concern about appearance doesn't seem to be a problem for most boys and men. A 2003 poll ("The Man Poll") revealed that 87% of men in America are very or somewhat satisfied with their appearance, and 50% of men don't worry at all about losing their physical attractiveness. Men who are concerned about physical appearance tend to focus more on achieving "good" musculature (for instance, "six-pack abs") than slimness per se (Boodman, 2007; Roosevelt, 2010). Action figures socialize boys at an early age to understand that the ripped look is the current body ideal for masculinity. Consider one example: the 1973 G.I Joe action figure, if a real man, would be 5-foot 10-inches tall, have a 31.7-inch waist, a 44.4-inch chest, and 12.2-inch biceps, but the more recent G.I. Joe Extreme, if a real man, would be 5-foot 10-inches tall, have a 36.5-inch waist, a 54.8-inch chest, and 26.8-inch biceps (Harrison, 2008).

Girls and women are more likely to be dissatisfied with their appearance than boys and men are. For women, especially Caucasians, dislike of their bodies often affects overall self-esteem (Bulik & Taylor, 2005; Schooler, Ward, Merriwether, & Caruthers, 2004). It's difficult for women not to feel that they look inadequate when they are bombarded daily with images that are unrealistic—and unreal. Many women, particularly young ones, find it nearly impossible to resist the pervasive pressure to be thin (Hesse-Biber & Leavy, 2006; Rhode, 2010). Many young women say they know that models and cover girls are digitally altered and not "real," but still they dislike their own bodies for not measuring up to the manufactured perfection (Bordo, 2003; Rhode, 2010).

EXPLORING GENDERED LIVES　　|　　**BEAUTY: HIS AND HERS**

Q: Isn't it mainly rich women who have cosmetic surgery?

A: Today, both sexes have cosmetic surgery. Women most often have facial surgeries, fat-reduction operations, and breast augmentation or lifting (Barrett & Soringsen, 2007; Rhode, 2010). The most popular surgeries for men are liposuction, eyelid surgery, and nose reshaping (Mishori, 2005). Both sexes also increasingly rely on noninvasive treatments, such as Botox and Dysport injections—4,795,357 doses in 2009 at the average cost of $405 per injection (Louis, 2010a). Between 1997 and 2003, the number of cosmetic procedures increased 293%—from 2.1 million to 8.3 million (Orecklin, 2004).

Wealth is no longer a major part of the profile of people who have cosmetic surgery or noninvasive procedures (Blum, 2003; Bordo, 2004). Age is also not a criterion for cosmetic techniques. Increasingly Americans beween 13 and 19 years old are having injections of botulinum toxin, which goes by the brand names Botox and Dysport. In 2009, 12,000 injections were sold to people in this age group (Louis, 2010b).

Communication scholar John Jordan (2004) says it's not just surgery that is plastic today—people increasingly regard their bodies as plastic and endlessly changeable. Confirming this, a 2010 poll showed that 69% of American adults would choose to have cosmetic surgery if they could afford it (Louis, 2010a).

Q: So what's wrong with having plastic surgery to look better?

A: All of us care about our looks. However, it isn't healthy to have excessive concerns about how we look or unrealistic ideals for appearance. Many plastic surgeons report that prospective patients come to them with pictures of celebrities they want to look like. Even more troublesome are the reasons some people seek cosmetic surgery. Many think others will like them better if they "fix" how they look. They haven't learned to value themselves for qualities more important than physical appearance.

Q: So what's the big deal? Maybe appearance shouldn't matter so much, but if you can afford to have cosmetic surgery, why not do it?

A: There are some risks. Injections to hide wrinkles and smile lines can shrink and distort the face and other areas. Skin resurfacing can cause inflammation and discoloration of skin. Eyelift surgeries can make it difficult or even impossible to close the eyes completely. Breast implants significantly decrease breasts' sensitivity to touch. Scarring, chronic pain, and nerve damage, are other possible complications. Botox and Dysport injections in facial areas can result in complications including facial nerve paralysis, an asymmetrical smile, and speech impairments (Louis, 2010b).

Another reason to think carefully about surgery that changes your appearance is that fashions change. Years ago, when a pencil-thin model named Twiggy was a supermodel, women had breast-reduction surgeries in record numbers. Larger breasts are part of the current physical ideal for women, which goes a long way toward explaining why breast enlargement surgery has increased more than 700% since 1992 (Levy, 2005; Rives, 2005). And it's probably no coincidence that when Angelina Jolie ascended to superstar status, between 2002 and 2003, there was a 21% increase in lip implants, which are more lasting that the plumping injections (Barrett, 2004). In 2009, more than 21,000 people had lip augmentation (Louis, 2010a). When fashions in breast and lip size change, more procedures may be needed to undo the original ones.

For many girls and women, especially Caucasians, concern about weight starts early. By third grade, 50 to 80% of girls say they want to lose weight (Rhode, 2010), and by the fourth grade, 40% of girls diet (Kilbourne, 2004, 2007, 2010). By age 13, 53% of American girls say they are "unhappy with their bodies"; and by age 17, 78% say this (National Institute on Media & the Family, 2007). Pressure to be thin contributes to the epidemic of eating disorders, which affect 7 to 10 million Americans of which 90 to 95% are girls and women. Today, 10% of college students suffer from an eating disorder and 15% of women have unhealthy attitudes and behaviors regarding food (National Association of Anorexia Nervosa and Associated Disorders, 2010; National Institute of Mental Health, 2010). Ten million women in the United States have an eating disorder (Crane, 2008). Anorexia has the highest mortality rate of all psychiatric disorders—up to 15.6% of anorexics die from the condition or problems related to it (Harrison, 2008). Without treatment, as many as 20% of anorexics die within 20 years of developing the disease as a direct result of the disease, but with treatment only 2 to 3% die (National Association of Anorexia Nervosa and Associated Disorders, 2010; National Institute of Mental Health, 2010). The prevalence of eating disorders in women shouldn't surprise us, given the pervasive messages that very thin women are the ideal.

Nikki   *When I was growing up, my mother and grandmother were always on diets. They think being ultra-thin is essential. Four years ago, when I came to college, I gained the "freshman 15." When I went home for the summer, my mother and grandmother commented on how much weight I'd gained and how bad I looked. Mother got her doctor to put me on FenPhen, the diet pill. I'd heard it could be dangerous (you've probably read about the lawsuits against it), but I took the pills for two months and lost a lot of weight—more than the 15 pounds I'd gained. Then, I started having echoing sounds in my ears. I went to a doctor, and he said it was the result of taking FenPhen. The ringing is with me all the time, even though I've quit taking that pill. Being thin is fine, but it's not worth risking your health. I actually feel sorry for my mother and grandmother because they obsess over their weight and never enjoy eating food.*

Many current models are anorexic.

When women are encouraged to focus so intensely on their bodies, they may give less attention to more important aspects of identity. For many young women in America, the body has become an all-consuming project that takes precedence over character, integrity, and other components of self worth (Barash, 2006; Brumberg, 1997; Davies-Popelka, 2011).

Kyle *For me, the issue of physical appearance is really complicated because I'm transgendered. Biologically, I am female, but psychologically and spiritually I am male. Every time I see my naked body or have my period, it's totally unsettling because I'm really a man and shouldn't have breasts or periods. Surgery scares me, but I may have it one day so that my body matches my self-concept.*

Perhaps you are wondering who is most likely to become obsessed with weight. Approximately 40% of new cases of anorexia are females between the ages of 15 and 19 (Boodman, 2007; Bulik & Taylor, 2005; Pope, Phillips, & Olivardia, 2002; Strout, 2007). Female athletes are vulnerable to eating disorders, particularly anorexia (Strout, 2007). Women who have internalized the culture's views of femininity are more susceptible than androgynous women to cultural ideals for women's weight (Northrup, 1995). In general, Western Caucasian women, who subscribe to conventional ideals of femininity, are particularly likely to strive to meet unrealistic body ideals (McRobbie, 2009; Mernissi, 2004).

In general, African-American women tend to be more satisfied with their bodies, less prone to eating disorders, and less extreme in pursuing unrealistic physical ideals (Banks, 2000; Schooler et al., 2004; Walker, 2007). African-American women who identify strongly with their ethnic heritage are less vulnerable to obsession with thinness than are African-American women who leave their communities or who don't have strong black identities. In a letter to me, Daneen, a black student from a northern college, described the ideology behind the views of physical beauty that she and other black women in her community learned:

> My family and my African American culture instilled pride in me. I was told that my full lips, round body, and rough hair encompassed the beauty and pride of my history. To want to be skinny or have straight hair or thin lips would be to deny my identity as a Black woman.

Because our culture is increasingly emphasizing men's bodies, more and more men are exercising, working out with weights, taking fitness supplements, and using potentially lethal steroids to develop the muscularity promoted as ideal (Pope, Phillips, & Olivardia, 2002; Roosevelt, 2010). One eating disorder, binge eating, seems to be increasing among men. Male model Ron Saxen (2007) details his battle with binge eating in his book, *The Good Eater*. One group of men is particularly likely to be concerned about appearance and to develop eating disorders: gay men. Physical appearance is linked more closely to self-worth for gay men than for straight men (Beren, Hayden, Wilfey, Grilo, 1996).

EXPLORING GENDERED LIVES | **THE BILL FOR KEEPING UP APPEARANCES**

In 2008, John McCain, the Republican candidate for the Presidency of the United States, chose little-known Sarah Palin, Governor of Alaska, as his running mate. Palin claimed to be a "regular person," and a "hockey mom." In Palin's case, however, being a "regular person" cost a lot of money. After being selected as the Republican Vice Presidential nominee, the campaign spent more than $175,000 on clothes for Palin, $54,000 on a fashion consultant, $68,400 for a makeup artist, and $42,225 for a hair stylist. The money paid is about what Hollywood studios spend to prepare a top actress for a premiere or publicity campaign (Luo & Horyn, 2008).

Calculate how much you spend to maintain your appearance: all cosmetics and toiletries, clothes and shoes, nail and hair salons, etc.

EXPLORING GENDERED LIVES | **RACE AND VIEWS OF PHYSICAL BEAUTY**

What's thin? What's fat? Is weight attractive on women? It turns out that the answers often depend on the race of the person answering. There is growing evidence that black and white girls and women view their bodies in different ways and that they have different ideals of feminine beauty.

At early ages, many white girls learn that being slender or even thin is considered desirable. When asked to describe a perfectly shaped female, young white women respond that she would be 5 feet 7 inches tall and weigh 100 to 110 pounds. Young black women's descriptions of physical ideals typically include full hips and thick thighs. Young black women also tend to emphasize that beauty is about more than weight and appearance: It's having the "right attitude." These differences in feminine ideals shed light on the reasons why anorexia and bulimia are less common among black girls and women, especially those who are strongly identified with African-American culture (Bocella, 2001; Molloy & Herzberger, 1998; Vobejda & Perlstein, 1998).

Thinness is not the only aspect of physical attractiveness that is race related. For years, European-American features have been represented as the only standard of female beauty (Edrut, 2000; Shandler, 1999). Tyra Banks, Naomi Campbell, and other women of color who are successful models have skin color, hair, and features that are more like those of European Americans than like members of their own ethnic groups. But Campbell is trying to change that—working with other black models, she's pushing the fashion industry to feature more black models on the runway and in magazines (Samuels, 2008).

Celebrity models challenges Caucasian standards of beauty by representing shapely black women models such as Buffie the Body, Esther Baxter, and Ki Toy, who appear in magazines and hip-hop music videos (Powell, 2007).

In summary, sex-related differences in nonverbal behavior reflect culturally constructed views of masculinity and femininity. In general, women are more sensitive to nonverbal communication; display more overt interest, attention, and affiliation; constrict themselves physically; are given and use less space; use touch for affiliative purposes but are touched more; and restrict body gestures more than men. Reflecting cultural messages about how to enact masculinity, men tend to use nonverbal communication to signal power and status, to assert themselves and their agendas, to command territories, and to veil their emotions from public display.

INTERPRETING NONVERBAL BEHAVIOR

Before leaving our discussion of gender and nonverbal communication, we should ask whether there are sex- or gender-related differences in skill at decoding others' nonverbal behaviors. The research that has addressed this question reports that women are generally more skilled than men at interpreting others' nonverbal communication to identify the emotions they are experiencing (Hall, 2006). Researchers report that females exceed males in the capacity to decode nonverbal behaviors and more accurately discern many emotions that others feel (Stewart et al., 1996). There is one exception to this generalization, and it's one that calls our attention to both biological and sociological influences on our gendered identities. Although overall women exceed men in their ability to decipher facial cues, in an experiment men were notably faster than women at noticing angry faces (Bakalar, 2006). One explanation for this is that historically men's survival depended on having a keen ability to detect anger and other signs of possible aggression.

Although researchers agree that women are generally more skilled than men at interpreting nonverbal behavior, they disagree on why this is so. It may be explained by biology, social learning and cognitive development (Richmond & McCroskey, 2000), or standpoint. The first explanation of women's generally strong ability to read feelings is sex-related brain differences—females' right brain specialization—may make them more adept at decoding emotions. Second, both cognitive development and social learning theories explain that, from childhood on, most females are encouraged to be sensitive to others and to relationships. Related to this is the third explanation, women's standpoint as caregivers who often take care of children and sick family members may make them more adept at decoding emotions. Women also far outnumber men in caring professions, such as social work, counseling, nursing, and human resources. Women's involvement in caring encourages them to develop a standpoint that prioritizes attending to others and being able to read their feelings and needs.

Krista   *I buy the power explanation for women's decoding skill. I know that I learned to do this from my mother. My father is very moody, and you have to know how to read him, or there's trouble ahead. I remember, when I was a little girl, my mother would tell me not to ask Daddy for something or not to tell him about things at certain times because he was in a bad mood. I asked her how she knew, and she gave me a blueprint for reading him. She told me, when he was mad he fidgeted and mumbled more and that he got real quiet when he was upset. Later, she taught me other things, like how to tell when he's getting angry about something—his eyebrows twitch. She made it seem like a science, and I guess it was in a way. But she sure knew how to read his moods, and that's how we stayed out of his way when he was on the warpath.*

Standpoint theory also suggests that women's decoding skill results from their standpoint as subordinate members of society. Those who are oppressed or who have little power learn to interpret others in order to survive (Hall, Halberstadt, & O'Brien, 1997; Henley, 1977; Henley & LaFrance, 1996). Bill Puka

(1990) found consistency between the emotional sensitivity typical of women and that of prisoners, slaves, and other oppressed groups. For members of oppressed groups, decoding is a survival skill. Women's decoding skills probably result from a combination of biology, socialization, and historic and current power discrepancies between the sexes.

You might think about your experiences and observations of others and ask which explanation of women's decoding ability makes most sense to you.

CULTURAL VALUES ASSOCIATED WITH GENDERED NONVERBAL COMMUNICATION

Nonverbal behaviors expected of women emphasize communality—building and sustaining relationships and community. Nonverbal behaviors considered appropriate for men emphasize agency—displaying power and initiative, achieving. How do these prescriptions for feminine and masculine nonverbal communication reflect broad cultural values?

We begin by noting that Western society values agency more than communality. In other words, Western culture places higher value on the behaviors associated with masculinity than on those associated with femininity.

The different values assigned to agency and communality were dramatically illustrated in a classic study. A research team (Broverman, Broverman, Clarkson, Rosenkrantz, & Vogel, 1970) prepared a list of traits that reflected a broad range of human qualities. They then asked 79 male and female psychiatrists, psychologists, and social workers to check the attributes they thought described "normal, healthy women." Next, the clinicians checked traits they associated with "normal, healthy men." Finally, clinicians selected characteristics of "normal, healthy adults." The findings were clear and startling: Normal women were described as dependent, oriented toward relationships, deferential, unassertive, concerned with appearance, submissive, emotional, and uncompetitive. In contrast, clinicians described normal men as independent, aggressive, competitive, more rational than emotional, and ambitious. Associated with normal adults were the same qualities used to describe normal men.

We can draw two conclusions from this study. First, the clinicians perceived stereotypically masculine characteristics as the standard, or norm, for healthy adults. Second, the qualities associated with normal, healthy women were seen as inconsistent with those of normal, healthy adults. The bias favoring masculine qualities continues in Western society (McCreary, Newcomb, & Sadava, 1998; Wetherell, 1997).

But cultural beliefs are not etched in stone. Instead, they are constructed, sustained, and sometimes altered as members of a society interact in ways that constantly remake social views of gender. We can resist our culture's unequal views of agency and communality if we recognize that different nonverbal styles are simply different—not better or worse, just different. We can also choose not to embody the gendered nonverbal style prescribed for our gender. If we find that social expectations restrict us, we may resist them. In doing so, we act as agents of change who alter cultural understandings of women's and men's behavior.

RESPECTING GENDERED STYLES OF NONVERBAL COMMUNICATION

What we've learned in this chapter also empowers us to be more effective in our communication and in our interpretation of others' communication. People who have been socialized in conventionally masculine speech communities may perceive a woman who defers as less confident of her ideas than a man who advances his views assertively. Similarly, someone socialized in conventionally feminine speech communities might view a man as insensitive and domineering if he looks impassive, offers little response to her talk, and promotes his agenda. And some people make negative judgments of anyone who defies conventional expectations of gender and performs outside of the usual identity categories. Yet, such judgments reflect the communication rules we have learned, ones that may not apply to others' ways of expressing themselves. If we impose our values on behaviors that emanate from an alternative standpoint that is not guided by the rules we take for granted, then we distort what others mean to communicate. Greater accuracy in interpreting others' nonverbal communication results from understanding and respecting differences in how people use it.

Respecting differences calls on us to suspend judgment based on our own perspectives and to consider more thoughtfully what others mean in their own terms, not ours. This might lead you to ask for clarification of intent from conversational partners whose nonverbal communication patterns diverge from yours. For example, it might be constructive to say to someone less facially expressive than you, "I don't know how you're feeling about what I just said, because your face doesn't show any reaction. Could you tell me what you feel?" Conversely, understanding may be enhanced when someone with a masculine, assertive, nonverbal style says to his or her more deferential partner, "I'm not sure where you stand, because you seem to be responding to my ideas rather than expressing your own. I'm interested in your opinion." Communicative techniques such as these allow you to minimize the potential for misunderstandings that grow out of gendered communication styles.

Understanding and respecting different forms of nonverbal communication require us to make an honest effort to appreciate what another says on his or her own terms. At first, this is difficult because we have to get past our own egocentric ways of perceiving the world in order to interpret other people from their standpoints. People who commit to doing this say that it becomes easier with practice.

There's another benefit to learning to understand and respect alternative styles of nonverbal communication. It enhances your personal effectiveness by increasing the range of options you have for communicating with different people in diverse contexts and for varied reasons. Now that you are aware of gendered patterns in nonverbal communication, you may reflect on your own behaviors. Do you fit the patterns associated with your gender? Are you comfortable with your style and its effects, or would you like to alter your nonverbal behavior in some respects? By reflecting on your own nonverbal communication, you empower yourself to consciously create a style that reflects the identity you assign to yourself.

SUMMARY

In this chapter, we have seen that nonverbal communication expresses cultural views of gender. Social definitions of women as deferential, decorative, and relationship-centered are reinforced through nonverbal communication that emphasizes their appearance, limits their space, and defines them as touchable. Views of men as independent, powerful, and in control are reflected in nonverbal behaviors that accord them larger territories and greater normative rights to touch others, particularly women, and to invade their space. Consistent with how nonverbal communication defines men and women are differences in how they use it. Whereas many women embody femininity by speaking softly, condensing themselves, yielding territory, and displaying responsive facial expressions, men are likely to command space and volume, defend their turf, and display little facial expression to keep feelings camouflaged.

Recognizing the value of alternative styles of communication, both verbal and nonverbal, enables you to reflect critically on the patterns esteemed in our society. In turn, this empowers you to resist those social meanings that you find unconstructive, to revise your own nonverbal communication to reflect the identity you want, and to work toward changing the values our society assigns to masculine and feminine modes of expression. In doing this, you participate in the processes of constructing the meanings of masculinity and femininity and the values assigned to different forms of communication.

Key Terms

The terms following are defined in this chapter on the pages indicated, as well as in alphabetical order in the book's glossary, which begins on page 325. The text's companion website (**http://www.cengage.com/communication/wood/genderedlives10e**) also provides interactive flash cards and crossword puzzles to help you learn these terms and the concepts they represent.

artifact 143	paralanguage 149
haptics 147	power 142
kinesics 148	proxemics 145
liking 142	responsiveness 141
nonverbal communication 140	territoriality 146

Gender Online

1. To learn more about race and cultural representations of female beauty visit this site: **http://www.pale-reflections.com.**
2. Online search terms: "cosmetic surgery, side effects," "gender, nonverbal communication," "ideal bmi."

Reflection and Discussion

1. Look at the ads in magazines you enjoy reading. Describe the feminine and masculine ideals that are reflected in them.

2. Reflect on your artifacts, including clothing, accessories, and items on your desk, in your car, and in other spaces where you spend time. To what extent are your artifacts consistent with those that research has found to be associated with your sex?

3. Observe people in your classes, in restaurants and stores, and walking around campus. To what extent do you see gendered patterns of nonverbal communication that were identified in this chapter? For example, do women smile and hold eye contact more than men? Do men use larger motions and command more space than women?

4. Violate an expectation for nonverbal communication for your sex. Analyze how people respond both verbally and nonverbally.

5. Visit a store and notice personal care products that are marketed to women and men. Note differences in similar products marketed to men and women. For instance, are deodorants marketed to men packaged in different colors with bolder designs and different words describing the products than deodorants marketed to women?

6. Conduct an informal survey to learn how students on your campus define the physical ideal for women and men:

   • Ask five men and five women of a single race (preferably your own race so they feel comfortable talking frankly with you) to describe their physical ideal for women and men.
   • Record their answers, and share your findings with those of classmates.
   • Compare physical ideals stated by people of different races and sexes.
   • To what extent are your findings consistent with those reported in this chapter?

Recommended Resources

1. *Tootsie*. (1994). Burbank, CA: RCA/Columbia Pictures. This is a classic film, featuring Dustin Hoffman as Michael Dorsey who adopts the persona of Dorothy Michaels in order to get work. Hoffman does a superb job of changing his nonverbal behaviors from masculine when he is Michael to feminine when he is Dorothy.

2. Sandra Metts. (2006). Gendered Communication in Dating Relationships. In B. Dow & J. T. Wood (Eds.), *Handbook of Gender & Communication* (pp. 25–40). Thousand Oaks, CA: Sage. This chapter offers a wealth of information on gendered patterns of nonverbal communication. Especially interesting are the detailed descriptions of nonverbal flirting behaviors.

A lot of people are waiting for Martin Luther King or Mahatma Gandhi to come back, but they are gone. We are it. It's up to us. It's up to you.

Marion Wright Edelman

BECOMING GENDERED: THE EARLY YEARS

CHAPTER 7

Knowledge Challenge:

1. How do mothers and fathers generally differ in their interaction with children?
2. Do today's fathers spend more time with their children than their own fathers spent with them?
3. Are males and females growing up at the same pace today as in previous eras?

What does it mean to be a man in America today? What does it mean to be a woman in America today? Write one or two paragraphs describing what it means to you personally to be of the sex you are. Later in this chapter, we'll return to what you've written.

The first six chapters of this book have provided you with a great deal of information about being gendered. But how do we *become* gendered? How do biological males, females, and intersexuals become feminine, masculine, or gendered in other ways? How do we learn to express, or perform, our gender and sexuality? To answer these questions, this chapter explores the early years of our lives. Our experiences as infants, children, and adolescents profoundly influence who we are. Although we continue to evolve throughout our lives, the foundations of our identities, including gender, are keenly shaped by the first few years of life.

Because parents are such a key influence on our identities, we will examine at length how parents' communication teaches children the cultural gender code. We will also consider contemporary college students' views of what it means to be a man or a woman in America today. Their descriptions give rich insights into the influence of social expectations and peer cultures on gender. By understanding the origins and implications of gender development, you will better understand how

161

you became who you are and perhaps how you might continue the ongoing process of creating your identity.

ENTERING A GENDERED SOCIETY

We are born into a gendered society that guides our understanding of gender and shapes our personal gendered identities. At birth, many hospitals provide pink blankets for baby girls and blue blankets for baby boys. From birth onward, gender messages besiege us. As children grow up, they see boy characters on television engaging in more adventurous, rugged play than girl characters. They see cereal boxes that feature girls with bows and boys with binoculars (Lamb & Brown, 2006). They play with peers who, because of their own socialization, exert peer pressure to conform to gender norms. For instance, research shows that young boys use mockery and name-calling to punish a boy who doesn't play with masculine toys (Banerjee & Lintern, 2000; Archer & Coyne, 2005). Adding to this are parents' distinctive interactions with sons and daughters. As infants and young children interact with family members, peers, media, and society, they engage in two processes central to developing a personal identity: conceiving the self-as-object and monitoring.

SELF-AS-OBJECT

Unlike many life forms, humans are able to reflect on themselves. We are able to notice, describe, and evaluate our own activities much as we would those of others. For instance, just as we can think that another person is attractive or strong, we can think, "I am attractive" or "I am strong." **Self-as-object** is the ability to think about, reflect on, and respond to ourselves. Perhaps you've had the experience of feeling as though you were watching yourself as you talked to a new acquaintance or conferred with a teacher. Even as you are involved in conversation, a part of you is watching and assessing what you do (Miller, 2003). That's what it means to take the self as an object.

We don't reflect on ourselves from a purely personal perspective. Instead, we look at ourselves through the eyes of others. At first, others' views of us are external. Your father says you are cute, smart, too sassy, and so forth. Your mother tells you that you should be nicer to playmates. At first, we hear such communication as others' views of us. Gradually, however, many of us internalize what others say about us, and their views become instrumental in how we see ourselves. In fact, we can experience self only after experiencing others and their views of us. How we come to understand and perform gender depends on our social location, culture, and era. Standpoint, anthropological, and queer performative theories demonstrate that there is great variation in what is considered feminine and masculine.

MONITORING

Because we can view the self as an object, we are able to monitor ourselves, which means we observe and regulate our attitudes and behaviors. We use symbols, usually language, to define who we are (*son, student, mother, attorney, kind, attractive, athletic, independent,* and so on).

Monitoring takes place inside of us, but it involves others. Monitoring happens as we have internal dialogues with others' perspectives that we have internalized. As we engage in internal dialogues, we remind ourselves what others have told us we are supposed to think, do, look like, and feel—that is, we tell ourselves what the others have told us is appropriate for our age, sex, and so forth. For instance, a five-year-old girl might think, "I want to go play in the yard" and then monitor that wish by repeating her mother's words to herself: "Nice girls don't get dirty." The little girl's voice and her internalization of her mother's voice engage in an internal dialogue through which the child decides what to do. Because we can take ourselves as objects and use others' perspectives to monitor ourselves, our personal identity is always, inevitably social; who we are and how we see ourselves is deeply influenced by our family and society. This is so even when we don't identify with or choose to follow prevailing social perspectives. For instance, a 10-year-old boy who identifies with femininity will likely be treated as male and encouraged to act in masculine ways. This child must negotiate between social perspectives and a personal sense of self.

Gabe/Gabby   *Growing up was not a piece of cake for me. My father was in the Army and he embraced a very rigid code of masculinity. Since I was five, I liked to dress up in my sister's clothes. By the time I was 12, I was stuffing tissues in my shirt so I looked like I had breasts—always in the privacy of my own room, of course. Dad expected me to be a fullback and I wanted to be a ballerina. As I said, not easy.*

GENDERING COMMUNICATION IN THE FAMILY

Families, particularly parents and stepparents, are a primary influence on gender identity. To understand how families contribute to gendering children, we will first elaborate on the largely unconscious process of internalizing gender, which was introduced in Chapter 2. Second, we will draw on social learning and cognitive development theories to examine more overt ways in which children learn gender in families.

UNCONSCIOUS PROCESSES: IDENTIFICATION AND INTERNALIZATION

The conscious level of human experience does not fully explain human personality, including gender identity. Insight into unobservable, yet very important unconscious dynamics, comes primarily from psychoanalytic theories, which claim that a person's core identity is shaped in the early years of life.

Psychoanalytic theory originated with Sigmund Freud, who lived from 1856 until 1939. Freud claimed that "anatomy is destiny," by which he meant that biology, particularly the genitals, determines with which parent a child will identify and, thus, how the child's psyche will develop. According to Freudian theory, children of both sexes focus on the penis from an early age. Boys identify with their fathers, who also have penises, whereas girls recognize their similarity to their mothers, who do not have penises. Freud theorized that girls regard their mothers as responsible for their "lack" of penises, whereas boys view their fathers as having the power to castrate them. Both children see the father and the penis as power.

▼

Eileen   *I don't buy this stuff about penis envy. I've never envied my brother his penis. I remember, when we were both little, we took baths together sometimes, and I saw that he was made differently than I was. I thought it looked strange, but I didn't want it myself. But I do remember being jealous of him, or of the freedoms my parents allowed him but not me. They let him go off all day long to play, but I had to stay in the yard unless my mother was with me. He could play rough and get dirty, but I'd get a real fussin' if I did it. I remember wishing I were a boy so that I could do all of the fun things, but I didn't wish I had a penis. Definitely not.*

As interesting as Freud's theory is, there is limited empirical support for it (Pleck, 1981). According to more recent thinkers (Chodorow, 1978, 1989; Goldner, Penn, Sheinberg, & Walker, 1990), females do not literally envy the penis. What they may envy is what the penis symbolizes—the privilege and power that our society bestows on males.

Although current psychoanalytic theorists reject some of Freud's ideas, they agree with the basic psychoanalytic view that families are critical to the formation of gender identity. During the earliest stage of life, children of both sexes tend to depend on and identify with the person who takes care of them. Usually, this is a woman, often the mother. Thus, children of both sexes usually form their first identification with an adult woman.

Yet, their common identification with a female does not mean that boys and girls pursue similar developmental paths. Around the age of three, male development and female development diverge dramatically. You'll recall from cognitive development theory that this is the time at which gender constancy is usually secured, such that children realize that their sex is an unchanging, continuous part of their identity. For most girls, development proceeds along the path initially established—identification with the mother. Through concrete, daily interactions with her mother, a daughter continues to crystallize her sense of self within the original primary relationship.

To develop masculine gender identity, however, boys need to lessen the early identification with the mother and focus on identifying with a male. This process is complicated by the fact that some fathers are not highly involved in boys' everyday lives and are often emotionally remote as well (Banerji, 1998; Keen, 1991; Way, 1998). Many young boys have difficulty finding an adult masculine gender model with whom they can identify. Fathers in our era spend more time with children than their fathers did (Bianchi, Robinson, & Milkie, 2006; Tarkan, 2009) and say they have closer relationships with their sons than their fathers had with them (Morman & Floyd, 2002). Interestingly, sons perceive their fathers as less affectionate than their fathers perceive themselves (Floyd & Morman, 2005).

▼

Adrienne   *I remember watching my mother fix her hair and makeup in the morning. I thought she was the most beautiful woman in the world, and I wanted to be just like her. Many days, I went into her dressing room when she was busy downstairs and practiced putting on makeup and fixing my hair just like she did.*

For boys who lack a strong, personal relationship with an adult male, masculine gender can be elusive and difficult to grasp (Tyre, 2008). This may help explain why boys typically define their masculinity predominantly in negative terms—as not feminine, not female, not like mother. They repress the original identification with mothers and deny feminine tendencies or feelings in themselves. By extension, this may be the source of young boys' tendency to devalue the feminine in general ("Ugh, girls are icky"), a pattern not paralleled by young girls' views of masculinity. Research suggests that young boys' forceful contempt for anything feminine is a means of assuring themselves that they are truly masculine (Chodorow, 1989; Kantrowitz & Kalb, 1998).

▼

Rich   *My father left us before I was even a year old, so I didn't know him at all. My mom worked all day and was too tired to date or anything else, so there wasn't a man around. I tried to help Mom, but she'd tell me I didn't have to do this stuff, because I was "her little man." I used to watch Mom doing stuff around the house, and I'd think, "That's not what I'm supposed to do," but I had a lot of trouble figuring out what it was that I was supposed to do. I just knew it wasn't girl stuff. Then, I got a Big Brother through a program at school. He was 17, and he spent most every Saturday with me and sometimes some time after school during the week. Michael was great. He'd let me hang out with him, and he'd show me how to do stuff like play ball and use tools to make things. Finally, I had a sense of what I was supposed to be like and what I should do. Michael really helped me figure out who I was.*

As development continues, girls are often given positive rewards for being "Mommy's helper" and interacting with their mothers, and they learn to see the mother as a role model for femininity. Boys, on the other hand, are more likely to be rewarded for being independent, so they tend to roam away from home to find companions. Boys' social development typically occurs in larger groups with temporary and changing memberships, whereas for many girls it unfolds within continuing, personal relationships with individuals, including mothers. These different developmental paths encourage boys to become achieving and independent and girls to become nurturing and relationally oriented (Chodorow, 1989).

Because most girls develop feminine identity within personal, ongoing relationships, they continue to seek close relationships and place importance on personal communication with others throughout their lives. Because most boys develop masculine identities that require separating from their initial relationship with their mothers, and because they tend to interact in activity-specific groups with changing members, they learn to define themselves relatively independently of others and to maintain some distance between themselves and others.

Children in single-parent families may have difficulty finding available models of both genders. Although some people think the majority of single-parent families are nonwhite, white women under 25 who have a child are more likely to be single than married (Coontz, 2005a, 2005b; Cose, 2005b). There has been little research on what happens when men, not women, are solo parents, perhaps because there are fewer single-father families. Preliminary research suggests that single-father families are highly cohesive and that father-child discussions are more elaborate and less competitive than discussions between fathers and children in two-parent families (Galvin, 2006).

It's important to remind ourselves that we are discussing gender, not sex. This means, first, preferences for how independent of or connected to others we want to be are not wholly innate. We develop preferences in the process of being socialized. Second, it means that both men and women with masculine inclinations tend to value independence and generally prefer some distance from others. Conversely, both women and men with feminine orientations place a premium on relationships and interpersonal closeness.

EXPLORING GENDERED LIVES | TEACHING ETHNIC IDENTITY

In raising children, many African-American parents emphasize racial-ethnic identity at least as much as gender identity. African-American parents are more likely to act as cultural advisors and to use more stringent discipline than European-American parents (Socha, Sanchez-Hucles, Bromley, & Kelly, 1995). African-American mothers are more likely than European-American mothers to characterize adolescent daughters as their "best friends." They also tend to set more hard-and-fast rules and to engage in more sarcasm than European-American mothers (Galvin, 2006; Pennington & Turner, 2004). Daughters in African-American families headed by single women frequently exhibit greater self-reliance and self-esteem than their Caucasian counterparts (Diggs, 1999; Julia, 2000). African-American parents also place more emphasis than European-American parents on teaching children racial identity and history and on encouraging children to have pride in their race but also to be aware of prejudice in the world (Mosley-Howard & Evans, 1997).

EGO BOUNDARIES

At the same time that we construct our gender identity, we also form **ego boundaries** (Chodorow, 1989; Surrey, 1983). An ego boundary is the point at which an individual stops and the rest of the world begins. They distinguish the self—more or less distinctly—from everyone and everything else. Because they are linked to gender identity and evolve concurrently with it, masculine and feminine ego boundaries tend to differ. Individuals who develop feminine gender identities, which emphasize interrelatedness with others, tend to have relatively permeable ego boundaries. Because girls do not need to differentiate sharply from their mothers in order to develop a feminine gender identity, they often do not perceive clear-cut or absolute lines between themselves and others.

> **Vince**   *My girlfriend is so strange about her friends. Like, the other night I went by her apartment, and she was all upset and crying. When I asked her what was wrong, she told me Linda, her best friend, had just been dumped by her boyfriend. I said she acted like it was her who'd broken up, not Linda, and she didn't need to be so upset. She got even more upset and said it felt like her problem too; couldn't I understand what Linda was going through? I said I could, but that she wasn't going through it; Linda was. She told me it was the same thing because when you're really close to somebody else you hurt when they hurt. It didn't make sense to me, but maybe this concept of ego boundaries is what that's all about.*

The relatively permeable ego boundaries associated with femininity may partially explain why many girls and women tend to be empathic—to sense the feelings of those close to them and to experience those feelings almost as their own (Hall, 2006). It may also explain why women, more than men, sometimes become so involved with others that they neglect their own needs. Finally, this may shed light on the tendency of many women to feel responsible for others and for situations that are not their own doing. When the lines between self and others are blurred, it's hard to make a clear distinction between your own responsibilities and needs and those of others.

Conventional masculine gender identity is premised on differentiating from a female caregiver and defining the self as "not like her." It makes sense, then, that masculine

Jump Start: © United Feature Syndicate, Inc.

individuals tend to have relatively firm, or rigid, ego boundaries. They generally have a clear sense of where they stop and others begin; they may sympathize with others but are less likely to experience others' feelings as their own. The firmer ego boundaries that usually accompany a masculine gender identity explain why, later in life, many men keep some distance from others. People with firm ego boundaries may care about others, but they generally experience others' feelings as distinct from their own.

After measuring ego boundaries in nearly 1,000 people, Ernest Hartmann (1993) concluded that women's ego boundaries are generally more permeable than those of men. He also found that people with permeable ego boundaries tend to be comfortable feeling connected to others, sensing that their lives are inter-woven with those close to them. They may be uneasy in relationships with people who want a high degree of independence.

People with masculine gender identities and firm ego boundaries tend to feel secure when autonomy and self-sufficiency are high, and they may feel suffocated in relationships that are extremely close. Permeable ego boundaries may be why women often create more emotionally intense same-sex friendships than men (Walker, 2004). With other women, they are often able to build intimate, personal connections that they value and generally find more difficult to develop with men (Monsour, 2006; Werking, 1997).

PARENTAL COMMUNICATION ABOUT GENDER

From Chapter 2, you'll recall that one way children learn gender roles is by receiv-ing rewards and punishments for various behaviors (social learning theory) and through observing and emulating others whom they see as models (cognitive devel-opment theory). Typically, girls are rewarded for being cooperative, helpful, nur-turing, and deferential—all qualities consistent with social views of femininity. Parents may also reward—or at least not punish—girls for being sensitive, athletic, and smart. For boys, rewards are more likely to come for behaving competitively, independently, and assertively (Archer & Coyne, 2005; Bruess & Pearson, 1996; Leaper, Anderson, & Sanders, 1998; Leaper, Leve, Strasser, & Schwartz, 1995).

Parents' communication toward sons and daughters often reflects the parents' gender stereotypes. In a classic study, researchers found that, within just 24 hours of birth, parents responded to their babies in terms of gender stereotypes (Rubin, Provenzano, & Luria, 1974). Although male and female babies were matched for size, weight, and level of activity, parents described boys with words like *strong, hardy, big, active,* and *alert.* Parents described the equally large, active girls as *small, dainty, quiet,* and *delicate.* Similar results were found in more recent experiments (Elliott, 2009).

Some parents communicate different expectations about achievement to sons and daughters. Middle-class Caucasian parents in the United States emphasize and encourage achievement more when talking to sons than to daughters (Flanagon, Baker-Ward, & Graham, 1995). Some Chicano/a families discourage educational achievement in daughters to the point of regarding daughters who attend college as *Chicana falsa*—false Chicanas (Leland & Chambers, 1999). Conversely, many Asian and Asian-American families tend to encourage high achievement in children of both sexes (Woo, 2001).

▼

Melissa   *In my family, I learned that thinking about boys was not a high priority. If I told my mama that I liked a boy or that I was afraid a boy I was dating was going to break up with me, she'd say "Get your mind off boys and on books." Mama made it very clear that I was supposed to get my education and learn to take care of myself. Period.*

Parents also convey distinct messages about assertiveness and aggressiveness to sons and daughters. As children, boys and girls don't differ a great deal with respect to feelings of anger or aggression. Because of gender socialization, however, they learn different ways of expressing those feelings (Butaine & Costenbader, 1997; Deffenbacher & Swaim, 1999; Kivel, 1999). Research shows that parents, particularly white middle-class parents, reward verbal and physical activity, including aggression, in sons and reward interpersonal and social skills in daughters (Leaper, Anderson, & Sanders, 1998; Mills, Nazar, & Farrell, 2002; Morrow, 2006). Because many girls are discouraged from direct, overt aggression yet still feel aggressive at times, they develop other, less direct ways of expressing aggression. We'll explore girls' ways of expressing aggression later in this chapter when we discuss gender dynamics among peers.

Parents, especially fathers, encourage in children what they perceive to be gender-appropriate behaviors, fostering more independence, competitiveness, and aggression in sons and more emotional expressiveness and gentleness in daughters (Bryant & Check, 2000; Fivush, Brotman, Buckner, & Goodman, 2000; Galvin, 2006). When interacting with children, fathers tend to talk more with daughters and to engage in activities more with sons (Buerkel-Rothfuss, Fink, & Buerkel, 1995). Mothers tend to talk more about emotions and relationships with daughters than with sons (Galvin, 2006; Segrin & Flora, 2005; Trad, 1995). Because both mothers and fathers usually talk more intimately with daughters than sons, it's not surprising that daughters tend to surpass sons in developing relationship awareness. Daughters also disclose significantly more information to parents than do sons (Pennington & Turner, 2004).

| EXPLORING GENDERED LIVES | FATHER-DAUGHTER PURITY BALLS |

For many years, young women aspired to attend debutante balls, also known as coming out parties. In recent times, debutante balls have become less popular. On the other hand, a new kind of ball is rising in popularity: Father-Daughter Purity Balls. At these formal, black tie events, attended by up to 100 father-daughter couples, fathers publicly pledge to protect their daughters' purity. Each father pledges to God to guard his daughter from premarital sex. The daughters, in turn, may make public or silent pledges to remain sexually pure until married (Banerjee, 2008).

Mothers tend to spend more time with children than fathers do (Bianchi et al., 2006; Hochschild with Machung, 2003). Consistent with what we learned in Chapter 5 about gendered speech communities, mothers are inclined to make communication the center of their relationships with children, especially daughters. Mothers use talk to give information, advice, encouragement, and support to children (Galvin, 2006; Segrin & Flora, 2005; Trad, 1995). Mothers also use communication to teach children about relating to others, building social connections, and becoming emotionally competent.

> **Mark**   *My father took me hunting and coached me in football. He taught me to be strong around other men and to treat any woman with respect. He taught me that a real man is tough when he needs to be, loyal to friends, and protective of women.*

When interacting with children, mothers typically focus on providing comfort, security, and emotional development. They engage in more eye contact and face-to-face interaction with children than do fathers. Further, mothers tend to repeat infant daughters' vocalizations more than those of infant sons (Trudeau, 1996). More than fathers, mothers tend to play with children at the children's level, which develops children's confidence and security in play.

Although fathers spend less time than mothers in one-on-one communication with children, today's fathers talk more with children than did fathers in previous generations (Bianchi et al., 2006; Pruett & Pruett, 2009; Silverstein, 2002; Tarkan, 2009). Fathers typically focus more on playing with children than on taking care of them (Popenoe, 1996). They tend to engage in play that is physically stimulating and exciting, and they encourage children to develop skills and meet challenges. Fathers, more than mothers, stretch children by urging them to compete, achieve, take risks, act independently, and move beyond their current levels of ability (Luster & Okagaki, 2005; Popenoe, 1996; Stacey, 1996). Perhaps because fathers tend to focus communication on abilities, accomplishments, and goals, they have a particularly strong impact on children's self-esteem (Webb, Walker, Bolis, & Hebbani, 2004).

Another notable difference between communication typical of mothers and fathers concerns talk about sexual activity. Mothers are much more likely than fathers to discuss sex topics with children, particularly daughters (Warren, 2003). Girls who talk to their mothers about sex are more likely to have conservative sexual values than girls who rely on friends for discussions of sex (Dilorio, Kelley, & Hockenberry-Eaton, 1999). Research also shows that when mothers encourage condom use if their daughters choose to engage in sex, their daughters are more likely to use condoms consistently (Hutchinson, 2002; Aronowitz, Rennells, & Todd, 2005). Although fathers are not generally inclined to talk directly about sex with their children, some fathers do talk with daughters about related issues such as "understanding men" and resisting pressure for sex (Hutchinson, 2002). Both parents are more likely to talk about sex with daughters than with sons.

Parents also communicate gender expectations through the toys and activities they encourage for sons and daughters. Some parents actively discourage their children's interest in toys and games that are associated with the other sex. For instance, boys may be persuaded not to play house, and girls may be dissuaded from engaging in sports that call for high levels of physical aggression. Different types of toys and activities promote distinct kinds of thinking and interaction. More "feminine" toys, such as dolls, encourage quiet, nurturing interaction with another, physical closeness, and verbal communication. More typically "masculine" toys, such as sports equipment and train sets, promote independent or competitive activities that require little verbal interaction. Parents who don't want to limit their children to sex-typed toys may encounter challenges. Many stores sell girls' bikes in pink and other pastels and boys' bikes in darker colors. Halloween costumes are also very sex-typed. Research reports that costumes for boys include characters with supernatural powers and great strength whereas costumes for girls are ball gowns, bridal gowns, and highly sexualized outfits (Nelson, 2000; Stereotypes, 2009).

Another way parents communicate gender expectations is through the household chores they assign to sons and daughters. Like toys, various tasks cultivate particular types of thinking and activity. Domestic chores, which are more often assigned to girls, emphasize taking care of others and taking responsibility for them (e.g., washing clothes, cooking, and making beds), whereas outdoor work and repair jobs, more typically assigned to boys, encourage independent activity (e.g., mowing the lawn, taking garbage to the curb, and raking). Domestic chores also tend to occur in small, interior spaces, whereas outside chores are frequently done in open spaces.

In general, gender socialization is more rigid for boys than for girls (DeFrancisco & Chatham-Carpenter, 2000), and fathers are more insistent on gender-stereotyped toys and activities, especially for sons, than are mothers. It's much more acceptable for girls to play baseball or football than for boys to play house or to cuddle dolls. Similarly, it's considered more suitable for girls to be strong than for boys to cry, and more acceptable for girls to act independently than for boys to need others. Overall, boys are more intensively and rigidly pushed to be masculine than girls are pushed to be feminine.

> **Taylor**   *My father always tried to encourage me to be strong, play sports, and do things that girls were not supposedly good at doing, like working on carpentry for example. I often tried my best to meet my father's expectations, but I often failed. Peers often teased me and called me names like "faggot," "wuss," because I was never good at playing sports and because of my size. I really enjoyed watching sports, but I was afraid to even try to get on teams in middle school because I was setting myself up for failure.*

In summary, parents play a major role in shaping children's understandings of gender in general and their own gender in particular. In general, mothers and fathers contribute to children's development in distinct and complementary ways. Fathers generally help children, especially sons, develop a sense of personal agency—independence, initiative, and achievement. Mothers are more likely to foster competence in relating to others—making connections with others and feeling emotionally secure.

PARENTAL MODELING

Another way parents communicate gender is through modeling masculinity, femininity, and, for heterosexual parents, male-female relationships. As you will recall from Chapter 2, cognitive development theory tells us that, once children have gender constancy, they actively look for role models of their sex and use those models to develop masculine or feminine qualities, behaviors, and so forth. For most children, parents are the single most visible and available models of masculinity and femininity. By observing parents, children of heterosexuals often learn the roles socially prescribed for women and men. In heterosexual families that adhere to traditional sex roles, children of both sexes are likely to learn that women are supposed to nurture others, clean, cook, and show emotional sensitivity, and that men are supposed to earn money, make decisions, and be emotionally controlled.

Not all families, however, adopt traditional sex roles; in fact, families in our era are highly diverse (Galvin, 2006). Many children have a single parent, at least for part of their lives. Single mothers provide children with more-multifaceted models of women's roles, and single fathers provide children with more-multifaceted models of manhood. A major reason for changes in forms of families is that most women now work outside the home. In fact, for the first time ever in the United States, more women live without a spouse than live with one. In 1950, 35% of American women lived without a spouse; in 2000, 49% did, and by 2007 that figure had risen to 51% (Roberts, 2007). The percentage of women who live without a spouse varies by race: 70% of black women live without one, 49% of Hispanic women do, and 55% of non-Hispanic white women do (Roberts, 2007).

Another departure from traditional families has to do with the breadwinner role. In the mid-1970s, only about 40% of married women worked outside the home (Galvin, 2006). By 2000, the percentages had reversed, and 40% of married women were *not* employed outside the home (Bond, Thompson, Galinsky, & Prottas, 2002). The recession that began in 2008 further affected proportions of women and men in the paid labor force. Significantly more men than women were laid off because men tended to work in industries that downsized. The number of women who are sole wage earners for families was the highest ever in 2009, and the number of men who were sole wage earners for families dropped to the lowest level in a decade (Yen, 2010). Today, about 53% of mothers with infants work outside the home and 75% of mothers with school-age children work outside of the home (Bonnett, 2007).

Gay and lesbian parents are a third family form that is becoming more visible. Whereas some same-sex partners choose to be child free, others have children through technology or adoption or parent older children from former heterosexual unions.

Blended families, too, have become very common. Because divorce is common, many children live either with a single parent or in a family that formed when one or both parents remarried or cohabited. Additional stepparenting occurs when single mothers marry for the first time. Being part of more than one family and

EXPLORING GENDERED LIVES | GLBT PARENTING

Estimates of the number of children who have gay, lesbian, bisexual, or transgendered (GLBT) parents range from 1 million to 16 million (Garner, 2004). One-third of lesbian couples and 22% of gay couples live with children (Galvin, 2006). The majority of research on GLBT families shows that the sexual orientation of parents is not relevant to children's mental, emotional, or social development or to their sexual orientation (Stacey & Biblarz, 2005; "The State," 2002). Like most families, GLBT families have joys, challenges, and problems, including many of the same ones that heterosexual families experience (Weston, 1999). Problems unique to GLBT families seem to arise primarily from social prejudice rather than from any lack of parenting skills (Snow, 2004). To learn more about same-sex parenting, go to **http://www.hrc.org**.

being able to observe multiple models of gender gives these children more diverse ideas about how families can work and how gender can be embodied.

Parents also model attitudes about gender and physical appearance. Fathers who work out and engage in vigorous physical activities and who encourage their sons to play sports may impart the message that physical strength is masculine. Mothers who make disparaging remarks about their weight or about eating communicate that to be feminine is to be thin and that daughters should strive for thinness.

Although the first few years are important in shaping gender, they are not absolute determinants of our gender across the life span. Our understanding of gender and of our personal gender identity changes over time as we develop personally and as we interact with diverse people who embody alternative versions of masculinity and femininity.

THE PERSONAL SIDE OF THE GENDER DRAMA

So far, this chapter has summarized research on gender socialization in the early years of life. Yet, gender is also deeply personal. Each of us grew up in a gendered society and each of us has worked—and continues to work—to define and express our own gender. We'll now translate the research we've considered into personal portraits of becoming gendered in contemporary Western society with particular attention to the influence of media and peers.

At the beginning of this chapter, I asked you what it means to be a man or woman in America today. In the pages that follow, you'll learn how other men and women in college answer that question. As you read their responses, consider how their ideas are like and unlike your own.

GROWING UP MASCULINE

What does it mean to be a man in the United States in the twenty-first century? A first answer is that there is no single form of manhood or masculinity. Although there is a dominant model of masculinity, there are also many variations on and challenges to that (Connell, 2005; Zinn, Hondagneu-Sotelo, & Messner, 2007). To understand the advantages, challenges, and issues of various masculinities, let's consider what five college men have to say. In their commentaries, Eric, Aaron, Steve, Clifford, and Derek focus as much on the pressures, expectations, and constraints of manhood as they do on its prerogatives and privileges. What these five men tell us is consistent with research (Doyle, 1997; Lindgren & Lélièvre, 2009; Manliness, 2000). We'll discuss six themes of manhood in America today. Five of these were first identified by Doyle (1997).

Don't Be Female   This seems to be the most fundamental requirement for manhood, but boys have to learn not to be feminine. At young ages many boys cherish their friends and talk openly and expressively with them about serious topics, including feelings (Way, 2010). Yet, as boys mature, many of them encounter pressure to "grow up," by embodying traditional norms of masculinity. To be accepted by peers, they become more closed off and less expressive. Any male who shows sensitivity or vulnerability is likely to be called a sissy, a crybaby, a mama's boy, or a wimp (Kantrowitz & Kalb, 1998; Pollack, 2000). Peer groups pressure males to be tough, aggressive, and not feminine (Lobel & Bar, 1997; Ponton, 1997). The antifemale directive is at least as strong for African-American men as for European-American men (Messner, 2007).

When a young boy wants to hurt another boy, he is likely to call him by a name that is associated with femininity directly *(girlie)* or indirectly *(sissy).* Even as adults, a favorite means of scorning or putting down men is to suggest that they are feminine, or like women. During the 2008 presidential campaign, Republican candidate John McCain mocked Democratic candidate Barack Obama for not supporting the war in Iraq. Linking himself to traditional images of manhood, McCain portrayed himself as a real man who "fought for America."

In an interview, Doyle (Manliness, 2000), said that not acting or thinking like a woman "is so basic to the male model, this whole area has grown around how to really insult a man—all one needs to do is question him in terms of his acting like a girl. For most men, that immediately becomes extremely upsetting" (p. 1).

▼

Eric   *Ever since I can remember, being a man has been about winning. When I was a kid, it was about winning in T-ball and then baseball. In high school, it was about being a star player on the team. Now that I'm a senior in college, it's about getting a really good job and then being better than the others in my profession. My father taught me that winning is important and being average equals being a loser.*

Be Successful   This is the second requirement for men. Through the teen years, boys are expected to be successful at sports and other activities. As adults, men are expected to achieve status in their professions, to "make it." Warren Farrell (1991) writes that men are regarded as "success objects," and their worth as marriage partners, friends, and men is judged by how successful they are at what they do. Training begins early with sports, where winning is stressed (Messner, 2007).

As Eric notes in his commentary, the theme of success translates into not just being good at what you do but being better than others, more powerful than peers, pulling in a bigger salary than your neighbors, and having a more expensive home, car, and so on, than your friends. Many men today, like Aaron, say that being a good provider is the primary requirement for manhood—an internalized requirement that appears to cut across lines of race and economic class (Eagly, 1996; Ranson, 2001). In his commentary, Steve expresses some anger about the unfairness of this expectation.

Aaron   *The one thing I know for sure is that a man takes care of his family. My dad had no respect—zero—for his cousin who had to go on unemployment and then got a job but didn't earn enough to support his family. My dad called him "lazy," "no 'count," and "freeloader." The whole reason I'm majoring in business is because students who graduate from the business school have higher starting salaries and higher salaries down the line.*

Steve   *I am sick of hearing about "male privilege." Where is it? That's what I'd like to know. I'm expected to pay for dates; girls get a free ride. I have to pay a cover charge to get into a bar; ladies nights are freebies for girls. If the draft comes back, I could be drafted and shipped to a war; women aren't subject to the draft. I have to get a job and make money; a woman can do that, but she doesn't have to. So tell me where male privilege is in all of this.*

Be Aggressive   A third injunction for masculinity is to be aggressive. In childhood and adolescence, boys are often rewarded for being daredevils and roughnecks. They are expected to take stands, be tough, and not run from confrontations (Newburger, 1999; Pollack, 2000). Later, participation in sports reinforces early training by emphasizing aggression and toughness (Messner, 2007). Coaches psych teams up with demands that they "make the other team hurt, hurt, hurt" or "make them bleed." In fact, the physical and psychological qualities that are linked to success in athletics have become an important requirement for status in most adolescent and preadolescent male peer groups (Messner & Sabo, 2006). Messner (2005) also found that, in addition to reproducing men's power over women, sport is used to assert higher-status men's dominance over other men. As adults, men are expected to be aggressive professionally and to beat the competition. The masculine code tells men to fight, defeat others, endure pain stoically themselves, and win, win, win.

Being tough means not showing pain. A boy or man who gets hurt is expected to "suck it up." Youths of both sexes engage in sports and sustain injuries, yet males are less likely than females to report pain or symptoms of injuries, including life-threatening brain injuries. Recent research reports that the most prominent features of ideal masculinity today are courage, risk-taking, and the ability to

Contact sports encourage aggressiveness and self-confidence.

withstand pain without crying, whining, or quitting (Lindgren & Lélièvre, 2009). Although not all men—perhaps not most men—measure up to this model, it remains the ideal. From an early age "we teach boys they have to be tough" and they have to "play through the pain" (Gregory, 2007, p. 70).

The aggressiveness encouraged in boys and men may be linked to violence, especially violence against women (Levant & Pollock, 2003; Messner, 1997a, 1997b). Because masculine socialization encourages aggression and dominance, some men regard it as appropriate to dominate women. This belief is expressed by men who abuse girlfriends and wives (Gelles & Straus, 1988; Wood, 2001b, 2004). One study (Thompson, 1991) reports that both college women and men who are violent toward their dates have masculine gender orientations, reminding us again that *gender* and *sex* are not equivalent terms.

Be Sexual   This is a fourth element of the male role. Men should be interested in sex—all the time, any time. They are expected to have a number of sexual partners; the more partners a man has, the more of a stud he is (Jhally & Katz, 2001). During rush, a fraternity sent out invitations with the notation "B.Y.O.A.," which one of my students translated for me: Bring your own ass, meaning female date. Cornell West (2007) notes that for black males, sexuality is particularly associated with a machismo identity and with being powerful.

Being sexual is a way to perform and prove masculinity—heterosexual masculinity, to be precise. A man who does not want a lot of sex with a lot of women may find his manhood questioned by other men (Kimmel, 2008). When discussing this issue in my class, one male student said, "A man who maintains his virginity until marriage would be seen as crazy ... or not really a man."

Be Self-Reliant   This is the final male role expectation, says Doyle. A "real man" doesn't need others, particularly women. He depends on himself, takes care of himself, and relies on nobody. Autonomy is central to social views of manliness. As we noted earlier, developing a masculine identity requires differentiation from others, especially the mother or mother figure. From infancy, most boys are taught to be self-reliant and self-contained (Newburger, 1999). Men are expected to be emotionally controlled, not to let feelings control them, and not to need others.

▼

Clifford   *Black men face their own issues with masculinity. You have to present yourself as manly and powerful. If you don't get that down, you won't be seen as a man by any other black men. For black men, being a man also means knowing that you're expected to be violent, not to support your family, and to know everything about music and sports. That's what whites expect and they put that on me all the time. But black women are looking for men who will stand their ground—be strong and be there for them all the time. So what it means to be a black man depends on whether you look from a white or black perspective.*

Michael Shelton coordinates youth camp programs for Philadelphia and is a national consultant on best practices for youth agencies. Shelton (2008) observes that when boys at residential camps get homesick, both counselors and parents expect and sometimes coerce them to stick it out and "become a man" by staying at camp. According to Shelton, "when a male child begins to exhibit signs of homesickness, he breaks many of the cardinal rules of masculinity. He exhibits emotions of vulnerability, he does not display expected toughness, and perhaps most damaging, he shows that he has not achieved independence" (p. 44).

Embody and Transcend Traditional Views of Masculinity   The sixth theme highlights the confusing messages about masculinity that confront many boys and men today. In his commentary, Derek expresses his frustration with the paradoxical expectations to be a "real man" in traditional ways and simultaneously to defy traditional views of men by being sensitive and egalitarian (Corbett, 2009).

For many males, a primary source of pressure to be conventionally masculine is peers—other boys and, later, men—who enforce the masculine code (Archer & Coyne, 2005; Messner, 2005). Boys and men encourage each other to be silent, tough, independent, daring and to not be controlled by females. Boys and men who don't measure up often face peer shaming ("You're a wuss," "Do you do everything she tells you to do?"). At the same time, many men feel other pressures—often from romantic partners, female friends, and mothers—to be more sensitive and emotionally open and to be a full partner in running a home and raising children. It's hard to be both traditionally masculine and not traditionally masculine. Just as women in the 1960s and 1970s were confronted with mixed messages about being feminine, men today are negotiating new terrain to new ways of defining themselves.

Media are another source of masculine socialization. Media put forward images of extreme masculinity such as the oversized, grotesquely muscled male figures in video games and the characters on programs such as *Man vs. Wild* who are dropped into wilderness locales and must forage and use survival techniques. Or consider men who are represented as ideal on the popular MTV series, *Jackass*, which aired from 2000 until 2002 and was followed by two Jackass movies. The men on the show—all white, presumptively straight, and young (20s)—subjected themselves to daredevil stunts, deliberate assaults on their bodies, and incessant displays of their genitals (Lingren & Lélièvre, 2009). These images of "real men," lead many sensitive young boys to decide they have to toughen up to make it (Brown, Lamb, & Tappan, 2009).

Derek   *It's really frustrating to be a man today. My girlfriend wants me to open up and show my feelings and talk about them and stuff like that. But the guys on the team get on my case whenever I show any feelings other than about winning a game. I'm supposed to be sensitive and not. I'm supposed to keep my feelings to myself and not. I'm supposed to open doors for girls and pay for dates but then respect them as equals. A lot of times it feels like a no-win situation.*

What happens when men don't measure up to the social expectations of manhood? Some counselors believe that men's struggles to live up to social ideals of masculinity has produced an epidemic of hidden male depression (Scelfo, 2007). Dr. Michael Miller (2003) says that many men don't seek help when they are depressed because their gender identity is "tied up with strength, independence, efficiency, and self-control" (p. 71). Researchers estimate that more than six million men in the United States are depressed (Scelfo, 2007). Because masculine socialization stresses emotional control and self-reliance, many men who are depressed are unwilling to seek help. Depression that is untreated and that does not go away on its own can be deadly—men commit suicide at least four times more frequently than women (Scelfo, 2007).

Other researchers identify a new trend among young men: A resistance to growing up and maturing in the ways that their fathers and grandfathers did. In his recent book *Guyland*, sociologist Michael Kimmel (2008) says that the rising generation of men is extending adolescence. Whereas their fathers left home, finished their educations, got married, started work, and became parents by age 30, increasing numbers of men today have not reached or wanted to reach those milestones by age 30. Based on hundreds of interviews with men in their 20s, most of whom had at least some college education, Kimmel concludes that many men today spend years—even a decade—drinking, smoking, having sex, and avoiding commitments to partners, causes, or jobs. Kimmel is not the only scholar noting this trend. Gary Cross (2008) and Guy Garcia (2008) also argue that many young men today resist maturity and the responsibilities that accompany it.

Society's expectations for both men and women continue to change, and these changes provoke anxiety and confusion about how to be a man today. Men's traditional role as provider and protector is no longer the solid anchor it once was, and strong new anchors have not been found or created (Dokoupil, 2008; Garcia, 2008). Agreeing, Doyle (2001) says that a key aspect of men's lives in our era is the "confusion that many men feel, because the rules that governed what their grand-fathers and fathers needed to be like to be considered men, those rules have been shunted aside, if not completely dismissed. There's been few models that have come forward that men can hold to. It's almost as if it's every man for himself now. That can be very scary" (p. 3).

The first five themes of masculinity clearly reflect gender socialization in early life and lay out a blueprint for what being a man means. Yet, we also see a sixth theme that points out and challenges the contradictions in traditional and emerging views of masculinity. Individual men have options for defining and embodying masculinity, and many men are crafting nontraditional identities for themselves. In later chapters, we'll discover examples of ways to revise masculine identity.

GROWING UP FEMININE

What does it mean to be feminine in the United States in the twenty-first century? Two quite different narratives of femininity coexist today. One suggests that women now have it all. They can get jobs that were formerly closed to them, have egalitarian marriages with liberated men, and raise nonsexist children.

At the same time, our culture sends us a different message. Women may be able to get jobs, but fewer than 20% will actually be given opportunities to advance to the highest levels of professional life. Even women graduating today with M.B.A.s make $4,600 less per year than men (Bennett, et al., 2010). Crime statistics remind us that rape occurs frequently, as does battering of women. We discover that married women may have careers, but most of them still do the majority of housework and child care. And media relentlessly carry the message that youth and beauty are women's tickets to success (Barash, 2006; Lamb & Brown, 2006; Levy, 2005). Prevailing images of women are conflicting and confusing, as the commentaries by Jeanne, Mala, Bonita, Rebecca, Emily, and Sharon demonstrate. We can identify five themes in current views of femininity and womanhood.

▼

Jeanne   *Hungry. That's what being a woman means to me. I am hungry all of the time. Either I'm dieting, or I'm throwing up because I ate too much. I am scared to death of being fat, and I'm just not made to be thin. I gain weight just by smelling food. I think about food all the time—wanting it but being afraid to eat, eating but feeling guilty. It's a no-win situation. I'm obsessed, and I know it, but I can't help it. How can I not think about my weight all the time, when every magazine, every movie, every television show I see screams at me that I have to be thin to be desirable?*

Appearance Still Counts   This is the first theme. As Jeanne notes in her commen-tary, women are still judged by their looks. To be desirable, they are urged to be pretty, slim, and well dressed. The focus on appearance begins in the early years of life, when girls are given dolls and clothes, both of which invite them to attend to appearance. Gift catalogues for children regularly feature makeup kits, adornments for hair, and even wigs, so girls learn early to spend time and effort on looking good. Dolls, like the ever-popular Barbie, come with accessories such as extensive wardrobes, so girls learn that clothes and jewelry are important. The Bratz dolls, introduced in 2001, model sexuality as the ideal for young girls (Setoodeh, 2006). Teen magazines for girls are saturated with ads for makeup, diet aids, and hair products. Romance novels for adolescent females, such as the *Gossip Girls* and *A List* series, send the message that popularity depends on wearing the right clothes, engaging in casual sex, and being rich, thin, and sexy (Johnson, 2007, 2011; Wolf, 2006). Central to current cultural ideals for women is thinness, which can lead to harmful and sometimes fatal eating disorders. Jeanne's comments show how tyrannical this expectation can be.

The ideals of feminine appearance are communicated to women when they enter retail stores. Most mannequins in stores are size 2, 4, 0, or minus sizes; these are not the sizes of most real-life women. Social prescriptions for feminine beauty are also made clear by the saleswomen, who are often hired because of their looks, not their experience or skills. Managers of stores that market to young women like to hire people who are young, sexy, and good-looking. According to Antonio Serrano, a former assistant store manager for Abercrombie & Fitch, he and other employees were told by upper management "to approach someone in the mall who we think will look attractive in our store. But if someone came in who had lots of retail experience and not a pretty face, we were told not to hire them at all" (Greenhouse, 2003, p. 10 YT). Elysa Yanowitz, who was a regional sales manager for L'Oreal, says she was pressured to hire physically attractive saleswomen and once told to fire a top-performing employee who was "not hot enough" (Greenhouse, 2003, p. 10 YT). The Equal Employment Opportunity Commission has brought suit against a number of companies for discriminating against women who do not meet the current ideals of attractiveness.

Angela McRobbie (2009) notes that women's disorders related to body image have reached new heights in the last decade. She argues that pathologies have become expected, even considered normal in young women. McRobbie says that the quest to achieve the cultural ideal of femininity makes girls ill. Advertising shows beautiful women in powerful poses—at work, at home, with men. Media further encourage women to remake their bodies through the make-over genre of television programming. In such programs a person, most often a woman, who begins as unattractive is made over into a person who is desirable. The transformation depends on using products and services to remake the person. To maintain the new "improved" image, she must become active in consumer culture—spending her money to continue buying the products and services that make her acceptable. The illusion that is being marketed is that women have real power. If women believe that and if they believe dieting and wearing the "right" clothes are the bases of that power, they will not venture into realms of *real* power.

Not just any kind of attractive will do. Women and even girls today are expected to look sexy, hot, and seductive. And there's only one way to achieve that look: buy products and services, then buy more and more and more. To achieve the current instantiation of feminine desirability, women and girls have to become serious consumers. They have to buy the right makeup, cologne, clothes, and shoes. They have to drink the right brands of drinks, own the right kind of possessions, shop in the cool stores, wear the right hairstyles, and have the right cosmetic treatments. Consumption is unending and never sufficient to secure lasting success (Johnson, 2007; Levin & Kilbourne, 2008; Levy, 2005). As Susan Barash notes in her insightful book, *Tripping the Prom Queen* (2006), "in the perpetual beauty contest any woman who wins the contest today must expect to lose it—if not tomorrow, then the day after, or the day after that" because "beauty is bound up inextricably with youth" (p. 110).

Women athletes sometimes feel special pressure to look and act feminine. Women athletes in my classes tell me that, if they don't look ultra-feminine, others think they are lesbians. Female Olympic competitors increasingly pose nude or nearly nude in *Sports Illustrated, FHM (For Him Magazine),* or *Playboy,* which resoundingly performs femininity (Levy, 2005). Yet engaging in athletic performances is one way women today defy traditional gender norms. Meân and Kassing's (2008) research on female soccer players found they saw themselves as different from other women and male athletes. Another recent study examining women who play ice hockey found similar results: the women believe there is a distinct difference between an ice hockey player, a female ice hockey player, and a female (Gilenstam, Karp, & Henriksson-Larsén, 2008).

Be Sensitive and Caring   This is the second cultural expectation of women. They feel pressure to be nice, deferential, and helpful, whereas men are not held to the same requirements (Simmons, 2002). In addition, girls and women are supposed to care about and for others. From assuming primary responsibility for young children to taking care of elderly, sick, and disabled relatives, women do the preponderance of hands-on caring (Cancian & Oliker, 2000; Ferguson, 2000).

By the time girls enter puberty, they are encouraged—by society, peers, and sometimes family—to focus on pleasing others (Lally, 1996). White females are especially pressured in this way (Julia, 2000). Girls are encouraged to lose weight, to dress well, and to use makeup so that others will find them attractive. They're taught to soften their opinions and to accommodate others, particularly males (Berger, 2006; Deveny, 2009). Girls learn not to stand up to boys at school because they fear being called "bitch" (Bennett, Ellison, & Ball, 2010; Deveny, 2009). The bottom line is that, for many girls, adolescence means shifting attention from developing and asserting identity to pleasing others.

When psychologist Barbara Kerr (1997) asked her undergraduates to describe their perfect day, she found a striking sex difference in responses. College men tend to describe their perfect day like this:

> I wake up and get into my car—a really nice, rebuilt '67 Mustang—and then I go to work—I think I'm some kind of manager of a computer firm—and then I go home, and when I get there, my wife is there at the door (she has a really nice figure), she has a drink for me, and she's made a great meal. We watch TV or maybe play with the kids. (p. B7)

Contrast the men's perfect day with this typical description from college women:

> I wake up, and my husband and I get in our twin Jettas, and I go to the law firm where I work. Then after work, I go home, and he's pulling up in the driveway at the same time. We go in and have a glass of nice wine, and we make an omelet together and eat by candlelight. Then the nanny brings the children in and we play with them until bedtime. (p. B7)

The man imagines returning home to a wife who has drinks and dinner ready for her husband. Fewer and fewer college-educated women see this as an ideal day—or life. Yet, women's fantasy of shared responsibilities for home and family are not likely to be met unless there are major changes in current patterns. A majority of women and men share the breadwinner role relatively equally, but few have managed to share the homemaker and parenting role equally (Coontz, 2005b; Wood, 2010).

▼

Mala   *Males are favored over females in Indian culture. It is custom for a girl's family to give a dowry to a man who marries the girl to make it worth his while. As a result, many poor families in India kill a newborn baby if it is female and rejoice if the baby is male. When my third sister was born, my great grandmother expressed her disappointment that we had no boys and so many girls.*

Negative Treatment by Others   This is the third persistent theme of femininity for women. Men students in my class sometimes challenge this as a theme of femininity. They say women are treated better than men. They point out that women—but not men—get free drinks at "Ladies' Night," they get their meals paid for by dates, and they can cry their way out of speeding tickets. However, these rather small advantages of being female don't compensate for more significant disadvantages such as being more subject to sexual assault, more likely to live in poverty, and more likely to face job and salary discrimination.

Early in life, many children learn how society values each sex. In the United States, parents generally prefer sons, although the preference seems less strong than in former eras. In some cultures the preference for males is so strong that female fetuses are often aborted, and female infants are sometimes killed after birth (Hegde, 1999a, 1999b; Parrot & Cummings, 2006; Pollitt, 2000). In other cultures, female and male children are equally valued; in still others, females are more valued (Cronk, 1993; Lepowsky, 1998).

▼

Bonita   *You asked us to think about whether we ever got the message that males are more valued than females. I know I did. I guess I got it in a lot of ways, but one really stands out. I remember, when I was nine, my mother was pregnant for the third time. When she went into labor, Daddy took her to the hospital with me and my sister. We all sat in the waiting room while they took Mom down the hall. Later, the doctor came in and went to my father. I still remember his exact words. He said, "I'm sorry, Mr. Chavis, it's another girl. Guess you'll have to try again."*

Devaluation and mistreatment of females is pervasive in Western culture. The Web teems with sites such as "Rough Sex" and "Where Whores Get Owned" that feature beatings and sexual assaults on women. Gangsta rap refers to women as bitches and "hos," and routinely shows men abusing them. Highly popular video games allow players to earn points by mauling women (Herbert, 2006).

Devaluation of femininity is not only built into cultural views but typically is internalized by individuals, including women. Negative treatment of females begins early and can be especially intense in girls' peer groups (Chesler, 2001; Lamb, 2002; Simmons, 2002; Tavris, 2002; Willer, 2011). Girls can be highly critical of other girls who are not pretty, thin, and otherwise feminine, as the Exploring Gendered Lives feature on page 184 demonstrates.

▼

Rebecca   *"Sugar and spice and everything nice" is not the whole picture about girls. They can be really mean, especially to other girls. In middle school, there was one girl who was a real bully. Sherry and I were friends until 7th grade, and then out of nowhere she started ignoring me and spreading rumors about me to make other people not want to be friends with me. Boys may fight physically with each other, but at least that's direct and honest. When Sherry decided she didn't like me, she was really underhanded and indirect in how she hurt me.*

Rebecca is right when she says that sugar and spice is not a full description of girls. Research (Archer & Coyne, 2005; Levy, 2005; Simmons, 2002, 2004; Underwood, 2003) shows that many young girls engage in social aggression toward other girls. As the term implies, social aggression involves attacking others using social, rather than physical, strategies. Unlike physical aggression, social aggression is usually indirect, even covert. It takes forms such as spreading hurtful rumors, excluding a girl from groups, and encouraging others to turn against a particular girl. Social aggression among girls reflects their internalization of negative social views of females. For instance, one of the most damaging forms of aggression is spreading a rumor that a girl is a slut. All these tactics rupture the relational network of the girls who are the targets of social aggression. Social aggression peaks in girls between the ages of 10 and 14 (Simmons, 2002).

Why do young girls rely on indirect strategies of aggression? One reason appears to be that, even at young ages, girls understand that they are supposed to be nice to everyone, so they fear that being overtly mean or competitive would lead to disapproval or punishment (Barash, 2006; Simmons, 2002). Instead of learning how to work through feelings of anger, dislike, and so forth, young girls learn to hide those feelings and express them only indirectly.

EXPLORING GENDERED LIVES | **SISTERHOOD?**

Sororities claim to be sisterhoods—communities in which unrelated women become caring sisters to one another. Carolyn Thatcher might disagree. In 2007, she and 22 other members of DePauw University's chapter of Delta Zeta were dropped from the sorority. Why? Some members of the chapter were upset that fewer students were pledging DZ, so they decided that the sorority would be more attractive if all members met what one of the remaining sisters called standards of "social image, appearance, and weight" (Adler, 2007, p. 47). The only black member of the sorority was ousted, as were two of the three Asian members, and all members who wore a size larger than eight. Only 12 of the original 35 members were allowed to stay. However, only half of those—six women—chose to stay. The other six left to show solidarity with their ousted sisters.

Do you think sororities have a right to exclude girls who don't meet a specific physical ideal?

Be Superwoman   This is a fourth theme emerging in cultural expectations of women. Sharon's exhilaration (see box on page 185) over the choices open to her is tempered by Emily's realization that women feel they are required to try to have it all. It's not enough to be just a homemaker and mother or to just have a career—young women seem to feel they are expected to do it all.

▼

Emily   *Women are expected to want to climb the business ladder, yet they are also expected to pick up the kids after school, make dinner, help with homework, and be a loving wife. I do not want a career that will ruin my family life or a family life that will ruin my career. How am I supposed to pick between my personal life and my career goals? Why is it that women are expected to sacrifice their careers or be superwomen who do it all but men don't have to be that way?*

Women students talk with me frequently about the tension they feel trying to figure out how to have a full family life and a successful career. They tell me that they want both careers and families and don't see how they can make it all work. The physical and psychological toll on women who try to do it all is well documented (Coltrane & Adams, 2001; Galvin, 2006; Harris, 2004; Greenberg, 2001), and it is growing steadily as women find that changes in the workplace are not paralleled by changes in home life.

There Is No Single Meaning of Feminine Anymore   This is the final theme of femininity in the current era. This theme reflects all the others and the contradictions inherent in them. A woman who is assertive and ambitious in a career is likely to meet with approval, disapproval, and curiosity from some people and to be applauded by others. At the same time, a woman who chooses to stay home while her children are young will be criticized by some women and men, envied by others, and respected by still others. Perhaps, as Sharon suggests in her commentary, there are many ways to be feminine, and we can respect all of them.

Prevailing themes of femininity in Western culture reveal both constancy and change. Traditional expectations of attractiveness and caring for others persist, as does the greater likelihood of negative treatment by others. Yet, today there are multiple ways to define femininity and womanhood, which allow women with different talents, interests, and gender orientations to define themselves in diverse ways and to chart life courses that suit them as individuals.

Sharon   *My mother and I talk about women, and she tells me that she's glad she didn't have so many options. She says it was easier for her than it is for me because she knew what she was supposed to do—marry and raise a family—and she didn't have to go through the identity crisis that I do. I see her point, yet I kind of like having alternatives. I know I wouldn't be happy investing my total self in a home and family. I just have to be out doing things in the world. But my best friend really wants to do that. She's marrying a guy who wants that, too, so as soon as they've saved enough to be secure, they plan for her to quit work to raise a family. I know someone else who says she just flat out doesn't want to marry. She wants to be a doctor, and she doesn't think she can do that plus take care of a home and family, so she wants to stay single. I don't really know yet if I will or won't have kids, but it's nice to know I can choose to go either way. My mother couldn't.*

GROWING UP OUTSIDE CONVENTIONAL GENDER ROLES

Not every person grows up identifying with socially prescribed gender, sex, or sexual orientation. For people who do not identify with and perform normative gender, sex, and sexuality, growing up can be particularly difficult. Gay men are often socially ostracized because they are perceived as feminine, and lesbians may be scorned for being masculine.

Social isolation also greets many people who are (or are thought to be) transgendered. They find themselves trapped in a society that rigidly pairs males with masculinity and females with femininity. There are no in-between spaces; there is no room for blurring the rigid lines; there are no options beyond the binary choices of male/female, masculine/feminine, and straight/gay. For people who do not fit the conventional sex and gender roles, it is hard to find role models and equally difficult to find acceptance from family, peers, and society (Fausto-Sterling, 2000; Feinberg, 1996; Glenn, 2002). Of the students who have studied gender and communication with me over the years, a few have volunteered commentaries on growing up outside of conventional gender roles. Ben, Zena, and Mike's commentaries appear on pages 186 and 187.

> **Ben**   *What it means to be a man depends totally on whether you're gay or straight. I'm gay—knew that since I was 9 or 10. And being gay is hell for a teenager. Other guys, the straight ones, called me names all through middle school and high school—fag, queer, girlie. It didn't matter that I was big and toned and good at baseball. They totally excluded me because I was gay.*

In 2007, a cover story of the mainstream magazine *Newsweek* was about trans-gendered people. The author of the story, Deborah Rosenberg, wrote that most people "have no quarrel with the 'M' or the 'F on our birth certificates …. But to those who consider themselves transgender, there's a disconnect between the sex they were assigned at birth and the way they see or express themselves" (2007, p. 50). Between 750,000 and 3 million Americans are estimated to be transgender (Rosenberg, 2007). Until very recently, transgendered (as well as transsexed and intersexed) people seldom made their identities or struggles public. That's changing as more and more people who don't fit in conventional identity boxes demand to be recognized and accepted on their own terms. One sign of changing attitudes toward transgender people is campus policies. By 2010 nearly 300 colleges had added gender identity and expression to their nondiscrimination policies, and a number of colleges and universities have passed gender-neutral housing policies so that transgender students are not forced to live with people with whom they don't identify (Tilsley, 2010).

> **Zena**   *I wear a tie always and a dress never. If I go to a doctor, I'm labeled "female," but in everyday life, most people think I'm a "male." The problem is, neither of those labels is right. Neither fits me. I'm both or nei-ther or maybe something that is totally different than those stupid catego-ries. Sexually, I'm attracted to both "males" and "females," although more often to "females." I have no interest in girlie things, but I'm sensitive to others and a very caring person. All I can say is that I'm Zena, and that's a name I gave myself.*

For individuals who don't fit into conventional categories for sex, gender, and sexual orientation, there are barriers and challenges that are difficult for many gender-conforming heterosexuals to imagine. For those of you whose bodies are consistent with your personal sense of identity, imagine this: You visit a doctor and learn that you are actually a different sex than you have believed yourself to be and that you identify with. If you think of yourself as a woman, you discover that medically you fit the socially designated category of man. If you think of your-self as a man, you learn that society defines you as a woman. Your body doesn't match your self-concept. Everything from how you dress to whom you date to which bathroom you can use suddenly becomes an issue, a struggle, a matter you have to negotiate.

▼

Mike   *I have no idea what it means to be a man. I've never felt I was one, never identified with men. As a kid, I liked to dress in my mother's clothes until my dad caught me and beat the—out of me! I still identify more with women, and I think that I was meant to be a woman. Growing up looking like a male but feeling like a female meant that I didn't belong anywhere, didn't fit with anyone. It's better now that I'm in college and have found some people like me, but there was nobody in my rural Southern hometown!*

Stay with this hypothetical situation. Would you want to have hormone treatments and surgery so that your body was consistent with the sex and gender you feel that you are? The surgery is expensive, extensive, and painful. Are you willing to tolerate that in order to fit into society's categories and be considered "normal?" Or would you choose, instead, to change how you dress, style your hair, move, speak, and so forth in order to perform more credibly as the sex and gender society assigns to you? Or would you continue living as you have, looking and acting as the sex and gender you identify with while knowing that by medical criteria you are actually a different sex and perhaps a different gender?

EXPLORING GENDERED LIVES | JOB (DIS)QUALIFICATION

When he reached his mid-40s, Steven Stanton, the former city manager of Largo, Florida, could no longer tolerate feeling that he was a female trapped in a male body. He decided to become the woman he had always felt he was. He began hormone treatments and planned to have sex-reassignment surgery. Then the roof fell in when a newspaper published a story about his planned sex-change. Almost immediately, on March 12, 2007, the city commissioners voted five to two to fire Stanton despite his 14 years of service and consistently excellent job evaluations. On May 30, Stanton—now Susan, wearing a skirt, high heels, and makeup, applied for the job from which Steven Stanton had been fired. Susan was not hired (Waddell and Campo-Flores, 2007).

Stanton isn't the only one to find that the professional world values men more than women even if they are the same person. Researchers Kristen Schilt and Matthew Wiswall studied the career implications of changing one's sex (Cloud, 2008). They found that men who become women earn significantly less after they change sex than women who become men. Even people who stayed in the same job after transitioning were regarded as more competent if they had become men than if they had become women.

Do you think Stanton experienced sex discrimination on the job?

SUMMARY

Communication plays a primary role in shaping our gendered identities. Through interaction with others, we come to understand how society defines masculinity and femininity. But we need to remember that socialization is not as deterministic as it may seem. Clearly, we are influenced by the expectations of our culture, yet these expectations endure only to the extent that individuals and institutions sustain them. Through our own communication and the ways we act, we reinforce or challenge existing views of gender. As we do so, we contribute to forming social views that affect the extent to which each of us can define ourselves and live our lives as we choose.

Key Terms

The terms following are defined in this chapter on the pages indicated, as well as in alphabetical order in the book's glossary, which begins on page 325. The text's companion website (**http://www.cengage.com/communication/wood/gendered lives 10e**) also provides interactive flash cards and crossword puzzles to help you learn these terms and the concepts they represent.

ego boundaries 167   self-as-object 162

monitoring 163

Gender Online

1. Go to Youtube.com and search for videos on "gender socialization children."
2. Statistics about diverse family forms are available from the Census Bureau at: **http://www.census.gov/population/www/socdemo/hh-fam.html**.
3. Online search terms: "father role," "feminine socialization," masculine socialization," "parental models, gender"

Reflection and Discussion

1. How did your parents and/or stepparents model masculinity and femininity? Does your own embodiment of gender reflect their influences?
2. To what extent do the themes of masculinity or femininity discussed in this chapter apply to you?
3. Analyze how your ego boundaries work in one particular relationship in your life. Identify specific situations in which your boundaries were permeable or firm. How do your ego boundaries both enhance and constrain that relationship?
4. I opened this chapter by asking you to write a few paragraphs describing what it means to you to be a man or a woman today in America. How does your response echo or differ from themes in the responses of student commentaries presented in this chapter? How does your response differ from or contradict themes in the commentaries presented in this chapter?

5. Return to the hypothetical scenario presented on pages 186–187. What choices would you make if the sex and gender you feel that you are were inconsistent with those society assigns to you?

Recommended Resources

1. *Tough Guise*. (1999). Media Education Foundation. 26 Center Street. Northampton, MA. This video offers a critical perspective on socialization that links masculinity with aggression and violence. It is a disturbing video and an important one.
2. Michael Messner is a scholar who studies gender, particularly as it relates to athletics. Visit his blog at Huffington Post: **http://www.huffingtonpost.com/**
3. Michael Kimmel. (2008). *Guyland: The Perilous World Where Boys Become Men*. New York: Macmillan. I cited this book within this chapter because Kimmel advances new thoughts about becom*ing a man in America today. The book is intended for* a general audience so it is very accessible.
4. Susan Barash (2006). *Tripping the Prom Queen*. New York: St. Martin's Griffin. This is a funny, sassy, and very insightful analysis of social expectations of girls and women and the competition between them that those expectations fuel.

The mind has exactly the same power as the hands; not merely to grasp the world, but to change it.

Colin Wilson

CHAPTER **8**

GENDERED EDUCATION: COMMUNICATION IN SCHOOLS

Knowledge Challenge:

1. Do boys perform better than girls in high school math classes?
2. Are female and male college athletes given equal support?
3. What differences are there in how college students evaluate male and female instructors?

From America's founding through much of the twentieth century, girls and women in the United States have had less educational opportunity than boys and men have had. By now, much of the historic discrimination against female students has been eliminated. In the United States today, women and men have relatively equal access to educational opportunities. Yet, today's schools continue to be marked by gendered dynamics—ones that differ from those of previous eras yet have great impact on our lives.

In this chapter, we'll examine gendered aspects of education in the United States. We will first discuss distinct gendered expectations and pressures that confront male and female students. Second, we will explore gendered attitudes and practices that affect faculty in America's schools. As we will see, although American schools no longer discriminate blatantly and primarily based on sex, gendered biases and issues continue to infuse educational institutions.

As you read this chapter, keep in mind what's at stake. Our experiences in schools do more than instruct us in various subjects. Schools are also powerful agents of gender socialization. They teach us what each sex is expected to be and to do; they teach which careers are open to women and men. But what schools teach us about sex and gender is not static. As social views of gender have changed, so have educational expectations and opportunities for women and men. As social views continue to change in the years ahead, so will educational practices.

GENDERED EXPECTATIONS AND PRESSURES FACING STUDENTS

To understand the range of gendered dynamics facing male and female students today, we'll examine academics, athletics, and peer cultures at colleges and universities.

ACADEMICS

Both males and females encounter gendered expectations and pressures in schools from kindergarten through graduate and professional school. We'll first consider gendered expectations affecting boys and men, and then we'll examine those facing girls and women.

Males   Child psychologists Dan Kindlon and Michael Thompson (1999) state that "the average boy is developmentally disadvantaged in the early school environment" (p. 23). They point out that kindergarten, preschool, and elementary school are all primarily feminine environments where adult females greatly outnumber adult males. Further, compared to same-aged girls, young boys tend to have more physical energy and less impulse control, so they have difficulty adjusting to school contexts where they are supposed to sit quietly, follow instructions, and not deviate from lesson plans (Garloch, 2009). Thus, elementary classrooms are not boy friendly, making the early years of school a time of frustration and often of failure for boys (Tyre, 2008). This provides a poor foundation for success later in school.

The mismatch between young boys' development and the demands of school may contribute to a significant difference in the sexes' academic success. In kindergarten and elementary school, boys lag behind girls in reading and other verbal skills ("Attention Deficit," 2008; Strauss, 2008; Tyre, 2006). Biology contributes to males' slower development of verbal skills—their cognitive abilities to work with words mature later than those of girls. In high school, female students tend to be more successful academically, which may explain why males are 33% more likely than females to drop out of high school (Tyre, 2006, 2008). The gap between males and females continues after high school. Today, there are approximately 10 female students for every 7 male students in two- and four-year colleges in the United States ("The Nation," 2009, p. 10). Currently, among 22-year-olds there are 185 female college graduates for every 100 male college graduates (Brooks, 2010). Women and men are relatively equal in earning master's degrees (Yen, 2010).

The trend toward women's educational achievements shows no signs of diminishing. The latest Census report issued in April of 2011 shows that, in the United States, currently 20.1 million women have college degrees compared to 18.7 million men who have college degrees. Women also outpace men in earning graduate degrees (Yen, 2011).

Even more than sex, race and socio-economic class are linked to success in higher education (Lewin, 2008a). Eighty-one percent of high school graduates in

EXPLORING GENDERED LIVES | A Short History of Gendered Education in America

Throughout America's history, schools have echoed cultural views of gender (Minnich, 1998). In America's earliest years, women were discouraged from advanced study because it was commonly believed that exposure to higher education might "unsex" women, as an educated woman was "unnatural" (Gordon, 1998). The few women who did pursue education beyond high school attended finishing schools, where they learned traditional skills such as sewing. In the 1800s, some female academies were established to train women as nurses and teachers, two professions considered appropriate for women.

The Morrill Act of 1862 established coeducational state universities and land grant colleges to educate women and men in liberal arts and practical skills. Practical education for men included the study of agriculture and mechanics, whereas practical education for women focused on home economics. By 1870, 30% of U.S. colleges enrolled students of both sexes. In 1920, fully 70% of U.S. higher education institutions enrolled women and men. The progressive education movement in the 1920s and 1930s led to the development of women's colleges that stressed intellectual development, personal independence, and creativity, emphases not offered to women by most coeducational institutions.

Throughout most of America's history, many colleges discriminated against women. When more women than men graduated with awards and honors from Stanford University in 1901, the school quickly figured a way to make sure that didn't happen again: Stanford instituted an enrollment ratio of three men to every one woman (Solomon, 1986). Even in the 1960s, many schools accepted only female applicants who were better qualified than male applicants. With passage of Title IX of the Education Act Amendments in 1972, all educational institutions that receive federal funds are required to treat boys and girls, men and women, equally.

families that are in the 20% highest income group enter college, 61% of high school graduates in families in the middle 60% of income level enter college, and 51% of high school graduates in families in the lowest 20% income level enter college ("The Nation," 2008). Of those who do enter college, 59.2% of women and 53% of men graduate ("The Nation," 2008). Only 6% of children from families with very low incomes earn undergraduate degrees (Corbett, Hill, & Rose, 2008; Golden, 2006; Sacks, 2007).

Rattiya   *I was born in Thailand and came here last year for college. In Thailand schools, girls were always encouraged to be passive, quiet, and ladylike at all times. Elective classes for girls were cooking, painting, and dancing. We were not offered classes such as soccer, self-defending, or machine repair.*

EXPLORING GENDERED LIVES | **GENDERED EDUCATION AROUND THE GLOBE**

There are significant differences in the education of males and females in countries around the globe. The gender gap is greatest in sub-Saharan Africa, North Africa, South Asia, and the Middle East. In India, for example, 33 million fewer girls than boys attend school. In rural Africa, only 3 of 10 girls complete elementary school ("Educating Girls," 2005). One barrier to girls' education in sub-Saharan Africa is difficult for Westerners to imagine: lack of toilets. Schools lack toilets and water, so students go to the bathroom behind scrub bushes that allow no sanitation or privacy. This becomes a significant issue when girls start menstruating (LaFraniere, 2005).

But there are other countries where girls are more likely than boys to progress through university-level education. In Mongolia, for instance, women make up 60% of students attending universities, and more women than men are top students in faculty opinion (Lin-Liu, 2005). In the Persian Gulf, opportunities for women to enroll in college have increased remarkably since the 1980s (Zoepf, 2006). Other countries where females are likely to receive good educations are Belgium, France, Canada, Finland, and Norway.

Race, sex, and economics don't tell the whole story. Personal choices also affect academic performance and success. During a typical week, 26.9% of first-year men college students study six or more hours a week, whereas 37.6% of first-year women do; and 22% of first-year men spend six or more hours playing video or computer games, whereas only 3.8% of first-year women do (Wilson, 2007). Choices of how to spend time—studying or engaging in recreation—contribute to different levels of academic accomplishment.

Schools reproduce gender stereotypes by not encouraging boys and men to develop traditionally feminine skills, such as caring for others, and by not encouraging males to enter traditionally feminine fields. Nel Noddings (2002), a distinguished education professor at Stanford University, argues that education at all levels should prepare everyone—males and females—to be responsible, caring family members. Noddings' ideal is schools that teach not only science, history, and math, but also how to care for others and build a satisfying family life.

Females   What about women students? What biases and pressures do they face academically? Despite much effort to eliminate biases against women, not all barriers have disappeared. Women still face biases and barriers in particular fields—namely, math and natural sciences.

The long-standing belief that females innately have less aptitude and ability in math and science has helped erect barriers to women's participation in science and math education, not to mention barriers to careers in those fields (Fogg, 2005; "Hothouse," 2006; Monastersky, 2005a; Rimer, 2005). In the early years of school, girls do just as well as boys in mathematics. Twenty years ago, high school boys outscored girls in math, but that is no longer true. Today, male and female high school students perform equally well on math tests. Why the change? Girls used to take fewer advanced math classes than boys, but today they take just as many: With equal training, the sexes do equally well on math tests (Ceci & Williams, 2009; Lewin, 2008b). Yet, females progressively drop out of math and science as they advance in their educations. Women earn 22.6% of undergraduate degrees in physics but only 15.5% of doctorates. Women earn nearly half (46.7%) of undergraduate degrees in mathematics but less than a third (29%) of doctorates (Cox & Alm, 2005); and only 10% of faculty in math and sciences are women (Kantrowitz, 2005).

One reason many women drop out of math and science is that they encounter faculty, as well as peers, who assume that females are less able than males in those fields (Dreifus, 2010). A noteworthy example of faculty attitudes that pose barriers to women in sciences surfaced in 2005. At an academic conference, Larry Summers, President of Harvard University, said that innate gender differences might explain why so few women major in the sciences. MIT biology professor Nancy Hopkins—who, coincidentally, is a Harvard alumna—explains it this way: "When the president of Harvard University [Summers] appears to support the theory of innate differences, that pushes the stereotype into the realm of fact and makes it acceptable to think that women are just a little dumber by nature" (Kantrowitz, 2005, p. 36).

Scarlett   *I always liked science. Right from the first grade, it was my favorite subject. The older I got, though, the more I felt odd in my science classes. Especially in college after the required courses, I felt odd. Sometimes, I was the only woman in a class. I was majoring in early education and just took science electives for fun. That changed when I had a woman professor in a course about unsolved problems in biology. She was really good, and so was the course, but to me the main thing was seeing a woman teaching science. That's when I decided to change my major and become a science teacher.*

Females in math and sciences may face another gender-related barrier. Because cultural stereotypes of femininity do not include being skilled at science and math, social disapproval may greet women who excel in those fields. Further, the drive and assertiveness required to succeed in historically male fields is inconsistent with social prescriptions for femininity. Consequently, women in the sciences often face a double bind: If they are not extremely successful, they are judged incompetent, but if they are successful, they are often perceived as cold and manipulative and unfeminine (Dean, 2006).

Personal choices and preferences also affect career choices. Recent research (Ceci & Williams, 2009) shows that, in general, males are more interested in working with inanimate objects and inorganic subjects such as math whereas females are more interested in working with people. This gender gap widens for women and men who become parents. Fathers often become more involved with their careers and mothers tend to focus more intensely on family (Tierney, 2010).

But is it possible that males really are innately more skilled at math and science? Let's check the evidence. Research suggests that sex-related differences in brains and hormones may give males an edge in some math and science skills (Lippa, 2005). For instance, males have an advantage at three-dimensional spatial thought, whereas females have an advantage at arithmetic (Pinker, 2002). Also, based on mean averages, males have stronger science and math skills than females. However, the higher mean average for males comes primarily from a very few males who have truly extraordinary ability. In other words, the few males who make exceedingly high scores pull up the overall average for all males such that it is higher than the average for females, whose scores are concentrated in the middle of the test range (Hulbert, 2005; Lewin, 2008b).

Yet, even researchers who think there are some innate differences in the sexes' math and science abilities think that innate differences are less important than cultural influences. In the United States, males are more likely than females to be encouraged to pursue careers in math and science, whereas females are more likely to be encouraged to enter careers that involve more direct interaction with people (Monastersky, 2005a). But that's not true in some other cultures. For instance, Chinese students of both sexes score better on math tests than American students (Monastersky, 2005b). In Turkey, it's not at all unusual for women students to major in math ("Women and Science," 2005). Observation of other cultures casts doubt over the existence of significant innate sex differences in math and science ability.

GENDER-STEREOTYPED CURRICULA

Although curricular content is less biased than in the past, gender stereotypes persist. Consider how history is taught. Accounts of wars, for instance, focus on battles and military leaders. Seldom noted are the contributions of women either on the battlefields or at home. Who kept families intact and food on the table while men fought? Who manufactured supplies for troops on the front? Chronicles of important events such as the civil rights movement focus on male leaders' speeches and press conferences and obscure the ways in which women contributed to the movements. We are taught about the leadership of Stokely Carmichael, Malcolm X, and the Reverend Martin Luther King Jr., but few of us learn about Ella Baker's pivotal work in organizing neighborhoods in support of civil rights (Parker, 2006; Ransby, 2003) or the activism that took place in African-American beauty shops during the Jim Crow era (Gill, 2010).

The few women who are highlighted in curricula tend to fall into two categories. First, there are women who fit traditional stereotypes of women. For example, most of us learned that Betsy Ross sewed the first American flag. A second group of women highlighted in curricula distinguished themselves on men's terms and in masculine contexts. Mother Jones, for example, was a powerful organizer for unions. Women in this category tend to be represented as exceptional cases—as atypical of women in general. This implies that most women can't do what a few notable ones did. Women such as Ella Baker, who achieve impact in other ways, remain hidden (Spitzack & Carter, 1987).

Historical epochs tend to be taught in terms of their effects on men while neglecting their impact on women and minorities. For instance, textbooks represent the Renaissance as a period of rebirth and progress in human life because it expanded men's options. The Renaissance is *not* taught in terms of its impact in reducing the status and opportunities of most women. The Enlightenment is taught as a time when reason ascended as the surest route to truth and human progress. The Enlightenment is *not* taught as a time when women were considered inferior because they were assumed to have limited capacity to reason. The Industrial Revolution is taught as a time when mechanization of production systems enabled mass production, which propelled factories as the primary workplace for men. The Industrial Revolution is *not* represented in terms of how it changed women's lives, work, and relationships with their husbands.

Even science, which we might think is a highly objective field, has gender stereotypes that can distort how science is taught. For instance, until recently science textbooks routinely misrepresented the process of human reproduction in ways that reflect social views of women and men: The active sperm were described as "invading" the passively waiting egg. When research proved that the egg is very active in controlling which sperm enter it, many science books revised their description of the process (Hammonds, 1998). As this example shows, gender stereotypes can be corrected when evidence disproves them. For this reason, curricula, including those in science, are less gender biased than in the past.

Sexism in education intersects with other forms of discrimination: racism, classism, and heterosexism. Not just any males are presented as the standard: White, heterosexual, able-bodied, middle- and upper-class men continue to be depicted as the norm in textbooks. How often have you studied contributions of lesbians and gays? How frequently did you learn about the lives and contributions of economically disadvantaged people? Have you learned about black women and men in journalism, Asian women and men in music, Hispanic scientists, or African writers? Along with women, minorities continue to be underrepresented in educational materials, where the reference point has been and remains white, heterosexual, able-bodied, middle- and upper-class males.

STONE SOUP   **BY JAN ELIOT**

Gender-stereotyped curricular material diminishes education for all students. When students learn primarily about straight, white, economically comfortable men and their experiences, perspectives, and accomplishments, they are deprived of understanding the perspectives and contributions of the majority of the population—women and minorities. On a more personal level, biases in instructional content encourage straight, white, able-bodied, middle-class men to see themselves as able to fulfill high ambitions and affect the course of events, and discourage women and minorities from those self-perceptions (AAUW, 1998; Smith, 2004b).

ATHLETICS

Today's female students enjoy unprecedented opportunities to participate in athletics. In large part, that is due to **Title IX**. There are three basic parts of Title IX as it applies to athletics (Title IX Q & A, 2008):

1. Women must be provided an equitable opportunity to participate in sports as men (not necessarily the identical sports but an equal opportunity to play).
2. Colleges must provide female athletes with athletic scholarship dollars proportional to their participation. For instance, if there are 100 male athletes and 50 female athletes at a school that has a $150,000 athletic scholarship budget, female athletes must receive $50,000 in scholarships.
3. Equal treatment includes more than playing time and scholarship. Schools are also required to provide female and male athletes with equivalent equipment and supplies, practice times, travel and daily allowance, tutoring, coaching, locker rooms and facilities, publicity and promotions, recruitment programs, and support services.

Despite Title IX, the playing field still is not exactly even—male athletes and coaches of men's teams continue to have more support, financial and otherwise, than female athletes and coaches of women's teams. In addition, male athletes are more likely than female athletes to get academic tutoring and prime times and venues for practice. In this chapter, we've noted that women's enrollment at colleges has increased. Yet the number of female athletes has not increased proportionately. Further, before passage of Title IX, more than 90% of coaches of women's sports were women. Following Title IX's passage, fewer women's sports are coached by women, and all Division I colleges pay male coaches more than women coaches (Wolverton, 2006).

Heather   *This school claims to go by Title IX, but the support for women athletes doesn't even come close to what men get. The school is fair about the number of women it recruits and funds with scholarships, but that's where the equity stops. The men have tutors who basically babysit them through their classes. We are expected to earn our own grades. They have the best practice times on the field; we get the leftover times. They get more travel allowance than we do, and they get a lot more publicity.*

EXPLORING GENDERED LIVES | **GENERIC MAXIMUM HEART RATE**

For years, we've all been told that the formula for calculating the maximum heart rate is 220 minus a person's age. Guess what? It turns out that formula isn't accurate for women because it was based on men. To remedy this, researchers at Northwestern Medicine in Chicago studied 5,500 healthy women. Based on these data, the researchers concluded that the correct formula to calculate women's maximum heart reate is 206 minus 88% of the woman's age. Maybe now women who work out will be less exhausted by effort to meet a rate that is too high for them (Parker-Pope, 2010b).

In 2005, the Supreme Court issued an important ruling that affects implementation of Title IX. The original law requires schools that receive federal funds to provide equal opportunities to female and male students to participate in intercollegiate competition. To meet Title IX requirements, schools have had to provide evidence that their present programs completely accommodate male and female students' interests and abilities. In 2005, the Supreme Court ruled that all a college was required to do was send students a survey, including one sent by e-mail, about athletic interests and abilities. Students who do not reply could be assumed to be satisfied with present policies (Suggs, 2005b). How often do you delete e-mails from unfamiliar senders without even opening them? How often do you open an e-mail, see that it's another survey, and delete it without replying? These criticisms of using e-mail surveys to demonstrate accommodation of all students led to repeal. In 2010 the U.S. Department of Education withdrew the policy allowing e-mail surveys to be used for Title IX purposes (Sander, 2010).

This ruling, however, has not ensured that colleges and universities receiving federal support actually meet the spirit of Title IX. In fact, a recent report in the *New York Times* (Thomas, 2011) documented a number of deceptive practices that colleges and universities use to appear to comply with Title IX while actually undermining gender equity in athletics. Some schools require women who are cross-country runners to join the indoor and outdoor track teams, which allows the schools to count each runner three times in tallying up the number of women athletes it has. Another deceptive practice that occurs at Division I schools as Cornell and Texas A & M is counting male players who practice with women as female athletes. Other schools pad the rosters of female athletes by including women who have returned their scholarships or who don't play or by adding the names of women students to teams when the numbers are counted and then cutting the players after the count is done.

Inequities in supporting athletics have consequences beyond the school years. Girls and women who participate in sports are more likely to pursue additional education and have higher earning power in their 20s and 30s (the latest ages for which data are available). They are also more likely to be healthy on many measures, including weight (Parker-Pope, 2010a).

EXPLORING GENDERED LIVES | **TITLE IX: FICTION AND FACT**

Although Title IX has been around for more than 30 years, it is still widely misunderstood. Check your understanding of Title IX (Messner, 2002; Neinas, 2002; Suggs, 2005a; Title IX Q & A, 2008).

Fiction: Title IX is binding on all schools in the United States.
Fact: Title IX is binding only on schools that accept federal funds.
Fiction: Title IX bans sex discrimination only in athletics.
Fact: Title IX bans sex discrimination of all sorts in federally supported schools. This applies to academics as well as athletics.
Fiction: Title IX has reduced opportunities for male college athletes.
Fact: Since the passage of Title IX, college men's sports opportunities have actually increased.
Fiction: Title IX requires identical athletic programs for males and females.
Fact: Title IX does not require that men's and women's teams receive identical support. Instead, it requires that they receive comparable levels of service, supplies, and facilities. Variations between men's and women's programs are allowed.
Fiction: Because of Title IX, colleges that receive federal funds provide fully equal support to women's and men's sports.
Fact: Compared to male athletes, female athletes receive fewer scholarship dollars, and their teams get fewer dollars for recruiting and operating teams.
Fiction: Most Americans don't support Title IX.
Fact: In a 2000 poll, 79% of Americans said that they approve of Title IX. Support for Title IX didn't vary much by sex; 79% of women and 73% of men supported it.

Are you satisfied with Title IX as it is currently implemented? If so, why? If not, how do you think it should be modified?

GENDER SOCIALIZATION IN PEER CULTURES

The power of peer pressure is no myth. To be accepted by peers, many students conform to social views of gender (Rudman & Glick, 2008). College is a training ground for adulthood, and peer groups are primary agents of socialization on campuses.

Scott   *On this campus, Greeks are cool. It took me just a few weeks on campus to figure out that if I wanted to be popular in college, I had to join a fraternity. So I rushed and pledged my first year. I like being part of the group and being considered cool, but I'm still uncomfortable with some of what goes on in the house. Some of the brothers talk about girls like they're all sluts, and if you don't go along with that talk, you're a jerk. Same with drinking—you have to drink a lot to be in with the group.*

Bill Frakes /Sports Illustrated/Getty Images

Title IX has created more opportunities for women athletes.

Pressures to Conform to Masculinity   As young boys grow into adolescence, male bonding in peer groups reinforces masculine identification (Cross, 2008; Messner, 2001, 2007). Males often engage in drinking and sexual activity to demonstrate their masculinity, and they encourage the same in peers (Cross, 2008; Kimmel, 2008). This was dramatically evident in a scandal surrounding the University of Colorado's football team. In 2004, the story broke: Women were exploited as part of the university's recruitment strategy. The recruiters not only provided female companions to the high school men they wanted to recruit, but they hired strippers (Jacobson, 2004b). Apparently, with at least tacit support from some members of the coaching staff, players treated women as sex objects. Six of the team's players were accused of rape, and others were accused of sexual harassment and assault.

Some male groups encourage members to embody extreme versions of masculinity that involve heavy drinking, having sex with as many women as possible, and talking about women in demeaning ways. To be accepted in the group, some men say and do things as part of the group that they would never consider doing as individuals.

Pressures to Conform to Femininity   Female peer groups tend to encourage and reward compliance with feminine stereotypes. Girls often make fun of or exclude girls who don't wear popular brands of clothing or who weigh more than what is considered ideal. (Adler, 2007; Barash, 2006).

▼

Spencer   *Tuition is nothing compared to what you have to spend to dress well! At this school, it's almost like there is a competition among girls to dress in the latest styles. If you're not wearing the cool boot or not layering the way models do in* Marie Claire, *you're just out of it. It takes a lot of money to buy all of the clothes and pay for haircuts and manicures. It also takes huge amounts of time that I could spend other ways.*

From the earliest years of school through college and graduate school, girls and women report that some male students routinely jeer at them, make lewd suggestions, and touch them without invitation or consent. Sexual discrimination and harassment are not confined to peer interactions. Some faculty harass and discriminate against women (Wilson, 2009). Ranging from compliments on appearance instead of on academic work to offers of higher grades for sexual favors, these actions make women students' sex more salient than their intellectual abilities and aspirations. In treating women as sexual objects, such actions tell women students that they are not taken seriously as members of an intellectual community.

▼

Bailey   *It's so unfair how professors treat women. I'm a serious student, and I plan a business career, but my professors have never asked me about my career plans. Even when I bring the subject up, all I get is really superficial stuff—like they really don't want to talk to me. One of my boyfriend's teachers invited him to have coffee and talk about graduate school. My boyfriend didn't even have to ask! They spent over an hour just talking about what he would do after undergraduate school. And my grades are better than his!*

The college years present new challenges for women. Studies of women students at colleges and universities report that they feel two sets of pressures: to be successful as women—attractive, fun to be with, and so forth—and to be smart and academically successful. A 2003 study at Duke University named the problem: Women feel compelled to achieve **effortless perfection**: to be beautiful, fit, popular, smart, and accomplished without any visible effort (Dube, 2004; Lipka, 2004). Many undergraduate women describe a relentless pressure to be all of that without ever seeming to work at it. According to the study, undergraduate women believe that being sexy or pretty is instrumental in being attractive to men, but that being smart, while also desirable, should not be too obvious.

EXPLORING GENDERED LIVES	**HOOKED UP**

Young people, particularly young women, are having more casual sexual contacts than ever before and at earlier and earlier ages, often as early as middle-school. On many college campuses dating has been largely replaced by "hooking up," short-term or even one-time sexual encounters between people who are not interested in romance or commitment (Stepp, 2007). Those who have studied this trend identify several contributing factors:

Fewer men than women attend college, which leads some women to lower their standards for heterosexual interaction (Whitmire, 2008).

Some women feel they must postpone love in order to prepare for and launch careers. Hooking up allows contact without commitment (Stepp, 2007).

Media increasingly teach women—and even very young girls—to view themselves as sexual objects for men. They see these sexual encounters not as sources of experience for themselves, but as sources of sexual pleasure for men. The result is that many young women say sex is something they do to fit in more than something they do for their own pleasure (Levin & Kilbourne, 2008; Levy, 2005).

To what extent do you think the factors identified by researchers account for hooking up?

Jacquie   *College is supposed to be a place for thinking and education, but the bottom line here is that you have to be really attractive if you want to be liked. Brains may get you good grades, but they won't get you friends or dates. Most of the girls I know spend as much time shopping for clothes and fixing their hair and nails as they do studying.*

In their book, *Educated in Romance,* Dorothy Holland and Margaret Eisenhart (1992) asked why so many young women who enter college with strong preparation and ambitious career goals wind up radically downsizing their ambitions during their college years. After spending 10 years studying women in college, Holland and Eisenhart concluded that two forces propel college women into a **culture of romance**. First, many women in college become discouraged by barriers to their academic achievement, such as lack of intellectual mentoring from professors and required readings and class discussions that emphasize important men and men's achievements and give little or no attention to important women and their achievements. The second factor propelling college women into a culture of romance is intense peer pressure that emphasizes attracting men as more important than anything else women can do.

SINGLE-SEX EDUCATIONAL PROGRAMS

Some educators, scholars, and social commentators think that single-sex schools, or programs in schools, might solve some of the problems we've discussed. For instance, in elementary school, boys generally lag behind girls in reading. If there were no girls in reading classes, teachers might be able to give young boys the help they need to develop reading skills. On campuses where there were no male students, heterosexual women might focus more on academics and less on the culture of romance. Faculty might also be more likely to mentor female students if there were no male students.

Is single-sex education effective? From elementary school through college, heterosexual males and females are more likely to make academics a priority in single-sex schools. Researchers think a primary reason for this is that, when students aren't focused on impressing members of the other sex, they will study more without worrying about seeming like nerds (Salomone, 2003). The facts on graduates of women's schools are also persuasive: Although women's colleges produce only about 5% of all female college graduates, a disproportionate number of women in the U.S. Congress and running top businesses graduated from women's colleges (Salome, 2007; Scelfo, 2006). When The Citadel was all male, its graduation rate was 70%—much higher than the 48% national average (AAUW, 2001).

But critics of single-sex education argue that sex-segregated education isn't the answer to gender inequities in schools. They think a better solution is to make sure that teachers in *all* schools treat all students equally so that males and females have the same educational opportunities and support. Also, single-sex schools tend to be private and too expensive for most families. Thus, although single-sex schools may benefit children from well-to-do families, they won't do much to help the majority of students.

GENDERED EXPECTATIONS AND PRESSURES FACING FACULTY

In addition to being educational institutions, schools are also workplaces, so we want to examine gendered attitudes and practices that affect employees, in this case faculty. We'll discuss gendered hierarchies, policies, and expectations in American educational institutions. As you will discover, gender dynamics faced by faculty often affect students as well.

GENDERED HIERARCHIES

The more prestigious institutions have greater proportions of male faculty members. In elementary schools, which have the least status in the hierarchy of educational institutions, the vast majority of teachers are female, but most superintendents and assistant superintendents are male. In high schools, which have more status, female teachers still outnumber male teachers, but the imbalance is less pronounced. At colleges and universities, which have higher status, the number of men increases. Table 8.1 shows that the proportion of women faculty compared to male faculty decreases as prestige of position increases ("The Profession," 2010, p. 20).

TABLE 8.1 | GENDERED HIERARCHIES AT COLLEGES AND UNIVERSITIES

Position	Number of Women	Number of Men	Prestige
Professor	45,571	126,515	most
Associate Professor	56,442	85,622	
Assistant Professor	78,119	86,796	
Instructor	53,546	45,533	least

Limited numbers of female and minority faculty mean that women and minority students have fewer role models among faculty. Recall cognitive development theory, which we discussed in Chapter 2. This theory notes that we look for models—preferably ones like us in sex, race, and so forth—to emulate as we develop identities. If more men than women are principals and full professors, students may infer that it's normal for men (but not for women) to rise to high levels in education.

▼

Morgan   *With so many male professors, I think it is difficult for some students to feel comfortable getting to know their professors and ask for help. Women are more likely to connect with a female teacher, minorities are more likely to connect with a teacher of their race, etc. Colleges always make a big deal about having a diverse campus, but what about the professors? Where are the female professors? Where are the LGBTQ professors? Where are the professors from other cultures and races? If colleges want to have a diverse student body, they should also have a diverse faculty that correlates with the students.*

GENDER BIAS IN EVALUATIONS

Are fewer women than men hired because of bias or because men are more qualified? Research shows that bias against women influences hiring decisions as well as performance reviews and promotions. Women and minorities are more likely to be hired when the selection process is blind with respect to applicants' sex, race, and other characteristics that sometimes are bases of discrimination (Reskin, 2003). Women are more likely to be hired in computerized application processes that do not identify sex (Richtel, 2000; Sturm, 2001). Hiring committees that are completely or predominantly male tend to hire fewer female faculty than committees with more sex-balanced membership (Valian, 1998; Wilson, 2004b).

Once hired, women faculty continue to face gender biases in evaluation. Researchers have identified three major sources of bias in the evaluation of faculty. First, women's performance tends to be more closely scrutinized than men's and judged by stricter standards. Second, men have to give more convincing demonstrations of incompetence to be judged by others as incompetent. Third, male candidates tend to be judged on whether they show promise, whereas female candidates tend to be judged on accomplishments, a form of bias that is particularly likely to affect hiring and promotion decisions (Wilson, 2004a, 2004b). All in all, different standards are used to evaluate men and women, and the way in which those standards are applied results in men being judged as more competent.

The subtlety and unintentional nature of gender bias in evaluation of faculty explains why it is called *invisible hand discrimination* (Haag, 2005). **Invisible hand discrimination** is unwitting discrimination in applying policies that are not inherently biased (Haag, 2005; Wilson, 2004a). It does not happen because a person consciously intends to discriminate or because a policy or practice is inherently discriminatory. The largely unconscious nature of invisible hand discrimination makes it particularly difficult to eliminate in evaluations of faculty and potential faculty.

Consider a few examples of how invisible hand discrimination works. Collegiality is a criterion many universities use when deciding whether faculty members deserve tenure. There is nothing inherently biased about the criterion, as it is reasonable to expect all faculty—men and women—to be civil, courteous, and reasonably easy to work with. So, how might a tenure committee evaluate the collegiality of Professor Smith, who is known to be very assertive? That often depends on whether Smith is male or female. Research shows that assertiveness in male faculty is likely to be taken as a sign of confidence and intelligence, whereas assertiveness in female faculty is often regarded as antagonistic or confrontational (Haag, 2005; Heilman, 2001). That's invisible hand discrimination.

Another example is the documented tendency to explain women's achievements as resulting from luck or help from others (her advisor included her name on his publication) while attributing men's achievements to competence (Heilman, 2001). So, male faculty who publish books may be judged "brilliant" but female faculty may be judged "lucky to have found a supportive editor." That's invisible hand discrimination. Gender biases in evaluation have material consequences, including discrepancies between the salaries paid to women and men faculty at American colleges and universities.

GENDERED POLICIES AND EXPECTATIONS

Like most institutions, colleges and universities are based on the outdated family model, in which the man is employed outside of the home to earn income and the woman takes care of the children and home. Colleges and universities based on that model assume that faculty don't have to worry about domestic life, which is the responsibility of the stay-at-home partner. That model, however, does not reflect today's faculty.

Earning Tenure   Women faculty face particular pressures arising from the outdated model. During the early years of an academic appointment, faculty members have probationary status—they are not permanent faculty until and unless they earn tenure. Thus, the early years require particularly long hours and heavy investments. For women, those years usually coincide with the ideal years for bearing children, a pressure that affects women faculty in ways it does not affect male faculty. The "tenure

---

EXPLORING GENDERED LIVES | **CATCH-22**

Administrators and other faculty aren't the only ones who engage in gender-biased evaluations. Students evaluate male and female faculty differently, particularly when male students rate female professors (Basow, 1998). Additionally, Caroline Turner (2003) has found that female faculty of color are frequently challenged and negatively evaluated by students, regardless of teaching ability.

In addition to averaged numerical rankings, written comments on evaluations often reflect sexism and even misogyny. At a Midwestern university where students post comments about faculty on a website, researchers found that it was not uncommon for students to criticize female faculty for appearance, describing them as "ugly," "dorky," or "frumpy." Students made virtually no comments about male professors' appearance. Also, it was commonplace for students to refer to female faculty as "bitches," "whores," and other derogatory names. Although male faculty were occasionally described as "jerks" or "assholes," they were not demeaned to the extent that female faculty were. The vast majority of explicit sexual comments and derogatory names were directed toward female faculty (Nelson, Trzemzalski, Malkasian, & Pfeffer, 2004).

Michael Messner (2000b) found that, although male faculty are evaluated for their skills and abilities as instructors, women faculty are first evaluated by their gender performance and then by their teaching performance. Women are caught in a catch-22 where they can't win. For example, if a woman tries to assert her authority in the classroom by wearing more formal attire and acting with authority, she may be seen as being less feminine and, therefore, not performing her appropriate gender role. As a result, students are critical because she is not conforming to their stereotypes of women as feminine, not authoritative. However, if she dresses and acts informally, it reinforces the stereotype that women aren't authorities.

To what extent do you use different criteria to evaluate female and male professors?

---

clock" is at odds with the biological clock, which creates tensions for faculty who are also parents (Kerber, 2005; Hayden & O'Brien Hallstein, 2010; Mason, 2007). The fact that this incompatibility affects female faculty more than male faculty may be another form of invisible hand discrimination.

Male faculty members are also penalized if their schools assume that a career is men's primary focus. Many male faculty want to spend time with families, particularly right after a child is born or adopted. Colleges that provide maternity leave but not paternity leave don't support male faculty's involvement in family life. Even so, some male faculty decide to be active partners and parents. Those who do are sometimes penalized professionally for not accomplishing more in terms of research and university service (Kerber, 2005; Mason, 2007).

Service Expectations   The limited number of women faculty generates another problem: excessive responsibilities for service and mentoring. Faculty committees are ubiquitous at universities, and committees are expected to be diverse—that is, to include women, men, and faculty of different races. Thus, the few women and minority faculty are asked to serve on more committees than their white male peers. The same goes for advising students, particularly women and minority students. If there is only one minority woman on the faculty of a department, she's likely to be besieged by requests from the majority of graduate and undergraduate students who are women of color.

SUMMARY

In this chapter, we've examined gendered aspects of American education from elementary school through graduate and professional schools. Today both sexes face gender-based issues, expectations, and biases in educational institutions. Males, especially boys in the early years of schooling, are disadvantaged by a system that doesn't accommodate their developmental status. As males progress through school, they are increasingly successful and are more likely than women students to attract faculty mentors, particularly in graduate and professional school. For female students, the reverse sequence is more common. They tend to be quite successful through high school and perhaps college, but they often hit barriers when they enter graduate and professional school, particularly in math and sciences.

The peer culture on college campuses further encourages male and female students to conform to particular gender ideals, which can be harmful. Male peer cultures tend to link masculinity with drinking, aggression, and sexual activity, including nonconsensual sex. Female peer cultures too often encourage campus women to attempt to meet the impossible ideal of effortless perfection.

We also looked at gender biases and pressures experienced by faculty. Both men and women are disadvantaged by current leave policies that make it nearly impossible to be both a good faculty member and a good parent. Further, male faculty often feel they cannot take family leave because doing so would lead others to perceive them as not living up to expectations of men. Discrimination in hiring, promotion, and salaries continues to be a problem at colleges and universities across the nation, as does the disparate expectations for service that women and men faculty members face.

Our examination warrants a mixed report card for America's schools. Discrimination and disadvantage based on sex and gender have been greatly reduced for students. There has been less progress for faculty.

Key Terms

The terms following are defined in this chapter on the pages indicated, as well as in alphabetical order in the book's glossary, which begins on page 325. The text's companion website (**http://www.cengage.com/communication/wood/genderedlives10e**) also provides interactive flash cards and crossword puzzles to help you learn these terms and the concepts they represent.

culture of romance 202   invisible hand discrimination 205

effortless perfection 201   Title IX 197

Gender Online

1. Learn more about Title IX by visiting: **http://www.titleix.info**.
2. Information about the United Nations' education initiative for girls can be found at: **http://www.ungei.org/**.
3. Online search terms: "effortless perfection," "peer pressure," "single-sex education."

Reflection and Discussion

1. Talk with male and female athletes on your campus to find out the extent to which they perceive that your school complies with Title IX.
2. If you could make three changes in elementary schools, with the goal of making them work better for boys and girls, what changes would you make?
3. Reread the material I present in the box Exploring Gendered Lives: Catch-22 on page 206. If your campus has a student-run website for evaluating faculty (often only students can access these), read the evaluations of male and female faculty. To what extent do you see patterns similar to those described in the box?
4. What is your opinion on the desirability of single-sex schools? What do you see as the advantages and disadvantages both for students in the schools and for society?

Recommended Resources

1. Peg Tyre. (2008). *The Trouble with Boys: A Surprising Report Card on our Sons, Their Problems at School, and What Parents and Educators Must Do*. New York: Crown. This book, which was a reference for the chapter, gives a thoughtful summary of barriers boys and men face in educational institutions. The book is written for general audiences.
2. Laura Sessions Stepp. (2007). *Unhooked: How Young Women Pursue Sex, Delay Love and Lose at Both*. New York: Penguin/Riverhead. Stepp's book gives in-depth portraits of young college women who participate in the "hook up culture" that is part of many campuses today.

The doors we open and close each day decide the lives we live.
Flora Whittenmore

GENDERED CLOSE RELATIONSHIPS

CHAPTER 9

Knowledge Challenge:

1. To what extent are talking and engaging in shared activities equally important for creating and sustaining intimacy?
2. Do women or men typically fall in love faster?
3. Are heterosexual or homosexual relationships more equitable?

Perhaps you have found yourself in situations such as those that Mark and Paige describe on page 210. For Mark, as for most people socialized into masculinity, communicating is important when you need to address an issue or solve a problem, but he doesn't see the point in talking extensively about small stuff. For Paige, it's incomprehensible that Ed can work on his paper when there is a problem between them. She doesn't realize that working on the paper is Ed's way of coping with his distress about their argument. If Paige and Mark do not figure out that their gendered viewpoints are creating misunderstandings, they will continue to experience frustration in their relationships.

In this chapter, we will focus on gender dynamics in close relationships. To begin our discussion, we will consider masculine and feminine ways of experiencing and expressing closeness. Then, we'll explore gendered patterns in friendships and romantic relationships. This chapter should give you insight into different ways that people build and communicate closeness.

THE MEANING OF PERSONAL RELATIONSHIPS

Of the many relationships we form, only a few become really personal. These are the ones that occupy a special place in our lives and affect us most deeply. **Personal relationships** are those in which partners depend on each other for various things from affection to material assistance. In personal relationships,

209

partners expect affection, companionship, time, energy, and assistance with the large and small issues in life. Also, partners in personal relationships regard each other as unique individuals who cannot be replaced. Most of our relationships are social or professional; we can replace the people in them, and the function of the relationship will continue. If a casual friend moves, a replacement may be found; if a business associate goes to another company, we can find a new work colleague; if your golfing buddy relocates, you can find another golfing partner. When a personal partner leaves or dies, however, the relationship ends, although we may continue to feel connected to the person who is no longer with us.

▼

Mark   *Sometimes I just don't know what goes on in Ellen's head. We can have a minor problem—like an issue between us, and it's really not serious stuff. But can we let it go? No way with Ellen. She wants "to talk about it." And I mean talk and talk and talk and talk. There's no end to how long she can talk about stuff that really doesn't matter. I tell her that she's analyzing the relationship to death, and I don't want to do that. She insists that we need "to talk things through." Why can't we just have a relationship, instead of always having to talk about it?*

▼

Paige   *Honestly, I almost left my boyfriend when we had our first fight after moving in together. It was really a big one about how to be committed to our relationship and also do all the other stuff that we have to do. It was major. And after we'd yelled for a while, there seemed to be nothing else to do—we were just at a stalemate in terms of conflict between what each of us wanted. So Ed walked away, and I sat fuming in the living room. When I finally left the living room, I found him working away on a paper for one of his courses, and I was furious. I couldn't understand how he could concentrate on work when we were so messed up. How in the world could he just put us aside and get on with his work? I felt like it was a really clear message that he wasn't very committed.*

MODELS OF PERSONAL RELATIONSHIPS

Differences in masculine and feminine orientations to close relationships usually—but not always—coincide with male and female approaches to relationships. Yet, researchers disagree about what the differences mean. Some scholars argue that masculine orientations are inferior to feminine ones, while others think that the two styles are different yet equally valid. We'll consider each of these viewpoints.

The Male Deficit Model   Because our society views women as interpersonally sensitive, it is widely assumed that feminine ways of forming relationships and interacting with others are "the right ways." Sharing the cultural assumption that women are better than men at relating to others, a number of researchers claim that a masculine style of building and maintaining relationships is inadequate. This view, the **male deficit model**, maintains that men are less skilled in developing and sustaining personal relationships.

The central assumption of the male deficit model is that personal, emotional talk is the hallmark of intimacy. With this assumption in mind, researchers began to study how women and men interact in close relationships. A classic investigation (Caldwell & Peplau, 1982) measured the intimacy of men's and women's same-sex friendships by the amount of intimate information disclosed between friends. As women generally self-disclose more than men, it is not surprising that the researchers concluded that women were more intimate than men. Such findings led to judgments that men's ways of relating are deficient. Some researchers called men's inexpressiveness "a tragedy of our society" (Balswick & Peek, 1976). Based on this line of research, men were advised to overcome their deficiencies, get in touch with their feelings, and learn to communicate openly and expressively.

Edwin   *I don't have any problem being emotionally sensitive or expressing my feelings. I may not go on forever about my feelings, but I know what they are, and I can express them fine. It's just that the way I express my feelings is different from the way most girls I know express their feelings. I'm not dramatic or sentimental or gushy, but I have ways of showing how I feel. not dramatic or sentimental or gushy, but I have ways of showing how I feel.*

The tendency to privilege feminine ways of relating and disparage masculine ways was strengthened by one of the men's movements we discussed in Chapter 4. Male feminists thought that men were generally emotionally repressed and would be enriched by becoming more aware and expressive of their feelings, and many men worked to develop and express emotions more openly in their relationships. In the 1980s, the male deficit model prevailed. Researchers claimed that men "feel threatened by intimacy" (Mazur & Olver, 1987, p. 533); that men are "lacking in mutual self-disclosure, shared feelings and other demonstrations of emotional closeness" (Williams, 1985, p. 588); that men suffer from "stunted emotional development" (Balswick, 1988); and that men do not know how to experience or express feelings (Aukett, Ritchie, & Mill, 1988).

Much academic and popular sentiment still holds that many men are deficient in their ability to express emotions and to care. A number of publications in the late 1990s and early part of this century state that personal disclosures are the crux of intimacy, that women have more intimate relationships than men do, that boys' friendships lack the emotional depth of girls' friendships, and that males focus on activities to avoid intimacy (Burleson, 1997; Oliker, 2001).

The assumption underlying the male deficit model is that verbal, emotional expressiveness and personal disclosures are the best ways to create closeness. Gradually, however, a few researchers began to question this assumption, leading to a second interpretation of differences between how men and women, in general, create and express closeness.

The Alternate Paths Model   The **alternate paths model** proposes that there are different and equally valid paths to closeness. This model agrees with the male deficit model that gendered socialization is the root of differences between feminine and masculine styles of relating. It departs from the deficit model, however, in two important ways. First, the alternate paths model does not presume that masculine people lack feelings or that emotional depth is unimportant to them. Rather, the alternate paths explanation suggests that masculine socialization leads most men to find it uncomfortable to verbally expressing some feelings and, further, that it limits men's opportunities to practice emotional talk.

Second, the alternate paths model argues that masculine people do express closeness, but in an alternate way than feminine people do. According to this model, masculine and feminine ways of expressing closeness are different, or alternate, and the two ways are equally valid.

The alternate paths model challenges the research used to support the male deficit model. Françoise Cancian (1987, 1989) claims that the ways in which we have learned to think about intimacy are heavily gendered. In Western culture, she suggests, we use a **"feminine ruler"** to define and measure closeness. She argues that using a specifically feminine ruler (emotional talk) misrepresents masculine modes of caring in the same way that using male standards to measure women's speech misrepresents women's communication. Cancian (1987) states that "there is a distinctive masculine style of love … but it is usually ignored by scholars and the general public" (p. 78).

Influenced by this viewpoint, Scott Swain (1989) studied men's perceptions of their close friendships. He discovered that many men develop a closeness "in the doing"—a connection that grows out of doing things together. For men, Swain concluded, engaging in activities is not an avoidance of intimacy but an alternate and equally legitimate way to create and express intimacy. Following Swain's lead, other studies showed that men's friendships are as intimate as women's, but closeness between men generally doesn't grow primarily out of emotional talk and self-disclosure and it is not primarily expressed in those ways (Clark, 1998; Sherrod, 1989). Research has also shown that father-son relationships are built largely on doing things together (Morman & Floyd, 2006). For many men, like Paige's boyfriend, talking about problems may be less effective than diversionary activities to relieve stress (Metts, 2006a; Riessman, 1990).

Additional research provides further insight into gendered communication in close relationships. In a study of how men and women communicate support, Daena Goldsmith and Susan Dun (1997) found that women tend to engage in emotional as well as instrumental forms of communication. Similarly, Françoise Cancian and Stacey Oliker (2000) found that women friends enjoy activities such as doing things together and helping each other out. In general, most men engage in less explicit emotional communication, yet most men do experience and express emotions in a range of ways (Chapman & Hendler, 1999). Further, as Paul Wright (2006) notes, many of the activities in which men engage enhance emotional closeness. Camping, for instance, provides a rich opportunity to share thoughts and feelings. Some current TV shows feature friendships between straight men that are emotionally close.

The gender of the person needing support may be as important as the gender of the person offering support. Communication scholars Jerold Hale, Rachael Tighe, and Paul Mongeau (1997) report that women typically engage in more sensitive comforting messages than men do. However, both sexes are more overtly sensitive when trying to comfort women than when trying to comfort men. Further, men offer more sensitive comforting communication in response to major stresses, whereas women tend to provide sensitive comfort for both major stresses and daily events.

From this research, we may conclude that masculine individuals less often express their feelings in feminine ways, just as feminine individuals less frequently express theirs in masculine ways. Notice that we are discussing the frequency with which each gender engages in particular behaviors. We are not saying that each gender engages exclusively in either instrumental or expressive behavior. As we've seen, there's a lot of overlap. This suggests that the most effective communicators are "bilingual"—they understand and use both ways of expressing and experiencing intimacy. As we explore feminine and masculine communication in friendships and romantic commitments, remember that there may be different but equally valuable ways to build and communicate closeness. The goal is to understand and learn from each orientation.

GENDERED STYLES OF FRIENDSHIP

Let's begin by noting that there are many similarities between the friendships of most men and most women. Both sexes value close friends and invest in them. Also, both sexes engage in instrumental and expressive modes of building and expressing closeness, although they differ in the extent to which they use each (Monsour, 2006). Against the backdrop of commonalities in approaches to friendship, there are some differences in how women and men typically—but not invariably—build friendships and interact within them. As you read about these differences, keep in mind that they are not absolute dichotomies. That is, most men do not engage exclusively in masculine styles of friendship and most women do not engage exclusively in feminine styles. Instead, most of us engage in both styles, although a majority of women more often engage in feminine style and a majority of men more often engage in masculine style. Figure 9.1 makes the point that dialogue and doing are on a continuum, rather than exclusive categories. Most of us fall in-between the ends of the continuum.

As early as 1982, Paul Wright pointed to interaction style as a key difference between women's and men's friendships. He noted that women tend to engage each other face to face, whereas men usually interact side by side. By this, Wright meant that women are more likely than men to communicate directly and verbally with each other to share themselves and their feelings. Men more typically engage in activities that do not involve facing each other. Wright suggested that the crux of

DOING/INSTRUMENTAL   DIALOGUE/EXPRESSIVE

FIGURE 9.1 | MODES OF BUILDING AND EXPRESSING AFFECTION

friendship differs between the sexes: For men, greater emphasis is placed on doing things together; for women, greater emphasis is placed on talking and being together. Wright's research gives us a foundation for exploring the qualities of friendship between women, between men, and between men and women.

FEMININE FRIENDSHIPS: CLOSENESS IN DIALOGUE

Regardless of race, ethnicity, or economic status, a majority of women regard talk as the primary way to build and enrich friendships (Veniegas & Peplau, 1997; Wood, 2011a; Wright, 2006; Yildirim, 1997). Typically they were socialized into feminine styles of expressing themselves. Consequently, many women share their personal feelings, experiences, fears, and problems in order to know and be known by each other. In addition, women talk about their daily lives and activities. By sharing details of lives, women feel intimately connected to one another. To capture the quality of women's friendships, Caroline Becker (1987) described them as "an evolving dialogue" through which initially separate worlds are woven together into a common one. The common world of women friends grows out of ongoing communication that is the crux of closeness between women.

Women friends want to know each other in depth. To achieve this, they talk about personal feelings and disclose intimate information (Braithwaite & Kellas, 2006; Johnson, 1996; Metts, 2006b; Oliker, 1989; Reisman, 1990; Walker, 2004). They are each other's confidantes, sharing personal vulnerabilities and inner feelings. Consistent with gender socialization, communication between women friends also tends to be expressive and supportive (Campbell, 2002; Kuchment, 2004). The more permeable ego boundaries encouraged by feminine socialization cultivate skill in empathizing (Campbell, 2002).

▼

Janice   *One of the worst things about being female is not having permission to be selfish or jealous or not to care about a friend. Usually, I'm pretty nice; I feel good for my friends when good things happen to them, and I want to support them when things aren't going well. But sometimes I don't feel that way. Like right now, all my friends and I are interviewing for jobs, and my best friend just got a great offer. I've had 23 interviews and no job offers so far. I felt good for Sally, but I also felt jealous. I couldn't talk about this with her, because I'm not supposed to feel jealous or to be selfish like this. It's just not allowed, so my friends and I have to hide those feelings.*

Because most women are socialized to be attentive, emotionally supportive, and caring, it is difficult for many women to deal with feelings of envy and competitiveness toward friends. It is not that women don't experience envy and competitiveness but rather that they think it's wrong to have such feelings, because they aren't consistent with cultural prescriptions for femininity (Simmons, 2002, 2004). Many women also find it difficult to override socialization's message that they are supposed to be constantly available and caring. Thus, when women lack the time or energy required to nurture others, they may feel guilty (Eichenbaum & Orbach, 1983). The responsiveness and caring typical of women's friendships both enrich and constrain people socialized into feminine rules of relating.

It is not unusual for women friends to talk explicitly about their relationship. The friendship itself and the dynamics between the friends are matters of interest and discussion (Winstead, 1986). Many women friends are comfortable stating affection explicitly or discussing tensions within a friendship. The ability to recognize and talk about problems allows women to monitor and improve their friendships.

A final quality typical of women's friendships is breadth. With close friends, women tend not to restrict their disclosures to specific areas but invite each other into many aspects of their lives. Because women talk in detail about varied aspects of their lives, women friends often know each other in complex and layered ways.

In summary, many women's friendships give center stage to communication, which fosters disclosure, verbal expressiveness, depth and breadth of knowledge, and attentiveness to the evolving nature of the relationship. Many women feel deeply connected to friends even when they are not physically together.

EXPLORING GENDERED LIVES | **WHEN FOCUSING ON FEELINGS MAKES US FEEL BAD**

In general, women pay more attention to feelings than men do. This allows women to be in touch with their emotions and to work through feelings. But there may be a down side.

Research shows that women generally have a greater tendency than men to brood about bad feelings. Excessive brooding can lead women to get stuck in unhappy feelings and to spiral downward emotionally into depression (Nolen-Hoeksema, 2003; Shea, 1998).

Some studies have found that extended discussion of problems may actually heighten anxieties rather than reduce them (Kershaw, 2008). Researchers have coined the term *co-rumination* to refer to frequent or excessive talk—face-to-face, e-mail, IMs, text messaging and posting on social networks—between friends about the same problem. A second danger of talking excessively about problems is emotional contagion in which the person listening to another's problem feels the anxieties and depression as if it is her own.

To what extent do you find talking with friends about problems heightens your anxiety? Have you ever experienced emotional contagion?

MASCULINE FRIENDSHIPS: CLOSENESS IN THE DOING

Like women, men value friendships and count on friends to be there for them. However, activities, rather than conversation, tend to be the center of masculine friendships. Beginning in childhood, friendships between males often revolve around shared activities, particularly sports. Scott Swain's (1989) phrase "closeness in the doing" captures the way many men build friendships. More than two-thirds of the men in Swain's study described activities other than talking as the most meaningful times with friends. Engaging in sports, watching games, and doing other things together cultivate camaraderie and closeness between men. Whereas women tend to look for confidantes in friends, men more typically seek companions (Chethik, 2008; Inman, 1996; Swain, 1989; Walker, 2004; Wood & Inman, 1993). Neil Chethik (2008) explains that women are more likely to share feelings, whereas men are more likely to share space. As a reminder, we're discussing tendencies, not absolute dichotomies. Of course, women friends sometimes share space and activities, and men friends sometimes talk and confide in each other.

Growing out of the emphasis on activities is a second feature of men's friendships: an instrumental focus. Many men like to do things for people they care about (Cancian, 1987; Sherrod, 1989); their friendships involve instrumental reciprocity. For example, one helps the other repair his car, and the other provides assistance with a computer problem—an exchange of favors that allows each man to hold his own while showing he cares about the other. The masculine inclination toward instrumentality also surfaces in how men help each other through rough times. Men are less likely to disclose feelings to other men than to women or than women are to other women (Burleson, Holmstrom, & Gilstrap, 2005). Rather than engaging in explicit talk about problems as women often do, men are more likely to suggest diversionary activities that take the friend's mind off his troubles (Cancian, 1987; Riessman, 1990).

▼

Keith   *My best friend and I almost never sit and just talk. Mainly, we do things together, like go places or shoot hoops or watch games on TV. When we do talk, we talk about what we have done or plan to do or what's happening in our lives, but we don't say much about how we feel. I don't think we need to. You can say a lot without words.*

The masculine emphasis on doing things together may explain why men's friendships are less likely than women's to last if one friend moves away. According to Mary Rohlfing (1995), women friends can sustain their closeness through phone calls, letters, and electronic mail. It's more difficult to shoot hoops or have jam sessions with someone who lives miles away.

Third, men's friendships often involve "covert intimacy" (Swain, 1989). Male friends tend to signal affection by teasing one another, engaging in friendly competition, and exchanging playful punches and backslaps. Most males learn very early in life that physical displays of affection between men are prohibited except in specific situations such as sports (Hunter & Mallon, 2000). According to Kory Floyd (1995, 1996a, 1996b, 1997a, 1997b), both women and men consider overt expressions of affection important, yet men are likely to restrict them to opposite-sex relationships, whereas women employ them in both same-sex and opposite-sex relationships. Compared to women friends, says Floyd, men "simply communicate affection in different, more 'covert' ways so as to avoid the possible ridicule that more overt expression might invite" (1997b, p. 78).

Finally, men's close friendships are often, although not always, more restricted in scope than women's close friendships. Men tend to have different friends for various spheres of interest (Wright, 1988). Thus, Jim might play racquetball with Mike, work on cars with Clay, and enjoy collaborating with Malcolm on work projects. Because men tend to focus friendships on particular activities, they may not share as many dimensions of their lives with friends as women tend to do. Overall, then, men's friendships emphasize shared activities, instrumental demonstrations of affection, covert intimacy, and defined spheres of interaction.

In summary, gender-linked communication patterns characterize most same-sex friendships. Women tend to rely on personal communication to share themselves and their lives and build friendships. Men more typically create and express closeness by sharing activities and interests and by doing things with and for each other. In other words, men tend to bond nonverbally through sharing experiences, whereas women typically become intimate through communicating verbally. These gender-linked tendencies, however, are not absolute, and men's and women's friendship styles are not dichotomous. As we've noted, most men engage in expressive communication and most women engage in instrumental communication.

Closeness in dialogue is common in friendships between women.

▼

Lee   *I don't know what girls get out of sitting around talking about problems all the time. What a downer. When something bad happens to me, like I blow a test or break up with a girl, the last thing I want is to talk about it. I already feel bad enough. What I want is something to distract me from how lousy I feel. That's where having buddies really matters. They know you feel bad and help you out by taking you out drinking or starting a pickup game or something that gets your mind off the problems. They give you breathing room and some escape from troubles; girls just wallow in troubles.*

FRIENDSHIPS BETWEEN WOMEN AND MEN

Friendships between the sexes pose unique challenges and offer special opportunities for growth. Because our culture so heavily emphasizes gender, it is difficult for women and men not to see each other in sexual terms. Even when cross-sex friends are not sexually involved, an undertone of sexuality often permeates their friendship.

Another tension in friendships between women and men arises from sex-segregated socialization. Beginning in childhood, males and females are often separated (Monsour, 2002, 2006). We have Boy Scouts and Girl Scouts rather than Scouts, and many athletic teams are still sex segregated. As boys and girls interact with same-sex peers, they learn the norms of gendered speech communities.

Despite these difficulties, many women and men do form friendships with each other and find them rewarding (West, Anderson, & Duck, 1996). In friendships between masculine and feminine people, each person has something unique to offer as the expert in particular areas. For many women, a primary benefit of friendships with men is companionship that is less emotionally intense than that with women friends. In a study of African-American men's friendships with feminist women, Aaronette White (2006) reported that the men found the friendships personally affirming and provided a context for them to practice interpersonal skills. For men, an especially valued benefit of closeness with women is access to emotional and expressive support, which tends to be less overtly communicated in friendships between men.

▼

Emily   *Last week Jay came by my place to talk. I've known Jay for a year—we're both in band—but we're not close friends or anything. He told me his parents are divorcing and he was really, really upset. He said it just tore him up, and he was crying and everything. Later, I saw Jay's closest friend Rob and asked how Jay was doing with his parents' divorce, but Rob didn't know a thing about it. I thought it was really strange that Jay hadn't told his closest friend but told me.*

Many men say they receive more emotional support and therapeutic release with women than with men friends. Women also say they receive more emotional support from women than from men friends (Koesten, 2004; Werking, 1997). There is also evidence that one reason some men are reluctant to be especially emotionally supportive of other men is because doing so is inconsistent with their views of masculinity and their personal masculine gender identity (Burleson, Holmstrom, & Gilstrap, 2005). In cross-sex friendships, men generally talk more and get more attention, response, and support than they offer. A majority of both sexes report that friendships with women are closer and more satisfying than those with men (Koesten, 2004; Werking, 1997). This may explain why both sexes tend to seek women friends in times of stress and why both women and men are generally more comfortable self-disclosing to women than to men (Monsour, 2006).

GENDERED ROMANTIC RELATIONSHIPS

Nowhere are gendered roles as salient as in heterosexual romantic relationships. The cultural script for romance is well known to most of us (Laner & Ventrone, 2002; Metts, 2006a; Mongeau, Serewicz, Henningsen, & Davis, 2006) and appears to be understood and followed in some other cultures. The script tells us:

- Feminine women and masculine men are desirable.
- Men should initiate, plan, and direct most activities in a relationship.
- Women should facilitate conversation, generally defer to men, but control sexual activity.
- Men should excel in status and earning money, and women should assume primary responsibility for the relationships.

As we will see, this script continues to be played out in many heterosexual relationships.

DEVELOPING ROMANTIC INTIMACY

Personal ads offer insight into what heterosexual men and women seek in romantic partners. Ads written by men looking for women often place priority on stereotypically feminine physical qualities, using words such as *attractive, slender, petite,* and *sexy.* Women's ads for male partners frequently emphasize status and success and include words such as *secure, ambitious, professional,* and *successful.* In reality, as in personal ads, our views of desirable partners often reflect cultural gender expectations—success and status in males, beauty and nurturing tendencies in females. That may explain why, in online communication, men are more likely than women to misrepresent their personal assets (e.g., financial worth), and women are more likely than men to misrepresent their weight (Hall, Park, Song, & Cody, 2010).

The conventional heterosexual dating script calls for men to take the initiative. Although many people claim they don't accept this pattern, most heterosexuals still conform to it. However, there are exceptions. Androgynous individuals, who break from rigid cultural definitions of masculinity and femininity, behave in more flexible, less stereotypical ways (DeLucia, 1987). And there is less role playing between gay men and even less between lesbian women (Kurdek & Schmitt, 1986b, 1986c, 1987; Patterson, 2000; Rutter & Schwartz, 1996).

Is one sex more romantic than the other? Contrary to popular beliefs, research indicates that men tend to fall in love faster and harder than women. They tend to be more active, impulsive, sexualized, and game-playing than women, whose styles of loving are more pragmatic and friendship-focused (Bierhoff, 1996; Cancian, 1987; Hendrick & Hendrick, 1986, 1996; Riessman, 1990). For instance, men may see love as taking trips to romantic places, spontaneously making love, and surprising their partners. Women more typically think of extended conversations, sharing deep feelings, and physical contact that isn't necessarily sexual.

Many things have changed in romantic relationships between women and men, but one thing that hasn't is attitudes toward sexual activity (Hill, 2002; Morr & Mongeau, 2004). Some members of both sexes enjoy casual sex, or "hook ups." Beyond that scene, women generally perceive sexual behavior as more closely linked to emotional involvement than men do (O'Sullivan & Gaines, 1998). Reflecting these same gendered patterns, lesbians tend to date for a while before becoming sexual, whereas gay men are more likely to have sex early in their relationships (Scrivner, 1997).

Women are more likely than men to focus on relationship dynamics—a pattern that holds regardless of sexual orientation (Metts, 2006a, 2006b; Patterson, 2000; Wood, 1993b). Lesbian partners tend to take mutual responsibility for nurturing and supporting relationships (Goldberg & Perry-Jenkins, 2007). Gay men, conversely, are less likely to focus on nurturing the relationship and providing emotional leadership (Kurdek & Schmitt, 1986b; Patterson, 2000; Wood, 1993b). Gay men's commitment to romantic relationships is more closely linked to intangible investments such as time, effort, and self-disclosure, whereas straight men's commitment to romantic relationships is more closely tied to tangible investments such as money and possessions (Lehmiller, 2010).

Committed heterosexual relationships, in general, continue to reflect traditional gender roles endorsed by the culture (Canary & Wahba, 2006; Wood, 2009a). Men tend to be perceived as the head of the family and are expected to be the major breadwinner; women tend to assume primary responsibility for domestic labor and child care; and men tend to have greater power.

Because gender distinctions are less salient, many gay and lesbian relationships do not follow the roles typical of heterosexual couples. Both gay and lesbian commitments often resemble best-friend relationships with the added dimensions of sexuality and romance. Following the best-friends model, long-term lesbian relationships tend to be monogamous and high in emotionality, disclosure, and support, and partners have the most equality of all types of relationships (Huston & Schwartz, 1996; Kurdek & Schmitt, 1986c; Murphy, 1997; Parker-Pope, 2008).

▼

Gina   *I consider myself a very independent, nontraditional woman. I plan a career in law, and I am very assertive. But when it comes to dating relationships, I fall into some really conventional patterns. I think a woman should be able to call a guy she likes and ask him out, but I can't bring myself to do that. I also kind of expect guys to pay for dates, at least until a relationship gets serious, even though I think it's more fair to split expenses. I expect the guy I'm with to make plans and decisions about a date, and I expect myself to be more interpersonally sensitive. I guess some of the old roles do persist.*

GENDERED PATTERNS IN COMMITTED RELATIONSHIPS

Gendered orientations influence four dimensions of long-term love relationships: modes of expressing care, needs for autonomy and connection, responsibility for relational maintenance, and power. As we will discover, these dynamics are influenced by the distinctive styles and priorities emphasized by masculine and feminine socialization.

▼

Phil   *What does my girlfriend want? That's all I want to know. She says, if I really loved her, I'd want to be together and talk all the time. I tell her all I do for her. I fix her car when it's broken; I give her rides to places; I helped her move last semester. We've talked about marriage, and I plan to take care of her then, too. I will work all day and overtime to give her a good home and to provide for our family. But she says, "Don't tell me what you do for me," like do is a bad word. Now, why would I do all this stuff if I didn't love her? Just tell me that.*

Gendered Modes of Expressing Affection   As we have seen, the masculine mode of expressing affection is primarily instrumental and activity-focused, whereas the feminine mode is more emotionally expressive and talk-focused. Women often feel hurt and shut out if men don't want to discuss feelings and the relationship. Conversely, some men feel resentful or intruded on when women push them to be emotionally expressive.

For many women, ongoing conversation about feelings and daily activities is a primary way to express and enrich personal relationships (Peretti & Abplanalp, 2004; Wood, 2011a). The masculine speech communities in which most men are socialized, however, regard the primary reasons to talk as solving problems and achieving goals. Thus, unless there is a problem, men often find it unnecessary to talk about a relationship, whereas many women feel that ongoing talk keeps problems from developing. Generally, men are more likely to express caring by doing things for and with their partners. Thus, the different genders may not recognize each other's ways of communicating care.

More feminine or androgynous ways of expressing care are valued by both sexes. Research shows that men as well as women are more satisfied with partners who are willing to engage in intimate self-disclosure, to give emotionally supportive responses, and to be sensitive and empathic (Lamke, Sollie, Durbin, & Fitzpatrick, 1994). Yet, most of us also count on traditionally masculine modes of caring—we feel cherished when a romantic partner does things for us and wants to do things with us.

The cultural bias favoring feminine modes of expressing love is illustrated by a classic study (Wills, Weiss, & Patterson, 1974). The researchers wanted to know how husbands' demonstrations of affection affected wives' feelings. To find out, they instructed husbands to engage in different degrees of affectionate behavior toward their wives, and then the wives' responses were measured. When one wife showed no indication of receiving affection, the researchers called the husband to see if he had followed instructions. Somewhat irately, the husband said he certainly

had—he had thoroughly washed his wife's car. Not only did his wife not experience this as affection, but the researchers themselves concluded that he had "confused" instrumental with affectionate behaviors. Doing something helpful was entirely disregarded as a valid way to express affection! This exemplifies the cultural bias toward feminine views of loving. It also illustrates a misunderstanding that plagues many heterosexual love relationships.

Sharon   *Most of this course has been a review of stuff I already knew, but the unit on how men and women show they love each other was news to me. I'm always fussing at my boyfriend for not showing me he cares. I tell him he takes me for granted and if he really loved me he'd want to talk more about personal, deep stuff inside him. But he bought me a book I'd been wanting, and a couple of weeks ago he spent a whole day fixing my car because he was worried about whether it was safe for me—I thought of that when we talked about the guy in the experiment who washed his wife's car. I guess he* has *been showing he cares for me, but I haven't been seeing it.*

Gay and lesbian couples tend to share perspectives about how to communicate affection. Gay men generally engage in more emotional and intimate talk than straight men but less than women of any sexual orientation. Lesbians, on the other hand, generally share responsibility for taking care of a relationship and build the most expressive and nurturing communication climates of any type of couple (Goldberg & Perry-Jenkins, 2007; Patterson, 2000; Wood, 1993b). Lesbian partners' mutual attentiveness to nurturing and emotional openness may explain why lesbians report more satisfaction with their romantic relationships than gays or heterosexuals do (Goldberg & Perry-Jenkins, 2007; Kurdek & Schmitt, 1986c).

Gendered Preferences for Autonomy and Connection   Autonomy and connection are two basic needs of all humans (Baxter, 1990). We all need to feel that we have both personal freedom and meaningful interrelatedness with others. Yet, gender affects how much of each of these we seek and find comfortable. Masculine individuals tend to want greater autonomy and less connection than feminine people, whose relative priorities are generally the reverse. We all want some autonomy and some connection, yet the proportionate weights that feminine and masculine people assign to each generally differ.

Desires for different degrees of autonomy and connection frequently generate friction in close relationships. Many couples are familiar with a pattern called *demand-withdraw* (Caughlin & Vangelisti, 2000; Christensen & Heavey, 1990; Wegner, 2005). In this pattern, one partner feels distant and tries to close the distance by engaging in personal, intimate talk, and the other partner withdraws from a degree of closeness that stifles his or her need for autonomy. The more one demands talk, the more the other withdraws; the more one withdraws from interaction, the more the other demands talk and time together. Both men and women are likely to withdraw when partners demand or request change; however, the intensity of withdrawal is greater when a woman requests change in a man than when a man requests change in a woman (Sagrestano, Heavey, & Christensen, 1998). Socialized toward independence, masculine individuals tend to be more comfortable when they have some distance from others, whereas feminine people tend to be more comfortable with close connections. Ironically, the very thing that creates closeness for one partner impedes it for the other.

▼

Jeff   *I get really frustrated talking about relationships with girls I've dated. It seems like they feel a need to discuss the relationship every time we're together. I don't get the point. I mean, why talk about a relationship if everything's going along fine? Why not just be in the relationship and enjoy it?*

▼

Karin   *I don't know why straight women put up with partners who don't work on their relationship. Angie and I both invest a lot of time and emotion in taking care of our relationship because it matters to both of us. I talk to straight friends and hear them complaining about how their partners never even notice the relationship. I would never settle for that.*

More hurtful than the demand-withdraw pattern itself, however, are partners' tendencies to interpret each other according to rules that don't apply to the other's behavior. For instance, to think that a man who wants time alone doesn't love his partner is to interpret his withdrawal according to a feminine rule. Similarly, to perceive as intrusive a woman who wants intimate conversation is to judge her by masculine standards. Although the demand-withdraw pattern may persist in relationships, we can eliminate the poison of misinterpretation by respecting different needs for autonomy and connection.

Gendered Responsibility for Relational Health   Lesbian couples tend to share responsibility for their relationships. Because most lesbians, like most heterosexual women, learn feminine ways of thinking and acting, both partners tend to be sensitive to interpersonal dynamics and interested in talking about their relationship and working through problems (Canary & Whaba, 2006; Schwartz & Rutter, 1998; Wood, 1993e).

Against the standard set by lesbians, heterosexual couples do not fare as well in distributing responsibility for relational health. In heterosexual relationships, both men and women tend to assume that women have primary responsibility for keeping relationships on track (Canary & Wahba, 2006; Cubbans & Vannoy, 2004; DeMaris, 2007; Stafford, Dutton, & Haas, 2000).

The expectation that one person should take care of relationships burdens one partner with the responsibility of keeping a relationship satisfying. In addition, it is difficult for one person to meet this responsibility if the other person doesn't acknowledge and work on matters that jeopardize relational health. The partner who is expected to safeguard the relationship may be perceived as a nag by the one who fails to recognize problems until they become very serious. Not surprisingly, research shows that the highest level of couple satisfaction exists when both partners share responsibility for the relationship (Cubbans & Vannoy, 2004; DeMaris, 2007).

Gendered Power Dynamics   Historically, the person who makes the money or the most money has had the greater power in heterosexual romantic relationships, and that person traditionally has been the male. As you might predict, problems fostered by believing that men should be more powerful are not prominent in lesbian relationships. Conversely, in some gay relationships partners constantly compete for status and dominance (Kurdek & Schmitt, 1986a, 1986b; Rutter & Schwartz, 1996).

As we noted in Chapter 7, the belief that men should be the primary breadwinners doesn't match reality for the growing number of two-worker households in which the woman earns as much as or more than the man. Among minorities, the trend toward greater achievement by women is especially strong. Minority women

EXPLORING GENDERED LIVES   **"I PROMISE NOT TO EXASPERATE MY HUSBAND." NOT!**

When Veronica Mendez and Gustavo Garcia married in Mexico City in 2006, their vows were not the same as those their parents took. Since 1859, the Epistle of Melchor Ocampo has been the official law for marriage ceremonies. According to the epistle, brides' vow not to exasperate their new husbands, and grooms vow to treat their new wives with "the magnanimity and generous benevolence that the strong must have for the weak" (Dellios, 2006, p. 16A). Ten years of lobbying were required to get Mexico's Congress to pass a resolution urging judges not to include the epistle in marriage services.

are twice as likely as minority men to earn college degrees (Goodman, 2006; Wilson, 2007). Further, the recession that began in 2008 has put more men than women out of work. The number of white professional men who are unemployed has doubled since 2007: More than a million of these men are unemployed, and that's not counting men who held sales jobs (another 300,000) (Marin & Dokoupil, 2011).

People who adhere to traditional views of gender in relationships are more likely to experience a decrease in both self-esteem and marital satisfaction if the woman earns more money (Helms, Prouiz, Klute, McHale, & Crouter, 2006; Waismel-Manor & Tolbert, 2010). How well couples adapt to a man earning less than a woman is influenced by the examples set by the couples' parents. Men whose fathers were actively involved in home life, sometimes as the primary home-maker, are more likely to see homemaking as compatible with masculinity. Women and men who had mothers who were successful in the paid labor force tend to see a woman's career success as consistent with femininity (Cose, 2003; Tyre & McGinn, 2003).

▼

Ernest   *As a male who was reared by a single mother, I see women differently from most of the white men I know. I and a lot of blacks see women as our equals more than most white men do. We treat the women in our lives with a lot more respect than middle-class white males. Men who were raised by a single mother understand women and their plight better than most white men. We know we and black women are in it together.*

In heterosexual relationships, the belief that men have more power than women is often reflected in the distribution of labor in the home. Although the majority of heterosexual families today have two wage earners, the housework and the care of children, parents, and other relatives continue to be done primarily by women (Baxter, Hewitt, & Western, 2005; Gerson, 2004; Medved, 2009; Sheehy, 2010; Wood, 2011b, c). This holds true even when women earn consider-ably more than their male partners (Baxter, et al., 2005; Tichenor, 2005). In fact, men who don't have jobs in the paid labor force and whose female partners work outside the home engage in *less* childcare and home maintenance than men who have jobs in the paid labor force (Dokoupil, 2009). As a point of comparison, unemployed women spend twice as much time on child care and housework as employed women (Dokoupil, 2009).

The reasons for women's and men's unequal contributions to domestic labor are complex. Al DeMaris and Monica Longmore (1996) have identified three primary reasons. The first is gender ideology. Men and women with more tradi-tional beliefs about gender are more likely than people with less traditional gen-der beliefs to perceive it as appropriate for women to do most of the domestic labor. The second reason is women's alternatives to a relationship. Women who have desirable alternatives to their current relationships have more leverage to persuade their partners to participate more in domestic labor. The third reason is equity. Most people prefer equitable relationships—ones in which they and their partners invest relatively equally and in which both partners benefit equally. The extent to which partners are committed to equity affects how they divide domestic chores. These three reasons often interact. For instance, women with more traditional gender ideology may perceive it as equitable for them to do the bulk of housework, whereas women with less traditional beliefs about gender may perceive it as inequitable for them to do more housework than their partners. Cultural factors may also affect the three reasons DeMaris and Longmore identified. Black and Hispanic men are less likely than white men to perceive it as inequitable when their female partners do the majority of housework (DeMaris & Longmore, 1996).

Dubbing the extra domestic labor that women typically do the "**second shift**," sociologist Arlie Hochschild (Hochschild with Machung, 2003) reports that the majority of wives employed outside their homes have a second-shift job in the home. Child care is a big part of the second shift for many women. Mothers with college educations spend an average of 21.2 hours a week with their children and mothers with less education spend 15.2 hours. Today's fathers are also spending more time with their children than did their own fathers. College-educated fathers spend an average of 9.6 hours a week with their children, and less educated fathers spend an average of 6.8 hours a week with children. That's more than double the amount of time fathers in 1977 spent with children. Fathers under 29 years of age spend more time with children than older fathers do (Council on Contemporary Families, 2010; Parker-Pope, 2010c; Ramey & Ramey, 2009).

As Lynn Hallstein (2008) points out, many women think that because becoming a mother is a choice, they are responsible for the consequences of that choice. In other words, many women who continue working in the paid labor force after becoming mothers accept the idea that they have to figure out how to manage motherhood and a career. They are reluctant to ask their workplaces to make accommodations and they often find their partners are not willing to invest as much time and effort in parenting as they are.

Men still do less housework than women (Council on Contemporary Families, 2010). In part, this may reflect masculine socialization, which emphasizes domestic chores less than feminine socialization. Because girls and young women are socialized to perform more traditionally "feminine" tasks such as laundry, cooking, and dusting, they typically have developed skill in these tasks by the time they set up an adult household. In addition, many women have higher standards for housekeeping than their male partners. This may lead women to criticize how their male partners perform the tasks and to redo or take over tasks that their male partners aren't performing to the women's satisfaction (Wiesmann, Boeije, van Doorne-Huiskes, & den Dulk, 2008). Responses like these understandably may discourage men from participating more actively in homemaking. Men may also feel that it's not fair for their partners to expect them to comply with housekeeping standards they don't endorse. Only when couples agree on a standard for housekeeping is it fair to expect both partners to follow that standard.

> **Gloria**   *I'm a mother and a professional and a part-time student, but I am not the only one who takes care of my home and family. That's a shared responsibility in our home. My daughter and son each cook dinner one night a week, and they switch off on chores like laundry and vacuuming. My husband and I share the other chores 50-50. Children don't resist a fair division of labor if their parents model it and show that it's expected of them.*

We should also note that much of the work women do in the home is generally more taxing and less gratifying. For instance, whereas many of the contributions men typically make are sporadic, variable, and flexible in timing (for example, mowing the lawn), the tasks women typically do are repetitive, routine, and constrained by deadlines (Canary & Wahba, 2006; Hochschild with Machung, 2003). Women are also more likely to do multiple tasks simultaneously (for example, helping a child with homework while preparing dinner). Whereas mothers tend to be constantly on duty, fathers more typically take responsibility for irregular tasks such as fixing broken appliances and doing car maintenance. Fathers are also more likely than mothers to engage in occasional fun child-care activities, such as trips to the park.

> **Aikau**   *My mother works all day at her job. She also cooks all of the meals for the family, does all of the housework, and takes care of my younger brother and sister. When my mother goes out of town on business, she fixes all of the family meals and freezes them before she leaves. She also arranges for day care and cleans very thoroughly before she leaves. My father expects this of her, and she expects it of herself.*

It's interesting to trace changes in men's participation in child care and household tasks. In the 1960s and earlier, few men did much to care for home and children. Between the mid-1970s and the mid-1980s, men's contributions increased considerably—and then stagnated at that level (Bronstein, 2004; Hochschild & Ehrenreich, 2003).

The recession that began in 2008 has propelled changes in men's involvement in home life. Between 2008 and 2010, millions of Americans lost jobs, and the majority of them were men. Currently, nearly 20% of men between the age of 25 and 54 are unemployed. This is the highest percentage of unemployed men during earning years since 1948 when the labor bureau began keeping track (Brooks, 2010; Marin & Dokoupil, 2011). As a consequence, many men who are out of work have become stay-at-home dads while their partners have become sole breadwinners. One estimate is that 2 million fathers (1 in 15) is currently a stay-at-home dad (Yen, 2011). The shift from fast-and-furious deal making and command decision making to picking children up from school and entertaining them is difficult. Laid off after 20 years in a Fortune

---

EXPLORING GENDERED LIVES | **SCIENTISTS AND THE SECOND SHIFT**

In 2009 Carol Greider got the call every scientist dreams of: The voice at the other end of the line was in Stokholm and told her she had won the Nobel Prize in Physiology or Medicine. Where was Dr. Greider when she got the call? In her lab? Writing a scientific paper? Nope, she was folding laundry, one of the many home responsibilities she assumes.

Greider isn't alone. According to a 2010 study of scientists in the United States, female scientists do twice as much cooking, cleaning, and laundry as male scientists (Schiebinger & Gilmartin, 2010). And then there's child care. Dr. Greider, for example, has two school-age children, and she takes much of the responsibility for going to their sports events, taking them to and from play dates, and so forth. And that's in addition to the 56 hours spent in paid labor in an average week (Laster, 2010; Philipsen, 2008).

Can you think of ways to reduce the second shift that many women experience?

---

500 company, Andrew Emery says, "It was a big part of my identity; it's who you are. It took me a long time to fill in the blank when people asked me what I do" (Kershaw, 2009, p. E6). Yet, after the initial adjustment, many men discover opportunities and satisfaction in being full-time fathers. In fact, many of them are hoping to find reemployment in careers that enable them to spend more time with their children (Kershaw, 2009). The benefits men receive from being engaged fathers include hormonal changes that increase their resourcefulness and their ability to handle stress (Kuchinskas, 2009a, 2009b).

Another way in which women's contributions to home life have been greater is in terms of **psychological responsibility**—the responsibility for remembering, planning, and making sure things get done (Hochschild with Machung, 2003). For

---

EXPLORING GENDERED LIVES | **FATHERING IN OTHER SPECIES**

Human fathers in most cultures may engage less in child care than human mothers, but fathering is a big time pursuit in some species (Angier, 2010). Among birds, males and females usually share the tasks of sitting on eggs to hatch them and fetching insects for the baby birds. In certain species of birds, such as emus and rheas, the males exclusively tend the nest.

And birds aren't the only active fathers. Male pipefish and seahorses become pregant and give birth. Some primates also emphasize the role and status of fathers. Male barbary macaques, for example, appear with infants to increase their standing in their social groups.

Can you think of reasons why males of other species might be more engaged fathers?

EXPLORING GENDERED LIVES | **THE MOMMY MYTH**

That's the title of Susan Douglas and Meredith Michaels' (2004) book. In it, they say that many American mothers today are brought up to expect motherhood to be an idyllic experience in which mothers and children spend their days engaged in happy adventures. This ideal mother enjoys her children endlessly, never wants time away from them, and certainly never raises her voice to the little darlings. Unfortunately, a lot of women find that real, day-to-day mothering is very different from the myth. They feel overwhelmed by what they are expected to do.

Judith Warner (2005b) agrees. She says the expectations of American mothers today are a recipe for the perfect madness, which is the title of her book. There is no way that any normal human being can be as endlessly patient and as engaged as today's mothers feel they are supposed to be. Because it is impossible to meet these expectations, many mothers feel inadequate and guilty. Warner, Douglas, and Michaels think that a number of factors have contributed to creating and sustaining the mommy myth. One is media. Many young mothers today were raised when "The Cosby Show" was popular. In it, the character, Clair Huxtable, Cosby's wife, was a successful attorney and an excellent mom, and she never looked at all stressed. And then there's "Dr. Laura" (Laura Schlessinger), who advises women to quit working outside the home, become full-time moms, and enjoy every minute of it. Another contributing factor is the relentless quest for perfection that characterizes American culture—whatever we do, we should do it perfectly. One way to address this, say Douglas and Michaels, is to learn what the mommy myth is and to name every instance of it you see.

What is your image of mothering?

instance, partners may agree to share responsibility for taking children to doctors and dentists, but typically the woman is expected to remember when various inoculations are due, to schedule appointments, to notice when the child needs attention, and to keep track of whose turn it is to take the child. Similarly, partners may share responsibility for preparing meals, but women usually take on the associated responsibilities of planning menus, keeping an inventory of food and cooking supplies, making shopping lists, and going to the grocery store. All of this planning and organization is a psychological responsibility that is often not counted in couples' agreements for sharing the work of a family.

The consequences of the second shift are substantial. Women who do most of the homemaking and child-care tasks are often extremely stressed, fatigued, and susceptible to illness (Babarskiene & Tweed, 2009; Hochschild with Machung, 2003), and they are at a disadvantage in their paid work because they have such heavy responsibilities at home (McDonald, Phipps, & Lethbridge, 2005). Similar stress has been found in single fathers who work a second shift (Baird, 2010; Ranson, 2001). Frustration, resentment, and conflict are also likely when only one person in a partnership bears the double responsibilities of jobs inside and outside the home (Cubbans & Vannoy, 2004; DeMaris, 2007; Erickson, 2005). In addition,

EXPLORING GENDERED LIVES | GLOBAL NANNIES

Two careers plus children may be too much! Many two-worker families find they can't fulfill all their responsibilities at home and in the workplace. One solution is to hire someone else to take care of the home, an option increasingly chosen by many dual-earner families. For the many people who want to minimize the cost of hiring full-time help for the home, the cheapest domestic labor is women from underdeveloped countries who will work for a fraction of the cost that Americans will. That solves one problem but creates another. Each year, millions of women leave Mexico, the Philippines, and other relatively poor countries to become maids and nannies for well-to-do families in the United States. Poor countries become even poorer as women migrate to the United States to work here rather than in their home countries. The result is a "care deficit" in countries that already have too few resources (Bronstein, 2004; Hochschild & Ehrenreich, 2003; Hondagneu-Sotelo, 2007).

the inequity of the arrangement is a primary source of relationship dissatisfaction and instability (Chethik, 2008; DeMaris, 2007).

Another clue to power dynamics is how couples manage conflict. Masculine individuals (whether female or male) tend to use more unilateral strategies to engage in and to avoid conflicts. They are more likely than feminine people to issue ultimatums, to refuse to listen or discuss an issue, or to assert that the partner is blowing things out of proportion, thus enacting the masculine tendency to maintain independence and protect the self. Feminine individuals more typically defer or compromise to reduce tension, and they employ indirect strategies when they do engage in conflict, which is consistent with feminine speech communities' emphasis on maintaining equality and building relationships (Rusbult, 1987; Stafford, Dutton, & Haas, 2000). As you might expect, the tension between masculine and feminine ways of exerting influence is often less pronounced in lesbian relationships, where equality is particularly high. For gay partners, power struggles are common and are sometimes a continual backdrop for the relationship (Kurdek & Schmitt, 1986b).

Finally, gendered power dynamics underlie violence and abuse, which are means of exercising dominance over others. We will cover the topic of violence in detail in Chapter 12, but we also need to acknowledge here that intimate partner violence is one manifestation of gendered power dynamics in romantic relationships. Not confined to any single group, violence cuts across race, ethnic, and class lines. Researchers estimate that at least 28% and possibly as many as 50% of women suffer physical abuse from partners, and even more suffer psychological abuse (Wood, 2001b).

Violence is inflicted primarily by men, most of whom have been socialized into masculine identities (Johnson, 2006; Wood, 2004). In the United States, every 12 to 18 seconds a woman is beaten by a man; four women each day are reported beaten to death; and women are 600% more likely to be brutalized by an intimate than are men (Wood, 2001b). Convincing evidence that violence is connected more closely to gender than to sex comes from a study by Edwin Thompson (1991). Based on reports from 336 undergraduates, Thompson found a high degree of violence in dating relationships. Sex alone, however, did not explain the violence. Thompson discovered that violence is linked to gender, with abusers—both male and female—being more masculine and less feminine in their gender orientation. This led Thompson to conclude that physical aggression is associated with the traditionally masculine emphasis on control, domination, and power.

We've seen that personal relationships reflect the expectations and orientations encouraged by feminine and masculine socialization. Gender differences surface in partners' expressions and experiences of caring, preferences for autonomy and connection, the distribution of responsibility for maintaining relationships, and power dynamics.

SUMMARY

Gendered ideas continue to shape friendships and romantic relationships. Yet, today many people feel that traditional gender roles aren't satisfying or realistic. As people discover the limits and disadvantages of traditional gender roles, they are experimenting with new ways to form and sustain relationships and their own identities within those relationships. For instance, some men choose to be stay-at-home dads because they find greater fulfillment in nurturing a family than in pursuing a career in the paid labor force. Some women discover that they are more effective and more fulfilled by work outside the home than by work inside it. And many people balance home and paid work in ways that transcend traditional roles. Examples such as these remind us that we can edit cultural scripts, using our own lives to craft alternative visions of women, men, and relationships.

Key Terms

The terms following are defined in this chapter on the pages indicated, as well as in alphabetical order in the book's glossary, which begins on page 325. The text's companion website (**http://www.cengage.com/communication/wood/genderedlives10e**) also provides interactive flash cards and crossword puzzles to help you learn these terms and the concepts they represent.

alternate paths model 212	personal relationships 209
feminine ruler 212	psychological responsibility 228
male deficit model 211	second shift 226

Recommended Resources

1. Look at personal ads on Match.com or eharmony.com. To what extent do the characteristics sought in men and women conform to gender stereotypes?
2. Online search terms: "cross-sex friends," "psychological responsibility," "second shift," "dual-worker families."

Reflection and Discussion

1. Reread the quotation on the opening page of this chapter. How could you apply this quotation to the idea of building and sustaining personal relationships?
2. To what extent do you agree with the male deficit and alternate paths models of closeness? How does the model you accept affect your behaviors and interpretations of others' behaviors?
3. Do you see gendered patterns of interaction in your romantic relationships? Does knowing about gender-linked patterns affect how you interpret what happens in your own relationships?
4. Expand your communication repertoire. If you have relied primarily on talk to build closeness, see what happens when you do things with friends. Do you experience "closeness in the doing?" If your friendships have tended to grow out of shared activities, check out what happens if you talk with friends without some activity to structure time.

Recommended Resources

1. Julia Wood & Chris Inman (1993). In a different mode: Recognizing male modes of closeness. *Journal of Applied Communication Research, 21* (pp. 279–295). This is the article that introduced the alternate paths model of closeness. At the time that we wrote the article, Chris Inman and I were team-teaching a course in gender and communication.
2. Sandra Metts. (2006). Gendered communication in dating relationships. In B. J. Dow & Julia T. Wood (Eds.), *The Sage handbook of gender and communication* (pp. 25–40). Thousand Oaks, CA: Sage.

The last of the human freedoms is to choose one's attitudes.
Victor Frankl

GENDERED ORGANIZATIONAL COMMUNICATION

CHAPTER **10**

Knowledge Challenge:

1. How much is the pay gap between women and men for full-time work?
2. Is the number of mothers with preschool children who work outside of the home increasing, decreasing, or staying the same?
3. To what extent are quotas consistent with affirmative action?

The Augusta National Golf Club had refused to admit women since it was established. This policy kept women from competing in one of the biggest tournaments—the Masters, which took place on the Augusta Club's grounds. As chair of the National Council of Women's Organizations, Martha Burk thought this was discrimination, so she organized and led a protest against the club. But the protest was not her first step. Initially, she tried more diplomatic measures. For instance, in her initial letter to the Augusta Club's chairman, Hootie Johnson, Burk politely asked him to review the club's policies and open the membership to women. Johnson's reply was not polite. He disparaged Burk in harsh language, and he dismissed her claim that not admitting women was discriminatory.

In her 2005 book, *Cult of Power,* Burk tells of her initial exchange with Johnson, and she chronicles her continued efforts to get the club to admit women members. She also shares with readers what she discovered while involved in this drama. She found out that several powerful corporate presidents were members of the club, and she learned of countless anecdotes of daily discrimination against women at their companies. She also learned that some men at the Augusta Club and elsewhere are committed to ending sex discrimination and work within their organizations to end it. Like most people who have studied sex and gender in organizations, Burk concludes that overt, blatant sex discrimination is rarely practiced in hiring, promotion, and salary decisions. Instead, the inequities between women and men in today's workplace are more subtle, more indirect, and much more difficult to name and address.

In this chapter, we discuss gender dynamics in the world of paid labor. We'll begin by identifying gender stereotypes that affect how women and men are perceived and treated in the workplace. Next, we'll examine gendered dynamics in formal and informal networks, and we'll see how these can result in inequitable treatment of women and men. Finally, we'll consider ways to redress sex and gender discrimination in organizations.

GENDERED STEREOTYPES IN THE WORKPLACE

Like all of us, people who work in organizations have views of women and men. Some of these views are gender stereotypes—broad generalizations that may or may not apply to particular women and men. We'll identify stereotypes of women and men in professional contexts.

STEREOTYPES OF WOMEN

Women in the workforce are often classified according to one of four roles, each of which reflects a deeply gendered stereotype: sex object, mother, child, or iron maiden (Aries, 1998; Jamieson, 1995; Kanter, 1977; Wood & Conrad, 1983).

Sex Object   This stereotype defines women in terms of their sex or sexuality. Frequently, it leads to judgments of women workers based on their appearance and actions. An example of this occurred when the premiere Bolshoi Theatre fired Anastasia Volochkova, one of Russia's best-known ballerinas. The reason? She was "too fat." Volochkova is at least 5′7″ tall (reports vary) and weighs 109 pounds (Kishkovsky, 2003). We saw other examples of this stereotype in the 2008 Presidential Primary. Some commentators described Republican Vice Presidential candidate, Governor Sarah Palin, as "a babe," and "hot." When Hillary Rodham Clinton campaigned in the Democratic Primary, she too was described in terms of her sexuality; however, Senator Clinton was criticized for not being sexy and feminine enough (Mandziuk, 2008).

▼

Maggie   *I worked at Hooters for a while. They had a manual you are given when you are hired at Hooters. It explains to you their discrimination policy and says they can discriminate based on age, weight and level of attractiveness. They also have make up and hair policies. Hair must be worn down and it must be done (curled or straightened), jewelry and tattoos are not allowed. Make up is required.*

Stereotyping women as sex objects contributes to sexual harassment, which roughly half the women who work outside the home have experienced (Rundblad, 2001). Harassing women is particularly prevalent in the military (Bourg & Segal,

2001; Herbert, 2009a; Smith 2006), as exemplified by the Tailhook and Aberdeen scandals in the 1990s, in which male military personnel mauled, violated, and verbally harassed female personnel. When The Citadel, a private military school in South Carolina, began admitting women, sexual assaults proliferated. According to a study that The Citadel itself conducted, 20% of the female cadets experienced sexual assault even years after women began being admitted (Smith, 2006). The just-released Pentagon data show a 9% (2,923 incidents) increase in the last year and a 25% increase in assaults reported by women serving in Iraq and Afghanistan (Herbert, 2009a). Incidents such as these reflect the continuing tendency to perceive and treat women as sex objects.

The sex-object stereotype is also used to define and harass gay men and lesbians. Like heterosexual women, gays and lesbians are often perceived primarily in terms of their sexuality and their conformity—or lack of conformity—to conventional gender roles.

▼

Milissa   *Women can use the sex-object stereotype to their advantage. I pay for my education by being an exotic dancer, and I make better money than any other student I know. A lot of people think all exotic dancers are sluts, but that's not true. There's no difference between me using my body to fund my education and an athlete's using his or her body to fund his or her education. Same thing.*

Mother   In institutional life, the stereotype of women as mothers has both figurative and literal forms. The figurative version of this stereotype is expressed when others expect women employees to take care of the "emotional labor" for everyone—to smile, exchange pleasantries, prepare coffee and snacks, and listen to, support, and help others (Basinger, 2001; Bellas, 2001).

Stereotyping women as mothers is one basis of job segregation by gender, a subtle and pervasive form of discrimination. Approximately 75% of women in the paid labor force are in traditionally female jobs or positions that support others (Goddess & Calderón, 2006; Watt & Eccles, 2008). Called "pink collar" positions, these are clerks, secretaries, administrative assistants, and so forth, whose job, like that of a mother, is to take care of others. Although at least half of the paid workforce in the United States is female, only 3% of Fortune 500 companies have women as CEOs, only one-third of board members of Fortune 500 companies are women, and less than 20% of members of Congress are women (Rudman & Glick, 2008; Salomone, 2007). The jobs that most women have—assisting others—generally have the least prestige and the lowest salaries.

The woman-as-mother stereotype also has a literal form. Women employees who have or plan to have children are often perceived as less serious professionals than men or than women who aren't mothers. In one experiment, two résumés were created for fictitious female job applicants. The résumés were identical in most respects—successful track record, uninterrupted career history, obvious ambition. The only difference was that one résumé noted that the applicant was active in the Parent-Teacher Association, a tip-off that the applicant was a mother, while the other résumé did not include mention of the PTA. Potential employers judged the applicant whose résumé mentioned her involvement with the PTA to be less competent and committed to work than the applicant whose résumé did not mention the PTA, and the PTA applicant was 44% less likely to be hired (Andronici & Katz, 2007b; Goodman, 2007). Men who are fathers are not judged as less committed or competent; in fact, fatherhood tends to improve perceptions of male workers (Andronici & Katz, 2007; Mock, 2005).

The mother stereotype can become a self-fulfilling prophecy. It is illegal to stereotype women in the workforce as mothers or to act toward them in ways that reflect the belief that work and motherhood are incompatible. Despite this ruling, stereotypes and their material consequences are still with us. Each year the Equal Employment Opportunity Commission receives thousands of complaints of pregnancy-based discrimination (Goddess & Calderón, 2006). Women also experience discrimination once they are mothers. Professor of Law, Joan C. Williams has studied the bias against mothers (Crosby, Williams, & Biernat, 2004; Williams, 2004; Williams & Calvert, 2005–2007). She coined the term **maternal wall** to refer to unexamined assumptions held by coworkers and superiors about how women will behave once they become mothers. For example, a supervisor may assume that mothers are always available to their children. Based on this assumption, the supervisor may decide not to promote Lynn Hall, a working mother, to a job with more responsibility and salary. Later, when the supervisor is looking for someone with a background and experience in a certain area, he notes that Ms. Hall is not qualified and attributes this to her focus on mothering. Assumptions such as these systematically disadvantage working mothers (Correll, Benard, & Paik, 2007).

▼

Charlotte   *I know the mother role all too well. Before coming back to college, I worked as an adjuster for an insurance company. In my office, there were eleven men and one other woman, Anne. I'll bet there weren't more than 10 days in the 3 years I worked there that one of the guys didn't come in to talk with me or Anne about some personal problem. Sometimes, they wanted a lot of time and sympathy; sometimes, they just wanted a few minutes, but always it was Anne and me they came to—never one of the guys. What really burns is that they went to each other to consult about professional matters, but they never came to Anne and me about those. They treated us like mothers, not colleagues.*

Child   A third stereotype sometimes imposed on women is that of child, or pet—cute but not to be taken seriously. This stereotype reflects a view of women as less mature, less competent, and less capable than adults. Stereotyping women as children often masquerades as "protecting" women. A few years ago, a company tried to bar all female employees of childbearing age from positions that exposed them to lead, because such exposure may affect fetuses. (It may also affect sperm, but men

EXPLORING GENDERED LIVES   **IN AND OUT OF STEREOTYPES**

In 2009, the Army announced it was consolidating its drill schools into a single campus. At the same time, the Army announced it had appointed a new commandant of the new drill school. For the first time in Army history, a woman will be in charge of basic training for enlisted soldiers.

Meet Sergeant Major Teresa L. King, the eighth of 12 children, who began her Army career as a postal clerk. Those who have worked with Sergeant Major King say she's perfect for the job. Colonel John Bessler who was her commander when she went through basic training describes her as "confident, no nonsense, but compassionate about what's right for the soldier" (Dao, 2009, p. A22). Others who've worked with King say she is gruff, yet shows surprising tenderness toward her soldiers. She is petite in stature yet can do 34 push-ups and 66 sit-ups, each in less than two minutes. In other words, King manages to conform to some expectations of femininity while defying others.

were not barred from the jobs.) Even if women did not intend to have children, the company insisted on "protecting" them from the dangers of these jobs, which, incidentally, were higher-paying jobs in that company. The policy was struck down when a court ruled that the company was wrong in treating adult women as children instead of respecting their ability to assess risks and make their own choices.

One argument against allowing women in combat is that they should be protected from the gruesome realities of war. This is ironic, as women have been involved in and killed in every war fought by our nation. "Protecting" women from challenging work often excludes them from experiences that lead to promotion and raises, as well as from the personal development that comes with new challenges. Within the military, for instance, combat duty is virtually essential for advancement to the highest levels.

Iron Maiden   If a woman is not perceived in terms of one of the three stereotypes we've discussed, she may be perceived as fitting a fourth. A female professional who is independent, ambitious, directive, competitive, and sometimes tough may be labeled an "iron maiden." She is generally perceived as competent but unlikeable and unfeminine (Heilman & Okimoto, 2007; Rudman & Glick, 2008). Hillary Clinton shows how this stereotype can be imposed on a woman. During the 2008 Democratic Primary, polls consistently showed that many people considered her experienced and competent but cold, insensitive, and unlikeable—qualities that violate expectations for femininity. Because Clinton does not fit into the conventional views of women and femininity, she was referred to as "ice queen," "ball breaker," and "castrating bitch" (Phelan, Moss-Racusin, & Rudman, 2007; Rudman & Glick, 2008, p. 162).

Another example of this occurred in 1990 when Ann Hopkins sued the accounting firm of Price Waterhouse for sex discrimination (Hopkins, 2001; Hopkins & Walsh, 1996). Hopkins brought in more money in new accounts than any

EXPLORING GENDERED LIVES | **GENDERED WAGES**

Chuck Kennedy/MCT/Newscom

Lilly Ledbetter (left) at signing of the Lilly Ledbetter Act.

In 1963, the U.S. Congress passed the Equal Pay Act. At the time, women earned 59 cents for every dollar men earned. By the turn of the century, women earned 72 cents for every dollar men earned. The most recent data show that women now earn 80.2 cents for each dollar a man earns (Yen, 2010b). But averages don't tell the whole story. Women in the top 20% of the workforce have made most of the gains, whereas women in the lower half are paid about what they were 30 years ago. And women in the workforce who are mothers are paid less than women who do not have children (Andronici & Katz, 2007).

Why does the wage gap persist? The President's Council of Economic Advisors reports that the difference isn't fully accounted for by training, experience, or performance. In other words, discrimination based on sex and gender continues to affect what people are paid for the work they do.

In an effort to correct gender discrimation in wages, Congress took up two bills in 2009. The first, the Lilly Ledbetter Fair Pay Act, passed and has been signed into law. Lilly Ledbetter worked 19 years as a supervisor at a Goodyear Tire and Rubber plant in Alabama. As she approached retirement, someone anonymously left her a pay schedule that showed she was making significantly less than men in the same position she held. Ledbetter sued, but the Supreme Court ruled against her because the law stated that she had to file her suit within 180 days of the first occurrence of pay discrimination (Abrams, 2009; Collins, 2009a). Ledbetter, of course, didn't know that her pay was less for all those years. The Lilly Ledbetter Fair Pay Act states that wage discrimination occurs whenever an empoyee receives discriminary pay.

The second bill is the Paycheck Fairness Act, which was still in hearings when I wrote this chapter (March, 2010). This act would close loopholes in the Equal Pay Act of 1963. It would also barr employers from retaliating against employees who disclose or ask about pay schedules (Pear, 2009).

Gender discrimination in wages is not a small matter. As the chart below shows, over time the difference in pay can amount to $22,232 a year (Winik & Massey, 2009).

	Age 15-24	Age 25-44	Age 45-64
Women	23,357	41,558	44,808
Men	26,100	55,286	67,040

of her 87 male peers, yet 47 of the men were made partner, whereas Hopkins was not. Describing Hopkins as "authoritative" and "too tough," executives told her that, if she wanted to be promoted, she should look and act more feminine.

I met with Ann Hopkins to discuss her case. In our conversation, she recalled that a senior man in the firm had advised her to fix her hair and wear more jewelry (2001). Hopkins was promoted after a federal district court ruled that she was the target of gender stereotyping, which is a form of sex discrimination and therefore illegal. Yet, many women who face discrimination lack the funds or confidence to fight for their rights.

These four stereotypes define women in terms of sex and gender instead of job qualifications and performance. Successful career women report that they escape being classified according to the stereotypes by being very careful not to be unfeminine yet not to act "too much like women" (Nadesan & Trethewey, 2000; Powell & Graves, 2006). For many women, the stereotypes are barriers to hiring, promotion, and equitable pay (Heilman, 2001).

STEREOTYPES OF MEN

Within institutional settings, men are also stereotyped. Like stereotypes of women, those applied to men reflect cultural views of masculinity and men's roles. Three stereotypes of men are particularly prevalent in organizations: sturdy oak, fighter, and breadwinner.

Sturdy Oak   The sturdy oak is a self-sufficient pillar of strength who is never weak or reliant on others. In politics, we see dramatic examples of the extent to which men are expected to be sturdy oaks. Arnold Schwarzenegger ran for election and governed as a hypermasculine man, catapulting his role in action movies into political life. The stereotype of the sturdy oak can hinder men in professional contexts. When others communicate that they think it is unmanly to admit doubts or ask for help, male workers may rule out consulting others for advice or assistance. When others discourage men from collaborating and supporting co-workers, men may feel forced to act independently (Rudman & Fairchild, 2004). One result can be decision making that is faulty because of lack of important input.

Fighter   Cultural stereotypes also cast men as fighters—brave warriors who go to battle, whether literally in war or metaphorically in professional life. Childhood training to be aggressive, to "give 'em hell," and to win at all costs translates into professional expectations to beat the competition. There is no room for being less than fully committed to the cause, less than aggressive, or less than ruthless in defeating the competition. Because fighters are not supposed to take time from work for family, men who do so risk disapproval from coworkers. Although many men working outside the home say they would like to spend more time with their families (Philipsen & Bostic, 2010; Schmidt, 2010), many fear that doing so would lead coworkers to see them as not fully committed to their jobs.

Gabe   *A man at the place where I work part-time asked for family leave when his wife had a baby. Our manager gave him two weeks—he had to by company policy—but he really put the guy down behind his back. I heard him kidding with some of the other managers, saying did the guy think he was a mother or something? Nobody has ever said anything when a woman took family leave.*

Breadwinner   Perhaps no other stereotype so strongly defines men in our society as that of breadwinner. Within organizations, stereotyping men as breadwinners has been used to justify paying them higher wages than women. Being the primary or sole breadwinner for a family is central to how our society has historically judged men, as well as how many men judge themselves. Men who tie their identity and worth to earning power are in danger in an uncertain economy where job security is not assured.

The stereotypes of women and men don't match the reality of today's workplace. Research clearly shows that most women in the paid labor force do not fit any of the four female stereotypes, and most men in the paid labor force can't be neatly classified as one of the three male stereotypes (Aries, 1998).

MASCULINE NORMS IN PROFESSIONAL LIFE

Because men historically have dominated institutional life, masculine norms infuse the workplace (Ashcraft & Mumby, 2004). We'll examine how masculine norms lead to three misperceptions that affect employment and advancement.

MISPERCEPTION 1: THINK MANAGER—THINK MALE

Within many organizations, there is a pervasive mindset that management scholars call the "think manager—think male" phenomenon (Atwater, Brett, Waldman, Dimare, & Hayden, 2004; Kunkel, Dennis, & Waters, 2003; Powell & Graves, 2006). Equating *male* with *manager* in the workplace poses a major barrier to women's advancement. The ability to manage and lead is widely associated with communication traits that are cultivated more in masculine speech communities than in feminine ones—assertiveness, independence, competitiveness, and confidence. To the extent that women engage in traditionally feminine communication, they may not be recognized as leaders or marked for advancement in professional settings.

There seem to be a few general differences in women's and men's approaches to work life. In general, women are more likely than men to base career choices to some extent on the desire to help others (Fletcher, 1999). Women are also more likely than men to engage in caring, personal communication on the job (Eagly, Johannesen-Schmidt, & van Engen, 2003; Otten, 1995; "Women Take Care," 2004). In leadership roles, women tend to exceed men in collaborative, participative communication that enables others (Aries, 1987).

Does this mean that women are less professional and less able to lead than men? Not according to research. Subordinates judge male and female leaders to be equally effective, and judge both masculine and feminine styles of communication to be important in leaders (Eagly & Carli, 2007; Eagly, et al., 2003; Fletcher, Jordan, & Miller, 2000). The most effective leadership style appears to incorporate both relationship-building and instrumental qualities (Eagly, et al., 2003; Fletcher, 1999). Leaders who support others and build team cohesion are complemented by people who focus on the task and ensure efficiency (Cleveland, Stockdale, & Murphy, 2000). Effective teams and organizations need both kinds of leadership communication. In fact, Fortune 500 companies that have strong records of promoting women to executive levels outperform other Fortune 500 companies. Beginning in 2001, 200 Fortune 500 companies were tracked. Those that promoted more women had overall profits and revenue higher than the industry average. And 10 firms that promoted the most women showed the highest profits (Adler, 2009).

There's one further insight to add. Men and women may be judged differently for enacting the *same* communication. This fact highlights the importance of distinguishing between how women and men *actually* behave and how others *perceive* them. If communication is perceived through gender stereotypes, then women and men may need to communicate differently to be equally effective.

EXPLORING GENDERED LIVES | WINNER TAKES ALL? NOT MY GAME

Recently, economists at the University of Pittsburgh conducted the following experiment (Tierney, 2005).

In step one, men and women worked individually to add numbers in their heads. The individuals received 50 cents for each correct computation they performed in five minutes.

In step two, they competed in four-person teams, with the winning team receiving $2 and the losing team receiving nothing. In both the individual and the team situations, men and women earned about equal amounts of money.

In step three, the people were offered the choice of taking the individual rate or competing in teams for the larger prize. Most women—even those who had done the best in the team competitions—chose to take the individual rate. Most men—even those who had done very poorly in the team competition—chose to compete. The men who weren't good at the task lost a little money by deciding to compete, whereas the women who were really good at the task lost more money by choosing not to enter competitions they would probably have won.

Why did women pass up the opportunity to make substantially more money? The researchers concluded that it was not because the women were insecure about their skill. Instead, it's more likely that they didn't enjoy competition and weren't willing to do something they didn't like just to make money.

It is also established that, in general, women, who are usually socialized in feminine speech communities, are less comfortable negotiating salaries because they perceive negotiations as competitions that threaten relationships. Men, who are usually socialized in masculine speech communities, see negotiating as just part of the game of business. In their speech communities, they learned that scrapping, competing, and pushing themselves are just parts of life that have nothing to do with relationships (Babcock & Laschever, 2003; Hildebrandt, 2004).

Choosing not to negotiate salaries may cost women big bucks—half a million or more over the course of a career (Babcock & Laschever, 2003). At the same time, by taking a less competitive approach to work life, women may spare themselves stress-related medical problems such as ulcers, high blood pressure, and heart attacks.

Have you ever negotiated a salary? Would you be comfortable doing so?

Because cultural views link femininity to friendly and supportive behavior, women who use assertive and instrumental communication may be branded "iron maidens" (Aries, 1998; Bennett, Ellison, & Ball, 2010). Coworkers who hold gender stereotypes may negatively evaluate women—but not men—who communicate assertively and who demand results.

EXPLORING GENDERED LIVES | **IF SHE'S A HE, HE'S BETTER AND PAID BETTER TOO!**

For years, researchers have tried to figure out whether differences in judgments of men and men in the workplace are due to sex biases or other variables. Finally, a group of scholars came up with a sure-fire way to test whether a person's sex affects judgments of competence (Schilt, 2007, 2010; Schilt & Wiswall, 2008; Wentley, Schilt, Windsor, & Lucal, 2008). They studied coworkers' perceptions and pay rates for people who were first one sex and then the other sex and continued to do the same job. By studying transsexuals, Schilt and Wiswall eliminated variables, even personality variables, other than sex. They found that men who become women earn, on average, 32% less after they transitioned.

In one study (Schilt & Wiswall, 2008), the authors described a particular case: Susan was an attorney who transitioned to being a man and took the name Thomas. Thomas stayed at the same firm and one of the other lawyers at the firm mistakenly thought that Susan had left and Thomas had been hired to replace her. The other lawyer told one of the senior partners in the firm that Susan had been incompetent but her replacement (Thomas) was excellent.

Tara   *When I first started working, I tried to act like the men at my level. I was pleasant to people, but I didn't talk with coworkers about my life or their lives. I did my work, led my team with firm, directive communication, and stressed results. When I had my first performance review, I got great marks on achieving tasks, but there was serious criticism of "my attitude." A number of people—both my peers and staff I supervised—complained that I was unfriendly or cold. People criticized me for not caring about them and their lives. I pointed out to my supervisor that nobody made those complaints about men, and she told me that I couldn't act like a man if I wanted to succeed in business.*

Thus, it may well be that women and men who communicate similarly may be judged very differently based on their coworkers' gendered expectations (Andronici & Katz, 2007).

MISPERCEPTION 2: COMMUNICATION STYLES DON'T CHANGE

Earlier chapters in this book demonstrated that our communication styles are learned. Feminine speech communities encourage creating and sustaining interpersonal connections and responding to others, whereas masculine speech communities emphasize competing and communicating to assert independence and status. But are we bound forever by what we learned in childhood? Can we change our communication styles? To answer these questions, we return to standpoint theory, which states that our ways of knowing and communicating are influenced by our contexts. Yet, standpoint theory also claims that, as our contexts change, so might our ways of thinking, communicating, and performing identity, including gender. If this is true, then as women enter into contexts that include masculine communication, they should become proficient in new skills. Similarly, as men interact with coworkers who use feminine communication styles, men should develop skills in collaboration and support.

Support for standpoint theory's claim comes from research showing that both men and women develop new communication skills that are needed for effectiveness on the job (Aries, 1998; Buzzanell & Lucas, 2006). All of us can develop communication skills when we find ourselves in positions that require abilities not emphasized in our early socialization.

MISPERCEPTION 3: CAREERS MUST FOLLOW LINEAR, FULL-TIME PATTERNS

Career paths are typically regarded as linear progressions. A new employee takes a beginning position and works his or her way up the ladder by demonstrating commitment and competence at each level of position. Career paths are also typically thought of as being full-time. A serious professional works eight or more hours at least five days a week and those eight-plus hours generally start at 8 or 9 a.m. and end at 5 or 6 p.m.

The assumption that serious careers are linear and full-time reflects social relations of previous eras in which most professionals were men who had stay-at-home wives to care for the home and children. Today, most women and men work outside of the home. Few people can afford full-time maids and nannies, so the responsibilities of taking care of home and family are not easily met when both partners work outside of the home.

Increasing numbers of people—both male and female—are arguing that organizations should be more flexible to accommodate the realities of today's families (Philipsen & Bostic, 2010). Why must everyone be at work by 8 or 9 a.m.? Why can't people take breaks of several months or years within a serious career? Why can't employees work part-time when there are young children or other family members who need attention and nurturing? Why can't organizations (at least large ones) provide on-site day care?

Beneath these questions lies a gender issue: Why do women's careers suffer more than men's when there are children or other family members who need care? When couples decide to have children, it is usually the woman who accommodates, often by taking time off from work. Most women don't want to quit work when they have children, but the inflexibility of the workplace and the inability or unwillingness of male partners to take half of the responsibility for parenting leaves women little choice (Goodman, 2008a; Stone, 2007). The cost of not providing significant support for families is substantial.

Although most women who leave paid labor to care for children plan to return to the workforce in a few years, they run into barriers when they are ready to return to work outside of the home. Many mothers can't find jobs when they are ready to return to work. Either employers prefer to hire women who are not mothers or the break from work leads employers to perceive mothers as less committed workers (Hewlett, 2007; June, 2010; Steiner, 2007; Tyre, 2006; Williams, 2004). Even those who do find jobs often discover that they are marginalized at work because colleagues and supervisors perceive working mothers as less than fully committed to their careers (Hayden & O'Brien Hallstein, 2010; Stone, 2007; Wood & Dow, 2010). Further, taking a few years off from work tends to reduce earning power. Women lose 18%, on average, of their earning power when they opt out of work for a few years, and only 40% of women who were in powerful positions get back to full-time work (Hirshman, 2007).

Perhaps you are thinking that people who step off the traditional career path should expect to be less well compensated than those who follow the conventional trajectory. If so, we would expect career losses to be experienced by both women and men who step out of full-time work for a period of time. That's not the case. A very recent report (Carter & Silva, 2010) shows that only women experience negative consequences for stepping off the traditional track. Studying the careers of top M.B.A. graduates in countries such as the United States, Asia, Canada, and England, researchers found that men who step off the traditional full-time career track do not take cuts in pay or position when they return to full-time work, but women do.

▼

Perry   *I'll admit I was against having a woman promoted to our executive board, but I'll also admit that I was wrong. I thought Linda wouldn't fit in or have anything to add. I voted for a junior male who I thought would fit in with the rest of us executives. But Linda is just superb. What I like most about having her in our group is that she's a real consensus builder, and nobody else is. Linda's first concern always seems to be finding common ground among us, and she has an absolutely amazing lack of ego invested in decisions. I'm not sure it's flattering to admit this, but the guys in the group, including me, operate from ego. Sometimes, winning a point is more important than crafting the best decision. Linda moves us away from that mindset.*

GENDERED PATTERNS IN ORGANIZATIONS

Organizations have both formal and informal practices. Formal practices include policies regarding leaves, work schedules, performance reviews, who reports to whom, who authorizes and evaluates whom, and so on. Informal practices include normative behaviors and understandings that are not covered by explicit policies: what is required to be on the fast track, gossiping and exchanging information, advising, mentoring, and so forth. As we will see, both formal and informal networks often entail gendered dynamics.

FORMAL PRACTICES

Leave Policies   In 1993, the Family and Medical Leave Act (FMLA) was passed so that U.S. employees could take up to 12 weeks of unpaid leave to care for new babies or sick family members. In 2010, President Obama announced that the right to family leave will be expanded to include workers in same-sex relationships who need time to care for a partner's child (Pear, 2010). Since the act was passed, more than 50 million Americans have taken family leave. The act, however, doesn't cover all workers. Only companies with 50 or more workers are required to grant family leaves, and some employees can be exempted from leave—FMLA covers only about 60% of employees in companies with 50 or more employees (Goodman, 2005). The minimum required leave is 12 weeks. Some individual states, however, do require companies with as few as 25 employees to grant family and medical leave (Bernstein, 1999), and two states—California and Washington—have laws requiring paid family leave ("Catching Up," 2008).

The FMLA is not a complete solution to the tension between work and family. Because FMLA does not require that companies pay workers who take leaves, many workers cannot afford a leave even if they qualify for it. When time must be taken for families, it is usually a woman who takes it. The mother stereotype of women combines with the breadwinner stereotype of men to create a situation in which it is difficult for men to become full partners in raising children (June, 2010). Even men who do take family leave spend considerably less of their leave time with children than do either females who take leave or females who don't. In other words, a woman who works full-time outside of home often spends more time with a child than does a man who is on family leave (Rhoads, 2004; Wilson, 2005a).

The United States lags behind other developed countries in providing family-friendly policies in the workplace. In fact, the United States is one of only four countries in a survey of 173 countries that does not guarantee some form of paid maternity leave to any working mother. The other three countries that do not guarantee paid maternity leave are Liberia, Papua New Guinea, and Swaziland (Crary, 2008). Further, 66 of the 173 countries surveyed give working fathers the right to paid paternity leave (Crary, 2008). Paid sick leave is provided by 145 countries, but the United States does not have a federal law guaranteeing paid sick leave (Crary, 2008). Most developed countries provide generous parental and family leave policies—from 7 to 51 weeks at 60% to 100% of salary ("Catching Up, 2008). The lack of real support that businesses in the United States provide to employees forces many workers to choose between taking care of families and earning income ("Catching Up," 2008; McGinn, 2006; Porter, 2006a, b). The lack of institutional support also influences some workers' career choices. Increasingly workers, predominantly women, are opting out of careers that don't provide support for families (Moe & Shandy, 2010; Quinn, 2010; Quinn & Litzler, 2009; Trower & Quinn, 2009).

Work Schedules   Another way in which organizational rules affect men and women employees stems from the rigid working schedules that are generally mandated. Increasingly, the 9-to-5 model of the workday is giving way to the expectation that 7 or 8 a.m to 7 or 8 p.m. is normal for "really committed professionals." Obviously, this model—or even the 9-to-5 model—doesn't accommodate families with young children. Even if parents can afford day care, children are sometimes too sick to attend; day-care centers also may be closed for a day or more, making it necessary for a parent to take responsibility for child care. Women are more likely than men to take time off to care for children, a pattern that reflects and reinforces gendered assumptions that women put families first and men put careers first.

Providing more leave time and flexible working hours can actually save employers money because it's less expensive to grant leaves than to replace employees. Family-friendly policies also enhance businesses' ability to recruit and keep talented workers they would otherwise lose (Quinn, 2010).

INFORMAL PRACTICES

In addition to formal policies, organizations operate with a number of informal, unwritten understandings that can make or break careers. Through a range of normative practices, some organizations emphasize gender differences, define one sex or gender as standard, or extend different opportunities to women and men.

Unwelcoming Environments for Women   In some organizations, language and behavior that emphasize men's experiences and interests are normative (Cheney, Christensen, Zorn, & Ganesh, 2004). Women are generally less familiar and less comfortable with terms taken from sports *(hit a home run, huddle on strategy, ballpark figures, second-string player, come up with a game plan, be a team player, line up, score a touchdown, put it in your court)*, sexuality or sex organs *(hit on a person, he has balls, he's a real prick, screw the competition, get into a pissing contest, stick it to them;* calling women employees "hon" or referring to women generally in sexual ways); and the military *(battle plan, mount a campaign, strategy, plan of attack, under fire, get the big guns)*. Intentional or not, language related to sports, sexuality, and the military binds men into a masculine community in which some women feel unwelcome (Messner, 2001).

There can be resistance to—and occasionally outright hostility toward—women who enter fields in which men predominate. Women may be given unrewarding assignments, isolated from key networks of people and information, and treated stereotypically as sex objects, mothers, or children. Each of these techniques contributes to a communication climate that defines women as "not real members of the team."

The Informal Network   Relationships among colleagues are important in creating a sense of fit and providing access to essential information that may not come through formal channels (Barreto, Ryan, & Schmitt, 2009). Because men have predominated in the workplace, many informal networks are largely or exclusively male, giving rise to the term *old boy network*. Hiring and promotion decisions are often made through informal communication within these networks. For example, while golfing, Bob tells Nathan about a job candidate; over a beer, Ed tells Joel about an impressive trainee, and thus, that trainee stands out later in Ed's mind when he selects people for an important assignment; Mike talks with Ben, John, and Frank about his new marketing plan, so when Mike introduces it formally in a meeting, he has support lined up. Informal communication networks are vital to professional success. At Rutgers University,

EXPLORING GENDERED LIVES | **THE VIRTUAL INFORMAL NETWORK**

A senior technology executive named Josephine recently gave this advice to younger women in her field: "If you want to be in the loop, get yourself a male alias" (Rose, 2008, p. 7G). There's a story behind that advice. Years earlier when she began working at a startup tech company, she asked her boss to call her "Finn," short for Josephine. She was routinely included on e-mails to and from colleagues in other locations. The e-mails to Finn were peppered with crude language and sexist comments and jokes, but they also contained under-the-radar information about markets, investments, and people in the field. E-mails to Josephine contained only general information and didn't provide the inside scoop that allowed Finn to be in the know and to use her knowledge to advance.

Do you think it's professionally smart for women to have male aliases? Do you think it's ethical?

faculty in political science had a longstanding tradition of Tuesday night dinners, hosted by senior faculty. The senior faculty happen to be male and only male faculty of any rank are invited. Female faculty members were routinely excluded from the Tuesday night dinners, which were the unofficial forum for decision making about departmental matters (Moser, 2008).

Women tend to be less involved than men in informal networks. Sometimes they are not invited to be part of the network or not made to feel welcome if they try to participate. When only one or two women are in a company or at a particular level, they stand out as different and unlike most of the employees. Only when a group reaches about 30% does it have critical mass, that is, sufficient size not to be marginalized (Rowling, 2002). A sense of difference is also experienced by transgender people and people of color in predominantly white organizations (Allen, 2006). In the face of communication that defines them as outsiders, women and minorities may avoid informal networks and thus lose out on these key sources of information and support.

Mentoring Relationships   A mentor is an experienced person who guides the development of a less experienced person. In the workforce, mentors are usually older employees who help younger employees build careers. A mentor is at least helpful, and sometimes indispensable, to career advancement. Women and minorities are less likely to have mentors than are white men.

Several factors account for the low number of women and minority people who have the benefit of mentors. First, the numbers game works against them. Lower numbers of women and minorities in senior positions means that there are few who might counsel new female and/or minority employees. Men are sometimes reluctant to mentor young women for a variety of reasons: They may fear gossip about sexual relations; they may assume that women are less serious than men about careers; or they may feel less comfortable with women than with men. This pattern perpetuates the status quo, in which white men get more help than women and minorities in climbing the corporate ladder.

In an effort to compensate for the lack of networks and mentors available in existing organizations, some professional women have formed their own networks, in which women share ideas, contacts, strategies for advancement, and information. In addition to furnishing information, these networks provide women with support and a sense of belonging with other professionals like themselves. As men and women become accustomed to interacting as colleagues, they may become more comfortable mentoring one another and forming sex-integrated communication networks.

▼

Tangia   *Where I used to work, the boss was always dropping in on the men who held positions at my level, but he never dropped in to talk with any of the women at that level. He also had a habit of introducing males in our division to visitors from the main office, but he never introduced women to them. It was like there was a closed loop and we weren't part of it.*

Glass Ceilings and Walls   Many women hit the **glass ceiling**, an invisible barrier that limits the advancement of women and minorities. More than a decade ago, in 1991, the glass ceiling was identified as a barrier to women's progress in professions ("Trouble at the Top," 1991). More recent research confirms the persistence of glass ceilings that limit women's careers (Andronici & Katz, 2007; Barreto, et al., 2009). Women's progress is often impeded by subtle discrimination that limits their opportunities. It might be the stereotype of women as mothers that leads an executive to assume that a working mother would not be interested in a major new assignment that could advance her career. It might be seeing a woman in sexual terms so that her competence is overlooked. It might be misinterpreting an inclusive, collaborative style of communication as lack of initiative. It might be assuming that women don't have math and science abilities so cannot handle positions that require these aptitudes (Ceci & Williams, 2007). These stereotypes can create a glass ceiling—an invisible barrier—that keeps women out of the executive suite.

But glass ceilings may be only part of the problem. The term **glass walls** is a metaphor for sex segregation on the job, in which women are placed in "pink collar" positions that require traditionally feminine skills (assistant, clerical, counseling, human relations) (Watt & Eccles, 2008). Typically, such jobs do not include career ladders, on which doing well at one level allows advancement to the next. In essence, many of the positions that women are encouraged to take have no advancement paths (Ashcraft, 2006; Correll et al., 2007; Wharton, 2004).

www.CartoonStock.com. Used by permission.

EXPLORING GENDERED LIVES | **MICROINEQUITIES**

Microinequities are pervasive and subtle forms of discrimination. They are verbal comments and behaviors that devalue members of a group but are not specific violations of laws prohibiting discrimination. Examples are speaking to male colleagues but not speaking to female ones, asking only a male worker to fill in as supervisor when the supervisor has to be away from the office, and not telling women workers what they need to do to improve job performance and qualify for promotions. Although microinequities don't cross the line of illegal actions, they have negative impact on morale, job performance, and opportunities for promotion and training.

EFFORTS TO REDRESS GENDERED INEQUITY IN INSTITUTIONS

A desire to correct discrimination based on sex, gender, and other factors has led to five efforts to reduce discrimination: equal opportunity laws, affirmative action policies, quotas, goals, and diversity training. It is important to understand these methods of redressing inequities and the differences among them so that we can evaluate arguments for and against them and decide our own positions. Although this chapter focuses specifically on the workplace, these remedies apply to both professional and educational settings, the two contexts in which efforts to end discrimination have been most pronounced.

Equal Opportunity Laws

Laws prohibiting discrimination began with the landmark legal case *Brown v. Board of Education of Topeka, Kansas*, which was tried in 1954. In that case, the U.S. Supreme Court overturned the "separate but equal" doctrine that had allowed separate educational systems for white and black citizens.

Following *Brown v. Board of Education,* a number of laws were passed in the 1950s and 1960s to prohibit discrimination against individuals who belong to groups that historically have faced discrimination. Two primary examples of **equal opportunity laws** are Title VII of the Civil Rights Act of 1964, which prohibits discrimination in employment, and the 1972 Title IX, which forbids discrimination in educational programs that receive federal aid. Other anti-discrimination laws are Title IV of the 1964 Civil Rights Act, the Women's Educational Equity Acts of 1974 and 1978, and an amendment to the 1976 Vocational Education Act.

Equal opportunity laws focus on discrimination against *individuals.* In other words, complaints filed with the Equal Employment Opportunity Commission (EEOC) must claim that a particular person has suffered discrimination because of sex, race, or other criteria named in laws. Equal opportunity law does not ask whether a group (for example, women or Hispanics) is underrepresented or is treated inequitably. Instead, it is concerned solely with discrimination against individuals.

Equal opportunity laws focus on *present* practices, so historical patterns of discrimination are irrelevant. For example, a university with a record of denying admission to women is not subject to suit unless a particular individual can prove she personally and currently suffered discrimination on the basis of her sex.

The scope of Title IX was weakened in 1984 when the Supreme Court narrowed its application from whole institutions to specific programs and activities that receive federal money.

Affirmative Action Policies

President Lyndon B. Johnson used his 1965 commencement address at Howard University to announce a new policy that would address historical prejudice, which equal opportunity laws ignored. He said, "You do not take a person who

---

EXPLORING GENDERED LIVES | **NEW IMPLICATIONS OF TITLE IX AND THE CIVIL RIGHTS ACT**

In 2007 Peggy Robertson applied for insurance with the Golden Rule Insurance Company. Robertson was rejected because she had previously had a caesarean, but she was told she would be eligible if she were sterilized (Grady, 2010).

Robertson's case is particularly dramatic, but "gender rating" has long been practiced by insurance companies. Individual policies often excluded maternity coverage, but covered treatment for prostate cancer. Some companies charged more in premiums to women who did not smoke than to men who did (Grady, 2010).

All of this ended with the health care plan signed into law in 2009. The basis for no longer allowing insurance companies to engage in gender rating is laws against sex discrimination, specifically the Civil Rights Act and Title IX, which say organizations (including insurance companies) that receive any federal money cannot deny participation or benefits because of sex.

---

for years has been hobbled by chains and liberate him, bring him to the starting line of a race, and then say, 'you are free to compete with all the others."

Affirmative action is based on three key ideas. First, because discrimination has systematically restricted the opportunities of *groups* of people, remedies must apply to entire groups, not just to individuals. Second, to compensate for the legacy of discrimination, there must be *preferential treatment* of qualified members of groups that have suffered discrimination. Third, the effectiveness of remedies is judged by *results,* not intent. If a law does not result in a greater presence of women and minorities, then it is ineffective in producing equality.

Some people think that aiming for greater numbers of women and minorities in companies and academic programs results in excluding better-qualified white males. Yet, the claim that affirmative action deprives whites of admission to schools is challenged by a study by William Bowen, president of the Mellon Foundation and former president of Princeton, and Derek Bok, former president of Harvard University (1998). After analyzing grades, SAT scores, and other data for 93,000 students of all races, Bowen and Bok found that eliminating affirmative action would raise whites' chances of admission by a mere 1.5%.

Many people do not realize that affirmative action includes two important limitations. First, affirmative action policies recognize the *limited availability* of qualified people from historically underrepresented groups. Because of long-standing discriminatory practices, fewer women and minorities may be qualified for certain jobs and academic programs.

Second, affirmative action aims to increase the number of *qualified* members of historically marginalized groups. It does not advocate admitting, hiring, or promoting women and minorities who lack necessary qualifications. To understand how affirmative action policies work, it's important to distinguish between *qualified* and *best qualified.* Consider an example: Jane Evans and John Powell are candidates for the last opening in a medical school that requires a 3.2 undergraduate grade point average and a score of 1200 on the medical aptitude exam. Jane's undergraduate average is 3.4, whereas John's is 3.6. On the entrance exam, she scores 1290, and he scores 1300. Although his qualifications are slightly better than hers, both individuals clearly meet the school's requirements, so both are qualified. Under affirmative action guidelines, the school would admit Jane because she meets the qualifications and does so despite historical patterns that discourage women from studying sciences and math.

Affirmative action attempts to compensate for the effects of a history of bias by giving preference to individuals whose qualification was achieved despite obstacles and discrimination. As Thomas Shapiro (2007) points out, one reason that many blacks are economically less well off than Caucasians is that "one generation passes advantage and disadvantage to the next" (p. 133). Thus, whites who owned property in the 1700s passed it along to their children who passed it along to their children and so forth. Blacks who were slaves owned no land, so they could not pass it on to future generations.

▼

Johnson   *I've never done anything to discriminate against members of other races, so I don't think I should have to step aside so they can have special advantages now. I don't owe them anything, and I earned everything I've got.*

▼

Sheretta   *I get so ripped off when I hear white guys badmouth affirmative action. They don't know what they're talking about. They speak totally from their self-interest and their ignorance. One thing that white guys say a lot is that they didn't hold blacks down in the past, so they shouldn't be penalized today. To that, I'd like to say they sure as hell don't mind taking a heap of advantages they didn't earn, like good schools and clothes and financial support. Do they think they earned those things? How do they think their daddies and granddaddies earned them? I'll tell you how: off the labor of black people that they were holding back, that's how.*

Ever since affirmative action policies were enacted, public debate about them has been vigorous. The debate is more about whether preferential treatment is fair than whether it works. The effectiveness of affirmative action is clear when we look at changes in proportions of minorities and whites. In 1955, only 4.9% of college students were black. In the 1970s, the number rose to 7.8%; in the 1980s, it was 9.1%, and in the 1990s it rose to 11.3% (Eisaguirre, 1999). In 1979, only 4% of the San Francisco Police Department's entry-level officers were female; by 1985, the number rose to 14.5%, largely as a result of affirmative action policies (Eisaguirre, 1999).

Let's look more closely at two key studies of the effectiveness of affirmative action. One study examined the records of students admitted to medical schools under affirmative action and a matched sample of students admitted using standard admission criteria (Dreier & Freer, 1997). Students admitted under affirmative action did equally well in their residencies and became equally successful physicians. Further, black men who graduated from selective schools were more likely than their white peers to become civic and community leaders (Bowen & Bok, 1998). A study of law students (Mangan, 2004) produced similar findings. Even though minority students began their professional study with lower grades and standardized scores, they wound up being just as successful in their careers as white students.

The Supreme Court has issued a number of rulings that clarify and refine affirmative action. In 2003, the Court ruled that race cannot be *the deciding factor*, but it may be a factor in admissions decisions because universities have "a compelling interest in a diverse student body" ("In Their Words," 2003, p. 5A).

The most recent case heard by the Supreme Court resulted in a rolling back of affirmative action policies for public elementary and high schools. In late June 2007 the Court ruled that public school districts cannot use race as a basis for assigning students to elementary and secondary schools. The vote was close—five justices voting to invalidate both schools' plans and four voting to allow them. The four justices who dissented from the ruling wrote an opinion that emphasized the compelling need to continue efforts to ensure diversity at all levels of education. Their sense that America has not yet gotten beyond segregation is supported by the fact that 75% of African-American, Latino, and Latina schoolchildren attend schools with predominantly minority populations, and an even greater percentage of white schoolchildren attend schools with predominantly white populations (Chemerinsky & Clotfelter, 2007). In coming years, we are likely to see additional cases that push the Court to clarify which ways of taking race into account will be allowed. This ruling does not affect admissions policies in higher education.

Lakisha   *I don't know how anyone can say the playing field is even today. It's not. I'm the first in my family to go to college. Actually, I'm the first to finish high school. My school didn't have SAT prep courses. My parents didn't know how to help me with my homework or apply to colleges. I didn't have any of the breaks that most students at this college did. So don't tell me the playing field is even. If it weren't for affirmative action, I wouldn't even be* on *the playing field!*

In 2005 the Supreme Court ruled that individuals who report suspected sex discrimination are protected from retaliation under federal law (Lipka, 2005). Without this protection, many people would not report suspected discrimination.

In recent years, there has been growing interest in revising affirmative action to give preference based on socioeconomic status rather than race-ethnicity (Bowen, Tobin, & Kurtzweil, 2005; Gose, 2005; Kahlenberg, 2010; Naughton, 2004). People who are economically disadvantaged face numerous barriers to advancement in education and the job market (Andersen & Collins, 2007b). For instance, a white high school student from a working- or poverty-class family who has a 3.6 grade point average and a 1200 on the SAT has worked against significant disadvantages and, thus, may merit some preferential treatment.

Protection for transgender workers is also underway. In 2009, President Obama authorized attorneys to begin drafting policy guidelines that prohibit workplace discrimination against transgender employees working in the federal government (Rutenberg, 2009). The new guidelines will be in the handbook for federal managers and supervisors and will explicitly warn against discriminating against transgender employees.

QUOTAS

Perhaps the most controversial effort to redress discrimination is the **quota**. Building on affirmative action's focus on results, a quota specifies that a number or percentage of women or minorities must be admitted, hired, or promoted. For instance, a company might stipulate that 30% of promotions must go to women. A binding quota requires a specified number or percentage of women regardless of issues such as merit. If there are not enough qualified women to meet the 30% quota, then women who lack qualifications must be promoted.

A famous case relevant to quotas was brought in 1978, when Alan Bakke sued the University of California at Davis's medical school for rejecting him, a white male, in favor of less-qualified minority applicants. Bakke won his case on the grounds that he had been a victim of "reverse discrimination" because the University of California at Davis violated his Fourteenth Amendment right to equal protection under the law. However, the Court did not outlaw the use of race as one factor in admissions decisions. It only ruled that schools may not set aside specific numbers of spaces for minorities. In other words, the Court allowed race to be a factor as long as it didn't result in a rigid quota. As we noted earlier, this position was reaffirmed in 2003, when the Supreme Court ruled that race can be one factor in admissions decisions but that no factor, including race, can be set as a quota or given a set advantage, such as points added to admission profiles ("In Their Words," 2003, p. 5A).

EXPLORING GENDERED LIVES	WHEN QUOTAS RAISE QUESTIONS — AND WHEN THEY DON'T

Some people think it's unfair to reserve places for women and minorities. They advocate evaluating all applicants on individual merit. It's interesting that questions aren't raised about a long-standing quota system that has benefited white and male students. Many, if not most, universities have legacy policies, which accord preferential consideration to the children of alumnae and alumni. For example, in recent years, Harvard admitted 40 percent of legacy applicants but only 11 percent of the total applicants. Princeton had an overall acceptance rate of 9 percent, but it acceptd 42 percent of legacy applicants. It's unlikely the legacy applicants were substantially stronger academically since they had lower SAT scores and grade point averages than the overall entering class (Kahlenberg, 2010).

Do you approve of schools giving preferential treatment to children of alumni?

Some states have banned race-conscious admissions policies. California, Florida, Michigan, and Washington state currently forbid racial preferences in admissions to colleges. California was the first state to ban affirmative action in admissions. Ten years after California enacted the ban, only 2% of first-year students at UCLA were black—the smallest percentage in 30 years (Lewin, 2007).

▼

Nicola   *The quota system is the only thing that can work. The laws aren't enforced, so they don't help, and affirmative action is just a bunch of talk. I've watched both my parents be discriminated against all of their lives just because of their skin color. All the laws and pledges of affirmative action haven't done a damned thing to change that. Quotas cut through all of the crap of intentions and pledges and say point-blank there will be so many African Americans in this company or this school or whatever. That's the only way change is ever going to happen. And when I hear white guys whining about how quotas are unfair to them, I want to throw up. They* **know** *nothing about unfair.*

GOALS

A goal is different from a quota, although the two are frequently confused. A **goal** is a stated intention to achieve representation of minorities or women. For instance, a company could establish the goal of awarding 30% of its promotions to women by the year 2015. But goals do not require results. If the company awarded only 13% of its promotions to women by 2010, there would be no penalty; the company could simply announce a new goal: to award 30% of its promotions to women by 2020. Members of groups that have historically experienced discrimination are often skeptical of goals because there are no penalties for not achieving them.

Ironically, both quotas and goals can work *against* women and minorities. The numbers specified by quotas and goals can be interpreted as a maximum number of women and minorities rather than a minimum. In our example, the 30% number could be used to keep more than 30% of promotions from going to women, even if 40% of qualified applicants were women. Departments may hire an African-American or transgender scholar and then cease to consider other female and transgender applicants for future openings—they've met their quota by employing one.

▼

Tyrone   *I resent the way so many people at this school assume that any minority student is here only because of affirmative action or quotas. I've heard people say that, if it weren't for racial quotas, there wouldn't be anyone here who isn't white. One of my suitemates even said to my face once that, since he hadn't had a quota to get him in here, he had to bust his butt to get into this school. I asked him what his SAT score was. He said 1080. I told him mine was 1164; then I walked out.*

Goals and quotas can work against women and minorities in a second way. When goals or quotas are in effect, members of institutions may assume that women and minorities got in only because of their sex or race. When this happens, individual women and people of color are not regarded as capable members of the school, business, or trade. Regardless of their qualifications, women and minorities may be perceived as underqualified.

DIVERSITY TRAINING

A final remedy for persistent discrimination—one that is often combined with one of the other four—is diversity training, which aims to increase awareness of and respect for differences that arise from distinct standpoints. This strategy assumes that many people are unaware of how their comments and behavior could be offensive to women, members of minority races, and people who have nontraditional gender identities. Raising awareness is what followed after Lawrence Summers, then-president of Harvard, made his infamous comment that innate differences in science and math explain the lower numbers of women in math and science faculty lines. In the five years since Summers made his comment, two task forces on women faculty have raised awareness of problems and helped Harvard implement solutions. As a result, today more than 25% of Harvard's faculty are women, the earth and planetary sciences and math have tenured their first women faculty, and professors can get up to $20,000 to help pay the costs of child care (Lewin, 2010).

Of course, not everyone cares about inequities, and many people are unwilling to make changes, especially changes that may limit their own privileges. Thus, an important drawback of diversity training is that it requires strong personal commitment from participants.

SUMMARY

In this chapter, we have considered a variety of ways in which institutional life intersects with cultural understandings of gender and communication. Cultural views of masculinity and femininity seep into the formal and informal life of organizations.

Yet, current views of gender won't necessarily be future views. You and your peers will make up and define the workplace of the future. One of the most pressing challenges for your generation is to remake our institutions to correspond to the lives of today's men and women. By recognizing and challenging inequities and the stereotypes behind them, you have the opportunity to contribute to changes that improve the conditions in which we all live and work.

Key Terms

The terms following are defined in this chapter on the pages indicated, as well as in alphabetical order in the book's glossary, which begins on page 325. The text's companion website (**http://www.cengage.com/communication/wood/genderedlives10e**) also provides interactive flash cards and crossword puzzles to help you learn these terms and the concepts they represent.

affirmative action 252

equal opportunity laws 251

glass ceiling 249

glass walls 249

goal 256

maternal wall 236

mentor 248

microinequities 250

quota 255

Gender Online

1. To learn more about efforts to reduce discrimination in the workplace, visit the Equal Employment Opportunity Commission's homepage: **www.eeoc.gov**.
2. Online search terms: "affirmative action," "glass ceiling," "Lilly Ledbetter."

Reflection and Discussion

1. Have you observed instances of classifying women or men workers into stereotypes identified in this chapter? How might workers resist being stereotyped?
2. Now that you understand distinctions among equal opportunity laws, affirmative action, goals, quotas, and diversity training, how do you evaluate each?
3. Interview some people involved in careers to learn how much they rely on informal networks. To what extent do women and men professionals report that they are equally welcomed into informal networks in their organizations and fields?
4. Talk with staff in the admissions office at your school to learn about admissions policies. Also ask about demographics—the number of students of different races and sexes. What is your opinion of your school's policies?
5. On your own or with several classmates, take a group of five men and five women through the three steps in the experiment discussed in the Exploring Gendered Lives: Winner Takes All? Not My Game box on page 242.

   - How many men and how many women chose the individual rate in step three? How many chose to compete?
   - Ask the men and women in your experiment why they made the choices they did in step three. Be sure to ask them individually so they don't influence one another's answers.

Recommended Resources

1. Dennis K. Mumby (2006). Introduction. In B. Dow & J. T. Wood (Eds.), *Handbook of Gender & Communication* (pp. 89–95). Thousand Oaks, CA: Sage. This essay introduces four surveys of current research on gendered aspects of the workplace. Dennis Mumby is one of the most influential scholars in the study of gendered organizational life.

2. Patrice Buzzanell and Kristen Lucas. (2006). Gendered Stories of Career. In B. Dow & J. T. Wood (Eds.), *Handbook of Gender & Communication* (pp. 161–178). Thousand Oaks, CA: Sage. This essay provides an excellent overview of material, psychological, and communicative influences on women's career opportunities and career experiences.
3. Peggy McIntosh. (2007). White privilege: Unpacking the invisible knapsack. In M. Andersen & P. H. Collins, *Race, Class & Gender* (pp. 98–102). Belmont, CA: Thomson Wadsworth. This is a classic article that makes more visible white privileges that are normalized.

The media we use and the stories they tell help to make us who we are.
Maria Mastronardi

CHAPTER **11**   GENDERED MEDIA

Knowledge Challenge:

1. To what extent do media represent male and female athletes in similar ways?
2. How do women and men differ in their use of media?
3. How does consuming media affect women's self-esteem and body image?

"That's some nappy-headed hos there," said Don Imus in reference to the Scarlet Knights, the Rutgers women's basketball team that made it to the 2007 NCAA championship game. Don Imus's comment during the sports segment of his April 4, 2007 show wasn't his first instance of racist or sexist remarks. His show, *Imus in the Morning,* frequently used the n-word to refer to blacks and favored ethnic slurs such as "ragheads" for Arabs (Kosova, 2007). More than a decade before the remarks that got him fired, "the I-Man," as Imus likes to call himself, referred to African-American reporter Gwen Ifill, who was covering the White House, as "the cleaning lady" (Ifill, 2007, p. 11A). Racist and sexist jokes and comments were the mainstay of his morning program. For instance, Hillary Clinton was referred to as "a bitch" and the program featured a song about her menstrual period (Herbert, 2007a).

When Imus made his remark about the Scarlet Knights, Ryan Chiachiere was taping the program. Chiachiere worked with Media Matters for America, a liberal watchdog group. After Chiachiere showed the tape to others involved with Media Matters, the group posted a video clip on its site and on YouTube, then notified journalists and civil rights and women's activists (Kosova, 2007). Response was swift and fierce. The public, including many people who tuned into Imus each morning, was outraged. Next, corporate sponsors of the show threatened to withdraw their advertising if Imus's show was not canceled. That led MSNBC then CBS to cancel the show—in effect, to fire Imus.

Clearly Imus should have been reprimanded for his racist, sexist statement, yet this incident is about more than one man whose speech was offensive. How could Imus have thought it would be acceptable to refer to serious, skilled athletes as "nappy headed hos?" What impulses in our culture could have led him to think he could say that?

As wrong as Imus may have been, he surely wasn't the only one at fault. What does it mean that his show was hugely popular, that millions of Americans wanted to hear what he had to say each day? Thoughtful commentators such as Bob Herbert (2007b) observe that Imus is a symptom of a larger problem. He says America is permeated by racism and sexism, and deeply racist and sexist language is no longer unusual; it is common. It fills the airwaves. Kathi Gray (2007) comments that it is unsurprising that a white man such as Imus would feel free to refer to black women as "hos" when black artists make millions with songs titled, "Can You Control Yo Ho?" "Smack My Bitch Up," "These Hos Like It Raw," and "Break a Bitch Til I Die." In 2009, two years after Imus' remarks, Eminem released "Relapse," which includes these lyrics: "See whore, you're the kinda girl that I'd assault and rape." Sexism, as well as racism, still pollute cultural life.

Although many rap songs and videos do degrade women, we should also note the presence of socially conscious rappers such as Common, Lupe Fiasco, and Mos Def, who manage to succeed without defiling women or blacks. The Reverends Al Sharpton and Jesse Jackson spoke against Imus's remarks and chastised black male rappers who degrade black women. Oprah, another talk show host, has made a fortune and earned a strong, positive public image without relying on sexist, racist language.

We can draw three lessons from the Imus incident. First, media advance representations of gendered and racial identities. Second, media have both progressive and regressive tendencies. And third, media content can be challenged and changed.

In this chapter, we explore how media shape our understandings of gender and how gender shapes our use of media. We begin by documenting the media-saturated character of our era. We then discuss how women and men use media and how media affect our views and expectations of women, men, and issues related to gender.

MEDIA SATURATION OF CULTURAL LIFE

People today are the most media-saturated and media-engaged people in history. Mass media are woven into our everyday lives. Nearly all (98.9%) of American homes have at least one television, and the average American home has more televisions than people—3.3 televisions and fewer than 3 people per household, and at least one of those televisions is on eight hours and 21 minutes a day (Media Trends Track, 2010).

Television is only one form of mass media. We watch films and read newspapers. Magazines abound, and each one is full of stories that offer us images of men and women and their relationships. Advertisements, which make up nearly half of some magazines, tell us what products we need if we are to meet cultural expectations of women and men. While walking, driving or biking, we take in an endless procession of billboards that advertise various products, services, people, and companies. Popular advice books and gothic novels are best sellers; pornographic print and visual media are increasingly popular.

And then there are the social media that we rely on to connect and interact with others. Today, personal and social media are seamlessly woven into our lives (Bohill, Owen, Jeong, Alicea, & Bocca, 2009; Potter, 2009). Many people, especially younger ones, consider cell phones, iPods, BlackBerries, MP3s, and PDAs essential to daily life (Kearney, 2006; Nunes, 2006). Most of us rely on the Web to meet people, chat with friends, collaborate, and participate in online communities. Today, 93% of adolescents in the United States use the Internet (Lenhart, Madden, Macgill, & Smith, 2007), and most use it daily (Jackson, 2008). More than half the teenagers in the United States are members of at least one social networking site (Lenhart, et al., 2007). Video games have become so popular that they often generate more revenue than top grossing films (Ivory, 2008).

As people become increasingly tech-savvy, many of us become not just consumer, but producers of media. In other words, unlike mass media, social media are often produced and consumed by the same people—regular people like you. People create personal blogs and podcasts. They give frequent updates on their lives on Facebook. They post videos on YouTube.

▼

Stephani   *I don't think the media influence who I am or what I do. I mean, sure, I watch a lot of shows and movies and read magazines like* Cosmo *and* Self, *but I think for myself. I like to see new styles of clothes and hair and makeup, and then I try them out for myself. That doesn't make me a dupe of the media.*

MEDIA INFLUENCES

Many people think they are immune to media effects or influences. In fact, surveys show that almost everyone thinks media affect others but not themselves, but scholars who study mass and social media say that they do affect most people's opinions, identities, choices, and lives (Kilbourne, 2007).

▼

Andrew   *Anyone who thinks media don't influence people just needs to spend five minutes on this campus. Everyone dresses alike and everyone changes how they dress when the media hawks new styles. Guys all wear the low slung jeans that nearly fall off their butts. All the girls wear pants so tight they look like they're painted on. Check out shoes. Check out hairstyles. Check out colors. Whatever the fashion gods say is in is what everybody wears. Tattoos? Earrings? If we're told they're cool, we all get them.*

From newspapers and television programs to video games and online communities, media shape our understandings of gender. They present images of women,

men, and relationships, and they shape our perspectives on events and issues relevant to gender.

We will consider five ways that media and gender affect our lives. The first concerns how men and women use media. The other four concern ways that media shape our views of men and women.

GENDERED MEDIA USE

There are general differences in how women and men tend to use media. Based on previous chapters in this book, you can probably make informed guesses about the nature of gendered patterns in media use.

In general, boys and men use media primarily for instrumental purposes. Matthew texts Carter if he wants to go out to dinner. Carter texts back "no" or "yes" and agrees on a time and place, and the call ends. They both stop texting at this point, having accomplished the task. Men are also more likely than women to read papers and watch television to get news and use the Internet to gather information (Consalvo, 2006) or accomplish tasks. Mike sends an IM to Bryan to see if Bryan has notes from a class Mike missed. Bryan IMs back. Two short messages take care of the task.

Men also tend to regard media as sources of entertainment. Watching football and basketball games on TV is part of many men's routines during seasons. Compared to girls and women, boys and men are more avid consumers of video games that are action-oriented or violent (Ivory, 2008). Boys and men also surpass girls and women in posting videos online (Rosenbloom, 2008).

Girls and women often use media to build relationships. Young girls (12–17 years old) are inclined to view social media as ways to connect with others. They spend a lot of online time sharing stories and developing relationships (Miller, 2008; Rosenbloom, 2008). Girls and women are also more likely to see phone conversations as ways to massage relationships. Katy calls Elizabeth to see if Elizabeth wants to go out to dinner. They talk for 20 minutes before Katy gets around to asking about dinner. They agree when and where to meet, then talk another 10 minutes before hanging up. Hannah sends an IM to Ashley, asking what Ashley's doing; she skypes Harrison to let him know she's planning to come to his recital; she texts Elaine to say she saw a great film that Elaine would like. In each case, Hannah is using IMs to connect with friends, to build relationships. Girls build online relationships that can be very intimate, in some ways more so than face-to-face relationships. On gURL.com many members say they disclose things to online friends that they cannot tell face-to-face friends.

Girls and women also perceive social media as allowing them to express themselves. They are more likely than boys to blog, create web content, and create profiles on social networking sites (Rosenbloom, 2008). In a recent study, Katy Bodey (2009; Bodey & Wood, 2009) explored how girls in their late teens use media to develop identities. She found that their blogs and pages on social sites are places where they talk about issues such as pressures to be skinny, drink (or not), have sex (or not), and dress particular ways. Bodey noticed that the girls were not just recording what they thought or did related to these pressures, but they were actually working out what they thought and wanted to do in the process of blogging or chatting online. In other words, social media were platforms for them to actively construct identities and get response from others. Many of the girls in Bodey's study said that getting responses to their posts helped them clarify their own thinking and also gain confidence in their ability to refuse to conform to gender norms they found troubling.

We also use media as platforms for discussing and sometimes challenging cultural expectations for femininity and masculinity. By 2004, 57% of teens in the United States had created their own media content (Pew, 2004). According to media scholar Henry Jenkins (2007), young people today use media as a means of "taking their culture apart and remixing it" (p. B10). For example, the 2010 Super Bowl featured several ads that derogated men for being weak. One was a fake injury report about a man who had his spine removed and went with his wife on a shopping trip, ending by telling the man to "Change out of the skirt." Another ad shows a thug giving a man in a car the ultimatum, "your Bridgestone tires or your life." The driver kicks the woman [his wife] out of his car, leaving the thug shouting "I said life, not wife." Within a few days of the broadcast of those ads, YouTube featured a number of parodies of them and satirical responses to them. Each of these videos challenged the assumption that real men must dominate others, particularly women.

Tell Us What's Important

Early theories of media's influence likened media to a hypodermic needle that injects a message into passive audiences (Campbell, Martin, & Fabos, 2005; Sparks, 2006). It didn't take scholars long to realize the hypodermic needle theory (also called direct effects theory and the magic bullet theory) was too simplistic. It didn't account for a number of factors that affect the impact of media. For instance, individuals differ in knowledge, education, experiences, and cognitive skills, all of which can affect the impact of any particular media message.

A more sophisticated approach to media influence is **agenda setting**, which claims media set our agenda by telling us what's important. Media, particularly mass media, have the ability to direct audience's attention to particular issues, events, and people and not to other issues, events, and people (Campbell, et al., 2005; Vivian, 2006). Media don't necessarily tell us what to think, but they do tell us what to think *about*—which issues, events, and people merit our attention; and which aspects of people and events are most important. By making certain phenomena more prominent than others, media focus our attention. A story on the front page of the newspaper seems more important than one on an inside page; the lead story on the evening news strikes us as more significant than a story covered at the end of the program; and an issue that is discussed on multiple blogs and chat rooms seems more consequential than an issue mentioned only a few times.

During the 2008 Presidential campaign, there were numerous issues that could have become the focus of attention. To which issues did the media direct our attention? You may recall the extensive coverage of the $150,000 the Republican National Committee spent on Vice Presidential candidate Sarah Palin's wardrobe and her role as mother. Less coverage was given to her stand on issues of the economy and national security.

The term **gatekeeper** refers to people and groups that control which messages get through to audiences of mass media. Gatekeepers include editors, owners, producers, and sometimes advertisers. The gatekeepers' newspapers and news programs shape our perceptions by deciding which stories to feature, how to represent issues and events, and how to depict women and men. Other gatekeepers are White House staff who decide which issues merit press releases and news conferences and which administration officials will appear on news programs. In making these decisions, the staff decides which topics will get coverage and thus be prominent in citizens' minds. By selectively regulating what we see, the news media influence how we perceive movements about gender and gender itself.

Beginning with the second wave of U.S. feminism in the 1960s, news media have consistently portrayed women's movements negatively. In the early days of radical feminism, media portrayed feminists as man-hating, bra-burning extremists. In 1970, thousands of women marched in cities around the world in the Strike for Equality. National news media did not present an interview with a single participant in the march. Not a single marcher's voice was included in national reporting on the event (Dow, 2004). In the early 1970s, an editor at *Newsday* gave these instructions to a reporter he assigned to research and write a story on the women's movement (Faludi, 1991): "Get out there and find an authority who'll say it's all a crock of shit" (pp. 75–76). Little wonder that the story that later appeared reported that the women's movement was a minor ripple without support or a future.

Communication scholars Lauren Danner and Susan Walsh (1999) analyzed newspaper coverage of the United Nations Fourth World Conference on Women and discovered that barely one-fourth of the stories focused on substantive issues at the conference. The majority of coverage emphasized conflicts among women at the conference (referred to as "bickering"), conferees' appearances (criticized for "letting themselves go" and having no sense of style), and feminism as the root problem for women. Further, most stories were placed in the inside pages or lifestyle sections—a location that would never be considered for stories on other United Nations conferences.

Another example of media bias in reporting on gender issues occurred in 1989 when Felice Schwartz, a management consultant, published an article in the prestigious *Harvard Business Review*. In that article, she argued that women who want to have children cost businesses too much money and should be placed on a separate track, in which they do not get the opportunities for advancement that go to men and women who are career-oriented. Dubbing this the **mommy track**, newspapers and magazines cited Schwartz's article as proof that women's place really is in the home and that they are lesser players in professional life. Once again, though, facts to support the claim were flimsy. Schwartz's article was speculative, as was her opinion that most women would willingly trade promotions and opportunities for more time with their families. Schwartz later retracted her advocacy of the mommy track, saying she had erred in claiming that women were more expensive as employees than men. Her retraction, however, got little coverage, because Schwartz's revised point of view did not support the media's bias regarding women's roles. Because there was virtually no coverage of Schwartz's retraction, many people read only the first article and continue to believe it.

EXPLPORING GENDERED LIVES | **BEAUTIFUL AND GRACEFUL AND, BY THE WAY, A GREAT ATHLETE**

How do the gatekeepers regulate television coverage of men's and women's sports and male and female athletes? For starters, men's sports get the lion's share of TV time. The limited coverage of women's sports that exists disproportionately focuses on sports in which athletes have the most conventional feminine appearance and behavior—ice skating and gymnastics, for instance (Eastman, 2004).

And then there's the issue of how women athletes are covered and what we are told is important about them. Announcers at the Summer Olympics routinely describe male athletes as having more skill and commitment than they describe female athletes as having (Eastman, 2004). Olympics announcers are 300% more likely to mention physical attractiveness when discussing female athletes than when discussing male athletes (Eastman, 2004). Also, greater coverage is given to particularly attractive female athletes, such as Maria Sharapova ("Celebrity 100," 2005). Sports writer Jane Gottesman describes mainstream media's coverage of women as "victims and vixens." As an example, she points to *Sports Illustrated.* In one year, the magazine had women on five covers: One was the annual swimsuit issue (vixens). The other four covers featured women who were victims: Monica Seles after she was stabbed, Nancy Kerrigan after being whacked, the widows of the Cleveland Indians players who died, and Mary Pierce who was portrayed as the victim of an unstable father (Araton, 2007).

Television and radio programs tend to negatively portray women who are identified as feminists. An analysis of news and public affairs television and radio programs on ABC, CNN, NPR, and PBS showed that women who are labeled "feminist" are more likely to be demonized than women who are not so labeled (Lind & Salo, 2004). After reviewing the *New York Times*'s coverage of stories about the feminist movement, media scholar Susan Douglas (2005) concluded that "bashing feminism" was prominent in the paper and that tells women that "feminism has been bad for them" (p. 15).

When the United States is engaged in war in the Gulf, Iraq or other places, newspapers and magazines feature poignant pictures of children watching mothers go to war, while talk shows ask, "Should a woman leave her baby to go to war?" Surely, this is a reasonable question to ask about any parent, but the media tend to ask it only about mothers and not about fathers. By doing this, media make motherhood central to how we think about women in the military service. In addition, media imply that women—good women—don't leave their children and that fathers aren't able to take care of children while mothers are overseas.

TELL US WHAT WOMEN AND MEN ARE/SHOULD BE

Media present us with images of what women and men are and should be. We'll focus on three aspects of how media portray the sexes. First, media underrepresent women, as well as minorities. Second, both sexes are portrayed primarily in stereotypical ways that reflect and reproduce conventional views of gender.

Underrepresent Women and Minorities   Mass media consistently underrepresent women and minorities relative to their presence in the population. Whether it is prime-time television, children's programming, or newscasts, males outnumber females. On Sunday-morning news programs only 10% of guests are women, and female guests are given less time to talk than males (Udell, 2005). The *Global Media Monitoring Project* (Gallagher, 2006) reports that in news programming "women are virtually invisible" (p. 17). Front pages of U.S. newspapers have more stories and photos about men than women (Lont & Bridge, 2004). In big box office films, women are underrepresented. Roughly 70% of major characters in top-grossing films are males (Jaimeson, More, Lee, Busse, & Romer, 2008). Although in reality women outnumber men, media (mis)representations would lead us to believe the opposite.

Beginning in 2001, The White House Project has researched the absence of women on Sunday morning talk shows on the five major networks: ABC, CBS, CNN, FOX, and NBC ("Who's Talking," 2001, 2002, 2005). The first "Who's Talking" report was released in 2001 and found that men outnumbered women 9 to 1 on these agenda-setting shows. A 2002 follow-up report noted that there had been little improvement—women only made up 13% of all guest appearances on the shows. The 2005 study, called Who's Talking Now, reported more than half of Sunday morning news shows still didn't include a single women. The lack of inclusion of qualified women on talk shows was particularly obvious after the 9/11 attacks. Kay Bailey Hutchison, who was the ranking member of the Senate Subcommittee on Aviation Operations, Safety, and Security, was not asked to appear once. Neither was Nancy Pelosi, the highest ranking Democrat on the House Intelligence Committee.

Minorities are also underrepresented and represented negatively in many cases. Members of minority groups appear in supporting roles, and they are likely to be shown in predominantly white cultures with their own racial culture and values obscured or devalued. Reality shows spotlight nonwhite characters, often representing them as dangerous or troublesome (Dubrofsky & Hardy, 2008; Hasinoff, 2008). Black characters have become more prominent in television programs, although they are often stereotyped as subordinate, athletic, lazy, criminal, or exotic (Dixon, 2006; Ramasubramanian, 2010; Wilson, Gutiérrez & Chao, 2003). Asians, Native Americans, and, with the exception of America Ferrara ("Ugly Betty"), Hispanics are underrepresented on prime-time television (Stroman & Dates, 2008). African Americans, Latinas, and Latinos are disproportionately cast in the roles of criminals with whites typically cast in the corresponding roles of law enforcers (Ramasubramanian, 2010). When they are presented, minority males usually appear as villains or criminals, and minority female characters are usually highly emotional and sexualized (Brooks & Hébert, 2006).

Portray Men Stereotypically   The majority of men on prime-time television are independent, aggressive, and in charge. Television programming for all ages disproportionately depicts men, particularly white, heterosexual men, as serious, confident, competent, and powerful (Brooks & Hébert, 2006; Walsh, 2008). Popular films such as *Fight Club, Armageddon,* and *Gladiator* exalt extreme stereotypes of masculinity: hard, tough, independent, sexually aggressive, unafraid, violent, totally in control of all emotions, and—above all—in no way feminine. Media also portray males as sexually active and as not responsible for sexual safety or pregnancies, should those result from having sex (Hust, Brown, & L'Engle, 2008; Kunkel, Eyal, Finnerty, Biely, & Donnerstein, 2005; L'Engle & Jackson, 2008).

Reality TV thrives on portraying men in the most traditional, stereotyped ways imaginable. One favored stereotype is the macho man, who proves his manliness by degrading women. For example, a man on *Joe Millionaire* was praised for ordering his dates, who were dressed elegantly, to shovel horse manure. A man on *Average Joes* was praised for calling his date a "beaver," and a contestant on *For Love or Money* forced a woman to bend over to pull off his boots while he kicked her bottom (Pozner, 2004). And the guiding premise of *Who Wants to Marry a Millionaire* is that being rich makes men desirable—the most traditional of all images of men. Notice that shows such as these not only advance degrading images of women, but also portray men negatively.

Equally interesting is how males are not typically portrayed. The most obvious misrepresentation is the scarcity of nonwhite men and nonwhite versions of masculinity. In the majority of media, white masculinity remains the norm—the unspoken and unquestioned standard for all men (Brooks & Hébert, 2006). One exception is hip-hop and rap music, which gives center stage to black men who are portrayed as independent, aggressive, and focused on sexual conquests (Weekes, 2004). News programs reinforce stereotypes of black men as angry and violent by giving greater attention to black men's violence than that of white men (Dixon & Azocar, 2006). Another absence is that men are seldom shown nurturing others or doing housework. With the notable exception of the 1983 film *Mr. Mom*—a comedy, not a serious drama—media tend to portray men as incompetent at homemaking, cooking, and child care (Vavrus, 2002). Although children's books sometimes depict women engaged in activities outside the home, there has been little parallel effort to show men involved in home life.

Yet, traditional representations of men are not the whole story. Media offer us some more complex portrayals of men—portrayals in which male characters combine qualities traditionally associated with masculinity and qualities traditionally associated with femininity. Toby Maguire, who starred in the *Spider-Man* movies, was kind and gentle when not ousting evildoers. Megastars such as Denzel Washington, Johnny Depp, and Tom Hanks have appeared as caring, sensitive men in many movies.

Contradictory images of masculinity are also embodied by rock and rap artists and their music. Some rappers uphold very traditional images of men, women, and relationships even as they claim to be alternatives to the mainstream. For instance, Eminem raps about violent, homophobic men who dominate and harm women. In one song, he raps about having 10 of his friends take his little sister's virginity (Goldstein, 2003). Rapper 50 Cent trades on his criminal past, and Nelly imitates gangsters with his gold tooth and yard fashions. At the same time, an LL Cool J video features a gospel choir and portraits of young children. In his video "Retrospect for Life," Common showed a young, pregnant black woman who faced single motherhood until the father returned to stay with her.

EXPLORING GENDERED LIVES | *The Man Show*

The Man Show, which ran from 1999 until 2004, was a half-hour television show on Comedy Central. Advertising itself as "a joyous celebration of chauvinism," the show premiered on June 16, 1999, with host Adam Carolla announcing that he was "a horrible misogynist" (Johnson, M., 2007, p. 171). Throughout its five-year history, the show was unabashedly and unapologetically sexist—erotic dancers who jumped on trampolines were called "juggies," powerful women such as Oprah were disparaged, and feminists were ridiculed. In one show, the host stated, "We are building a dam. A dam to hold back the tidal wave of feminization that is flooding this country. ... A dam to urinate off of when we're really drunk. We call this dam *The Man Show*" (cited in Johnson, M., 2007, p. 173).

The Man Show was very successful, receiving strong ratings throughout its run. It ended in 2004, not because it had lost audience, but because the two hosts, one of whom was the show's primary writer, left the show for other opportunities.

Do you think any network would air a show that viciously demeans a group other than women—a show demeaning Jews, whites, blacks, Hispanics?

Portray Women Stereotypically Media continue to portray girls and women primarily in ways consistent with traditional stereotypes. Media aimed at youth show female characters shopping, grooming, being emotional, and engaging in domestic activities, whereas male characters tend to be shown working, building, fighting, and thinking (Walsh & Ward, 2008). Also there is an increasing trend for media to portray women and even young girls in highly sexualized ways.

Like media representations of men, those of women tend to assume that whiteness is both the norm and the ideal. In media for adults, depictions of black women often rely on negative stereotypes of mammies, jezebels, matriarchs, and welfare mothers (Brooks & Hébert, 2006; Collins, 2004; Manatu, 2003). The prominence of white norms for female attractiveness is demonstrated by the tendency for black women who are portrayed as desirable to have lighter skin and straighter hair than is typical of their race (Perry, 2003). Asian women and Latinas are usually represented as exotic and sexualized (Brooks & Hébert, 2006). Amy Hasinoff's (2008) analysis of *America's Next Top Model* provides further evidence of media's normalization of whiteness. Hasinoff found that judges described women of color as having "an exotic look" or "an urban vibe," but described white women as "classic" and "American" (p. 334).

The most traditional stereotype is woman as sex object, and that continues to dominate media. Highly sexual portrayals of women and, increasingly girls, of all races pervade programming, advertising, and music videos (Brooks & Hébert, 2006; Rich, 2008; Walsh & Ward, 2008). The feminine ideal is young and extremely thin (Harrison, 2008), preoccupied with men, children and shopping. Music videos and magazines predominantly show women with impossibly perfect bodies, which have often been digitally altered (Rich, 2008), who are subservient to men. Traditional views of femininity even find their way into news shows, where female newscasters are young, attractive, and less outspoken than males (Jenkins, 2003; Thornham, 2007).

▼

Jill   *I hate reading magazines or watching TV anymore. All they tell me is what's wrong with me and what I should do to fix it. I think my butt is too big; my roommate has decided hers is too little. Doesn't anybody have a butt that is right? Same for breasts. I wonder if I should have breast enlargement surgery. It sounds stupid, but I keep thinking that I would look better and be more popular. I pluck my eyebrows and wax my legs and streak my hair. I wonder if it will ever be okay for women to look like they really look!*

Media's sexualization of women and girls has reached new levels. The highly sexualized portrayals of women have led some media commentators to refer to the pornification of mainstream media (Atwood, 2006; McRobbie, 2004; Paul, 2005). Ironically, even as media encourage girls to model themselves after hyper-sexualized female characters, media also send the message that girls and women—and not boys and men—are responsible for consequences of sexual activity (Hust, et al., 2008; Kunkel, Eyal, et al., 2005; L'Engle & Jackson, 2008).

Makeover reality shows strongly reinforce traditional views of women and what makes women desirable. In 2009, more than 250 makeover shows aired in U.S. broadcast media ("The Big Reveal," 2009). Judges on *America's Next Top Model* lavish praise on anorexic contestants and call normal-sized contestants (130 pounds at 5'8") "plus sized" (Pozner, 2004). *The Swan* and *Extreme Makeover* shine the spotlight on women who are willing to undergo as many as 14 cosmetic surgeries to meet unrealistic and unhealthy ideals for feminine beauty (Pozner, 2004; Weber, 2009). The message for women is clear: Your worth is based on your attractiveness. If you aren't gorgeous, then it's your job to make yourself over until you are (Bodey & Wood, 2009; Weber, 2009).

Another gendered pattern in media is portrayal of girls and women as relatively passive. From children's programming, in which a majority of female characters typically spend their time watching males do things, to MTV, which routinely shows women being sexually dominated, who enjoy being dominated and sometimes abused (Jhally & Katz, 2001; Rich, 2008; Walsh & Ward, 2008), media repeat the cultural view of women as dependent, ornamental objects who exist to look good, to please men, to care for children, and to be sexually desirable and available. Current popular magazines aimed at women provide better coverage than women's magazines of a decade ago on issues such as managing money, social projects, and obtaining credit. However, they also continue to advise women how to look better, lose weight, appeal to men, cook nice meals, maintain relationships, keep the home clean, and care for families (Kuczynski, 2001; Walsh & Ward, 2008).

A good example of media's gender stereotyping comes from reports just after the 9/11 attacks on America. There were approximately three male victims for

every one female victim, but media gave far more coverage, especially visual, to female victims. Why? Because showing women victims conformed to widely held social perceptions of women as passive victims, whereas showing men as victims would be inconsistent with social perceptions. Media also showed women grieving, mourning, and emoting. On the other hand, media virtually erased women's acts of heroism immediately following the 9/11 attacks. Women were involved in rescuing and providing medical help to victims, but they were nearly absent in coverage of the heroism displayed by Americans following the attacks (Faludi, 2007).

Media favor two opposite prototypes of women: good and bad. These polar opposites are often juxtaposed to dramatize differences in the consequences that befall good and bad women. Good women are pretty, deferential, faithful, and focused on home and family. Subordinate to men, they are usually cast as victims, angels, martyrs, and loyal helpmates.

Media also offer us the "bad woman"—the opposite of the "good woman." Versions of this image are the witch, bitch, whore, and iron maiden. In children's literature, we encounter witches and mean stepmothers as bad women and beautiful, passive females like Snow White and Sleeping Beauty as good women.

The criteria for the good woman have been challenged in some recent films and TV shows. For instance, Camryn Manheim on *The Practice* was heavier than social ideals of femininity prescribe. The character of Dr. Melfi on *The Sopranos* was middle-aged and not especially thin or sexy. Princess Fiona in *Shrek* was an overweight, green ogre who changed into a beautiful princess but then chose to return to being an ogre. In *Sailor Moon,* a children's show, a female lead character gets involved in amazing adventures (Leaper, 2000). And Marina, the lead character in Disney's *Sinbad,* decides not to marry the prince. Instead, she chooses the adventurous life of a pirate and saving her crew and ship from dangers. The runaway hit *Crouching Tiger, Hidden Dragon* told the story of Jen Yu, a strong woman who resists the marriage that has been arranged for her. Jen Yu fights fiercely, never needs to be rescued, and calls her own shots. Although Jen Yu, like Thelma and Louise, went over a cliff to avoid being controlled by others, she was nonetheless a strong, self-made character.

But aren't we seeing some images of good women who don't fit the old stereotypes? For instance, in the *Charlie's Angels* films, three very smart, aggressive women are portrayed positively, and *Titanic* features Rose, a woman who takes charge of her life. However, if we look more closely at these allegedly nontraditional images of women, we see that a desirable woman can be strong and

---

EXPLORING GENDERED LIVES | **VIRGIN OR WHORE; VIRGIN AND WHORE**

Sut Jhally is a professor of communication at the University of Massachusetts. Jackson Katz is a former all-star football player and founder-director of the U.S. Marine Corps gender violence prevention program. Both men are committed to research and education to reduce men's violence. In a recent comment on pop culture's normalization of violence, they made the following observations (Jhally & Katz, 2001, p. 30):

> While the forced choice between "virgin" and "whore" has been around for a long time— at least as far back as the Old Testament—today a new twist has been added: Girls now have to be both virgin and whore. Along with the cultural imperative that "sexuality is everything" is the equally powerful message that "good girls don't." Thus, teenage pop star Britney Spears presented herself as highly sexualized in appearance and music but also claimed to be a good girl who "saved herself for marriage." Young women caught in this catch-22 are constantly negotiating an impossible balance between virgin and slut, constantly concerned that admiration may change to contempt. If girls are confused about their sexual identities and appropriate ways to behave, it is because the culture itself tells a contradictory story about female sexual identity.

Do you agree that young women today are encouraged to be simultaneously innocent and sexual?

---

successful if and only if she also meets traditional stereotypes of femininity—that is, if she is beautiful, compassionate, and identified with one or more men. The women in *Charlie's Angels* were very sexy and were often shown with minimal clothing—dancing in underwear, wrapped in bath towels, and exposing cleavage even as they engaged in fights. They fought the movie's villains in leather outfits and high heels and never broke a sweat. In *Charlie Wilson's War* Joanne Herring, played by Julia Roberts, believes the United States is not doing what it should to aid Afghan Freedom Fighters. To give them more aid, she has to depend on a man, Charlie Wilson, played by Tom Hanks. What at first appear to be radically different images of women are still entwined with some very familiar, very traditional images.

Some of my students asserted that *Sex and the City* portrayed women in progressive, unconventional ways. *Sex and the City* did show women aggressively going after what they wanted, but what did they want? Clothes, shoes, purses, and men. The program did show women being sexually active, but what is unconventional about heterosexual sex between two consenting adults? *Sex and the City* did not show women exerting power outside of the bedroom and did not show women being ambitious about much other than shopping. In one episode, Carrie, the sex columnist, discovered she had less than $1,000 in her bank account but $40,000 worth of designer shoes—what is new or progressive about depicting a woman whose life centers on fashion and shopping?

Similarly, many viewers perceive *Desperate Housewives* as showing strong, smart women who know what they want and go for it with a take-no-hostages style. Yes, the plot lines are campy, there's lots of wit, and the show offers more than an occasional wink toward gays and lesbians. But the women who are the desperate housewives don't provide new or unconventional images of women (Pozner & Seigel, 2005). When not cheating on her husband with her teenaged gardener, Gabrielle mows the lawn in an elaborate evening gown and high heels—an amusing caricature, but the underlying idea is that women must look sexy no matter what they are doing. She is the only minority woman, and she embodies the stereotype of the oversexed, materialistic Latina. In fact, all the desperate housewives echo very conventional depictions of women as sex objects who are obsessed with clothes, money, and men.

Nowhere is commodified sexuality more prominent than in reality TV shows (Lundy, Ruth, & Park, 2008). In fact, it is central to the plot lines of shows such as *The Bachelor, Shot at Love with Tila Tequila,* and *Rock of Love.* Or consider *The Girls Next Door,* another reality TV show. This one features three young women who explicitly use their sexuality to gain power and get ahead. Yes, the women are powerful and are advancing, but they are doing so because and only because they are glamorous, sexy babes. E! Network's very popular *Keeping Up with the Kardashians* follows the lives of young women who are successful in their careers—again because they unabashedly use their sexuality to advance. The hypersexual identity they are urged to cultivate is one that women can only achieve—and, in fact, can only attempt to achieve—by consuming products and services. Marketers tell girls they can maximize their potential through consumption (Gill, 2008; McRobbie, 2000, 2004; Morreale, 2007).

Perhaps the most interesting trend in media is combining traditional and nontraditional images of gender in a single character. For instance, in *Erin Brockovich* Julia Roberts met the conventional feminine image of sexiness, but she defied prevailing expectations of femininity by refusing to put her children ahead of her own goals. Likewise, in *Charlie Wilson's War,* Roberts portrayed a beautiful, desirable woman, yet she was also highly engaged in political matters. Jack in *Titanic* is traditionally masculine in his adventurous spirit and independence, yet he is also nurturing and gentle. In *Mr. and Mrs. Smith,* Angelina Jolie's character was hypersexualized and, thus, feminine, but she was also a cold-blooded assassin, which is not consistent with conventional femininity. In *Saving Private Ryan,* Tom Hanks's character fulfills dominant views of masculinity by being a soldier and engaging in the violence of war; at the same time, he disputes conventional views of masculinity by showing nurturance and tenderness. In *Public Enemies,* Johnny Depp is a cold-blooded killer, but he is also very tender with his sweetheart.

Gendered Images in Advertising   The stereotypical portrayals of women and men we've discussed appear not only in stories and programs but also in advertising. There are several reasons why advertising's influence on our views of women and men may be even more powerful than that of programmed media content (Kilbourne, 2007). First, advertisements on TV, in magazines, on billboards, and so forth are repeated multiple times, so we are exposed repeatedly to the messages. Second, a majority of ads emphasize visual images, which are less subject to conscious analysis than verbal claims. Third, advertising can affect us significantly because we think we're immune to it. Although many people think they don't buy

| EXPLORING GENDERED LIVES | GIRLS GONE WILD |

The "Girls Gone Wild" videos show young women—often college students, usually intoxicated—baring their breasts and sometimes more. Some of the women who have appeared on Girls Gone Wild videos say they felt freed and empowered by the partial striptease. They say doing it makes them feel liberated, even though they are embodying the most conventional script for women (Pitcher, 2006).

Joe Francis feels more than liberated; he feels rich. Since he began producing the videos, they have generated more than $100 million in direct mail sales (Pitcher, 2006). He's bought two mansions, a ski resort, and a jet (Navarro, 2004). And what do the women—who make the videos sell—get? A GGW T-shirt.

But, says Francis, Mantra Films, Inc., which distributes GGW videos, has a policy not to film girls under 18. In 2006, however, he pleaded guilty to filming two 17-year-olds baring their breasts ("Girls Gone Wild," 2006).

To what extent do you perceive being in a GGW video as liberating for girls?

a particular brand of jeans or beer because of ads, research suggests differently—ads do affect what people purchase and what they consider attractive, feminine, masculine, and so forth. We buy not just products but also the images that advertisers sell us (Kilbourne, 2007, 2010).

Consistent with traditional views of masculinity, advertising generally portrays men as independent, successful, engaged in activities, and strong. In some ads, males appear angry—often in the roles of rebels against authority (Katz, 2003). The men in ads tend to have muscular bodies, perfect hair and skin, and brilliantly white teeth. The message to men is that this is the ideal of masculinity. According to Michael Rich (2008), these unrealistic images can contribute to negative self-images and to extreme, sometimes dangerous behaviors aimed at achieving the ideals.

Advertising directed at men often links products with hypermasculinity and violence. For example, leading brands of condoms bear the names of ancient warriors (Trojans) and kings (Ramses). Super-athlete Michael Jordan advertises Hanes underwear for men. Other athletes are used to advertise yogurt, deodorant, and light beers—if a star athlete will eat yogurt and drink light beer, these products must be manly. Men's dominance is also emphasized by positioning. In commercials, men are usually shown positioned above women, and women are more frequently pictured in varying degrees of undress. Such nonverbal cues represent men as powerful and women as vulnerable and submissive.

Just as prime-time television ignores or ridicules men's domestic activities, ads for cooking and cleaning products caricature men as incompetent klutzes in the kitchen and no better at taking care of children. Ads often represent men in home situations as lazy dolts who care only about beer, cars, and sports.

▼

Kaleb   *What burns me up is those programs and commercials that show men as absolute idiots. One of the worst is that one where the mother gets sick, and the kids and husband just fall apart without her to fix meals and do laundry. Give me a break. Most guys can do the basic stuff just as well as women, and I'm tired of seeing them made into jokes anytime they enter a nursery or kitchen.*

Although ads generally portray women as more competent at homemaking tasks, men still tend to be defined as authorities. Women are routinely shown anguishing over dirty floors and bathroom fixtures, only to be relieved of their distress when Mr. Clean shows up to tell them how to keep their homes spotless. Even when commercials are aimed at women and are selling products intended for them, most of the time a man's voice is used to explain the value of what is being sold. Male **voice-overs** reinforce the cultural view that men are authorities and women depend on men to tell them what to do.

▼

Regina   *The ad that just kills me is the one where a woman is cleaning her carpet with whatever product is being advertised—something you sprinkle on your rug and then vacuum up. This woman is dancing around with her vacuum and seems deliriously happy—like this is what she most loves to do in the world. We may do cleaning, but only a total bimbo would get ecstatic about it. That ad makes women look silly and stupid and trivial.*

Central to advertising is sexual objectification of women. Women, usually with minimum clothes and in highly sexual poses, are used to sell everything from jeans to fishing line (Zimmerman & Dahlberg, 2008). The women in the ads, like those in programming, have perfect faces, bodies, and hair. By linking incredibly sexy women with products, advertisers hope we will buy the product thinking that it will either make us more like the women in the ads or more likely to be appealing to them.

Advertising plays a key role in promoting appearance and pleasing others as foci of women's lives. Advertising tells women how to be "me, only better" by coloring their hair; how to lose weight and get rid of wrinkles so "you'll still be attractive to him"; and how to prepare gourmet meals so "he's always glad to come home." Advertisements for makeup, cologne, shampoo, and clothes often show women attracting men because they have used the products to make themselves irresistible. The ads and articles emphasize that women need to change themselves to be adequate—they need to fix, improve, repair, rejuvenate, disguise, and correct some or all parts of themselves. Beneath these ads is the warning that, if a woman fails to look good and please her man, he might leave (Kilbourne, 2007).

There are more subtle ways in which ads influence our understandings of women and men. Sometimes advertising and content are blurred. One way this happens is when an advertiser pays for an ad in a magazine, and, in return, the magazine gives **complimentary copy**—one or more articles that increase the market appeal of its product (Turner, 1998). A soup company that places an ad might be given a three-page story on how to prepare meals using that brand of soup; an ad for hair-coloring products might be accompanied by an article based on interviews with famous women who color their hair. A second way in which advertising and content are blurred is **product placement,** showing or mentioning a particular brand or product in a show, story, film, or other form of media. For example, Coca-Cola could pay to have characters in a film drink Cokes instead of another soft drink. If complimentary copy and product placement blur the line between advertising and content, immersive advertising completely erases the line. **Immersive advertising** incorporates a product or brand into actual storylines in books, television programs, and films (Lamb & Brown, 2006). For instance, Naomi Johnson (2007, 2010, 2011) critically analyzed romance novels marketed to young girls. She found that storylines in series such as *A List* and *Gossip Girl* revolved around buying products such as La Perla lingerie and Prada bags and relying on services to glamorize the face and body. The characters' identities were defined by particular products and services.

Several years ago, Dove introduced a new and very different campaign focused on "real beauty." Instead of showing only young, thin women with perfect bodies, faces, and hair, ads showed women of various ages, sizes, and appearances (Pozner, 2005). Within this campaign Dove has included ads showing how the perfect women usually featured in media are created. For instance, one ad begins with a regular-looking woman seated. Viewers see how makeup and hairstyling change her appearance, making her beautiful. This ad is innovative in revealing the techniques used to create a "natural" beauty.

In sum, media, including advertising, tell us what women and men are and should be. Although media sometimes portray men and women in nontraditional roles or with nontraditional qualities, most media images reflect long-established cultural stereotypes of masculinity and femininity. Let's now consider what media tell us about relationships between women and men.

TELL US HOW WOMEN AND MEN RELATE TO EACH OTHER

Occasionally, media offer nontraditional images of relationships between men and women. Most of the time, however, media tell us that women and men relate to each other in traditional ways. We'll discuss four traditional images of relations between the sexes that are prominent in media.

Women's Dependence/Men's Independence   Media continue to portray women primarily as domestic and dependent on powerful, independent men. Consider first the prevalence of depictions of girls and women as dependent and boys and men as independent. In Disney's award-winning animated film *The Little Mermaid,* the mermaid quite literally gives up her identity as a mermaid in order to be with a man. Similarly, Disney's *The Lion King* features female lions that depend on a male lion to save them, and the heroine of *Pocahontas* is portrayed as a beautiful, sexy maiden rather than as the courageous, strong Native American girl she actually was.

Books aimed at adolescent females, such as the *Gossip Girls* and *A-List* series, emphasize the importance of being pretty, sexy, and popular in order to win the attention of males (Johnson, 2007, 2011; Wolf, 2006). Women, as well as minorities, are still more often cast in supporting roles than leading ones in television shows aimed at children and adults. Beauty is more emphasized than health in women's magazines (Walsh & Ward, 2008). Even magazines such as *Working Woman* and *Savvy*, which are aimed at professional women, give substantial space to appearance and dress, along with articles on career topics. Magazines aimed at preadolescent and adolescent girls brim over with advice on how to lose weight, look better, and be interesting to boys.

A great many music videos portray females as strippers, nymphomaniacs, or prostitutes who exist only for men and spend their lives waiting for men's rescue or attention, whereas males are shown ignoring, exploiting, or directing women (Walsh & Ward, 2008). In the digital world of video games, women are routinely sexualized and infantilized (Flanagan, 2004).

But there are exceptions worth noting. *Law and Order: Special Victims Unit* breaks away from many norms in media representations of women and violence against women. The program rarely shows actual rape scenes, highlights the role of rape culture in violence against women, and challenges myths that most rapes are committed by minority men (Cuklanz & Moorti, 2006). ABC's hit show, *Ugly Betty*, features America Ferrara as Betty Suárez, a working-class Latina who is portrayed as clumsy and unattractive. Betty, however, seems comfortable with who she is and how she looks. She's much more interested in succeeding in her career than in dieting or wearing makeup (Rivero, 2007).

Women's Incompetence/Men's Authority   A second prevalent theme in media's representations of relationships is men as the competent authorities who save or take care of less-competent women. Children's literature vividly implements this motif by portraying females who are rescued by males. Sleeping Beauty's resurrection depends on Prince Charming's kiss, and Snow White has to rely on a prince of her own. One of the most popular adolescent book and TV series began with the novel, *Twilight*. In the twilight world, Bella is a lovely but clumsy young woman who is constantly getting in danger. Always there to rescue her is Edward, the handsome, inhumanly strong vampire. He takes care of Bella, repeatedly saving her from various dire fates.

As with other stereotypes, this one is being challenged by occasional resistant media images. The children's film *Sinbad* tells the story of a young woman who decides not to marry a prince. Instead, she follows her heart to sail the seas and becomes a pirate. Jen Yu in *Crouching Tiger, Hidden Dragon* takes care of herself instead of waiting for a man to rescue her. The same is true of Buffy on *Buffy the Vampire Slayer*. Suzanne Collins' *Hunger Games* and *Chasing Fire* feature a strong female protagonist.

Newspapers also convey the message that men are authorities and—by their near absence or lack of power—women are not. More than two-thirds of cited sources in newspaper stories are male. Similarly, women are unlikely to be represented as experts on topics, and blacks are still too often cast in racially stereotyped roles (Brooks & Hébert, 2006). An analysis of front pages in newspapers revealed that women are far more often represented as victims than as leaders, role models, success stories, or heroes (Lont & Bridge, 2004). As noted earlier in this chapter, there were approximately three male victims for every one female victim in the aftermath 9/11 attacks on the United States, but media portrayed far more women victims than men (Faludi, 2007). Even when newspapers do cover powerful women, such as Oprah Winfrey, the stories often focus more on women's appearance and personal lives than on their success and power (Lont & Bridge, 2004). During the 2008 Presidential primary, commentators talked extensively about Hillary Clinton's appearance—what clothes she wore, her hairstyle, lines on her face. Parallel comments were not made about the appearance of male contenders in the primary. During the election campaign, there was much conversation about Governor Sarah Palin's appearance with some commentators noting she was "a babe."

Women as Primary Caregivers/Men as Breadwinners   A third perennial theme in media is that women are caregivers and men are breadwinners. Since the 1980s, in fact, this gendered arrangement has been broadcast with renewed vigor. Media portrayals of career women often give little or no attention to their career activities. Although these characters have titles such as lawyer or doctor, they are shown predominantly in their roles as homemakers, mothers, and wives. We knew more about the shoes (Jimmy Choo, usually) than about the careers of *Sex in the City's* four main characters!

Women's roles in the home and men's roles outside it are reinforced by newspapers and television news. Stories about men focus on work and on their achievements (Lont & Bridge, 2004), reiterating the cultural message that men are supposed to *do,* to perform. Meanwhile, the fewer stories about women tend to emphasize their roles as wives, mothers, and home-makers. Women's professional status can be erased by on-air comments that demean women's professionalism and emphasize their sexuality. For example, the *New York Post* referred to foreign correspondent Christiane Amanpour as a "war slut," and the *Wall Street Journal* criticized her choice of clothing; the *Wall Street Journal* had earlier criticized CNN's Paula Zahn's hairstyle (Jenkins, 2003). In August of 2007, presidential primary candidate Hillary Clinton spoke while wearing a V-necked top and a conservative jacket. Media coverage of Clinton's speech was so focused on the hint of cleavage revealed by the V-necked top that what Clinton said was virtually ignored.

Even stories about women who are in the news because of achievements and professional activities typically mention marriage, family life, and other aspects of women's traditional roles. For example, when Margaret Thatcher became prime minister of England, newspapers repeatedly referred to her as "a housewife," a label that ignored her long and active role in politics (Romaine, 1999). Virtually every story on Governor Sarah Palin included information about her family as well as her appearance.

Women as Victims and Sex Objects/Men as Aggressors   A final theme in media's representations of relationships is that women continue to be portrayed as sex objects for men's pleasure. In this representation, the very qualities women are encouraged to develop (beauty, sexiness, passivity, and powerlessness) in order to meet cultural ideals of femininity contribute to objectifying and dehumanizing them (Hust, et al., 2008; Kunkel, Eyal, et al., 2005; L'Engle & Jackson, 2008). Also, the qualities that men are urged to exemplify (aggressiveness, sexuality, and strength) are the same qualities that are linked to abuse of women (Johnson, 2006; Wood, 2001b).

Prevalent in media of all types are images of desirable men as aggressive and dominant and of desirable women as young, pretty, sexual, and vulnerable. Whereas men are seldom shown nude, women routinely are. Portrayals of women as sex objects and of men as sexual aggressors are common in many rap and rock music videos and video games. Typically, MTV portrays females dancing provocatively in scanty or revealing clothing. Frequently, men are seen coercing women into sexual activities or physically abusing them (Smith, 2005). These portrayals, in carrying to extremes the long-standing cultural views of masculinity as aggressive and femininity as passive, encourage us to see violence as erotic (Romer 2008). Some of the most popular video games require violence to win (Ivory, 2008; Romer, 2008).

Hip-hop, rap, and especially gangsta rap also carry messages about relationships between women and men. They portray women as sex objects—often only particular body parts instead of whole human beings—and portray men as egocentric, insensitive abusers of women (Collins, 2007; Gray, 2007). Some of the most extreme rap videos appear on *Uncut*, which is broadcast on Black Entertainment Television and features endless shots of women's butts wriggling in thongs and occasional shots of a rapper swiping a credit card between the cheeks of a woman's behind (Wright, 2004). After studying teenagers for more than two years, researchers report that adolescents who listen to music with the highest levels of sexually degrading lyrics (defined as representing women as sex objects, men as sexually voracious, and sex as casual and meaningless) are more likely to engage in sex (Parker-Pope, 2007).

▼

Tiffany   *It makes black guys angry when I say it, but I think gangsta rap is totally sexist and destructive. Some of my girlfriends say they like rap and don't take the anti-woman lyrics personally. The way I see it, though, calling women bitches and whores is as hateful as you can get. It totally disses women. If black men talk that way about black women, how can we respect ourselves or expect others to?*

Along with the disrespect of women, much of rap and gangsta rap glorifies violence. This conveys messages not only about gender but also about race. According to *New York Times* commentator Brent Staples (2005), African-American teenagers are being fed a dangerous myth that "defines middle-class normalcy and achievement as 'white' while embracing violence, illiteracy and drug dealing as

---

EXPLORING GENDERED LIVES | **HIP-HOP WITHOUT THE MISOGYNY**

"I love hip-hop, but it upsets me that young boys treat girls like objects. I feel like I don't have a voice," said 17-year-old Tempestt Young (Dawson, 2005, p. 18). So she became a key organizer for the 2005 Feminism and Hip-Hop Conference, which was attended by more than 2,000 people, including music industry professionals. Young is just one of many young black women who have decided to change the game in hip-hop (Morgan, 1999).

Young is not alone. In 2005, *Essence*, a leading magazine aimed at blacks, announced it was sponsoring a year-long campaign called "Take Back the Music." The campaign's goal is to challenge and change the antiwoman stance of much rap music (Childress, 2005). Women students at historically black Spelman College chimed in by voting male rap artist Nelly as "Misogynist of the Month." The women had long resented the antiwoman attitudes in his songs, but it was the last straw when he released "Tip Drill," an urban slang term for a woman who has an attractive body but an unattractive face (Farrell, 2004). Al Sharpton added his support by asking the FCC to ban rappers who disrespect women (Childress, 2005). Many of those who protest rappers like Nelly point to progressive rappers such as Mos Def and Common who, they say, "resist dick-swinging bravado" ("Ms. Musings," 2004, p. 13).

Queen Latifa has similarly insisted that music doesn't have to degrade women to be cool. She believes that rap can maintain its strong, distinctive character without demeaning women. Her own music, as well as other rap that she praises, portrays women as strong and able people.

Do you think rap and gangsta rap music can maintain its character without disparaging women?

'authentically' black" (p. A26). The glorification of violence is evident in the name of the record company that Dr. Dre cofounded: Death Row Records; it's obvious in the title of 50 Cent's album, *The Massacre*; it's apparent in gang-style rivalries that resulted in the deaths of Tupac Shakur and Notorious B.I.G. Patricia Hill Collins (2007) notes that the "pimp-playa-bitch-ho" representations "encourage youth who listen to rap music, watch hip-hop music videos and chase the latest hip-hop fashions to think of themselves in these terms" (p. 74).

MOTIVATE US TO CONSUME

Media encourage us to consume. In fact, some media analysts say that the primary purpose of media is to convince us we need to own more things, buy more products and services, spend, spend, spend. According to Diane Levin and Jean Kilbourne (2008), television, films, music, and the Internet encourage us to think that owning the right things will make us sexy, cool, and desirable. If we buy certain clothes, we'll look sexy. If we drink certain drinks, we'll be cool. If we undergo certain surgeries, we'll be beautiful. If we shop in certain stores and go to certain clubs, we'll be with it.

When we see perfect bodies in magazines and on television, we may feel our body is not good enough. When we watch *Extreme Makeover,* we witness someone being transformed from ordinary looking to extraordinary looking, and we learn it's possible to transform ourselves. Advertising plays on that insecurity by telling us that if we buy a certain product or have a certain procedure, we will look better. If a woman uses Pantene shampoo, her hair will be as luxurious as that of the model in the television ad for that product. If a man drinks Michelob, he'll get the gorgeous woman that is with the man in the Michelob ad. If we buy our clothes at the Gap, we'll look like the cover girl on *Marie Claire.*

The whole purpose of advertising is to convince us that buying whatever is advertised will make us happier, more attractive, more successful, and so forth. Sometimes ads tell us about products and services that claim to help with some need we have already identified. But that's not all media do. They actively cultivate desire in us by convincing us we have problems we weren't aware of that can be solved by products and services we had never thought of.

Media encourage us to perceive normal bodies and normal physical functions as problems that can be solved by buying something (McRobbie, 2009). It's understandable to wish we weighed a little more or less, had better-developed muscles, and never had pimples or cramps. What is not reasonable, however, is to regard normal, functional bodies as unacceptable or defective. Yet, this is precisely the perception cultivated by the predominant media portrayals of women and men.

In recent years, advertising has increasingly focused on young girls. In *Packaging Girlhood,* Sharon Lamb and Lyn Brown (2006) argue that for many girls today girl power is reduced to purchasing power. There's nothing new in marketing campaigns that focus on (improving) women's appearance and attractiveness (to men). What is new and noteworthy is the kind of image girls are told is ideal, the kind of image they are encouraged to embody. Aggressive marketing aimed at girls who are

---

EXPLORING GENDERED LIVES | CHALLENGING THE INSECURITY FACTORY

In 2007, Anna Holmes had had enough! She was disillusioned with women's magazines that function as an "insecurity factory"—making women feel insecure about their bodies, clothes, and behaviors and then advising women to "fix" the insecurity by buying various products. Holmes decided to do something. She founded Jezebel.com, a women's interest blog. Now run by executive editor, Jessica Coen, the blog criticizes digitally altered pictures that present unrealistic ideals of beauty; it offers commonsense advice on matters such as how to dress for internships; it calls out sexism in media and in celebrities; and offers inexpensive alternatives to the high-end products hyped in most women's magazines. With 37 million page views a month and about 200,000 distinct visitors each day, Jezebel.com has established its niche (Mascia, 2010).

just reaching puberty encourages them to aspire to a highly sexualized image of femininity (Durham, 2008; Lamb & Brown, 2006). According to Levy (2005), in *Female Chauvinist Pig*, "we live in a time when self-empowerment is sold to women and girls as packaged, magazine-cover 'beauty.' ... American society teaches girls that their value and success are tied to their appearance" (p. 4). So too is power tied to consumption; girl power defines girls as consumers since buying the right products and services is the primary, perhaps the only, route to status and success.

Buying products to improve ourselves is not restricted to women. Media also pathologize normal male bodies, telling them that they are deficient but can fix that by buying something. No longer is it good enough to be healthy and active. The bodybuilding trend has created unrealistic and unhealthy ideals for masculine bodies. The desire to have a very muscular body contributes to the increasing abuse of steroids among men. Although media's idealization of extreme musculature and strength is not the only cause of steroid use, we should not dismiss the influence of portrayals of muscle-bound men as ideal (Lindgren, & Lélièvre, 2009).

Normal changes in men's sexual vigor are also represented as problems to be solved. In recent years, Viagra, Levitra, and Cialis have become blockbuster drugs, making millions for the companies that can solve the "problem." The "problem," of course, was not a problem until drug companies decided they could make money by pathologizing normal changes in male sexual vitality.

In 2010, the news broke that there was a pill that the maker claimed can "restore depressed female sex drive" in premenopausal women (Wilson, 2010, p. A1). The maker, German drug company Boehringer Ingelheim, tried to get the pill approved in the United States. The Food and Drug Administration (FDA), however, has not approved the drug. A review by FDA staff concluded that the possible benefits do not outweigh side effects, which include dizziness, nausea, and fatigue. Critics further pointed out that a marketing campaign that would follow approval would try to convince normal women that they have a problem they need to treat. Dr. Fugh-Berman of Georgetown University's medical school notes that this is a classic case of "medicalizing normal conditions" (Wilson, 2010, p. 2A).

Media have convinced millions of American women that what every medical source considers "normal body weight" is really abnormal and cause for severe dieting (Harrison, 2008; Levin & Kilbourne, 2008; National Institute of Mental Health, 2010). Similarly, gray hair, which naturally develops with age, is now something all of us, especially women, are encouraged to cover up. Facial lines, which indicate that a person has lived a life and accumulated experiences, now can be removed so that we look younger—a prime goal in a culture that glorifies youth.

The belief that women (and increasingly men) should remove body hair grows out of a media campaign to persuade us that something normal is really abnormal. In 1915, a sustained marketing campaign informed women that underarm hair was unsightly and socially incorrect. (The campaign against leg hair came later.) *Harper's Bazaar,* an upscale magazine, launched the crusade against underarm hair with a photograph of a woman whose raised arms revealed clean-shaven armpits. Underneath the photograph was this caption: "Summer dress and modern dancing combine to make necessary the removal of objectionable hair" (Adams, 1991). By 1922, razors and depilatories were firmly ensconced in middle America, as evidenced by their inclusion in the women's section of the Sears & Roebuck

She is never embarrassed because of—

those insistent and obvious growths of superfluous hair which so completely take away a woman's charm and rob her of daintiness. Like nearly two million other women she has learned that Veet Cream offers a most satisfactory solution to the perplexing problem almost every woman faces, of how best to get rid of such disfiguring hair. If you are a slave to the razor, or have to resort to old-fashioned, bothersome depilatories, you will do well to try this perfumed, velvety cream. Whereas the old-fashioned methods employed merely remove hair *above* the skin surface, Veet melts the hair away *beneath* it. Veet is put up in a tube and is ready for instant use. You simply spread it on, wait a few minutes, rinse it off and the hair is gone. Entirely satisfactory results are guaranteed in every case, or money refunded. It may be obtained for 3/- and 1/6 at chemists, hairdressers and stores, or direct by post upon receipt of purchase price, plus 6d. for postage and packing. (A trial tube sent for 6d. in stamps.) Dae Health Laboratories, Ltd., (Dept 381P), 68, Bolsover St., London, W.1.

Beware of imitations and inferior substitutes — they are often more expensive too!

VEET CREAM

REMOVES HAIR LIKE MAGIC.

3/- and 1/6 per tube

Advertising Archives

Advertising aims to create needs that new products can fulfill.

catalogue. In recent years, the hair removal campaign has targeted men—promoting the clean (usually waxed) chest as the ideal of masculinity. With that, companies expand the market of people who will pay for products and services that increase their profits.

Many women's natural breast size exceeded the cultural ideal in the 1960s, when thin, angular bodies were represented as desirable. Thus, breast reduction surgeries increased. By the 1980s, cultural standards had changed to define large breasts as the feminine ideal. Consequently, breast augmentation surgeries accelerated in an effort to meet the new cultural standards for beautiful bodies. To achieve constructed and arbitrary ideals, many women continue to endure surgery that sometimes leads to disfigurement and loss of sensation.

Surgeries to conform to white ideals of beauty are also on the rise. In 2006, one of the most popular plastic surgeries for Asians was surgery to transform eyes from ovals, typical of Asians, to orbs, typical of Caucasians. For African Americans surgery to make the nose less broad was the number-one procedure (Cognard-Black, 2007).

Media images encourage us to measure up to impossible ideals. When we fail, as inevitably we must, we feel bad about our bodies and ourselves. Accepting media messages about our bodies and ourselves, however, is not inevitable: Each of us has the ability to reflect on the messages and resist those we consider inappropriate or harmful.

▼

Christi   *When I used to diet, I remember thinking that I was in control. I believed what all the ads said about taking charge of myself, exerting control. But I was totally* not *in control. The advertisers and the companies making diet products were in control. So was society with the idea that "you can't be too thin" and that it's more important for girls to look good (read "thin") than to feel good (read "not hungry"). Society and its views of women were in control, not me. I was totally a puppet who was just doing what they told me to do.*

Media efforts to pathologize natural physiology can be very serious. As we have seen in previous chapters, the emphasis on excessive thinness contributes to severe and potentially lethal dieting and eating disorders, especially in Caucasian women. Nonetheless, most of the top female models are skeletal. Seeing anorexic models as the ideal motivates many college women to diet excessively in an effort to force their bodies to fit a socially constructed ideal that is unrealistic and unhealthy. Dangers—including heart attack, stroke, and liver disease—also exist for men who use steroids or diet in an effort to meet the ideal masculine form promoted by media.

We've now considered five ways that media—mass, social, and personal—intersect our lives and, particularly, how we understand and embody gender in our lives. In the final pages of this chapter, we'll discuss two broad implications of gendered media.

EXPLORING GENDERED LIVES | **IS CENSORSHIP THE ANSWER?**

Should we ban violent, misogynistic media that celebrate violence against women? Even those who are most outraged by the objectification and sexism of media seldom advocate censorship. The U.S. Constitution provides strong protections of freedom of speech, and for good reason. The problem with censoring is that somebody decides what all of us can watch, hear, and see. Who has the right to make this decision for all of us? A better answer may be to demand that media offer us multiple, diverse images of women and men. Instead of banning what we don't like, perhaps we work to enlarge the range of ways in which people and relationships are portrayed (Clemetson & Samuels, 2000). Acting on this idea, Marta Lamas in Mexico founded *Debate Feminista,* a periodical that provides alternatives to mainstream South American views of gender and relationships between women and men (Navarro, 2005).

Under what conditions, if any, would you support censorship of media?

IMPLICATIONS OF GENDERED MEDIA

ASSESS OURSELVES UNFAIRLY

The unrealistic images of men, women, and relationships that media advances encourage us to see ourselves, by comparison, as inadequate. Media, including advertising, bombard us with unrealistic images of women, men, and relationships—images that few real people can ever achieve. Regardless of how many products we buy and how many surgeries we have, few women are going to look like Evan Rachel Wood, Halle Berry, or Kiera Knightley, and few men are going to look like Zac Efron or Elijah Kelley. These are not images against which to measure ourselves. Yet many people do compare themselves to actors and models, and the result is low self-esteem.

Media portrayals of relationships between women and men are also unrealistic and not fair standards for assessing our own relationships. Most of us will not meet the man or woman of our dreams who has no flaws. Most of us encounter problems in our relationships that cannot be solved in 30 minutes (minus time for commercial interruptions). Most of us will not be able to pursue a demanding career and still be as relaxed and available to family and friends as media characters are. And most of us will not have a rich, charming, and devastatingly attractive man or woman fall in love with us as happens in many novels. Yet the portrayals in media create expectations, and if we have unrealistic expectations of what relationships are and can be, we are likely to be dissatisfied with real, normal relationships.

You might think that, because we all know the difference between fantasy and reality, we don't accept media images as models for our own lives and identities.

Research, however, suggests that the unrealistic ideals in popular media do influence how many of us feel about ourselves and our relationships. For centuries, the people of Fiji were a food-loving society. People enjoyed eating and considered fleshy bodies attractive in both women and men. In fact, when someone seemed to be losing weight, acquaintances would chide her or him for "going thin." All that changed in 1995, when television stations in Fiji began to broadcast American programs, such as *Melrose Place, Seinfeld,* and *Beverly Hills 90210.* Within three years, an astonishing number of Fijian women began to diet and developed eating disorders. When asked why they were trying to lose weight, young Fijian women cited characters such as Amanda (Heather Locklear) on *Melrose Place* as their model (Becker & Burwell, 1999; Becker, Burwell, Gilman, Herzog, & Hamburg, 2002).

NORMALIZE VIOLENCE AGAINST WOMEN

Violence is so pervasive in contemporary life that all of Chapter 12 is devoted to examining it. Yet, it would be irresponsible not to mention violence in the context of media. Although it would be naïve to claim that media *cause* violence, there is mounting evidence that violence in media contributes to increasing male violence in real life. Research shows that, after watching sexually explicit films that degrade women (not just sexually explicit films), men become more dominant toward women with whom they interact (Mulac, Jansma, & Linz, 2003). Studies have also shown that men who watch music videos and pro wrestling are more likely to believe that forcing a partner to have sex is sometimes okay (Browne & Hamilton-Giachritis, 2005; Kaestle, Halpern, & Brown, 2007). When we continually see violence in media, we may come to view it as commonplace, normal, and increasingly acceptable as part of ordinary life (Harris, 2005).

Miriam   *My kids are so much more violent than I was or than my friends were when we were young, and I think the violence they see on television is a big part of the reason. When I caught my three-year-old trying to hit our dog, he told me that he'd seen that on a cartoon show—a cartoon show! I try to screen what my children watch, but it's getting so there are very few programs that don't include violence. How can kids think it is anything but normal when they see it every day?*

Video games push the envelope of mediated violence. Although some researchers think violent video games are harmless (Johnson, 2005), a majority of scholars think they are dangerous because they invite players not just to watch violence (as with films and TV) but to engage virtually in violence, including violence against women (Ivory, 2008; Romer, 2008). *Grand Theft Auto: San Andreas* is a video game that glorifies sexual violence against women. One way players earn points is by having sex with prostitutes and then killing them. In the summer of 2005, it was revealed that within the game is a hidden scene in which players can use a joystick to control a character who is having sex with a nude woman. When a website published instructions for unlocking the scene, the video's rating went immediately from M (Mature) to AO (Adults Only)—but not before more than six million copies had been sold (Levy, 2005).

Several theories about gender development offer insight into the relationship between mediated violence and real-life violence. Social learning theory claims we engage in behaviors that are rewarded and avoid behaviors that are punished. What happens when boys and men watch music videos that show men being rewarded for exploiting and violating women? Cognitive development theory focuses on our use of role models on which to base our behaviors and identities. If girls and women watch programs and videos in which women allow or invite violence against them, are they more likely to think they should accept violence to be desirable women? Symbolic interactionism highlights the importance of social views in shaping individuals' identities. When disrespect toward women and "pimp-ho" versions of male-female relationships pervade music videos, is it any wonder that Imus thought he could call the Scarlet Knights "nappy-headed hos?"

SUMMARY

From children's cartoons to video games, media influence how we perceive men and women in general and ourselves in particular. Media also shape our views of what's normal and right in relationships between women and men. The historical trend of emphasizing gender-stereotyped roles and images continues today; yet it is sometimes challenged by alternative images of women, men, and relationships. Below the surface, however, most media products continue to reflect traditional views of women and men on a deeper level. Media representations of gender foster unrealistic gender ideals in men and women, encourage us to pathologize normal human bodies and functions, and normalize violence against women.

Understanding the overt and subtle gender messages in media empowers us to be more critical consumers. As individuals and citizens, we have a responsibility to criticize media representations that demean men and women and that contribute to attitudes that harm us and our relationships.

And we—each of us—can make a difference. Increasingly, regular people like you can use media to challenge expectations of gender and to craft our own gendered identities in ways that don't fully conform to current social norms. Criticism of dangerously thin fashion models led to new standards that require they have a body mass index that is within the healthy range. In 2005 Nike launched a campaign that celebrated normal-sized bodies. In one ad, a woman comfortably noted "My butt is big;" in another ad, a woman affirmed her "thunder thighs" (Klimkiewicz, 2006). Dove developed a line of ads that positively portrayed women of all ages, races, and sizes. Changes such as these don't just happen. They happen for a reason: because consumers—on whom the companies making ads and selling fashions depend—demand new images of themselves.

Key Terms

The terms following are defined in this chapter on the pages indicated, as well as in alphabetical order in the book's glossary, which begins on page 325. The text's companion website (**http://www.cengage.com/communication/wood/genderedlives10e**) also provides interactive flash cards and crossword puzzles to help you learn these terms and the concepts they represent.

agenda setting 264	mommy track 265
complimentary copy 276	product placement 276
gatekeeper 265	voice-overs 275
immersive advertising 276	

Gender Online

1. If you want to learn more about gender and media, or if you want to become active in working against media that devalue women, visit these websites:

   Media Watch: **http://www.mediawatch.com**

   Off Our Backs: **http://www.offourbacks.org**

   Girls, women + media Project: **http://www.mediaandwomen.org**

2. Visit this website: **http://www.genderads.com**. Does it help you understand how advertisers use gender ideals to sell products and images of how we are supposed to be?
3. Online search terms: "girls gone wild," "gender and media," "media effects."

Reflection and Discussion

1. Some people think that the violence in some rap music and video games is harmless. Other people think it encourages, or normalizes, violence in real life. Where do you stand on this issue?
2. Watch children's programming on Saturday morning. Are male characters more prominent than female characters? What differences, if any, do you see in the activities of male and female characters?
3. Watch morning and evening news programming. What kinds of stories do male and female reporters and newscasters present? Are there differences in story content? Are there differences in the communication styles of male and female newscasters?
4. Bring advertisements from magazines to class, and discuss the images of women, men, and relationships in them. Are these healthy? What are your options as a reader and a consumer?
5. Watch prime-time coverage of sports on ESPN or another channel (during the Olympics, most channels have extensive sports programming). Make a record of how much time is devoted to women's and men's sports and how often

reporters comment on male and female athletes' dress and appearance. Are the patterns you identify consistent with those discussed in this chapter?

Recommended Resources

1. Diane Levin and Jean Kilbourne (2008). *So Sexy, So Soon.* New York: Ballantine. Alicia Quart. (2003). *Branded: The Buying and Selling of Teenagers.* New York: Basic. Both of these books provide accessible analyses of the increasing number of ads aimed at very young girls that encourage the girls to become heavy consumers in order to appear sexy.
2. **http://www.about-face.org** This is an excellent site for getting informed and taking action. About-face.org is devoted to media literacy about gender and self-esteem. Among its features is an ever-changing list of "Top Ten Offenders," which shows ads that destructively stereotype women and men and, in some cases, condone violence toward women. About-Face provides the addresses of companies featured in each ad so you can contact the companies directly.
3. **http://www.genderads.com** This site offers education on how to analyze ads critically.

The world is a dangerous place to live, not because of the people who are evil, but because of the people who don't do anything about it.

Albert Einstein

CHAPTER **12**

GENDERED POWER AND VIOLENCE

Knowledge Challenge:

1. What is "street harassment?"
2. How common are false reports of rape?
3. Would victims of intimate partner violence be safer leaving abusive partners?

- In the United States, every nine seconds a woman is beaten by an intimate partner; at least three women are murdered by their husbands or boyfriends every day.

- In some countries, it is not uncommon for female fetuses to be aborted and for female infants to be neglected until they die.

- More than two million girls a year—about 16,000 per day—are subjected to female genital mutilation.

- Someone (most often, a female) is sexually assaulted every two minutes in the United States. Female college students are four times more likely than other people to be raped.

- Males are the least likely to report a sexual assault, though they make up about 10% of all victims.

This chapter focuses on the distressing topic of gendered violence. As the opening statistics indicate, gendered violence is widespread (Statistics, 2009). In the pages that follow, we'll discuss the nature and extent of gendered violence and identify social structures, practices, and attitudes that cultivate and condone it. We will also ask how we can be part of reducing gendered violence—how ordinary people like you and me can diminish gendered violence in our communities and around the world.

THE SOCIAL CONSTRUCTION OF GENDERED VIOLENCE

Many people explain acts of gendered violence by saying that the perpetrators are sick individuals. It's true that isolated incidents of violence may occur because of individual pathologies. However, individual pathologies can't explain why violence is pervasive and why it is disproportionately inflicted on certain groups. Widespread violence reflects social definitions of femininity, masculinity, and relationships between women and men.

Because gendered violence is a worldwide problem, we will discuss its occurrence in both developing and industrialized countries. What happens beyond the borders of the United States is relevant to us because we belong to a world that is larger than our own country.

THE MANY FACES OF GENDERED VIOLENCE

What comes to mind when you hear terms such as *gendered violence* and *sexual violence?* Most people think of rape, intimate partner violence, and perhaps sexual harassment. That trilogy of abuses, however, doesn't include all the forms gendered violence takes. The term **gendered violence** refers to physical, verbal, emotional, sexual, and visual brutality that is inflicted disproportionately or exclusively on members of one sex. In the following pages, we'll discuss six types of gendered violence.

GENDER INTIMIDATION

Gender intimidation occurs when members of one sex are treated in ways that make them feel humiliated, unsafe, or inferior because of their sex (Kramarae, 1992). *Street harassment* is a common form of gender intimidation. Probably all of us feel unsafe at times. Gender intimidation, however, exists when members of one sex are treated in ways that lead them to feel more vulnerable or unsafe than members of the other sex.

Gender intimidation includes lewd remarks and requests made in public spaces. A number of women students at my university often take longer, less-direct routes around campus to avoid workmen who assault them with sexual comments and suggestions. In the first 11 months of 2009, there were 587 reported incidents of verbal or physical assaults on New York City subways. Frustrated that officials did nothing about ogling, grouping, flashing, and verbal assaults on subways, a citizen group formed New Yorkers for Safe Transit to address the problem (Lee, 2009). Understandably, women feel unsafe and uncomfortable in areas where others can violate them with verbal propositions, comments, and evaluations. Even if a woman doesn't have a desire to go out, the knowledge that it would be dangerous to go out alone restricts her.

> **Tim**   *I think gay-bashing is a kind of gender intimidation. I've been a victim of insults and really gross remarks just because I'm gay. I'll be just walking along minding my own business, and someone will shout "fag" at me or even come at me screaming, "We don't want any queers around here." When I go into bathrooms on campus, I usually see gay-bashing graffiti. I have to tolerate these hassles strictly because I'm gay. That makes it gender intimidation.*

Tim's commentary highlights another form of gender intimidation: treating gays and trans people (or people suspected of being gay or trans) in ways that make them feel unsafe, humiliated, or inferior. Simply because someone is assumed not to be straight, the person becomes a target of intimidation.

SEXUAL ASSAULT

Sexual assault is sexual activity that occurs without the informed consent of at least one of the people involved. Rape is one type of sexual assault, but it isn't the only one. In fact, what *rape* means isn't as clear-cut as you might think. For many years, marital rape was not recognized as a crime in the United States. It was assumed that once a woman married, she didn't have the right not to consent to sex with

---

EXPLORING GENDERED LIVES | **HOLLA BACK!**

Tired of having strangers comment on your body? The advice of Holla Back, a grassroots organization in New York City, is to turn the tables and embarrass people who engage in street harassment. Created in 2005, Holla Back encourages victims of street harassment to shoot the harassers—with cameras. The photos can then be posted, along with the photographer's comments, on Holla Back's site: **http://www.hollabacknyc.com**. The worst incidents are posted in the Holla Shame on the site (Fiske, 2006).

Women in India have come up with a similar response to street harassment. "Eve-teasing" is what Indians call street harassment in which men whistle at, leer at, and sometimes stalk women who have not invited their attention. Unwilling to continue tolerating Eve-teasing, a group of Indian women created Blank Noise—blank for the silence that has surrounded Eve-teasing; noise for breaking the silence. Blank Noise has developed several responses to Eve-teasing. One is posting "Unwanted" photos of perpetrators on the Blank Noise blog (**www.blanknoiseproject.blogspot.com**). Another is "Did You Ask for It?," a collection of items of clothing worn by women who were Eve-teased. The fact that most of the items are modest or very modest (burqas) testifies that women's dress is not the cause of Eve-teasing (Girish, 2007).

her husband. Some countries still don't recognize that married women have a right to not consent to sex with their husbands. Only in 2009 did Afghanistan change its laws so that married women do not have to consent to sex with their husbands (by law, married women still must do housework!) ("Law on Marital Rape," 2009). In many states, first-degree rape is limited to forced vaginal intercourse. This means that forced anal and oral intercourse are not considered first-degree rape. According to this definition, a man who is forced to have sex with another man has not been raped.

Sexual assault includes rape and other forced sexual activities with strangers; sex that is coerced by "friends" or dates; forced sex in marriage; incest; and sexual activities with children. In other words, sexual assault occurs whenever one person doesn't give **informed consent** for sexual activity. Informed consent can be given only by an adult who has normal mental abilities, who is not being coerced, and whose judgment is not impaired by alcohol, other drugs, or circumstances. Informed consent cannot be given by children. The 33% of children—both boys and girls—who experience sexual activity before reaching the age of legal consent are legally victims of sexual assault (Davis, 2004). Whenever sex occurs without informed consent, it is sexual assault.

Sexual assault is not confined to civilian contexts. In 2011, a group of more than 24 women and 2 men filed a federal class-action lawsuit against the current and former Defense Secretaries. They claim that servicemen are allowed to get away with forms of sexual abuse ranging from obscene verbal attacks to gang rape. They also claim that victims are either involuntarily discharged or encouraged or even ordered to continue to serve with the men who violated them while those men are not even reprimanded. Current Defense Secretary Robert Gates has acknowledged that sexual assault is a substantial problem in the U.S. military (Hefling, 2011).

Lawrence Korb, former President Reagan's assistant secretary of defense, acknowledges that the government and military services have "treated military women like prostitutes" (Moniz & Pardue, 1996, p. 22A). The 2002–2003 sexual assault scandal at the Air Force Academy revealed that male cadets raped female cadets with horrifying frequency and that investigations and punishments were rare (Quindlen, 2003a).

▼

Abby   When people think of rape, they think about strangers jumping out of bushes at night. But that's not how it usually happens. Most of the women in my victims' support group were raped by friends or dates—guys they knew and trusted. In some ways, that's worse because it makes you afraid to trust anyone.

Sexual assault is prevalent on college campuses. In a recent study, Laurel Crown and Linda Roberts (2007) found that one-third of undergraduate women they surveyed reported one or more unwanted sexual interactions, ranging from kissing to intercourse, during a single year; one-half of college women in their senior year reported one or more unwanted sexual interactions during their college careers. In another study, 20.9% of undergraduate women reported experiencing unwanted sexual interactions during a six-month period (Banyard, Plante, Cohn, Moorhead, Ward, & Walsh, 2005). These studies, as well as other research (Christopher & Kisler, 2004; Seely, 2007), also report that most incidents of sexual violation are perpetrated by people known to victims. In fact, the most recent report shows that 73% of rape victims know their assailant (Statistics, 2009). Kate Harris (2009, 2011) interviewed women who had engaged in nonconsensual sex with acquaintances or dates. She found that many of these women felt confused because they couldn't associate "rape" with friends. For that reason, they seldom called the nonconsensual sex "rape" or reported it.

A number of researchers suggest that rapes are so common at colleges and universities because of what they call the "rape culture" of campuses (Burnett, Mattern, Herakova, Kahl, Tabola, & Bornsen, 2009; Forbes, Adams-Curtis, Pakalka, & White, 2006; Sanday, 2007). According to Burnett et al. (2009), following date rape, perceived ambiguity mutes many college women. Ambiguity may arise because women believe rape myths so they think "Did I 'ask for it'?" "Was I responsible?" "Will others blame me for what happened?" In addition, if a victim talks with others about the rape, others may respond in ways that reflect a campus rape culture: "Did you say 'no' forcefully?" "What were you wearing?"

Researchers estimate that one in six women and one in thirty-three men will be raped in their lifetimes (Statistics, 2009). Research indicates that one reason for the prevalence of rape is that a substantial number of people regard forced sex as acceptable. In a study of 520 undergraduate students, Grace Kim and Michael Roloff (1999) found that both women and men tend not to judge forced intercourse as rape if it occurs with an acquaintance or friend and is not "violent"—that is, it doesn't involve physical force or injury other than the rape itself. This may reflect a "rape script" (Berrington & Jones, 2002; Livingston & Testa, 2000), which is the belief—conscious or unconscious—that dates and friends can't rape because rape is a violent act imposed by a stranger. Research also suggests that there is a link between endorsing views of traditional masculinity and power, and perpetrating rape (Marine, 2004).

▼

Carrie   *I went to a club with some friends, and we were dancing in a circle. I was wearing this great top that makes me feel really sexy and pretty. This guy I had met once pulled me out of the group and started to dirty dance. Then he groped me, my genitals. I backed off, and he said "What?" like he hadn't done anything wrong. I know he violated me, but I can't help thinking that maybe I was "asking for it" because I was wearing a sexy outfit and all. I know my mother would say I was asking for it because I was dressed in a sexy way.*

Austin   *What do girls expect if they go to a club where hookups happen, and they're wearing revealing clothes that are meant to excite and provoke guys, and they are dancing suggestively? It's like sending out an invitation to a guy. So why, when a guy accepts, do they blame him for responding to their invitation?*

Approximately 60% of rape victims choose not to prosecute or even report rape because they fear that families and friends will blame them for the rape (Anderson & Doherty, 2008; Burnett et al., 2009; Statistics, 2009). Saying that rape happens because of the way a woman is dressed or the places she goes is **blaming the victim:** holding a harmed person responsible for the harm that another person has inflicted. The commentaries by Carrie and Austin offer insight into how some people perceive women who dress and behave provocatively or who are out alone at night, particularly in isolated places. Carrie clearly enjoys being sexually attractive, which she does not see as inviting sexual assault. Yet, she has internalized the myth that, if she is dressed or acting provocatively, she is to blame if a male assaults her. Austin thinks a woman who looks and acts sexy is inviting him to do more than look.

Although rape involves sex, it isn't motivated primarily by sexual desire. Rape is an act of aggression intended to humiliate and dominate another person. This explains why rape is one way in which male prison inmates brutalize one another and establish a power hierarchy. Recognizing rape as an act of aggression also sheds light on why soldiers routinely rape women in areas they capture—it is a means of claiming the territories, shaming the men who lost the war, and impregnating women so that the conquered people's genetic line is disrupted (Nolen, 2005).

In 2008, the United Nations officially designated rape a "weapon of war." In 2007, the humanitarian group Refugees International released a report documenting the systematic use of rape as a means of ethnic cleansing in Darfur. The government-backed Janjaweed military routinely rape women without fear of consequence because Sudanese laws include harsh punishments for women who have sex—even against their wills—outside of marriage (Boustany, 2007). In Zimbabwe, hundreds of women have been raped by opposition soldiers. Some of the rape victims are children who have not even reached puberty; others are pregnant women (Zukerman, 2009). Increasingly, males are also victims of rape in the Congo. Oxfam, Human Rights Watch, and the United Nations estimate that war in the Congo and Rwanda has resulted in hundreds of thousands of female rape victims, and rape is now a weapon used to humiliate and demoralize men (Gettleman, 2009a). According to Pulitzer Prize winning journalists, Nicholas Kristof and Sherryl WuDunn (2009) 90% of women and girls over the age of three were sexually abused during civil wars in Liberia and 75% of women in some areas of the Congo have been raped. Kristof and WuDunn report that "In one instance, soldiers raped a three-year-old girl and then fired their guns into her. When surgeons saw her, there was no tissue left to repair" (p. 84).

EXPLORING GENDERED LIVES | THE VICTIM

One of my students adapted this story from one he found on the Web. A version of the story was previously posted on the Men Ending Rape site at **http://www.menendingrape.org/Rape**. It makes the point that, although many people still blame victims of rape for being raped, we would find it ridiculous to blame a victim of robbery for being robbed.

Bob Smith was robbed by John Jones. Jones was caught, and Smith pressed charges. Following is the transcript of the defense attorney's cross-examination of Mr. Smith.

"Mr. Smith, were you held up on the corner of 16th and Locust by Mr. Jones?"

"Yes."

"Did you struggle with Mr. Jones?"

"No."

"Why not?"

"He had a gun to my head and told me he'd kill me if I didn't give him my wallet."

"So you decided to comply with his demands instead of resisting. Did you at least scream for help?"

"No. I was afraid."

"Is it true that, earlier on the evening of the alleged robbery, you gave money to some friends who asked for it?"

"Yes."

"Isn't it true that you often give money to others?"

"Yes, I like to help people I care about."

"In fact, don't you have quite a reputation for generosity—for giving money away? How was Mr. Jones supposed to know you didn't want to give him money? I mean, you give it away to lots of people, so why shouldn't Mr. Jones have assumed you would give him some?"

"What are you getting at?"

"Never mind. When did the robbery take place?"

"About 11 p.m."

"11 p.m.? You were out walking alone at 11 p.m. at night? You know it's dangerous to be out on the streets alone at night. Why were you there at that time of night?"

"I just felt like walking home instead of taking a cab."

"Okay. What were you wearing?"

"A suit. I'd worked late at the office, gone out to dinner with friends, and was walking home."

"A suit. An expensive suit, right?"

"Well, yes. It is a very nice suit. What's your point?"

"So, you were walking around a deserted street late at night in an expensive suit that practically advertised you had money. The way you were dressed was really provocative, isn't that so? In fact, we could think that, being dressed that way and out on the streets alone late at night, you were asking to be robbed."

Why do you think most people would not think the man in this story asked to be robbed but might think a woman wearing sexy clothes and was out late at night asked to be raped?

Sexual assault includes forced prostitution, also called sexual slavery. During World War II, the Japanese forced countless women to be "comfort women" for Japanese soldiers. They were forced to have sex with 20 to 30 Japanese soldiers a day. The repeated and sometimes brutal rapes caused some of these women to become sterile. Those who became pregnant were given injections of Terramycin, which caused their bodies to swell and usually induced abortions. Many committed suicide. After the war, the Japanese government denied it had forced women to work at comfort stations. However, in 1992, wartime documents were found that confirmed that Japanese forces had operated comfort stations. In 1995, the Japanese government acknowledged that it had forced women to serve in comfort stations (Onishi, 2007).

Sexual slavery is not confined to the past. Even today, in countries such as the Philippines, India, Albania, Afghanistan, and Thailand, some women are sold by their families or kidnapped and forced to be prostitutes in their countries or other countries (Monroe, 2005; Owen, 2007; Samuel, Kisimir, & Schenk, 2007). It is estimated that 480,000 to 640,000 girls and women are trafficked into sexual slavery ("Human Trafficking," 2006) and that 50,000 to 100,000 of those are trafficked into the United States (Goddess & Calderón, 2006). The trafficking industry generates an estimated $15 billion per year (Samuel, Kisimir, & Schenk, 2007). Women and young girls, some who have not even gone through puberty, are sold to be wives of older men or to be prostitutes who work in brothels in the sex industry. Virgins bring particularly high prices, because in some countries men with HIV-AIDS believe that having sex with a virgin will cure them (Kristof, 2006a; Norlund & Rubin, 2010). The men are wrong in that belief, but they are likely to pass their lethal disease to the girl or woman who is the sex slave.

EXPLORING GENDERED LIVES | CORRECTIVE RAPE

Jeremy Schaap is an ESPN anchor, Emmy-award winning journalist, and a national news correspondent. One of his most recent journalistic projects is a documentary video on "corrective rape" in South Africa. Corrective rape is rape of lesbians that is intended to punish them for being lesbian and correct their sexual orientation. Preceding and during the rape, the women are usually beaten, often brutally. Lesbian soccer players have been particular targets of corrective rape. Eudy Simelane, an acclaimed Banyana national female soccer player, was raped and murdered. The intention of "corrective" rapists, in addition to the domination and humiliation characteristic of other rapes, is to teach a lesbian that she should stop "acting like a man" and act like a woman and want sex with men.

In the documentary Schaap comments that the authorities often don't seem to pursue these crimes with the same energy they invest in crimes against heterosexual women.

I am providing a link so that you can view the video, but please be aware that it is very disturbing: **http://espn.go.com/video/clip?id=5181871**.

| EXPLORING GENDERED LIVES | MYTHS AND FACTS ABOUT RAPE |

Myth	Fact
Rape is motivated by sexual urges.	Rape is an aggressive act used to dominate another person.
Most rapes occur between strangers.	More than 75% of rapes are committed by a person known to the victim.
Most rapists are African-American men, and most victims are European-American women.	More than three-fourths of all rapes occur within races, not between races.
False reports of rapes are frequent.	False reports of rapes constitute only 2% of all reported rapes.
The way a woman dresses affects the likelihood that she will be raped.	Most rapes are planned in advance, without knowledge of how victims will be dressed.
Women who don't drink too much are alert enough to protect themselves from being raped.	Date rape drugs such as Rohypnol, GHB (gamma hydroxybutyric acid), and Ketamine have no color, smell, or taste, so you can't tell if you are being drugged. The drugs can make you become weak and confused—or even pass out—so that you are unable to refuse sex or defend yourself.

INTIMATE PARTNER VIOLENCE

Intimate partner violence is the most common form of violence committed against women in the United States (Haynes, 2009). At least 28% and possibly as many as 50% of women suffer **intimate partner violence,** which is physical, mental, emotional, verbal, or economic power used by one partner against the other partner in a romantic relationship (Jackman, 2003). National surveys report that nearly 25% of women and 30% of men regard violence as a normal and even positive part of marriage (Johnson, 2006), which suggests substantial acceptance of marital violence in our culture (Wood, 2001b, 2006). Intimate partner violence is also on the rise in dating relationships, including those of very young people (Capaldi, Shortt, & Crosby, 2003; Wolfe & Feiring, 2000).

Paula   *The worst thing I ever went through was being stalked by my ex-boyfriend. We'd dated for about a year when I broke up with him. He was so jealous—wouldn't let me go out with friends or anything, so I just decided to end the relationship. But he didn't want it to end. He followed me around campus, showed up at movies when I was out with other guys, and called at all hours of the night. Sometimes, he would tell me he loved me and beg to get back together; other times, he would threaten me. I finally called the police, and that put an end to his terrorism.*

Among heterosexuals, intimate partner violence is inflicted primarily by men against women. Men make up an estimated 15% of all victims of intimate partner violence (France, 2006). Researchers note that 26% of all female murder victims are killed by husbands or boyfriends, whereas only 3% of male murder victims are killed by wives or girlfriends (Hammer, 2002). Although a majority of perpetrators of intimate partner violence are men, the vast majority of men do not inflict violence on girlfriends and wives, and they would not consider doing so.

Sex is less important than gender in explaining intimate partner violence. A study of 336 undergraduates showed that both men and women who abused their partners had strong masculine gender orientations (Thompson, 1991). Research also documents intimate partner violence in lesbian relationships, making it clear that sex—maleness, in this case—doesn't explain this phenomenon (Giorgi, 2002). The more strongly an individual identifies with traditional masculinity, the more likely he or she is to engage in violence, including violence against intimate partners (Messner, 2001; Williamson & Silverman, 2001; Wood, 2004, 2006). This may explain why intimate partner violence is especially widespread in countries such as Egypt, South Africa, and Spain, which accord men substantial power over women (Rosenthal, 2006).

In 2009, President Obama's administration recommended that political asylum be granted to a Guatemalan woman who had battled immigration courts since 1995. Rody Alvarado had come to the United States to escape a brutally abusive husband. Married at 16, she was routinely the target of her husband's violence. He beat and kicked her, dislocated her jaw, pistol whipped her, and threatened her with a machete (Preston, 2009a, b). The administration's recommendation is ground breaking because it recognizes that intimate partner violence is a basis for asylum.

Most people do not enter intimate relationships expecting them to involve violence. Instead, people generally become intimate with people who seem loving and good. Once the relationship is established and the partners are psychologically committed to each other, violence may begin. Intimate partner violence typically follows a cyclical pattern (Johnson, 2006). In the first stage, the perpetrator experiences mounting tension. Perhaps the individual has problems at work or feels insecure or frustrated. As tension mounts, verbal and emotional abuse may occur. In

---

EXPLORING GENDERED LIVES | **GENDERED VIOLENCE IS A MEN'S ISSUE**

In a chapter that discusses men's violence toward women, it's easy to forget that most men are not violent toward women. These men have a stake in speaking out against men who are violent toward women and in challenging social views that link violence and masculinity. Sut Jhally and Jackson Katz (2001, p. 31) put it this way:

The majority of men are in fact nonviolent. ...The silence of nonviolent men in the face of other men's violence is a key factor that allows masculinity to be coded in narrow and destructive ways. ... What we have to do now is offer more resources to these men—the majority—in order to help them intervene in male culture in a productive fashion...to become, in the words of Pearl Jam's Eddie Vedder, "better men."

EXPLORING GENDERED LIVES | **THE CYCLE OF INTIMATE PARTNER VIOLENCE**

Stage 1: Tension builds, and the abusive partner blames the other for problems or for not being supportive. Typically, the abuser begins psychological battering with insults, threats, taunts, and intimidation. Especially in chronically abusive relationships, victims learn to spot cues, to become extremely compliant, and to refrain from doing anything to annoy the partner. This seldom helps, because the abuser is looking for an excuse to relieve frustration by exerting power over another.

Stage 2: An explosion occurs. Tension erupts into physical violence. The abuser may wait until the victim is relaxing or even asleep and then attack. Often victims require hospital care. Sometimes they are pregnant and miscarry.

Stage 3: The abuser appears contrite and remorseful. The abuser may apologize to the victim and typically promises it will never happen again. The victim sees the "good person" inside and remembers what led to commitment or marriage.

Stage 4: This is the honeymoon phase. The abuser acts courtly and loving. The victim becomes convinced the abuse was an aberration that will not recur—even if it has repeatedly. And then the whole cycle begins anew.

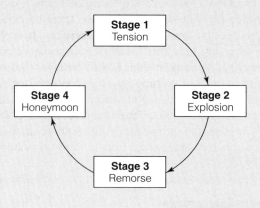

the second stage, there is a violent explosion involving physical assault—kicking, beating, throwing the victim against a wall, cutting, or shooting. The third stage in the cycle of abuse is called remorse because the perpetrator typically acts ashamed, apologizes, and promises never to do it again. In the fourth stage, the honeymoon phase, the abuser acts lovingly and often brings gifts to the battered partner. The apologies of stage three and the loving acts of stage four often have strong psychological effects such as reviving faith in the abuser and the possibility of a loving relationship. They convince victims to stay with abusive partners. Thus, the cycle continues.

Brice *Growing up, I saw my father shove Mom around whenever he was having a rough time at work. Sometimes, it was more than shoving—he would actually hit her. Always, the next day he would be Mr. Nice, and things would go along fine for a while until he got upset about something else; then it would start all over again. I hated him because of what he did to Mother, and I swore I would never be like him. But last year, when I was going through a really rough time, the girl I was dating kept nagging me, and I hauled off and hit her. I never thought I could do that.*

Brice's experience, as presented in his commentary, is not unusual. There is a strong relationship between growing up in a family with one or more abusive adults and becoming an abuser (Wood, 2006). In our families of origin, we learn what is normal and allowable in relationships between men and women. What we learn in families, however, need not be the blueprint for our lives. We can choose not to repeat destructive patterns that we have observed in our families.

There are general differences in the frequency, motivation, and type of violence committed by women and men. Men commit at least 90% of documented acts of physical intimate partner violence in the United States (Johnson, M., 2006, 2008; Wood, 2004). Men and women also differ in the severity of violence they inflict on others. Abusive women most often verbally abuse or push, slap, or shove partners. In contrast, abusive men are more likely to use their bodies, weapons, and even acid to commit brutal, sometimes deadly, assaults (Johnson, M., 2006, 2008). Although both sexes may engage in violence, men more often inflict moderate to severe physical injuries. Men who engage in domestic violence tend justify their violence by overestimating how common such behavior is or underestimating the damage their violence does (Olson & Rauscher, 2011). According to a recent study, men who perpetrate intimate partner violence overestimate the commonness of what they do by two to three times the actual rates of behaviors ranging from throwing something at a partner to rape (Neighbors, Walker, Mbilinyi, O'Rourke, Edleson, Zegree, & Roffman, 2010).

In comparing feminine and masculine individuals' abusive tendencies, we should also consider differences in motives. Feminine people can be violent in self-defense. They slap a partner who has beaten them or throw an object at a partner who has slugged them. Other than in self-defense, feminine people tend to aggress only when they can't resolve issues through strategies prescribed for women, such as crying, talking with friends, and turning anger inward (Johnson, 2006).

Men who inflict violence on others are generally motivated by reasons different from those that motivate women to be violent. Many male abusers use physical aggression to gain or sustain self-esteem, to win the respect of others, and to maintain control over people and situations. Among children aged four to seven, girls aggress primarily to protect themselves and their property, whereas boys aggress to dominate others and increase their status (Bordo, 1998). As boys become men, they are most likely to resort to violence when they feel they need to prove their toughness or feel they need to gain control (May, 1998a; Messner, 2001; Wood, 2004). In Asian

EXPLORING GENDERED LIVES	MYTHS AND FACTS ABOUT VIOLENCE BETWEEN INTIMATES
Myth	**Fact**
Victims of battering can just leave the abusive relationship.	Many victims of battering have nowhere to go and no means of supporting themselves and their children.
Abuse of intimates often stops on its own.	Abuse of intimates seldom stops without intervention or other radical measures.
Abuse is confined primarily to the working and poverty classes.	Abuse occurs in relationships between members of the upper and middle classes as well as members of the working and poverty classes.
Victims of battering would be safer if they left abusive relationships.	Victims of battering are most likely to be murdered by abusive partners if they try to leave.

countries such as Pakistan and Cambodia, men use acid attacks to punish women who refuse to be subservient to men. When Naeema Azar, a Pakistani woman, decided she wanted to divorce her husband, he agreed but later poured acid on her face. The acid blinded her and burned away her left ear, her eyelids and the flesh on her face. Acid burnings are seldom prosecuted (Kristof, 2008).

Increasingly, stalking is recognized as a form of intimate partner violence. Stalking is repeated, intrusive behavior that is uninvited and unwanted, that seems obsessive, and that makes the target concerned for her or his safety (Cupach & Spitzack, 2011). In studies on college campuses, 13% of women students and 2% of male students reported having been stalked during the previous year (Bazar, 2007; Brownstein, 2000). About half of female victims are stalked by ex-partners and another 25% by men they have dated at least once (Meloy, 2006). Stalking is particularly common on campuses because it is easy to monitor and learn others' routines. Further, IMing and social networking sites, such as MySpace and Facebook, give stalkers more ways to learn about (potential) victims' habits and patterns.

SEXUAL HARASSMENT

Sexual harassment is unwelcome verbal or nonverbal behavior of a sexual nature that links academic or professional standing or success to sexual favors or that interferes with work or learning.

Prior to the 1970s, the term *sexual harassment* was not used (Wise & Stanley, 1987). Once sexual harassment was named, those who were targets of it had a way to define their experience and demand institutional and legal redress. Although women are the predominant targets and men the predominant harassers, the Supreme Court has recognized that either sex can be the target or the perpetrator.

Further, in the spring of 1998 the U.S. Supreme Court unanimously ruled that federal law protects employees from being sexually harassed by people of their own sex in the workplace. Within the intent of Title VII of the Civil Rights Act of 1964, stated Justice Scalia, equal protection exists for victims of both heterosexual and homosexual harassment.

Two broad categories of sexual harassment are widely recognized today: *quid pro quo harassment* and *hostile environment harassment*.

Quid Pro Quo   Quid pro quo harassment is the actual or threatened use of professional or academic rewards and/or punishments to gain sexual compliance from a subordinate or student. *Quid pro quo* is a Latin phrase that means "this for that." For instance, a professor might promise a student a good grade in exchange for a date, or a manager might offer a subordinate a promotion in exchange for sex. Quid pro quo harassment may also involve punishing someone for not providing sexual favors. For example, a manager might withhold a promotion from an employee who refuses to have sex.

Quid pro quo sex depends on power differences. The person seeking sexual favors must have some kind of power over the other person—the power to assign a grade, give a promotion, or control wages. Quid pro quo harassment works because of this power difference—the person with less power may be reluctant or unable to say "no" (Lane, 2006).

Hostile Environment   Hostile environment harassment is unwelcome conduct of a sexual nature that interferes with a person's ability to perform a job or to gain an education, and/or conduct that creates a hostile, intimidating, or offensive working environment because of sexualized conduct. In 2009, the *Chronicle of Higher Education* reported that nearly 20% of undergraduates said they had experienced sexual harassment from faculty and staff (Wilson, 2009). Both women and men have brought suits for hostile environment sexual harassment. In one case, a jury awarded $3.75 million to a male prison guard whose employer did nothing to stop a female coworker who harassed him by calling his home, following him at work, and making repeated sexual comments and invitations to him ("Sexually Harassed Male," 1999).

Hostile environment sexual harassment may involve making lewd remarks, using language that demeans one sex, hanging pinups, and circulating rumors about an individual's real or speculated sexual activities. Particularly common is sexual banter or suggestions. An example is Amanda Nichols, who took a summer job at a Steak 'n Shake restaurant after completing 11th grade. She spent much of her shift each day trying to evade an older male cook who touched her, pulled her apron, and constantly made sexually explicit remarks and suggestions. Nichols successfully sued the company for failing to provide a reasonable working environment. Similar cases have been won against companies such as Jiffy Lube (the company paid $300,000 to settle), Red Lobster ($60,000 to settle), and Jack in the Box, Inc. ($300,000 to settle) (Joyce, 2004).

Another form of hostile environment does not involve sexual suggestions and comments. Instead, it exists when members of one sex (usually women) are disrespected, demeaned, ignored, and/or told directly or indirectly that they aren't welcome. One example involved the Physics Department at Duke University. The problem at Duke came into the national spotlight when a 23-year-old female graduate student in physics, who had planned to earn her doctorate, left Duke with only a master's degree. Why did she leave? Because, she says, she was ignored because she was female. Men in the department refused to include her in work sessions. Some faculty in the department agreed that it was a hostile environment for women. Said Joshua Socolar, "The discipline has been a men's club. ...Whatever chauvinistic tendencies people might have are amplified" (Wilson, 2004, p. A7). Members of either sex may be harassed for not living up to gendered expectations—men for not being independent, strong, and competitive (Berdahl, 2007a); women for not being deferential and nurturing (Berdahl, 2007b).

I sometimes consult with attorneys who are trying sexual harassment cases. In one instance, a woman sued her former supervisor for subjecting her to continuous comments about her body and questions about her sexual activities. The supervisor's constant sexualized communication interfered with the woman's ability to concentrate on her job and to feel safe in her job. In another case, a woman had become the first woman in a region to be appointed high school principal. On her first day in her high school, a male faculty member told her, "We're renaming the school Hen-House High because you're principal." Another male faculty member said, "Having a woman in charge is like a cancer on our school." A subscription to *Playboy* was anonymously given to her. These and other incidents formed a pattern of abusive conduct of a sexual nature that undercut the principal's authority and created a climate that was offensive and hostile to her and other women in the school.

A hostile environment is created by a pattern of behavior. A single action, even if it is unwelcome and inappropriate, is unlikely to meet the legal standard for sexual harassment. Instead, there must be a pervasive pattern of unwelcome conduct related to a person's sex, and that pattern must create conditions that are so intolerable a reasonable person would resign (Greenhouse, 2004). This standard ensures that isolated misconduct, which might be deliberate or inadvertent, doesn't result in excessive penalties.

In 2006, the U.S. Supreme Court issued an important ruling that offers further protection to victims of sexual discrimination of all sorts. The landmark case was *Burlington Northern & Santa Fe Railway Co. v. White*. The plaintiff, White, sued the railway company because, after she complained about sexist statements made by her supervisor, she was reassigned to less desirable duties and then suspended. The Court ruled that the company could not suspend or reassign workers who complained about sexist treatment to less desirable work because such retaliatory actions would discourage other workers from complaining about sexist treatment and, thus, would undercut laws protecting workers against sexual harassment (Andronici & Katz, 2007).

Whose Perspective Counts?   Research shows that women and men, in general, differ in how they perceive sexist comments and jokes in the workplace. Many men regard such acts as harmless or even complimentary. In contrast, many women perceive such acts as demeaning or intimidating (Kurth, Spiller, & Travis, 2000; Levy & Paludi, 1997).

The courts have struggled with the question of whose perspective counts ever since sexual harassment cases first appeared on trial dockets (Collier, 2008; MacKinnon, 2005; Renzetti, 2008). Within Western legal traditions, the convention for judging behavior has been the "reasonable man" standard; for example, to determine whether a homeowner who shot a burglar behaved appropriately, the court would ask, "What would a reasonable man do if someone broke into his home?" The *reasonable man* standard prevailed in early sexual harassment cases. For example, in *Rabidue v. Osceola Refining Company* (1986), the majority opinion of the Sixth Circuit Court was that behavior that might offend many women was "an everyday occurrence... [that] is natural, acceptable, and part of the fabric of society's morality" (Pollack, 1990, p. 65). In *Rabidue,* men's perceptions were declared to be the standard.

A few years after *Rabidue,* courts dealt with the question of whether pinups in public areas of a workplace create an offensive working environment. In this case, the judge ruled that, although nude and near-nude photos of women might not offend a reasonable man, they could well offend a reasonable woman (Tiffs & VanOsdol, 1991). Since that ruling, the *reasonable woman* standard has been used to judge sexual harassment in a number of cases (Farrell & Matthews, 2000). This legal criterion draws on the logic of standpoint theory, which we discussed in Chapter 2.

Regardless of which standard is used, the law insists on the criterion of reasonableness. This provides a safeguard against idiosyncratic perceptions. Courts assess whether perceptions of behaviors as harassing reflect commonly held perceptions of particular behaviors.

GENITAL SURGERY

Some people have never heard of genital surgery (also called genital mutilation). Of those who have, many think it is an ancient procedure that is no longer practiced. Yet, genital surgery is practiced in many parts of the world today. More than two million girls a year—about 16,000 per day—are subjected to female genital mutilation (Heyl, 2005; Marton, 2004) in an effort to control their sexual activities by making them unpleasurable (Rudman & Glick, 2008). In this section, we'll discuss forms of genital surgery and their consequences. I'll warn you in advance that you may find the pages that follow very disturbing.

Male Circumcision   Male circumcision is the removal of the sheath, or prepuce, of the penis. In many countries, including the United States, male babies are routinely circumcised. The rationale for male circumcision is that it makes it easier to keep the penis clean and reduces the likelihood of infections. According to recent findings from medical research, male circumcision reduces the incidence of HIV, herpes simplex virus Type 2, and human papilloma virus (Bakalar, 2009).

Sunna   The word **sunna** comes from the Arabic word for "religious duty" (Trangsrud, 1994). Sunna, or female circumcision, is practiced primarily in African countries. It is usually performed on girls between the ages of 4 and 14, although it is sometimes performed on infants (Johnson, A., 2008). Sunna involves removing both the sheath and the tip of the clitoris. Although you might think sunna and male circumcision are equivalent, they are different in severity and consequence. Removal of the foreskin of a penis doesn't preclude a man's sexual pleasure, but removal of the prepuce and tip of the clitoris often leaves a woman unable to experience sexual excitement or orgasm. Sunna also has greater potential for medical complications.

Excision or Clitoridectomy   A second type of female genital surgery is excision or **clitoridectomy,** in which the entire clitoris and parts of the labia minora are removed. This operation greatly diminishes women's ability to experience sexual pleasure, so it is thought to reduce the likelihood that a woman will be sexually active before marriage or unfaithful after marriage. Of lesser concern to those who endorse the practice is that it often has medical complications and increases pain and danger in childbirth.

You might be surprised to learn that clitoridectomies were performed in the United States and Europe as late as the twentieth century. In the United States, some physicians also removed women's ovaries in the belief that eliminating all sources of women's sexual sensation would "cure" masturbation and prevent orgasm, which was considered an "ailment" that good women didn't have (Dreifus, 2000). Reminding us again of the power of social constructions of gender, views that women should be sexually "pure" were, and still are, used to justify mutilating women.

Infibulation   The most radical form of genital surgery is **infibulation**. In this operation, which is usually performed on girls between ages five and eight, the clitoris and labia minora are removed. Next, the flesh of the labia majora is scraped raw and sewn together to form a hood over the vagina, with a small opening left for urination and menstruation (Toubia, 1994). When a female who has been infibulated marries, an opening is cut to permit intercourse. Sometimes the opening is deliberately made extremely small to increase male sexual pleasure, although it makes intercourse painful for women. Husbands may order their wives resewn when they go on journeys or to prevent pregnancy.

This technique seems to have been first used by ancient Upper Egyptians, who fastened a clasp (fibula) through the large genital lips of slave women to keep them from having children, which would interfere with their work. Today, infibulation is practiced primarily in some Muslim and West African societies that believe women who are not infibulated are unclean.

Women who have been infibulated report that the process is excruciatingly painful (Finnerty, 1999; Ziv, 1997). A woman from Somalia who was infibulated at the age of six reported that four women held her down, and a razor blade was used to amputate her clitoris and all of her vaginal lips. Then, thorns were used to close the wound, and her legs were bound together from her heels to her thighs. As in this case, genital surgery is performed by people with little or no medical training who operate in unsanitary conditions and without anesthesia. The immediate consequences may include excruciating pain, hemorrhage, tetanus, gangrene, blood poisoning, and fractured bones from the force needed to hold girls down during the operation. Long-term consequences include sterility, agonizing pain

EXPLORING GENDERED LIVES | DEFINING HUMAN RIGHTS

Fauziya Kasinga grew up in Togo, Ghana. Unlike most men in Togo, Fauziya's father was progressive. He didn't believe in polygamy, forced marriage, or denying education to women. He also refused to let any of his five daughters be circumcised as was the custom in Togo. But when her father died, Fauziya was scheduled for genital surgery. She managed to escape and came to the United States, where she asked for asylum on the grounds that she would be subjected to genital mutilation if she returned home.

The judge who heard her case concluded that her story was "unbelievable" and that Fauziya was not credible. Her case was investigated and then supported by Amnesty International and other human rights groups. On appeal, she was granted asylum—the first time the United States acknowledged that forced genital surgery could be considered a violation of human rights (Goodman, 1996; Kassindja, 1998).

during intercourse, difficulty delivering babies, permanent incontinence, and still-births of babies who cannot emerge through birth canals that have been scarred and deformed by genital operations (Browne, 2003/2004).

Consider another example of cultural traditions that changed only when members of the culture resisted them. In China, for centuries women's feet were bound. Yet, this practice was eliminated in a mere 17 years (1895–1912) in urban China when progressive Chinese citizens launched an education campaign against foot binding. Also critical to ending the practice was the formation of associations of fathers who refused to bind their daughters' feet and prohibited their sons from marrying women whose feet had been bound (Lorber, 1997). When enough fathers made these commitments, it affected marriage patterns and made women with unbound feet attractive as marriage partners.

Even though we should be hesitant to apply the standards of our culture to the practices of other cultures, troubling questions about genital surgery cannot be ignored. We must realize that genital surgery increases a woman's status in societies that endorse this practice. Yet, we also must ask why this painful and dangerous procedure is needed for a woman to have status (Dirie, 1998; Lacey, 2004). We should also recognize the gender inequity that exists when men don't have to suffer genital surgery to gain status.

GENDER-BASED MURDER

Consider two facts: (1) When both sexes are given adequate care, there are more females than males in the population; and (2) in many countries today, men substantially outnumber women. How can both of these facts be true? Because millions of females are killed before or after birth.

One way to reduce the number of women is to selectively abort female fetuses, a common practice in some countries today (Patel, 2006; Shepherd, 2008). If a female child is born, cultures that don't value females condone female infanticide, the active or passive killing of female children. Active female infanticide is sometimes practiced by smothering a newborn female or drowning her in a bucket of water kept by the birthing bed. More passive methods of female infanticide include feeding girl babies little or nothing and denying them essential medical care (Hegde, 1999a, 1999b; Patel, 2006).

Women who survive to adulthood aren't necessarily safe. **Femicide** is the killing of women. In many places, including India, Pakistan, Albania, Mexico, and United Arab Emirates, adult women disappear or are killed. Governments do little to investigate cases of women who are found dead or who simply disappear (de Alba & Guzmán, 2010; Panther, 2008). Femicide also takes the form of dowry deaths, or bride burnings. Some groups in India still follow the custom in which a woman's parents give a sum of money or other goods to the bridegroom when he marries their daughter. After the marriage, the new husband sometimes makes demands for additional payments from the bride's parents. If the demands aren't met, the husband's family may hold the bride near the cooking stove until her sari catches fire and she burns to death. The husband is then free to get another wife and another dowry. Hundreds of thousands of women have been victims of bride burning. Currently, it's estimated that there is a dowry death in India every 1 hour and 44 minutes (Shott, 2008). Tim Muehlhoff (2007), a communication professor at Biola University, went to India to interview women about gender relations in their culture. Repeatedly women told him that the largest wing in hospitals was the burn unit, which is where women who have "accidents" in the kitchen go for help.

From abortions of female fetuses to killing of female infants to femicide, females around the world are being murdered daily. These practices are dramatic evidence of the devaluation of girls, women, and femininity. By now, the body count produced by these values is in the millions and still growing.

Throughout this book, we have seen that what is considered acceptable or normal is a matter of social negotiation and communication in a culture. Years ago, it was considered normal that women did not have the right to vote or to pursue higher education and careers. Today, in some countries genital mutilation, female infanticide, and femicide are regarded as normal. In the next section of this chapter, we discuss social processes that allow or encourage gendered violence.

THE SOCIAL FOUNDATIONS OF GENDERED VIOLENCE

Although particular individuals commit violent acts and should be held responsible for them, causes are broader than individual psychology and circumstances. To unravel cultural forces that cultivate tolerance for violence toward women and people who do not conform to conventional sex and gender roles, we will consider how media, institutions, and language normalize gendered violence.

THE NORMALIZATION OF VIOLENCE IN MEDIA

There is fairly convincing evidence that exposure to sexual violence in media is linked to increased tolerance, or even approval, of violence in actual relationships (Cuklanz, 1996; Jackson, 2008; May, 1998a; Rich, 2008; Romer, 2008). As we noted in Chapter 11, violence is customary—not unusual—in films, on MTV and television programs, and in popular music and video games. Gangsta rap includes lyrics that refer to women as "hos" (whores) and "bitches" and glorify killing for sport, which reflects a widespread and deeply ensconced cultural ideology that esteems violence.

Pornography often includes violence against women that may encourage those who consume it to think violence in real relationships is acceptable or normal. Before going further with this discussion, we need to distinguish pornography from **erotica**. Pornography is not simply sexually explicit material. Rather, it is material that favorably shows subordination and degradation of individuals by presenting sadistic behaviors as pleasurable, pain as enjoyable, and forced sex as positive. Erotica, on the other hand, depicts consensual activities that are desired by and pleasurable to all parties. Erotic material doesn't cultivate violence in relationships, whereas pornographic media are linked to violence between intimates.

Pornography is a multibillion-dollar business in the United States. A majority of X-rated films include scenes in which one or more men dominate and aggress on one or more women, and explicit rape scenes are common. Researchers report that repeated exposure to sexual violence may lead viewers to see it as acceptable and enticing (Harris, 2005; Jensen, 2007; Sparks, 2006).

Newspaper coverage of intimate partner violence focuses on individual incidents, often giving very detailed accounts of what went wrong in a relationship (Carlyle, Slater, & Chakroff, 2008). Focusing on specific episodes of violence diverts attention from larger patterns and the social context that supports them (Carlyle, Slater, & Chakroff, 2008).

THE NORMALIZATION OF VIOLENCE BY INSTITUTIONS

There is growing consensus that many of the basic structures and institutional practices of Western culture tolerate or uphold violence, including violence toward women. They do this in a variety of ways, such as refusing to interfere in domestic disputes, praising men for aggression, advising victims not to prosecute batterers, and encouraging women to fulfill social prescriptions for femininity by standing by their men.

Family   One of the most important institutions shaping cultural consciousness, including perspectives on violence, is the family. In families where violence exists, daughters and sons may grow up assuming that violence is part of marriage. In a recent study I conducted, one woman explained why she stayed with a man who physically and sexually brutalized her: "Once, when I told my mama that Gerald was sometimes mean, she said that all men are and that's just how they are—that all of them have bad spells—that's what Mama called them—and sometimes you just have to overlook those" (Wood, 2001b, p. 254).

Tolerance of intimate partner violence is greater in cultures that emphasize family cohesiveness and masculine superiority. In many countries, cultural norms maintain that men have a right to abuse women and that women should tolerate abuse and remain loyal. Some African-American and Asian-American women don't report intimate partner violence because family cohesiveness is culturally important and because they don't want to fuel negative stereotypes of their race (Dasgupta, 2007; Meyers, 2004).

When masculine socialization is extreme, it can promote appalling violence, such as the assaults in Central Park at the National Puerto Rican Day Parade on June 11, 2000. Four or five dozen men groped and stripped at least 47 women while yelling, "Get that bitch" and "You know you want it" (Campo-Flores & Rosenberg, 2000). More than 900 police officers were on duty in the park at the time, but they were unresponsive to pleas for help. One of the men who had participated shrugged off what he and others did to women, saying that it was "an innocent water fight that got out of hand" (Cloud, 2000, p. 32). The June 26, 2000, issue of *Time* included a two-page story on the Central Park incident. The same issue gave five pages to coverage of an architect and seven pages to an article on television voyeurism.

Law Enforcement   Families are not the only social institution that upholds tolerance of violence. Some law enforcement officers also reflect and sustain cultural acceptance of violence. Police officers are often reluctant to intervene in violence in families.

A highly publicized case was that of O. J. Simpson and Nicole Brown Simpson (Bordo, 1997). After Nicole Brown Simpson was found murdered, O. J. Simpson was accused of her murder. The jury found him not guilty, and he was released. This was not the first time O. J. had been suspected of violence toward Nicole. In 1989, while they were still married, police entered the Simpsons' home and found Nicole Brown Simpson badly beaten and fearful for her life. The officers accepted O. J.'s statement that he and his wife were involved in "a family matter ... we can handle it" (Hunt, 1994). Judge Ronald Schoenberg didn't sentence repeated abuser O. J. Simpson to any prison time or to counseling.

Another case, this one in New Hampshire in 1993, involved a man who smashed his partner's face so badly that she needed 17 stitches. Acknowledging that the man had battered the woman, the judge nonetheless ruled, "I can't conclude that it was completely unprovoked" (Hunt, 1994). In Denver in 2007, a judge refused to have a man fired for violence against his partner because the partner, a woman, "does not present a mousy appearance" so did not fit the judge's expectations of a victim (Osher, 2007).

Compared to previous eras, officers of the law—from police to judges—are more aware of violence against women and more willing to hold perpetrators accountable. Also, laws have been passed that increase victims' and potential victims' ability to protect themselves. Despite this progress, the current legal system does not offer sufficient safeguards for victims (Johnson, M., 2008).

Language   Another cultural practice that reflects and sustains tolerance of violence is the use of language that obscures the seriousness of the issue. Much of the language used to describe violence between intimates conceals the brutality of what happens. Why do newspapers and news programs use inappropriately gentle terms, such as *domestic dispute* or *spousal conflict*, to camouflage acts such as smashing women's faces with fists and hammers, slashing women with knives, and breaking bones by throwing or stomping on women (Lamb, 1991, 1999)?

Commonly used language about gendered violence also obscures moral responsibility. Terms such as *spousal conflict* and *family problems* distort reality by representing the issue as one for which partners share culpability. Responsibility for violence is also diminished by passive language that fails to name aggressors—for example, "The battery occurred on Sunday," "Women are abused frequently," or "Many women are beaten." The horror of intimate partner violence is also diminished when the language of love is used to describe physical abuse. Media accounts of battering of women often include phrases such as "He loved her too much," "She was the victim of love," and "It was love that went too far" (Meyers, 1994, 2004).

Cultural acceptance of gendered violence is supported—subtly and overtly, deliberately and inadvertently—by a number of social practices and institutions. But violence is not innate, and acceptance of it is not inevitable. Individual attitudes and cultural ideologies can be transformed.

RESISTING GENDERED VIOLENCE: WHERE DO WE GO FROM HERE?

I suspect that this chapter has been as distressing for you to read as it was for me to research and write. However, if we are only distressed about the extent of gendered violence, we will not lessen it. We must ask how we can be agents of change who resist gendered violence and who compel revisions in cultural attitudes toward it.

PERSONAL EFFORTS TO REDUCE GENDERED VIOLENCE

Each of us can do something to lessen gendered violence. The most basic personal choice is to decide that you will not engage in or tolerate violence in your relationships. You can also make conscious choices about the language you use. You can heighten others' awareness of the extent and brutality of violence against women by selecting words that accurately represent the ugliness and inhumanity of violent actions.

Another choice, one emphasized by Mentors in Violence Prevention, is to refuse to be a silent bystander. In 2009, a homecoming dance in Richmond, California turned into a horrific tragedy when a 15-year-old girl was beaten and gang-raped for more than two hours. More than a dozen people stood by and watched during this extended attack. None of them choose to intervene to stop the brutal assault ("California," 2009). You can make a different choice; you can speak out against violence and intervene in situations such as the one in Richmond, California. If a woman you know verbally abuses her boyfriend, you can remain silent, or you can let her know that you think what she's doing is wrong. You can also speak against others who inflict violence or threaten to do so. You may be able to intervene in some situations to prevent violence.

Jimmy Carter made the choice to speak out. A born-again Christian, the former President and winner of the Nobel Peace Prize had belonged to the Southern Baptist Church for more than 60 years. But in 2009, Carter broke with the church because it refused to ordain women and insisted that women should be subordinate to their husbands. Explaining what he called a "torturous decision," Carter said, "At its most repugnant, the belief that women must be subjugated to the wishes of men excuses slavery, violence, forced prostitution, genital mutilation and national laws that omit rape as a crime. ... The truth is that male religious leaders have had—and still have—an option to interpret holy teachings either to exalt or subjugate women. They have, for their own selfish ends, overwhelmingly chosen the latter. Their continuing choice provides the foundation or justification for much of the pervasive persecution and abuse of women throughout the world" (Carter, 2009, n.p.).

▼

Denny   *Cindy and I were at a bar, and it was pretty late, and most folks had been drinking for hours. I overheard a group of guys talking about this one girl who had danced with lots of the men during the evening. One of the guys said he bet she'd had enough to drink that she wouldn't be able to put up much of a fight. The other guys agreed and then started talking about who would take the next dance and move her outside. I kind of eased my beer down on the bar and went over to dance with the girl. When the song ended, I guided her back to where Cindy was, and we just kind of hung out with her until closing time. I saw* The Accused, *so I knew what could happen in a bar with guys who'd been drinking.*

There are other ways you personally can take a stand against gendered violence. You might volunteer to work with victims of violence. Most campuses and communities have a number of women's groups that offer outreach programs to educate citizens about violence toward women. Men on many campuses work to get other men involved in combating violence toward women. Becoming a community educator is a way to be an active agent of change. You can also make a personal statement by writing or calling in to object to magazine stories, radio programs, and televisions shows that present violence as normal or acceptable. If you are a parent or plan to be one, you can teach your children that nobody has a right to touch them in a violent or sexual way without their permission. And all children should learn that it is not appropriate or acceptable to be violent toward others or to coerce others into sexual activities.

You can use your voice to resist gendered violence by supporting friends and acquaintances who are victims of violence. For too many years, people have looked away from sexual harassment and violence between intimates. We've pretended not to see bruises, looked the other way when there was on-the-job harassment. If you suspect that a friend or colleague is experiencing violence, don't tell yourself, "it's none of my business." It *is* your business. Speaking up to support someone who is being harmed is a concrete way to use your voice to resist violence.

SOCIAL EFFORTS TO REDUCE GENDERED VIOLENCE

We must also change cultural practices and structures. Here, too, there are many ways to be an agent of change. You can vote for bonds and tax increases to underwrite more education and counseling. If you have skills as an educator or administrator, you may be able to help design and implement educational programs. You can also get involved with international efforts to reduce violence toward women.

EXPLORING GENDERED LIVES | STUDENT INITIATIVES TO LESSEN GENDERED VIOLENCE

When I travel to other schools, students and faculty often ask me how I teach my class, Gender, Communication, and Culture. They are particularly interested in how I approach the unit on gendered violence. For me, the highlight of the unit is an assignment that asks each student in my class to identify one action that she or he can take to diminish one type of gendered violence. In introducing this assignment, I caution my students not to discuss a great idea that *someone* could implement. Instead, the goal is to identify something that an individual student can do, given his or her personal location and resources. Below are four of the personal interventions generated by students in my class. As you read their ideas, notice how each student's action takes advantage of her or his particular position and resources.

- Pat is a 20-year-old drama major. "For two years I've worked with Players, which presents shows on campus. I proposed that next fall we do a show about street harassment, specifically the place on the quad where guys line up and call out ratings of girls who walk by. I don't think a lot of guys who do this have any idea how humiliating and offensive their 'game' is to girls. Our show will spotlight how girls feel when this happens. I think if guys see how much it hurts girls, a lot of them will stop doing it."

- Katelyn is a 20-year-old cross-country runner. "I talked with my teammates and coach, and we agreed to sponsor a race that I'm calling 'Put Your Best Foot Forward to End Violence.' Each of us is going to ask people to sponsor us at 10, 20, 50 cents or even a dollar per mile we run and all proceeds go to the county women's shelter."

- Courtney is a 21-year-old resident advisor for her residence hall. "I've proposed that next year each R.A. organizes a program on sexual assault that would happen in the dorm. A lot of people who won't go to a campus-wide program might attend one in their own dorm. The program will cover precautions to avoid assault and also resources on campus and in town for people who are assaulted."

- Kenny is a 19-year-old college student who belongs to a fraternity. "I've started noticing the language we use in the house [his fraternity]. There is a lot of trash talk about women that I really hadn't paid attention to before. I've decided not to engage in it and not to be silent when brothers do. Last week one of the brothers said something about a girl's 'fine ass,' and I said, 'I know that girl and she's not just 'an ass.' She's really smart and funny.' It might not sound like much, and it surely isn't going to win me a popularity contest, but it's making me more conscious of my own language about women and also putting my brothers on notice."

Do you think initiatives such as these four could have impact on your campus?

Many organizations work against violence, and they welcome volunteers and financial support. For example, Southeast Asian women formed *Saheli,* which protests dowry deaths. *Saheli* was successful in getting a law passed that requires thorough investigation of any "accidental death" of a woman during the first seven years of marriage. Eve Ensler (2000, 2001), who won the coveted Obie award for her play, *Vagina Monologues,* has founded Vday (Ensler, 2004). This organization works to stop all kinds of violence against women, including rape, incest, female genital mutilation, and sexual slavery. Groups such as these could use support, both personal and financial, from women and men in less hazardous circumstances.

Gendered violence, particularly violence against women, is pervasive. As Bob Herbert (2009a) recently commented after a man gunned down nine women, killing three, "there would have been thunderous outrage if someone had separated potential victims by race or religion and then shot, say, only the blacks, or only the whites or only the Jews. But if you shoot only the girls or only the women—not so much of an uproar. ... We should take particular notice of the staggering amounts of violence brought down on the nation's women and girls each and every day for no other reason than *because they are female*" (p. A17).

Sometimes, when I am overwhelmed by the extent of violence against women, I inspire myself by reading accounts of resistance by women and girls in cultures that radically degrade women. Girls at a rural high school in Zimbabwe were routinely harassed and sexually abused by boys and male teachers. They formed a group named Girl-Child Network and set up the first safe house in their country for abused girls (The Global Fund for Women, 2005). In India, a group of women formed *Vimochana,* an organization that helps battered women get legal assistance. In addition to responding to the symptoms of violence (battered women), *Vimochana* tackles the structural causes of it by organizing consciousness-raising groups that help women work together to redefine battering and dowry murders as unacceptable. Asian men have formed "Men Oppose Wife Abuse" to end intimate partner violence (Cuklanz & Moorti,

EXPLORING GENDERED LIVES	THE BANDIT QUEEN OF INDIA

Phoolan Devi was born into Dalit, a low caste of boat rowers in India. At 11, she was married to a man 20 years her senior who was chosen by her parents. Her husband beat her, and later, while under detention, Devi was raped. Instead of accepting this as the fate of women in her society, Devi rebelled. She took up a gun and formed a gang that killed men who harmed women. In 1983, she turned herself in—in exchange for the government's promise of an eight-year jail sentence. Devi was jailed without trial for 11 years, then released without comment in 1994. Within a year of her release, women elected her to federal parliament (Schmetzer, 1997). She became a very powerful advocate for women in India. To her followers, she was the reincarnation of Kali, a Hindu goddess, and a symbol of women's rights in a country that historically has not recognized that women have rights. In 2001, at the age of 38, Devi was gunned down in India by Sher Singh Rana, a 22-year-old student.

2009). Chilean women are risking imprisonment and death to demand that *desaparecidas,* "disappeared women," be returned. If high school girls in Zimbabwe and women in India can claim a voice in resisting violence, you and I can, too.

I want to close this chapter with a story that highlights the horrific nature of gendered violence and gives us an inspiring example of personal dignity, courage, and commitment to change. The Exploring Gendered Lives box below presents this story.

EXPLORING GENDERED LIVES | REFUSING TO BE DEFEATED

Mukhtar Mai.

This is the story of Mukhtar Mai, a Pakistani woman (Moreau & Hussain, 2005; Pennington, 2005; Strauss & Walsh, 2005). In June 2002, when Mukhtar was 32, her 12-year-old brother was accused of having sexual relations with the daughter in a higher-caste family. Later reports found no basis for the claim against Mukhtar's brother (Shah, 2011). The village council found him guilty and decided to punish his family by sentencing Mukhtar to be gang raped. A group of men stripped her, carried out the sentence, then forced her to walk home naked while

300 villagers watched. A woman who has been raped in Pakistan is dishonored (Minhas, 2009) so Mukhtar was expected to commit suicide.

She didn't. Instead, she fought back—and not just for herself. She prosecuted her rapists in another court that convicted them and awarded her $8,300. She used that money to start two schools in her village, one for boys and one for girls. Mukhtar believes that education is the best way to change the attitudes that led a council to punish her family by sentencing her to be gang raped and led her neighbors to commit the assault. *New York Times* columnist Nicholas Kristof (2005a, b, c, d) brought the case to the world's attention and continually updated the story. On March 3, 2005, a Pakistani appeals court overturned the death sentences of six of the men convicted of attacking her and set five of them free to live in her neighborhood. Almost immediately, an Islamic court, reinstated the convictions. A few days after that, Pakistani authorities declared that the Islamic court did not have jurisdiction (Pennington, 2005). The Pakistani authorities placed Mukhtar under house arrest and refused to let her make a planned visit the United States (Kristof, 2005c).

In June 2005, the Pakistani Supreme Court reopened inquiry into Mukhtar's case. Perhaps yielding to international pressure, the court freed her from house arrest and allowed her to return to her village, where she continues her efforts to provide educational opportunities to children. But Mukhtar is far from safe. She lives under threats on her life, yet continues her work providing education to Pakistanis and supporting Pakistani women who want to prosecute rapes and acid attacks. In 2011, Pakistan's Supreme Court freed five of the six men who were imprisoned for gang raping Mukhtar (Shah, 2011).

Mukhtar's story is presented in her autobiography, *In the Name of Honor* (Mai, Cuny, Kristof, & Coverdale, 2006) and in "Shame," a documentary produced by Showtime in 2007. If you wish to know more about her work or contribute to it, contact Mercy Corps at 3015 S.W. First St., Portland, OR 97201.

SUMMARY

In this chapter, we've examined forms of gendered violence and some of the ways in which communication sustains and normalizes violence, especially violence toward women. We do not have to accept the current state of affairs. We can do much to reduce gendered violence in our personal lives and to contribute to broader changes in the social structures and practices that sustain cultural acceptance of gendered violence. All that is required is to decide that you will assume an active role in improving the world.

We need to work together to provide safe refuges for victims of violence and to provide counseling to both victims and abusers. In addition, we need to develop educational programs that teach very young children that violence toward others is unacceptable. These and other changes in social structures and practices can reform cultural attitudes toward gendered violence. The changes will not be easy, but they are possible. Continuing to live with pervasive and relentless violence is not acceptable.

In the time it has taken you to read this far in the chapter, at least one woman has been raped and at least two have been beaten by a friend, lover, or family member.

Key Terms

The terms following are defined in this chapter on the pages indicated, as well as in alphabetical order in the book's glossary, which begins on page 325. The text's companion website (**http://www.cengage.com/communication/wood/genderedlives10e**) also provides interactive flash cards and crossword puzzles to help you learn these terms and the concepts they represent.

blaming the victim 295

clitoridectomy 306

erotica 309

femicide 308

gender intimidation 291

gendered violence 291

hostile environment harassment 303

infibulation 306

informed consent 293

intimate partner violence 298

male circumcision 305

pornography 309

quid pro quo harassment 303

sexual assault 292

sexual harassment 302

sunna 305

Gender Online

1. For more information, go to the National Coalition Against Domestic Violence's site at **http://www.ncadv.org**.
2. These are organizations that provide up-to-date information on ways you can help stop gendered violence around the world. For starters, try these websites: Office of Violence Against Women: **http://www.usdoj.gov/ovw**; National Domestic Violence Hotline: **http://www.ndvh.org**.
3. To learn more about men who are committed to stopping men's violence, visit this website: **http://menstoppingviolence.org**.
4. The Department of Justice has a special office that focuses exclusively on violence against women. Its website is: **http://www.ovw.usdoj.gov**. You might want to pay particular attention to the "Campus Grants" link, which is a relatively new feature that emphasizes dealing with and reducing violence against women on campuses.
5. Online search terms: "bride burning," "informed consent," "sexual harassment."

Reflection and Discussion

1. Do you support the reasonable man standard, the reasonable woman standard, or another standard? How is this issue linked to our discussion of generic language?
2. To understand how sexual harassment affects individuals, read the stories of people who have personally experienced it. The Fall 1992 issue of the *Journal*

of Applied Communication Research includes a special symposium that features the stories of survivors of sexual harassment.

3. Invite an attorney to talk with your class about your state's laws concerning rape charges and trials. What counts as rape in your state? What insights can the attorney offer about juries' attitudes toward plaintiffs who bring rape charges? Are juries equally sympathetic toward plaintiffs who bring charges of stranger versus acquaintance rape?

4. Conduct a survey to see if students on your campus believe the rape myths discussed in this chapter.

   - On the left-hand side of a sheet of paper, type the five myths about rape that are listed in the Exploring Gendered Lives: Myths and Facts about Rape box. To the right of the statements, type five categories of answer: strongly agree; somewhat agree; not sure; somewhat disagree; strongly disagree.
   - Make 15 copies of the sheet. Use two different colors of paper; give one color to women students and the other color to men students. Ask the students to respond anonymously. Ideally, members of the class should poll students at different places, such as the library, the student center or union, a fraternity house, and so forth.
   - Compile and analyze the data gathered by all the students in your class.

Recommended Resources

1. Mukhtar Mai, Nicholas Kristof, and Neil Coverdale. (2006). *In the Name of Honor*. New York: Simon Schuster/Atria. This is Mukhtar Mai's autobiography.
2. *Shame* (2007). Showtime, Producer. This is the documentary on Mukhtar Mai's schools and her commitment to social change.
3. Nicholas Kristof and Sherryl WuDunn. (2009). *Half the Sky*. New York: Knopf.

If you don't like something, change it.
Maya Angelou

Looking Backward, Looking Forward

This book is ending, yet the cultural conversation about gender will continue. It is carried on in living rooms, blogs, legislative chambers, classrooms, church groups, zines, barbershops, newspapers, personal relationships, video games, and boardrooms. It is a conversation in which we all participate; each generation edits what's been said before and adds new themes to the dialogue.

What you've learned about communication, gender, and culture will affect how you participate in the ongoing conversation about gender, communication, and culture. Your decisions of how to participate will shape and reflect your personal identity and the collective world we share. In this epilogue, we'll consider some of the choices that will be open to you in the years ahead.

Throughout this book, we've seen that society communicates gendered expectations that affect the rights, roles, and opportunities available to each of us. Yet, we are not only receivers of cultural communication about gender. We also shape our culture's views of men and women. We fortify or resist prevailing views as we enact our own gendered identities and as we respond to the communication and expressed identities of others.

A central theme of *Gendered Lives* is that current views of gender and existing gender relations are socially constructed. This means that they are not the only possible ones or necessarily the best ones. In this book, I've invited you to notice how dramatically cultural views of gender have changed over time. I've also encouraged you to think critically about current views of gender and to challenge those that limit our individual and collective lives. You and others of your generation will revise what gender means to you and to society. Given the profound impact of gender on personal and social life, this is no small responsibility.

You have inherited opportunities and definitions of gender that were crafted by the generations that preceded you. In the 1800s and early 1900s, women and some men changed laws and the Constitution to give women basic rights. My generation challenged restrictive definitions of women and men, and we demanded changes in social practices that limited the opportunities available to both sexes. We devoted much of our energy to identifying gender inequities and fighting to change economic, political, professional, and social subordination of women. The legacy of our efforts is substantial, and it has altered the educational, social, professional, and legal rights that are available to you.

▼

Taft   *I wonder if it's possible that we'll see a movement for gender equality that involves a lot of men and women. It seems to me that it would be good for us to work together instead of in separate movements. After all, a lot of the issues men face have to do with women and vice versa. Couldn't we get a lot more accomplished by talking with each other and combining forces to work for change?*

Your generation faces its own challenges, ones that are distinct to your era. To meet those challenges, you will need to define different priorities from those that motivated previous generations. Framing the issues of your era is a growing awareness of how the interaction of communication, gender, and culture privileges some people and oppresses others. All around us are inequities—some glaringly obvious, others more subtle. In shaping the future, you individually and your generation collectively will decide how to respond to social practices that produce differences in the quality of life and opportunities available to various groups in our culture.

You will have opportunities to influence policies and laws that affect work-life balance. Do you plan to take a voice on public issues, such as laws to ensure family leave policies for men and women who work outside the home? Do you plan to make commitments within your personal relationships that lead to greater gender equity than have traditional norms for relationships? In the places you work, will you speak out for policies that provide equitable opportunities, working environments, and rewards for women and men on the job? In influencing government and business policies regarding families, your generation will play a critical role in redesigning institutional practices that have an impact on every citizen.

CREATING THE FUTURE

The future is open. You and others in your generation will decide what it becomes. Your choices—in personal, social, and professional life—will contribute to defining gender in the years ahead and to the ways our society deals with the range of people it comprises.

EXPLORING GENDERED LIVES | REMAKING OURSELVES

Freedom ... is characterized by a constantly renewed obligation to remake the Self, which designates the free being.

—Jean Paul Sartre (1966)

DEFINING MASCULINITY AND FEMININITY

Are you comfortable with how masculinity and femininity are currently defined?

If you are a man, are you satisfied with the views of masculinity that are emphasized today? How will you define masculinity for yourself? What will your actions say about what it means to be a man? How will they shape others' views of manhood? If you have children, will you define active fathering as integral to masculinity? Will you assume a fair share of responsibility for housework and child care? You may also want to consider the traditional relationship between violence and manhood. Like all social views, this one can be changed, but only if you and others take a role in creating versions of masculinity that do not include violence (Kirby & Krone, 2002).

You may want to rethink the long-standing connection between masculinity and breadwinning because an increasing number of men of your generation form relationships with women who earn higher salaries and have more professional prestige. If your view of manhood remains tied to status and power, this will create enormous tension in your relationships and your identity. Through your personal and collective choices, your generation will author its own vision—or visions—of manhood, one that has the potential to revise and enlarge how women and men view masculinity.

If you are a woman, how do you define femininity for yourself? How does your embodiment of femininity affect others' views of what women are and can be? If you have children, how will you define mothering and, if you have a partner, parenting? Would you be comfortable earning a greater salary and having more professional status than your partner? Would your view of a man be affected by whether he earns more or less money than his partner? How do your behaviors and appearance reinforce or challenge media images that encourage women to starve themselves or to undergo cosmetic surgery in order to meet cultural standards? You have the capacity to resist the images of women that marketers advance. As a woman, the femininity that you personally embody and perform will contribute to the diversity of images of women that is available to everyone.

As women and men, you can affect what society expects of and admires in each sex.

RESPONDING TO DIFFERENCES

Growing out of what we have discussed is perhaps the most urgent challenge for your generation: to enlarge recognition of and respect for differences that include and go beyond differences between men and women. Diversity can be a source of strength or divisiveness, and you will influence which it is in the future. Will you respect men who give up careers to be homemakers and primary parents *and* men who find fulfillment in intense entrepreneurial ventures? Will you encourage your sons and daughters to be caring and strong? Will you respect and work and socialize with trans people? Understand that your real answers to these questions will be found not in what you say in this moment, but in how you live your life.

We should also attend to the ongoing debate about how different men and women really are and, by implication, whether they should be treated differently. How we resolve this question profoundly affects our material lives, particularly in terms of legal rights and institutional policies. For example, our courts are currently hearing cases in which one attorney argues for equal treatment of women and opposing counsel argues for equitable, not equal, treatment that is responsive to women's distinct biological qualities. A specific example is pregnancy: Should it be defined as a uniquely female condition that requires special provisions, or should it be defined as one of many medical conditions that affect people? Should someone who has transitioned from one sex to another have the legal and social rights of the identity to which the person transitioned?

As your generation remakes social meanings of women, men, gender identity, and differences among people, you will simultaneously influence our collective vision of ourselves as a culture. Our country has always included people of varied gender identities, sexual orientations, sexes, socioeconomic classes, and races. Yet, our language and the dominant cultural ideology advocate a single cultural ideal that some people embody more fully than others. Within this perspective, differences are matters of better and worse, and we are encouraged to use a single standard to evaluate ourselves and others. Historically, the white, middle-class, heterosexual, able-bodied male has been that standard.

The aspiration toward a single cultural ideal is reflected in the melting-pot metaphor that has long been used to describe America. This metaphor encourages people to erase their differences—including facets of their identity that they cherish—and become alike in order to assimilate into a single, homogeneous culture. The painful divisions in our society suggest that the melting pot is an inappropriate ideal for us. It no longer works—if indeed it ever did.

Perhaps it is time to abandon the melting-pot metaphor and inaugurate a new one that acclaims differences as valuable and desirable, one that remakes the cultural ideal to include all citizens instead of trying to remake diverse citizens to fit a single, narrow ideal. Maybe your generation will replace the melting-pot metaphor with one that recognizes commonality without obliterating real and valuable differences among people. To create a new vision, we must realize that we participate in a common world, yet each of us experiences it somewhat differently from locations shaped by intersections among gender, race, class, and sexual orientation. What sort of metaphor might capture this as our national character?

In her history of the second wave of feminism in the United States, Flora Davis (1991) used the metaphor of a salad bowl to describe our society. She pointed out that a salad consists of many different ingredients that retain their individual tastes, textures, and colors and at the same time contribute to a whole that is more complex, interesting, and enjoyable than the individual parts or some fusion of those parts. The Reverend Jesse Jackson offered the compelling metaphor of our nation as a family quilt made up of patches of various colors and design. Another metaphor is that of a collage, in which distinct patterns stand out in their individual integrity while simultaneously contributing to the character and complexity of the whole. If your generation is able to affirm diversity in sex, race, class, ethnicity, sexuality, and sexual orientation, then you will have inaugurated a bold new theme in the cultural conversation—one with the potential to make our society richer and more equitable for all. That is a responsibility and an opportunity that belongs to each of you.

TAKING A VOICE

Men and women like you will be key players in the next stage of the cultural conversation about gender. You cannot escape participating or the responsibilities it entails. Just as speaking out against discrimination is a choice, so, too, is silence. You can't avoid having influence. Instead, your only options are to decide what influence you will exert and how and where you will do it. There are multiple ways in which you can influence our cultural views of gender and gender-related issues. In his study of how people respond to toxic chemical disasters, Michael Reich (1991) identified three ways in which citizens affect public awareness, public policy, and redress for victims of chemical disasters. Translating his ideas to our concern with gender, we can identify three forms of influence on cultural views of gender: direct power, agenda setting, and voice.

Direct power is the ability to make others do what they would not do on their own. If you become an executive or own a company, you will have many opportunities to exercise direct power. For instance, you may be able to establish policies that affect family leave, work schedules, and criteria for promotion. Parents exercise direct power when they allow or don't allow children to play with particular toys or to engage in various kinds of activities. Teachers exercise direct power when they assign readings and projects. And citizens exercise direct power when they enter politics, cast votes, and lobby legislators on gender-related issues.

A second form of power is gate keeping or agenda setting. As we saw in Chapter 11, newspaper editors and television producers set agendas when they decide what stories to cover and how to represent the issues and people involved in those stories. If you pursue a career in advertising, public relations, popular music, or journalism, you will have opportunities to shape the public agenda. You can also participate in agenda setting by writing letters to editors or calling in to talk shows to state your opinions and to get issues on the public agenda. Likewise, you can engage in agenda setting in your professional and social relationships by putting on the table issues that operate covertly to sustain gender inequities.

The third way to exercise power is through voice—communicating with others and engaging in everyday acts of resistance and principled stances. One example of the power of voice is adopting a traitorous identity, which we discussed in Chapter 4. Queer performative work, which we first discussed in Chapter 2, is another means of using voice to challenge conventional categories of sex, gender, and sexuality. Other examples of voice come from third-wave feminists who challenge sexist attitudes and practices in everyday life. They challenge the supervisor who calls female employees "hon" or "sweetheart"; they refuse to diet excessively to meet unrealistic and unhealthy ideals of femininity; they speak up in classes to challenge racist, sexist, and homophobic comments; they participate in protests and rallies; and they use their voices to challenge inequities and to introduce new perspectives in everyday conversations with friends, coworkers, and acquaintances.

It's important to realize that voice and resistance are processes. We tend to see the outcomes of extended processes—for example, we notice a protest, or rally, or strike. But those specific, visible results grow out of processes of listening, reading, reflecting, and talking with others. We are often cultivating our voices in quiet moments, even private moments. Making time to think about issues raised in this book is part of developing your voice.

Your capacity for influence is great because society is a human creation that we continuously remake through communication in private and public settings. You can take a voice in shaping the meaning of gender and what it means to be men and women in the years ahead. You will also influence attitudes toward diversity, either by advancing the view that differences are divisive or by endorsing the view that differences are sources of individual and collective strength.

On April 9, 2009, President Obama spoke about the economic crisis that gripped the globe. He said that some of us are to blame for the crisis, but all of us are responsible for it. Those words apply equally to other facets of our lives, including gender. We are all responsible. We owe it to ourselves and to each other to take responsibility for our shared future.

What gender and culture will mean in the future is up to you. In your personal and social relationships, professional interactions, and civic activities, you will create and communicate visions of who we can be and how we can live.

The most radical step you can take is your next one.
James Baldwin

REFLECTION AND DISCUSSION

1. What do you see as the future of women's and men's movements? Do you think one branch will come to predominate in each movement? Will new kinds of movements emerge? Will men and women come together in a single movement?
2. After reading this book and completing the course it accompanies, how do you now define feminism? Has your view changed at all as a result of your studies this term?
3. If you could write the script, how would you define masculinity and femininity in the year 2050? Ideally, what would each gender be like? Or would there be no need for two distinct genders? Or would there be more than two? If gender is a linchpin of culture, then changing gender changes culture. How would the ideals you have in mind affect the character of social life?
4. The textbook closes by discussing metaphors for the United States that might replace the melting-pot metaphor. Do you like the alternatives suggested here: a family quilt, a salad bowl, or a collage? Can you come up with other metaphors that simultaneously represent diversity and commonality among members of our society?

Glossary

affirmative action Collective term for policies that go beyond equal opportunity laws to redress discrimination. Assumes that historical patterns of discrimination against groups of people justify the preferential treatment of members of those groups; focuses on results, not on the intent of efforts to redress inequities; and attempts to increase the number of qualified members of minorities in education and the workplace, commensurate with their availability.

agenda setting Claims media set the public agenda by telling us what's important or what we should think about.

alternate paths model A relationship theory according to which masculine and feminine ways of creating and expressing closeness are viewed as different from each other and equally valid.

androgyny Combination of qualities society considers both masculine and feminine. Androgynous people tend to identify with and enact qualities socially ascribed both to women and to men.

antifeminism A movement opposing any measures that advance women's equality, status, rights, or opportunities; also called the *backlash against feminism.*

antisuffrage movement A movement that aimed to prevent women from gaining the right to vote in the United States. Opposition to women's suffrage was evident as early as 1848 and was formalized in organizations by 1911.

artifact A personal object that influences how we see ourselves and how we express our identities.

backlash A countermovement that seeks to repudiate and contain feminism by arguing two contradictory claims: (1) that women have never had it so good, so there is no longer any need for feminism; and (2) that feminism has caused serious problems in women's lives and family relationships. Also called *antifeminism.*

biological theory The theory that biological characteristics of the sexes are the basis of differences in women's and men's thinking, communicating, feeling, and other functions.

blaming the victim Holding a harmed person responsible for the harm inflicted on him or her by another person.

cis Prefix that designates someone whose gender identity is consistent with what society considers appropriate for the sex assigned at birth.

clitoridectomy Removal of the entire clitoris. Part or all of the labia minora may also be removed. Also called excision.

cognitive development theory A developmental theory according to which children participate in defining their genders by acting on internal motivations to be competent, which in turn lead them to seek out gender models that help them to sculpt their own femininity or masculinity.

communication A dynamic, systemic process in which meanings are created and reflected in and through humans' interactions with symbols.

complimentary copy An article or section of writing about an advertiser's product or service that is placed in a magazine by the publisher at no cost to the advertiser, to increase the market appeal of the product or service.

content level of meaning The literal meaning of communication. Content-level meanings are the formal, or denotative, meanings of messages.

critical research methods Identification and challenge to inequities and problems in social life.

cultural feminism The viewpoint that women and men differ in fundamental ways, including biology, and that, in general, women and men have distinct standpoints that foster different experiences, perspectives, skills, and knowledge (for instance, nurturance in women and independence in men).

culture The structures and practices, especially those relating to communication, through which a particular social order is produced and reproduced by legitimizing certain values, expectations, meanings, and patterns of behavior.

culture of romance Created when forces in higher education encourage women students to regard being attractive to men as more important than academics and career preparation.

ecofeminism A movement that integrates the intellectual and political bases of feminist theorizing with ecological philosophy. The specific oppression of women is seen as a particular instance of a larger ideology that esteems violence and domination of women, children, animals, and the Earth.

effortless perfection The pressure felt by many women students at colleges to be beautiful, fit, popular, smart, and accomplished, all without visible effort.

ego boundary Psychologically, the point at which an individual stops and the rest of the world begins; an individual's sense of the line between herself or himself and others. Ego boundaries range from permeable (a sense of self that includes others and their issues, problems, and so on) to rigid (a sense of self as completely distinct from others).

equal opportunity laws Laws that prohibit discrimination on the basis of race, color, religion, sex, or national origin. Equal opportunity laws seek to protect *individual* members of groups that have been targets of discrimination; they redress only current discrimination, not historical bias.

erotica Depictions of sexual activities that are agreed to and enjoyed by the parties participating in the activities.

essentializing The reduction of a phenomenon to its essential characteristics, which are generally presumed to be innate or unchangeable. To essentialize the sexes is to imply that all women are alike in basic respects, that all men are alike in basic respects, and that the two sexes are distinct from each other because of fundamental, essential qualities.

excision See *clitoridectomy*.

father hunger From the mythopoetic men's movement, men's yearning to be close to other men and to build deep, enduring bonds with them; based on the mythopoetic belief that most young boys have distant relationships with the primary man in their lives—the father—and that the hunger for meaningful contact with men, of which they were deprived in youth, continues throughout life.

Fathers 4 Justice A British fathers' rights group that relies on the two rhetorical strategies of humor and dramatic stunts to raise public awareness about the custody rights of separated and divorced fathers.

femicide The killing of girls and women.

feminine ruler Measuring closeness, or intimacy in a way that gives priority to behaviors more typical of women than men.

Free Men A branch of the men's movement that seeks to restore the traditional image of men by celebrating and encouraging the qualities of competitiveness, independence, and ruggedness in men.

gatekeeper Person or group that controls which messages get through to audiences of mass media.

gender Also called gender role. A social, symbolic construction that expresses the meanings a society associates with biological sex. Gender varies across cultures, over time within any given society, and in relation to other genders.

gender constancy A person's understanding, which usually develops by age three, that her or his sex is relatively fixed and unchanging.

gender identity A person's own identification as male or female. It is the personal perception of one's sex.

gender schema An internal mental framework that organizes perceptions and directs behavior related to gender.

gender schema theory Claims that cognitive processes are central to our learning what gender means in our culture and to learning how to perform our gender competently. Related to cognitive development theory.

gendered violence Physical, verbal, emotional, sexual, or visual brutality inflicted disproportionately or exclusively on members of one sex. Includes gender intimidation, sexual assault, violence between intimates, sexual harassment, genital mutilation, and gender-based murder.

gender intimidation The treatment of members of one sex in ways that make them feel humiliated, unsafe, or inferior because of their sex.

gender linked-language effect Asserts that differences between women's and men's communication are influenced by a variety of factors including topics, speaker status, salience of gender in a communication situation, and other people present.

glass ceiling An invisible barrier, made up of subtle, often unconscious prejudices and stereotypes, that limits the opportunities and advancement of women and minorities.

glass walls A metaphor for sex segregation on the job. Glass walls exist when members of a group, such as women, are placed in positions based on stereotypes of that group. Typically, such positions do not entail advancement ladders.

goal A stated intention to achieve a defined representation of minorities or women.

haptics Touch as a form of nonverbal communication.

hermaphrodite A person who possesses aspects of physical genitalia from both sexes. Currently, *intersexual* is the preferred term.

heteronormativity The assumption that heterosexuality is normative and all other sexual identities are abnormal.

hostile environment harassment Conduct that has sexual overtones and that interferes with a person's ability to perform a job or gain an education or that creates a hostile, intimidating, or offensive working environment.

immersive advertising Incorporating a particular brand or product into entertainment.

infibulation Removal of the clitoris and labia minora and subsequent joining of the lips of the labia majora so that they fuse together.

informed consent Consent given by a legal adult with normal mental abilities whose judgment is not impaired by circumstances, including alcohol or other drugs.

intersexed Having both male and female biological sexual characteristics.

intimate partner violence The use of physical, mental, emotional, verbal, or economic power by one partner against the other partner in a current or past romantic relationship.

invisible hand discrimination The inadvertent application, in discriminatory fashion, of policies that are not inherently biased.

kinesics Facial and body movements; one type of nonverbal communication.

lesbian feminists Feminists whose sexual preference is women, who define themselves as woman identified, and who are committed to fighting for legal rights for all woman-identified women.

liberal feminism A form of feminism that maintains that women and men are alike in important respects and that women should have the same economic, political, professional, and civic opportunities and rights as men. NOW (the National Organization for Women) is the best-known organization representing liberal feminism.

liking The dimension of relationship-level meaning that expresses affection for another.

male circumcision Removal of the sheath, or prepuce, of the penis.

male deficit model A relationship theory according to which men are deficient in forming and participating in close relationships; holds that most men's ways of experiencing and expressing closeness are not simply different from, but inferior to, those of women.

male feminists Men who believe that women and men are alike in important respects and that the sexes should enjoy the same privileges, rights, opportunities, and status in society. Male feminists join liberal women feminists in fighting for equitable treatment of women. In addition, many male feminists seek to rid themselves of what they regard as toxic masculinity promoted in men by socialization, and to develop sensitivities more typically inculcated in women. Also called *profeminist men.*

male generic language Words and phrases that are claimed to refer to both women and men yet are denotatively masculine; for example, the word *man* used to refer to all human beings.

masculinist A category of men's movement that sees men as oppressed and seeks to preserve men's freedom from women and feminization.

maternal wall Unexamined assumptions held by coworkers and superiors about how women will behave once they become mothers.

matriarchal Of or pertaining to matriarchy, "rule by the mothers." The term *matriarchy* is generally used to refer to systems of ideology, social structures, and practices that are created by women and reflect the values, priorities, and views of women as a group.

men's rights activists Members of a men's movement whose goal is to restore traditional roles for men and women and, with that, the privileges men have historically enjoyed.

mentor A more experienced person who helps a less experienced person develop.

Mentors in Violence Prevention (MVP) A male antiviolence program that educates men about socialization that links masculinity to violence and aggression; motivates men to reject violence in themselves and in other men.

microinequities Verbal comments and behaviors that devalue members of a group but do not violate antidiscrimination laws; can affect morale, job performance, and career advancement.

Million Man March A branch of the men's movement that began with a march in Washington, D.C., in 1995, in which black men atoned for sins and committed themselves to spiritual transformation and political action. Annual marches were also held in subsequent years.

Million Woman March A grassroots gathering of African-American women launched in Philadelphia in 1997 to celebrate and foster solidarity among black women.

minimal response cues Nominal indicators of listening or attending. "Um" and "yeah" are minimal response cues.

mommy track Informal term for the practice of placing women on a separate career path that limits their career opportunities and advancement.

monitoring The process of observing and regulating our own attitudes and behaviors, which is possible because humans can reflect on themselves from others' perspectives (self-as-object).

multiracial feminism A branch of the women's movement that is concerned with race and the racial oppression of women.

mythopoetic movement A branch of the men's movement headed by poet Robert Bly and active in the 1990s. Mythopoetics believe that men need to rediscover their distinctively masculine modes of feeling, which they regard as rooted largely in myth.

NOMAS (National Organization for Men Against Sexism) An activist men's organization that promotes personal, political, and social changes that foster equality of men and women and gay and straight people through workshops and informal group discussions, public speaking, educational outreach programs, and enactment of traitorous identities.

nonverbal communication All elements of communication other than words themselves. Estimated to carry 65% to 93% of the total meaning of communication; includes visual, vocal, environmental, and physical aspects of interaction.

paralanguage Vocal cues that accompany verbal communication, such as accent, volume, and inflection.

patriarchal Of or pertaining to patriarchy, "rule by the fathers." The term *patriarchy* generally refers to systems of ideology, social structures, and practices, created by men, that reflect the values, priorities, and views of men as a group.

performative theory Claims that identity, including gender, is not something individuals have, but rather something they do through performance or expression.

personal relationships Connections in which partners are interdependent, consider each other irreplaceable, and are strongly and specifically connected to each other as unique individuals.

physical appearance Aspects of personal appearance; often evaluated according to cultural standards.

polarized thinking Conceiving things in terms of opposites (e.g., good or bad, right or wrong).

pornography Written, oral, or visual material that favorably shows subordination and degradation of individuals by presenting sadistic behaviors as pleasurable, pain as enjoyable, and forced sex as positive. Distinct from erotica, which depicts consensual activities desired by and pleasurable to all parties.

power Dimension of relationship-level meaning that expresses the degree to which a person is equal to, dominant over, or deferential to others.

power feminism A movement that emerged in the 1990s as a reaction to feminist emphasis on women's oppression. Urges women to take the power that is theirs and to reject seeing themselves as victims of men or society.

product placement Showing or mentioning a particular brand or product in a show, story, film, or other form of media.

profeminist See *male feminists.*

Promise Keepers Begun in 1990, a Christian branch of the men's movement that calls men together to pray and commit to Christ-centered living.

proxemics Space and the human use of space, including personal territories.

psychodynamic theory The theory that family relationships, especially between mother and child during the formative years of life, have a pivotal and continuing impact on the development of self, particularly gender identity.

psychological responsibility The responsibility to remember, plan, think ahead, organize, and so forth. In most heterosexual relationships, even when physical labor is divided between partners, women assume greater psychological responsibility for the home and children.

qualitative research methods Aim to understand the nature or meaning of experiences, which cannot be quantified into numbers.

quantitative research methods Way of gathering data that can be quantified and analyzing the data to draw conclusions.

queer performative theories Integration of queer and performative theories into a perspective on performances as means of challenging and destabilizing conventional cultural categories and the values attached to them.

queer theory Critique of conventional categories of identity and cultural views of "normal" and "abnormal," particularly in relation to sexuality. Queer theory argues identities are not fixed, but fluid.

quid pro quo harassment Actual or threatened use of professional or academic rewards or punishments to gain sexual compliance from a subordinate or student.

quota A particular number or percentage of women or minorities who must be admitted to schools, hired in certain positions, or promoted to certain levels in institutions.

radical feminism A branch of feminism that grew out of New Left politics and demanded the same attention to women's oppression that New Left organizations gave to racial oppression and other ideological issues. Radical feminists pioneered revolutionary communication techniques such as consciousness raising, leaderless group discussion, and guerrilla theater.

relationship level of meaning The nonliteral meaning of communication. Expresses how a speaker sees the relationship between self and other. May provide cues about how to interpret the literal meaning of a message, for instance, as a joke.

responsiveness The dimension of relationship-level meaning that expresses attentiveness to others and interest in what they say and do.

revalorists Feminists who focus on valuing traditionally feminine skills, activities, and perspectives and their contributions to personal, interpersonal, and cultural life.

role Social definitions of expected behaviors and the values associated with them; typically internalized by individuals in the process of socialization.

second shift The work of homemaking and child care performed by a member of a dual-worker family after and in addition to that person's job in the paid labor force.

self-as-object The ability to reflect on the self from the standpoint of others. Because humans are able to take others' perspectives, their views of self are necessarily social.

separatists Feminists who believe that, because patriarchal culture cannot be changed or reformed, women who find it oppressive must create and live in their own women-centered communities separate from the larger culture.

sex A personal quality determined by biological and genetic characteristics. *Male, female, man,* and *woman* indicate sex.

sexual assault Sexual activity to which at least one participant has not given informed consent.

sexual harassment Unwelcome sexualized conduct that is linked to the target's academic or professional standing.

sexual orientation A person's preferences for romantic and sexual partners.

social learning theory Theory that individuals learn to be masculine and feminine (among other things) by observing and imitating others and by reacting to the rewards and punishments others give in response to imitative behaviors.

speech community A group of people who share assumptions regarding how, when, and why to communicate and how to interpret others' communication.

spotlighting Highlighting a person's sex rather than other, more relevant characteristics; for example, the headline "Woman Elected Mayor."

standpoint theory A theory that focuses on the influence of gender, race, class, and other social categories on circumstances of people's lives, especially their social positions and the kinds of experiences fostered within those positions. According to standpoint theory, political consciousness about social location can generate a standpoint that affects perspective and action.

stereotype A broad generalization about an entire class of phenomena, based on some knowledge of limited aspects of certain members of the class.

sunna Genital mutilation involving removal of the sheath and tip of the clitoris. Also called *female circumcision.*

symbolic interactionism The theory that individuals develop self-identity and an understanding of social life, values, and codes of conduct through communicative interactions with others in a society.

territoriality An aspect of proxemics; the sense of personal space that one does not want others to invade.

theory A way to describe, explain, and predict relationships among phenomena.

third-wave feminism An emergent movement asserting that feminism for the current era is not just an extension of second-wave feminism. Aims (1) to be inclusive of diverse peoples; (2) to use personal life and personal action for political impact; and (3) to work to build coalitions with other groups that struggle against oppression.

Title IX The section of the Educational Amendment of 1972 that makes it illegal for schools that accept federal funds to discriminate on the basis of sex.

traitorous identity A group member's criticism of particular attitudes and actions—for example, sexist jokes—that are accepted and normative within the group.

transgendered Individual who feels that her or his biologically assigned sex is inconsistent with her or his true sexual identity.

transsexual Individual who has had surgery and/or hormonal treatments to make his or her body more closely match the sex with which he or she identifies.

transvestites People who enjoy wearing clothing of the other sex.

voice-over A technique used in audiovisual media, particularly television commercials; over the action on the screen, viewers hear a voice that makes claims about the product, gives advice, or explains the action.

White Ribbon Campaign (WRC) An international group of men who work to end men's violence against women.

womanists A group of women who define their identities and goals as reflecting both race and gender oppression. The womanist movement arose out of dissatisfaction with mainstream feminism's focus on white, middle-class women and their interests.

women's rights movement From the mid-1800s to the 1920s, a movement that focused on gaining basic rights for women, such as the rights to vote, to pursue higher education, and to enter professions.

REFERENCES

Abrams, J. (2009, January 23). Bill lifting limits on equal-pay lawsuits clears Senate. *Raleigh News & Observer*, p. 6A.

Acitelli, L. (1988). When spouses talk to each other about their relationship. *Journal of Social and Personal Relationships, 5*, 185–199.

Adams, C. (1991, April). The straight dope. *Triangle Comic Review*, p. 26.

Addington, D. W. (1968). The relationship of selected vocal characteristics to personality perceptions. *Speech Monographs, 35*, 492–503.

Adler, J. (2007, March 12). The great sorority purge. *Newsweek*, p. 47.

Adler, R. (2009, March-April). Profit, thy name is ... woman? *Miller-McCune*, pp. 33–35.

Allen, B. (2006). Communicating race at Weigh Co. In J. T. Wood & S. W. Duck (Eds.), *Composing relationships: Communication in everyday life* (pp. 156–165). Belmont, CA: Thomson.

Allis, S. (1990, Fall). What do men really want? *Time*, pp. 80–82.

Almaguer, T. (1993). Chicano men: A cartography of homosexual identity and behavior. In H. Abelove, M. Barale, & D. Halperin (Eds.), *The lesbian and gay studies reader* (pp. 255–273). London: Routledge.

American Association of University Women (AAUW). (1991). *Shortchanging girls, shortchanging America*. Washington, DC: Greenberg-Lake Analysis Group.

American Association of University Women (AAUW). (1998). *Gender gaps: Where schools still fail our children*. Washington, DC: American Association of University Women Educational Foundation.

American Association of University Women (AAUW). (2001). *Beyond the "gender wars": A conversation about girls, boys, and education*. Washington, DC: American Association of University Women Educational Foundation.

Andelin, H. (1975). *Fascinating womanhood*. New York: Bantam.

Andersen, M., & Collins, P. H. (Eds.). (2007a). *Race, class, and gender: An anthology* (6th ed.). Belmont, CA: Thomson.

Andersen, M., & Collins, P. H. (2007b). Systems of power and inequality. In M. Andersen & P. H. Collins (Eds.), *Race, class, and gender: An anthology* (6th ed., pp. 61–90). Belmont, CA: Thomson.

Andersen, P. (2006). The evolution of biological sex differences in communication. In K. Dindia & D. Canary (Eds.), *Sex differences and similarities in communication* (pp. 117–135). Mahwah, NJ: Erlbaum.

Anderson, I., & Doherty, K. (2008). *Accounting for rape*. New York: Routledge.

Anderson, K., & Leaper, C. (1998). Meta-analyses of gender effects on conversational interruption: Who, what, when, where, and how. *Sex Roles, 39*, 225–252.

Andronici, J. F., & Katz, D. S. (2007, Winter). Scaling the maternal wall. *Ms.*, pp. 63–64.

Angier, N. (2007a, May 1). For motherly X chromosome, gender is only the beginning. *The New York Times*, pp. D1, D6.

Angier, N. (2007b, June 12). Sleek, fast and focused: The cells that make dad dad. *The New York Times*, pp. D1, D6.

Angier, N. (2010, June 15). Paternal bonds, special and strange. *New York Times*, pp. D1, D2.

331

Anzaldúa, G. (1999). *Borderlands/la frontera: The new mestiza.* San Francisco: Spinsters/Aunt Lute.

Anzaldúa, G. (2002, October 11). Beyond traditional notions of identity. *The Chronicle of Higher Education,* pp. B11–B13.

Anzaldúa, G., & Keating, A. (Eds.). (2002). *This bridge called home.* New York: Routledge.

Aptheker, B. (1998). Cultural feminism. In W. Mankiller, G. Mink, M. Navarro, B. Smith, & G. Steinem (Eds.), *The reader's companion to U.S. women's history* (pp. 205–206). New York: Houghton Mifflin.

Araton, H. (2007, November 9). Amid inequity in coverage, Rutgers women turn page. *The New York Times,* p. C13.

Archer, J., & Coyne, S. M. (2005). An integrated review of indirect, relational, and social aggression. *Personality and Social Review, 9,* 212–230.

Aries, E. (1987). Gender and communication. In P. Shaver & C. Hendrick (Eds.), *Sex and gender* (pp. 149–176). Newbury Park, CA: Sage.

Aries, E. (1998). Gender differences in interaction. In D. Canary & K. Dindia (Eds.), *Sex differences and similarities in interaction: Critical essays and empirical investigations* (pp. 65–81). Mahwah, NJ: Erlbaum.

Aronowitz, T., Rennells, R. E., & Todd, E. (2005). Heterosocial behaviors in early adolescent African American girls: The role of mother-daughter relationships. *Journal of Family Nursing, 11,* 122–139.

Ashcraft, K. (2006). Back to work: Sights/sites of difference in gender and organizational communication studies. In B. Dow & J. T. Wood (Eds.), *Handbook of gender and communication* (pp. 97–122). Thousand Oaks, CA: Sage.

Ashcraft, K., & Mumby, D. (2004). *Reworking gender: A feminist communicology of organization.* Thousand Oaks, CA: Sage.

Atwater, L. E., Brett, J. F., Waldman, D., Dimare, L., & Hayden, M. V. (2004). Men's and women's perceptions of the gender typing of management subroles. *Sex Roles, 50,* 191–200.

Atwood, F. (2006). Sexed up: Theorizing the sexualization of culture. *Sexualities, 9,* 77–94.

Aukett, R., Ritchie, J., & Mill, K. (1988). Gender differences in friendship patterns. *Sex Roles, 19,* 57–66.

Avery, S. (1999, November 19). Whatever happened to the men's movement? *Raleigh News & Observer,* pp. 1E, 3E.

Babarskiene, J., & Tweed, R. (2009). Marital adjustment in post-Soviet Eastern Europe: A focus on Lithuania. *Personal Relationships, 16,* 647–658.

Babcock, L., & Laschever, S. (2003). *Women don't ask.* Princeton, NJ: Princeton University Press.

Bagemihl, B. (2000). *Biological exuberance: Animal homosexuality and natural diversity.* Boston: St. Martin's Press.

Bailey, A. (1994). Mothering, diversity, and peace politics. *Hypatia, 9,* 188–198.

Baird, J. (2010, April 19). Beyond the bad boys. *Newsweek,* p. 24.

Bakalar, N. (2006, June 13). Men are better than women at ferreting out that angry face in a crowd. *The New York Times,* p. D5.

Bakalar, N. (2009, March 27). Circumcision is found to curb two S.T.D.'s. *New York Times,* p. A17.

Baker, J. (2006). *Sisters: The lives of America's suffragists.* New York: Hill and Wang.

Balswick, J. O. (1988). *The inexpressive male.* Lexington, MA: Lexington Books.

Balswick, J. O., & Peek, C. W. (1976). The inexpressive male: A tragedy of American society. In D. Brannon & R. Brannon (Eds.), *The forty-nine percent majority: The male sex-role* (pp. 55–57). Reading, MA: Addison-Wesley.

Bandura, A. (2002). Social cognitive theory of mass communication. In J. Bryant & D. Zillmann (Eds.), *Media effects: Advances in theory and research* (2nd ed., pp. 121–153). Mahwah, NJ: Erlbaum.

Bandura, A., & Walters, R. H. (1963). *Social learning and personality development.* New York: Holt, Rinehart & Winston.

Banerjee, N. (2008, May 19). Fathers and daughters dance the night away, with a higher purpose. *New York Times,* p. A13.

Banerjee, R., & Lintern, V. (2000). Boys will be boys: The effect of social evaluation concerns on gender-typing. *Social Development, 9,* 397–408.

Banerji, A. (1998, July 10). Telling the stories of everyday youths. *The Chronicle of Higher Education,* p. A7.

Banks, I. (2000). *Hair matters: Beauty, power, and black women's consciousness.* New York: New York University Press.

Banyard, V. L., Plante, E. G., Cohn, E. S., Moorhead, C., Ward, S., & Walsh, W. (2005). Revisiting unwanted sexual experiences on campus: A 12-year follow-up. *Violence Against Women, 11,* 426–446.

Barash, D. (2002, May 24). Evolution, males, and violence. *The Chronicle of Higher Education,* pp. B7–B9.

Barash, D., & Lipton, J. (2002). *Gender gap: The biology of male-female differences.* New Brunswick, NJ: Transaction Publishers.

Barash, S. (2006). *Tripping the prom queen.* New York: St. Martin's Griffin.

Barreto, M., Ryan, M., & Schmitt, M. (Eds.). (2009). *The glass ceiling in the 21st century.* Washington, DC: American Psychological Association.

Barnett, R., & Rivers, C. (1996). *She works, he works: How two-income families are happier, healthier, and better off.* San Francisco: HarperCollins.

Barnett, R., & Rivers, C. (2004). *Same difference: How gender myths are hurting our relationships, our children, and our jobs.* New York: Basic Books.

Barres, B. (2006, July). Does gender matter? *Nature, 442,* 133–136.

Barrett, J. (2004, May 10). No time for wrinkles. *Newsweek,* pp. 82–85.

Barrett, J., & Springen, K. (2007, December 24). *Newsweek,* p. 18.

Barry, K. (1998). Radical feminism. In W. Mankiller, G. Mink, M. Navarro, B. Smith, & G. Steinem (Eds.), *The reader's companion to U.S. women's history* (pp. 217–218). New York: Houghton Mifflin.

Bartkowski, J. (2004). *The Promise Keepers: Servants, soldiers and godly men.* New Brunswick, NJ: Rutgers University Press.

Bartlett, T. (2009, November 27). The puzzle of boys. *Chronicle of Higher Education,* pp. B6–B9.

Basinger, J. (2001, April 27). Struggling for a balanced life as a president. *The Chronicle of Higher Education,* pp. A37–A39.

Basow, S. A. (1990). Effects of teacher expressiveness: Mediated by sex-typing? *Journal of Educational Psychology, 82,* 599–602.

Basow, S. A. (1998). Student evaluations: The role of gender bias and teaching styles. In L. H. Collins, J. C. Chrisler, & K. Quina (Eds.), *Career strategies for women in academe: Arming Athena* (pp. 135–156). Thousand Oaks, CA: Sage.

Basow, S. A., & Rubenfeld, K. (2003). "Troubles talk": Effects of gender and gender-typing. *Sex roles, 48,* 183–187.

Batman scales wall near palace balcony (2004, September 14). *Raleigh News & Observer,* p. A2.

Baumgardner, J., & Richards, A. (2000). *Manifesta: Young women, feminism, and the future.* New York: Farrar, Straus & Giroux.

Baxter, J., Hewitt, B., & Western, M. (2005). Post-familial families and the domestic division of labor. *Journal of Comparative Family Studies, 36,* 583–600.

Baxter, L. A. (1990). Dialectical contradictions in relational development. *Journal of Social and Personal Relationships, 7,* 143–158.

Bazar, E. (2007, April 24). Stalking "definitely a problem" for women at college. *USA Today,* p. 5A.

Bearak, B. (2009, August 26). Inquiry about sprinter's sex angers South Africans. *New York Times,* p. A6.

Beate, L. (Ed.). (2001). *Feminist perspectives: Environment and society.* Englewood Cliffs, NJ: Prentice Hall.

Beatie, T. (2008). *Labor of love: The story of one man's extraordinary pregnancy.* Boston: Seal.

Beck, R. (2008, January 23). When they couldn't even vote. *Raleigh News & Observer,* p. A14.

Becker, A., & Burwell, R. (1999, May 19). Acculturation and disordered eating in Fiji. Paper presented at the American Psychiatric Association Conference, Washington, DC.

Becker, A., Burwell, R., Gilman, S., Herzog, D., & Hamburg, P. (2002). Eating behaviours and attitudes following prolonged exposure to television among ethnic Fijian adolescent girls. *British Journal of Psychiatry, 180,* 509–514.

Becker, C. S. (1987). Friendship between women: A phenomenological study of best friends. *Journal of Phenomenological Psychology, 18,* 59–72.

Begley, S. (2009, June 29). Don't blame the cavemen. *Newsweek,* pp. 50–62

Bellas, M. (2001). The gendered nature of emotional labor in the workplace. In D. Vannoy (Ed.), *Gender mosaics* (pp. 269–278). Los Angeles: Roxbury.

Bem, S. L. (1983). Gender schema theory and its implications for child development: Raising gender-aschematic children in a gender-schematic society. *Signs, 8,* 598–616.

Bem, S. (1993). *The lenses of gender: Transforming the debate on sexual inequality.* New Haven, CT: Yale University Press.

Benenson, J., Del Bianco, R., Philippoussis, M., & Apostoleris, N. (1997). Girls' expression of their own perspectives in the presence of varying numbers of boys. *International Journal of Behavioral Development, 21,* 389–405.

Bennett, J., Ellison, J., & Ball, S. (2010). Are we there yet? *Newsweek,* pp. 42–46.

Berdahl, J. (2007a). Harassment based on sex: Protecting social status in the context of gender hierarchy. *Academy of Management Review, 32,* 641–658.

Berdahl, J. (2007b). The sexual harassment of uppity women. *Journal of Applied Psychology, 92,* 425–437.

Beren, S. Hayden, H, Wilfey, D., Grilo, C. (1996). The influence of sexual orientation on body dissatisfaction in adult men and women. *The International Journal of Eating Disorders, 20,* 135–141.

Berger, E. (2006). *Raising kids with character.* New York: Rowman & Littlefield.

Bernstein, A. (1999, February 1). Why the law should adopt more family leave. *Business Week,* p. 48.

Bernstein, F. (2004, March 17). On campus, rethinking Biology 101. *The New York Times,* pp. 9–1, 9–6.

Berrington, E., & Jones H. (2002). Reality vs. myth: Constructions of women's insecurity. *Feminist Media Studies, 2,* 307–323.

Bianchi, S., Robinson, J., & Milkie, M. (2006). *Changing rhythms of American family life.* New York: Russell Sage Foundation.

Bierhoff, H. (1996). Heterosexual partnerships: Initiation, maintenance and disengagement. In A. E. Auhagen & M. von Salisch (Eds.), *The diversity of human relationships* (pp. 173–196). New York: Cambridge University Press.

The Big Reveal. (2009, October 29). *Chronicle of Higher Education*, p. B18.

Bilefsky, D. (2008, June 25). Albanian Custom Fades: Woman as Family Man. http://www .nytimes.com/2008/06/25/world/europe/ 25virgins.html?ex=1372132800&en= 8668ba514ff6f5fd&ei=5124&partner= permalink&exprod=permalink. Accessed July 7, 2008.

Birdwhistell, R. (1970). *Kinesics and context.* Philadelphia: University of Pennsylvania Press.

Blackless, M., Charuvastra, A., Derryek, A., Fausto-Sterling, A., Lauzanne, K., & Lee, E. (2000). How sexually dimorphic are we? Review and synthesis. *American Journal of Human Biology, 12,* 151–166.

Blades, J., & Rowe-Finkbeiner, K. (2006). *The motherhood manifesto.* New York: Nation Books.

Blum, D. (1997). *Sex on the brain: The biological differences between women and men.* New York: Penguin.

Blum, D. (1998, September/October). The gender blur: Where does biology end and society take over? *Utne Reader,* pp. 45–48.

Blum, V. (2003). *Flesh wounds: The culture of cosmetic surgery.* Berkeley: University of California Press.

Bly, R. (1990). *Iron John: A book about men.* Reading, MA: Addison-Wesley.

Bocella, K. (2001, January 31). Eating disorders spread among minority girls, women. *Raleigh News & Observer,* p. 5E.

Bodey, K. (2009). Exploring the Possibilities of Self Work: Girls Speak about their Lives. Ph.D. Dissertation. Department of Communication Studies. The University of North Carolina at Chapel Hill.

Bodey, K. R., & Wood, J. T. (2009). Whose voices count and who does the counting? *Southern Communication Journal, 74,* 325–337.

Bohill, C, Owen, C., Jeong, E., Aliea, B., & Bocca, F. (2009). Virtual reality. In W. F. Eadie (Ed.), *21st century communication: A reference handbook* (pp. 534–542). Thousand Oaks, CA: Sage.

Bond, J. T., Thompson, C., Galinsky, E., & Prottas, D. (2002). Highlights of the national study of the changing workforce: Executive summary. *Families and Work Institute,* No. 3, pp. 1–4.

Bonnett, A. (1996). The new primitives: Identity, landscape and cultural appropriation in the mythopoetic men's movement. *Antipode, 28,* 273–291.

Bonnett, C. (2007, May 13). What's up with mom? *Raleigh News & Observer,* pp. 23A–24A.

Boodman, S. (2007, March 15). Eating disorders strike men. *Raleigh News & Observer,* pp. 1E, 3E.

Bordo, S. (1997). *Twilight zones: The hidden life of cultural images from Plato to O. J.* Berkeley: University of California Press.

Bordo, S. (1998, May 1). Sexual harassment is about bullying, not sex. *The Chronicle of Higher Education,* p. B6.

Bordo, S. (2003, December 19). The empire of images in our world of bodies. *The Chronicle of Higher Education,* pp. B6–B9.

Bordo, S. (2004). *Unbearable weight: Feminism, western culture, and the body.* Berkeley: University of California Press.

Borenstein, S. (2010, January 14). Ladies first? Chromosomes say no. *Raleigh News & Observer,* p. 4A.

Boston Women's Health Club Book Collective. (1976). *Our bodies/ourselves* (2nd ed.). New York: Simon & Schuster.

Bourg, C., & Segal, M. (2001). Gender, sexuality, and the military. In D. Vannoy (Ed.), *Gender mosaics* (pp. 332–342). Los Angeles: Roxbury.

Boustany, N. (2007, July 4). Rape called a weapon in Sudan. *Raleigh News & Observer,* p. 7A.

Bowen, W., & Bok, D. (1998). *The shape of the river.* Princeton, NJ: Princeton University Press.

Bowen, W., Tobin, E., & Kurtzweil, M. (2005). *Equity and excellence in American higher education.* Charlottesville, VA: University of Virginia Press.

Boyd, A. (2002). Truth is a virus: Meme warfare and the billionaires for Bush (or Gore). In S. Duncombe (Ed.), *Cultural resistance reader* (pp. 369–378). New York: Verso.

Boyd, H. (2007). *She's not the man I married: My life with a transgender husband.* Boston: Seal.

Braithwaite, D., & Kellas, J. (2006). Shopping for and with friends: Everyday communication at the shopping mall. In J. T. Wood & S. W. Duck (Eds.), *Composing relationships: Communication in everyday life* (pp. 86–95). Belmont, CA: Thomson/Wadsworth.

Breines, W. (2006). *The trouble between us: An uneasy history of white and black women in the feminist movement.* New York: Oxford University Press.

Brizendine, L., (2007). *The female brain.* New York: Doubleday/Broadway.

Bronstein, Z. (2004, Spring). Nowhere woman. *Dissent,* pp. 90–97.

Brooks, D. (2010, February 16). The lean years. *New York Times,* p. A23.

Brooks, D. E., & Hébert, L. P. (2006). Gender, race and media representation. In B. Dow & J. T. Wood (Eds.), *Handbook of gender and communication* (pp. 297–317). Thousand Oaks, CA: Sage.

Broverman, I., Broverman, D. M., Clarkson, F. E., Rosenkrantz, P. S., & Vogel, S. R. (1970). Sex-role stereotypes and clinical judgments of mental health. *Journal of Consulting and Clinical Psychology, 34,* 1–7.

Brown, L. (1997). *Two-spirit people*. Binghamton, NY: Haworth Press.

Brown, L. M., Lamb, S., & Tappan, M (2009). *Packaging boyhood*. New York: St. Martin's Press.

Browne, K. (2003/2004, Winter). Fighting fistula. *Ms.*, p. 20.

Browne, K., & Hamilton-Giachritsis, C. (2005). The influence of violent media on children and adolescents: A public-health approach. *Lancet, 365,* 702–710.

Brownstein, A. (2000, December 8). In the campus shadows, women are stalkers as well as the stalked. *The Chronicle of Higher Education,* pp. A40–A42.

Bruess, C., & Pearson, J. (1996). Gendered patterns in family communication. In J. T. Wood (Ed.), *Gendered relationships: A reader* (pp. 59–78). Mountain View, CA: Mayfield.

Brumberg, J. (1997). *The body project: An intimate history of American girls*. New York: Random House.

Bryant, A., & Check, E. (2000, Fall/Winter). How parents raise boys and girls. *Newsweek,* pp. 64–65.

Buerkel-Rothfuss, N. L., Fink, D. S., & Buerkel, R. (1995). Communication in the father-child dyad: The intergenerational transmission process. In T. J. Socha & G. H. Stamp (Eds.), *Parents, children, and communication: Frontiers of theory and research* (pp. 63–85). Mahwah, NJ: Erlbaum.

Bulik, C., & Taylor, N. (2005). *Runaway eating.* New York: Rodale Books.

Burgoon, J. K., Buller, D. B., & Woodall, G. W. (1996). *Nonverbal communication: The unspoken dialogue* (2nd ed). New York: Harper & Row.

Burgoon, J. K., & Hale, J. L. (1988). Nonverbal expectancy violations: Model elaborations and application to immediacy behaviors. *Communication Monographs, 55,* 58–79.

Burk, M. (2005). *Cult of power: Sex discrimination in corporate America and what can be done about it.* New York: Scribner.

Burleson, B. (1997, November). Sex-related differences in communicative behavior: A matter of social skills, not gender cultures. Paper presented at the National Communication Convention, Chicago.

Burleson, B. R., Holmstrom, A. J., & Gilstrap, C. M. (2005). "Guys can't say that to guys": Four experiments assessing the normative motivation account for deficiencies in the emotional support provided by men. *Communication Monographs, 72,* 468–501.

Burn, J. (1996). *The social psychology of gender.* New York: McGraw-Hill.

Burnett, A., Mattern, J., Herakova, L., Kahl, Jr., D., Tabola, C., & Bornsen, E. (2009). Communicating/muting date rape: A co-cultural theoretical analysis of communication factors related to rape culture on a college campus. *Journal of Applied Communication Research, 37,* 435–465.

Buss, D. (1994). *The evolution of desire: Strategies of human mating.* New York: Basic Books.

Buss, D. (1995). Evolutionary psychology: A new paradigm for psychological science. *Psychological Inquiry, 6,* 1–30.

Buss, D. (1996). The evolutionary psychology of human social strategies. In E. Higgins & A. Druglanski (Eds.), *Social psychology: Handbook of basic principles* (pp. 3–38). New York: Guilford.

Buss, D. (1999). *Evolutionary psychology: The new science of the mind.* Boston: Allyn & Bacon.

Buss, D., & Kenrick, D. (1998). Evolutionary social psychology. In D. Gilbert, S. Fiske, & G. Lindzey (Eds.), *The handbook of social psychology: Vol. 2* (4th ed., pp. 982–1026). Boston: McGraw-Hill.

Butaine, R., & Costenbader, V. (1997). Self-reported differences in the experience and expression of anger between girls and boys. *Sex Roles, 36,* 625–637.

Butler, J. (1990). Performative acts and gender constitution: An essay in phenomenology and feminist theory. In S. Case (Ed.), *Performing feminisms: Feminist critical theory and theater* (pp. 270–282). Baltimore: Johns Hopkins University Press.

Butler, J. (1993a). *Bodies that matter: On the discursive limits of "sex."* New York: Routledge.

Butler, J. (1993b). *Gender trouble: Feminism and the subversion of identity.* New York: Routledge.

Butler, J. (2004). *Undoing gender.* London: Routledge.

Buzzanell, P. M., & Lucas, K. (2006). Gendered stories of career: Unfolding discourses of time, space, and identity. In B. Dow & J. T. Wood (Eds.), *Handbook of gender and communication* (pp. 161–178). Thousand Oaks, CA: Sage.

Caldwell, M., & Peplau, L. (1982). Sex differences in same-sex friendship. *Sex Roles, 8,* 721–732.

California: Gang Rape Is Investigated. (2009, October 27). *New York Times,* p. A21.

Callimachi, R. (2007, February 5). Here, women woo, men wait. *Raleigh News & Observer,* p. 10A.

Campbell, A. (2002). *A mind of her own.* Oxford: Oxford University Press.

Campbell, K. (2005). Agency: Promiscuous and protean. *Communication and Critical/Cultural Studies, 2,* 1–19.

Campbell, K. K. (1989a). *Man cannot speak for her: I. A critical study of early feminist rhetoric.* New York: Praeger.

Campbell, K. K. (1989b). *Man cannot speak for her: II. Key texts of the early feminists.* New York: Greenwood.

Campbell, K. K. (Ed.). (1993). *Women public speakers in the United States: A biocritical sourcebook.* Westport, CT: Greenwood.

Campbell, R., Martin, C., & Fabos, B. (2005). *Media and culture: An introduction to mass communication,* 4th ed. Boston: Bedford-St. Martin's.

Campo-Flores, A., & Rosenberg, Y. (2000, June 26). A return to wilding. *Newsweek,* p. 28.

Canary, D., & Wahba, J. (2006). Do women work harder than men at maintaining relationships? In K. Dindia & D. Canary (Eds.), *Sex differences and similarities in communication* (2nd ed., pp. 359–377). Mahwah, NJ: Erlbaum.

Cancian, F. (1987). *Love in America.* Cambridge, MA: Cambridge University Press.

Cancian, F. (1989). Love and the rise of capitalism. In B. Risman & P. Schwartz (Eds.), *Gender and intimate relationships* (pp. 12–25). Belmont, CA: Wadsworth.

Cancian, F., & Oliker, S. (2000). *Caring and gender.* Thousand Oaks, CA: Sage.

Cantœ, L. (2004). De ambiente: Queer tourism and the shifting boundaries of Mexican male sexualities. In J. Spade & C. Valentine (Eds.), *The gender kaleidoscope* (pp. 521–531). Belmont, CA: Thomson/Wadsworth.

Capaldi, D., Shortt, J., & Crosby, L. (2003). Physical and psychological aggression in at-risk young couples: Stability and change in young adulthood. *Merrill-Palmer Quarterly, 49,* 1–27.

Carlyle, K., Slater, M., & Chakroff, J. (2008). Newspaper coverage of intimate partner violence: Skewing representations of risk. *Journal of Communication, 58,* 168–186.

Carter, C., Branston, G., & Allan, S. (Eds.). (1998). *News, gender and power.* New York: Routledge.

Carter, N. M., & Silva, C. (2010). *Broken promises.* New York: Catalyst.

Carter, J. (2009, July 15). Losing my religion for equality. http://www.theage.com.au/opinion/losing-my-religion-for-equality-20090714-dk0v.html?page=1. Accessed April 18, 2010.

Cassidy, T. (2004, July 5). Proper whites? *Raleigh News & Observer,* p. 3B.

Catching Up on Family Values. (2008, February 26). *New York Times,* p. A18.

Caughlin, P., & Caughlin, P. (2005). *No more Christian nice guy.* Minneapolis, MN: Bethany House.

Caughlin, J., & Vangelisti, A. (2000). An individual differences explanation of why married couples engage in the demand/withdraw pattern of conflict. *Journal of Social and Personal Relationships, 17,* 523–551.

Ceci, S. J., & Williams, W. M. (Eds.). 2007). *Why aren't more women in science?* Washington, DC: American Psychological Association.

Ceci, S. J., & Williams, W. M. (2009). *The mathematics of sex.* New York: Oxford University Press.

Cegela, D., & Sillars, A. (1989). Further examination of nonverbal manifestations of interaction involvement. *Communication Reports, 2,* 39–47.

Celebrity 100. (2005, July 4). *Forbes,* pp. 102–111.

Channell, C. (2002, May). The Tatau: A bridge to manhood. *Faces: People, Places and Culture,* pp. 18–22.

Chapman, M., & Hendler, G. (Eds.). (1999). *Sentimental men: Masculinity and the politics of affect in American culture.* Berkeley: University of California Press.

Chatham-Carpenter, A., & DeFrancisco, V. (1998). Women construct self-esteem in their own terms: A feminist qualitative study. *Feminism & Psychology, 8,* 467–489.

Chaudhry, L. (2005, November 21). Babes in Bushworld. *In These Times,* pp. 38–39.

Chemerinsky, E., & Clotfelter, C. (2007, July 3). The death of desegregation. *Raleigh News & Observer,* p. 11A.

Cheney, G., Christensen, L., Zorn, T., & Ganesh, S. (2004). *Organizational communication in an age of globalization.* Prospect Heights, IL: Waveland.

Chernik, A. F. (1995). The body politic. In B. Findlen (Ed.), *Listen up: Voices from the next generation of feminists* (pp. 75–84). Seattle: Seal Press.

Chesler, E. (1992). *Woman of valor: Margaret Sanger and the birth control movement in America.* New York: Simon & Schuster.

Chesler, P. (2001). *Woman's inhumanity to woman.* New York: Thunder's Mouth Press/ Nation Books.

Chethik, N. (2001). *FatherLoss: How sons of all ages come to terms with the deaths of their dads.* New York: Hyperion.

Chethik, N. (2008). *VoiceMale: What husbands really think about their marriages, their wives, sex, housework and commitment.* New York: Simon & Schuster.

Childress, S. (2005, May 9). Anti-misogyny message. *Newsweek,* p. 13.

Chodorow, N. J. (1978). *The reproduction of mothering: Psychoanalysis and the sociology of gender.* Berkeley: University of California Press.

Chodorow, N. J. (1989). *Feminism and psychoanalytic theory.* New Haven, CT: Yale University Press.

Chodorow, N. J. (1999). *The power of feelings: Personal meaning in psychoanalysis, gender, and culture.* New Haven, CT: Yale University Press.

Christensen, A., & Heavey, C. (1990). Gender and social structure in the demand/withdraw pattern in marital conflict. *Journal of Personality and Social Psychology, 59,* 73–81.

Christopher, F., & Kisler, T. S. (2004). Sexual aggression in romantic relationships. In J. H. Harvey, A. Wenzel, & S. Sprecher (Eds.), *The* handbook of sexuality in close relationships (pp. 287–309). Mahwah, NJ: Erlbaum.

Clark, R. A. (1998). A comparison of topics and objectives in a cross section of young men's and women's everyday conversations. In D. J. Canary & K. Dindia (Eds.), Sex differences and similarities in communication: Critical essays and empirical investigations of sex and gender in interaction (pp. 303–319). Mahwah, NJ: Erlbaum.

Clarey, C., & Kolata, G. (2009, August 21). Godl is awarded, but dispute over runner's sex intensifies. New York Times, P. B9.

Clatterbaugh, K. (1997). Contemporary perspectives on masculinity. Boulder, CO: Westview Press.

Clemetson, L., & Samuels, A. (2000, December 18). We have the power. Newsweek, pp. 54–60.

Cleveland, J., Stockdale, M., & Murphy, K. (2000). Women and men in organizations. Mahwah, NJ: Erlbaum.

Clift, E. (2003). Founding sisters and the nineteenth amendment. New York: John Wiley & Sons.

Clinton, K. (2001, May). Unplugged: Surrendered wives. The Nation, p. 17.

Cloud, J. (2000, June 26). The bad Sunday in the park. Time, pp. 32–33.

Cloud, J. (2008, October 7). If women were more like men: Why females earn less. Time online: http://www.time.com/time/nation/article/0,8599,1847194,00.html. Retrieved October 7, 2008.

Coates, J. (1986). Women, men, and language: Studies in language and linguistics. London: Longman.

Coates, J. (Ed.). (1997). Language and gender: A reader. London: Basil Blackwell.

Coates, J., & Cameron, D. (1989). Women in their speech communities: New perspectives on language and sex. London: Longman.

Cognard-Black, J. (2007, Summer). Extreme makeover: Feminist edition. Ms., pp. 46–49.

Colapinto, J. (2006). As nature made him. New York: HarperPerennial.

Cole, J. B., & Guy-Sheftall, B. (2003). The struggle for women's equality in African American communities. New York: Random House.

Collier, R. (2008) Essays on law, men, and masculinities. New York: Routledge.

Collins, G. (2009a, January 29). Lilly's big day. New York Times, p. A21.

Collins, G. (2009b). When everything changed: The amazing journey of American women from 1960 to the present. New York: Little, Brown, & Co.

Collins, P. H. (1986). Learning from the outsider within. Social Problems, 33, 514–532.

Collins, P. H. (1998). Fighting words: Black women and the search for justice. Minneapolis: University of Minnesota Press.

Collins, P. H. (2004). Black sexual politics: African Americans, gender, and the new racism. New York: Routledge.

Collins, P. H. (2007, Spring). The lust generation. Ms., pp. 73–74.

Coltrane, S. (1996). Family man: Fatherhood, housework, and gender equity. New York: Oxford University Press.

Coltrane, S., & Adams, M. (2001). Men, women and housework. In D. Vannoy (Ed.), Gender mosaics (pp. 145–154). Los Angeles: Roxbury.

Consalvo, M. (2006). Gender and new media. In B. Dow & J. T. Wood (Eds.), The handbook of gender & communication (p. 355–369). Thousand Oaks, CA: Sage.

Coontz, S. (2005a, February 14). Historically incorrect canoodling. The New York Times, p. A23.

Coontz, S. (2005b). Marriage: A history. New York: Viking Adult.

Cooper, A. (2006, November-December). One of the guys: Transgender performance artist Scott Turner Schofield explores gender issues for the average Joe. Utne Reader, pp. 34–35.

Connell, R. W. (2005). Masculinities, 2nd ed. Cambridge, UK: Polity.

Corbett, K. (2009). Boyhoods: Rethinking masculinities. New Haven, CT: Yale University Press.

Corbett, C., Hill, C., & Rose, A. (2008). Where the girls are: The facts about gender equity in education. Washington, DC: American Association of University Women.

Correll, S., Benard, S., & Paik, I. (2007). Getting a job: Is there a motherhood penalty? American Journal of Sociology, 112, 1297–1338.

Cose, E. (1997, October 13). Promises. Newsweek, pp. 30–31.

Cose, E. (2003, March 3). The black gender gap. Newsweek, pp. 46–51.

Cose, E. (2005b, March 14). Long after the alarm went off. Newsweek, p. 37.

Cote, J. (1997). A social history of youth in Samoa: Religion, capitalism, and cultural disenfranchisement. International Journal of Comparative Sociology, 38, 207–222.

Council on Contemporary Families (2010). Unconventional wisdom. http://www.contemporaryfamilies.org/all/unconventional-wisdom-issue-3.html?q=unconventional+wisdom. Accessed April 14, 2010.

Cowley, G. (2003a, June 16). Why we strive for status. Newsweek, pp. 66–70.

Cowley, G. (2003b, September 8). Girls, boys, and autism. Newsweek, pp. 40–50.

Cox, M., & Alm, R. (2005, February 28). Scientists are made, not born. The New York Times, p. A25.

Crane, K. (2008, August 21). Older women battle eating disorders. Raleigh News & Observer, pp. 1D, 3D.

Crary, D. (2008, December 8). Family-friendly laws face uncertain times. *Raleigh News & Observer*, p. 7A.

Crawford, B. J. (2007). Toward a third-wave feminist legal theory: Young women, pornography and the praxis of pleasure. *Michigan Journal of Gender & Law, 14*, p. 99.

Cronk, L. (1993). Parental favoritism toward daughters. *American Scientist, 81*, 272–279.

Crosby, F. J., Williams, J.C., & Biernat, M. (2004). The maternal wall. *Journal of Social Issues, 60*, 675–682.

Cross, G. (2008). *Men to boys: The making of modern immaturity.* New York: Columbia University Press.

Crouch, R. (1998). Betwixt and between: The past and the future of intersexuality. *Journal of Clinical Ethics, 9*, 372–384.

Crown, L., & Roberts, L. (2007). Against their will: Young women's nonagentic sexual experiences. *Journal of Social and Personal Relationships, 24*, 385–405.

Crowston, K., & Kammeres, E. (1998). Communicative style and gender differences in computer-mediated communications. In B. Ebo (Ed.), *Cyberghetto or cybertopia* (pp. 185–202). Westport, CT: Praeger.

Cubbans, L. A., & Vannoy, D. (2004). Division of household labor as a source of contention for married and cohabiting couples in Metropolitan Moscow. *Journal of Family Issues, 25*, 182–185.

Cudworth, E. (2005). *Developing ecofeminist theory: The complexity of difference.* New York: Palgrave Macmillan.

Cuklanz, L. (1996). *Rape on trial: How the media construct legal reforms and social change.* Philadelphia: University of Pennsylvania Press.

Cuklanz, L. M., & Moorti, S. (2006). Television's "new" feminism: Prime-time representations of women and victimization. *Critical Studies in Media Communication, 23*, 301–321.

Cuklanz, L. M., & Moorti, S. (Eds.). (2009). *Local violence, global media.* New York: Peter Lang.

Cupach, W., & Spitzberg, B. (2011). Unilateral union: Obsessive relational intrusion and stalking in a romantic context. In D. O. Braithwaite & J. T. Wood (Eds.), *Casing interpersonal communication* (pp. 157–164). Dubuque, IA: Kendall-Hunt.

Danner, L., & Walsh, S. (1999). "Radical" feminists and "bickering" women: U.S. media coverage of the United Nations Fourth World Conference on Women. *Critical Studies in Mass Communication, 16*, 63–84.

Dao, J. (2009, September 22). Drill sergeant at heart, she ascends to a top spot in the Army. *New York Times*, pp. A1, A22.

Dasgupta, S. D. (Ed.). (2007). *Body evidence: Intimate violence against South Asian women in America.* NJ: Rutgers University Press.

Davies-Popelka, W. (2011). Mirror, mirror on the wall. In D. O. Braithwaite & J. T. Wood (Eds.), *Casing interpersonal communication* (pp. 25–32). Dubuque, IA: Kendall Hunt.

Davis, F. (1991). *Moving the mountain: The women's movement in America since 1960.* New York: Simon & Schuster.

Davis, J. E. (2004). *Accounts of innocence: Sexual abuse, trauma, and the self.* Chicago: University of Chicago Press.

Davis, S., & Gergen, M. (1997). Toward a new psychology of gender: Opening conversations. In M. Gergen & S. Davis (Eds.), *Toward a new psychology of gender* (pp. 1–27). New York: Routledge.

Davison, K., & Birch, L. (2001). Weight, status, parent reaction, and self-concept in five-year-old girls. *Pediatrics, 107*, 42–53.

Dawson, I. (2005, Summer). Good rap, bad rap. *Ms.*, p. 18.

De Alba, G. A., & Guzmán, G. (2010). *Making a killing: Femicide, free trade, and la frontera.* Austin, TX: University of Texas Press.

Dean, C. (2006, December 19). Women in science: The battle moves to the trenches. *The New York Times*, pp. D6–D7.

D'eaubonne, F. (1974). *Le féminisme ou la mort.* Paris: Pierre Horay.

Deaux, K., & LaFrance, M. (1998). Gender. In D. Gilbert, S. T. Fiske, & G. Lindzey (Eds.), *Handbook of social psychology* (pp. 788–827). New York: McGraw-Hill.

Deffenbacher, J., & Swaim, R. (1999). Anger expression in Mexican-American and white non-Hispanic adolescents. *Journal of Counseling Psychology, 46*, 61–69.

DeFrancisco, V., & Chatham-Carpenter, A. (2000). Self in community: African American women's views of self-esteem. *Howard Journal of Communication, 11*, 73–92.

Degler, C. N. (1980). *At odds: Women and the family in America from the Revolution to the present.* New York: Oxford University Press.

Dellios, H. (2006, May 24). Mexican law no longer sees bride as "weak creature." *Raleigh News & Observer*, p. 16A.

DeLucia, J. L. (1987). Gender role identity and dating behavior: What is the relationship? *Sex Roles, 17*, 153–161.

DeMaris, A. (2007). The role of relationship inequity in marital disruption. *Journal of Social and Personal Relationships, 24*, 177–195.

DeMaris, A., & Longmore, M. A. (1996). Ideology, power, and equity: Testing competing explanations for the perception of fairness in household labor. *Social Forces, 74*, 1043–1071.

De Ruijter, E., Treas, J. K., & Cohen, P. N. (2005). Outsourcing the gender factory: Living arrangements and service expenditures on female and male tasks. *Social Forces, 84*(1), 305–322.

DeVault, M. (1990). Conflict over housework: A problem that (still) has no name. In L. Kreisberg (Ed.), *Research in social movements, conflict, and change*. Greenwich, CT: JAI Press.

Deveny, K. (2009, June 30). We're bossy—and proud of it. *Newsweek*, p. 58.

Devor, H. (1997). *FTM: Female-to-male transsexuals in society*. Bloomington: Indiana University Press.

de Waal, F. (1998). *Bonobo: The forgotten ape*. Berkeley, CA: University of California Press.

The Diagram Group. (1977). *Woman's body: An owner's manual*. New York: Bantam.

Diamond, E. (1960, March 7). Young wives. *Newsweek*, pp. 57–60.

Dicker, R., & Piepmeier, A. (2003). *Catching a wave: Reclaiming feminism for the 21st century*. Boston: Northeastern University Press.

Digby, T. (Ed.). (1998). *Men doing feminism*. New York: Routledge.

Diggs, R. C. (1999). African-American and European-American adolescents' perceptions of self-esteem as influenced by parent and peer communication and support environments. In T. J. Socha & R. C. Diggs (Eds.), *Communication, race, and family* (pp. 105–146). Mahwah, NJ: Erlbaum.

Dilorio, C., Kelley, M., & Hockenberry-Eaton, M. (1999). Communication about sexual issues: Mothers, fathers, and friends. *Journal of Adolescent Health, 24*, 181–189.

Dirie, W. (1998). *Desert flower*. New York: Morrow.

Dixon, T. L. (2006). Psychological reactions to crime news portrayals of black criminals: Understanding the moderating roles of prior news view and stereotype endorsement. *Communication Monographs, 73*, 162–187.

Dixon, T. L., & Azocar, C. L. (2006). The representation of juvenile offenders by race on Los Angeles area television news. *Howard Journal of Communication, 17*, pp. 143–161.

Dokoupil, T. (2008, September 8). Why I am leaving guyland. *Newsweek*, pp. 70–71.

Dokoupil, T. (2009, March 2). Men will be men. *Newsweek*, p. 50.

Dominus, S. (2005, May 8). The fathers' crusade. *The New York Times Magazine*, pp. 25–33, 50, 56–58.

Douglas, A. (1977). *The feminization of American culture*. New York: Knopf.

Douglas, S. (2005, December 19). The Times disses women. *In These Times*, p. 15.

Douglas, S., & Michaels, M. (2004). *The mommy myth: The idealization of motherhood and how it has undermined women*. New York: The Free Press.

Dow, B. (2004, April 1). Framing feminism: Early television news coverage of the women's liberation movement. *The Brigance Forum*. Crawfordsville, IN: Wabash College.

Dow, B., & Condit, C. (2005). The state of the art in feminist scholarship. *Journal of Communication, 55*, 448–478.

Dow, B., & Tonn, M. B. (1993). Feminine style and political judgment in the rhetoric of Ann Richards. *Quarterly Journal of Speech, 79*, 286–302.

Dow, B. J., & Wood, J. T. (Eds.). (2006). *The handbook of gender and communication*. Thousand Oaks, CA: Sage.

Dowd, M. (2005, March 20). X-celling over men. *The New York Times*, p. 4–13.

Doyle, J. (1997). *The male experience* (3rd ed.). Dubuque, IA: Brown & Benchmark.

Doyle, L. (2001). *The surrendered wife: A practical guide for finding intimacy, passion and peace with a man*. New York: Fireside.

Dreier, P., & Freer, R. (1997, October 24). Saints, sinners, and affirmative action. *The Chronicle of Higher Education*, pp. B6, B7.

Dreifus, C. (2000, July 11). A conversation with Nawal Nour. *The New York Times*, p. D7.

Driefus, C. (2010), June 22). A conversation with Elaine Fuchs. The *New York Times*, p.D3.

Dresser, N. (1996). *Multicultural manners*. New York: Wiley.

Dube, K. (2004, June 18). What feminism means to today's undergraduates. *The Chronicle of Higher Education*, p. B5.

Dubois, D., Serbin, L., & Derbyshire, A. (1998). Toddlers' intermodal and verbal knowledge about gender. *Merrill-Palmer Quarterly, 44*, 338–351.

Dubrofsky, R. E., & Hardy, A. (2008). Performing race in *Flavor of Love* and *The Bachelor*. *Critical Studies in Media Communication, 25*, 373–392.

Duenwald, M. (2005, March 8). Aspirin is found to protect women from strokes, not heart attacks. *The New York Times*, p. D5.

Dunn, J. (1999). Siblings, friends, and the development of social understanding. In W. A. Collins & B. Laursen (Eds.), *Relationships as developmental contexts* (pp. 263–279). Mahwah, NJ: Erlbaum.

DuPlessis, R., & Snitow, A. (Eds.). (1999). *The feminist memoir project: Voices from women's liberation*. Three Rivers, MI: Three Rivers.

Durham, M. G. (2008). *The Lolita effect: The media sexualization of young girls and what we can do about it*. New York: Overlook Press.

Dyer, G. (2007, January 26). France gives birth to a trend. *Raleigh News & Observer*, p. 13A.

Eagly, A. H. (1996). Differences between women and men. *American Psychologist, 51*, 158–159.

Eagly, A. H., & Carli, L. L. (2007). *Through the labyrinth: The truth about how women become leaders*. Boston, MA: Harvard Business School Press.

Eagly, A. H., Johannesen-Schmidt, M. C., & van Engen, M. L. (2003). Transformational, transactional, and laissez-faire leadership styles: A meta-analysis comparing women and men. *Psychological Bulletin, 108,* 233–256.

Eastman, S. (2004). Favoritism and identity in the mediation of sports. In R. Lind (Ed.), *Race/gender/media* (pp. 110–117). Boston: Pearson/Allyn & Bacon.

Edrut, O. (Ed.). (2000). *Body outlaws.* Seattle, WA: Seal Press.

Educating Girls. (2005, June 25). *The New York Times,* p. A28.

Eichenbaum, L., & Orbach, S. (1983). *Understanding women: A feminist psychoanalytic approach.* New York: Basic Books.

Eisaguirre, Lynne. (1999). *Affirmative action: A reference handbook.* Santa Barbara, CA: ABC-CLIO.

Eisenberg, N. (2002). Empathy-related emotional responses, altruism, and their socialization. In R. Davidson & A. Harrington (Eds.), *Visions of compassion: Western scientists and Tibetan Buddhists examine human nature* (pp. 131–164). London: Oxford University Press.

Elliott, L. (2009). *Pink brain, blue brain: How small differences grow into troublesome gaps—and what we can do about it.* Boston, MA: Houghton Mifflin-Harcourt.

Ensler, E. (2000). *The vagina monologues: The V-Day edition.* New York: Random House: Villard.

Ensler, E. (2001). *Necessary targets: A story of women and war.* New York: Random House: Villard.

Ensler, E. (2004). *The good body.* New York: Random House: Villard.

Ensler, E. (2011). *I am an emotional creature.* New York: Random House: Villard

Erickson, R. J. (2005). Why emotion work matters: Sex, gender and the division of household labor. *Journal of Marriage and the Family, 67,* 337–351.

Espiritu, Y. L. (1997). *Asian American women and men.* Thousand Oaks, CA: Sage.

Estioko-Griffin, A., & Griffin, P. (1997). Woman the hunter: The Agta. In C. Brettell & C. Sargent (Eds.), *Gender in crosscultural perspectives* (pp. 123–149). Englewood Cliffs, NJ: Prentice Hall.

Faludi, S. (1991). *Backlash: The undeclared war against American women.* New York: Crown.

Faludi, S. (1999). *Stiffed: The betrayal of the American man.* New York: Morrow.

Faludi, S. (2007). *The terror dream: Fear and fantasy in post-9/11 America.* New York: Metropolitan.

Farrell, C., & Matthews, D. (2000). *The reasonable woman as a standard for men.* New York: New York University Press.

Farrell, E. F. (2004, June 4). "It's getting hot in here." *The Chronicle of Higher Education,* pp. A27–A28.

Farrell, W. (1991, May/June). Men as success objects. *Utne Reader,* pp. 81–84.

Fattah, H. (2006, June 30). Kuwaiti women join the voting after a long battle for suffrage. *Raleigh News & Observer,* p. A9.

Fausto-Sterling, A. (2000). *Sexing the body: Gender politics and the construction of sexuality.* New York: Basic Books.

Federman, D. D., & Walford, G. A. (2007, January 15). Is male menopause real? *Newsweek,* pp. 58–60.

Feinberg, L. (1996). *Transgender warriors: Making history from Joan of Arc to RuPaul.* Boston, MA: Beacon.

Ferguson, S. (2000). Challenging traditional marriage: New married Chinese-American and Japanese-American women. *Gender and Society, 14,* 136–159.

Ferraro, S. (2001, February 15). Gender affects the course of disease, researchers say. *Raleigh News & Observer,* p. 2E.

Fiebert, M. (1987). Some perspectives on the men's movement. *Men's Studies Review, 4,* 8–10.

Fields, A. (2003). *Katharine Dexter McCormick: Pioneer for women's rights.* Westport, CT: Praeger.

Findlen, B. (Ed.). (1995). *Listen up! Voices from the next feminist generation.* Seattle: Seal Press.

Finnerty, A. (1999, May 9). The body politic. *The New York Times Magazine,* p. 22.

Fisher, H. (2000). *The first sex.* New York: Bantam.

Fishman, P. M. (1978). Interaction: The work women do. *Social Problems, 25,* 397–406.

Fiske, E. (2006, Summer). Do-it-yourself mug shots. *Ms.,* p. 16.

Fivush, R., Brotman, M., Buckner, J., & Goodman, S. (2000). Gender differences in parent-child emotion narratives. *Sex Roles, 42,* 223–253.

Fixmer, N. (2003). Revisioning the political: Feminism, difference, and solidarity in a new generation. Unpublished master's thesis, University of North Carolina at Chapel Hill.

Fixmer, N., & Wood, J. T. (2005). The political is personal: Difference, solidarity, and embodied politics in a new generation of feminists. *Women's Studies in Communication, 28,* 235–257.

Flanagan, M. (2004). Next level: Women's digital activism through gaming. In G. Liestøl, A. Morrison, & T. Rasmussen (Eds.), *Digital media revisited* (pp. 82–106). Cambridge: MIT Press.

Flanagon, D., Baker-Ward, L., & Graham, L. (1995). Talk about preschool: Patterns of topic discussion and elaboration related to gender and ethnicity. *Sex Roles, 32,* 1–15.

Fletcher, J. (1999). *Disappearing acts: Gender, power and relational practice at work.* Cambridge: MIT Press.

Fletcher, J., Jordan, J., & Miller, J. (2000). Women and the workplace: Applications of a psychodynamic theory. *American Journal of Psychoanalysis, 60,* 243–261.

Floyd, K. (1995). Gender and closeness among friends and siblings. *Journal of Psychology, 129,* 193–202.

Floyd, K. (1996a). Brotherly love I: The experience of closeness in the fraternal dyad. *Personal Relationships, 3,* 369–385.

Floyd, K. (1996b). Communicating closeness among siblings: An application of the gendered closeness perspective. *Communication Research Reports, 13,* 27–34.

Floyd, K. (1997a). Brotherly love II: A developmental perspective on liking, love, and closeness in the fraternal dyad. *Journal of Family Psychology, 11,* 196–209.

Floyd, K. (1997b). Communicating affection in dyadic relationships: An assessment of behavior and expectancies. *Communication Quarterly, 45,* 68–80.

Floyd, K., & Morman, M. (2005). Fathers' and sons' reports of fathers' affectionate communication: Implications of a naïve theory of affection. *Journal of Social and Personal Relationships, 22,* 99–109.

Fogg, P. (2005, March 25). Board backs Harvard chief after a faculty thumbs down. *The Chronicle of Higher Education,* pp. A1, A12.

Forbes, G., Adams-Curtis, L., Pakalka, A., & White, K. (2006). Dating aggression, sexual coercion, and aggression-supporting attitudes among college men as a function of participation in aggressive high school sports. *Violence Against Women, 12,* 441–455.

Foss, K., Edson, B., & Linde, J. (2000). What's in a name? Negotiating decisions about marital names. In D. O. Braithwaite & J. T. Wood (Eds.), *Case studies in interpersonal communication* (pp. 18–25). Belmont, CA: Wadsworth.

Foucault, M. (1978). *The history of sexuality, volume 1: An introduction.* (R. Hurley, Trans.). New York: Pantheon.

Fowler, R., & Fuehrer, A. (1997). Women's marital names: An interpretive study of name retainers' concepts of marriage. *Feminism & Psychology, 7,* 315–320.

France, D. (2006, January & February). Domestic violence. *AARP Magazine,* pp. 84–85, 112–118.

Franzoi, S. L., & Koehler, V. (1998). Age and gender differences in body attitudes: A comparison of young and elderly adults. *International Journal of Aging and Human Development, 47,* 1–10.

Frawley, T. J. (2008). Gender schema and prejudicial recall: How children misremember, fabricate, and distort gendered picture book information. *Journal of Research in Childhood Education, 22,* 291–303.

Freeman, E. (2002). *No turning back.* New York: Ballantine.

Friedan, B. (1963). *The feminine mystique.* New York: Dell.

Gallagher, M. (2006). *Who makes the news? Global Media Monitoring Project, 2005.* www.whomakesthenews.org. Accessed November 15, 2008.

Galvin, K. (2006). Gendered communication in families. In B. Dow & J. T. Wood (Eds.), *Handbook of gender and communication* (pp. 41–55). Thousand Oaks, CA: Sage.

Garcia, G. (2008). *The decline of men: How the American male is tuning out, giving up, and flipping off his future.* New York: Harper.

Garloch, K. (2009, September 29). Saving our sons. *Raleigh News & Observer,* p. D1.

Garner, A. (2004). *Families like mine: Children of gay parents tell it like it is.* New York: HarperCollins.

Garrett, W. (2001). Personal communication.

Gastil, J. (1990). Generic pronouns and sexist language: The oxymoronic character of masculine generics. *Sex Roles, 23,* 629–643.

Gelles, R., & Straus, M. (1988). *Intimate violence.* New York: Simon & Schuster.

Gender gap starts with household chores, study finds. (2006, December 8). *Raleigh News & Observer,* p. 3A.

Gerson, K. (2004). Moral dilemmas, moral strategies, and the transformation of gender: Lessons from two generations of work and family change. In J. Spade & C. Valentine (Eds.), *The kaleidoscope of gender: Prisms, patterns, and possibilities* (pp. 413–424). Belmont, CA: Thomson/Wadsworth.

Gettleman, J. (2009a, August 5). Latest tragic symbol of an unhealed Congo: Male rape victims. *New York Times,* pp. A1, A7.

Gettleman, J. (2009b, September 7). Sudanese court to define indecent dress for women. *New York Times,* p. A5.

Gilenstam, K., Karp, S., & Henriksson-Larsén, K. (2008). Gender in ice hockey: Women in a male territory. *Scandinavian Journal of Medicine & Science in Sports, 18,* 235–249.

Gill, R. (2008). Empowerment/sexism: Figuring female sexual agency in contemporary advertising. *Feminism & Psychology, 18,* 35–60.

Gill, T. (2010). *Beauty shop politics: African American women's activism in the beauty industry.* Urbana, IL: University of Illinois Press.

Gilley, B. J. (2006). *Becoming two-spirit: Gay identity and social acceptance in Indian country.* Lincoln: University of Nebraska Press.

Gilligan, C. (1982). *In a different voice: Psychological theory and women's development.* Cambridge, MA: Harvard University Press.

Gilligan, C., & Pollack, S. (1988). The vulnerable and invulnerable physician. In C. Gilligan, J. V.

Ward, & J. M. Taylor (with B. Bardige) (Eds.), *Mapping the moral domain* (pp. 245–262). Cambridge, MA: Harvard University Press.

Giorgi, G. (2002). Speaking silence: Definitional dialogues in abusive lesbian relationships. *Violence Against Women, 8,* 1233–1259.

Girish, U. (2007, Spring). Don't "tease" these Eves. *Ms.,* p. 27.

"Girls Gone Wild" leader pleads guilty. (2006, December 14). *Raleigh News & Observer,* p. 3A.

Givhan, R. (2006, December 11). Thin is not in on runways. *Raleigh News & Observer,* p. 3C.

Glenn, D. (2002, November 22). Practices, identities, and desires. *The Chronicle of Higher Education,* pp. A20–A21.

Glover, D., & Kaplan, C. (2009). *Genders,* 2nd ed. New York: Routledge.

Goddess, R., & Calderón, J. L. (Eds.). 2006. *We got issues!* Makawao, Maui, HI: Inner Ocean Publishing, Inc.

Goldberg, A., & Perry-Jenkins, M. (2007). The division of labor and perceptions of parental roles: Lesbian couples across the transition to parenthood. *Journal of Social and Personal Relationships, 24,* 297–318.

Golden, D. (2006). *The price of admission: How America's ruling class buys its way into elite colleges—and who gets left outside the gates.* New York: Crown.

Goldner, V., Penn, P., Sheinberg, M., & Walker, G. (1990). Love and violence: Gender paradoxes in volatile attachments. *Family Process, 19,* 343–364.

Goldsmith, D., & Fulfs, P. (1999). "You just don't have the evidence": An analysis of claims and evidence in Deborah Tannen's *You Just Don't Understand.* In M. Roloff (Ed.), *Communication Yearbook, 22,* pp. 1–49.

Goldstein, R. (2003, March 24). Neo-macho man: Pop culture and post-9/11 politics. *The Nation,* pp. 16–19.

González, A., Houston, M., & Chen, V. (2007). *Our voices: Essays in culture, ethnicity, and communication,* 4th ed. Los Angeles, CA: Roxbury.

Gonzales, A., & Kertész, J. (2001). Engendering power in Native North America. In D. Vannoy (Ed.), *Gender mosaics* (pp. 43–52). Los Angeles: Roxbury.

Good, S. (2000, February 28). As it turns out, you haven't come a long way, baby. *Insight on the News, 16,* 4.

Goodman, E. (1996, April 9). Freedom from mutilation. *Raleigh News & Observer,* p. 9A.

Goodman, E. (2005, February 15). No sick pay makes us ill at ease. *Raleigh News & Observer,* p. 9A.

Goodman, E. (2006, July 10). Boys and girls and school. *Raleigh News & Observer,* p. 11A.

Goodman, E. (2007). Our other office ceiling. *Raleigh News & Observer,* p. 15A.

Goodman, E. (2008a, August 4). How equality's adding up. *Raleigh News & Observer,* p. 9A.

Goodwin, M. H. (1990). *He said, she said: Talk as social organization among black children.* Bloomington: Indiana University Press.

Goodwin, M. H. (2006). *The hidden life of girls.* Maiden, MA: Blackwell Publishing.

Gordon, L. (1976). *Woman's body, woman's right: A social history of birth control in America.* New York: Grossman.

Gordon, L. (1998). Women's colleges. In W. Mankiller, G. Mink, M. Navarro, B. Smith, & G. Steinem (Eds.), *The reader's companion to U.S. women's history* (pp. 642–644). New York: Houghton Mifflin.

Gordon, L (2007). *The moral property of women: A history of birth control politics in America.* Chicago: University of Illinois Press.

Gorman, C., & Cole, C. (2004, March 1). Between the sexes. *Newsweek,* pp. 54–56.

Gorski, E. (2003, October 6). Promise Keepers to shift direction under new chief. *Denver Post,* pp. 1B, 3B.

Gose, B. (2005, February 25). The chorus grows louder for class-based affirmative action. *The Chronicle of Higher Education,* pp. B5–B6.

Grady, D. (2010, March 30). Overhaul will lower the costs of being a woman. *New York Times,* p. D2.

Gray, J. (1992). *Men are from Mars, women are from Venus: A practical guide for improving communication and getting what you want in your relationships.* New York: HarperCollins.

Gray, J. (1995). *Mars and Venus in the bedroom: A guide to lasting romance and passion.* New York: HarperCollins.

Gray, J. (1996a). *Mars and Venus in love.* New York: HarperCollins.

Gray, J. (1996b). *Mars and Venus together forever.* New York: HarperCollins.

Gray, J. (1998). *Mars and Venus on a date: A guide for navigating the five stages of dating to create a loving and lasting relationship.* New York: HarperCollins.

Gray, K. (2007, April 13). Speaking of shockers, what about rap artists? *Raleigh News & Observer,* p. 17A.

Gray, P. (2010). *Fatherhood: Evolution and human paternal behavior.* Cambridge, MA: Harvard University Press.

Gray, P., & Feldman, J. (1997). Patterns of age mixing and gender mixing among children and adolescents at an ungraded democratic school. *Merill-Palmer Quarterly, 43,* 67–86.

Greenberg, S. (2001, January 8). Time to plan your life. *Newsweek,* pp. 54–55.

Greenhouse, L. (2004, June 15). Rules are set for some harassment cases. *The New York Times,* p. A16.

Greenhouse, S. (2003, July 13). Going for the look, but risking discrimination. *The New York Times International,* p. 10YT.

Gregory, S. (2007, December 10). Head games. *Time*, pp. 69–70.

Griffith, R. (1997, October 17). The affinities between feminists and evangelical women. *The Chronicle of Higher Education*, pp. B6, B7.

Gross, D. (1990, April 16). The gender rap. *New Republic*, pp. 11–14.

Guerrero, L. (1997). Nonverbal involvement across interactions with same-sex friends, opposite-sex friends, and romantic partners: Consistency or change? *Journal of Social and Personal Relationships, 14*, 31–58.

Guerrero, L., DeVito, J., & Hecht, M. (Eds.). (1999). *The nonverbal communication reader: Classic and contemporary readings* (2nd ed.). Prospect Heights, IL: Waveland Press.

Guerrero, L., Jones, S., & Boburka, R. (2006). Sex differences in emotional communication. In K. Dindia & D. Canary (Eds.), *Sex differences and similarities in communication* (pp. 242–261). Mahwah, MJ: Erlbaum.

Guerrilla Girls. (1995). *Confessions of the Guerrilla Girls*. New York: HarperPerennial.

Gurian, M. (2006). *The wonder of boys*. New York: Penguin/Tarcher.

Gurian, M., & Stevens, K. (2007). *The minds of boys*. San Francisco: Jossey-Bass.

Guy-Sheftall, B. (2003). African American women: The legacy of black feminism. In R. Morgan (Ed.), *Sisterhood is forever* (pp. 176–187). New York: Washington Square Press.

Haag, P. (2005, February 11). Navigating the new subtleties of sex-discrimination cases in academe. *The Chronicle of Higher Education*, p. B20.

Hale, J., Tighe, R., & Mongeau, P. (1997). Effects of event type and sex on comforting messages. *Communication Research Reports, 14*, 214–220.

Hall, D., & Langellier, K. (1988). Storytelling strategies in mother-daughter communication. In B. Bate & A. Taylor (Eds.), *Women communicating: Studies of women's talk* (pp. 107–126). Norwood, NJ: Ablex.

Hall, J. (2006). How big are nonverbal sex differences? The case of smiling and nonverbal sensitivity. In K. Dindia & D. Canary (Eds.), *Sex differences and similarities in communication* (2nd ed., pp. 59–81). Mahwah, NJ: Lawrence Erlbaum.

Hall, J., Park, N., Song, H., & Cody, J. (2010). Strategic misrepresentation in online dating: The effects of gender, self-monitoring, and personality traits. *Journal of Social and Personal Relationships, 27*, 117–135.

Hall, J. A., Halberstadt, A. G., & O'Brien, C. E. (1997). "Subordination" and nonverbal sensitivity: A study and synthesis of findings based on trait measures. *Sex Roles, 37*, 295–317.

Hallstein, D. L. O. (2008). Silences and choice: The legacies of white second wave feminism in the new professoriate. *Women's Studies in Communication, 31* 143–150.

Halperin, D. (2004). *How to do the history of homosexuality*. Urbana: University of Illinois Press.

Halperin, D. (2007). *What do gay men want? An essay on sex, risk, and subjectivity*. Ann Arbor: University of Michigan Press.

Halpern, D. (1996). Public policy implications of sex differences in cognitive abilities. *Psychology, Public Policy, and Law, 2*, 561–574.

Hamilton, M. C. (1991). Masculine bias in the attribution of personhood: People-male, male-people. *Psychology of Women Quarterly, 15*, 393–402.

Hammer, J. (2001). *What it means to be a daddy: Fatherhood for black men living away from their children*. New York: Columbia University Press.

Hammer, R. (2002). *Antifeminism and family terrorism: A critical feminist perspective*. New York: Rowman & Littlefield.

Hammonds, E. (1998). Science and gender. In W. Mankiller, G. Mink, M. Navarro, B. Smith, & G. Steinem (Eds.), *The reader's companion to U.S. women's history* (pp. 521–522). New York: Houghton Mifflin.

Hanisch, C. (1970). What can be learned? A critique of the Miss America protest. In L. Tanner (Ed.), *Voices from women's liberation* (pp. 132–136). New York: Signet Classics.

Harding, S. (1991). *Whose science? Whose knowledge? Thinking from women's lives*. Ithaca, NY: Cornell University Press.

Harding, S. (1998). *Is science multicultural?* Ithaca, NY: Cornell University Press.

Harris, A. (Ed.). (2004). *All about the girl*. London: Routledge.

Harris, J. (1998). *The nurture assumption*. New York: Simon & Schuster/Free Press.

Harris, K. (2009). The next problem that has no name: The discourse and politics of "rape." M. A. Thesis, Department of Communication Studies, The University of North Carolina at Chapel Hill.

Harris, K. (2011). Peanut butter sandwiches: Making sense of acquaintance rape in ongoing relationships. In D. O. Braithwaite & J. T. Wood (Eds.), *Casing interpersonal communication* (pp. 181–285). Dubuque, IA: Kendall-Hunt.

Harris, R. (2005). *A cognitive psychology of mass communication* (4th ed.). Mahwah, NJ: Erlbaum.

Harrison, C. E. (1988). *On account of sex: The politics of women's issues, 1945–1968*. Berkeley: University of California Press.

Harrison, K. (2008). Adolescent body image and eating in the media: Trends and implications for adolescent health. In P. E. Jamieson &

D. Romer (Eds.), *The changing portrayal of adolescents in the media since 1950* (pp. 165–197). New York: Oxford University Press.

Hartmann, E. (1993). *Boundaries in the mind: A new psychology of personality.* New York: Basic Books.

Hasinoff, A. (2008). Fashioning race for the free market on *America's Next Top Model. Critical Studies in Media Communication, 25,* 324–343.

Hayden, S. (2003). Family metaphors and the nation: Promoting a politics of care through the Million Mom March. *Quarterly Journal of Speech, 89,* 196–215.

Hayden, S., & O'Brien Hallstein, L. (Eds.). (2010.) *Contemplating maternity in an era of choice: Exploring discourses of reproduction.* New York: Lexington.

Haynes, J. (2009). Exposing domestic violence in country music videos. In L. Cuklanz & S. Moorti (Eds.), *Local violence, global media* (pp. 201–221). New York: Peter Lang.

Heath, D. (1991). *Fulfilling lives: Paths to maturity and success.* San Francisco: Jossey-Bass.

Helfling, K. (2011, February 16). Veterans sue over rape cases. *Raleigh News & Observer,* p. 5A.

Hegde, R. (1999a). Sons and m(others): Framing the maternal body and the politics of reproduction in a south Indian context. *Women's Studies in Communication, 22,* 1–20.

Hegde, R. (1999b). Marking bodies, reproducing violence: A feminist reading of female infanticide in south India. *Violence Against Women, 5,* 507–524.

Hegde, R. (2006). Globalizing feminist research in communication. In B. Dow & J. T. Wood (Eds.), *Handbook of gender and communication* (pp. 433–449). Thousand Oaks, CA: Sage.

Hegel, G. W. F. (1807). *Phenomenology of mind.* (J. B. Baillie, Trans.). Germany: Wurzburg & Bamburg.

Heilbrun, A. B. (1986). Androgyny as type and androgyny as behavior: Implications for gender schema in males and females. *Sex Roles, 14,* 123–139.

Heilman, M. E. (2001). Description and prescription: How gender stereotypes prevent women's ascent up the organizational ladder. *Journal of Social Issues, 57,* 657–674.

Heilman, M. E., & Okimoto, T. G. (2007). Averting penalties for women's success: Rectifying the perceived communality deficiency. *Journal of Applied Psychology, 92,* 81–92.

Helms, H., Prouix, C., Klute, M., McHale, S., & Crouter, A. (2006). Spouses' gender-typed attributes and their links with marital quality: A pattern analytic approach. *Journal of Social and Personal Relationships, 23,* 343–364.

Hendrick, C., & Hendrick, S. (1986). A theory and method of love. *Journal of Personality and Social Psychology, 50,* 392–402.

Hendrick, C., & Hendrick, S. (1996). Gender and the experience of heterosexual love. In J. T. Wood (Ed.), *Gendered relationships: A reader.* Mountain View, CA: Mayfield.

Henley, N. M. (1977). *Body politics: Power, sex and nonverbal communication.* Englewood Cliffs, NJ: Prentice-Hall.

Henley, N. M., & Freeman, J. (1995). The sexual politics of interpersonal behavior. In J. Freeman (Ed.), *Women: A feminist perspective* (5th ed., pp. 79–91). Mountain View, CA: Mayfield.

Henley, N. M., & LaFrance, M. (1996). On oppressing hypotenses: Or differences in nonverbal sensitivity revisited. In L. Radtke & H. Stam (Eds.), *Power/gender: Social relations in theory and practice. Inquiries in social construction* (pp. 287–311). Thousand Oaks, CA: Sage.

Henry, A. (2004). *Not my mother's sister.* Bloomington: Indiana University Press.

Herbert, B. (2006, October 16). Why aren't we shocked? *The New York Times,* p. A23.

Herbert, B. (2007a, April 12). Paying the price. *The New York Times,* p. A21.

Herbert, B. (2007b, April 16). Signs of infection. *The New York Times,* p. A23.

Herbert, B. (2009a, March 21). The great shame. *New York Times,* p. A17.

Herbert, B. (2009b, August 8). Women at risk. *New York Times,* p. A17.

Herdt, G. (1997). *Same sex, different cultures.* Boulder, CO: Westview.

Hernández, D., & Rehman, B. (Eds.). (2002). *Colonize this! Young women of color on today's feminism.* Seattle: Seal Press.

Hesse-Biber, S. N., & Leavy, P. (2006). *The cult of thinness* (2nd ed.). New York: Oxford University Press.

Hewitt, N. A. (Ed.). (2010). *No permanent waves: Recasting histories of U. S. feminism.* Piscataway, NJ: Rutgers University Press.

Hewlett, S. (2007). *Off-ramps and on-ramps.* Boston, MA: Harvard Business School Press.

Heyl, M. (2005, Spring). Female genital mutilation. *Patchwork,* pp. 14–15.

Hildebrandt, K. (2004, April 16). Tradition, personality can be barriers. (Sioux Falls, SD) *Argus News Leader,* pp. 1A, 7A.

Hill, C. A. (2002). Gender, relationship stage, and sexual behavior: The importance of partner emotional investment within specific situations. *Journal of Sex Research, 39,* 228–240.

Hine, D., & Thompson, K. (1998). *A shining thread of hope: The history of black women in America.* New York: Broadway.

Hines, M. (1992, April 19). [Untitled report]. *Health Information Communication Network, 5,* 2.

Hines, S. (2006). Intimate transitions: Transgender practices of partnering and parenting. *Sociology, 2,* 353–371.

Hirschfeld, S., & Wolf, S. (2005, May 27). Sex, religion, and politics: New challenges in discrimination law. *The Chronicle of Higher Education,* pp. B10–B14.

Hirshman, L. (2007, April 25). Off to work she should go. *The New York Times,* p. A31.

Hise, T. (2004). *The war against men.* Oakland, OR: Elderberry Press.

Hochschild, A. (with Machung, A.). (2003). *The second shift: Working parents and the revolution at home* (Rev. ed.). New York: Viking/Penguin Press.

Hochschild, A., & Ehrenreich, B. (Eds.). (2003). *Global women: Nannies, maids and sex workers in the new economy.* New York: Metropolitan.

Holland, D., & Eisenhart, M. (1992). *Educated in romance: Women, achievement, and college culture.* Chicago: University of Chicago Press.

Holmes, M. (2008). *Gender and everyday life.* New York: Routledge.

Hondagneu-Sotelo, P. (2007). *Domestica: Immigrant workers cleaning and caring in the shadows of affluence.* Berkeley: University of California Press,

hooks, b. (1990). *Yearning: Race, gender, and cultural politics.* Boston: South End Press.

hooks, b. (2000). *Feminist theory: From margin to center* (2nd ed.). Boston: South End Press,

hooks, b. (2002). *Feminism is for everybody.* Boston: South End Press.

Hopkins, A. (2001). Personal communication.

Hopkins, A., & Walsh, M. (1996). *So ordered: Making partner the hard way.* Amherst: University of Massachusetts Press.

A hothouse for female students. (2006, May 5). *The Chronicle of Higher Education,* p. A12.

Howey, N. (2002). *Dress codes: Of three girlhoods: My mother's, my father's and mine.* New York: Picador USA.

Howry, A., & Wood, J. T. (2001). Something old, something new, something borrowed: Themes in the voices of a new generation of feminists. *Southern Journal of Communication, 66,* 323–336.

Hudson, B. (2001). *African American female speech communities: Varieties of talk.* Westport, CT: Bergin & Garvey/Greenwood Press.

Hulbert, A. (2005, April 3). Boy problems. *The New York Times Magazine,* pp. 13–14.

Human Trafficking Fact Sheet. (2006, April 16). Sexual Trafficking: Breaking the Crisis of Silence. Conference held at the University of North Carolina at Chapel Hill.

Hunt, A. (1994, June 23). O. J. and the brutal truth about marital violence. *The Wall Street Journal,* p. A15.

Hunter, J., & Mallon, G. P. (2000). Lesbian, gay and bisexual adolescent development: Dancing with your feet tied together. In B. Greene & G. Croom (Eds.), *Education,* *research, and practice in lesbian, gay, bisexual, and transgendered psychology* (pp. 226–243). Thousand Oaks, CA: Sage.

Hurlemann, R., Patin, A., Onur, O., Cohen, M., Baumgartner, T., Metzler, S., Dziobek, I., Gallinat, J., Wagner, M., Maier, W., & Kendrick, K. (2010). Ocytocin enhances amygdala-dependent, socially reinforced learning and emotional empathy in humans. *Journal of Neuroscience, 30,* 4999–5007.

Hust, S. J. T., Brown, J., & L'Engle, K. L. (2008). Boys will be boys and girls better be prepared: An analysis of the rare sexual health messages in young adolescents' media. *Mass Communication & Society, 11,* 3–23.

Huston, M., & Schwartz, P. (1996). Gendered dynamics in gay and lesbian relationships. In J. T. Wood (Ed.), *Gendered relationships: A reader* (pp. 89–121). Mountain View, CA: Mayfield.

Hutchinson, M. (2002). The influence of sexual risk communication between parents and daughters on sexual risk behaviors. *Family Relations, 51,* 238–247.

Hyde, J. S. (1984). Children's understanding of sexist language. *Developmental Psychology, 20,* 697–706.

Ickes, W. (1993). Traditional gender roles: Do they make and then break our relationships? *Journal of Social Work, 49,* 71–85.

Ifill, G. (2007, April 11). Too far for Imus, not far enough for us. *Raleigh News & Observer,* p. 11A.

In their words. (2003, June 24). *Raleigh News & Observer,* p. 5A.

Ingraham, L. (1997, July 15). Feminists welcome the Promise Keepers. *Raleigh News & Observer,* p. 11A.

Inman, C. (1996). Friendships between men: Closeness in the doing. In J. T. Wood (Ed.), *Gendered relationships: A reader* (pp. 95–110). Mountain View, CA: Mayfield.

Ivory, J. D. (2008). The games, they are a-changin'. In P. E. Jamieson & D. Romer (Eds.), *The changing portrayal of adolescents in the media since 1950* (pp. 347–376). New York: Oxford.

Jackman, M. R. (2003). Violence in social life. *Annual Review of Sociology, 28,* 387–415.

Jackson, L. A. (2008). Adolescents and the internet. In P. E. Jamieson & D. Romer (Eds.), *The changing portrayal of adolescents in the media since 1950* (pp. 377–411). New York: Oxford University Press.

Jacobson, J. (2001, March 9). Why do so many female athletes enter ACL hell? *The Chronicle of Higher Education,* p. A45.

Jacobson, J. (2004a, May 7). At the women's march: 2 students, 2 hearts, 2 minds. *The Chronicle of Higher Education,* pp. A38–A39.

Jacobson, J. (2004b, February 27). Sex and football. *The Chronicle of Higher Education,* pp. A33–A34.

Jagger, G. (2008). *Judith Butler: Sexual politics, social change and the power of performance.* New York: Routledge.

Jamieson, K. H. (1995). *Beyond the double bind: Women and leadership.* New York: Oxford University Press.

Jamieson, P. E., More, E., Lee, S. S., Busse, P., & Romer, D. (2008). It matters what young people watch: Health risk behaviors portrayed in top-grossing movies since 1950. In P. E. Jamieson & D. Romer (Eds.), *The changing portrayal of adolescents in the media since 1950* (pp. 107–131). New York: Oxford.

Jamieson, P. E., & Romer, D. (Eds.). (2008). *The changing portrayal of adolescents in the media since 1950.* New York: Oxford University Press.

Jamila, S. (2002). Can I get a witness? Testimony from a hip-hop feminist. In D. Hernández & D. Rehman (Eds.), *Colonize this! Young women of color on today's feminism* (pp. 382–394). New York: Seal Press.

Janeway, E. (1971). *Man's world, woman's place: A study in social mythology.* New York: Dell.

Jegalian, K., & Lahn, B. (2001). Why the Y is so weird. *Scientific American, 284,* 56.

Jenkins, H. (2007, February 10). From YouTube to YouNiversity. *Chronicle of Higher Education,* pp. B9–10.

Jensen, R. (2007). *Getting off: Pornography and the end of masculinity.* Boston: South End Press.

Jhally, S., & Katz, J. (2001, Winter). Big trouble, little pond: Reflections on the meaning of the campus pond rapes. *UMass,* pp. 26–31.

Johnson, A. (2007). The subtleties of blatant sexism. *Communication and Critical/Cultural Studies, 4,* 166–183.

Johnson, A. (2006). *Privilege, power, and difference,* 2nd ed. New York: McGraw-Hill.

Johnson, A. (2008, August 4). One by one, women in Egypt fight female circumcision. *Raleigh News & Observer,* p. 7A.

Johnson, F. (1996). Friendships among women: Closeness in dialogue. In J. T. Wood (Ed.), *Gendered relationships: A reader* (pp. 79–94). Mountain View, CA: Mayfield.

Johnson, F. (2000). *Speaking culturally: Language diversity in the United States.* Thousad Oaks, CA: Sage.

Johnson, J. W. (1912/1989). *Autobiography of an ex-coloured man.* New York: Vintage-Random.

Johnson, M. (2006). Gendered communication and intimate partner violence. In B. Dow & J. T. Wood (Eds.), *Handbook of gender and communication.* Thousand Oaks, CA: Sage.

Johnson, M. (2008). *A typology of domestic violence.* Boston: Northeastern University Press.

Johnson, M. L. (Ed.). (2007). *Third-wave feminism and television: Jane puts it in a box.* New York: Palgrave Macmillan.

Johnson, N. R. (2010). Consuming desires: Consumption, romance, and sexuality in best-selling teen romance novels. *Women's Studies in Communication, 33,* 54–73.

Johnson, N. (2007). *All I Want Is Everything: A Feminist Analysis of Consumption in Bestselling Teen Romance Novels.* PhD Dissertation. The University of North Carolina at Chapel Hill.

Johnson, N. (2011). The whole package: Commodifying the self. In D. O. Braithwaite & J. T. Wood (Eds.), *Casing interpersonal communication* (pp. 9–15). Dubuque, IA: Kendall-Hunt.

Johnson, S. (2005). *Whatever is bad for you is good for you.* New York: Riverhead Hardcover.

Jordan, J. (2004). The rhetorical limits of the "plastic body." *Quarterly Journal of Speech, 90,* 327–358.

Joseph, R. (2000). The evolution of sex differences in language, sexuality and visual-spatial skills. *Archives of Sexual Behavior, 29,* 55–66.

Joyce, A. (2004, December 3). Working teens face harassment. *Raleigh News & Observer,* p. 6A.

Julia, I. (Ed.). (2000). *Constructing gender: Multicultural perspectives in working with women.* Belmont, CA: Thomson/Brooks/Cole.

June, A. W. (2010, February 19). Family-friendly policies fall short when professors worry about backlash. *Chronicle of Higher Education,* p. A12.

Kaestle, C., Halpern, C., & Brown, J. (2007). Music videos, pro wrestling, and acceptance of date rape among middle school males and females: An exploratory analysis. *Journal of Adolescent Health, 40,* 185–187.

Kahlenberg, R. (2010). *Affirmative action for the rich: Legacy preferences in college admissions.* New York: Century/Foundation.

Kahlenberg, R. (2010) (Ed.). *Rewarding strivers: Helping low-income students succeed in college.* New York: Century Foundation Press.

Kailey, M. (2006). *Just add hormones: An insider's guide to the transsexual experience.* Boston: Beacon.

Kanter, R. M. (1977). *Men and women of the corporation.* New York: Basic Books.

Kantrowitz, B. (2005, January 31). Sex and science. *Newsweek,* pp. 36–38.

Kantrowitz, B., & Kalb, C. (1998, May 11). How to build a better boy. *Newsweek,* pp. 55–60.

Kaschak, E. (1992). *Engendered lives.* New York: Basic Books.

Kassindja, F. (1998). Do *they hear you when you cry?* New York: Delacorte.

Katz, J. (2000). MVP trainer's guide for working with male high school students. MVP strategies: Gender violence prevention education and training. Retrieved November 20, 2007, from http://www.eurowrc.org/05.education/education_en/1 1 .edu_en.htm.

Katz, J., & Jhally, S. (1999, May 2). The national conversation in the wake of Littleton is missing the mark. *The Boston Globe*, p. E1.

Katz, J., & Jhally, S. (2000, June 25). Put the blame where it belongs: On men. *The Los Angeles Times*, p. M5.

Kearney, M. C. (2006). *Girls make media*. London: Routledge.

Keen, S. (1991). *Fire in the belly: On being a man*. New York: Bantam.

Kerr, B. (1997). *Smart girls: A new psychology of girls, women, and giftedness*. Scottsdale, AZ: Gifted Psychology Press.

Kerber, L. (2005, March 18). We must make the academic workplace more humane and equitable. *The Chronicle of Higher Education*, pp. B6–B9.

Kershaw, S. (2008, September 11). Girl talk has its limits. *New York Times*, pp. E1, E6.

Kershaw, S. (2009, April 23). Mr. Moms (by way of Fortune 500). *New York Times*, pp. E1, E6.

Kilbourne, J. (2010). *Still killing us softly/4*. Northampton, MA: Media Education Foundation.

Kilbourne, J. (2004). The more you subtract, the more you add: Cutting girls down to size. In J. Spade & C. Valentine (Eds.), *The kaleidoscope of gender: Prisms, patterns, and possibilities* (pp. 234–244). Belmont, CA: Thomson/Wadsworth.

Kilbourne, J. (2007). "You talkin' to me?" In M. Andersen & P. H. Collins (Eds.), *Race, class, and gender: An anthology* (6th ed., pp. 228–233). Belmont, CA: Thomson.

Kim, G., & Roloff, M. (1999). Attributing sexual consent. *Journal of Applied Communication Research, 27*, 1–23.

Kimbrell, A. (1991, May/June). A time for men to pull together. *Utne Reader*, pp. 66–71.

Kimmel, M. (1996). *Manhood*. New York: Free Press.

Kimmel, M. (2000a). *The gendered society*. Cambridge, MA: Oxford University Press.

Kimmel, M. (2000b, January 12). What about the boys? Keynote speech at the Center for Research on Women's 6th Annual Gender Equity Conference, Boston, MA.

Kimmel, M. (2003). Introduction. In Kimmel, M. (Ed.) (with Aronson, A.), *The gendered society reader* (pp. 1–6). New York: Oxford University Press.

Kimmel, M. (2005). *Manhood in America*. New York: Oxford University Press.

Kimmell, M. (2008). *Guyland: The perilous world where boys become men*. New York: Macmillan.

Kimura, D. (1999). *Sex and cognition*. Cambridge: MIT Press.

Kindlon, D., & Thompson, M. (1999). *Raising Cain: Protecting the emotinal life of boys*. New York: Ballentine.

Kinney, T. A., Smith, B. A., & Donzella, B. (2001). The influence of sex, gender, self-discrepancies, and self-awareness on anger and verbal aggressiveness among U.S. college students. *Journal of Social Psychology, 141*, 245–276.

Kirby, E., & Krone, K. (2002). "The policy exists but you can't really use it": Communication and the structuration of work-family policies. *Journal of Applied Communication Research, 30*, 50–77.

Kishkovsky, S. (2003, September 17). Bolshoi decides it's over before "fat lady dances." *The New York Times*, pp. A1, A6.

Klimkiewicz, J. (2006, October 29). Airbrushed ideals of beauty under attack. *Charlotte Observer*, p. 14A.

Kline, S., Stafford, L., & Miklosovic, J. (1996). Women's surnames: Decisions, interpretations, and associations with relational qualities. *Journal of Social and Personal Relationships, 13*, 593–617.

Kneidinger, L. M., Maple, T. L., & Tross, S. A. (2001). Touching behavior in sport: Functional components, analysis of sex differences, and ethological considerations. *Journal of Nonverbal Behavior, 25*, 43–62.

Koesten, J. (2004). Family communication patterns, sex of subject, and communication competence. *Communication Monographs, 71*, 226–244.

Kohlberg, L. (1958). The development of modes of thinking and moral choice in the years 10 to 16. Unpublished doctoral dissertation, University of Chicago.

Kollwitz, K., & Kahlo, F. (2003). Women and the art world: Diary of the feminist masked avengers. In R. Morgan (Ed.), *Sisterhood is forever* (pp. 437–444). New York: Washington Square Press.

Konner, M. (2003, June 16). Bridging our differences. *Newsweek*, pp. 74, 77.

Kosova, W. (2007, April 23). The power that was. *Newsweek*, pp. 24–32.

Kovacs, P., Parker, J., & Hoffman, L. (1996). Behavioral, affective and social correlates of involvement in cross-sex friendships in elementary school. *Child Development, 67*, 2269–2286.

Kramarae, C. (1992). Harassment and everyday life. In L. F. Rakow (Ed.), *Women making meaning: New feminist directions in communication* (pp. 100–120). New York: Routledge.

Kristof, N. (2005a, June 21). The 11-year-old wife. *The New York Times*, p. A23.

Kristof, N. (2005b, June 19). A free woman. *The New York Times*, section 4, p.13.

Kristof, N. (2005c, June 14). Raped, kidnapped and silenced. *The New York Times*, p. A19.

Kristof, N. (2005d, March 5). When rapists walk free. *The New York Times,* p. A27.

Kristof, N. (2006a, December 12). A Cambodian girl's tragedy: Being young and pretty. *The New York Times,* p. A31.

Kristof, N. (2008, December 5). Women the victims, acid the weapon. *Raleigh News & Observer,* p. 17A.

Kristof, N., & WuDunn, S. (2009). *Half the sky.* New York: Knopf.

Kuchinskas, S. (2009a, May-June). Benefits of the daddy brain. Miller-McCune, pp. 20–23.

Kuchinskas, S. (2009b). *The chemistry of connection.* Oakland, CA: Harbinger.

Kuchment, A. (2004, May 10). The more social sex. *Newsweek,* pp. 88–89.

Kuczynski, A. (2001). *Beauty junkies.* New York: Doubleday.

Kunkel, A., Dennis, R., & Waters, E. (2003). Contemporary university students' ratings of characteristics of men, women, and CEOs. *Psychological Reports, 93,* pp. 1197–1213.

Kunkel, A., Hummert, M., & Dennis, M. (2006). Social learning theory: Modeling and communication in the family context. In D. Braithwaite & L. Baxter (Eds.), *Engaging theories in family communication* (pp. 260–275). Thousand Oaks, CA: Sage.

Kunkel, D. Eyal, K., Finnerty, K., Biely, E., & Donnerstein, E. (2005). *Sex on TV4: A biennial report of the Kaiser Family Foundation.* Menlo Park, CA: Henry J. Kaiser Family Foundation.

Kurdek, L. A., & Schmitt, J. P. (1986a). Early development of relationship quality in heterosexual married, heterosexual cohabiting, gay, and lesbian couples. *Developmental Psychology, 22,* 305–309.

Kurdek, L. A., & Schmitt, J. P. (1986b). Interaction of sex-role self-concept with relationship quality and relationship belief in married, heterosexual cohabiting, gay, and lesbian couples. *Journal of Personality and Social Psychology, 51,* 365–370.

Kurdek, L. A., & Schmitt, J. P. (1986c). Relationship quality of partners in heterosexual married, heterosexual cohabiting, and gay and lesbian relationships. *Journal of Personality and Social Psychology, 51,* 711–720.

Kurdek, L. A., & Schmitt, J. P. (1987). Partner homogamy in married, heterosexual cohabiting, gay, and lesbian couples. *Journal of Sex Research, 23,* 212–232.

Kurth, S., Spiller, B., & Travis, C. B. (2000). Consent, power and sexual scripts: Deconstructing sexual harassment. In C. B. Travis & J. W. White (Eds.), *Sexuality, society, and feminism* (pp. 323–354). Washington, DC: American Psychological Association.

Labov, W. (1972). *Sociolinguistic patterns.* Philadelphia: University of Pennsylvania Press.

Lacey, M. (2004, June 8). Genital cutting shows signs of losing favor in Africa. *The New York Times,* p. A3.

Lacey, M. (2008, December 7). A lifestyle distinct: The muxe of Mexico. *New York Times,* p. WK4.

L'Engle, K. & Jackson, C. (2008). Socialization influences on early adolescents' cognitive susceptibility and transition to sexual intercourse. *Journal of Research on Adolescence, 18,* 353–378.

LaFraniere, S. (2005, December 23). Another school barrier for African girls: No toilet. *The New York Times,* pp. A1, A10.

LaFraniere, S. (2007, July 8). If obesity is beauty, health is a low priority. *Raleigh News & Observer,* p. 20A.

Lakoff, R. (1975). *Language and woman's place.* New York: Harper & Row.

Lally, K. (1996, January 7). For girls now, adolescence a perilous rite. *Richmond Times Dispatch,* pp. G1, G2.

Lamb, S. (1991). Acts without agents: An analysis of linguistic avoidance in journal articles on men who batter women. *American Journal of Orthopsychiatry, 61,* 87–102.

Lamb, S. (Ed.). (1999). *New versions of victims.* New York: New York University Press.

Lamb, S. (2002). *The secret lives of girls: What good girls really do—sex play, aggression, and their guilt.* New York: Free Press.

Lamb, S., & Brown, L. (2006). *Packaging girlhood: Rescuing our daughters from marketers' schemes.* New York: St. Martin's Press.

Lamke, L., Sollie, D., Durbin, R., & Fitzpatrick, J. (1994). Masculinity, femininity, and relationship satisfaction: The mediating role of interpersonal competence. *Journal of Social and Personal Relationships, 11,* 535–554.

Lane, A. J. (2006, May 5). Gender, power, and sexuality: First, do no harm. *The Chronicle of Higher Education,* pp. B10–B13.

Laner, M. R., & Ventrone, N. A. (2002). Dating scripts revisited. *Journal of Family Issues, 21,* 488–500.

Lang, S. S. (1991, January 20). When women drink. *Parade,* pp. 18–20.

Langer, S. K. (1953). *Feeling and form: A theory of art.* New York: Scribner's.

Langer, S. K. (1979). *Philosophy in a new key: A study in the symbolism of reason, rite and art* (3rd ed.). Cambridge, MA: Harvard University Press.

Langreth, R. (1997, June 12). Hey guys, for the next party, try borrowing women's genes. *The Wall Street Journal,* p. B1.

Lansberg, M. (2000). White Ribbon Campaign: Canadian feminists' uneasy alliance with men challenging violence. *Voice Male,* p. 15.

Laster, J. (2010, January 29). Unlike men, female scientists have a second shift: Housework. *Chronicle of Higher Education,* p. A10.

Law on Marital Rape Revised. (2009, July 10). *Raleigh News & Observer*, p. 3A.

Leaper, C. (Ed.). (1994). *Childhood gender segregation: Causes and consequences.* San Francisco: Jossey-Bass.

Leaper, C. (1996). The relationship of play activity and gender to parent and child sex-typed communication. *International Journal of Behavioral Development, 19,* 689–703.

Leaper, C. (2000). The social construction and socialization of gender. In P. Miller & E. Scholnick (Eds.), *Towards a feminist developmental psychology* (pp. 127–152). New York: Routledge.

Leaper, C., Anderson, K., & Sanders, P. (1998). Moderators of gender effects on parents' talk to their children: A meta-analysis. *Developmental Psychology, 34,* 3–27.

Leaper, C., & Ayres, M. (2007). A meta-analytic review of gender variations in adults' language use: Talkativeness, affiliative speech, and assertive speech. *Personality & Social Psychology Review, 11,* 328–363.

Leaper, C., Leve, L., Strasser, T., & Schwartz, R. (1995). Mother-child communication sequences: Play activity, child gender, and marital status effects. *Merrill-Palmer Quarterly, 41,* 307–327.

Lee, J. (2009, November 20). Sex offences on subways are widespread, city officials are told. *New York Times,* p. A28

Lee, S. (Director). (1997). *Get on the Bus.* [Motion picture]. United States: Columbia/Tristar.

Lehmiller, J. J. (2010). Differences in relationship investments between gay and heterosexual men. *Journal of Personal Relationships, 17,* 81–96.

Leland, J., & Chambers, V. (1999, July 12). Generation N. *Newsweek*, pp. 52–58.

Lelchuk, I. (2007, May 20). Being Mr. Dad. *San Francisco Chronicle Magazine*, pp. 8, 9, 19.

Lenhart, A., Madden, M., Macgill, A. R., Smith, A. (2007, December 19). Teens and social media. Retrieved April 4, 2008 from *Pew Internet and American Life Project:* http://www.ibiblio.org/fred/inls_490/readings/Week2/Recommended/Lenhart2007Teens-and-Social-Med.pdf.

LePoire, B. A., Burgoon, J. K., & Parrott, R. (1992). Status and privacy restoring communication in the workplace. *Journal of Applied Communication Research, 4,* 419–436.

Lepowsky, M. (1998). The influence of culture on behavior and the case of aggression: Women, men, and aggression in an egalitarian society. In D. Anselmi & A. Law (Eds.), *Questions of gender: Perspectives and paradoxes* (pp. 159–172). New York: McGraw-Hill.

Levant, R., & Pollock, W. (Eds.). (2003). *A new psychology of men.* New York: Basic.

Levin, D., & Kilbourne, J. (2008). *So sexy, so soon.* New York: Ballantine.

Levy, A. (2005). *Female chauvinist pigs.* New York: Free Press.

Levy, A., & Paludi, M. (1997). *Workplace sexual harassment.* Englewood Cliffs, NJ: Prentice Hall.

Levy, G. D. (1998). Effects of gender constancy and figure's height and sex on young children's gender-type attributions. *Journal of General Psychology, 125,* 65–89.

Levy, S. (2005, August 1). Sex, secret codes, and videogames. *Newsweek*, p. 14.

Lewin, T. (2007, January 26). Colleges regroup after votes ban race preferences. *The New York Times*, pp. A1, A13.

Lewin, T. (2008a, May 20). Girls' gains have not cost boys, report says. *New York Times,* p. a17.

Lewin, T. (2008b, July 25). Math scores show no gap for girls, study finds. *New York Times.* http://www.nytimes.com/2008/07/25/education/25math.html?_r=1&oref=slogin. Accessed October 26, 2008.

Lewin, T. (2010, March 13). Women making gains on faculty at Harvard. *New York Times,* p. A12.

Lind, R., & Salo, C. (2004). Framing feminism. In R. Lind (Ed.), *Race/gender/media* (pp. 160–168). Boston: Pearson/Allyn & Bacon.

Lindgren, S., & Lélièvre, M. (2009). In the laboratory of masculinity: Renegotiating gender subjectivities in MTV's *Jackass. Critical Studies in Media Communication, 26,* 393–410.

Lin-Liu, J. (2005, February 4). Mongolia's reverse gender gap. *The Chronicle of Higher Education,* p. A39.

Lipka, S. (2005, April 8). High court expands protections of Title IX. *The Chronicle of Higher Education,* pp. A1, A36.

Lippa, R. (2005). *Gender, nature, and nurture* (2nd ed.). Mahwah, NJ: Erlbaum.

Livingston, J., & Testa, M. (2000). Qualitative analysis of women's perceived vulnerability to sexual aggression in a hypothetical dating context. *Journal of Social and Personal Relationships, 17,* 729–741.

Lobel, T., & Bar, E. (1997). Perceptions of masculinity and femininity of kibbutz and urban adolescents. *Sex Roles, 37,* 283–289.

Logwood, D. (1998, Winter). One million strong. *Hues*, pp. 15–19.

Lont, C., & Bridge, M. (2004). The face of the front page: A content analysis of U.S. newspapers. In R. Lind (Ed.), *Race/gender/media* (pp. 140–146). Boston: Pearson/Allyn & Bacon.

Looy, H., & Bouma III, H. (2005). The nature of gender: Gender identity in persons who are intersexed or transgender. *Journal of Psychology and Theology, 3,* 166–178.

Lorber, J. (1997). A woman's rights/cultural conflict. *Democratic Left, 2,* 3–5.

Lorber, J. (2001). *Gender inequality: Feminist theories and politics* (2nd ed.). Los Angeles: Roxbury.

Louis, C. S. (2010a, April 29). Cosmetic surgery gets a nip and tuck. *New York Times*, p. E3.

Louis, C. S. (2010b, August 12). This teenage girl uses botox. And, no, she's not alone. *New York Times*, pp. E1, E3.

Loury, G. (1996, January/February). Joy and doubt on the mall. *Utne Reader*, pp. 70–71.

Lugones, M., & Spelman, E. (1983). Have we got a theory for you! Feminist theory, cultural imperialism, and the demand for "the woman's voice." *Women's Studies International Forum, 6*, 573–581.

Lundy, L, K., Ruth, A. M., & Park, T. D. (2008). Simply irresistible: Reality TV consumption patterns. *Communication Quarterly, 56*, 208–225.

Luo, M., & Horyn, C. (2008, December 6). 3 Palin stylists cost campaign more than $165,000. *New York Times*, pp. A9, A11.

Luster, T., & Okagaki, L. (Eds.). (2005). *Parenting: An ecological perspective* (2nd ed.). Mahwah, NJ: Erlbaum.

Lynch, J., & Kilmartin, C. (1999).*The pain behind the mask: Overcoming masculine depression*. Binghamton, NY: Haworth Press.

Maccoby, E. E. (1998). *The two sexes: Growing up apart, coming together*. Cambridge, MA: Belknap Press of the Harvard University Press.

MacGeorge, E., Gillihan, S. J., Samter, W., & Clark, R. A. (2003). Skill deficit or differential motivation? Accounting for sex differences in the provision of emotional support. *Communication Research, 30*, 272–293.

Mai, M., Cuny, M., Kristof, N., & Coverdale, L. (2006). *In the name of honor*. New York: Simon & Schuster/Atria.

MacKinnon, C. A. (2005). *Women's lives, men's laws*. Cambridge, MA: Harvard University Press.

Major, B., Schmidlin, A. M., & Williams, L. (1990). Gender patterns in social touch: The impact of setting and age. *Journal of Personality and Social Psychology, 58*, 634–643.

Maltz, D. N., & Borker, R. (1982). A cultural approach to male-female miscommunication. In J. J. Gumperz (Ed.), *Language and social identity* (pp. 196–216). Cambridge, UK: Cambridge University Press.

Manatu, N. (2003). *African American women and sexuality in the cinema*. Jefferson, NC: McFarland.

Mandziuk, R. (2008). Dressing down Hillary. *Communication and Critical/Cultural Studies, 5*, 312–316.

Mangan, K. (2004, November 12). Does affirmative action hurt black law students? *The Chronicle of Higher Education*, pp. A35–A36.

Manliness in the Twenty First Century with James Doyle (2000, June 1). *WebMD Live Events Transcript*, 4 pages. http://www.medicinenet.com/script/main/art.asp?articlekey=53987. Accessed October 25, 2008.

Mangan, K. (2004, November 12). Does affirmative action hurt black law students? *The Chronicle of Higher Education*, pp. A35–A36.

Manji, I. (2005). *The trouble with Islam*. Boston: St. Martin's Press.

Mansbridge, J. (1986). *Why we lost the ERA*. Chicago: University of Chicago Press.

Mansfield, H. (2007). *Manliness*. New Haven, CT: Yale University Press.

Mapstone, E. (1998). *War of words: Women and men argue*. London: Random House.

March of Dimes. (2006, October). Chromosomal abnormalities. Retrieved November 12, 2007, from http://www.marchofdimes.com/pnhec/4439_1209.asp.

Marcus, S. (2007). *Between women: Friendship, desire, and marriage in Victorian England*. Princeton, NJ: Princeton University Press.

Marine, S. (2004, November 26). Waking up from the nightmare of rape. *The Chronicle of Higher Education*, p. B5.

Marin, R., & Dokoupil, T. (2011, April 25). Dead suit walking. *Newsweek*, pp. 30–36.

Martin, C. (1997). Gender cognitions and social relationships. Paper presented at the meeting of the American Psychological Association, Chicago.

Martin, C., & Halverson, F. Jr. (1981). A schematic processing model of sex typing and stereotyping in children. *Child Development, 52*, 1119–1134.

Martin, C., & Ruble, D. (2004). Children's search for gender cues: Cognitive perspectives on gender development. *Current Directions in Psychological Science, 13*, 67–70.

Martin, T., & Doka, K. (2000). *Men don't cry... women do: Transcending gender stereotypes of grief*. Philadelphia: University of Pennsylvania Press.

Marton, K. (2004, May 10). A worldwide gender gap. *Newsweek*, p. 94.

Marx, J. (2004, August 29). He turns boys into men. *Parade*, pp. 4–7.

Marx, K. (1975). *Capital* (Vol. 1). (B. Fowles, Trans.). New York: Vintage.

Marx, K. (1977). Early writings. (Ed. Q. Hoare). New York: Vintage.

Mascia, J. (2010, July 12). A Web site that's not afraid to pick a fight. *New York Times*, pp. B1, B4.

Mason, M.A. (2007). *Mothers on the fast track: How a new generation can balance family and careers*. Cambridge, MA: Yale University Press.

May, L. (1998a). Many men still find strength in violence. *The Chronicle of Higher Education*, p. B7.

Mazur, E. (1989). Predicting gender differences in same-sex friendships from affiliation motive and value. *Psychology of Women Quarterly, 13,* 277–291.

Mazur, E., & Olver, R. (1987). Intimacy and structure: Sex differences in imagery of same-sex relationships. *Sex Roles, 16,* 533–558.

McCann, C., & Kim, S. (Eds.). (2003). *Feminist theory reader.* London: Routledge.

McClelland, C. (2004, May 14). Man raised as a girl commits suicide at 38. *Raleigh News & Observer,* p. 9B.

McClish, G., & Bacon, J. (2002)."Telling the story her own way": The role of feminist standpoint theory in rhetorical studies. *Rhetoric Society Quarterly, 32,* 27–55.

McCloskey, D. (1999). *Crossing: A memoir.* Chicago: University of Chicago Press.

McCreary, D., Newcomb, M., & Sadava, S. (1998). Dimensions of the male gender role: A confirmatory analysis in men and women. *Sex Roles, 39,* 81–95.

McDonald, M., Phipps, S. & Lethbridge, L. (2005). Taking its toll: The influences of paid and unpaid work on women's well being. *Feminist Economics, 11,* 63–94.

McDonald, T. (2005, June 19). The rite to be men. *Raleigh News & Observer,* pp. 1B, 2B.

McGinn, D. (2003, September 25). Getting back on track. *Newsweek,* pp. 62–66.

McGuffey, S., & Rich, L. (2004). Playing in the gender transgression zone: Race, class, and hegemonic masculinity in middle childhood. In J. Spade & C. Valentine (Eds.), *The kaleidoscope of gender: Prisms, patterns, and possibilities* (pp. 172–183). Belmont, CA: Wadsworth.

McKee, M. (2006, April). Al mousawat (equality) for Iraqi women. *Raising our voices: News from the Global Fund for Women,* n.p.

McRobbie, A. (2000). *Feminism and youth culture.* New York: Routledge.

McRobbie, A. (2004). Post-feminism and popular culture. *Feminist Media Studies, 4,* 255–264.

McRobbie, A. (2009). *The aftermath of feminism: Gender, culture and social change.* Thousand Oaks, CA: Sage.

Mead, M. (1935/1968). *Sex and temperament in three primitive societies.* New York: Dell.

Mealy, L. (2000). *Sex differences: Development and evolutionary strategies.* San Diego: Academic Press.

Meân, L. J., & Kassing, J. W. (2008). "I would just like to be known as an athlete": Maintaining hegemony, femininity, and heterosexuality in female sport. *Western Journal of Communication, 72*(2), 126–144.

Mechling, E., & Mechling, J. (1994). The Jung and the restless: The mythopoetic men's movement. *Southern Communication Journal, 59,* 97–111.

Media Trends Track. (2010). http://www.tvb.org/rcentral/mediatrendstrack/tvbasics/ 02_TVHouseholds.asp. Accessed April 22, 2010.

Medved, C. E. (2009). Crossing and transforming occupational and household gendered divisions of labor. *Communication Yearbook, 33,* 301–341.

Mehrabian, A. (1981). *Silent messages: Implicit communication of emotion and attitudes* (2nd ed.). Belmont, CA: Wadsworth.

Meloy, R. (2006). *The psychology of stalking: Clinical and forensic perspectives* (2nd ed.). New York: Academic Press.

Men use half a brain to listen, study finds. (2000, November 29). *Raleigh News & Observer,* p. 8A.

Mernissi, F. (2004). Size 6: The Western woman's harem. In J. Spade & C. Valentine (Eds.), *The kaleidoscope of gender: Prisms, patterns, and possibilities* (pp. 297–301). Belmont, CA: Thomson/Wadsworth.

Messner, M. (1997a). Boyhood, organized sports, and the construction of masculinities. In E. Disch (Ed.), *Reconstructing gender* (pp. 57–73). Mountain View, CA: Mayfield.

Messner, M. (1997b). *Politics of masculinities: Men in movements.* Thousand Oaks, CA: Sage.

Messner, M. (2000a). Barbie girls versus sea monsters: Children constructing gender. *Gender and Society, 7,* 121–137.

Messner, M. A. (2000b). White guy habitus in the classroom: Challenging the reproduction of privilege. *Men and Masculinities, 2,* 457–469.

Messner, M. (2001). When bodies are weapons: Masculinity and violence in sports. In D. Vannoy (Ed.), *Gender mosaics* (pp. 94–105). Los Angeles: Roxbury.

Messner, M. (2002, December 6). Needed: A fair assessment by a "budgetary umpire." *The Chronicle of Higher Education,* pp. B8–B9.

Messner, M. A. (2005). Still a man's world?: Studying masculinities and sport. In M. A. Messner, J. Hearn, & R. W. Connell (Eds.), *Handbook of studies on men & masculinities* (pp. 313–325). Thousand Oaks, CA: Sage Publications.

Messner, M. (2007). Masculinities and athletic careers. In M. Andersen & P. H. Collins (Eds.), *Race, class, gender: An anthology* (6th ed., pp. 172–184). Belmont, CA: Thomson.

Messner, M. A., & Sabo, D. F. (2006). Sport in the social construction of masculinity. In S. M. Whitehead (Ed.), *Men and masculinities: Critical concepts in sociology* (pp. 303–316). New York: Routledge.

Metts, S. (2006a). Gendered communication in dating relationships. In B. Dow & J.T. Wood (Eds.), *Handbook of Gender & Communication* (pp. 25–40). Thousand Oaks, CA: Sage.

Metts, S. (2006b). Hanging out and doing lunch: Enacting friendship closeness. In J. T. Wood & S. W. Duck (Eds.), *Composing relationships:*

Communication in everyday life (pp. 76–85). Belmont, CA: Thomson/Wadsworth.

Meyers, D. (2007). *Nature, nurture, and human diversity.* New York: Worth Publishers.

Meyers, M. (1994). News of battering. *Journal of Communication, 44,* 47–62.

Meyers, M. (2004). African American women and violence: Gender, race, and class in the news. *Critical Studies in Media Communication, 21,* 95–118.

Mihalic, S., & Elliot, D. (1997). A social learning theory model of marital violence. *Journal of Family Violence, 12,* 21–47.

Miller, C. (2008, August 14). Woman to woman, online. *New York Times,* pp. C1, C9.

Miller, M. (2003, June 16). Stop pretending nothing's wrong. *Newsweek,* pp. 71–72.

Miller, W. I. (2003). *Faking it.* New York: Cambridge University Press.

Miller-Day, M. & Fisher, C. (2006). Communication in mother-adult daughter relationships. In K. Floyd & M. Morman (Eds.), *Widening the family circle: New research on family communication* (pp. 15–38). Newbury Park, CA: Sage.

Million, J. (2003). *Woman's voice, woman's place: Lucy Stone and the birth of the women's rights movement.* Westport, CT: Praeger.

Million Family March picks up where men's march ended 5 years before. (2000, October 14). *Raleigh News & Observer,* p. 6B.

Mills, J. (1985, February). Body language speaks louder than words. *Horizon,* pp. 8–12.

Mills, R., Nazar, J., & Farrell, H. (2002). Child and parent perceptions of hurtful messages. *Journal of Social and Personal Relationships, 19,* 731–754.

Mills, S. (1999). Discourse competence: Or how to theorize strong women. In C. Hendricks & K. Oliver (Eds.), *Language and liberation* (pp. 81–97). Albany: State University of New York Press.

Minhas, S. F. (2009). The politics of rape and honor in Pakistan. In L. Cuklanz & S. Moorti (Eds.), *Local violence, global media* (pp. 65–78). New York: Peter Lang.

Minnich, E. (1998). Education. In W. Mankiller, G. Mink, M. Navarro, B. Smith, & G. Steinem (Eds.), *The reader's companion to U.S. women's history* (pp. 163–167). New York: Houghton Mifflin.

Mischel, W. (1966). A social learning view of sex differences in behavior. In E. E. Maccoby (Ed.), *The development of sex differences* (pp. 93–106). Stanford, CA: Stanford University Press.

Mishori, R. M. D. (2005, June 10). Is cosmetic surgery right for you? *Parade,* pp. 10–11.

The Missile Dick Chicks. Home. [Lyrics]. Retrieved March 29, 2004, from http://www.missiledickchicks.net/index.html.

Missile Dick Chicks's YouTube Channel. (2009). http://www.youtube.com/user/

MissileDickChicks?gl=GB&hl=en-GB. Accessed 21 April, 2009.

Mock, M. S. (2005, November 5). Confined by the stained-glass ceiling. *The Chronicle of Higher Education,* p. B24.

Moe, K., & Shandy, D. (2010). *Glass ceilings & 100-hour couples: What the opt-out phenomenon can teach us about work and family.* Athens, GA: University of Georgia Press.

Moller, L., & Serbin, L. (1996). Antecedents of toddler gender segregation: Cognitive consonance, gender-typed toy preferences and behavioral compatibility. *Sex Roles, 35,* 445–460.

Molloy, B., & Herzberger, S. (1998). Body image and self-esteem: A comparison of African-American and Caucasian women. *Sex Roles, 38,* 631–643.

Monastersky, R. (2005a, March 4). Studies show biological differences in how boys and girls learn math, but social factors play a big role too. *The Chronicle of Higher Education,* pp. A1, A12–A19.

Monastersky, R. (2005b, March 4). Why Chinese students score high in math. *The Chronicle of Higher Education,* p. A19.

Mongeau, P., Serewicz, M., Henningsen, M., & Davis, K. (2006). Sex differences in the transition to a heterosexual romantic relationship. In K. Dindia & D. Canary (Eds.), *Sex differences and similarities in communication* (2nd ed., pp. 337–358). Mahwah, NJ: Lawrence Erlbaum.

Moniz, D., & Pardue, D. (1996, June 23). Uncounted casualties. *Raleigh News & Observer,* pp. 21A, 22A.

Monroe, J. (2005, April). 21st century slavery: A new reality. *Boiling Point,* pp. 8, 9, 11.

Monsour, M. (2002). *Women and men as friends: Relationships across the life span in the 21st century.* Mahwah, NJ: Erlbaum.

Monsour, M. (2006). Gendered communication in friendships. In B. Dow & J. T. Wood (Eds.), *The SAGE handbook of gender and communication.* Thousand Oaks, CA: Sage.

Moreau, R. & Hussain, Z. (2005, March 28). "I decided to fight back." *Newsweek,* p. 36.

Morgan, J. (1999). *When chickenheads come home to roost: My life as a hip-hop feminist.* New York: Simon & Schuster.

Morgan, M. (1973). *The total woman.* New York: Pocket.

Morgan, R. (Ed.). (2003). *Sisterhood is forever: The women's anthology for a new millennium.* New York: Washington Square Press.

Morgan, R. (2003/2004, Winter). Infecting our souls. *Ms.,* p. 95.

Mongeau, P., Serewicz, M., Henningsen, M., & Davis, K. (2006). Sex differences in the transition to a heterosexual romantic relationship. In K. Dindia & D. Canary (Eds.),

Sex differences and similarities in communication (pp. 337–358). Mahwah, NJ: Erlbaum.

Morman, M. T., & Floyd, K. (2002). A "changing culture of fatherhood": Effects on affectionate communication, closeness, and satisfaction in men's relationships with their fathers and their sons. *Western Journal of Communication, 66,* 395–411.

Morman, M. T., & Floyd, K. (2006). The good son: Men's perceptions of the characteristics of sonhood. In K. Floyd & M. T. Morman (Eds.), *Widening the family circle: New research on family communication* (pp. 37–55). Thousand Oaks, CA: Sage.

Morr, M. C., & Mongeau, P. A. (2004). First date expectations: The impact of sex of initiator, alcohol consumption, and relationship type. *Communication Research, 31,* 3–35.

Morreale, J. (2007). Faking it and the transformation of identity. In D. Heller (Ed.), *Makeover television: Realities remodeled* (pp. 6–22). New York: Palgrave Macmillan.

Morrow, V. (2006). Understanding gender differences in context: Implications for young children's everyday lives. *Children & Society, 20,* 92–104.

Moser, K. (2008, October 17). Women accuse Rutgers political-science department of bias and hostility. *Chronicle of Higher Education,* p. A14.

Mosley-Howard, S., & Evans, C. (1997). Relationships in the African American family. Paper presented at the 1997 Conference of the International Network on Personal Relationships, Oxford, OH.

Ms. Musings. (2004, Spring). *Ms.,* p. 13.

Muehlhoff, T. (2007, March 18). Personal communication.

Mulac, A. (1998). The gender-linked language effect: Do language differences really make a difference? In D. J. Canary & K. Dindia (Eds.), *Sex differences and similarities in communication: Critical essays and empirical investigations of sex and gender in interaction* (pp. 127–153). Mahwah, NJ: Erlbaum.

Mulac, A. (2006). The gender-linked language effect: Do language differences really make a difference? In K. Dindia & D. Canary (Eds.), *Sex differences and similarities in communication* (pp. 219–239). Mahwah, NJ: Erlbaum.

Mulac, A., Jansma, L., & Linz, D. (2003). Men's behavior toward women after viewing sexually explicit films: Degradation makes a difference. *Communication Monographs, 69,* 311–328.

Mulac, A., Wiemann, J. M., Widenmann, S. J., & Gibson, T.W. (1988). Male/female language differences and effects in same sex and mixed-sex dyads: The gender-linked language effect. *Communication Monographs, 55,* 315–335.

Murphy, B., & Zorn, T. (1996). Gendered interaction in professional relationships. In J. T. Wood (Ed.), *Gendered relationships: A reader* (pp. 213–232). Mountain View, CA: May field.

Murphy, B. C. (1997). Difference and diversity: Gay and lesbian couples. In M. Duberman (Ed.), *A queer world* (pp. 345–357). New York: New York University Press.

Murphy, C. (2005, February 25). Grass-roots men's ministries growing. *Raleigh News & Observer,* p. 5E.

Murrow, D. (2004). *Why men hate going to church.* Nashville, TN: Thomas Nelson.

Muwakkil, S. (2005, December 19). Jump-starting a movement. *In These Times,* p. 13.

Myers, P. N., & Biocca, F. A. (1992). The elastic body image: The effect of television advertising on body image distortion in young women. *Journal of Communication, 3,* 108–133.

Nadesan, M., & Trethewey, A. (2000). Performing the enterprising subject: Gendered strategies of success. *Text and Performance Quarterly, 20,* 223–250.

Namaste, V. (2000). *Invisible lives: The erasure of transsexual and transgendered people.* Chicago: University of Chicago Press.

Nanda, S. (2004). Multiple genders among North American Indians. In J. Spade & C. Valentine (Eds.), *The kaleidoscope of gender* (pp. 64–70). Belmont, CA: Thomson/Wadsworth.

Natalier, K. (2003). 'I'm not his wife': Doing gender and doing housework in the absence of women. *Journal of Sociology, 39,* 253–269.

National Association of Anorexia Nervosa and Associated Disorders. (2010). http://www. anad.org/getInformation/abouteatingdisorders. Accessed April 22, 2010.

National Coalition Against Domestic Violence. [Website]. Accessed July 10, 1999, at http: www.ncadv.org.

National Domestic Violence Hotline. (n.d.). Abuse in America. In *Break the silence, make the call.* Retrieved December 8, 2005, from http://www. ndvh.org/educate/abuse_in_america.html.

National Institute on Media and the Family. Retrieved June 8, 2007, from http://www. mediafamily.org/facts/facts_mediaeffect.shtml.

National Institute of Mental Health. (2010). http:// www.nimh.nih.gov/health/publications/eating-disorders/what-are-eating-disorders.shtml. Accessed April 22, 2010.

Naughton, K. (2004, January 5). A new campus crusader. *Newsweek,* pp. 78–79.

Navarro, M. (2004, April 4). The very long legs of "Girls Gone Wild." *The New York Times,* Sec.

Navarro, M. (2005, Spring). Mexico: Activism and reflection. *Ms.,* p. 29.

Neighbors, C., Walker, D., Mbilinyi, L., O'Rourke, A., Edleson, J., Zegree, J., & Roffman, R. (2010). Normative misperceptions of abuse among perpetrators of intimate partner violence, *Violence against Women, 16*, 370–389.

Neinas, C. M. (2002, December 6). Can we avoid unintended consequences for men? *The Chronicle of Higher Education*, p. B8.

Nelson, A. (2000). The pink dragons are female. *Psychology of Women Quarterly, 24*, 137–144.

Nelson, C., Trzemzalski, J., Malkasian, K., Pfeffer, K. (2004, April). Expressions of incompetence, sexual fantasies, and sexualized hostility toward male and female faculty: A qualitative analysis of student comments on an anonymous faculty evaluation Web site. Presentation at Multicultural Psychology (Psy 493W/Psy 992), Michigan State University, East Lansing, MI.

Newburger, E. (1999). *The men they will become: The nature and nurture of male character*. Cambridge, MA: Perseus Books.

Newcombe, N. (2002, December 14). Is sociobiology ready for prime time? *The Chronicle of Higher Education*, pp. B10–B11.

No Comment. (2004, March). *The Progressive*, p. 11.

Noddings, N. (2002). *Starting at home: Caring and social policy*. Berkeley: University of California Press.

Nolen, S. (2005, Spring). "Not women anymore...": The Congo's rape survivors face pain, shame and AIDS. *Ms.*, pp. 56–58.

Nolen-Hoeksema, S. (2003). *Women who think too much*. New York: Henry Holt.

Norlund, R., & Rubin, A. (2010, May 31). Escaping marriage, but not lashes. *The New York Times*, p. A4.

Northrup, C. (1995). *Women's bodies, women's wisdom*. New York: Bantam.

Nunes, M. (2006). *Cyberspaces of everyday life*. Minneapolis: University of Minnesota Press.

O'Kelly, C. G., & Carney, L. S. (1986). *Women and men in society* (2nd ed.). Belmont, CA: Wadsworth.

Oliker, S. (1989). *Best friends and marriage: Exchange among women*. Berkeley: University of California Press.

Oliker, S. (2001). Gender and friendship. In D. Vannoy (Ed.), *Gender mosaics* (pp. 195–204). Los Angeles: Roxbury.

Olson, L., & Rauscher, E. (2011). We'll never be that kind of couple: The variability of intimate violence. In D. O. Braithwaite & J. T. Wood (Eds.), *Casing interpersonal communication* (pp. 149–156). Dubuque, IA: Kendall-Hunt.

Olyslager, F., & Conway, L. (2007). On the calculation of the prevalence of transsexualism. Paper presented at the WPATH 20th International Symposium, Chicago, Illinois, September 5–8.

O'Neill, R., & Colley, A. (2006). Gender and status effects in student e-mails to staff. *Journal of Computer Assisted Learning, 22*, 360–367.

Onishi, H. (1998). Women in Japan and the USA: Identity status and its relationship to depression. Unpublished doctoral dissertation, University of Connecticut.

Onishi, N. (2007, April 28). Japan court rules against sex slaves and laborers. *The New York Times*, p. A5.

Orecklin, M. (2004, March 1). At what cost beauty? *Newsweek*, pp. 50–51.

Osher, C. (2007, June 4). Cop's firing over abuse claim reversed. *The Denver Post*, pp. 1A, 5A.

Ostrow, N. (2010, May 19). Men, too, suffer postpartum depression. *Raleigh News & Observer*, p. 5A.

O'Sullivan, L. F., & Gaines, M. E. (1998). Decision making in college students' heterosexual dating relationships: Ambivalence about engaging in sexual activity. *Journal of Social and Personal Relationships, 15*, 347–363.

Otten, A. L. (1995, January 27). Women and men still see things differently. *The Wall Street Journal*, p. B1.

Owen, D. (2007, Spring). A tragic tradition. *World Vision*, p. 25.

Painter, N. (1996). *Sojourner Truth: A life, a symbol*. New York: W. W. Norton.

Palomares, N. (2008). Gender salience and language. *Human Communication Research, 34*, 263–286.

Palomares, N. A. (2010). Gender-based language use: Understanding how and why men communicate similarly and differently. In M. B. Hinner (Ed.), *The interrelationship of business and communication* (pp. 74–96). Frankfurt, Germany: Peter Lang.

Panee, B. (1994). Defending the "date-rape crisis": A critical discussion of Katie Roiphe's *The morning after: Sex, fear, and feminism on campus*. Paper submitted in Communication Studies 111, University of North Carolina-Chapel Hill.

Panther, N. (2008). *Violence against women and femicide in Mexico*. Saarbruken, Germany: VDM Verlag.

Parker, P. (2006). *Race, gender, and leadership: Re-envisioning organizational leadership from the perspective of African American women*. Mahwah, NJ: Erlbaum.

Parker-Pope, T. (2007, November 6). For clues on teenage sex, experts look to hip-hop. *The New York Times*, pp. D5, D8.

Parker-Pope, T. (2008, June 10). Gay unions shed light on gender in marriage. *New York Times*, p. D1.

Parker-Pope, T. (2010a, February 16). As girls become women, sports pay dividends. *New York Times*, p. D5.

Parker-Pope, T. (2010b, July 6). Recalibrated formula eases women's workouts. *New York Times*, p. D5.

Parker-Pope, T. (2010c, April 6). Surprisingly, family time has grown. *New York Times*, p. D5.

Parks, S. (2010). *Fierce angels: The strong black woman in American life and culture.* New York: Random House.

Parlee, M. B. (1979, May). Conversational politics. *Psychology Today,* pp. 48–56.

Parrot, A., & Cummings, N. (2006). *Forsaken females: The global brutalization of women.* Lanham, MD: Rowman & Littlefield.

Patel, T. (2006). *Sex-selective abortion in India.* Thousand Oaks, CA: Sage.

Patterson, C. J. (2000). Family relationships of lesbians and gay men. *Journal of Marriage and the Family, 62,* 1052–1069.

Paul, P. (2006). *Pornified: How pornography is damaging our lives, our relationships and our families.* New York: Owl Books.

Pear, R. (2009, January 10). House passes 2 measures on job bias. *New York Times,* p. A13.

Pear, R. (2010, June 22). Gay workers get time to care for partner's sick child. *The New York Times,* p. A13.

Pearson, J., West, R., & Turner, L. (1995). *Gender and communication* (3rd ed). Dubuque, IA: Brown and Benchmark.

Pearson, J. C. (1985). *Gender and communication.* Dubuque, IA: William C. Brown.

Pennington, B. A., & Turner, L. H. (2004). Playground or training ground? The function of talk in African American and European American mother-adolescent daughter dyads. In P. M. Buzzanell, H. Sterk, & L. H. Turner (Eds.), *Gender in applied contexts* (pp. 275–294). Thousand Oaks, CA: Sage Publications.

Pennington, M. (2005, June 28). Rape victim pursues appeal. *Raleigh News & Observer,* p. 7A.

Peretti, P. O., & Abplanalp, R. R., Jr. (2004). Chemistry in the college dating process: Structure and function. *Social Behavior and Personality, 32,* 147–154.

Perry, I. (2003). Who(se) am I? The identity and image of women in hip-hop. In G. Dines & J. Humez (Eds.), *Gender, race, and class in media: A text reader* (2nd ed., pp. 136–148). Thousand Oaks, CA: Sage.

Pew Internet and American Life Project. (2004). Retrieved August 2, 2005, from http://207.21.232.103/pdfs/PIP_2004_Campaign.pdf.

Phelan, J. E., Moss-Racusin, C. A., & Rudman, L. A. (2007). *Competent yet out in the cold: Shifting standards reflect backlash toward agentic women.* Manuscript submitted for publication. Cited in Rudman & Glick, 2008.

Philipsen, M. I. (2008). *Challenges of the faculty career for women.* San Francisco: Jossey-Bass, Wiley.

Philipsen, M. I., & Bostic, T. P. (2010). *Helpping faculty find work-life balance: The path toward life-friendly institutions.* San Francisco: Jossey-Bass, Wiley.

Piaget, J. (1932/1965). *The moral judgment of the child.* New York: Free Press.

Piepmeier, A. (2009). *Girl zines: Making media, doing feminism.* New York: New York University Press.

Pinker, S. (2002). *The blank slate: Modern denial of human nature.* New York: Penguin.

Pinsky, L., Erickson, R., & Schimke, R. (Eds.). (1999). *Genetic disorders of human sexual development.* New York: Oxford University Press.

Pinsky, M. (2007, February 2). Churches ramp up to bring in men. *Raleigh News & Observer,* p. 4E.

Pitcher, K. C. (2006). The staging of agency in *Girls Gone Wild. Critical Studies in Media Communication, 23,* 200–218.

Pleck, J. H. (1981). *The myth of masculinity.* Cambridge: MIT Press.

Pollack, W. (1990). Sexual harassment: Women's experience vs. legal definitions. *Harvard Women's Law Review, 13,* 35–85.

Pollack, W. (2000). *Real boys: Rescuing ourselves from the myths of boyhood.* New York: Owl Books.

Pollitt, K. (1994). *Reasonable creatures: Essays on women and feminism.* New York: Knopf.

Pollitt, K. (2000, May 1). Abortion History 101. *The Nation,* p. 8.

Ponton, L. (1997). *The romance of risk: Why teenagers do the things they do.* New York: Basic Books.

Pope, H., Phillips, K., & Olivardia, R. (2002). *The Adonis complex: The secret crisis of male body obsession.* New York: Simon & Schuster.

Popenoe, D. (1996). *Life without father.* New York: Free Press.

Porter, B. (2007, Spring). Changing his name. *Ms.,* p. 17.

Porter, E. (2006a, March 3). Fewer women entering workplace. *Raleigh News & Observer,* p. 3A.

Porter, E. (2006b, March 2). Stretched to limit, women stall march to work. *New York Times,* pp. A1, C2.

Potter, W. J. (2009). Media literacy. In W. F. Eadie (Ed.), *21st century communication: A reference handbook* (pp. 534–542). Thousand Oaks, CA: Sage.

Powell, G., & Graves, L. (2006). Gender and leadership: Perceptions and realities. In K. Dindia & D. Canary (Eds.), *Sex differences and similarities in communication* (pp. 83–97). Mahwah, NJ: Erlbaum.

Powell, J. (2007, June 26). Curves resurge. *Raleigh News & Observer,* pp. 1E, 3E.

Powlishta, K., Serbin, L., & Moller, L. (1993). The stability of individual differences in gender typing: Implications for understanding gender segregation. *Sex Roles, 29,* 723–788.

Pozner, J. (2004, Fall). The unreal world. *Ms.,* pp. 50–53.

Pozner, J. (2005, Fall). Dove's "real beauty" backlash. *Bitch*, p. 15.

Pozner, J., & Seigel, J. (2005, Spring). Desperately debating housewives. *Ms.*, pp. 40–43.

Preston, J. (2009a, October 30). Officals endorse asylum for abuse. *New York Times*, pp. A12, A20.

Preston, J. (2009b, July 16). New policy permits asylum for battered women. *New York Times*, pp. A1, A18.

Preves, S. (2004). Sexing the intersexed: An analysis of sociocultural responses to intersexuality. In J. Spade & C. Valentine (Eds.), *The kaleidoscope of gender: Prisms, patterns, and possibilities* (pp. 31–45). Belmont, CA: Thomson/Wadsworth.

The Profession. (August 27, 2010). *The Chronicle of Higher Education*, pp. 20–24.

Promise Keepers: "Men have dropped the ball." (1997, October 1). *USA Today*, p. 14A.

Pruett, M. K., & Pruett, K. (2009). *Partnership parenting*. Cambridge, MA: DaCapo Lifelong Books.

Puka, B. (1990). The liberation of caring: A different voice for Gilligan's different voice. *Hypatia*, 5, 59–82.

Putney, C. (2003). *Muscular Christianity*. Cambridge, MA: Harvard University Press.

Quindlen, A. (2003a, April 7). Not so safe back home. *Newsweek*, p. 72.

Quinn, K. (2010). Tenure Clock Extension Policies: Who uses them and to what effect? *Journal about Women in Higher Education, 3*, 182–206.

Quinn, K. & Litzler, E. (2009). Turning away from academic careers: What does work-family have to do with it? *Journal about Women in Higher Education, 2*, 66–90.

Rabidue v. Osceola Refining Company. 805F 2nd 611, 626 Cir. (6th Cir. 1986).

Radford-Hill, S. (2000). *Further to fly: Black women and the politics of empowerment*. Minneapolis: University of Minnesota Press.

Ramasubramanian, S. (2010). Television viewing, racial attitudes, and policy preferences: Exploring the role of social identity and intergroup emotions in influencing support for affirmative action. *Communication Monographs, 77*, 102–120.

Ramey, G., & Ramey, V. A. (2009, August). The rug rat race. NBER Working Paper No. w15284. Available at http://ssrn.com/abstract=1459585. Accessed April 6, 2010.

Ransby, B. (2003). *Ella Baker and the Black Freedom Movement: A radical democratic vision*. Chapel Hill: University of North Carolina Press.

Ranson, G. (2001). Men at work: Change—or no change?—in the era of the "new father." *Men and Masculinities, 4*, 3–26.

Rasmussen, J. L., & Moley, B. E. (1986). Impression formation as a function of the sex

role appropriateness of linguistic behavior. *Sex Roles, 14*, 149–161.

Reich, M. (1991). *Toxic politics: Responding to chemical disasters*. Ithaca, NY: Cornell University Press.

Reisman, J. M. (1990). Intimacy in same-sex friendships. *Sex Roles, 23*, 65–82.

Reiss, D. (2000). *The relational code: Genetic and social influences on social development*. Cambridge, MA: Harvard University Press.

Renzetti, C. (2008). *Feminist criminology*. New York: Routledge.

Reskin, B. (2003). Including mechanisms in our models of ascriptive inequality. *American Sociological Review, 6*, 1–21.

Retherford, R. D., Ogawa, N., & Matsukura, R. (2001). Late marriage and less marriage in Japan. *Population and Development Review, 27*, 65–102.

Reuther, R. R. (Ed.). (1974). *Religion and sexism: Images of woman in the Jewish and Christian traditions*. New York: Simon & Schuster.

Reuther, R. R. (1983). *Sexism and Godtalk: Toward a feminist theology*. Boston: Beacon.

Reuther, R. R. (2001). Ecofeminism and healing ourselves, healing the earth. In D. Vannoy (Ed.), *Gender mosaics* (pp. 406–414). Los Angeles: Roxbury.

Rhoads, S. E. (2004). *Taking sex differences seriously*. San Francisco: Encounter Books.

Rich, M. (2008). Music videos: Media of the youth, by the youth, for the youth. In P. E. Jamieson & D. Romer (Eds.), *The changing portrayal of adolescents in the media since 1950* (pp. 78–102). New York: Oxford University Press.

Richmond, V., & McCroskey, J. (2000). *Nonverbal behavior in interpersonal relations* (4th ed). Boston: Allyn & Bacon.

Richtel, M. (2000, February 6). Online revolution's latest twist: Computers screening job seekers. *The New York Times*, p. A1.

Rhode, D. (2010). *The beauty bias: The injustice of appearance in life and law*. New York: Oxford University Press.

Riessman, C. K. (1990). *Divorce talk: Women and men make sense of personal relationships*. New Brunswick, NJ: Rutgers University Press.

Rimer, S. (2005, February 19). Rift deepens as professors at Harvard see remarks. *The New York Times*, p. A10.

Risman, B., & Godwin, S. (2001). Twentieth-century changes in economic work and family. In D. Vannoy (Ed.), *Gender mosaics* (pp. 134–144). Los Angeles: Roxbury.

Risman, B. J. (1989). Can men mother? Life as a single father. In B. J. Risman & P. Schwartz (Eds.), *Gender in intimate relationships* (pp. 155–164). Belmont, CA: Wadsworth.

Rivero, Y. (2007, Winter). Beautiful Betty. *Ms.*, pp. 65–66.

Rives, K. (2005, May 22). Keep up appearances. *Raleigh News & Observer*, p. 1A.

Roberts, S. (2007, January 16). 51% of women are now living without spouse. *The New York Times*, pp. A1, A19.

Rohlfing, M. (1995). "Doesn't anybody stay in one place anymore?": An exploration of the understudied phenomenon of long-distance relationships. In J. T. Wood & S. W. Duck (Eds.), *Understanding personal relationships, 6: Understudied relationships: Off the beaten track* (pp. 173–196). Thousand Oaks, CA: Sage.

Roiphe, K. (1993). The morning after: Sex, *fear, and feminism on campus*. Boston: Little, Brown.

Romaine, S. (1999). *Communicating gender*. Mahwah, NJ: Erlbaum.

Romer, D. (2008). Introduction: Mass media and the socialization of adolescents since World War II. In P. E. Jamieson & D. Romer (Eds.), *The changing portrayal of adolescents in the media since 1950* (pp. 3–24). New York: Oxford University Press.

Roosevelt, M. (2010, January 14). When the gym isn't enough. *New York Times*, pp. E1, E8.

Rose, B. (2008, June 8). Even the geeks are sexist. *Raleigh News & Observer*, p. 7G.

Rose, N. S. (2007). *The politics of life itself: Biomedicine, power, and subjectivity in the twenty-first century*. Princeton: Princeton University Press.

Rosenberg, D. (2007, May 21). (Rethinking) gender. *Newsweek*, pp. 50–57.

Rosenbloom, S. (2008, February 21). Sorry, boys, this is our domain. *New York Times*, pp. E1, E8.

Rosenthal, E. (2006, October 6). Women face greatest threat of violence at home, study finds. *The New York Times*, p. A5.

Roth, B. (2003). *Separate roads to feminism in America's second wave*. Cambridge, UK: Cambridge University Press.

Rowe-Finkbeiner, K. (2004). *The F word: Feminism in jeopardy*. Emeryville, CA: Seal Press.

Rowling, M. (2002, July 22). Europe crawls ahead. *In These Times*, pp. 15–17.

Rubin, J. Z., Provenzano, F. J., & Luria, Z. (1974). The eye of the beholder: Parents' views on sex of newborns. *American Journal of Orthopsychiatry, 44*, 512–519.

Ruble, D., & Martin, C. (1998). Gender development. In W. Damon (Ed.), *The handbook of child psychology* (pp. 933–1017). New York: Wiley.

Ruddick, S. (1989). *Maternal thinking: Toward a politics of peace*. Boston: Beacon.

Rudacille, D. (2006). *The riddle of gender*. New York: Anchor.

Rudman, L. A., & Fairchild, K. (2004). Reactions to counterstereotypic behavior: The role of backlash in cultural stereotype maintenance. *Journal of Personality and Social Psychology, 87*, 157–176.

Rudman, L. A., & Glick, P. (2008). *The social psychology of gender*. New York: Guilford Press.

Rudman, L. A., & Phelan, J. E. (2007). The interpersonal power feminism: Is feminism good for relationships? Sex *Roles, 57*, 787–799.

Rundblad, G. (2001). Gender, power, and sexual harassment. In D. Vannoy (Ed.), *Gender mosaics* (pp. 352–362). Los Angeles: Roxbury.

Rusbult, C. (1987). Responses to dissatisfaction in close relationships: The exit-voice-loyalty-neglect model. In D. Perlman & S. W. Duck (Eds.), *Intimate relationships: Development, dynamics, and deterioration* (pp. 209–238). London: Sage.

Rutenberg, J. (2009, June 24). Obama team to add protections for transgender federal employees. *New York Times*, p. A15.

Rutter, V., & Schwartz, P. (1996). Same-sex couples: Courtship, commitment, and context. In A. Auhagen & M. von Salisch (Eds.), *The diversity of human relationships* (pp. 197–226). New York: Cambridge University Press.

Ryan, B. (2004). Identity politics in the women's movement. In J. Spade & C. Valentine (Eds.), *The kaleidoscope of gender: Prisms, patterns, and possibilities* (pp. 104–113). Belmont, CA: Thomson/Wadsworth.

Ryan, K., & Kanjorski, J. (1998). The enjoyment of sexist humor, rape attitudes, and relationship aggression in college students. *Sex Roles, 38*, 743–755.

Sacks, P. (2007, January 12). How colleges perpetuate inequality. *The Chronicle of Higher Education*, pp. B9–B10.

Sagrestano, L., Heavey, C., & Christensen, A. (1998). Theoretical approaches to understanding sex differences and similarities in conflict behavior. In D. J. Canary & K. Dindia (Eds.), *Sex differences and similarities in communication: Critical essays and empirical investigations of sex and gender in interaction* (pp. 287–302). Mahwah, NJ: Erlbaum.

Sales, K. (1987, September 26). Ecofeminism—a new perspective. *The Nation*, pp. 302–305.

Salomone, R. (2003). *Same, different, equal: Rethinking single-sex schooling*. New Haven, CT: Yale University Press.

Salome, R. (2007, February 16). A place for women's colleges. *The Chronicle of Higher Education*, p. B20.

Samovar, L., Porter, R., & Stefani, L. (1998). *Communication between cultures* (2nd ed). Belmont, CA: Wadsworth.

Samuel, R., Kisimir, J., & Schenk, J. (2007, Spring). Sex trafficking. *World Vision*, p. 27.

Samuels, A. (2008, July 7–14). A new color clash on the catwalk. *Newsweek*, p. 12.

Sanday, P. (2007). *Fraternity gang rape: Sex, brotherhood, and privilege on campus*, 2nd ed. New York: New York University Press.

Sander, L. (2010, April 30). Education Department ends Bush-era policy on Title IX compliance. *Chronicle of Higher Education*, p. A14.

Sandler, B. (2004). The chilly climate: Subtle ways in which women are often treated differently at work and in classrooms. In J. Spade & C. Valentine (Eds.), *The kaleidoscope of gender: Prisms, patterns, and possibilities* (pp. 187–190). Belmont, CA: Thomson/Wadsworth.

Sanger, M. (1914, June). Suppression. *The Woman Rebel*, p. 1.

Sarkela, S. J., Ross, S. R., & Lowe, M. A. (2003). *From megaphones to microphones: Speeches of American women, 1920–1960*. Westport, CT: Praeger.

Sartre, J. P. (1966). *Being and nothingness: An essay in phenomenological ontology*. New York: Citadel.

Saucier, D., & Kimura, D. (1998). Intrapersonal motor, but not extra-personal targeting skill is enhanced during the midluteal phase of the menstrual cycle. *Developmental Neuropsychology, 14*, 385–398.

Saxen, R. (2007). *Good eater: The true story of one man's struggle with binge eating disorder*. Oakland, CA: New Harbinger Publications.

Scelfo, J. (2002, December 9). Kneed to know. *Newsweek*, pp. 88, 90.

Scelfo, J. (2006, November 6). Extreme makeovers. *Newsweek*, pp. 56–57.

Scelfo, J. (2007, February 26). Men & depression: Facing darkness. *Newsweek*, pp. 42–47.

Schaap, J. (2010). "Corrective rape." Video shown on ESPN May 10, 2010. http://espn.go.com/video/clip?id=5181871

Schechter, T. (2005). *I was a teenage feminist: A documentary about redefining the F-word* [Motion picture]. Cambridge, MA: Trixiefilms. (Available from http://www.trixiefilms.com).

Schiebinger, L., & Gilmartin, S. K. (2010, January-February). Housework is an academic issue. *Academe*, 39–44.

Schiff, S. (2006, October 13). Desperately seeking Susan. *The New York Times*, p. A27.

Schilt, K. R. (2007, August 11) "Doing Gender in Open Workplace Transitions: The Power of Homosocial Reproduction." Paper *presented at the annual meeting of the American Sociological Association*, New York City, New York.

Schilt, K. (2010). *Just one of the guys? Transgender men and the persistence of inequality*. Chicago: University of Chicago Press.

Schilt, K. R., & Wiswall, M. (2008). Before and after: Gender transitions, human capital, and workplace experiences. *Berkeley Electronic Journal of Economic Analysis & Policy*. http://www.bepress.com/bejeap/vol8/iss1/art39/ Accessed October 28, 2008.

Schmetzer, U. (1997, August 13). From abused wife to India's avenging angel. *Raleigh News & Observer*, p. 13A.

Schmidt, P. (2010, March 26). Male professors face their own challenges in balancing work and home. *Chronicle of Higher Education*, p. A8–A10.

Schneider, J., & Hacker, S. (1973). Sex role imagery and use of the generic "man" in introductory texts: A case in the sociology of sociology. *American Sociologist, 8*, 12–18.

Schroeder, L. O. (1986). A rose by any other name: Post-marital right to use maiden name: 1934–1982. *Sociology and Social Research, 70*, 290–293.

Schooler, D., Ward, M., Merriwether, A., & Caruthers, A. (2004). Who's that girl: Television's role in the body image of young white and black women. *Psychology of Women Quarterly, 28*, 38–47.

Schwalbe, M. (1996). *Unlocking the cage: The men's movement, gender, politics, and American culture*. Cambridge, MA: Oxford University Press.

Schwartz, B., & Cellini, H. (1995). Female sex offenders. In B. Schwartz & H. Cellini (Eds.), *The sex offender: Corrections, treatment, and legal practice* (Vol. 1, pp. 51–52). Kingston, NJ: Civic Research Institute.

Schwartz, F. (1989, January/February). Management women and the new facts of life. *Harvard Business Review*, pp. 65–76.

Schwartz, P., & Rutter, V. (1998). *The gender of sexuality*. Newbury Park, CA: Pine Forge Press.

Scrivner, R. (1997). Gay men and nonrelational sex. In R. Levant & G. Brooks (Eds.), *Men and sex* (pp. 229–257). New York: Wiley.

Seattle Times, July 9, 2009. http://seattletimes.nwsource.com/html/books/2009437319_steinem10.html

Sedgwick, E. (1990). *Epistemology of the closet*. Berkeley: University of California Press.

Seely, M. (2007). *Fight like a girl*. New York: New York University Press.

Segerstråle, U. (2000). *Defenders of the truth: The battle for science in the sociobiology debate and beyond*. Oxford, UK: Oxford University Press.

Segrin, C., & Flora, F. J. (2005). *Family communication*. Mahwah, NJ: Erlbaum.

Seligman, K. (2007, May 20). The motherhood movement. *San Francisco Chronicle Magazine*, pp. 10–15, 19.

Sen, J., & Saini, M. (2005). *Are other worlds possible? Talking new politics*. New Delhi, India: Zubaan.

Setoodeh, R. (2006, December 11). Get ready to rumble. *Newsweek*, p. 46.

Sexually harassed male guard awarded $3.75 million. (1999, May 30). *Raleigh News & Observer*, p. 9A.

Shah, S. (2011, April 22). Pakistan frees 5 accused in court-ordered gang rape. *Raleigh News & Observer*, p. 4A.

Shandler, S. (1999). *Ophelia speaks: Adolescent girls write about their search for self*. New York: HarperPerennial.

Shapiro, T. (2007). The hidden cost of being African American. In M. Andersen & P. H. Collins (Eds.), *Race, class, & gender*, 6th ed (pp. 127–135). Thousand Oaks, CA: Sage.

Shea, C. (1998, January 30). Why depression strikes more women than men: "Ruminative coping" may provide answers. *The Chronicle of Higher Education*, p. A14.

Sheehy, G. (2010). *Passages in caregiving*. New York: William Morrow.

Shelton, M. (2008, May-June). Forced into manhood: Males and homesickness at camp. *Camping Magazine*, pp. 41–45.

Shepard, B. (2008). *Queer political performance and protest*. New York: Routledge.

Shepherd, M. E. (2008). *Sex-selective abortion in India*. Amherst, NY: Cambria Press.

Sheridan-Rabideau, M. P. (2009). *Girls, feminism, and grassroots literacies: Activism in the Girlzone*. New York: SUNY Press.

Sherrod, D. (1989). The influence of gender on same-sex friendships. In C. Hendrick (Ed.), *Close relationships* (pp. 164–186). Newbury Park, CA: Sage.

Shimron, Y. (1997, January 22). Men unite to live their faith. *Raleigh News & Observer*, pp. 1A, 6A.

Shimron, Y. (2002, July 21). Promise Keepers fill the house—and heart. *Raleigh News & Observer*, pp. 1A, 17A.

Shimron, Y. (2006, June 16). Promise Keepers return. *Raleigh News & Observer*, p. 1E.

Shimron, Y. (2007, May 10). Christians test masculine side. *Raleigh News & Observer*, pp. 1B, 7B.

Shugart, H. A., Waggoner, C. E., & Hallstein, D. L. O. (2001). Mediating third-wave feminism: Appropriation as postmodern media practice. *Critical Studies in Media Communication, 18*, 194–210.

Silverstein, L., Auerbach, C., Grieco, L., & Dunkel, F. (1999). Do Promise Keepers dream of feminist sheep? *Sex Roles, 40*, 665–688.

Silverstein, L. B. (2002). Fathers and families. In J. P. McHale & W. S. Grolnick (Eds.), *Retrospect and prospect in the psychological study of families* (pp. 35–64). Mahwah, NJ: Erlbaum.

Simmons, R. (2002). *Odd girl out: The hidden culture of aggression in girls*. New York: Harcourt.

Simmons, R. (2004). *Odd girl speaks out: Girls write about bullies, cliques, popularity, and jealousy*. Orlando, FL: Harvest Books.

Sloop, J. (2004). *Disciplining gender: Rhetorics of sex identity in contemporary U.S. culture*. Amherst: University of Massachusetts Press.

Sloop, J. (2006). Critical studies in gender/ sexuality and media. In B. Dow & J. T. Wood (Eds.), *Handbook of gender and communication* (pp. 319–333). Thousand Oaks, CA: Sage.

Smeal, E. (2004, May 10). A crucial coalition. *Ms.*, pp. 25, 35.

Smith, B. (1998). Black feminism. In W. Mankiller, G. Mink, M. Navarro, B. Smith, & G. Steinem (Eds.), *The reader's companion to U.S. women's history* (pp. 202–204). New York: Houghton Mifflin.

Smith, B. (2006, August 24). Women at the Citadel report sexual assaults. *Raleigh News & Observer*, p. 7A.

Smith, D. (2004a, February 8). Gay animals not uncommon. *Raleigh News & Observer*, p. 7A.

Smith, D. (2004b). Schooling for inequality. In J. Spade & C. Valentine (Eds.), *The kaleidoscope of gender: Prisms, patterns, and possibilities* (pp. 183–186). Belmont, CA: Thomson/ Wadsworth.

Smith, N. (1998). Guerrilla girls. In W. Mankiller, G. Mink, M. Navarro, B. Smith, & G. Steinem (Eds.), *The reader's companion to U.S. women's history* (p. 250). New York: Houghton Mifflin.

Smith, S. (2005). From Dr. Dre to Dismissed: Assessing violence, sex, and substance use on MTV. *Critical Studies in Media Communication, 22*, 89–98.

Smith, V. (1998). *Not just race, not just gender: Black feminist readings*. New York: Routledge.

Snow, J. (2004). *How it feels to have a gay or lesbian parent*. New York: Harrington Park Press.

Socha, T. J., Sanchez-Hucles, J., Bromley, J., & Kelly, B. (1995). Invisible parents and children: Exploring African-American parent-child communication. In T. J. Socha & G. H. Stamp (Eds.), *Parents, children and communication: Frontiers of theory and research* (pp. 127–145). Mahwah, NJ: Erlbaum.

Solomon, B. (1986). *In the company of educated women*. New Haven, CT: Yale University Press.

Sommers, C. (2000). *The war against boys: How misguided feminism is harming our young men*. New York: Simon & Schuster.

Sparks, G. (2006). *Media effects research* (2nd ed.). Belmont, CA: Thomson.

Spence, J., & Buckner, C. (2000). Instrumental and expressive traits, trait stereotypes and sexist attitudes: What do they signify? *Psychology of Women Quarterly, 24*, 44–62.

Spender, D. (1984a). *Man-made language*. London: Routledge and Kegan Paul.

Spender, D. (1984b). Defining reality: A powerful tool. In C. Kramarae, M. Schultz, & W. O'Barr

(Eds.), *Language and power* (pp. 195–205). Beverly Hills, CA: Sage.

Spitzack, C., & Carter, K. (1987). Women in communication studies: A typology for revision. *Quarterly Journal of Speech, 73,* 401–423.

Stacey, J. (1996). *In the name of the father: Rethinking family values in a postmodern age.* Boston: Beacon.

Stacey, J., & Biblarz, T. (2005). How does the sexual orientation of parents matter? *American Sociological Review, 63,* 18–33.

Stafford, L., Dutton, M., & Haas, S. (2000). Measuring routine maintenance: Scale revision, sex versus gender roles, and the prediction of relational characteristics. *Communication Monographs, 67,* 306–323.

Stafford, L., & Kline, S. (1996). Women's surnames and titles: Men's and women's views. *Communication Research Reports, 13,* 214–224.

Stansell, C. (2010). *The feminist promise.* New York: Random House.

Statistics. (2009). Rape, Abuse, and Incest National Network. Retrieved November 22, 2009, from http://www.rainn.org.

Stanton, E. C., Anthony, S. B., & Gage, M. J. (Eds.). (1882). *History of woman suffrage* (Vol. 1, p. 116). New York: Fowler & Wells.

Staples, B. (2005, May 12). How hip-hop music lost its way and betrayed its fans. *The New York Times,* p. A26.

Starling-Lyons, K. (2003, October 21). The gender game. *Raleigh News & Observer,* pp. 1E, 3E.

The state of the family. (2002). Washington, DC: Human Rights Foundation.

Steiner, L. M. (2007). *Mommy wars: Stay-at-home and career moms face off on their choices, their lives.* New York: Random House.

Stepp, L. S. (2007). *Unhooked: How young women pursue sex, delay love and lose at both.* New York: Penguin/Riverhead.

Stereotypes in costume. (2009, September-October). *Miller McCune,* p. 83.

Stewart, L. P., Stewart, A. D., Friedley, S. A., & Cooper, P. J. (1996). *Communication between the sexes: Sex differences and sex role stereotypes* (3rd ed.). Scottsdale, AZ: Gorsuch Scarisbrick.

Stone, P. (2007). *Opting out?: Why women really quit careers and head home.* Berkeley, CA: University of California Press.

Straus, S. (2004). Escape from animal house. In J. Spade & C. Valentine (Eds.), *The kaleidoscope of gender* (pp. 462–465). Belmont, CA: Thomson/Wadsworth.

Strauss, C., & Walsh, D. (2005, March 7). The courage to fight back. *People,* pp. 119–122.

Strauss, V. (2008, May 20). 'Boys crisis' in education debunked. *Raleigh News & Observer,* p. 5A.

Stroman, C. A., & Dates, J. L. (2008). African Americans, Latinos, Asians, and Native Americans in the media. In P. E. Jamieson &

D. Romer (Eds.), *The changing portrayal of adolescents in the media since 1950.* (pp. 198–219). New York: Oxford.

Strout, E. (2007, February 16). What the stopwatch doesn't tell. *The Chronicle of Higher Education,* pp. A44–A46.

Stryker, S. (1997). Over and out in academe: Transgender studies come of age. In G. Israel & D. Tarver II (Eds.), *Transgender care: Recommended guidelines, practical information, and personal accounts* (pp. 241–244). Philadelphia: Temple University Press.

Stryker, S. (1998). The transgender issue: An introduction. *GLQ: A Journal of Lesbian and Gay Studies, 4,* 145–158.

Study reveals new differences between the sexes. (2005, March 17). *The New York Times,* p. A23.

Sturm, S. (2001). Second generation employment discrimination. *Columbia Law Review, 101,* 458–568.

Suggs, W. (2005a, July 1). Gender quotas? Not in college sports. *The Chronicle of Higher Education,* pp. A24–A26.

Suggs, W. (2005b, April 15). New developments may alter enforcement of Title IX. *The Chronicle of Higher Education,* pp. A33–A34.

Sullivan, P. J., & Short, S. E. (2001). Furthering the construct of effective communication: A second version of the Scale for Effective Communication in Team Sports. Paper presented at the North American Society for the Psychology of Sport and Physical Activity (NASPSPA), St Louis, MO.

Superson, A., & Cudd, A. (Eds.). (2002). *Theorizing backlash: Philosophical reflections on the resistance to feminism.* Oxford, UK: Rowman & Littlefield.

Surrey, J. L. (1983). The relational self in women: Clinical implications. In J. V. Jordan, J. L. Surrey, & A. G. Kaplan (Speakers), *Women and empathy: Implications for psychological development and psychotherapy* (pp. 6–11). Wellesley, MA: Stone Center for Developmental Services and Studies.

Suter, E. (2004). Tradition never goes out of style: The role of tradition in women's naming practices. *Communication Review, 7,* 57–87.

Suter, E., & Oswald, R. (2003). Do lesbians change their last names in the context of a committed relationship? *Journal of Lesbian Studies, 7,* 71–83.

Swain, S. (1989). Covert intimacy: Closeness in men's friendships. In B. J. Risman & P. Schwartz (Eds.), *Gender and intimate relationships* (pp. 71–86). Belmont, CA: Wadsworth.

Switzer, J. Y. (1990). The impact of generic word choices: An empirical investigation of age- and sex-related differences. *Sex Roles, 22,* 69–82.

Tannen, D. (1990a). Gender differences in conversational coherence: Physical alignment and topical cohesion. In B. Dorval (Ed.), *Conversational organization and its development.* (Vol. XXXVIII, pp. 167–206). Norwood, NJ: Ablex.

Tannen, D. (1990b). *You just don't understand: Women and men in conversation.* New York: Morrow.

Tannen, D. (1995). *Talking 9 to 5: Women and men in the workplace.* New York: Avon.

Tanouye, E. (1996, June 28). Heredity theory says intelligence in males is "like mother, like son." *The Wall Street Journal,* p. B1.

Tarkan, L. (2009). Fathers gain respect from experts (and mothers). *New York Times,* pp. D5–D6.

Tavris, C. (1992). *The mismeasure of woman.* New York: Simon & Schuster.

Tavris, C. (2002, July 5). Are girls really as mean as books say they are? *The Chronicle of Higher Education,* pp. B7–B9.

Taylor, S. (2002). *The tending instinct: How nurturing is essential for who we are and how we live.* New York: Times Books.

Taylor, V., & Rupp, L. (1998). Lesbian organizations. In W. Mankiller, G. Mink, M. Navarro, B. Smith, & G. Steinem (Eds.), *The reader's companion to U.S. women's history* (pp. 330–332). New York: Houghton Mifflin.

Thomas, K. (2008, July 30). A lab is set to test the gender of some female athletes. *New York Times,* p. C9.

Thomas, K. (2011, April 26). College teams, relying on deception, undermine gender equity. *New York Times,* pp. A1, A18.

Thompson, E. H., Jr. (1991). The maleness of violence in dating relationships: An appraisal of stereotypes. *Sex Roles, 24,* 261–278.

Thornham, S. (2007). *Women, feminism, and media.* Edinburgh: Edinburgh University Press.

Tichenor, V. (2005). Maintaining men's dominance: Negotiating identity and power when she earns more. *Sex Roles, 53,* 191–205.

Tierney, J. (2005, May 24). What women want. *The New York Times,* p. A25.

Tierney, J. (2010, June 15). Legislation won't close gender gap in sciences. *New York Times,* p. D4.

Tiffs, S., & VanOsdol, P. (1991, February 4). A setback for pinups at work. *Time,* p. 61.

Tilsley, A. (2010, July 2). New policies accommodate transgender students. *Chronicle of Higher Education,* pp. A19–A20.

Timmers, M., Fischer, A. H., & Manstead, A. S. (1998). Gender differences in motives for regulating emotions. *Personality and Social Psychology Bulletin, 24,* 974–985.

Title IX Q & A. http://www.womenssports foundation.org/Content/Articles/Issues/Title%20IX/T/Title%20IX%20Q%20%20A.aspx. Accessed October 26, 2008.

Tootsie. (1994). Burbank, CA: RCA/Columbia Pictures.

Toubia, N. (1994). Female circumcision as a public health issue. *New England Journal of Medicine, 331,* 712–716.

Tough Guise. (1999). Media Education Foundation. Northampton, MA.

Townsley, N. (2006). Love, sex, and tech in the global workplace. In B. Dow & J. T. Wood (Eds.), *Handbook of gender and communication* (pp. 143–160). Thousand Oaks, CA: Sage.

Trad, P.V. (1995). Adolescent girls and their mothers: Realigning the relationship. *American Journal of Family Therapy, 23,* 11–24.

Trangsrud, K. (1994). Female genital mutilation: Recommendations for education and policy. *Carolina Papers in International Health and Development,* 1, n.p.

Trinh, M. (1989). *Woman, native, other: Writing postcoloniality and feminism.* Bloomington: Indiana University Press.

Trouble at the top. (1991, June 17). *U.S. News and World Report,* pp. 40–48.

Trower, C., & Quinn, K. (2009). Generation matters: What department chairs need to know about Gen X and Boomer pre-tenure faculty. *The Department Chair, 20,* 10–12.

Trudeau, M. (1996, June 4). *Morning edition.* Public Broadcasting System.

Turner, C. S. (2002). Women of color in the academe: Living with multiple marginality. *The Journal of Higher Education, 73,* 74–93.

Turner, C. S. (2003). Incorporation and marginalization in the academy: From border toward center for faculty of color? *Journal of Black Studies, 34,* 112–125.

Turner, R. (1998, December 14). Back in the Ms. biz. *Newsweek,* p. 67.

Tyre, P. (2006a, January 30). The trouble with boys. *Newsweek,* pp. 44–52.

Tyre, P. (2006b, March 6). Smart moms, hard choices. *Newsweek,* p. 55.

Tyre, P. (2008). *The trouble with boys: A surprising report card on our sons, their problems at school, and what parents and educators must do.* New York: Crown.

Tyre, P., & Scelfo, J. (2006, July 31). Why girls will be girls. *Newsweek,* pp. 46–47.

Udell, E. (2005, May 9). Where are the women? *In These Times,* p. 32.

Ueland, B. (1992, November/December). Tell me more: On the fine art of listening. *Utne Reader,* pp. 104–109.

Ugwu-Oju, D. (2000, December 4). My turn: Should my tribal past shape Delia's future? *Newsweek,* p. 14.

Underwood M. (2003). *Social aggression among girls.* New York: Guilford.

Unger, R. (1998). *Resisting gender: Twenty-five years of feminist psychology.* Thousand Oaks, CA: Sage.

Valentine, D. (2007). *Imagining transgender: An ethnography of a category*. Durham, NC: Duke University Press.

Valian, V. (1998). *Why so slow? The advancement of women*. Boston: MIT Press.

Vargas, V. (2003). Feminism, globalization and the global justice and solidarity movement. *Cultural Studies 17*, 905–920.

Vavrus, M. D. (2002). Domesticating patriarchy: Hegemonic masculinity and television's Mr. Mom. *Critical Studies in Media Communication, 19*, 352–375.

Veniegas, R., & Peplau, L. (1997). Power and the quality of same-sex friendships. *Psychology of Women Quarterly, 21*, 279–297.

Vincent, N. (2006). *Self made man: One woman's journey into manhood and back*. New York: Viking.

Vivian, J. (2006). *The media of mass communication,* 8th ed. Boston: Allyn & Bacon.

Vobejda, B., & Perlstein, L. (1998, June 7). Girls catching up with boys in ways good and bad, study finds. *Raleigh News & Observer*, pp. 1A, 14A.

Voice of the Shuttle. http://vos.ucsb.edu/browse.asp?id=1810. Accessed March 22, 2010.

Waddell, L., & Campo-Flores, A. (2007, March 12). A case of gender blues. *Newsweek,* p. 51.

Wade, N. (2009, September 15). New clues to sex anomalies in how Y chromosomes are copied. *New York Times,* p. D4.

Wadsworth, B. (1996). *Piaget's theory of cognitive and affective development*. New York: Addison-Wesley.

Wagenheim, J. (1990, September/October). The secret life of men. *New Age Journal,* pp. 40–45, 106–118.

Wagenheim, J. (1996, January-February). Among the Promise Keepers. *Utne Reader,* pp. 74–77.

Waismel-Manor, R., & Tolbert, P. (2010). Earnings differences in dual earner couples. International Sociological Association Conference. Gothenburg, Sweden.

Walker, A. (1983). *In search of our mothers' gardens*. New York: Harcourt Brace Jovanovich.

Walker, K. (2004). Men, women, and friendship: What they say, what they do. In J. Spade & C. Valentine (Eds.), *The kaleidoscope of gender: Prisms, patterns, and possibilities* (pp. 403–413). Belmont, CA: Thomson/Wadsworth.

Walker, S. (2007). *Style and status: Selling beauty to African American women*. Lexington, KY: University of Kentucky Press.

Walsh, J. L., & Ward, L. M. (2008). Adolescent gender role portrayals in the media: 1950 to the present. In P. E. Jamieson & D. Romer (Eds.), *The changing portrayal of adolescents in the media since 1950* (pp. 132–164). New York: Oxford.

Warin, J. (2000). The attainment of self-consistency through gender in young children. *Sex Roles, 42,* 209–231.

Warner, J. (2005). *Mommy madness*. New York: Penguin/Riverhead Books.

Warren, C. (2003). Communicating about sex with parents and partners. In K. M. Galvin & P. J. Cooper (Eds.), *Making connections: Readings in relational communication* (pp. 317–324). Los Angeles: Roxbury.

Warren, K. (2000). *Ecofeminist philosophy: A Western perspective on what it is and why it matters*. Lanham, MD: Rowman & Littlefield.

Wartik, N. (2002, June 23). Hurting more, helped less? *The New York Times,* pp. 15–1, 15–6, 15–7.

Watt, H. M. G., & Eccles, J.S. (Eds.). (2008). *Gender and occupational outcomes*. Washington, DC: American Psychological Association.

Watzlawick, P., Beavin, J., & Jackson, D. D. (1967). *Pragmatics of human communication*. New York: W. W. Norton.

Way, N. (1998). *Everyday courage*. New York: New York University Press.

Way, N. (2010). *Deep secrets: The hidden landscape of boys' friendships*. Cambridge, MA: Harvard University Press.

Webb, L. M., Walker, K. L., Bollis, T. S., & Hebbani, A. G. (2004). Perceived parental communication, gender, and young adults' self-esteem. In O. M. Backlund & M. R. Williams (Eds.), *Readings in gender communication* (pp. 197–224). Belmont, CA: Thomson/Wadsworth.

Weber, B. R. (2009). *Makeover TV: Selfhood, citizenship, and celebrity*. Durham, NC: Duke University Press.

Weekes, C. (2004). Where my girls at? Black girls and the construction of the sexual. In A. Harris (Ed.), *All about the girl* (pp. 141–153). London: Routledge.

Wegner, H., Jr. (2005). Disconfirming communication and self-verification in marriage: Associations among the demand/withdraw interaction pattern, feeling understood, and marital satisfaction. *Journal of Social and Personal Relationships, 22,* 19–31.

Weiss, D. M., & Sachs, J. (1991). Persuasive strategies used by preschool children. *Sociology, 97,* 114–142.

Welter, B. (1966). The cult of true womanhood: 1820–1960. *American Quarterly, 18,* 151–174.

Wentley, T., Schilt, K., Windsor, E., & Lucal, E. (2008). Teaching transgender issues. *Teaching Sociology,* 49–57.

Werking, K. (1997). *We're just good friends: Women and men in nonromantic relationships*. New York: Guilford.

West, C. (2007). Black sexuality: The taboo subject. In M. Andersen & P. H. Collins (Eds.),

Race, class, gender: An anthology (6th ed., pp. 247–252). Belmont, CA: Thomson.

West, C., & Zimmerman, D. H. (1983). Small insults: A study of interruptions in cross-sex conversations between unacquainted persons. In B. Thorne, C. Kramarae, & N. Henley (Eds.), *Language, gender and society* (pp. 102–117). Rowley, MA: Newbury House.

West, L., Anderson, J., & Duck, S. W. (1996). Crossing the barriers to friendship between women and men. In J. T. Wood (Ed.), *Gendered relationships: A reader* (pp. 111–127). Mountain View, CA: Mayfield.

Weston, K. (1999). *Love makes a family: Portraits of lesbian, gay, bisexual, and transgender parents and their families.* Amherst: University of Massachusetts Press.

Wetherell, M. (1997). Linguistic repertoires and literary criticism. New directions for a social psychology of gender. In M. Gergen & S. Davis (Eds.), *Toward a new psychology of gender* (pp. 149–165). New York: Routledge.

Wharton, A. S. (2004). Feminism at work. In J. Spade & C. Valentine (Eds.), *The kaleidoscope of gender: Prisms, patterns, and possibilities* (pp. 347–356). Belmont, CA: Thomson/Wadsworth.

Whitaker, S. (2001). Gender politics in men's movements. In D. Vannoy (Ed.), *Gender mosaics* (pp. 343–351). Los Angeles: Roxbury.

White, A. M. (2006). "You've got a friend": African American men's cross-sex feminist friendships and their influence on perceptions of masculinity and women. *Journal of Social and Personal Relationships, 23,* 523–542.

White, A. M. (2008). *Ain't I a feminist? African American men speak out on fatherhood, friendship, forgiveness, and freedom.* New York: State University of New York Press.

Whitehead, B. (1997, October 3). Soccer dads march on Washington. *The Wall Street Journal,* p. A10.

Whitehead, S. (Ed). (2006).*Men and masculinities.* New York: Routledge.

White Ribbon Campaign. (n.d.). Retrieved May 20, 2003, from http://www.whiteribbon.com.

Whitmire, R. (2008, July 25). A tough time to be a girl: Gender imbalance on campuses. *Chronicle of Higher Education,* p. A23.

Who's Talking Research. (2001). The White House Project. New York. Available at: www.thewhitehouseproject.org.

Who's Talking Research. (2002). The White House Project. New York. Available at: www.thewhitehouseproject.org.

Who's Talking Research. (2005). The White House Project. New York. Available at: www.thewhitehouseproject.org.

Wiesmann, S., Boeije, H, van Doorne-Huiskes, A, & den Dulk, L. (2008). 'Not worth mentioning': The implicit and explicit nature of decision-making about the division of paid and domestic work. *Community, Work & Family, 11,* 341–363.

Willer, E. (2011). The queen and her bee: Social aggression in female friendship. In D. O. Braithwaite & J. T. Wood (Eds.), *Casing interpersonal communication* (pp. 189–196). Dubuque, IA: Kendall-Hunt.

Williams, D. (1985). Gender, masculinity, femininity, and emotional intimacy in same-sex friendship. *Sex Roles, 12,* 587–600.

Williams, J. C. (2004). Hitting the maternal wall. *Academe, 90,* 16–20.

Williams, J. C., & Calvert, C. T. (2005–2007). *Worklife Law's guide to family responsibilities discrimination.* University of CA College of Law: Center for Worklife Law.

Williamson, G., & Silverman, J. (2001). Violence against female partners: Direct and interactive effects of family history, communal orientation, and peer-related variables. *Journal of Social and Personal Relationships, 18,* 535–549.

Willis, E. (1992). *No more nice girls: Counter-cultural essays.* Hanover, NH: Wesleyan University Press.

Wills, T. A., Weiss, R. L., & Patterson, G. R. (1974). A behavioral analysis of the determinants of marital satisfaction. *Journal of Consulting and Clinical Psychology, 42,* 802–811.

Wilson, C., Gutiérrez, F., & Chao, L. (2003). *Racism, sexism, and the media.* Thousand Oaks, CA: Sage.

Wilson, D. (2010, June 17). Big push of pill to marketplace stirs debate on sexual desire. *The New York Times,* pp. A1, A2.

Wilson, E. (1975). *Sociobiology: The new synthesis.* Cambridge, MA: Harvard University Press, Belknap.

Wilson, E. (2010, January 14). The triumph of the size 12's. *New York Times,* pp. E1, E6.

Wilson, M. (2004, Summer). Closing the leadership gap. *Ms.,* pp. 14–15.

Wilson, R. (2004a, January 23). Louts in the lab. *The Chronicle of Higher Education,* pp. A7, A9.

Wilson, R. (2004b, October 29). Report shows difficulty of sex-discrimination lawsuits. *The Chronicle of Higher Education,* p. A12.

Wilson, R. (2005a, January 7). On parental leave, men have it easier. *The Chronicle of Higher Education,* p. A25.

Wilson, R. (2005c, October 7). Second sex. *Chronicle of Higher Education,* pp. A10–A12.

Wilson, R. (2007, January 26). The new gender divide. *Chronicle of Higher Education,* pp. A36–A39.

Wilson, R. (2009, February 20). Notoriety yields to tragedy in Iowa sexual harassment cases. *Chronicle of Higher Education,* pp. A1, A8–A13.

Winik, L. W., & Massey, M. (2009, January 18). A new push for equal pay. *Parade,* p. 8.

Winstead, B. A. (1986). Sex differences in same-sex friendships. In V. J. Derlega & B. A. Winstead

(Eds.), *Friendship and social interaction* (pp. 81–99). New York: Springer-Verlag.

Wise, S., & Stanley, L. (1987). *Georgie Porgie: Sexual harassment in everyday life.* New York: Pandora.

Wolf, N. (1991). *The beauty myth.* New York: Morrow.

Wolf, N. (1993). *Fire with fire: The new female power and how it will change the 21st century.* New York: Random House.

Wolf, N. (2006, March 12). Wild things. *New York Times Book Review,* pp. 22–23.

Wolfe, D., & Feiring, C. (2000). Dating violence through the lens of adolescent romantic relationships. *Child Maltreatment, 5,* 360–363.

Wolverton, B. (2006, July 28). Crying foul over postseason opportunities. *The Chronicle of Higher Education,* pp. A26–A27.

Women and Science. (2005, Spring/Summer). *The Stone Center Report,* pp. 9–11.

Women "Take Care," Men "Take Charge": Stereotyping of U.S. Business Leaders Exposed. Catalyst report. Retrieved November 9, 2005, from http://www.catalyst.org/xcart/product.php?productid=16181.

Woo, D. (2001). The gap between striving and achieving: The case of Asian American women. In M. Anderson & P. H. Collins (Eds.), *Race, class, and gender: An anthology* (4th ed., pp. 243–251). Belmont, CA: Wadsworth.

Wood, J.T. (1993b). Engendered identities: Shaping voice and mind through gender. In D. Vocate (Ed.), *Intrapersonal communication: Different voices, different minds* (pp. 145–167). Hillsdale, NJ: Erlbaum.

Wood, J. T. (1993e). Gender and relationship crises: Contrasting reasons, responses, and relational orientations. In J. Ringer (Ed.), *Queer words, queer images: The (re) construction of homosexuality* (pp. 238–264). New York: New York University Press.

Wood, J. T. (1994b). *Who cares: Women, care, and culture.* Carbondale: Southern Illinois University Press.

Wood, J. T. (1996a). Dominant and muted discourses in popular representations of feminism. *Quarterly Journal of Speech, 82,* 171–185.

Wood, J. T. (Ed.). (1996b). *Gendered relationships: A reader.* Mountain View, CA: Mayfield.

Wood, J. T. (1998). *But I thought you meant... Misunderstandings in human communication.* Mountain View, CA: Mayfield.

Wood, J. T. (2001a). A critical response to John Gray's Mars and Venus portrayals of men and women. *Southern Communication Journal, 67,* 201–210.

Wood, J. T. (2001b). The normalization of violence in heterosexual romantic relationships: Women's narratives of love and violence. *Journal of Social and Personal Relationships, 18,* 239–262.

Wood, J. T. (2004). Monsters and victims: Male felons' accounts of intimate partner violence. *Journal of Social and Personal Relationships, 21,* 555–576.

Wood, J. T. (2005). Feminist standpoint theory and muted group theory: Commonalities and divergences. *Women & Language, 28,* 61–64.

Wood, J. T. (2006). Gender, power and violence in heterosexual relationships. In D. Canary and K. Dindia (Eds.), *Sex differences and similarities in communication* (2nd ed., pp. 397–411). Mahwah, NJ: Erlbaum.

Wood, J. T. (2008). Critical, feminist theories of interpersonal communication. In L. A. Baxter & D. O. Braithwaite (Eds.), *Engaging theories in interpersonal communication* (pp. 323–334). Thousand Oaks, CA: Sage.

Wood, J. T. (2009a). Gender as an area of study. In W. Eadie (Ed.), *21st century communication: A reference handbook* (pp. 371–379). Thousand Oaks, CA: Sage.

Wood, J. T. (2009b). Gender differences in communication. In S. Hendrick & C. Hendrick (Eds.), *The encyclopedia of human relationships.* Thousand Oaks, CA: Sage.

Wood, J. T. (2010). The can-do discourse and young women's anticipations of future. *Women & Language.*

Wood, J. T. (2011a). He says/she says: Misunderstandings in communication between women and men. In D. O. Braithwaite & J. T. Wood (Eds.), *Casing interpersonal communication* (pp. 59–65). Dubuque, IA: Kendall-Hunt.

Wood, J. T. (2011b). Which ruler? What are we measuring?: Thoughts on theorizing the division of domestic labor. *Journal of Family Communication, 11,* 39–49.

Wood, J. T. (2011c). Who's the parent now? In D. O. Braithwaite & J. T. Wood (Eds.), *Casing interpersonal communication* (pp. 197–202). Dubuque, IA: Kendall-Hunt.

Wood, J. T. (In press, b). Becoming gendered: Theories of gender development in families. In M. Fine & F. Fincham (Eds.), *Family theories: A content-based approach.* New York: Routledge.

Wood, J. T., & Conrad, C. R. (1983). Paradox in the experience of professional women. *Western Journal of Speech Communication, 47,* 305–322.

Wood, J. T., & Dow, B. J. (2010). The invisible politics of "choice" in the workplace: Naming the informal parenting support system. In S. Hayden & L. Obrien Hallstein (Eds.), *Contemplating maternity in an era of choice: Contemplating discourses of reproduction* (pp. 203–225). Lanham, MD: Lexington Books.

Wood, J. T., & Inman, C. (1993). In a different mode: Recognizing male modes of closeness. *Journal of Applied Communication Research, 21,* 279–295.

Wood, W., Christensen, P., Hebl, M., & Rothgerber, H. (1997). Conformity to sex-typed norms, affect, and the self-concept. *Journal of Personality and Social Psychology, 73,* 523–535.

Woolls, D. (2006, September 9). Too-thin models can't walk the catwalk at Madrid fashion show. *Raleigh News & Observer,* p.3A.

Wright, K. (2004, October). Hip-hop kids these days. *The Progressive,* pp. 40–42.

Wright, P. H. (1982). Men's friendships, women's friendships, and the alleged inferiority of the latter. *Sex Roles, 8,* 1–20.

Wright, P. H. (1988). Interpreting research on gender differences in friendship: A case for moderation and a plea for caution. *Journal of Social and Personal Relationships, 5,* 367–373.

Wright, P. H. (2006). Toward an expanded orientation to the comparative study of women's and men's same-sex friendships. In K. Dindia & D. Canary (Eds.), *Sex differences and similarities in communication* (pp. 37–57). Mahwah, NJ: Erlbaum.

Yardley, J. (2008, August 13). In grand Olympic show, some sleight of voice. *New York Times,* pp. A1, A12.

Yen, H. (2010, January 16). More moms become breadwinners. *Raleigh News & Observer,* p. 3A.

Yen, H. (2010, April 21b). Women even with men in degrees. *Raleigh News & Observer,* p. 6A.

Yen, H. (2011, April 27). As more women earn degrees, more men stay home. *Raleigh News & Observer,* pp. 1A, 6A.

Yildirim, A. (1997). Gender role influences on Turkish adolescents' self-identity. *Adolescence, 32,* 216–231.

Zack, N. (2005). *Inclusive feminism: A third wave theory of women's commonality.* Lanham, MD: Rowman & Littlefield.

Zimmerman, A., & Dahlberg, J. (2008). The sexual objectification of women in advertising: A contemporary cultural perspective. *Journal of Advertising Research, 48,* 71–79.

Zimmerman, A. & Geist-Martin, P. (2006). The hybrid identities of gender queer: Claiming neither/nor, both/and. In L. A. Samovar, R. E. Porter, & E. R. McDaniel (Eds.), *Intercultural communication: A reader* (11th ed., pp. 76–82). Belmont, CA: Thomson.

Zinn, M., & Dill, B. (1996). Theorizing difference from multiracial feminism. *Feminist Studies, 22,* 321–331.

Zinn, M., Hondagneu-Sotelo, P., & Messner, M. (2007). Sex and gender through the prism of difference. In M. Andersen & P. H. Collins (Eds.), *Race, class, gender: An anthology* (6th ed., pp. 147–156). Belmont, CA: Thomson.

Ziv, L. (1997, May). The horror of female genital mutilation. *Cosmopolitan,* pp. 242–245.

Zoepf, K. (2006, April 14). Universities for women push borders in Persian Gulf. *The Chronicle of Higher Education,* pp. A45–A47.

Zukerman, J. C. (2009, March 22). We must stop the rape and terror. *Parade,* pp. 6–7.

Index